Houghton Mifflin
English

Shirley Haley-James   John Warren Stewig

Marcus T. Ballenger   Jacqueline L. Chaparro   Nancy C. Millett

June Grant Shane   C. Ann Terry

HOUGHTON   MIFFLIN   COMPANY   BOSTON

Atlanta   Dallas   Geneva, Illinois   Palo Alto   Princeton   Toronto

Acknowledgments

"The Dinner Party" by Mona Gardner. Reprinted by permission of Bill Berger Associates, Inc., and *The Saturday Review*, January 31, 1942.

"The Drum" from *Spin a Soft Black Song* by Nikki Giovanni. Copyright © 1971 by Nikki Giovanni. Reprinted by permission of Farrar, Straus and Giroux, Inc.

"Early Theories of Flight," from *Dreams and Realities of the Conquest of the Skies* by Beril Becker. Copyright © 1967 Beril Becker, author of *Mechanical Man, Jules Verne, Paul Gauguin, Victoria Woodhull*, and *Around the World Underwater*. Reprinted with permission of the author.

"Geography Lesson" from *Jets from Orange* by Zulfikar Ghose. Copyright © 1967 by Zulfikar Ghose. Reprinted by permission of Macmillan Co., and Dufours Editions Inc., Chester Springs, Pa.

"Greek Gods and Mortals," from *Greek Myths* by Olivia Coolidge. Copyright © 1964 by Houghton Mifflin Company. Study material by George Hillocks, Jr., adapted by permission of the publishers.

"Growing Up," from *Growing Up* by Russell Baker. Copyright © 1982 by Russell Baker. Reprinted by permission of Congdon & Weed, Inc. and Don Congdon Associates, Inc.

"Icarus and Daedalus," from *Old Greek Folk Stories Told Anew* by Josephine Preston Peabody (New York: Houghton Mifflin Company, 1897).

"Imagination" in *The Girl from Yamhill: A Memoir* by Beverly Cleary. Copyright © 1988. Reprinted by permission of William Morrow & Co.

"An Introduction to Greek Mythology," from *Greek Myths* by Olivia Coolidge. Copyright 1949 and copyright © renewed 1977 by Olivia E. Coolidge. Reprinted by permission of Houghton Mifflin Company.

"Lincoln's Letter to His Step-brother," from *A Treasury of the World's Great Letters* by M. Lincoln Schuster, ed. Copyright © 1940, 1968 by Simon and Schuster, Inc. Reprinted by permission of Simon and Schuster, Inc.

"The River Took My Sister," from *South Dakota Review* Vol. 7, No. 2, Summer, 1969. Copyright © 1969, University of South Dakota. Reprinted by permission.

"The Road Not Taken," from *The Poetry of Robert Frost* edited by Edward Connery Lathem. Copyright 1916, © 1969 by Holt, Rinehart & Winston. Copyright 1944 by Robert Frost. Reprinted by permission of Holt, Rinehart & Winston, Publishers, and Jonathan Cape Ltd.

(Acknowledgments continued on page 668.)

Table of Contents

UNIT 4 LITERATURE AND WRITING

Comparison and Contrast

UNIT 5 LANGUAGE AND USAGE

Verbs

Description

Capitalization and Punctuation

Persuasive Letter

Pronouns

UNIT 12 LITERATURE AND WRITING

Research Report

UNIT 13 LANGUAGE AND USAGE

Phrases

UNIT 14 LANGUAGE AND USAGE:

Clauses

STUDENT'S HANDBOOK

STRATEGIES HANDBOOK
Study Strategies

WRITER'S HANDBOOK

There is nothing to write about, you say.
Well then, write and let me know just this—
that there *is* nothing to write about. . . .
    Pliny the Younger
    from *Letters*

LITERATURE

Can a class assignment show you something new about yourself?

Imagination

By Beverly Cleary

Miss Smith also gave unusual assignments. Once, without warning, she said, "I want you to pretend you live in George Washington's time and write a letter to someone describing an experience."

Write something we had not learned in a book? This was unheard of. "But that's not fair," some protested.

Miss Smith assured us that such an assignment was perfectly fair. We knew she was right. Miss Smith was always fair. Strict, but fair.

"You mean *now?*" someone asked.

"Now." Miss Smith was always firm.

"But how?" someone else asked.

"Use your imaginations," said Miss Smith, unconcerned by the consternation she had created.

I was excited. All my life, Mother had told me to use my imagination, but I had never expected to be asked, or even allowed, to use it in school. After a moment of pencil chewing, I wrote to an imaginary cousin, telling how I had sacrificed my pet chicken to help feed Washington's starving, freezing troops at Valley Forge.

The next day, Miss Smith read my letter to the class, praised me for using my imagination, and said everyone else in the class had to try again. At Fernwood any written work, even practice sentences, that did not measure up to teachers' standards was rewritten—sometimes more than once. Smugly I read a library book while my classmates struggled with letters about their sacrifices of pet lambs and calves for Washington's troops. Copycats, I thought with contempt. Mother had told me authors found their ideas in their own minds, not in the words of others. Besides, who ever heard of lambs and calves in the middle of winter? In Yamhill, they were born in springtime.

Next Miss Smith gave us homework: writing an essay about our favorite book character. This brought forth groans and sighs of resignation from most of the class. Nobody wanted to do homework, especially original homework.

That weekend, Mother happened to be visiting her parents in Banks, where Grandpa Atlee had bought back his store. (When he was seventy, after two years of retirement, he decided he was too young to be idle.) After I put together a Sunday dinner for my father, who gamely ate it and was enjoying his pipe and the Sunday paper, I sat down to write the essay. Which favorite character when I had so many? Peter Pan? Judy from *Daddy-Long-Legs*? Tom Sawyer? I finally solved this problem by writing about a girl who went to Bookland and talked to several of my favorite characters. I wrote on and on, inventing conversations that the characters might have had with a strange girl. As rain beat against the windows, a feeling of peace came over me as I wrote far beyond the required length of the essay. I had discovered the pleasure of writing, and to this day, whenever it rains, I feel the urge to write. Most of my books are written in winter.

Beverly Cleary kept writing. Eventually she wrote the *Ramona* books. This story is from her autobiography, *A Girl from Yamhill: A Memoir.*

Think and Discuss
1. What did Beverly Cleary learn from the first "unusual assignment" her teacher gave her?
2. Why does Cleary always feel the urge to write when it rains?
3. What are some situations when it is appropriate to use your imagination? When is it not so appropriate?

The Writing Process

STEP 1: PREWRITING

How to Get and Explore Ideas

How do you write when you can't think of anything to write about? Your own brain is a storehouse of information and ideas. Pick it! You'll be surprised what you find. Try these techniques to find or explore a topic, or to discover more ideas when you're stuck.

Brainstorming Get together with a group or a partner. Start with a word, an object, or an idea. What does it bring to mind? Throw out ideas as quickly as you can. Express them in a word, a phrase, or a sentence. Have one person record, writing down all the thoughts, feelings, and memories in the order they are spoken. Don't censor anything! Don't evaluate ideas. Just think!

Journal Writing Do you keep a journal? If not, start now. Record not only daily events but also your thoughts, feelings, and reactions to anything—to a book you just read, to a picture you really liked, to someone you talked to. Whenever you have a thought that you'd like to hold onto, write it in your journal. When you are looking for a writing topic, look back in your journal. You're sure to find plenty of ideas.

Listing Brainstorm on your own. List whatever comes to mind. Don't write complete sentences, and don't even think about punctuation, capitalization, spelling, or grammar. Don't stop—just keep listing. Your goal is to capture as many ideas on paper as quickly as possible.

Clustering A cluster shows relationships between ideas. First, write your topic in the middle of your paper. Circle it. Around the word, write words or phrases that flash to your mind. Circle them and draw lines to connect them to your topic. Do these words now suggest other ideas? Write them.

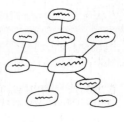

Cubing Make a cube. On each side write a different instruction to yourself. You may want to use some of the instructions in dark print below. On a piece of paper, write your thoughts about your topic in response to the instructions. For each instruction, write for about three minutes.

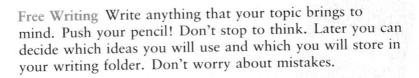

- **Describe it.** What do you see?
- **Compare it.** What is it similar to? different from?
- **Associate it.** What does it bring to mind?
- **Analyze it.** What is it made of? What parts does it have?
- **Apply it.** How could you use it?
- **Argue for or against it.** What are the pros and cons? (You don't have to be serious.)

Free Writing Write anything that your topic brings to mind. Push your pencil! Don't stop to think. Later you can decide which ideas you will use and which you will store in your writing folder. Don't worry about mistakes.

Interviewing Working with a partner, discover as much as you can about your topics. Take turns asking each other questions with *who, what, when, where, why,* and *how.*

Prewriting on Your Own

Choose a topic Find a writing topic that presents two opposing courses of action. Use at least two of the techniques above. How many ideas can you write?

Explore your topic Use at least two of these techniques to help you get ideas about your topic. Circle the ideas you will use to write your first draft.

How to Write a First Draft

Think of a sculptor working with clay. The first task is to make the shape. When you write your first draft, you are a sculptor. In your first draft, you shape your composition.

GUIDELINES FOR DRAFTING

- Keep in mind your purpose and your audience.
- Write your ideas on paper as fast as you can. You can make crossouts, leave blanks, use abbreviations.
- Skip lines, leaving room to add or make changes.
- Don't worry about errors. You can correct them later.

Rachel wanted to persuade her classmates that to be better writers they should write in their journals every day at a certain time rather than write only when they felt inspired. First, she presented the two courses of action. Here is her second paragraph.

> ~~A good writer~~ I always write at five every day, just before dinner. If you set aside a regular time you won't forget to write. If you want to be a good writer, you will set aside a specific time each day for writeing. Getting in the habit will make you remember to write every day at that time.

Think and Discuss

- How did Rachel change the beginning of her paragraph?
- Which parts of her paragraph are unclear?

Drafting on Your Own

Write your first draft. In it, discuss two courses of action. Then show your audience why one is better. Use the notes you took when you explored your topic.

How to Have a Writing Conference

Congratulations! You've written your first draft. Have you said everything you wanted to say? Have you stated all your ideas clearly and in a sensible way? Sometimes it's difficult to judge your own writing. A conference with a classmate can help you see how you might make your writing more effective.

Rachel read her second paragraph to Maria.

You can have a writing conference at any stage of your writing. After writing your first draft, a writing conference can show you where you've left gaps or where you need to revise. Think about these points as you confer with a partner.

GUIDELINES FOR A WRITING CONFERENCE

As the writer:
- Read slowly and clearly enough to be easily understood.
- Answer your partner's questions politely.
- Think of ways to improve points that seem confusing.
- Respond to your partner's criticism by taking out unnecessary information or adding information that is needed.
- Thank your partner for his or her help.

As the listener:
- Listen carefully.
- Help the writer feel at ease by telling what you liked about the writing or by retelling what you heard.
- Be polite at all times.
- Offer suggestions for changes only if the writer asks for them.
- Ask questions that begin with *who, what, when, where, why,* and *how* to help clarify the writing and get more information.

When you are listening to persuasive writing, consider questions such as these:
- Is the writer's opinion stated clearly?
- Is the opinion supported by factual reasons?
- Does each paragraph have a topic sentence?
- What other reasons or examples could be added?
- Are any reasons or examples not related to the writer's argument?
- Are the reasons presented in the best order?

Having a Writing Conference

Work with a partner. Hold a writing conference about your first drafts. Follow the guidelines above.

How to Revise Your Draft

Now is your chance to take up your pencil, to chisel away at your sculpture, to define its shape and make it your own. As you revise your first draft, you will think about your partner's suggestions, add ideas, take away words and sentences, rearrange, and rewrite.

GUIDELINES FOR REVISING

- Add parts by writing between the lines and in the margins.
- Move parts by circling them and drawing arrows to show where you want them to be.
- Take out parts by crossing them out.
- Don't worry about mistakes. You can fix them later.

~~A good writer~~ I always write at five every day, just before dinner. If you set aside a regular time *get busy doing other things and* you won't forget to write. If you want to be a good writer, you will set aside a specific time each day for writeing. Getting in the habit will make you remember to write every day at that time. *Atheletes and musishuns practice every day at a set time, why shouldn't writers?*

Think and Discuss

- How did Rachel change the order of her sentences?
- Where did she add new information?
- Which sentence did she take out? Why?

Revising on Your Own

Revise your first draft, using the guidelines above.

How to Proofread Your Writing

You've completed your masterpiece, but it needs a bit of polishing. Follow these steps to put on the finishing touches.

GUIDELINES FOR PROOFREADING

- Check any spellings you are unsure of in a dictionary.
- Indent all paragraphs.
- Check for punctuation.
- Check for capitalization.
- Check for grammar errors.
- Use proofreading marks.

Proofreading Marks

- ¶ Indent
- ∧ Add
- ⌃ Add a comma
- ⩓⩓ Add quotation marks
- ⊙ Add a period
- ℓ Take out
- ≡ Capitalize
- / Make a small letter
- ∿ Reverse the order

A good writer I always write at five every day, just before dinner. If you set aside a regular time get busy doing other things and you won't forget to write. If you want to be a good writer, you will set aside a specific time each day for writing. Getting in the habit will make you remember to write every day at that time. Athletes and musicians practice every day at a set time, why shouldn't writers?

Think and Discuss

- Which words did Rachel correct for spelling?
- What punctuation mark did she add? Why?
- How did she correct a run-on sentence?

Proofreading on Your Own

Using the proofreading marks on this page, proofread your paper. Polish it. Make it shine!

How to Publish Your Writing

Now is your chance to share your masterpiece with the world. But before you do, put it in final form.

GUIDELINES FOR PUBLISHING

- Copy your writing onto a clean piece of paper.
- Add an attention-getting title.
- Reread it to make sure you haven't made any errors in copying. If you catch any other errors, this is your last chance to fix them, too.
- Share your writing with an audience.

Rachel typed her paper neatly and put it in a folder with her classmates' writing. Later they made this into a book, *Let Us Convince You.* They added illustrations and presented a copy to the school library.

Ideas for Publishing

- Mount your final copy on colored paper. Add photographs, pictures from old magazines, or hand-drawn illustrations. Display your poster on the class bulletin board.
- Get together with a partner and present two courses of action, based on your paper. Stage a debate for your class.

Publishing on Your Own

Unveil your masterpiece. Present it to the world! Use an idea from this page or one of your own.

Language and Usage

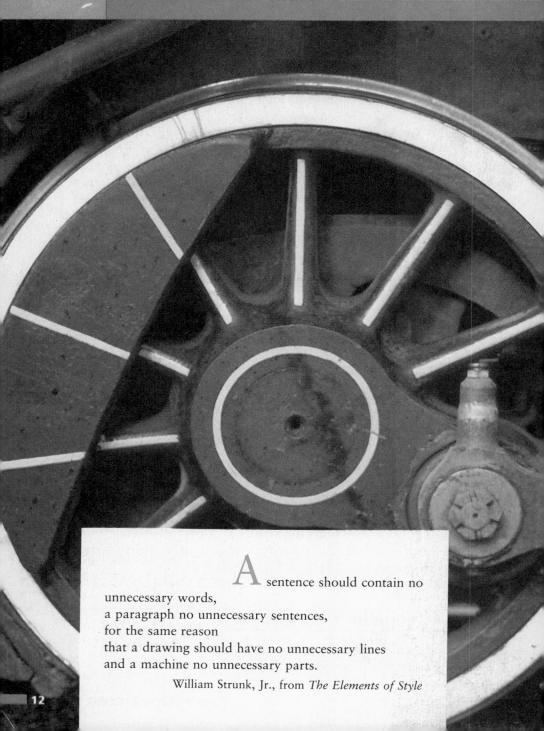

A sentence should contain no unnecessary words,
a paragraph no unnecessary sentences,
for the same reason
that a drawing should have no unnecessary lines
and a machine no unnecessary parts.

William Strunk, Jr., from *The Elements of Style*

The Sentence

Getting Ready We use sentences in both our speaking and our writing. What we do *not* always do is create sentences that are clear and easy to understand. How often have you heard or read a sentence that leaves you saying *What?* instead of *Oh, I see!* In this unit you will learn more about writing clear sentences in which every word works.

ACTIVITIES

Listening Listen as the quotation on the opposite page is read. What does the writer mean by "unnecessary words"? Write a sentence, just as it comes to your mind. Look at it. Does your sentence contain any unnecessary words?

Speaking Look at the picture. What do you see? If this picture showed the whole machine, what would it be? Make up different kinds of sentences about the picture: (1) one that ends with an exclamation point, (2) one that ends with a question mark, (3) one that contains the word *but,* (4) one that includes the word *although.*

Writing What does this wheel remind you of? Write your thoughts in your journal.

1 | Kinds of Sentences

A **sentence** is a group of words that express a complete thought. A sentence begins with a capital letter and ends with a punctuation mark. There are four kinds of sentences.

1. A **declarative sentence** makes a statement and ends with a period.

   Ben is a great singer.   Music is enjoyable.

2. An **interrogative sentence** asks a question and ends with a question mark.

   Isn't Ben a great singer?   Who is singing tonight?

3. An **imperative sentence** makes a command or a request and ends with a period.

   Come in, please.   Maria, don't be late.

4. An **exclamatory sentence** expresses strong feeling and ends with an exclamation point.

   What a great concert that was!   These distractions must end!

   You can make any type of sentence exclamatory by punctuating it with an exclamation point to express strong feeling.

   Music is enjoyable!   Isn't Ben a great singer!

Do not overuse the exclamation point, however. Too many exclamation points can make your writing ineffective.

Guided Practice

A. What kind of sentence is each of the following?

Example: Is that our cue? *interrogative*

1. We're late.
2. Please stay calm, Arnold.
3. Couldn't we start?
4. How impatient you are!

B. What punctuation mark should end each sentence? What kind of sentence is it?

Example: Will Ida remember her lines
   question mark   interrogative

5. Watch her face carefully
6. The lights are on her
7. Is her voice quivering
8. How radiant she looks

▶ **Declarative sentences** make statements and end with periods.
▶ **Interrogative sentences** ask questions and end with question marks.
▶ **Imperative sentences** make commands or requests and end with periods.
▶ **Exclamatory sentences** express strong feelings and end with exclamation points.

Independent Practice Write each sentence, adding the correct end punctuation. Then label each sentence *declarative, interrogative, imperative,* or *exclamatory*.

Example: Are you watching the play
  Are you watching the play? **interrogative**

9. Please pay attention
10. Why are you making a face
11. How great this performance is
12. Don't applaud yet
13. Good drama certainly is thrilling
14. It's exciting and entertaining
15. Try to see more plays
16. You seem to like the theater
17. Have you seen the comedy at the Plaza
18. What an amusing play it is
19. Good comedy makes me feel terrific
20. Musicals are a lot of fun too
21. I prefer serious plays
22. They give you more to think about
23. Go see *The Baileys*
24. Tell me what you think of it
25. Did you like it
26. It was the best play I've ever seen

Writing Application: A Review Imagine that you are the entertainment critic for your local or school newspaper. Describe a play, a movie, or a TV show that you have seen recently. Use each kind of sentence—*declarative, interrogative, imperative,* and *exclamatory*—at least once. Use correct punctuation.

For Extra Practice, see p. 42.

2 | Complete Subjects and Complete Predicates

In order to express a complete thought, a sentence must have two parts, a subject and a predicate. The **subject** tells whom or what the sentence is about. The **predicate** tells what the subject is, does, has, or feels.

SUBJECT	PREDICATE
People	eat.
Most people in America	eat three meals every day.
Many kinds of foods	are eaten around the world.

The **complete subject** includes a noun or a pronoun and the words and phrases that describe it. The **complete predicate** contains a verb or a verb phrase and all the words that complete its meaning.

People in some countries	eat seafood.
Prince Edward Island	is famous for its oysters.
You	should try this specialty.

Sometimes the complete subject or the complete predicate or both are just one word.

Fish	swim.

Guided Practice What are the complete subject and the complete predicate in each sentence?

Example: The fair at school will definitely be tomorrow.
      complete subject: The fair at school
      complete predicate: will definitely be tomorrow

1. Students in every class are now preparing projects.
2. Two English classes are performing *Julius Caesar.*
3. Some of the students in Ms. Solano's social studies class have collected flags of many nations.
4. One of the students has built a miniature house.
5. Susan's class baked whole-wheat bread in the shape of hearts and cloverleaves.
6. Julia has designed colorful programs.
7. Students from other schools will be coming.
8. We are looking forward to the event.

▶ Every sentence has a **subject** and a **predicate**.
▶ The **complete subject** tells whom or what the sentence is about.
▶ The **complete predicate** tells what the subject is, does, has, or feels.

Independent Practice Write each sentence. Draw a line between the complete subject and the complete predicate.

Example: The people of Clayville were unprepared for the storm.
The people of Clayville|were unprepared for the storm.

9. The weather had been beautiful.
10. The storm didn't begin until nightfall.
11. Mist turned to light rain.
12. The light rain had become a downpour by dawn.
13. A steady rain fell for almost two days.
14. The rain was extremely welcome after so many weeks of dry weather.
15. A few of the residents of Clayville had been worried about the lack of rain.
16. The heavy rainfall had many good results for the farmers and their crops.
17. Corn plants grew greener and taller.
18. Small tomato plants suddenly blossomed.
19. A few fruit trees produced new buds.
20. Both grape vines and squash vines looked healthier and fuller.
21. Even the cows benefited from the greener grass.
22. The children of Clayville enjoyed the results of the rain too.
23. Many of them swam in the pond for the first time that summer.
24. Several of the townspeople did not water their lawns and gardens for a week.

Writing Application: A Description Remember or imagine being a child experiencing your first thunderstorm. You are amazed and curious about what is happening outside. You watch for the lightning and are struck with wonder by what you see. Write a paragraph about this experience. Be sure that each sentence has a subject and a predicate.

For Extra Practice, see p. 43.
Complete Subjects and Predicates **17**

3 | Simple Subjects and Simple Predicates

You have learned that the complete subject contains the words that name and describe the subject. The key word or words in the complete subject are called the **simple subject**. The simple subject tells whom or what the sentence is about and is usually a noun or a pronoun.

Peanuts in their natural state   are good for you.
Carver's discoveries   made peanuts important.
They   grow in shells.

The simple subject may be the same as the complete subject.

Oil   is a peanut product.
George Washington Carver   experimented with peanuts.

The **simple predicate** is the key word or words in the complete predicate that tell what the subject is, does, has, or feels. The simple predicate is always either a verb or a verb phrase.

Peanut products   contain many natural resources.
Peanuts   have been important for years.

The simple predicate may be interrupted by other words.

We do not know the origin of peanuts.

In some sentences the simple predicate and the complete predicate may be the same.

Peanut crop pests must be controlled

Guided Practice Find the simple subject and the simple predicate in each sentence. The complete subject and the complete predicate are separated by a line.

Example: One potato|can supply half your daily vitamin C.
   simple subject: potato
   simple predicate: can supply

1. Many B vitamins|are found in a potato as well.
2. It|does not contain much fat.
3. Sailors|once ate raw potatoes as prevention against disease.
4. A research institute in Peru|feeds potatoes to babies.
5. A medium potato without butter|does not have many calories.

▸ The **simple subject** is the key word in the complete subject. It is usually a noun or a pronoun.

▸ The **simple predicate** is the verb or verb phrase in the complete predicate.

Independent Practice

A. Write each sentence. Underline the simple subject once and the simple predicate twice. The complete subject and the complete predicate are separated by a line.

Example: A popular vegetable|was first grown in Peru.
A popular vegetable|was first grown in Peru.

   6. The potato|is a familiar vegetable.
   7. South America|was the birthplace of the potato.
   8. It|was brought to Spain by sixteenth-century explorers.
   9. The vegetable|seemed strange to Europeans.
   10. This product|is now grown in many countries.
   11. It|grew particularly well in Ireland.
   12. The people's diet|became dependent on the potato.
   13. The potato crop|failed in the 1840s because of disease.
   14. Thousands of Irish|were forced to go elsewhere.

B. Write the simple subject and the simple predicate of each sentence. Draw a line between them.

Example: Many people left Ireland for America. *people|left*

   15. Russia now grows more potatoes than any other country.
   16. The people of Russia call potatoes their second bread.
   17. Every state in the United States grows potatoes.
   18. Most potatoes are raised on large northern farms.
   19. An amazing variety of potatoes can be found in Peru.
   20. Farmers in Peru grow potatoes in many shapes and colors.
   21. The native language of Peru contains over one thousand words for the potato.
   22. Some form of potato has been growing in Peru for three thousand or more years.

Writing Application: Food Review You are a waiter in a restaurant. Write a paragraph recommending your favorite dish to a customer. Underline each simple subject once and each simple predicate twice.

4 | Finding the Subject

Most sentences that you write are in **natural order:** the subject comes before the predicate. Sometimes you write sentences in **inverted order:** the subject follows all or part of the complete predicate.

> Into the tree flew a bird.
> Out of the woods came the Mad Hatter.
> Lying on top of a mushroom was a caterpillar.

Interrogative sentences are usually in inverted order.

> Was the caterpillar blue?
> When would it speak to Alice?

Whenever you want to find the subject of an inverted sentence, try rearranging the words into their natural order.

> The Mad Hatter came out of the woods.
> A caterpillar was lying on top of a mushroom.
> The caterpillar was blue.
> It would speak to Alice when?

Sentences that begin with the introductory word *there* or *here* are also in inverted order.

> There was a caterpillar near Alice.
> Here is a butterfly.

To find the subject of a sentence beginning with *there* or *here,* locate the verb and ask the question *who?* or *what?* about it.

> What was near Alice? A caterpillar was.

Imperative sentences are in natural order, but the subject usually does not appear in the sentence. The subject *you* is understood. The subject remains *you* even when the name of the person is used.

> (You) Peer through the looking glass.
> Alice, (you) watch the cat.

Some sentences in natural order begin with words other than the subject.

> In the book a strange character appears.
> At the end of the story, Alice awakens.

Again, to find the subject, locate the verb first and ask the question *who?* or *what?* about it.

Guided Practice What is the simple subject of each sentence?

Example: Imagine the tale about Alice in a dreamland. *(You)*

1. On a branch of the tree sat a cat.
2. To his right lived the Mad Hatter.
3. There was the March Hare to the left.
4. Also attending the party was a dormouse.
5. How does the book end?
6. Read the book for the complete story.

Independent Practice Write the simple subject of each sentence.

Example: There is my mother's copy of *Alice's Adventures in Wonderland* by Lewis Carroll. *copy*

7. On the second page is a picture of the author.
8. Do you know his real name?
9. Inez, tell me his name. *you*
10. Have you read the book?
11. Please lend it to me. *you*
12. When will you return it?
13. On this paper I have written the date.
14. There is no name on the paper.
15. Here is my signature on the other side.
16. Do you have any other children's books?
17. On the top shelf is a great book.
18. Who wrote it?
19. Here is the author's name on the spine.
20. Did E. B. White write many children's books?

Writing Application: A Poster Write some sentences for a poster that advertises a book for children. Begin one sentence with *here* or *there*. Begin one sentence with *in* or *at*. Make one of your sentences a question. Your poster can be about a real or an imaginary book.

For Extra Practice, see p. 45.

5 | Compound Subjects and Compound Predicates

A sentence can include two or more simple subjects, two or more simple predicates, or both. Two or more simple subjects with the same predicate form a **compound subject**.

> Pancho and Erin are running.

Two or more simple predicates with the same subject form a **compound predicate**.

> Sue Lee tried out and made the team.
> Cindy Page tried out but did not make it.

A sentence may also have both a compound subject and a compound predicate.

> The captain, the co-captain, or the coach ran and fell.

Sentences in inverted order also may have compound subjects and predicates.

COMPOUND SUBJECT: Here are Oxbow and Chun.
COMPOUND PREDICATE: Are they laughing or crying?

The parts of a compound subject or of a compound predicate are usually joined by *and, but,* or *or.*

Guided Practice What are the compound subjects and the compound predicates in these sentences?

Example: Ed and the trainer watched and coached the team.
  compound subj.: Ed   trainer
  compound pred.: watched   coached

1. Alissa and Ed ran but did not jump.
2. Martha Perkins will not practice or work on her form tonight.
3. There may be rain, sleet, or snow for tomorrow's meet.
4. Jill and Joe left the house quite early today.
5. Here are their new track shoes and shirts for the meet.
6. Jill and Joe have been planning a team trip for weeks.
7. Did the coach or a teacher go along?
8. Mr. Wills will go but will not stay the whole time.
9. Are the runners, the gymnasts, or the jumpers competing now?

▶ A **compound subject** is made up of two or more simple subjects that have the same predicate.

▶ A **compound predicate** is made up of two or more simple predicates that have the same subject.

Independent Practice Write each sentence. Underline each simple subject once and each simple predicate twice. Label each sentence *compound subject, compound predicate,* or *both.*

Example: The runner crossed the finish line and grinned.
> *The runner crossed the finish line and grinned.*
>
> **compound predicate**

10. Would Horace, Karen, Donald, or Elsa be the runner-up?
11. Here are my cousin and her friend.
12. Kelly trained, ran, and finished the race alone.
13. Watching from the sidelines were my parents and my cousin.
14. The meet began with the coach's lengthy speech and ended with an hour-long parade.
15. A man and a woman led the procession.
16. Four bands and a juggler were part of the parade.
17. The parade honored the team and lasted for an hour.
18. David and Kathleen go to the parade every year but stay only a very short time.
19. Did Phil and Carmen give their report on parades to you?
20. They gave an oral report and also showed a filmstrip.
21. In 3000 B.C., citizens built special streets and held processions.
22. A religious festival or a military display was quite often an occasion for a parade.
23. Circus performers marched and danced in the processions.
24. In the 1880s and 1890s, political parades were very popular in the United States but are not as common today.
25. Parades are vivid events and are usually well attended.
26. Band music and floats are often the main features of a parade.
27. Trained animals and colorful costumes will attract an audience to any parade.
28. Are you going to the parade tomorrow or staying home?

Writing Application: A Description Write a paragraph about a track meet or a parade that you have watched. Include a sentence with a compound subject, a sentence with a compound predicate, and a sentence with both.

6 | Combining Sentences: Compound Sentences

A simple sentence expresses one complete idea. When the ideas of two or more simple sentences are related, you may combine the simple sentences into a **compound sentence**.

SIMPLE SENTENCES	COMPOUND SENTENCE
The stage door is locked.	The stage door is locked,
The theater looks dark.	and the theater looks dark.

Join simple sentences with a conjunction, or connecting word, like *and, but,* or *or.* Use a comma between the joined sentences unless the sentences are very short.

| People shouted. | People shouted and confetti flew. |
| Confetti flew. | |

| Will the performance end? | Will the performance end, or |
| Will it continue? | will it continue? |

The actress curtsied.	The actress curtsied, the
The actor bowed.	actor bowed, and they left
They left the stage.	the stage.

You may also join two simple sentences with a semicolon.

| The curtain fell. | The curtain fell; |
| Applause followed. | applause followed. |

Do not confuse compound sentences with simple sentences that have a compound subject, a compound predicate, or both. A compound sentence can always be separated into two or more sentences.

SIMPLE SENTENCE: The curtain swayed and fell.

COMPOUND SENTENCE: The curtain swayed and it fell.

Guided Practice

A. Which sentences are simple sentences? Which are compound?

Example: Comedy is happy, but tragedy is sad. *compound*

1. Comedy and tragedy were two forms of ancient Greek drama.
2. Both originated as songs, but each developed differently.
3. Animals, humans, gods, and monsters appeared in plays.

B. Write each pair of sentences as a compound sentence. Use the conjunction in parentheses. Where do commas belong?

Example: A myth is a tale. Mythologists study myths.   (and)
A myth is a tale, and mythologists study myths.

4. Greek drama was based on myth. Playwrights could choose from a variety of stories.   (and)
5. Greek myths came from many sources. Men, women, gods, and goddesses were the subjects of all these myths.   (but)
6. Were the characters real? Did writers make them up?   (or)
7. No one really knows. The characters seemed real.   (but)

Summing up

▶ You may combine two or more related simple sentences into a **compound sentence.** You usually join the sentences with a conjunction, adding a comma before the conjunction.

Independent Practice Rewrite each pair of sentences as one compound sentence. Use the conjunction in parentheses, and add commas where necessary.

Example: Edith Hamilton was born in Germany. Her parents were from the United States.   (but)
Edith Hamilton was born in Germany, but her parents were from the United States.

8. She loved to study. Many people in the late 1800s did not consider that appropriate for a woman.   (but)
9. Her father was not one of those people. He introduced her to the study of the classics.   (and)
10. At the age of seven, Edith was already studying Latin. She learned Greek soon afterward.   (and)
11. At the University of Munich, she had to sit apart from the male students. She could not attend classes.   (or)
12. Her interest in the classical world was great. She taught about Greece and Rome nearly all her life.   (and)
13. She did not write about ancient Greece and Rome until her retirement. Then she produced many books about them.   (but)
14. Edith Hamilton received many honors. In her ninetieth year, she was made an honorary citizen of Athens, Greece.   (and)

Writing Application: A Summary Write about a myth, folk tale, or legend. Use some compound sentences.

Compound Sentences   **25**

7 || Conjunctions

You have seen how a connecting word, or a conjunction, connects two or more simple sentences in a compound sentence. You can also use conjunctions to join other kinds of words. A **conjunction** is a word that joins words or groups of words. A **coordinating conjunction** connects related words or word groups that have the same function in a sentence.

COMPOUND SUBJECT: Carol and Brian have arrived.
COMPOUND PREDICATE: Carol may dance but will not sing.
COMPOUND MODIFIER: The guests are happy yet quiet.
COMPOUND SENTENCES: Ron will sing, for Carol will play piano.
Sam will not dance, nor will he juggle.

Coordinating Conjunctions					
and	but	or	nor	for	yet

Like coordinating conjunctions, **correlative conjunctions** join words or word groups. Correlative conjunctions appear in pairs and are more forceful and precise than coordinating conjunctions.

Neither Lin nor Thom has arrived.
Either the car will start, or Jim will jump-start it.
Whether it rains or snows, we will go.

Correlative Conjunctions	
either . . . or	not only . . . but (also)
neither . . . nor	whether . . . or
both . . . and	just as . . . so

Guided Practice

A. What are the conjunctions in these sentences?

Example: The elephant is large, but its brain is small. *but*

1. The molar tooth of an elephant measures about a foot and weighs eight or nine pounds.
2. Both cow elephants and bull elephants have tusks.
3. An elephant eats over five hundred pounds of food and drinks fifty gallons of water a day.

B. Complete the sentences with appropriate conjunctions.

> Example: Indian elephants _____ African elephants are the most common elephants. *and*

4. The Indian elephant is about nine feet tall, _____ the African elephant can be as tall as thirteen feet.
5. Both Indian _____ African elephants can be tamed.
6. The Indian elephant makes a good circus elephant, _____ it can be tamed more easily than the African elephant.

Summing up

> ▶ **Coordinating conjunctions**, such as *and, but,* and *or,* join words or word groups that have the same function.
> ▶ **Correlative conjunctions**, such as *neither . . . nor,* are pairs of conjunctions that connect related words or word groups.

Independent Practice

A. Write the conjunctions from these sentences.

> Example: Tigers once roamed much of Asia, but now some species are extinct. *but*

7. Their numbers have decreased, yet some survive.
8. Many people admire tigers and work to protect them.
9. Today many tigers live either in zoos or in large protected wildlife areas.
10. Since the 1970s, wildlife groups have been trying to save tigers, and the number of tigers is growing.

B. Write conjunctions to complete the sentences. Some sentences have more than one possible answer.

> Example: Not only hot rain forests _____ cold mountains are suitable for tigers. *but (also)*

11. Continental _____ island parts of Asia have wild tigers.
12. Tigers usually live near water _____ swim very well.
13. Young tigers do not harm people, _____ they do damage the environment.
14. An animal park _____ reserve is a good home for a tiger.

Writing Application: Creative Writing Imagine that you are an animal confronting a person. Write sentences about what you see, hear, smell, wonder, and think. Use both coordinating and correlative conjunctions, and underline them.

For Extra Practice, see p. 48.   Conjunctions   **27**

8 | Complex Sentences

A **clause** is a group of words that has a subject and a predicate. One kind of clause that you already know is a simple sentence. A simple sentence has a subject and a predicate and expresses a complete thought. A simple sentence that is joined to another clause is called a main or **independent clause**. When you join two independent clauses together, you form a compound sentence.

               indep. clause   indep. clause
COMPOUND SENTENCE: A tree matures, and it bears fruit.

A clause that does not express a complete thought is a dependent, or **subordinate clause**.

       When a tree matures,

A subordinate clause depends on an independent clause to complete its meaning. One or more subordinate clauses joined to an independent clause form a **complex sentence**.

             sub. clause   indep. clause
COMPLEX SENTENCE: When a tree matures, it bears fruit.

Subordinate clauses can be in different places in a complex sentence. Always use a comma after a subordinate clause that begins a sentence. Do not use a comma before a subordinate clause that ends a sentence.

    When you go to the library, read about trees.
    Read about trees when you go to the library.

Subordinate clauses often begin with words like *although, when,* and *after.* Such words that connect subordinate clauses to independent clauses are called **subordinating conjunctions**.

Common Subordinating Conjunctions

after	as long as	if	unless	where
although	as though	since	until	whereas
as	because	so that	when	wherever
as if	before	than	whenever	while

You can combine related simple sentences with subordinating conjunctions to form complex sentences.

SIMPLE SENTENCES	COMPLEX SENTENCE
All trees produce sap.	Although all trees produce sap,
Not all sap produces syrup.	not all sap produces syrup.

Different conjunctions express different relationships.

> After I climbed the tree, Charles whistled.
> Whenever I climbed the tree, Charles whistled.
> While I climbed the tree, Charles whistled.
> If I climbed the tree, Charles whistled.

Be sure to use the subordinating conjunction that expresses the meaning you intend.

Guided Practice

A. Is each sentence *simple, compound,* or *complex*? Identify each subordinating conjunction and subordinate clause.

> Example: You can tell the age of a tree if you count its rings.
> *complex   subordinating conjunction: if*
> *subordinate clause: if you count its rings*

1. Some kinds of trees produce rings every year whereas other kinds of trees don't.
2. Because some trees do not produce rings annually, their age cannot be determined exactly.
3. Although no one has counted more than 3,200 rings on a tree, some trees may be even older.
4. The largest trees in the world are in California.
5. These trees are nearly three hundred feet high and thirty-five feet in diameter.
6. The fruit of some trees is hard and dry, but the fruit of others is soft and fleshy.
7. Some fruit weighs as much as forty pounds while other fruit weighs less than an ounce.

B. Which clauses are independent and which are subordinate? Add an independent clause to each subordinate clause to form a complex sentence. Where do commas belong?

> Example: since the buckets are full
> *subordinate clause: since the buckets are full*
> *Since the buckets are full, we will have to get more.*

8. when the snow falls
9. although we will get there early
10. the trees don't have leaves yet
11. wherever squirrels are
12. if you look closely at this tree
13. Harriet will collect nuts and fruit
14. as soon as it gets warmer

Summing up

- An **independent clause** can stand alone.
- A **subordinate clause** cannot stand alone.
- A subordinate clause usually begins with a **subordinating conjunction**.
- A sentence with one or more subordinate clauses and an independent clause is a **complex sentence**.

Independent Practice

A. Write *simple, compound,* or *complex* to describe each sentence. Write each complex sentence, underlining the subordinate clause once and the subordinating conjunction twice.

Example: Some maple trees are grown for wood while others are cultivated for their sap.

complex *Some maple trees are grown for wood <u>while</u> others are cultivated for their sap.*

15. The Norway and Japanese maples are decorative trees.
16. Since some hard maple trees have a beautiful grain, they are selected for furniture.
17. The wood of soft maples is good for small wooden articles.
18. The big-leaf maple can be one hundred feet high, and its leaves are sometimes one foot wide.
19. The silver maple has beautiful leaves so that it is often used for street planting.
20. Maple trees have more varieties than most people imagine.

B. Write complex sentences by adding independent clauses to these clauses. Add commas where necessary.

Example: because it was autumn
Because it was autumn, the leaves were falling.

21. while the sun shone
22. when the boys arrived
23. before we left
24. whenever it snows hard
25. if you come at three o'clock
26. as soon as we finish our work

Writing Application: A Description Describe a tree, its leaves, its shape, and anything else you can see when you look at the tree. Use several complex sentences.

For Extra Practice, see p. 49.

9 | Correcting Fragments and Run-ons

The capital letter and end punctuation of a sentence show where a thought begins and ends. You can confuse your reader if you use sentence punctuation for an incomplete thought or if you run your sentences into each other.

Sentence Fragments

A **sentence fragment** is any word group that does not have both a subject and a predicate or does not express a complete thought. Most fragments leave you with the question *who?* or *what?* unanswered.

> In the river. *(Who did what in the river?)*
> Because I like water. *(What did you do?)*

Notice how each fragment below is corrected by adding a subject or a predicate, or by completing a thought.

FRAGMENT	CORRECTED SENTENCE
Went to the lake.	We went to the lake.
But he likes boats.	Joe doesn't row, but he likes boats.
After the race.	Prizes were awarded after the race.

Guided Practice

A. Is each group a sentence or a fragment?

Example: Some canoes are plastic. *sentence*

1. Canoed on the ocean.
2. Although it was an important means of transportation.
3. But it is also a lot of fun.
4. While they floated down the rapids.

B. Which item below is a sentence? Which items are fragments? How would you correct the fragments?

Example: White water canoeing. *fragment*
        Bob has done a lot of white water canoeing.

5. Canoeing a popular sport.
6. Because he likes adventure.
7. Bob doesn't plan to do any canoeing next weekend.

Run-on Sentences

Be careful not to run your sentences together. A **run-on sentence** consists of two or more sentences that are run together with commas or without any punctuation.

> Dean looked, he didn't see the flashlight. He looked again the flashlight had appeared from nowhere.

You can correct a run-on sentence in one of three ways.

1. Divide it into separate sentences by using end punctuation and a capital letter.

> Dean looked. He didn't see the flashlight.

2. Rewrite it as a compound sentence, using a comma and a coordinating conjunction.

> Dean looked, but he didn't see the flashlight.

3. Rewrite it as a complex sentence, using a subordinating conjunction.

> Although Dean looked, he didn't see the flashlight. When he looked again, the flashlight had appeared from nowhere.

Guided Practice

A. Which two items below are run-on sentences?

Example: Sonja Henie was a well-known ice skater she came from Norway. *run-on*

8. She won medals for figure skating in the Winter Olympics of 1928, 1932, and 1936.
9. Later Miss Henie became an actress, she skated in films.
10. She made over a dozen films she died in 1969.

B. How would you correct these run-ons?

Example: Mimi put on the ice skates, it was her first time.
Mimi put on the ice skates. It was her first time.

11. Mimi stood up she felt a little unsteady.
12. She felt nervous, she didn't fall.
13. Slowly she glided over the ice Sue smiled at her.
14. She knew she needed a lot of practice, Sue agreed.
15. Mimi went home happy, she would skate again tomorrow.
16. Sue would be there to help her they were good friends.
17. They had known each other since childhood they lived next door to each other now.
18. They weren't in the same class, they always ate together.

> ▶ A **sentence fragment** does not have both a subject and a predi-
> cate or does not express a complete thought.
> ▶ A **run-on sentence** is two or more sentences that run together.
> Rewrite a run-on as separate simple sentences, as a compound
> sentence, or as a complex sentence.

Independent Practice

A. Rewrite the sentences, correcting the fragments.

Example: The sport of rowing.
The sport of rowing goes very far back in history.

19. In 1840 the first Henley Royal Regatta.
20. Held yearly at Henley-on-Thames in England.
21. Now an Olympic sport for men and women.
22. Sculling and sweep-oar rowing.

B. Rewrite the items below, correcting the run-on sentences.

23. One old race is the "Doggett Coat and Badge" it began in the
1700s in England, it is still held.
24. Professional oarsmen used to row small ferries, some trans-
ported businessmen to meet trans-Atlantic ships.
25. Intercollegiate rowing races were popular for many years the
first Harvard-Yale race was held in 1852.

C. (26–33) Rewrite the paragraphs, correcting all sentence
fragments and all run-on sentences.

Example: Canoeing can be challenging. When the water flows fast.
Canoeing can be challenging when the water flows fast.

Many of the rivers in Canada near Hudson Bay are excellent for canoeing, there are also certain rivers. Where the sport
would be quite dangerous. For the rapids are long and swift.
For example, a small river with rapids. Feeds into the Moose
River, people fear them because the water moves so swiftly.

If you want to watch a very different kind of water race,
might find sailing races interesting, the first America's Cup
race in 1851 in England. In 1983, breaking a 132-year winning streak by American yachts. Australia won the cup, the
yacht *Australia II* the defeat of the American yacht *Liberty*.

Writing Application: A Paragraph Write a paragraph of
at least five sentences about a real or imaginary canoeing trip.
Check your paper carefully. Correct any fragments or run-ons.

For Extra Practice, see p. 50. Correcting Fragments and Run-ons

10 | Interjections

You know that an exclamatory sentence expresses strong feeling, indicated by an exclamation point. Certain words can also be exclamatory. A word or a group of words that expresses feeling is called an **interjection**. Interjections express emotions such as anger, surprise, pain, happiness, and relief.

Common Interjections

ah	goodness	oh dear	ow	uh oh
aha	hey	oh my	phew	well
bam	hooray	oh yes/no	pow	whee
bravo	hurrah	okay	shh	whoops
good grief	oh	ouch	ugh	wow

An interjection is not a sentence and has no grammatical relationship to the other words around it. Use an exclamation point after an interjection that expresses strong feeling. Use a comma after an interjection that expresses mild feeling.

Hooray! I got the part.   Shh! I can't hear.
Oh, I forgot my lines.   Okay, let's continue.

An interjection may represent a sound.

Bam! That was a loud noise.

Like exclamation points, interjections should not be overused. Too many interjections make your writing or speaking ineffective.

Guided Practice
Find the interjection in each sentence. How should each sentence be punctuated?

Example: Oh my I've never seen such a beautiful ballerina.
          Oh my! / Oh my,

1. Hey do you know her name?
2. Wow She leaps across the stage with such ease.
3. Oh I'll never be able to dance like that.
4. Goodness she's spinning so gracefully.
5. Bravo She's terrific.

▶ An **interjection** is a word or a group of words that expresses feeling or represents a sound. Use an exclamation point after an interjection that expresses strong feeling. Use a comma after an interjection that expresses mild feeling.

Independent Practice Rewrite each sentence, adding the correct punctuation. Underline each interjection.

Example: Hey are you going to the baseball game?
         Hey, are you going to the baseball game? / _Hey! Are . . ._

6. Well I'm not sure.
7. Goodness the team is quite good this year.
8. Okay I'll go.
9. Bam The bat really whacked the ball.
10. Wow Andrea really hit that ball high.
11. Pow It went right over the pitcher's head.
12. Whoops Phil shouldn't have swung at that one.
13. Phew The catcher almost tagged Sara out at home plate.
14. Ugh The umpire really missed that call.
15. Oh dear Did you see the other team's new pitcher?
16. Wow He really throws the ball fast.
17. Oh no That ball hit Mike's shoulder.
18. Ow That hurt.
19. Bravo That was quite a hit.
20. Whoops The shortstop just missed that ball by an inch.
21. Hey Coach Walker, can you tell us the score?
22. Shh Be quiet.
23. Uh oh We're behind, eleven to twelve.
24. Oh no We'll probably lose this game.
25. Phew Janie's home run came just in time.
26. Hooray We won after all.
27. Phew That was a close one.
28. Ugh I hope the next game won't be so hair-raising.

Writing Application: Creative Writing Imagine that you are in a theater. The curtain has just fallen on an exciting performance, and the audience is reacting. Write sentences that tell what audience members are saying. Use an interjection in each sentence to express emotions such as anger, surprise, happiness, disppointment, and relief.

Grammar-Writing Connection

Varying Your Sentences

Sentences of different form and length can make your writing clearer and more interesting.

SIMPLE SENTENCES: The wind blows along the shore. It picks up sand. The sand is blown against rocks. The rocks are smoothed. Winds pick up soil. They carry it away. In such ways, the wind reshapes the land.

VARIED SENTENCES: When the wind blows along the shore, it picks up sand. The sand is blown against rocks, and the rocks are smoothed. Winds pick up soil and carry it away. In such ways, the wind reshapes the land.

The first passage is monotonous and unclear, for related ideas are not connected. In the second passage, the rhythm is interesting, and the relationship between ideas is clear.

When you write, use a variety of sentences. When you revise, look for simple sentences that can be combined.

COMPLEX SENTENCE: When the wind blows along the shore, it picks up sand.

COMPOUND SENTENCE: The sand is blown against rocks, and the surface of the rocks is smoothed.

COMPOUND PREDICATE: Winds pick up soil and carry it away.

SIMPLE SENTENCE: In such ways, the wind reshapes the land.

Revising Sentences

Rewrite the sentences, combining some of them to produce a variety of sentence types.

1. The glaciers of the Ice Age melted. They left a layer of mud. This mud formed a rich soil.
2. Winds swept up the soil. They carried it away. That soil is now found all over the world.
3. Waves change the shoreline. So do tides. They wear away the shore in one place. They build it up in another.
4. People thought the ocean floor was flat. They were wrong. Scientists explored it. They found mountains and valleys.
5. The earth quakes under the ocean. Volcanoes erupt there, too. One volcano erupted. It formed the islands of Hawaii.

Creative Writing

Vincent van Gogh, *Vincent's Bedroom at Arles*
Musée du Louvre, courtesy Réunion des Musées Nationaux

Instead of using color to show this room realistically, Vincent van Gogh has used color to express his feelings.

- How do you think van Gogh felt when he made this painting? Why do you think this? What colors did he use to show how he felt?
- What does the painting tell you about van Gogh's life at this time? Do you think he was living in the country or in the city? Why?

Activities

1. **Paint a picture with words.** Think of a room that is special to you. Describe the room as if it were a painting, not as it actually appears. Use adjectives and similes to tell how it feels to the touch, what it sounds like, what it smells like, and how it looks.

2. **Pretend you are here.** Pretend that you are coming to this room during or after a long journey. Where have you been? How do you feel when you arrive here? Why were you traveling? Can you stay here awhile? Where will you go after you leave? Is this your home? Who lives here?

Check-up: Unit 1

A Kinds of Sentences *(p. 14)* Write and punctuate each sentence. Label it *decl., int., imp., or excl.*

1. What a thrill it is to go to Washington
2. I leave here next Saturday morning
3. Have you ever been there at cherry blossom time
4. Come to the airport with me
5. I won't see you for a week after that

B Complete Subjects and Predicates *(p. 16)* Write each sentence. Draw a line between the complete subject and predicate.

6. The first excursion will be next week.
7. Both experienced and inexperienced hikers are invited.
8. Everyone should bring binoculars.
9. Flat, comfortable shoes are needed.
10. The trails can be steep and rocky.

C Simple Subjects and Predicates *(p. 18)* Write the sentences. Underline simple subjects once and simple predicates twice.

11. Japan is composed of many islands.
12. Two air currents influence the climate.
13. The northern islands can be cool in the summer.
14. Most summers are hot and humid in the south.
15. The city of Tokyo lies near the middle of Japan.

D Finding the Subject *(p. 20)* Write each simple subject.

16. How do you find the area of this triangle?
17. Please pay attention to the problem, Bob.
18. There are no tricks to this problem.
19. Is the base equal to the height?
20. Divide the product by two for the correct answer!

E Compound Subjects and Predicates *(p. 22)* Write each sentence. Underline each simple subject once and simple predicate twice. Label each compound subject and compound predicate.

21. Kathy and some other students made plans for their report.
22. They went to the library and borrowed some books.
23. Each person read one book and wrote a short summary of it.
24. The group gathered and traded ideas for their report.
25. Lin and Brad reported on the solar system and showed slides.

Combining Sentences: Compound Sentences (*p. 24*) Rewrite each pair of sentences as one compound sentence. Use the conjunction in parentheses, and add commas where necessary.

26. The swimmers gathered. A storm broke. (and)
27. Some looked glum. Others were more cheerful. (but)
28. The rain had to end. The coaches would cancel the meet. (or)
29. Many competitors had practiced long and hard. They might not get a chance to compete. (but)
30. In ten minutes the sun came out. The meet began. (and)

Conjunctions (*p. 26*) Write each conjunction.

31. Ping and I like to make big tuna sandwiches for picnics.
32. We add either grated carrots or chopped celery to the tuna.
33. The sandwiches are not only tastier but also more nutritious.
34. Both lettuce and tomatoes make bread soggy.
35. There are fancier picnic foods, yet I like tuna best.

Complex Sentences (*p. 28*) Write each complex sentence. Underline each subordinate clause once and each subordinating conjunction twice. Add commas where needed.

36. Whenever I am tired from homework I take a quick jog.
37. If I continue my work my mind wanders.
38. I dash out of the house before I grow too sleepy.
39. While I jog I don't think about my homework at all.
40. After I've jogged for ten minutes I feel refreshed.

Correcting Fragments and Run-ons (*p. 31*) Rewrite the sentences, correcting the fragments and run-ons.

41. India has a variety of climates they follow a pattern.
42. Cool, hot, and rainy seasons.
43. During the rainy summer.
44. Monsoon winds blow in from the Indian Ocean they bring rains.
45. Although the crops need rain.

Interjections (*p. 34*) Rewrite each sentence, adding one of these interjections: *golly, hey, hurrah, wow, well*. Use each only once, and capitalize and punctuate each interjection.

46. _____ Have you seen *Galaxy* yet?
47. _____ it is so exciting.
48. _____ What a terrific ending it had!
49. _____ we hardly ever see such good movies.
50. _____ We should be happy for even one.

Enrichment

Storytellers

Tell a story with two or three classmates. One person writes a simple sentence. Each person continues the story by writing another simple sentence. Take turns adding simple sentences until you finish the story. Then revise it by combining some of your sentences to make them compound.

Endangered Species

Make a chart listing three endangered species. (Possibilities include wild turkeys, Atlantic salmon, the bald eagle, the jaguar, the Indian python, and the tiger.) Read about them in an encyclopedia. For each animal, bird, fish, or reptile, write one simple sentence on each of the following: physical description, habits or characteristics, habitat, and population.

First Aid

Make a first-aid chart to hang in your kitchen. Tell about treatment for injuries that result from cooking accidents. Use your health book or a library book for reference. Divide your chart into two columns. Write *Supplies* on the left. Under this, list first-aid supplies

you should have on hand. After each item write a declarative sentence explaining its purpose. Then write *Procedures* on the right. Under this, write imperative sentences that tell what to do when an injury occurs. Illustrate your chart if you wish.

Dog Dollars

Imagine that you are a representative to the town council and that you have to raise money for the government. You propose to increase the cost of dog licenses. These currently cost $5.00, and the town issues approximately 750 a year. Make a chart showing how much you could increase the town's income if you increased the cost of dog licenses by 10%, 20%, and 30%. Then write a paragraph to read to the town council. Include a summary of the information on the chart and a statement telling the council what you recommend. Use coordinating conjunctions where possible, and underline them. Include also at least one correlative conjunction in your paragraph.

Famous People

Think of a period in American history that interests you, such as Colonial days, the Depression era, or World War II. Look up five people from that period whom you admire. Then write the following kinds of sentences about each person: (1) a declarative sentence about the most significant thing this person did; (2) an interrogative sentence about where this person lived or went to school; (3) an exclamatory sentence about why or how much you admire this person; and (4) an imperative sentence about where others can learn more about this person.

Display this information by making a chart, a poster, or a mural. You may wish to illustrate it with pictures that you have drawn or cut out of an old magazine.

Theodore Roosevelt

Harriet Tubman

Extra Practice: Unit 1

Kinds of Sentences (p. 14)

● Write *declarative, interrogative, imperative,* or *exclamatory* to describe each sentence.
Example: Why is opening night so exciting? *interrogative*
   1. An actor's voice is an important tool.
   2. Performers must learn to speak loudly and clearly.
   3. Try speaking higher, lower, louder, and softer.
   4. Could the audience understand you?
   5. Don't slam the door.
   6. Watch out for falling scenery!
   7. Can you walk like a lame duck?
   8. That was such a wonderful imitation!

▲ Write each sentence, adding the correct end punctuation. Label each sentence *declarative, interrogative, imperative,* or *exclamatory.*
Example: Mime is an expressive form of acting
              Mime is an expressive form of acting. **declarative**
   9. The actors tell their stories with gestures instead of sound
  10. Use your hands and face to show your feelings
  11. Marcel Marceau is the best known mime in the world
  12. How amazing he is
  13. Have you ever seen a mime with white face makeup
  14. Practice looking happy, angry, and surprised
  15. Can you pretend to walk and still stay in the same place
  16. I would love to learn the art of mime

■ Rewrite each sentence to make the kind of sentence shown in parentheses. Use the correct end punctuation.
Example: Was Agatha Christie a mystery writer? (declarative)
              Agatha Christie was a mystery writer.
  17. Did she write sixteen plays? (declarative)
  18. Have you seen *The Mousetrap*? (imperative)
  19. It is London's longest-running play. (interrogative)
  20. I know what a "red herring" is. (interrogative)
  21. That was an obvious clue. (exclamatory)
  22. Did the butler do it? (exclamatory)
  23. Is Miss Marple your favorite character? (declarative)
  24. Can you picture what she looks like? (imperative)

2 | Complete Subjs. and Preds. (p. 16)

● Write each sentence. Draw a line between the complete subject and the complete predicate.

Example: About one hundred million Americans ride bicycles.

About one hundred million Americans|ride bicycles.

1. Bicycles are found almost everywhere.
2. Many city streets have special lanes for bicycles.
3. The earliest bicycle was made of wood.
4. A different bicycle appeared in the 1880s.
5. It was called the high-wheeler.
6. This bicycle had a huge front wheel and a small rear wheel.
7. Bicycles became very popular in the 1880s.
8. The popularity of cars caused a decline in bicycle riding.

▲ Write each sentence. Draw a line between the complete subject and the complete predicate.

Example: The popular bicycle can be seen all over the world.

The popular bicycle|can be seen all over the world.

9. Many people ride bicycles today for exercise.
10. The Olympic games include bicycling as an event.
11. The parts of a bicycle have now become more complicated.
12. The basic design of the bicycle has not changed, however.
13. Bicycles all over the world have as many as ten speeds.
14. The United States is full of bicycles of all sizes.
15. Other countries with many bike riders are China and France.

■ Write *complete subject, complete predicate,* or *sentence* to describe each group of words. Write each incomplete sentence, adding a subject or a predicate to make it complete. Draw a line between the complete subject and the complete predicate.

Example: Bicycle competitions.

complete subject *Bicycle competitions|are popular.*

16. Most bicycle races.
17. Are held on public roads and highways.
18. Often cover more than fifty miles.
19. Special bicycles are used.
20. The annual *Tour de France.*
21. The name of the most popular road race of all.
22. Cyclists race through the French countryside.
23. Another European road race is the race from Paris to Brussels.
24. People ride from twenty-five hundred to three thousand miles in twenty-one days.

3 | Simple Subjs. and Preds. (p. 18)

● The complete subject and the complete predicate are separated by a line in each sentence. Write the simple subject and the simple predicate for each sentence.

Example: People in Colonial times|ate one big hot meal a day.

   People   ate

1. Dinner|was their main meal.
2. They|ate it in the early afternoon.
3. Hot, healthy food|gave workers energy for the afternoon.
4. Supper|was the last meal of the day.
5. The usual supper|was bread and soup.
6. Workers in the 1830s|did not have time for big midday meals.
7. A quick lunch at noon|became more common.
8. Twentieth-century workers|have also adopted this custom.
9. Most people|now eat a big hot meal at night.

▲ Write each sentence. Draw a line between the complete subject and the complete predicate. Underline the simple subject once and the simple predicate twice.

Example: The style of breakfast has changed over the years.

   The style of breakfast|has changed over the years.

10. A colonial breakfast was often oatmeal or mush.
11. Mush was made with cornmeal and hot milk.
12. Large breakfasts were once popular.
13. Such meals included fruit, eggs, meat, potatoes, and toast.
14. People of today may not have time for big breakfasts.
15. Many people are also choosing foods with fewer calories.
16. A healthful meal at the start of the day is important.
17. A well-balanced breakfast will give you energy for hours.
18. You might include juice, cereal, milk, and eggs in your meal.

■ Rewrite the sentences, expanding each subject and predicate with additional words and phrases. Then underline the simple subject once and the simple predicate twice.

Example: Colonists farmed.

   The early Colonists farmed the land.

19. They harvested wheat.
20. Corn grew.
21. Coal was used.
22. Cattle grazed.
23. People labored.
24. Disease existed.
25. Times have changed.
26. Machinery was invented.
27. Oil is used.
28. Medicine has improved.

4 | Finding the Subject (p. 20)

● Write the simple subject of each sentence. If the subject *you* is understood, write *(you)*.

Example: Lying on my desk is a notebook. *notebook*

1. Under it is a book.
2. Hand it to me, please.
3. On the cover is a frightening picture.
4. Here is the title of the book.
5. Is it *Dr. Jekyll and Mr. Hyde*?
6. Have you read this book by Robert Louis Stevenson?
7. There are other good books by the same author.
8. Lying on that table is another book.
9. When did Stevenson write?

▲ Write the simple subject of each sentence. If the subject *you* is understood, write *(you)*.

Example: Did Stevenson write in the late 1800s? *Stevenson*

10. Where do you keep your adventure stories?
11. In that bookcase are several novels.
12. Show me one of the books, please.
13. Here is a well-known book by Stevenson.
14. Sitting next to it is a copy of another good book.
15. Read *Treasure Island* soon.
16. There are many great scenes of adventure in it.
17. Is *Kidnapped* your favorite book by Stevenson?
18. In that book David Balfour tells his story.

■ Rewrite each sentence, following the directions in parentheses. Change the word order if necessary. Write the simple subject.

Example: Three books are on your desk.   (Begin with *There.*)
          There are three books on your desk. books

19. Two more books are on the chair.   (Begin with *On.*)
20. You have read all of them.   (Make interrogative.)
21. You should finish them one at a time.   (Make imperative.)
22. You have a favorite author.   (Make interrogative with *Do.*)
23. You should read many different authors for variety. (Make imperative.)
24. My library card is in my wallet.   (Begin with *In.*)
25. A reading room is located in the library.   (Begin with *Located.*)
26. The library closes at nine.   (Make interrogative with *When.*)
27. You shouldn't stay too late.   (Make imperative.)
28. The library is closed on Saturday.   (Make interrogative.)

5 | Compound Subjs. and Preds. (p. 22)

● Write the sentences. Underline the compound subjects once and the compound predicates twice.

Example: Washington and Lincoln were born in February.

    Washington and Lincoln were born in February.

1. The day and the year were different, of course.
2. Lincoln became President in 1861 and was in office until 1865.
3. Lincoln was shot and killed in 1865.
4. We might not recognize or understand those times.
5. There were fewer people and no cars.
6. Were the East and the West connected by telegraph in 1861?
7. Thirteen stripes and thirty-three stars were on the flag.
8. Did the Civil War begin and end in the 1860s?

▲ Write each sentence. Underline each simple subject once and each simple predicate twice. Then label the sentences *compound subject* or *compound predicate* or *both*.

Example: Has Ada or Don written or spoken about Lincoln?

    Has Ada or Don written or spoken about Lincoln?   both

9. Lincoln's boyhood was hard but does not seem unusual for then.
10. His parents were farmers and lived in a log cabin.
11. Lincoln first lived in Kentucky but moved to Indiana.
12. There were few schools or books in those days.
13. Lincoln and other children studied alone and wrote on boards.
14. He chopped wood for the fire and split logs for fences.
15. Lincoln and his wife had four sons.
16. Lincoln's speeches and letters are famous for their style.

■ Rewrite each sentence. Add one or more subjects or predicates to make a compound subject or a compound predicate. Underline each simple subject once and simple predicate twice.

Example: Pioneer men in Lincoln's day grew their food.

    Pioneer men and women in Lincoln's day grew their food.

17. Long hours of work did not bother these frontiersmen.
18. Laboring in the fields were children of all ages.
19. Oxen dragged plows through the soil.
20. Horses were the primary means of transportation.
21. There were few railroads until the 1850s.
22. Many novels have been written about pioneer life.
23. Families in covered wagons traveled west.
24. Can you imagine a world without modern technology?

6 | Combining: Compound Sentences (p. 24)

● Write *simple* or *compound* to describe each sentence.
   Example: Mr. Wu travels often, and he is now in Greece.   *compound*
   1. Greece is a small country, but it has a long history.
   2. Ancient Greece has greatly influenced our way of life.
   3. Artists and scientists lived in Greece three thousand years ago.
   4. The writers were brilliant, and we still read their works.
   5. Boys but not girls went to school in ancient Greece.
   6. The Greeks were athletic and loved sports.
   7. Every town had a place for sports, and people gathered there.
   8. Government by the people began there, and all of the citizens were active in it.

▲ Write each pair of sentences as a compound sentence. Use the conjunction in parentheses. Add commas where necessary.
   Example: Olympic games may seem modern. They are very old.   (but)
      Olympic games may seem modern, but they are very old.
   9. These games began in 776 B.C. They are still popular.   (and)
   10. The Olympics began in Olympia, Greece. Citizens from all parts of Greece participated.   (and)
   11. There were only four races at first. Other sports were introduced later.   (but)
   12. Winners received wreaths. Celebrations were held.   (and)
   13. The Olympics are now held every four years. People from many countries attend.   (and)
   14. Athletes from at least twelve nations must enter an event. The event will not be held.   (or)
   15. Can the participants be professional athletes? Must they be amateurs?   (or)

■ Add a sentence to each simple sentence to form a compound sentence. Use the conjunctions *and*, *but*, and *or* at least once.
   Example: Greece is a beautiful country.
      Greece is a beautiful country, and thousands of tourists go there every year.
   16. Have you ever traveled to a foreign country?
   17. A trip to a foreign land can be very educational.
   18. There are many fascinating customs in every nation.
   19. Faraway places interest most of us.
   20. Our lives have been influenced by foreign cultures.
   21. Many English words have Greek or Latin roots.
   22. We eat many different foods from other lands.

7 | Conjunctions (p. 26)

● Write the coordinating or correlative conjunctions from each sentence.

Example: A camel can go for weeks not only without food but also without water. *not only . . . but also*

1. The camel's hump does not carry water, but it stores fat.
2. A camel can hear but often disregards commands.
3. Camels are sometimes mean, yet they can be very gentle.
4. Camels may bite or spit at their masters.
5. A camel will lie down and refuse to carry a heavy load.
6. Not only one but three sets of eyelashes protect the camel's eyes.

▲ Write the best coordinating and correlative conjunctions to complete these sentences. Some sentences have more than one answer.

Example: Gorillas eat leaves, buds, barks, _____ fruits. *and*

7. Gorillas have broad shoulders, long arms, _____ short legs.
8. Gorillas look fierce, _____ they are actually shy.
9. They like companionship _____ attention.
10. A gorilla will harm a human only if provoked _____ attacked.
11. Gorillas make nests _____ on the ground _____ in trees.
12. Gorillas are not too intelligent, _____ a gorilla named Koko has been taught sign language.
13. Young gorillas wrestle each other _____ swing from vines.

■ Combine each set of sentences to form one sentence. Use an appropriate conjunction to connect compound parts. Add commas where necessary.

Example: The protection of wild animals is necessary. Management of their environment is necessary too.
The protection of wild animals and the management of their environment are necessary.

14. Certain species of animals are diminishing. Certain species are becoming extinct.
15. The destruction of habitat threatens wildlife. The reduction of animals' food supply threatens wildlife.
16. The pollution of water harms animals. The pollution of air harms them too.
17. We must practice conservation efforts. We will lose many of our natural resources.
18. Land animals are in danger of extinction. Sea animals are in danger of extinction. Birds are in danger of extinction.

8 | Complex Sentences (p. 28)

● Write the subordinate clause from each complex sentence.
Example: Although some people dislike cities, others are happy there.
Although some people dislike cities

1. Some people enjoy a city where life is constantly busy.
2. When you live in a big city, you can always find entertainment.
3. People and traffic surround you wherever you go.
4. You can browse as you walk along the street.
5. After the sun goes down, the lights of the city sparkle.
6. As long as you don't mind noise, you will enjoy city life.
7. The city is also exciting unless you prefer peace and quiet.
8. If you had a choice, would you live there or in the country?

▲ Write each complex sentence. Underline the subordinate clause once. Underline the subordinating conjunction twice. Add a comma where necessary.
Example: After the leaves change color they fall from the trees.
After the leaves change color, they fall from the trees.

9. The countryside in New England is beautiful when all the leaves have turned.
10. Although the color of the leaves changes the brightness of the color depends on the weather.
11. When the weather is sunny and cool the colors are very bright.
12. If the weather is warm and wet the colors are muddy and dull.
13. As the leaves begin to die the green color breaks down.
14. The hidden yellow or orange-red appears after this has happened.
15. The red maple received its name because its leaves are bright red especially in the fall.

■ Write a complex sentence by adding a subordinate clause to each sentence. Use appropriate subordinating conjunctions and underline them. Add commas where necessary.
Example: Ida lived on a farm.
Before she went to Chicago, Ida lived on a farm.

16. Her father preferred the country.
17. The family visited the nearby city often.
18. Everyone always enjoyed the visits.
19. The family also welcomed the peace of the country.
20. The nights were peaceful and quiet there.
21. Ida took a job in the city.
22. Would you prefer to live in the city or in the country?

9 | Fragments and Run-ons (p. 31)

● Label each item *fragment, run-on,* or *sentence.*
  Example: Made up of rocks or the remains of animals.   ***fragment***
  1. If you see very black soil.
  2. Most of the land on Earth is covered with soil.
  3. Plants and crops grow on it, soil produces most of our food.
  4. Although soil is deep in some places, it is shallow in others.
  5. When you are in Georgia.
  6. Each layer of soil has color and thickness.
  7. Dead plants decompose.
  8. A mixture of soil and sand makes sandy loam, it is good for grow-
     ing some kinds of plants.

▲ **(9-19)**   Rewrite the passage to correct all fragments and run-ons.
  Example: Soil supports the growth of plants, it is important.
           Soil supports the growth of plants. It is important.
If the soil cannot produce good crops. Not enough food will be produced. Rain and wind wash soil away, it takes a long time to make
more. Rocks become softer over the years, they break down into
soil. Wind blows sand against rocks, the rocks wear down slowly.
When a river runs over rocks for years. Wears them away. Water
freezes in cracks in rocks. And it breaks the rocks, this is called
weathering. These pieces of rock get smaller, they become part of the
soil. Wind, water, or glaciers carry soil from one place to another.

■ **(20-28)**   Rewrite the passage to correct all fragments and
run-ons.
  Example: Although we depend on soil to grow food. We have not
           always taken proper care of it.
           *Although we depend on soil to grow food, we have not
           always taken proper care of it.*
Soil is built up over hundreds of years. But rain and wind can carry
it away quickly. The early colonists and later pioneers did not know
how to care for the soil. They grew crop after crop on the same soil
they failed to fertilize it. When they cleared land for their farms.
They cut down trees that had protected soil from water and wind,
more recently farmers plowed down grassland and replaced it with
wheat they also damaged the soil. Grass keeps soil from being blown
away by the wind. We must protect our supply of good soil. Or our
food supply will be affected.

10 | Interjections (p. 34)

● Write the interjections.

Example: Oh dear, I'm always so nervous before a performance.
Oh dear

1. Shh! The curtain is about to go up.
2. Oh no, I lost my wig!
3. Good grief! You'll miss your entrance!
4. Hey! Someone help look for her wig.
5. Phew, that was a close call.
6. Well, let's hope nothing else unexpected happens.
7. Ugh! Something always seems to go wrong.
8. Ah, you should always expect the unexpected.
9. Goodness, I didn't expect anything like that to happen.
10. Oh well, worse things than that could happen.

▲ Rewrite each sentence, adding the correct punctuation. Underline each interjection.

Example: Oh I hope I get the part! <u>Oh!</u> *I hope I get the part.*

11. Hey are you going to try out for the school play?
12. Oh yes I want the lead role.
13. Hooray I'll be a star at last.
14. Oh no Spare me the details for a change.
15. Well I'll try to keep my head on straight.
16. Goodness I will never memorize this speech.
17. Wow this scenery is really quite heavy.
18. Shh I'm trying to learn my lines before morning.
19. Bravo You got them right finally.

■ Rewrite each sentence adding an appropriate interjection from the box. Punctuate and capitalize your sentences correctly.

Example: You are a very good actor.
Bravo! You are a very good actor.

20. Pay attention to me.
21. Think about the personality of your character.
22. I can't say the line that way.
23. I don't understand this speech.
24. Why would your character say that?
25. I understand this now!
26. I'll speak these lines in a deep voice.
27. Your gestures added a lot to this scene.
28. That was really terrific.

| aha |
| okay |
| bravo |
| hey |
| well |
| no |
| oh yes |
| goodness |
| wow |
| hooray |

O ne afternoon, I took another
way home, a way that brought me through Market Street.
Market Street was where all the stores were, and I
passed by slowly, staring into the shop windows. . . . What
I was really looking at was my own reflection in the
glass, though it was a while before I knew that.

Jamaica Kincaid
from *Annie John*

Personal Narrative

Getting Ready Did you ever catch sight of your reflection in a mirror and, for a moment, not recognize yourself? That is probably as close as you can get to seeing yourself as others see you—as a stranger! You know yourself best, and the things you know most about are those that you have experienced. You may not have had earth-shaking adventures, but you have interesting stories to tell. Other people will want to hear them. In this unit you will read a personal narrative and you will write one of your own. Start thinking now about the kind of experience you'd like to share.

ACTIVITIES

Listening Listen as the excerpt on the opposite page is read. It is taken from the middle of a personal narrative. What does it tell you about the writer? What kinds of questions does it leave unanswered?

Speaking Look at the picture. What is this girl thinking about? Has something in the window caught her eye, or is she daydreaming? Will she notice her reflection?

Writing Try to put this girl's thoughts into words. In your journal, write what you imagine she is thinking.

The Road Not Taken

By Robert Frost

Two roads diverged in a yellow wood,
And sorry I could not travel both
And be one traveler, long I stood
And looked down one as far as I could
To where it bent in the undergrowth;

Then took the other, as just as fair,
And having perhaps the better claim,
Because it was grassy and wanted wear;
Though as for that, the passing there
Had worn them really about the same,

And both that morning equally lay
In leaves no step had trodden black.
Oh, I kept the first for another day!
Yet knowing how way leads on to way,
I doubted if I should ever come back.

I shall be telling this with a sigh
Somewhere ages and ages hence:
Two roads diverged in a wood, and I—
I took the one less traveled by,
And that has made all the difference.

Think and Discuss

1. What choice does the traveler face? What decision does he make?

2. A **symbol** is something that represents something else. The Statue of Liberty, for example, represents freedom and democracy. A storm can represent anger; a rock can stand for strength. In "The Road Not Taken," Frost uses the two roads as a symbol. What do the two roads stand for?

3. Frost's poem is divided into four stanzas. A **stanza** is a section of at least two lines of a poem. Usually stanzas follow the same pattern of rhythm and rhyme, and each stanza often expresses one main idea. With each stanza, the poet leads the reader closer to the meaning of the whole poem. What is the main idea in each stanza of "The Road Not Taken"? Explain the poet's ideas in your own words.

4. The speaker doubts that he will ever come back to try the other road. Do you think decisions are always final? Explain your answer.

Is there any hope for a boy with "no gumption"?

Growing Up

By Russell Baker

I began working in journalism when I was eight years old. It was my mother's idea. She wanted me to "make something" of myself and, after a level-headed appraisal of my strengths, decided I had better start young if I was to have any chance of keeping up with the competition.

The flaw in my character which she had already spotted was lack of "gumption." My idea of a perfect afternoon was lying in front of the radio rereading my favorite Big Little Book, *Dick Tracy Meets Stooge Viller*. My mother despised inactivity. Seeing me having a good time in repose, she was powerless to hide her disgust. "You've got no more gumption than a bump on a log," she said. "Get out in the kitchen and help Doris do those dirty dishes."

My sister Doris, though two years younger than I, had enough gumption for a dozen people. She positively enjoyed washing dishes, making beds, and cleaning the house. When she was only seven she could carry a piece of short-weighted cheese back to the store, threaten the manager with legal action, and come back triumphantly with the full quarter-pound we'd paid for and a few ounces extra thrown in for forgiveness. Doris could have made something of herself if she hadn't been a girl. Because of this defect, however, the best she could hope for was a career as a nurse or schoolteacher, the only work that capable females were considered up to in those days.

This must have saddened my mother, this twist of fate that had allocated all the gumption to the daughter and left her with a son who was content with Dick Tracy and Stooge Viller.

Fifty years ago parents still asked boys if they wanted to grow up to be President, and asked it not jokingly but seriously. Many parents who were hardly more than paupers still believed their sons could do it. Abraham Lincoln had done it. We were only sixty-five years from Lincoln. Many a grandfather who walked among us could remember Lincoln's time. Men of grandfatherly age were the worst for asking if you wanted to grow up to be President. A surprising number of little boys said yes and meant it.

I was asked many times myself. No, I would say, I didn't want to grow up to be President. My mother was present during one of these interrogations. An elderly uncle, having posed the usual question and exposed my lack of interest in the Presidency, asked, "Well, what *do* you want to be when you grow up?"

I loved to pick through trash piles and collect empty bottles, tin cans with pretty labels, and discarded magazines. The most desirable job on earth sprang instantly to mind. "I want to be a garbage man," I said.

My uncle smiled, but my mother had seen the first distressing evidence of a bump budding on a log. "Have a little gumption, Russell," she said. Her calling me Russell was a signal of unhappiness. When she approved of me I was always "Buddy."

When I turned eight years old she decided that the job of starting me on the road toward making something of myself could no longer be safely delayed. "Buddy," she said one day, "I want you to come home right after school this afternoon. Somebody's coming and I want you to meet him."

When I burst in that afternoon she was in conference in the parlor with an executive of the Curtis Publishing Company. She introduced me. He bent low from the waist and shook my hand. Was it true as my mother had told him, he asked, that I longed for the opportunity to conquer the world of business?

My mother replied that I was blessed with a rare determination to make something of myself.

"That's right," I whispered.

"But have you got the grit, the character, the never-say-quit spirit it takes to succeed in business?"

My mother said I certainly did.

"That's right," I said.

Again he studied me as though debating whether I was worthy of a knighthood. Finally: "Are you trustworthy?"

My mother said I was the soul of honesty.

"That's right," I said.

The caller smiled for the first time. He told me I was a lucky young man. He admired my spunk. Too many young men thought life was all play. Those young men would not go far in this world. Only a young man willing to work and save and keep his face washed and his hair neatly combed could hope to come out on top in a world such as ours. Did I truly and sincerely believe that I was such a young man?

"He certainly does," said my mother.

"That's right," I said.

He said he had been so impressed by what he had seen of me that he was going to make me a representative of the Curtis Publishing Company. On the following Tuesday, he said, thirty freshly printed copies of the *Saturday Evening Post* would be delivered at our door. I would place these magazines, still damp with the ink of the presses, in a handsome canvas bag, sling it over my shoulder, and set forth through the streets to bring the best in journalism, fiction, and cartoons to the American public.

The following Tuesday I raced home from school, put the canvas bag over my shoulder, dumped the magazines in, and, tilting to the left to balance their weight on my right hip, embarked on the highway of journalism.

We lived in Belleville, New Jersey, a commuter town at the northern fringe of Newark. It was 1932, the bleakest year of the Depression. My father had died two years before, leaving us with a few pieces of furniture and not much else, and my mother had taken Doris and me to live with one of her younger brothers. This was my Uncle Allen. Uncle Allen had made something of himself by 1932. As salesman for a soft-drink bottler in Newark, he had an income of $30 a week; wore pearl-gray spats, detachable collars, and a three-piece suit; was happily married; and took in threadbare relatives.

With my load of magazines I headed toward Belleville Avenue. That's where the people were. There were two filling stations at the intersection with Union Avenue, as well as a grocery, a fruit stand, a bakery, a barber shop, Zuccarelli's drugstore, and a diner shaped like a railroad car. For several hours I made myself highly visible, shifting position now and then from corner to corner, from shop window to shop window, to make sure everyone could see the heavy black lettering on the canvas bag that said *The Saturday Evening Post*. When the angle of the light indicated it was suppertime, I walked back to the house.

I told my mother I'd changed my mind about wanting to succeed in the magazine business.

"If you think I'm going to raise a good-for-nothing," she replied, "you've got another think coming." She told me to hit the streets with the canvas bag and start ringing doorbells the instant school was out next day.

And so I set forth with my sack of magazines. I was afraid of the dogs that snarled behind the doors of potential buyers. I was timid about ringing the doorbells of strangers, relieved when no one came to the door, and scared when someone did. Despite my mother's instructions, I could not deliver an engaging sales pitch. When a door opened I simply asked, "Want to buy a *Saturday Evening Post*?" In Belleville few persons did. It was a town of 30,000 people, and most weeks I rang a fair majority of its doorbells. But I rarely sold my thirty copies. Some weeks I canvassed the entire town for six days and still had four or five unsold magazines on Monday evening; then I dreaded the coming of Tuesday morning, when a batch of thirty fresh *Saturday Evening Posts* was due at the front door.

One rainy night when car windows were sealed against me I came back soaked and with not a single sale to report. My mother beckoned to Doris.

"Go back down there with Buddy and show him how to sell these magazines," she said.

Brimming with zest, Doris, who was then seven years old, returned with me to the corner. She took a magazine from the bag, and when the light turned red she strode to the nearest car and banged her small fist against the closed window. The driver, probably startled at what he took to be an assault on his car, lowered the window to stare, and Doris thrust a *Saturday Evening Post* at him.

"You need this magazine," she piped, "and it only costs a nickel."

Her salesmanship was irresistible. Before the light changed half a dozen times she disposed of the entire batch. I didn't feel humiliated. To the contrary. I was so happy I decided to give her a treat. Leading her to the vegetable store on Belleville Avenue, I bought three apples, which cost a nickel, and gave her one.

"You shouldn't waste money," she said.

"Eat your apple." I bit into mine.

"You shouldn't eat before supper," she said. "It'll spoil your appetite."

Back at the house that evening, she dutifully reported me for wasting a nickel. Instead of a scolding, I was rewarded with a pat on the back for having the good sense to buy fruit instead of candy. My mother reached into her bottomless supply of maxims and told Doris, "An apple a day keeps the doctor away."

By the time I was ten I had learned all my mother's maxims by heart. Asking to stay up past normal bedtime, I knew that a refusal would be explained with, "Early to bed and early to rise, makes a man healthy, wealthy, and wise." If I whimpered about having to get up early in the morning, I could depend on her to say, "The early bird gets the worm."

The one I most despised was, "If at first you don't succeed, try, try again." This was the battle cry with which she constantly sent me back into the hopeless struggle whenever I moaned that I had rung every doorbell in town and knew there wasn't a single potential buyer left in Belleville that week. After listening to my explanation, she handed me the canvas bag and said, "If at first you don't succeed . . ."

Three years in that job, which I would gladly have quit after the first day except for her insistence, produced at least one valuable result. My mother finally concluded that I would never make something of myself by pursuing a life in business and started considering careers that demanded less competitive zeal.

One evening when I was eleven I brought home a short "composition" on my summer vacation which the teacher had graded with an A. Reading it with her own schoolteacher's eye, my mother agreed that it was top-drawer seventh grade prose and complimented me. Nothing more was said about it immediately, but a new idea had taken life in her mind. Halfway through supper she suddenly interrupted the conversation.

"Buddy," she said, "maybe you could be a writer."

I clasped the idea to my heart. I had never met a writer, had shown no previous urge to write, and hadn't a notion how to become a writer, but I loved stories and thought that making up stories must surely be almost as much fun as reading them. Best of all, though, and what really gladdened my heart, was the ease of the writer's life. Writers did not have to trudge through the town peddling from canvas bags, defending themselves against angry dogs, being rejected by surly strangers. Writers did not have to ring doorbells. So far as I could make out, what writers did couldn't even be classified as work.

I was enchanted. Writers didn't have to have any gumption at all. I did not dare tell anybody for fear of being laughed at in the schoolyard, but secretly I decided that what I'd like to be when I grew up was a writer.

Think and Discuss

1. How does the author let us know that the boy with "no gumption" might succeed someday?
2. The author lets us get to know Russell's mother through her words and her actions. What is she like? Find three examples of words or actions that support your impression of her.
3. Russell Baker did grow up to be a well-known writer. The selection you have just read is from his book of the same title, *Growing Up*. The book is an **autobiography** —a true story of the author's own life. Near the beginning of his autobiography, Baker gives his reasons for writing the book: "I thought that someday my own children would . . . want to know what the world was like when my mother was young and I was younger . . ." What might be some other reasons why people write autobiographies?

the drum
By Nikki Giovanni

daddy says the world is
a drum tight and hard
and i told him
i'm gonna beat
out my own rhythm

Think and Discuss

1. The speaker uses the poem to tell something about her-self. Give your impression of the speaker. Do you think you would like her? Tell why or why not.
2. What does the drum stand for in the poem?
3. Poetry is meant to be read aloud. The **sound** of a poem brings out the poem's meaning. For example, a love poem often has soft, gentle sounds, and an angry poem often sounds harsh.

   The sound of a poem depends on
   a. the **rhythm**—the pattern of accented and unac-cented beats
   b. the **sounds of the words** themselves

   In this poem, the words *tight* and *hard* sound like what they mean. They are short, quick, and closed. Read "the drum" aloud. Listen to the length and sounds of the words and to the rhythm of the poem. How do they fit the poem's meaning?

RESPONDING TO LITERATURE

The Reading and Writing Connection

Personal response Write about a time when you faced a choice, like the traveler did in "The Road Not Taken." Your choice may have been any kind of choice—important, easy, or even silly. Tell what you decided and what happened as a result.

Creative writing The speaker in one poem you read is "gonna beat out my own rhythm." The speaker in the other poem takes the road "less traveled." Write a poem or essay about someone you know who does not follow the crowd —someone who strikes you as a true individual.

Creative Activities

Make a collage Choose one stanza from "The Road Not Taken." Using magazine pictures, make a collage that expresses the main idea of those lines. Show either what the poet describes or how the idea relates to your own life.

Read aloud Practice reading aloud "the drum" and the last stanza of "The Road Not Taken" until you can recite them from memory. Be sure to make your pace, rhythm, and tone of voice fit the meaning of what you are saying. Be prepared to recite the poem or stanza to the class.

Vocabulary

Look up the word *autobiography*. What are its three parts? How do they explain its meaning? From what you have learned about *autobiography,* figure out the parts and meanings of *automobile* and *autograph*. Check the meanings in a dictionary.

Looking Ahead

Personal narrative Many writers keep a journal, or diary, of their lives. They gather story ideas from their journals. In the lessons that follow, you will be writing a story about yourself. Start keeping a journal of your own thoughts, memories, and activities.

VOCABULARY CONNECTION
Denotation and Connotation

When you write, you need to be aware of the two kinds of meanings of the words you use. The **denotation** of a word is the meaning that you would find in your dictionary. The **connotation** of a word is the feeling or mental picture that people associate with that word.

> Writers did not have to **trudge** through the town peddling from canvas bags, defending themselves against angry dogs, being rejected by surly strangers.
>
> *from "Growing Up" by Russell Baker*

- What mental picture or feeling does *trudge* suggest?
- How does that picture change if you replace *trudge* with *stroll*?
- How does it change if you replace *trudge* with *walk*?

The words *trudge, stroll,* and *walk* have different connotations. *Trudge* has a negative connotation. It makes you think about walking with great effort, perhaps walking when you are very tired. *Stroll* suggests a positive connotation, walking because you feel like it. *Walk* is neither positive nor negative. Its connotation is neutral.

Think carefully about the connotations of the words you use. Connotations can have an important effect on your writing and the meaning that a word conveys to your reader.

Vocabulary Practice

A. Write each word in the pairs below. Label each one *positive* or *negative* to describe its connotation.

1. notorious, famous
2. debate, quarrel
3. instantly, hastily
4. odor, fragrance
5. snoop, investigate
6. attract, lure

B. For each of the following words from "Growing Up," write a word that has a similar denotation but a different connotation. You may use your Thesaurus Plus. Then write a sentence for each word in the pair.

7. exposed   8. spunk   9. sad   10. rejected

Prewriting
Personal Narrative

Listening and Speaking:
Signals of Meaning

When people speak or read aloud, they rely not only on words but also on voice, hand, face, and posture signals to get across their meaning. For example, imagine that you are hearing Russell Baker read this passage about his mother.

> Seeing me having a good time in repose, she was powerless to hide her disgust. "You've got no more gumption than a bump on a log," she said. "Get out in the kitchen and help Doris do those dirty dishes."
>
> *from* Growing Up *by Russell Baker*

- When he reached his mother's dialogue, might Baker's tone of voice have changed? his expression?
- What gestures might Baker have used as he read his mother's words?

Guides for Using and Detecting Signals of Meaning

1. Use gestures, facial expressions, and stance to convey meaning, and pay attention to these when you listen to a speaker. An arm movement may signal an important point; a serious or smiling face shows feeling or attitude.
2. Use changes in your speaking pace and volume to get your meaning across, and notice these changes when you listen to a speaker. The changes can be used to signal a new subject or to emphasize an important point.
3. Use the tone of your voice to indicate meaning, and pay attention to a speaker's tone. The same words spoken in a different tone can have a different meaning. For example, the sentence "Look at this!" can signal delight, anger, or wonder, depending on the speaker's voice.

Prewriting Practice

With a partner, take turns telling a personal experience. Use gestures, facial expressions, posture, pace, volume, and tone to signal your meaning. Take notes on your partner's signals.

Listening and Speaking **65**

Thinking: Sequencing

Sequential or **chronological order** is the order in which events happen. A personal narrative usually presents a set of events in sequential order. Sometimes order words are used to make the sequence clear.

> One evening when I was eleven I brought home a short "composition" on my summer vacation which the teacher had graded with an A. Reading it with her own schoolteacher's eye, my mother agreed that it was top-drawer seventh grade prose and complimented me. Nothing more was said about it immediately, but a new idea had taken life in her mind. Halfway through supper she suddenly interrupted the conversation.
>
> *from* Growing Up *by Russell Baker*

The words *when, immediately, halfway,* and *suddenly* tell you the order of events. But writers do not always use order words.

> I would place these magazines, still damp with the ink of the presses, in a handsome canvas bag, sling it over my shoulder, and set forth through the streets to bring the best in journalism, fiction, and cartoons to the American public.
>
> *from* Growing Up *by Russell Baker*

- What was the sequence of events?

Guidelines for Sequencing

1. Fit each event into the narrative. Determine that each event leads logically to the next.
2. Use order words if they are necessary to make the sequence perfectly clear.

Prewriting Practice

What challenging experience did you have as a child? List the events in sequential order. Then write each event on a slip of paper. Give the slips to a partner and see if he or she can arrange them in sequential order. Discuss reasons for any mistakes.

Composition Skills
Personal Narrative

Writing a Good Beginning ☑

> I began working in journalism when I was eight years old.
> *from* Growing Up *by Russell Baker*

Were you surprised by the first sentence in "Growing Up"? How many eight-year-olds are "in journalism"? Baker's opening sentence succeeds in its purpose—to capture your interest.

A story can begin in different ways. Whatever the beginning, it must catch the readers' attention and make them want to read on.

Here are some different ways to begin a story. All of them are from the book *Growing Up* by Russell Baker.

1. Start with details about the setting.

> Ep Ahalt's farm looked down across sloping cornfields toward a small village a quarter mile to the south.

This sentence gives a clear picture of a graceful country landscape. Like the opening shot in a movie, it draws you into the story by showing you where the action will begin.

2. Start with an action.

> Uncle Hal arrived in the night with three boards. This was after Uncle Allen had moved us to New Street, . . .

Who could resist finding out more about this strange arrival? Starting with an action makes the reader wonder why it happened and what will follow.

3. Start with dialogue.

> "Something will come along."
> That became my mother's battle cry as I plowed into the final year of high school.

Opening with dialogue sweeps the reader right into the story. At the same time, the reader may learn something about the character and perhaps about the plot.

4. Start with details about yourself or someone else in the story.

> For my mother, a trip outside Ida Rebecca's territory was worth a little risk.

This opening statement gives you a hint about a relationship between two characters in the story. You read on to find out just what the problem is.

5. Start in the middle or at the end of the plot.

> At the age of eighty, my mother had her last bad fall, and after that her mind wandered free through time.

This sentence begins the book. From here, the story jumps backward to a time when Baker's mother was much younger. Jumping from the present to the past in a story is called a **flashback**. Baker uses a flashback to show how the past ties in with the present.

6. Start with a general statement.

> The thrill of a new life in a home of our own in Baltimore was short-lived.

This is a general statement about a period of time. It makes a good opening sentence because it raises a question in the reader's mind: What spoiled Russell's happiness?

Prewriting Practice

Read the following summary of a story.

> My friend Duane and I were riding our bikes to the park on a nice summer evening. Near the playground a car sped toward us and swerved. It jumped the curb, knocked over a sign, hit someone, and raced off. I stayed with the woman, who was hurt but conscious, while Duane went for help. The police arrived and questioned us, and an ambulance rushed off with the woman. My heart raced— I had never seen an accident before.

What kind of beginning would you add to this story? Write three different beginnings. Then exchange beginnings with a partner. Discuss which is best and why.

Supplying Details ☑

Good writers *show* rather than *tell*. They do this by supplying the reader with details about places, people, things, and events. In "Growing Up," Baker *could* have said, "My mother arranged for me to be interviewed by a magazine salesman, but she did all the talking." Instead, he *shows* his mother arranging the meeting, handling the interview, and stating her opinions firmly. By supplying these details, Baker lets us see for ourselves what happened.

Baker also shows what he was like as a boy. Why is the second sentence below better at showing Baker's "lack of gumption"?

1. I wasn't very active. Whenever I could, I just lay around and read.

2. My idea of a perfect afternoon was lying in front of the radio and rereading my favorite Big Little Book, *Dick Tracy Meets Stooge Viller.*

from Growing Up *by Russell Baker*

The second example is better because it *shows* rather than tells what Baker was doing. It provides details that allow you to picture him in the scene.

Prewriting Practice

A. Think of a person you have known. *Show* what that person is like by writing two or more details for each of the following.

1. The person's appearance
2. Something the person would be likely to do
3. Something the person would be likely to say

B. The following sentences *tell* about something that happened. Replace each one with two or three sentences that use details to *show* what happened.

1. Brad got angry when the door wouldn't open.
2. The car came up the street too fast.
3. It was a great day for the game.
4. Kathryn nearly fell out of the tree.
5. The singers were wearing crazy outfits.

The Grammar Connection

Varying Sentence Length

One way to make your writing flow smoothly is by varying the lengths of your sentences. Too many short sentences in a row can make a paragraph sound choppy. A series of long sentences can be hard to follow. Read these two paragraphs.

> **1.** I was enchanted. Writers didn't have to have any gumption at all. I didn't dare tell anybody. I was afraid of being laughed at in the schoolyard. Secretly I decided what I'd be when I grew up. I would be a writer.

> **2.** I was enchanted. Writers didn't have to have any gumption at all. I did not dare tell anybody for fear of being laughed at in the schoolyard, but secretly I decided that what I'd like to be when I grew up was a writer.

> *from* Growing Up *by Russell Baker*

- How many sentences are there in each paragraph?
- Why does the second paragraph read more smoothly?

Practice Improve each of the following paragraphs by varying sentence lengths.

1. I woke up this morning. I went downstairs. I had breakfast. I had scrambled eggs. I had cereal. I had fruit. It was a gloomy day. I was in a good mood.

2. Last Saturday I went to the zoo. I wanted to see the monkeys because I was writing a report on chimpanzees, and I wanted to take some pictures so that I could include them in my report, and I also wanted to ask the zookeeper what the chimps eat, and I wanted to know what happens to them in the winter, since the zoo is closed in the winter

Writing Dialogue ☑

How could the following scene be made more interesting?

> Every Sunday they all commented on Cousin Edwin's column in the *New York Times*, but only Uncle Charlie read it. Everybody else just passed it along.

One way to make a story more interesting is to use conversation, or **dialogue**. Dialogue in a story makes the characters and actions seem real. Here is how Baker used dialogue to bring the scene to life.

> Aunt Pat, bustling in from the kitchen, would ask Uncle Allen, "Have you read Edwin's column yet, Dad?"
>
> "Not yet. I gave it to Charlie."
>
> Uncle Charlie had always read it. My mother never had. "I'll get to it later. Let Hal read it," she said.
>
> Uncle Hal, the sense of family obligation sitting strong upon him, would pick it up and after a paragraph or two say, "Edwin always had a good way of expressing himself," and lay it down casually and say, "I remember the time Aunt Sallie brought Edwin over to visit Mama and . . ."
>
> Then, interrupting his reminiscence, he handed the paper to Aunt Pat, saying, "Here, Pat, take it out in the kitchen with you and read it while you're making dinner."
>
> "Oh, you read it first, Lucy," Aunt Pat would say to my mother.
>
> "I'm too busy right now," my mother would say, "but don't lose it."
>
> *from* Growing Up *by Russell Baker*

- What does the dialogue show you that these family members really feel about Edwin's column?
- Does this dialogue sound like the way people really speak? Which lines sound the most natural?

In real life, people usually use informal language; they start sentences without finishing them or don't speak in sentences at all. Good dialogue captures the way people really speak.

Prewriting Practice

Replace each of the following statements with two or three sentences of dialogue between two characters.

1. We tried to figure out who had left the mysterious package.
2. I was surprised to get a phone call from my old friend Brook.
3. The sales clerk tried to talk me into buying the orange sweater.
4. Grandpa revealed an old family secret to me.
5. Marion told me all about her surprise party.

Writing a Good Ending ☑

A good beginning, as you know, captures the readers' attention. A good ending makes readers feel that their attention was worthwhile. It winds up the action in a way that makes sense with the rest of the story, and it leaves the readers feeling that they have been told just enough—not too much and not too little.

Once again, the best way to end a story is to *show* rather than tell the outcome. Why is the second ending better?

1. As her mind was drifting away, my mother no longer knew who I was. She did not even recognize my name or my wife's name.

2. She got her eyes open. "Who?"

"Russell," I said. "Russell and Mimi."

She glared at me the way I had so often seen her glare at a dolt. "Never heard of them," she said, and fell asleep.

from Growing Up *by Russell Baker*

The second version ends Baker's book. This version is more powerful because, through dialogue and details, it *shows* you what happens. You feel as if you are there.

The ending also leaves you with a feeling—a sense of growing up and older—that fits the rest of the book. Although the book has ended, the feeling remains for a while. Some questions remain as well. When did the mother actually die? How did Russell feel about it? A good ending does not answer everything; it leaves you with some questions to think about.

An ending may do even more. It may not only bring the present story to a close but foreshadow a future time.

> For many years I wondered about this incident . . . and never told another soul about it. I tell it now because now I believe it was in truth an omen, the forecasting of another day, another time, when I would hear that voice again and meet the secret face to face.
>
> *from* A Whale for the Killing *by Farley Mowat*

- The "voice" that Mowat speaks of was the voice of a whale, which led his ship to safety in a blinding fog. How does this ending leave you with something to think about?

When you write your own story, remember these points.

Your ending should

1. complete the action of the story
2. *show* rather than *tell*
3. fit the mood of the story
4. leave the readers feeling that they have been told just enough—not too much or too little

Prewriting Practice

A. Rewrite each of these story endings so that it shows rather than tells what happens. You may want to use more than one sentence.

1. Now that our fight was over, Nick and I were best friends.
2. Everybody wanted to leave the party as quickly as possible.
3. I was really happy to have won the race.
4. After all our troubles, we finally arrived just as the gates were starting to close.

B. Read the plot summary in the Prewriting Practice on page 68 again. Then decide how you might answer the following questions.

1. Did you and Duane feel frightened? calm? angry? curious?
2. In your role as witness, were you nervous? helpful? shy?
3. Afterward, did you feel like going to the park? going home?

Using the answers to one or more of these questions, write two different endings for the story. You might want to use dialogue, description, an action, or all three. Which ending do you prefer? See if a partner agrees with you.

The Writing Process
How to Write a Personal Narrative

Step 1: Prewriting—Choose a Topic

Brian made a list of interesting things that had happened to him when he was younger. Then he thought over these events and added two that had happened recently.

elementary school — This topic was too broad.

my first day at a new school — He couldn't remember this in enough detail.

the death of my dog Fred — This was too private to write about.

learning to play the saxophone — He couldn't narrow this to one incident.

getting braces on my front teeth — He remembered this clearly, and it could be funny.

Brian circled the last topic on his list.

On Your Own

1. **Think and discuss** Make a list of experiences from your own life that you could write about. Turn to the Ideas page for help. Discuss your ideas with a partner.
2. **Choose** Ask yourself these questions about the topics on your list.
   Which can I remember in detail?
   Which would I really enjoy writing about?
   Which topic is narrow enough to cover in a short story?
   Circle the topic you will write about.
3. **Explore** What will you write in your personal narrative? Do one of the activities under "Exploring Your Topic" on the Ideas page.

Ideas for Getting Started

Choosing a Topic

Topic Ideas
My first job
A difficult choice
My first plane ride
The most important dis-
covery I ever made
Learning to . . .
How my enemy became
my friend
How embarrassing!
My first trip alone
My most terrifying child-
hood experience
The joke was on me
A terrible, horrible, dread-
ful, bad day
My saddest day

Story Starters
Read these starters for
ideas.

Not a single face was fa-
miliar. Even the usual
school odors seemed for-
eign to me.
Some days are easily for-
gotten; others you can
never forget.
I had dreamed of this for
years. Finally, I was
boarding a train for . . .
"Watch out!" I heard the
warning clearly, but it
was too late.

Exploring Your Topic

Narrow Your Topic
Write a list showing the
main events that will make
up your story. Now look
at each item on your list.
Could any one of them be
a story in itself? Decide
whether you could write a
better story by narrowing
your topic to that item
alone.

Talk About It
Pretend that your story is a
movie you have just seen.
Tell a friend what happens
in this movie. Try to make
your friend *see* the movie
just as you remember it in
your mind. What details
should you add?

Step 2: Write a First Draft

Since many of his classmates wore braces, Brian chose his class as the audience for his story. He wanted to show the humorous side of his experience.

Brian wrote his first draft without worrying about mistakes in spelling and grammar. He would correct any mistakes in a later draft.

The beginning of Brian's first draft

> I'm going to tell you about the day I got braces. My mom drove me to the dentist. I was very nervous. The ~~nurse~~ receptionist called my name. She showed me into a different room, on the table was a book called <u>Braces: Owner's Mannual</u>. Seemed pretty wierd to me. It made me even more nervous.

Think and Discuss ☑

- How could Brian make his beginning more interesting?
- What do you learn about the people? the setting? Brian's particular experience?
- Where could Brian add dialogue?
- Where could he add more details?
- How could Brian make his story funnier?

On Your Own

1. **Think about purpose and audience** Answer these questions.
   Whom do I want my story to interest?
   How can I capture my readers' interest?
   What is my purpose? Do I want to amuse my readers? to make them understand how I felt?
2. **Write** Write your first draft. Use details and dialogue to make your story seem real. Write on every other line to leave room for changes. Do not worry about mistakes; just write all you can about your topic.

Step 3: Revise

Brian read his first draft. He decided his beginning was too boring, so he wrote a new one with some dialogue in it.

Brian wanted to find out how real his story would seem to someone else. He read it to Daniel.

Reading and responding

Daniel: I was just as scared as you when I got my braces!

Brian: Can you think of anything I've left out?

Daniel: Well, dentists' offices are always so quiet. Would you want to mention that?

Brian: Good idea. Was there any part you didn't understand?

Daniel: I wasn't sure why that book made you nervous.

Brian: Now that you mention it, that part does need more detail. Thanks.

Brian added a sentence about the silence. Then he tried to remember exactly why the book had bothered him. He added some of the thoughts that had gone through his mind.

The beginning of Brian's revision

~~I'm going to tell you about the day I got~~ "Brian Coty? Please follow me," said the nurse. ~~braces. My mom drove me to the dentist. I was~~ "Yes, Ma'am," I said. My voice squeaked. ᴧvery nervous. The ~~nurse~~ receptionist called ~~my name~~. She showed me into a different room, on the table was a book called <u>Braces: Owner's Mannual</u>. Seemed pretty wierd to me.ᴧ ~~It made~~ Did it mean I would have to tune and oil them? Could a piece ~~me even more nervous.~~ rust off and slip down my throat?

I jumped because the waiting room had been absolutely silent.

Think and Discuss ✓

- How did Brian make his beginning more interesting?
- What details did he add that showed how he felt?
- How did Brian add to the humor of his story?

Revising checklist

☑ How could I make the beginning more interesting?
☑ Where could I add more details? What could they be?
☑ Have I used dialogue effectively?
☑ How could I improve my ending?

1. **Revise** Make changes in your first draft. Cross out any parts that are boring or unclear. Write new details or dialogue between the lines or in the margins. Use the thesaurus below or the one at the back of this book.

2. **Have a conference** Read your story to someone else—a classmate.

WRITING
CONFERENCE

Ask your listener:	As you listen:
"Did the details and dialogue seem real?" "Which parts were the most interesting?" "Should I add or cut anything?"	I must listen closely. Which details are especially vivid? Is any part confusing? What would I like to know more about?

3. **Revise** Think about your listener's suggestions, and decide if you have any other ideas for improving your story. Make those changes on your paper.

Thesaurus

experience *v.* feel, sense, go through
funny *adj.* hilarious, witty, comical
happy *adj.* joyful, radiant, blissful
hurry *v.* dash, rush, scramble, fly
sad *adj.* forlorn, wretched, melancholy
say *v.* mention, declare, pronounce
shout *v.* holler, bellow, yell

Step 4: Proofread

Brian proofread his story for mistakes in spelling, grammar, and punctuation. He checked his spellings in a dictionary and used proofreading marks to make his changes.

Here is the way Brian's story looked after proofreading.

The beginning of Brian's proofread story

"Brian Coty? Please follow me," said the nurse.
~~braces.~~ My mom drove me to the dentist. I was
"Yes, Ma'am," I said. My voice squeaked.
^very nervous. The ~~nurse~~ receptionist called
~~my name.~~ She showed me into a different room,
on the table was a book called Braces: Owner's
                    That
Mann̷ual. ^Seemed pretty wie̷rd to me. ~~It made~~   Did it mean
I would have to tune and oil them? Could a piece
~~me even more nervous.~~
rust off and slip down my throat?
I jumped because the waiting room had
been absolutely silent.

Think and Discuss
- Which words did Brian correct for spelling?
- Which run-on sentence did he correct? How?
- How did he correct a sentence fragment?

On Your Own

1. **Proofreading Practice** Proofread this paragraph for mistakes in grammar and spelling. There are three spelling errors, one sentence fragment, and one run-on sentence. Write the paragraph correctly.

"Come on, Carlos," I yelled. I got this funny feeling Carlos wasn't with me. I jumped onto my "sled." Which was a peice of cardboard. Then I saw Carlos's sled shooting down the hill way ahead of me. My sled sped up, I fell off and rolled into some frozan bushes, the branches skratched me.

2. Proofreading Application Now proofread your paper. Use the Proofreading Checklist and the Grammar and Spelling Hints below. Check your spellings in a dictionary. You may use a colored pencil to make your corrections.

Proofreading Checklist	Proofreading Marks
Did I	⊅ Indent
☑ 1. indent?	∧ Add
☑ 2. use capitals and punctuation correctly?	⋏ Add a comma
	⌄⌄ Add quotation marks
	⊙ Add a period
☑ 3. correct fragments or run-ons?	ℓ Take out
	≡ Capitalize
☑ 4. spell all words correctly?	/ Make a small letter
	⌒ Reverse the order

The Grammar/Spelling Connection

Grammar Hints

Remember these hints when you are writing sentences.

• A word group that lacks a subject or predicate is not a sentence. It is a sentence fragment. Avoid sentence fragments in your writing. (Sentence fragment: *A new car, red and sparkling.* Sentence: *A new car, red and sparkling, drove up.*)

• Two or more sentences that run together with commas or without any punctuation are a run-on sentence. Avoid run-on sentences in your writing. (Run-on sentence: *Jon phoned me, I wasn't home.* Sentences: *Jon phoned me. I wasn't home. Jon phoned me, but I wasn't home. When Jon phoned me, I wasn't home.*)

• When combining two sentences, use a comma plus a conjunction. *(I tried the door, but it was locked.)*

Spelling Hints

Remember these principles when adding *-ing*.

• For most words ending in *e*, drop the *e* before adding *-ing*. *(flaming, admiring, competing)*

• For most one-syllable words ending in a single vowel and a consonant, double the consonant before adding *-ing*. *(flipping, plotting, stunning)*

Step 5: Publish

Brian shared his story in two ways. First, he read it to his class. Then he mailed it to his dentist, along with cartoons of himself "before" and "after."

On Your Own

1. **Copy** Write or type a neat copy of your story.
2. **Give it a title** Your title should tell what your story is about and catch your readers' interest.
3. **Check** Reread your story to be sure you have not omitted anything or made any mistakes in copying.
4. **Share** Think of a way to share your story.

Ideas for Sharing

- "Broadcast" your story as though it were a radio drama.
- Make a magazine article of your story. Create illustrations. Use special lettering for the title.
- Make a poster showing pictures of the story's setting, plot, and characters. Display the poster as you read the story to your class.
- Pretend your story is a movie, and make a poster to advertise it. Attach your story to the poster.

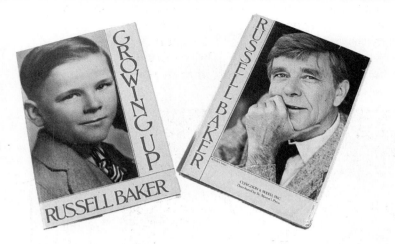

Literature and Creative Writing

In "Growing Up," Russell Baker tells about his first business venture—when he was eight years old. He failed dismally as a salesman, yet the experience led him to discover what he did want to be—a writer.

You have already tried writing about your own past. Now use what you learned to complete one of these activities.

1. **Write about a discovery.** Think of a time in your life when you, like young Russell Baker, made a discovery about yourself. Write a story about how you made the discovery and how it affected you.

2. **Write about a business venture.** Have you ever tried selling something? What was difficult, funny, or surprising about the experience? Write a story about it.

3. **Write about a perfect day.** As a boy, Russell Baker spent his free time relaxing in front of the radio and reading. How do you spend yours? Recall a day that you spent doing just as you pleased. Write a story about it.

Remember these things ☑
- Get the reader's interest in your beginning.
- *Show* rather than *tell* with details and dialogue.
- Write an ending that fits the story.

Writing Across the Curriculum
Drama

People who write drama for TV, movies, or theater often draw ideas from their own lives. The characters represent people they have known; the conflicts are similar to ones they have gone through; the dialogue contains bits and pieces of conversations they have heard or taken part in.

1. **Write about putting on a play.** Did you ever act in a play, help backstage, or work on costumes or scenery? Write a story about the experience.

Word Bank

script
spotlight
footlight
upstage
downstage
prompt
understudy

2. **Write a story through dialogue.** Before television was invented, radio dramas were a major form of entertainment. The writers relied mainly on dialogue to tell their stories. Think of an incident from your life in which conversation played an important part. Try telling the story almost entirely through dialogue.

3. **Write a story for TV.** Writers of TV episodes often present their ideas to a program director before they write the script. Suppose there were a TV series about your life. Think of an incident that would make a good half-hour episode. Write it into a brief story that would win the program director's "go-ahead."

Nicole really liked reading "Growing Up." For her next book report, she chose another autobiography—*Anne Frank: The Diary of a Young Girl*. This book was also about growing up, but Anne Frank's world was a very different one.

TITLE

Anne Frank: The Diary of a Young Girl

AUTHOR

Anne Frank

INTRODUCTION

Anne kept this diary during the two years she and her family hid from the Nazis in Amsterdam, Holland. Anne died in a concentration camp. The diary was found later and published in her memory.

BODY

Anne's diary was a gift for her thirteenth birthday. Although the Nazis had been making life more and more dangerous for the Jews, Anne's family was still living a fairly normal life. Her first entries are about school, friends, and family activities.

One day, everything changed forever. Mr. and Mrs. Frank, with Anne and her older sister Margot, moved into secret rooms above the warehouse where Mr. Frank had worked. Another family hid with them— Mr. and Mrs. Van Daan and their son.

Though living in fear and isolated in a small world, Anne was very much alive and lived a very intense life. When she wrote about herself and her feelings, she never dreamed that millions of people would someday read her diary.

CONCLUSION

Anne's diary is fascinating to read in many ways. You learn about history, you feel the danger and suspense of the family in hiding, and you get to know and care about all of the characters, especially Anne herself.

Think and Discuss
• What did you learn about Anne?
• What did you learn about the world she lived in?

Share Your Book

Write a Book Report

1. Write the **title** and **author**.
2. In your **introduction,** tell whether the book is fiction or nonfiction, and give a hint about the story that will catch your reader's interest.
3. In the **body** of your report, tell about the plot, characters, and setting. Use these guidelines:

   Plot: Describe the major conflict in the book. However, do not tell enough to give away the story.
   Characters: Mention the main characters.
   Setting: Briefly describe where the story takes place.

4. In your **conclusion,** tell why you consider the book to be worth reading. If you would not recommend the book, explain why.

Other Activities

- Choose one eventful day in the life of a character in your book. Write a diary entry for that day as the character might have written it.
- Use an almanac to find out what else happened in the world on that day. Make up a page of the day's newspaper, featuring world and national events, movie or book advertisements, sports events, and weather.
- Was there a character in the book toward whom you felt anger, sympathy, admiration, or any other strong emotion? Write a "letter" to that character. Express your feelings and explain why you feel as you do.

 # The Book Nook

The Endless Steppe *by Esther Hautzig* When her family is deported to Siberia, Esther's happy childhood ends as abruptly as Anne Frank's, but Esther's life is very different.	**All Creatures Great and Small** *by James Herriott* A veterinarian in Yorkshire, England, describes his often-comical adventures with his patients— and their owners.

Language and Usage

Now think of words. Take
sky
And ask yourself just why—
Like sun, moon, star, and cloud—
It sounds so well out loud,
And pleases so the sight
When printed black on white.

David McCord
from "Take Sky"

Nouns

Getting Ready Nouns are the names of the things we see around us, of ourselves and other people, and of the very place we live. Some nouns are general, such as *cat*. If you are thinking *cat* and someone uses a more specific noun like *tiger* or *kitten*, the picture in your mind changes. In this unit you will learn more about these all-important words.

ACTIVITIES

Listening Listen while the quotation on the facing page is read. What nouns has the poet singled out for our attention? Think of the particular picture each one makes in your mind. Are all of them pleasant pictures for you? Do any—like cloud, for instance—have a darker image?

Speaking Look at the picture. How many of the poet's words are in it? What other nouns are represented? List them all. Then say each one aloud. Do they have a good sound to your ear?

Writing Imagine yourself in this picture. What would you do here? Bring a picnic? Play a game? Write your ideas in your journal, noticing the nouns you use.

A **noun** names a person, a place, a thing, or an idea.

Bob visited Fresno and saw an exhibition of horses.

PERSON: Mr. Gomez, friend   THING: pencil, Statue of Liberty
PLACE: Utah, crossroad   IDEA: love, labor

Common and Proper Nouns

All nouns are either proper or common. A **proper noun** names a particular person, place, thing, or idea. Always capitalize a proper noun. If it consists of more than one word, capitalize only the important words. A **common noun** names a general class of person, place, thing, or idea.

PROPER: The National Horse Show was held in April in New York.
COMMON: The annual horse show was held last month in the city.

Guided Practice What are the common nouns and the proper nouns in these sentences? Which nouns should be capitalized?

Example: A parade began the ohio horse show.
       common: *parade*   **proper:** *Ohio Horse Show*

1. Horses feel tension.
2. A pony lost a shoe.
3. His name was gremlin.
4. Lynn held the reins.
5. A smile hid her fear.
6. Teams from utah competed.

Concrete and Abstract Nouns

All nouns are also either concrete or abstract. **Concrete nouns** refer to material things, to people, or to places. **Abstract nouns** name ideas, feelings, or qualities.

CONCRETE: This pony is small.   ABSTRACT: Lou wept in sorrow.

CONCRETE: people, Mexicans, Mount Hood, book, *Tom Sawyer*
ABSTRACT: love, relief, patriotism, language, Labor Day

Nouns, therefore, have several classifications. All nouns are either proper or common and either concrete or abstract.

Memorial Day: proper, abstract   happiness: common, abstract
Blue Nile: proper, concrete   box: common, concrete

Guided Practice What are the concrete nouns and the abstract nouns in these sentences?

Example: Richard Berg lives in fear of tardiness.
> **concrete:** *Richard Berg* **abstract:** *fear* *tardiness*

7. Where is your hotel?
8. Honesty is best.
9. Ann told us her idea.
10. What day is it?
11. The team visited Paris.
12. Jan sighed in relief.
13. Hopes are made of dreams.
14. Rain fell on the roofs.

Summing up

- ▶ **Nouns** name persons, places, things, or ideas.
- ▶ **Common nouns** name general classes of things.
- ▶ **Proper nouns** name particular things and are capitalized.
- ▶ **Concrete nouns** refer to material things.
- ▶ **Abstract nouns** name ideas, feelings, or qualities.

Independent Practice Write each noun. Label it *common or proper*, and *concrete* or *abstract*. Capitalize the proper nouns.

Example: The shetland is known for its gentleness.
> *Shetland* **proper concrete**
> *gentleness* **common abstract**

15. Does mrs. jones live in delaware?
16. Children have hopes and dreams.
17. What is your idea of justice?
18. The statue of liberty symbolizes freedom.
19. Will the skis fit into such a small trunk?
20. The winners felt enormous satisfaction.
21. Is your signature on this questionnaire?
22. The colonists opposed taxation without representation.
23. Democracy supports equality.
24. Did john hancock sign the declaration of independence?
25. Is your class studying history?
26. Did lincoln write the gettysburg address?

Writing Application: A Paragraph Write a paragraph about a show or a competition that you have watched or would like to watch. Underline the proper nouns once and the common nouns twice. Circle the abstract noun. Remember to capitalize all proper nouns.

For Extra Practice, see p. 107.   Kinds of Nouns **89**

2 | Compound and Collective Nouns

Compound Nouns

A noun of two or more words is a **compound noun**.

White House   software   Mrs. Wu
high school   forget-me-not   Professor Woodman

Some compound nouns are written as one word, some are written as two or more words, and some are written with hyphens. Check your dictionary to be sure of the spelling.

ONE WORD	SEPARATE WORDS	HYPHENATED WORDS
bookcase	Edgar Allan Poe	father-in-law
bridegroom	commander in chief	passer-by

Guided Practice Which nouns are compound?

Example: White Sox *compound*

1. airplane
2. happiness
3. lunchtime
4. sister-in-law
5. backpack
6. playpen
7. imitation
8. classroom
9. high school
10. sorrow
11. houses
12. sadness

Collective Nouns

A **collective noun** names a group or a collection of people, animals, or things that act as a unit.

Common Collective Nouns					
crew	orchestra	committee	flock	fleet	group
class	chorus	family	herd	jury	team

Guided Practice Which nouns are collective nouns?

Example: Our family went to the game last night. *family*

13. The team played poorly.
14. The crowd sounded like a herd of elephants.
15. Overhead we saw a flock of geese.
16. The band played the national anthem.
17. The staff included professionals and nonprofessionals.

Summing up

▶ A **compound noun** is a noun that is made up of more than one word. A compound noun may be written as one word, as separate words, or as hyphenated words.

▶ A **collective noun** names a group of people, animals, or things that act as a unit.

Independent Practice Write a collective noun or a compound noun from the box to complete each sentence.

Example: The _____ included many actors. *cast*

18. A _____ of wolves howled in the distance.
19. The class president and representatives made up the _____.
20. The _____ wore a tuxedo to his wedding.
21. Each _____ has its own set of dictionaries.
22. The _____ of ships was seen in the harbor.
23. *Cinderella* is a famous _____.
24. The lawyer presented his case to the _____.
25. Jill's favorite sport is _____.
26. Try to organize your notes into a _____.
27. The _____ of geese is flying in formation.
28. The _____ of ten has made a good decision.
29. The Pages have an old _____ in their bathroom.
30. How many can ride in the _____ at one time?
31. _____ is in Florida.
32. Warren used his _____ in the dark tunnel.
33. Some of Marta's _____ still live in Mexico.
34. The airplane's _____ has a layover in New York.
35. A _____ of bees flew above the picnic table.
36. The _____ of reporters gave the editor a gift.

Miami Beach
flock
staff
class
bathtub
fairy tale
fleet
jury
notebook
pack
bridegroom
cast
council
committee
station wagon
swarm
crew
basketball
flashlight
family

Writing Application: A News Report Your newspaper has sent you out to report on homecoming events of your school twenty-five years ago. You enter a time machine and go back. Write a short article reporting on the homecoming events. Use at least three collective nouns and three compound nouns. You may use the words from the Word Box if you wish.

crew
hometown
mob
home run
association
football

For Extra Practice, see p. 108.   **Compound and Collective Nouns**   91

3 | Singular and Plural Nouns

Most nouns change form to show number. A **singular noun** names one person, place, thing, or idea. A **plural noun** names more than one. You form the plural of most nouns by simply adding *s* to the singular. Other plural forms involve spelling changes. Look up a word in your dictionary when you are not sure of its plural form.

Regular Forms

Rules for Forming Plurals		
Add *s* to form the plural of these nouns:		
1. Most singular nouns	globes	Michaels
2. Most nouns ending in *o* preceded by a vowel	radios	stereos
3. Many nouns ending in *o*	pianos	altos
4. Nouns ending in *y* preceded by a vowel	donkeys	valleys
5. Proper nouns ending in *y*	Bradys	Malloys
6. Some nouns ending in *f* or *fe*	hoofs	safes
Add *es* to form the plural of these nouns:		
1. Nouns ending in *s, x, sh, ch, z*	boxes	buzzes
2. Some nouns ending in *o* preceded by a consonant	echoes	heroes
3. Nouns ending in *y* preceded by a consonant (change *y* to *i* first)	fly—flies	
4. Some nouns ending in *f* or *fe* (change *f* to *v* first)	calf—calves	

Guided Practice What is the plural form of each noun?

Example: toy *toys*

1. Harry	**7.** life	**13.** clay	**19.** rope
2. veto	**8.** bunch	**14.** bush	**20.** month
3. monkey	**9.** belief	**15.** history	**21.** potato
4. soprano	**10.** mess	**16.** safe	**22.** guy
5. ax	**11.** tax	**17.** Sally	**23.** solo
6. Ron	**12.** tornado	**18.** valley	**24.** leaf

Irregular Forms

Some nouns have unusual singular or plural forms. Check your dictionary if you cannot remember a special form.

Unusual Noun Forms

1. Some plurals are formed by irregular spelling changes.

child—children	foot—feet	mouse—mice
woman—women	tooth—teeth	man—men

2. Some nouns have the same singular and plural forms.

deer	sheep	grapefruit

3. Some nouns are used only in the plural form.

clothes	scissors	odds
slacks	pliers	pants

4. Some nouns end in *s* but have a singular meaning.

physics	measles	economics
mumps	mathematics	series

5. Some nouns from other languages are made plural as in the original language.

analysis—analyses	alumnus—alumni

6. Compound nouns usually are made plural by adding *s* to the most important word in the compound.

commanders in chief	brothers-in-law

7. Compound nouns that are written as one word or that do not have a noun part are made plural by adding *s* at the end.

cupfuls	forget-me-nots

8. Letters, numbers, symbols, and words used as words are made plural by adding an apostrophe and an *s*.

a's	8's	&'s	but's

Guided Practice What is the plural form of each item? Use your dictionary if you need help.

Example: foot *feet*

25. mouse	**33.** series	**41.** bookcase
26. basis	**34.** patch	**42.** physics
27. salmon	**35.** story	**43.** German measles
28. *?*	**36.** cupful	**44.** sister-in-law
29. *3*	**37.** maid of honor	**45.** goose
30. stimulus	**38.** crisis	**46.** tablespoonful
31. deer	**39.** *and*	**47.** lady's-slipper
32. grapefruit	**40.** analysis	**48.** *&*

▶ A **singular noun** names one person, place, thing, or idea.
▶ A **plural noun** names more than one.
▶ The plurals of nouns are formed in different ways. Check your dictionary if you are unsure about the spelling of a plural noun.

Independent Practice

A. Write the plural form of each item. If it is already plural, write *plural*. Use your dictionary if you need help.

Example: echoes   *plural*

49. bucketful	**55.** briefcase	**61.** odds
50. turkeys	**56.** church	**62.** potato
51. *20*	**57.** great-aunt	**63.** torpedoes
52. +	**58.** cousin	**64.** leaves
53. grandchild	**59.** trophies	**65.** clothes
54. crash	**60.** foxes	**66.** crises

B. Write the incorrect singular or plural nouns correctly.

Example: Blackbird is the name given to some thrushs.
          thrushes

67. Red-winged blackbirds spend their lifes in marshs.
68. They often sing while they sit in treeses or on fence postes and spread their wings and tailes.
69. For food they eat flys and seedes but not mouses.
70. Females look like large dark sparrowes with sharp bills.
71. Females are heavily striped on their bodys but have light stripes over their eyes.
72. Male blackbirds have colored patchs on their shoulders.
73. From the eggs that each female lays every year hatch four to five babys.
74. Another species of blackbird is often found on ranchs and corrales in the West.

Writing Application: Sentences

Imagine that animals wear clothes and that you design their clothing. Choose one animal that you like. Write five to eight sentences describing some clothing that you have designed for this animal. Use at least three noun plurals in your sentences. You may use the words in the Word Box.

clothes
pants
dresses
cuffs
geese
sheep
mice

4 | Possessive Nouns

You already know how to make nouns plural. You can also make them possessive. **Possessive nouns** show ownership or relationship. A possessive noun always has an apostrophe (').

Jade's scissors (the scissors that belong to Jade)
the dog's whiskers (the whiskers of the dog)
the workers' demands (the demands that the workers made)
Mike's new address (the new address that Mike has)

Rules for Forming Possessive Nouns

1. Most singular nouns: Add an apostrophe and *s*.	Mr. Bass—Mr. Bass's Tom—Tom's
2. Plural nouns ending with *s*: Add only an apostrophe.	girls—girls' babies—babies' Joneses—Joneses'
3. Other plural nouns: Add an apostrophe and *s*.	children—children's geese—geese's
4. Compound nouns: Add an apostrophe and *s* to the end.	sister-in-law—sister-in-law's sisters-in-law—sisters-in-law's

If two or more people own a single thing, place the apostrophe after the last person's name.

Doug and Scott's basketball

If each owns a thing separately, make each noun possessive.

Doug's and Scott's basketballs

Guided Practice
How would you change each word group into another word group that has a possessive noun?

Example: the pawprints of the dog *the dog's pawprints*

1. the bikes that Ted and Nick each has
2. the color of the rabbits
3. the cat that Lewis and Doris own together
4. the German shepherd that the Johnsons have
5. the apartment building of Mr. Dix
6. the glances of the passers-by
7. the tractor trailers of her son-in-law
8. the jack-in-the-box that the children own

> ▸ A **possessive noun** shows ownership or relationship.
> ▸ To form the possessive of a singular noun, a plural noun not ending in *s*, or a compound noun, add an apostrophe and *s*.
> ▸ To form the possessive of a plural noun ending in *s*, add an apostrophe only.

Independent Practice

A. Rewrite each word group as another word group with a possessive noun.

Example: the photographs that the Rogers have
the Rogers' photographs

9. the clocks that my brother-in-law owns
10. the spaghetti dinner that my cousins made
11. the application that Alison made
12. the wedding bouquet that my mother had
13. the request that our teachers made
14. the old computer of the instructor
15. the mathematics book that my brother has
16. the meow of the cat
17. the car that my mother and father own
18. the pets that Jerry and Eva each has

B. Write the singular possessive, plural, and plural possessive forms of each noun.

Example: mother **singular possessive:** *mother's* **plural:** *mothers*
plural possessive: *mothers'*

19. bear	25. chief	31. class
20. man	26. grandfather	32. deer
21. Cass	27. sheep	33. woman
22. Max	28. Carlos	34. alumnus
23. Darcy	29. commander in chief	35. child
24. weasel	30. mink	36. chorus

Writing Application: A Comparison Imagine that you are visiting the imaginary country Xanadu, and you meet two inhabitants, Gus and Jus, who are very different from each other and from people you know. Write a paragraph comparing and contrasting the characteristics of the two people with each other or with friends of yours. Use at least four possessive nouns in your paragraph.

5 | Combining Sentences: Appositives

You have seen how you can combine simple sentences into compound sentences and complex sentences. Another way to combine two or more sentences is by changing one sentence into an appositive. An **appositive** is a noun that identifies, describes, or renames another noun or pronoun that it follows.

Mozart was a wonder child. ⟶ Mozart, a composer,
    He was a composer. was a wonder child.

An appositive may be a noun alone or a noun with words that modify it.

Mozart and his sister were clever. ⟶ Mozart and his sister, Maria
    His sister was Maria Anna. Anna, were clever.

Don Juan appears in Mozart's ⟶ Don Juan, a legendary hero
work. Don Juan is a legendary ⟶ from Spain, appears in
    hero from Spain. Mozart's work.

Do not use commas with an appositive that is needed to identify the noun it follows.

> Mozart's son Franz wrote music. (Mozart had more than one son.)

Use commas to set off an appositive that is not needed to complete the meaning of a sentence. Commas indicate that the appositive gives extra information about the noun.

> *The Magic Flute,* an opera, became Mozart's most popular work. Mozart studied in Italy, the land of music

Guided Practice

A. Identify the appositives. Where should commas be added?

> Example: George Gershwin an American composer of serious and popular music lived from 1898 to 1937.
> *George Gershwin, an American composer of serious and popular music, lived from 1898 to 1937.*

  1. Gershwin worked as a songwriter and as a pianist in Tin Pan Alley the music district of New York.

  2. The lyrics for most of Gershwin's songs were written by Ira Gershwin one of his brothers.

3. The song "Swanee" made Gershwin famous in 1919.
4. "Rhapsody in Blue" a piano piece brought the Brooklyn composer world-wide recognition.
5. The opera *Porgy and Bess* contains Gershwin's finest music.
6. Adapted from a play by DuBose Heyward, the three-act folk opera *Porgy and Bess* was produced in 1935.
7. Blues and jazz the styles of music in this work had not been played very often in Broadway musicals.
8. "Summertime" perhaps the most famous song from *Porgy and Bess* has been performed by many musicians.

B. Combine each pair of sentences by changing the second sentence into an appositive. Where are commas needed?

9. *Porgy and Bess* has been revived recently. It is an American classic.
10. Gershwin wrote another musical. This musical was *An American in Paris.*
11. The musical takes place in Paris. Paris is the capital of France.
12. *An American in Paris* shows the impressions of an American visitor to Paris. It is a ballet.
13. The musician introduced Gershwin to the world. The musician was Paul Whiteman.
14. Paul Whiteman commissioned Gershwin to write a jazz piece. Paul Whiteman was a bandleader.
15. This piece brought the attention of serious musicians to jazz. Jazz was the popular music of that time.
16. Gershwin's life story was told in a movie. The movie was *Rhapsody in Blue.*
17. Gershwin died at the age of thirty-nine. Gershwin is a musical legend of our century.
18. Gershwin's music is still popular today. His music is a mixture of serious pieces and musical comedy.
19. *Les Misérables* is based on a novel by a Frenchman. *Les Misérables* is a recent popular musical.
20. The Frenchman was Victor Hugo. Victor Hugo was a writer in the nineteenth century.
21. The musical is performed on a revolving stage. The musical is an opera.
22. Claude-Michel Schönberg wrote the score. The score is a powerhouse of emotions and drama.

▶ You may combine sentences by changing one sentence into an appositive.

▶ An **appositive** is a noun, with or without accompanying words, that identifies another noun.

Independent Practice Rewrite the sentences, combining each pair by changing the second sentence into an appositive. Add commas if needed.

Example: Emma Lazarus was born in 1849. She was a writer.
Emma Lazarus, a writer, was born in 1849.

23. Lazarus began writing poetry early. She was a clever child.
24. Ralph Waldo Emerson liked her poems. Emerson was a poet.
25. Her first prose work was impressive. It was a novel.
26. Lazarus wrote a sonnet. A sonnet is a poem of fourteen lines.
27. The sonnet is inscribed on the Statue of Liberty. The Statue of Liberty is the gateway to the port of New York.
28. She wrote a book in 1882. The book was *Songs of a Semite*.
29. Lazarus died in New York. New York was her birthplace.
30. Robert Burns was born in Scotland. Robert Burns was a poet.
31. He wrote many lyrics. Lyrics are poems set to music.
32. Burns wrote much of his work in Scots. Scots is a dialect of English that many Scottish people spoke in the eighteenth century.
33. While still a boy, Burns developed heart trouble. Heart trouble was his killer when he was only thirty-seven.
34. Burns was considered a radical for his outspoken opinions on religion and politics. Burns was an admirer of the American Revolution.
35. Burns had a large circle of friends with whom he socialized regularly. Burns was a devoted family man and father.
36. Burns wrote three hundred songs about friendship, work, and patriotism. He was a productive songwriter.
37. Burns became the songwriter for all English people. He was his country's national poet.
38. Every New Year's Eve many of us sing a famous song by Burns. The song is "Auld Lang Syne."

Writing Application: A Paragraph Write a paragraph of at least six sentences about your favorite musician or poet. Use appositives in your sentences and use commas where needed.

For Extra Practice, see p. 111.   Combining Sentences: Appositives

Grammar-Writing Connection

Using Exact Nouns

Nouns name persons, places, things, and ideas. Exact nouns make your writing vivid and clear.

GENERAL: The individual bought the article at that location.
MORE EXACT: The woman bought the clothing at that store.
MOST EXACT: Mrs. Wilder bought the raincoat at Dudley's.

General nouns like *individual, article,* and *location* can name many different things. They do not help the reader to form a clear picture. *Woman, clothing,* and *store* are somewhat clearer, but they can still name many things. Exact nouns like *Mrs. Wilder, raincoat,* and *Dudley's* name exact things. They give the reader the clearest picture of all.

Compare these lists of nouns.

GENERAL	MORE EXACT	MOST EXACT
person	man	Mr. Warshaw
thing	machine	lawnmower
place	room	bedroom
food	vegetable	carrot
furniture	seat	couch

When you write, try to avoid *thing* and other general nouns. Use the noun that names exactly what you mean.

Revising Sentences

Rewrite each sentence twice. First, change each general noun to an exact noun. Then change each noun again to make it more exact. Make sure that your subjects and verbs agree.

1. Some things were buzzing around the place.
2. Does this thing belong to that person?
3. The furniture in that place was new but uncomfortable.
4. The people were extremely busy with the things that time.
5. That person's place is always cluttered with things.
6. My animals prefer that food, but it is not in that store.
7. Whose clothing and things are in my place?
8. My relatives enjoyed the music in that place.
9. Carefully the man arranged the food on each thing.
10. People carried the stuff from one place to the other place.

Creative Writing

Helen Lundeberg, *Double Portrait of the Artist in Time (1935)*, National Museum of American Art Smithsonian Institution

Through a trick of art, Helen Lundeberg bridges time and makes her childhood and adult selves inhabit the same room.

- Why does the shadow seem out of place? How does it contribute to the picture's mood?
- What do you think the clock and the flowers symbolize?

Activities

1. **Describe your portrait.** If you were to paint a self-portrait, how would you portray yourself? What special objects would you include to give viewers a sense of your personality? Write a description of your imaginary self-portrait.
2. **Explain how you've changed.** How have you changed in the past five years? Write about how your present self is different from your self of five years ago.

Check-up: Unit 3

Kinds of Nouns *(p. 88)* Write each noun and label it either *common* or *proper* and either *concrete* or *abstract*. Capitalize the proper nouns.

1. bridge
2. sadness
3. thanksgiving day
4. stripe
5. gulf of mexico
6. emma
7. north america
8. cousin
9. salt
10. sir francis drake
11. honor
12. truth
13. argentina
14. squash
15. detroit
16. year
17. joy
18. paper

Compound and Collective Nouns *(p. 90)* Write the compound nouns and the collective nouns. Label each one *compound* or *collective.*

19. Mrs. Romero is the best teacher of mathematics in our junior high school.
20. Yesterday she explained the difference between plane geometry and solid geometry to our class.
21. After the slide presentation, Mrs. Romero passed out some math problems to the audience.
22. We divided into small groups and worked on the problems.
23. Our math teachers served as onlookers and checked our work-sheets while we worked.
24. Even members of our math club thought that some of the problems were difficult!

Singular and Plural Nouns *(p. 92)* Write the correct form of the incorrectly spelled singular or plural nouns in these sentences. If a sentence has no incorrectly spelled word, write *correct*. Use your dictionary if you need help.

25. When you work with computers, you learn new wayes to use common words.
26. You have heard of a mouse or a disk, but computer mouses and disks have very particular uses.
27. Daisy wheels look a little like daisys or like spokes that have tooths on them.
28. Daisy wheels function like typewriter keyes.
29. Almost all professions have uses for the computer.
30. Doctors can use them to compare reactions to stimuluses.

31. Computers make it easier for doctors to make diagnosises.
32. Earth scientists might even use computers to analyze the different layers of rocks.
33. Farmers can keep track of their sheeps, pigs, and oxes.
34. Using a computer, a women's college would know where its alumnas lived and worked.
35. Be sure that the factes you put into computers are correct.
36. A saying of computer science is "Garbage in, garbage out."
37. The computer is one of the wonders of modern science.

Possessive Nouns *(p. 95)* For each singular noun, write the plural form, the possessive form, and the plural possessive form. Use your dictionary if you need help.

38. Iris
39. deer
40. father-in-law
41. gentleman
42. Bernstein
43. librarian
44. great-aunt
45. whale
46. hostess
47. author
48. Chong
49. firefighter
50. German shepherd

51. studio
52. Caroline
53. bird
54. Paco
55. chief
56. Ross
57. finch
58. Brock
59. mouse
60. editor
61. bass
62. teacher
63. May

64. Max
65. soprano
66. alto
67. baby
68. Estrada
69. sheep
70. ox
71. Victoria
72. Penny
73. beetle
74. alumnus
75. O'Malley
76. chorus

Combining Sentences: Appositives *(p. 97)* Combine each pair of sentences by changing the second sentence into an appositive. Write the sentence, and add commas where necessary.

77. Egypt has around forty-eight million people. Egypt is the second most populated country in Africa.
78. Egypt has an area of around one million square kilometers. Egypt is a medium-sized African country.
79. The capital of Egypt is Cairo. Cairo is one of the largest cities in the world.
80. There are more than twelve million Cairenes. Cairenes are residents of Cairo.
81. Cairo also has an Arabic name. The Arabic name is El-Qahira.
82. Two famous Egyptian sights are in Giza. They are the pyramids and the Sphinx.

Unit 1: The Sentence

Kinds of Sentences, Interjections *(pp. 14, 34)* Write each sentence, adding the correct end punctuation. Label each sentence *declarative, interrogative, imperative,* or *exclamatory.* Underline the interjections.

1. Put these two fingers on your wrist
2. Can you feel your pulse
3. Wow What a strong pulse you have
4. Well, this is really an amazing fact
5. Blood moves through your arteries
6. How does oxygen travel to your heart

Subjects and Predicates *(pp. 16, 18, 20, 22)* Write each sentence. Draw a line between the complete subject and the complete predicate. Underline each simple subject once and each simple predicate twice. Label the *compound subjects* or the *compound predicates.*

7. Alexander Hamilton, John Jay, and James Madison published *The Federalist.*
8. *The Federalist* is a series of eighty-five essays.
9. These essays explained republican government and encouraged acceptance of the Constitution.
10. Hamilton wrote most of the essays.
11. These essays argued against the existing government.
12. The strongest argument for acceptance of the Constitution must have been the need for law and order.

Compound Sentences, Conjunctions, Complex Sentences *(pp. 24, 26, 28)* Write each sentence, and label it *simple, compound,* or *complex.* Draw a line under a subordinate clause. Draw another line under the subordinating conjunctions.

13. Byron's friend is a dancer, and she is performing on Friday.
14. I would like to go, but I don't have the money.
15. If you lend me the money, I shall go.
16. Byron's friend is a talented dancer and singer.
17. Her skill has increased because she has practiced for years.
18. When she dances, she looks so graceful.
19. You practice, but you should practice more.
20. Dancers are tall and thin, yet their muscles are well developed.

Correcting Fragments and Run-ons (p. 30) Rewrite these sentences, correcting each fragment and run-on.

21. A triangle has three sides a quadrilateral has four sides.
22. Because there are different kinds of quadrilaterals.
23. A square has four equal sides they join at right angles.
24. A rhombus has four equal sides. But no right angles.
25. Which quadrilaterals have right angles which ones do not?
26. A triangle with a right angle a right triangle.
27. An obtuse angle is more than ninety degrees, a triangle can have only one obtuse angle.

Unit 3: Nouns

Kinds of Nouns (p. 88) Write the nouns. Label each one *concrete* or *abstract* and *common* or *proper*.

28. Sailors greet a lighthouse with respect.
29. Keepers of these buildings lead solitary but useful lives.
30. The light warns boats of the danger of rocks or reefs.
31. Ancient Libyans hung baskets of burning coal from towers.
32. Boats on the Mediterranean received these warnings.
33. Now the operation of these lights is automatic.
34. The structures often use radio beacons that send out signals.

Singular, Plural, and Possessive Nouns (pp. 92, 95) For each singular noun, write the plural, singular possessive, and plural possessive forms. Use a dictionary if you need help.

35. moth	38. Gus	41. America
36. son-in-law	39. Willis	42. squirrel
37. fly	40. May	43. fox

Combining Sentences: Appositives (p. 97) Combine each pair of sentences by changing the second sentence to an appositive. Write the sentence, and add commas where necessary.

44. AMPAS gives the Academy Award. AMPAS is the Academy of Motion Picture Arts and Sciences.
45. The award is Oscar. Oscar is a small gold statue.
46. Oscar got its name from Margaret Herrick in 1931. Margaret Herrick was executive secretary of the Academy.
47. The statue looked like her uncle. His name was Oscar.
48. One actress has won four Oscars. She is Katharine Hepburn.
49. John Ford also won four gold statues. He was a director.
50. *Ben Hur* won eleven Oscars in all. *Ben Hur* was the Academy's Best Picture of 1959.

Enrichment

Time Line

Choose five important contributions or discoveries made by Americans after 1865. Make a time line to show the order in which these events occurred. Under each date write a brief note about what happened. Write the inventor's name as a possessive noun in each note.

1879
|
Thomas Edison's invention of the light bulb

Medicines & Remedies

Create a chart to paste on the inside of your medicine cabinet at home. List six medicines, remedies, or other first-aid items. Write a short sentence about the use of each. Include an appositive in each sentence to tell more about each noun.

CURE-IT-ALL

Cure-it-all, a pain reliever, is good for headaches and backaches.

Noun Connection

Players—2. **You need**—paper, pencils. **How to play**—One player writes down a general category of concrete nouns, such as *bird*. The other player writes down a precise concrete noun, such as *dove*, that relates to the general noun and begins with the last letter of the general noun. The first player looks at the last letter of that precise noun and writes another related precise noun starting with that letter.

bird dove eagle

Continue to take turns until you run out of precise nouns. Then start again with another general noun, and repeat this game as many times as you wish. **Scoring**—If you wish, keep track of the number of times each player gets stumped. The person with the lowest score wins.

1 | Kinds of Nouns (p. 88)

● Write each noun. Then label it either *common* or *proper* and either *concrete* or *abstract*.

Example: horse **common** **concrete**

1. beauty	**7.** Ms. Ling	**13.** tablet
2. rider	**8.** France	**14.** molar
3. trophy	**9.** idea	**15.** cousin
4. July	**10.** love	**16.** elegance
5. table	**11.** book	**17.** kindness
6. Chicago	**12.** tuba	**18.** Lake Erie

▲ Write each noun, and label it either *common* or *proper* and either *concrete* or *abstract*.

Example: The Olympics include gymnastics.

Olympics **proper** **concrete**
gymnastics **common** **concrete**

19. These exercises develop balance and strength.
20. Movements include handsprings and somersaults.
21. The gymnast did a cartwheel with ease.
22. Silence filled the room, and the tension grew.
23. Mary Lou Retton won a medal.
24. A team from the United States won an award.
25. The whistles, shouts, and applause were deafening.
26. The woman from China performed with confidence.

■ Write each sentence. Underline the nouns. Capitalize the proper nouns. Add the kind of noun in parentheses to complete each sentence.

Example: My favorite event in the olympics is _____. (concrete)
My favorite <u>event</u> *in the* <u>Olympics</u> *is* <u>archery</u>.

27. It takes _____ to perform in front of a crowd. (abstract)
28. Did greg louganis make a perfect _____? (concrete)
29. A(n) _____ from west germany won a medal for the one-hundred-meter butterfly. (concrete)
30. The swimmers dived with style and _____. (abstract)
31. The summer _____ were in los angeles. (proper, concrete)
32. A(n) _____ from japan won a medal for judo. (concrete)
33. The winner cried tears of _____. (abstract)
34. The runners jumped over the _____. (concrete)

2 | Compound and Collective Nouns (p. 90)

● Write each underlined noun. Label it *compound* or *collective*.
Example: A group of hikers walked up the path. *group* **collective**

1. A campground lay ahead.
2. The hikers were walking through Yellowstone National Park.
3. A flock of birds flew noisily in the branches overhead.
4. The birds sounded like a band of trumpets.
5. Was that a crowd of skiers above the hikers in the distance?
6. A single passer-by waved to the hikers.
7. They were approaching the mountaintop.
8. The hikers reached the top of the mountain by lunchtime.
9. Another group of hikers greeted them.

▲ Write the compound nouns and the collective nouns. Label each one *compound* or *collective*.
Example: A crowd was gathering near the bandstand.
    crowd **collective** *bandstand* **compound**

10. The playground across the path was empty and dark.
11. A team of horses for the carriages stood near the bikeway.
12. Central Park welcomed a swarm of people this weekend.
13. A German shepherd and a cocker spaniel slept under a bench.
14. The moonlight shone through a cluster of surrounding trees.
15. Then the chattering audience grew quiet.
16. The woodwinds in the orchestra began to play.
17. New York City is always pleasant in the springtime.
18. Have you ever heard mockingbirds sing there?

■ Write a compound noun or a collective noun to complete each sentence. Label the noun *compound* or *collective*.
Example: Today is Charles's fourteenth _____.
    birthday **compound**

19. His parents and the rest of his _____ are coming to dinner.
20. Even his seventy-year-old _____ will be there.
21. Charles's older sister is a student at _____.
22. A _____ of her friends has just returned from a camping trip.
23. They spent three days in _____.
24. They carried their belongings in _____ on their shoulders.
25. At night they slept in the outdoors in a public _____.
26. Of course, they all had brought their _____.
27. A _____ of mosquitoes kept them awake one night.
28. The group often sang by the warm, roaring _____.

3 | Singular and Plural Nouns (p.92)

● Write the correct plural noun from each pair. Use your dictionary if you need help.

Example: memorys, memories *memories*

1. plates, platees
2. foxes, foxs
3. peachs, peaches
4. radioes, radios
5. pianoes, pianos
6. heros, heroes
7. stories, storys
8. tooths, teeth

9. bushs, bushes
10. chiefs, chieves
11. leafs, leaves
12. foots, feet
13. mans, men
14. wishes, wishs
15. sheeps, sheep
16. chefs, cheves

17. alumnuses, alumni
18. studios, studioes
19. childs, children
20. boxs, boxes
21. posts, postes
22. cupsful, cupfuls
23. 5es, 5's
24. cellos, celloes

▲ Write the plural form of each noun in parentheses. Use your dictionary if you need help.

Example: Two _____ in the chorus brought their _____. (alto, cello)
           altos   cellos

25. Use these _____ to cut those _____ of bread. (knife, loaf)
26. All the _____ ran, but the _____ walked. (child, woman)
27. Did you catch many _____ or _____ on your fishing trips? (salmon, trout)
28. Two of the _____ escaped over the _____. (thief, roof)
29. My _____ have visited faraway _____. (brother-in-law, country)
30. All of the _____ on those two _____ play _____. (music box, bookshelf, waltz)
31. _____ flew around the _____ of the _____. (Bee, hoof, donkey)
32. The _____ grow _____ and _____. (Rooney, potato, broccoli)
33. These _____ cut a hole in my _____. (scissors, pants)

■ Rewrite each sentence, correcting the spelling errors in the plural nouns. Use your dictionary if you need help.

Example: The sopranoes gave forget-me-nots to the alumnuses.
           The sopranos gave forget-me-nots to the alumni.

34. My great-uncles raise gooses and turkies on their farms.
35. The Kellys have modern theorys about farming.
36. My sister-in-laws have won many trophys at the state fair.
37. They grow the best tomatos, zucchinis, and beetes.
38. Our sheep and lambes lead peaceful lifes.
39. The womans carried bucketsful of water to the horseses.
40. Some rabbites were hiding under the bushs near the vegetables.
41. The mens put on old trouserses and sweaters.
42. The childs have had measles but not chicken pox.

4 | Possessive Nouns (p. 95)

● Rewrite each word group, adding an apostrophe where necessary to form a possessive noun.

Example: peoples choice   *people's choice*

1. sheeps wool
2. foxs color
3. Besss idea
4. ladies hats
5. the Smiths house
6. childrens toys
7. calfs foot
8. calves feet
9. mouses claws
10. flies wings
11. flys wings
12. sister-in-laws gloves
13. sisters-in-laws gloves
14. thieves goods
15. womans blouse
16. womens blouses
17. the basss voice
18. the basses voices
19. mices claws
20. thiefs escape

▲ Rewrite each word group, using a possessive noun.

Example: sneakers of the boy   *boy's sneakers*

21. swim team for boys
22. clothing for men
23. words of Alex
24. voice of the alto
25. sweater of Tess
26. cold of James
27. room of Hank and Jack
28. house of the Evanses
29. beard of Mr. Murray
30. desks of the girls
31. success of Mr. Tory
32. successes of the Torys
33. offices of the women
34. reign of King Charles
35. work of the doctor
36. poems by Pound and Frost
37. novels of Robert Peck
38. ties of her sons-in-law
39. test that Ms. Peters gave
40. caps of two nurses

■ Rewrite each incorrect phrase correctly. If a phrase has no errors, write *correct*.

Example: this firefighters' helmet   *this firefighter's helmet*

41. a man's sock
42. my sister Beths lunch
43. Uncle Boris' wig
44. this partie's conversation
45. that ladys' goldfish
46. my friend Carols's decision
47. the maid of honor's dress
48. the two girl's records
49. foxe's tail
50. one jurys' decision
51. three mens' beliefs
52. all witnesses's testimony
53. each witness's testimony
54. the bosses' secretaries
55. a poets rhyme
56. a heros' welcome
57. the geeses' honks
58. Bess's scarf
59. each boys' shoes
60. the three lawyerses cases

5 | Combining Sentences: Appositives (p. 97)

● Write each appositive.

Example: Rachel Carson, a biologist, wrote about science.

a biologist

1. In her birthplace, Pennsylvania, her career began.
2. Rachel, a talented young girl, published her first story at the age of ten.
3. One required college course, biology, changed her life.
4. She decided to combine writing and science, her two loves.
5. She had a special interest, the life of the seas.
6. Her book *The Sea Around Us* won the National Book Award.
7. Her most important work, *Silent Spring*, made the public aware of some important issues.

▲ Combine each pair of sentences by changing the second sentence into an appositive. Write the sentence, and add commas where necessary.

Example: Mary Pickford was "America's Sweetheart." She was a Canadian.

Mary Pickford, a Canadian, was "America's Sweetheart."

8. A term was first used for her. The term was *film star.*
9. Her real name wasn't theatrical enough. It was Gladys Smith.
10. By 1920 everyone knew the name. The name was Mary Pickford.
11. Mary first appeared on the movie screen at the age of sixteen. Mary was a lovely girl.
12. Her height allowed her to play children's roles. Her height was only five feet.
13. By the age of twenty-three, Mary had formed her own production company. Mary was a fine businessperson.

■ (14–22) Rewrite the paragraph, combining some of the sentences by forming appositives. Add commas where necessary.

Example: Leonard Bernstein is a conductor. He is also a pianist.

Leonard Bernstein, a conductor, is also a pianist.

Bernstein has taught many people about music. He is a skilled teacher. His position as the conductor of the New York Philharmonic Orchestra lasted from 1958 to 1969. He often performed in another role during that time. His role was composer. He wrote the music for *Wonderful Town* and *West Side Story*. These shows are famous Broadway musicals. In 1971 Leonard Bernstein composed a special work for a special event. The special event was the opening of the Kennedy Center for the Performing Arts.

Settings for myths and heroes are scattered all over the island of Crete. Eastern Crete always draws the most attention; visitors swarm the ruins at Knossos, palace of legendary King Minos. On the other hand, western Crete is dotted with traces of even earlier cities, and its mountains echo little-known stories of mythological figures.

Marie Gaudette
from "The Gorge of Samaria"

Comparison and Contrast

Getting Ready We compare and contrast often in our everyday conversations. We are always adding up pluses and minuses or weighing one thing against another. In this unit, you will be writing your own comparison and contrast paragraph.

ACTIVITIES

Listening Listen while the paragraph about Crete is read. What two areas are being compared and contrasted? What do both areas have in common? How do they differ? Does this mean one area is preferable to the other?

Speaking Look at the picture. It shows some of the partly reconstructed ruins in the rolling hills around Knossos. What might you see in a picture of the other area?

Writing Look at the landscape. In your journal, compare and contrast it with your own area.

LITERATURE

When is it dangerous to fly high?

Icarus and Daedalus

Retold by Josephine Preston Peabody

Among all those mortals who grew so wise that they learned the secrets of the gods, none was more cunning than Daedalus.[1]

He once built, for King Minos of Crete, a wonderful Labyrinth of winding ways so cunningly tangled up and twisted around that, once inside, you could never find your way out again without a magic clue. But the king's favor veered with the wind, and one day he had his master architect imprisoned in a tower. Daedalus managed to escape from his cell; but it seemed impossible to leave the island, since every ship that came or went was well guarded by order of the king.

At length, watching the sea-gulls in the air—the only creatures that were sure of liberty—he thought of a plan for himself and his young son Icarus,[2] who was captive with him.

Little by little, he gathered a store of feathers great and small. He fastened these together with thread, moulded them in with wax, and so fashioned two great wings like those of a bird. When they were done, Daedalus fitted them to his own shoulders, and after one or two efforts, he found that by waving his arms he could winnow the air and cleave it, as a swimmer does the sea. He held himself aloft, wavered this way and that with the wind, and at last, like a great fledgling, he learned to fly.

Without delay, he fell to work on a pair of wings for the boy Icarus, and taught him carefully how to

---

[1]Daedalus (dĕd′l-əs) [2]Icarus (ĭk′ər-əs)

use them, bidding him beware of rash adventures among the stars. "Remember," said the father, "never to fly very low or very high, for the fogs about the earth would weigh you down, but the blaze of the sun will surely melt your feathers apart if you go too near."

For Icarus, these cautions went in at one ear and out by the other. Who could remember to be careful when he was to fly for the first time? Are birds careful? Not they! And not an idea remained in the boy's head but the one joy of escape.

The day came, and the fair wind that was to set them free. The father bird put on his wings, and, while the light urged them to be gone, he waited to see that all was well with Icarus, for the two could not fly hand in hand. Up they rose, the boy after his father. The hateful ground of Crete sank beneath them; and the country folk, who caught a glimpse of them when they were high above the treetops, took it for a vision of the gods—Apollo, perhaps, with Cupid after him.

At first there was a terror in the joy. The wide vacancy of the air dazed them—a glance downward made their brains reel. But when a great wind filled their wings, and Icarus felt himself sustained, like a halcyon-bird in the hollow of a wave, like a child uplifted by his mother, he forgot everything in the world but joy. He forgot Crete and the other islands that he had passed over: he saw but vaguely that winged thing in the distance before him that was his father Daedalus. He longed for one draught of flight to quench the thirst of his captivity: he stretched out his arms to the sky and made towards the highest heavens.

Alas for him! Warmer and warmer grew the air. Those arms, that had seemed to uphold him, relaxed. His wings wavered, drooped. He fluttered his young hands vainly—he was falling—and in that terror he remembered. The heat of the sun had melted the wax from his wings; the feathers were falling, one by one, like snowflakes; and there was none to help.

He fell like a leaf tossed down the wind, down, down, with one cry that overtook Daedalus far away. When he returned, and sought high and low for the poor boy, he saw nothing but the bird-like feathers afloat on the water, and he knew that Icarus was drowned.

The nearest island he named Icaria, in memory of the child; but he, in heavy grief, went to the temple of Apollo in Sicily, and there hung up his wings as an offering. Never again did he attempt to fly.

You can read more myths in *Old Greek Folk Stories Told Anew*, by Josephine Preston Peabody.

Think and Discuss

1. What dangers did Daedalus warn Icarus about? How did the attitudes of the father and son differ?
2. In early times, people created stories to explain the world around them. These stories are called **myths**. Some myths explained events in nature; others told people how they should or should not behave. Which kind of myth is the story of Icarus and Daedalus? Explain your answer.
3. "Icarus and Daedalus" is a Greek myth. The ancient Greeks believed strongly in moderation, or avoiding extremes. Explain how the myth shows this belief.

Why did early people create myths?

An Introduction to Greek Mythology

By Olivia Coolidge

This article is from the author's book *Greek Myths*.

Greek legends have been favorite stories for many centuries. They are mentioned so often by famous writers that it has become impossible to read widely in English, or in many other literatures, without knowing what the best of these tales are about. Even though we no longer believe in the Greek gods, we enjoy hearing of them because they appeal to our imagination.

The Greeks thought all the forces of nature were spirits, so that the whole earth was filled with gods. Each river, each woodland, even each great tree had its own god or nymph. In the woods lived the satyrs,[1] who had pointed ears and the shaggy legs of goats. In the sea danced more than three thousand green-haired, white-limbed maidens. In the air rode wind gods, cloud nymphs, and the golden chariot of the sun. All these spirits, like the forces of nature, were beautiful and strong, but sometimes unreliable and unfair. Above all, however, the Greeks felt that they were tremendously interested in mankind.

From very early times the Greeks began to invent stories to account for the things that went on—the change of seasons, the sudden storms, the good and bad fortune of the farmer's year. These tales were spread by travelers from one valley to another. They were put together and altered by poets and musicians, until at last a great body of legends arose from the whole of Greece. These did not agree with one

---

[1]satyrs (sā′tərz)

another in details, but on the whole gave a clear picture of who the chief gods were, how men should behave to please them, and what their relationships had been with heroes of the past.

The ruler of all the gods was Zeus, the sky god, titled by courtesy father of gods and men. He lived in the clouds with most of the great gods in a palace on the top of Mount Olympus, the tallest mountain in Greece. Lightning was the weapon of Zeus, thunder was the rolling of his chariot, and when he nodded his head, the whole earth shook.

Zeus, though the ruler of the world, was not the eldest of the gods. First had come a race of monsters with fifty heads and a hundred arms each. Next followed elder gods called Titans, the leader of whom, Cronos, had reigned before Zeus. Then arose mighty giants, and finally Zeus and the Olympians. Zeus, in a series of wars, succeeded in banishing the Titans and imprisoning the giants in various ways. One huge monster, Typhon, lay imprisoned under the volcano of Aetna,[2] which spouted fire when he struggled. Atlas, one of the giants, was forced to stand holding the heavens on his shoulders so that they should not fall upon the earth.

Almost as powerful as Zeus were his two brothers, who did not live on Olympus: Poseidon,[3] ruler of the sea, and Hades,[4] gloomy king of the Underworld, where the spirits of the dead belong. Queen of the gods was blue-eyed, majestic Hera. Aphrodite,[5] the laughing, sea-born goddess, was queen of love and most beautiful of all. Apollo and Artemis were twins, god of the sun and goddess of the moon. Apollo was the more important. Every day he rode the heavens in a golden chariot from dawn to sunset. The sun's rays could be gentle and healing, or they could be terrible. Apollo, therefore, was a great healer and the father of the god of medicine. At the same time he was a famous archer, and the arrows from his golden bow were arrows of infection and death. Apollo was also god of poetry and song; his instrument was a

---

[2]Aetna (ĕt′nə)   [3]Poseidon (pō-sīd′n)   [4]Hades (hā′dēz)
[5]Aphrodite (ăf′rə-dī′tē)

golden lyre, and the nine Muses, goddesses of music and the arts, were his attendants. He was the ideal of young manhood and the patron of athletes.

Apollo was also god of prophecy. There were temples of Apollo, known as oracles, at which a man could ask questions about the future. The priestesses of Apollo, inspired by the god, gave him an answer, often in the form of a riddle which was hard to understand. Nevertheless, the Greeks believed that if a man could interpret the words of the oracle, he would find the answer to his problem.

Artemis, the silver moon goddess, was goddess of unmarried girls and a huntress of wild beasts in the mountains. She also could send deadly arrows from her silver bow.

Gray-eyed Athene,[6] the goddess of wisdom, was patron of Athens. She was queen of the domestic arts, particularly spinning and weaving. Athene was warlike too; she wore helmet and breastplate, and carried a spear. Ares,[7] however, was the real god of war, and the maker of weapons was Hephaestus,[8] the lame smith and metalworker.

The Greeks have left us so many stories about their gods that it hardly would be possible for everyone to know them all. We can still enjoy them because they are good stories. In spite of their great age we can still understand them because they are about nature and about people. We still need them to enrich our knowledge of our own language and of the great masterpieces of literature.

Think and Discuss

1. What sorts of things did ancient people try to explain through their myths?
2. Make a list of the natural events and activities that the different gods represented. What sorts of things seem to have been important in Greek culture?
3. Explain this statement: In modern times, science has taken over the role of the ancient myths.

---

[6]Athene (ə-thē′nē) [7]Ares (âr′ēz) [8]Hephaestus (hĭ-fĕs′təs)

How much were the Greek gods like people?

Greek Gods
and Mortals

By George Hillocks

At some point in their early history, the Greeks
began to attribute human characteristics to their
gods. Statues of the Greek gods resemble ideal human beings, graceful and majestic. In character and
temperament too, the gods were all too human,
sometimes appearing jealous, quick tempered, self-
centered, even treacherous—altogether, rather un-
godlike.

Humans, however, were expected to be loyal,
honest, and respectful before the gods—in short, to
possess all those virtues we admire. One of the
greatest offenses a person could commit against the
gods was that of *hubris*, or excessive pride, an of-
fense which inevitably led to disastrous consequences
for the mortal.

Because of their many high achievements in politics, literature, science, and the arts, the Greeks may
sometimes have been tempted to imagine themselves
gods. Such stories as that of Daedalus and Icarus,
both believable and human characters, would serve
to remind Greek mortals of their human limitations.

Think and Discuss

1. In what ways were the Greek gods like people?
2. According to the author, stories like "Icarus and
   Daedalus" were used to show the dangers of trying
   to imitate the gods. How did the story show this?
   Use details from the myth in your answer.
3. In the ancient Greek way of thinking, would recent
   developments in technology such as space travel
   and modern medicine be seen as "hubris"? Explain
   your answer.

RESPONDING TO LITERATURE

The Reading and Writing Connection

Personal response In the Greek myth about the escape of Daedalus and Icarus, the father and son attempted something unusual. When have you tried out something you had never done before? What made you do it? How did you go about it? Did it turn out well or badly? Tell about the experience.

Creative writing Early people used myths to explain things that they did not understand. Imagine that you are an ancient Greek who returns to Earth in modern times. How would you explain airplanes, a rock band, or television? Choose one of the wonders that you encounter and write a myth that explains it.

Creative Activities

Design an ad Suppose that Daedalus decides to sell his wings. Design a magazine ad for them. How will you illustrate it? What will the headline say? You can include details on their expert construction, quality materials, and fine performance.

Dramatize Choose a partner. One person will take the role of Daedalus and the other the role of Icarus. Make up the conversation the father and son might have had when they first talked about their plan of escape. Try to capture the difference in their attitudes.

Vocabulary

Some of the words we use today come from the names of characters in the myths of Greece and Rome. Find the origins of the words *mercurial, titanic, hypnosis, martial, volcano.* Tell how their meanings are based on figures in ancient myths.

Looking Ahead

Comparison and contrast Later in this unit, you will be writing paragraphs of comparison and contrast. Look back at the article "Greek Gods and Mortals," by George Hillocks. In what ways were the gods and humans alike? In what ways were they different?

VOCABULARY CONNECTION

Context Clues

Often you can figure out the meanings of unfamiliar words from the **context,** the words and the sentences around it. The context of a word may contain a comparison that helps explain the words.

> He held himself aloft, wavered this way and that with the wind, and at last, like a great **fledgling,** he learned to fly.
> *from "Icarus and Daedalus" retold by Josephine Peabody*

Daedalus is being compared to something that learns to fly, so you probably concluded that *fledgling* means "a young bird learning to fly."

Synonyms and antonyms can also be context clues.

> Apollo's **melancholy** mood matched the *gloomy* temple.
> He **feigned** interest in the talk, but he *really felt* bored.

Melancholy and *gloomy* are synonyms; their meanings are very similar. *Feigned* and *really felt* are antonyms; they are opposite in meaning.

The context can also contain examples or explanations of the unfamiliar word.

> People listened to **oracles,** *wise priests with messages from the gods.*

An *oracle* relayed information from the gods to the people.

Vocabulary Practice

A. Use context clues to figure out the meaning of each underlined word from the literature in this unit. Write the meaning of each word. Check your dictionary.

1. Zeus looked <u>majestic</u> and stately as he presided over the banquet of the gods.
2. Two <u>mortals</u>, not gods, told exciting tales.
3. Hera played the <u>lyre</u>, an instrument like a harp.

B. Find five unfamiliar words from the literature in this unit. Look them up in a dictionary. For each word, write a sentence that provides clear context clues.

Prewriting
Comparison and Contrast

Listening: To Take Notes

Suppose that "An Introduction to Greek Mythology" were read aloud to you. Even if you listened very carefully, you probably could not remember all the facts. When you *listen* for information, you cannot go back and review the facts, as you can when you read. Taking notes will help you remember information during a class, a meeting, a speech, or even a conversation. You will be able to concentrate better and retain more facts. Also, your notes will be a guide for later review or study.

When you take notes, do not try to write every word you hear. Write the speaker's main points and any important details that support them. Then write any questions that you may need to ask the speaker later.

A student named Alicia took notes while listening to an oral report given by her classmate, Michael. In his report, Michael compared and contrasted two Greek gods. Read the report and the notes Alicia took.

Michael's report

Poseidon and Hades were two important gods in Greek mythology. They were both brothers of Zeus, the ruler of all the gods, and they were mighty gods themselves. Both Poseidon and Hades helped Zeus gain control of the world by defeating the Titans. Then the three brothers divided the world among themselves. Zeus chose the sky and made his home at Mount Olympus. Poseidon took the sea, and Hades lived in the underworld and ruled over the dead.

In many ways, Poseidon and Hades were very different. As ruler of the sea, Poseidon carried a trident as his weapon. As ruler of the underworld, Hades wore a weapon called the helmet of darkness, which made him invisible. Poseidon was responsible for storms at sea and earthquakes, and he was known for his fury and violent temper. He was also the subject of many Greek myths and rituals. Hades, on the other hand, was portrayed as cold and grim, and few myths were written about him.

Listening **123**

Alicia's notes

Topic: Poseidon and Hades

<u>similarities</u>
- brothers of Zeus
- mighty gods
- fought to control world by defeating Titans
- shared in division of world

<u>differences</u>
- P. ruled the sea, H. the underworld & dead
- P. "known for his fury & violent temper"
- H. "cold and grim"
- P. subject of many myths & rituals, H. of few

Q: How did Zeus, Poseidon, & Hades **defeat** Titans

- What did Alicia decide were the main points?
- What abbreviations did Alicia use?
- Which of Michael's words did Alicia use exactly?
- What question does Alicia want to ask Michael?

Guidelines for Taking Notes

1. Note the date, place, speaker's name, and topic, if known.
2. Listen for the speaker's purpose and topic.
3. Write only the main points and important details. Listen for words such as *first, next, important, both, alike,* and *different.* These words signal important points.
4. Use abbreviations that you will be able to understand later.
5. Put quotation marks around words you quote exactly.
6. If the speaker gives a summary, check your notes to be sure you have included the important points.
7. Note any questions you want to ask the speaker later.
8. Write neatly so that you can read your notes.
9. Read your notes as soon as possible to be sure you still remember what they mean. Rewrite any unclear notes.

Prewriting Practice

Take notes as your teacher reads aloud a passage comparing and contrasting Greek and Roman myths. Use the guidelines.

Thinking: Comparing and Contrasting ☑

When you first saw an airplane, you probably noticed that it was similar to—but not exactly like—a bird. When you noted the ways in which the two items were alike, you were **comparing** them. When you noted ways in which the items were different, you were **contrasting** them. Since your childhood you have learned about new things by comparing and contrasting them with familiar things.

By comparing or contrasting people, places, and things mentioned in your reading with people, places, and things you know, you can gain a better understanding of what you read. For example, have you ever known anyone who ignored a warning or good advice and suffered the consequences? By comparing that person with Icarus, you will probably be able to imagine Icarus's character more clearly. Similarly, using comparison and contrast in your writing allows you to emphasize the details that you think will be particularly valuable to your readers. As a result, your readers will better understand your meaning and remember what they read.

The passage below uses comparison and contrast to describe the god Apollo and the goddess Artemis. As you read it, think of the deities' similarities and differences. Then study the lists that follow the passage.

> Apollo and Artemis were twins, god of the sun and goddess of the moon. Apollo was the more important. Every day he rode the heavens in a golden chariot from dawn to sunset. The sun's rays could be gentle and healing, or they could be terrible. Apollo, therefore, was a great healer and the father of the god of medicine. At the same time he was a famous archer, and the arrows from his golden bow were arrows of infection and death. Apollo was also god of poetry and song.
>
> Artemis, the silver moon goddess, was goddess of unmarried girls and a huntress of wild beasts in the mountains. She also could send deadly arrows from her silver bow.
>
> *from "An Introduction to Greek Mythology" by Olivia Coolidge*

SIMILARITIES—Comparing Apollo and Artemis

1. figures in Greek myths
2. twins
3. rulers of heavenly bodies
4. sent out deadly arrows

DIFFERENCES—Contrasting Apollo and Artemis

Apollo	Artemis
1. male	1. female
2. god of sun	2. goddess of moon
3. more important	3. less important
4. associated with gold	4. associated with silver
5. healer	5. huntress
6. god of poetry and song	6. goddess of unmarried girls

Notice that these lists compare and contrast the two figures point by point. Certain features are left out because there is no corresponding information for the other figure. For example, nothing is included about Apollo's daily trip around the heavens, for there is no comparable piece of information about Artemis.

When you compare and contrast, be sure that the two things have something in common. It makes sense, for example, to compare and contrast two figures in mythology or two ideas about the sun or two writers of short stories. However, it makes little sense to compare a myth with a table or a sea gull with a telephone pole, unless you are interested in achieving some special literary effect.

These guidelines will help you to compare and contrast.

Guidelines for Comparing and Contrasting

1. Be aware of your purpose for comparing and contrasting.
2. Be sure the items you have chosen to compare and contrast have something in common.
3. List the items' similarities and differences.
4. Omit from your lists any features that do not correspond from one item to the other.

Prewriting Practice

Compare and contrast four pairs of items below by listing their similarities and differences.

1. Greek god, modern hero
2. myth, personal experience
3. two species of birds
4. two sporting events
5. two towns you have lived in
6. palace, apartment

Composition Skills
Comparison and Contrast

Main Idea and Supporting Details ☑

Writing is like building. You put different parts together to create something new. You build words into sentences, sentences into paragraphs, and paragraphs into stories, reports, or letters.

A writer, like a builder, needs to put the parts together in certain ways. Not every group of words makes a sentence, and not every group of sentences makes a paragraph. A **paragraph** is a group of sentences that has one main idea. All the sentences in the paragraph must support that idea.

The following sentences all support one main idea.

> In one Greek myth, stones tossed onto the earth became men and women. In another, the teeth of a wild beast turned into warriors. The daughter of a Greek river god was saved from an unhappy marriage when her father turned her into a laurel tree. A woman famous for her weaving was turned into a spider for competing with a jealous Greek goddess.

Which statement best expresses the main idea?

1. In Greek myths, people sometimes turn into animals.
2. A story does not have to be realistic to be interesting.
3. Transformations occur frequently in Greek myths.

The first choice is too narrow. It applies only to one sentence in the paragraph. The second is too general. Only Greek myths are mentioned in the paragraph. The third choice best expresses the main idea. All the sentences support it.

Which of these sentences could best be added to the paragraph about Greek myths?

1. In a well-known Greek myth, a handsome young man turned into a flower.
2. Greek gods often fell in love with humans.
3. Magic clothing and weapons often play an important part in Greek myths.

The first sentence could be added because it gives another example to support the main idea.

Prewriting Practice

Here are sentences for a paragraph. One of the sentences does not support the main idea. Write that sentence. Then write the main idea expressed by the remaining sentences.

1. The planet Venus was named after the Roman goddess of love.
2. The largest planet in our solar system, Jupiter, was named after the Roman god who ruled all gods and mortals.
3. Today's writers still draw on ideas and images from the ancient myths.
4. The planet Neptune was named after the Roman god of the sea, and distant Pluto was named after the Roman god of the underworld.
5. Mercury, the smallest planet, was named after the Roman messenger god, and Mars was the Roman god of war.

Topic Sentences ☑

In a paragraph, a topic sentence tells you what the paragraph is about. The topic sentence states the main idea of the paragraph.

Not every paragraph has a topic sentence. Sometimes, especially in a longer piece of writing, the main idea is clear without it. Furthermore, the topic sentence does not always have to be at the beginning of the paragraph. It can occur in the middle or at the end.

Where is the topic sentence in this paragraph?

Minerva was the favorite child of Jupiter, the king of the Roman gods. She was born out of Jupiter's forehead, fully grown and dressed in armor. Minerva represented many different skills and became the goddess of wisdom. As the goddess of wisdom in warfare, she carried a magic shield. Minerva wore her armor proudly as one of the most important goddesses of ancient Rome.

The last sentence gives a clear, vivid statement of the main idea. It is the topic sentence. A good topic sentence states the main idea clearly and expresses that idea in lively, exact language. Would either of the following be a *better* topic sentence for the paragraph about Minerva?

> **1.** Minerva was important.
>
> **2.** Because she was the goddess of wisdom and warfare and the favorite child of the king of the gods, along with her many skills, Minerva certainly was an important goddess of ancient Rome.

The first sentence does not clearly state the main idea. It does not give enough information. Furthermore, the sentence is dull.

The second sentence repeats the details of the paragraph rather than just stating the main idea. It is boring, too, because it is hard to follow.

Prewriting Practice

A. Choose the better topic sentence of each pair. Give a reason for each choice.

1. **(a)** A marriage between a Greek god and goddess was not always a perfect match.
   (b) The Greek goddess of spring married the god of the gloomy underworld.
2. **(a)** Certain games are very enjoyable.
   (b) Chess can be an exciting game.
3. **(a)** Icebreakers have strong hulls and powerful engines to break through the Arctic ice and let ships pass from the Atlantic to the Pacific.
   (b) Sturdy ships called icebreakers make channels so ships can sail the Arctic Ocean.

B. Make up two topic sentences for each idea. Try to capture the idea in lively, exact language.

1. Why you do or do not enjoy reading myths
2. Why you would like to have wings
3. The Greek god or fantasy hero you would most like to be

The Grammar Connection

Exact Nouns

Sometimes you can make your writing more powerful by replacing several descriptive words with a single noun that "says it all." Notice the difference between the two sentences in each pair below.

> The downfall of King Midas was his desire for gold; he was never satisfied no matter how rich he grew.
> *The downfall of King Midas was his greed for gold.*

> As a weaver, the Greek maiden Arachne was extremely talented and highly skilled.
> *As a weaver, the Greek maiden Arachne was an expert.*

Practice In each sentence below, replace the underlined section with a single noun.

1. Icarus was enchanted by the bright, flickering shine of the ocean beneath him.
2. When Icarus fell into the sea, Daedalus was filled with feelings of loss and sorrow.
3. People enjoy playing games involving physical exercise.
4. A very large group of people had gathered in the stadium.
5. The benches above the playing field were packed with fans.
6. Her bat hit the ball with a loud, sharp sound.
7. Fans gave ear-splitting yells.
8. The setting sun lit the tall buildings of steel and concrete.

Organizing Comparison and Contrast Paragraphs ☑

Earlier in this unit you read two paragraphs in which the twin gods Apollo and Artemis were compared and contrasted. Apollo's features were described in one paragraph and those of Artemis in another.

When you write comparison and contrast paragraphs, it is important to organize your information so that it makes sense. Your topic sentence—which tells your reader that you are going to compare, contrast, or do both—may come at the beginning or at the end of a paragraph. Supporting sentences point out similarities and differences and include examples of ways in which your subjects are alike and different.

Read the following paragraph of comparison.

> At some point in early history, the Greeks began to attribute human characteristics to their gods. Statues of the Greek gods resemble ideal human beings, graceful and majestic. In character and temperament, too, the gods were all too human, sometimes appearing jealous, quick-tempered, self-centered, even treacherous— altogether rather ungodlike.
>
> *from "Greek Gods and Mortals" by George Hillocks*

- Which sentence is the topic sentence?
- To what are the Greek gods compared?
- What examples are given to make the comparison clear?

Now read the paragraph of contrast below.

> In Norse myths, twelve gods and twenty-four goddesses lived in Asgard. Only five Greek gods and five goddesses lived on Olympus, however. No Greek god matches Loki, the Norse god of mischief, who caused the overthrow of the gods. The Greek gods could not be destroyed; they were immortal. The Norse gods, on the other hand, knew that they would be destroyed.
>
> *adapted from* Anthology of Children's Literature

- What clue words make the contrast clear?
- How many points of contrast are given? What are they?

Remember these points when you compare and contrast.

1. You can write one paragraph for comparison and one for contrast, or one that both compares and contrasts.
2. Begin or end with a topic sentence.
3. Make each similarity or difference a separate point.
4. Add examples and details to illustrate each point.
5. Use words such as *similarly, like, however, but,* and *on the other hand* to make your comparison or contrast clear.

Prewriting Practice

For each pair of items below, write a topic sentence for (1) a paragraph of comparison, (2) a paragraph of contrast, and (3) a paragraph of both comparison and contrast. Then list three examples or details to support each topic sentence.

1. two friends   2. a tornado and a hurricane

Step 1: Prewriting—Choose a Topic

Celia made a list of all the pairs of things she could think of to compare and contrast. Then she made notes about each topic.

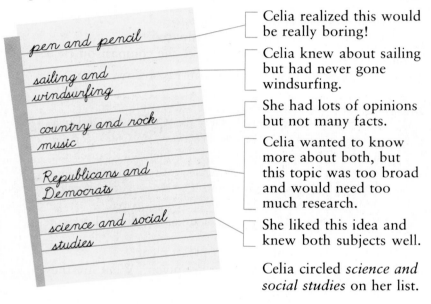

pen and pencil — Celia realized this would be really boring!

sailing and windsurfing — Celia knew about sailing but had never gone windsurfing.

country and rock music — She had lots of opinions but not many facts.

Republicans and Democrats — Celia wanted to know more about both, but this topic was too broad and would need too much research.

science and social studies — She liked this idea and knew both subjects well.

Celia circled *science and social studies* on her list.

On Your Own

1. **Think and discuss** Make a list of the pairs of things you can compare and contrast. Use the Ideas page to help you. Discuss your list with a partner.

2. **Choose** Ask these questions about each pair on your list.
   Do I know enough about each item?
   Can I come up with enough similarities and differences?
   Can I make specific comparisons and contrasts?
   Which topic would I most enjoy writing about?
   Circle the topic you choose.

3. **Explore** What will you cover in your paper? To help you decide what to write, do one of the activities under "Exploring Your Topic" on the Ideas page.

Ideas for Getting Started

Choosing a Topic

Topic Ideas

An ancient Greek and a modern explanation of a storm

Music videos and TV commercials

Newspapers and television news

Television and films

Jogging and cycling

Automatic and manual transmissions

Dolphins and porpoises

. . . Or Try These

Read these topic sentences for ideas.

Gospel and soul music do not sound identical, but they both have the same origins.

If you play racquetball, you can learn squash, though rules and equipment differ.

English and Western riding saddles differ in both appearance and use.

Plays and films entertain, but they affect an audience differently.

Exploring Your Topic

Match Game

Write the names of two things you are comparing at the top of a sheet of paper. Below each, list seven or eight characteristics. Draw red lines between the lists to connect similar characteristics. Draw blue lines to connect interesting differences.

Talk About It

Play "Compare-and-Contrast Tennis." Take your topic, and "serve" your partner a similarity between the two items. Your partner "returns" by stating a difference. Then your partner "serves" a similarity, and you "return" a difference. When a player cannot return a serve, the opponent wins a point.

Step 2: Write a First Draft

Since Celia was going to compare and contrast science and social studies, she decided to write her paper for her science and social studies teachers. She knew her classmates might read it too.

Without worrying about mistakes, Celia wrote a first draft. She would be able to make corrections and changes later.

Celia's first draft

~~Science~~ In science, you learn about the natural world. You study the makeup of things
like chemical elaments, cells, and organizms, you learn how they group together to
form plants, animals, and minerals. In
social studies, you learn how people work
together.

Think and Discuss ☑
- How could Celia make her main idea clearer?
- What details does Celia use to make her point?
- What details are unclear? How could Celia make them clearer?

On Your Own

1. **Think about purpose and audience** Answer these questions.
   For what audience am I writing?
   What is my purpose? What do I want my readers to get from this paper? What will I learn from it?
2. **Write** Write your first draft. Remember to write a topic sentence that clearly states your main idea. Make the other sentences in the paragraph support that idea. Write all you can; do not worry about mistakes, but write on every other line to leave room for changes and corrections you will make later.

Step 3: Revise

When Celia read her first draft, she discovered a problem. She had not made it clear that she was comparing and contrasting science and social studies. Her main idea did not become clear until the last sentence. She decided to add a topic sentence to the beginning.

Celia wanted to make sure that her point was now clear. She read her paper to Brooke.

Reading and responding

Celia: Do my ideas make sense?

Brooke: I never thought science and social studies were alike before. Now I see they are, so yes.

Celia: Are there any parts I need to change?

Brooke: The part about science was a lot clearer than the part about social studies. Maybe you could add more about social studies.

Celia agreed with Brooke that she had not been very specific about social studies. She added more details, using words that would show exactly what she meant.

Celia's revision

In both science and social studies, you learn about the world and how parts of it work together.

~~Science~~ In science, you learn about the natural world. You study the makeup of things like chemical elements, cells, and organizms, you learn how they group together to form plants, animals, and minerals. In

social studies, you learn *that people also* ~~how people work~~ *form groups. They interact to form* ~~together.~~ *families, communities, and countries.*

Think and Discuss ☑
- How did Celia make her main idea clearer?
- What else did she make clearer?
- What specific words and details did she add?

On Your Own

Revising checklist

☑ Have I clearly stated my main idea in a topic sentence?
☑ Do all my sentences support the main idea?
☑ Have I used specific details and exact words?
☑ Have I organized my details in a way that makes sense?
☑ Are my comparisons or contrasts clear?

1. **Revise** Make changes in your first draft. Cross out any parts that could be improved, and write your changes between the lines or in the margins. Add supporting details. If you need to find exact words, use the thesaurus below or the one at the back of this book.

2. **Have a conference** Read your paper to someone else—a teacher or a classmate. Write down their comments and suggestions.

WRITING

CONFERENCE

Ask your listener:	As you listen:
"How could I improve my topic sentence?" "Do you understand my points?" "Where could I use more details?"	I must listen carefully. What is the main idea? Are any points unclear? What do I want to learn more about?

3. **Revise** After thinking about your listener's suggestions, do you have any other ideas? Make those changes on your paper.

Thesaurus

alike *adj.* similar, comparable, equivalent
characteristic *n.* trait, quality, feature
contrast *v.* distinguish, differentiate
examine *v.* inspect, study, observe
main *adj.* principal, central, basic, primary
think *v.* believe, consider, reason, speculate

Step 4: Proofread

Celia proofread her paper for spelling, capitalization, and punctuation errors. She used a dictionary to check her spellings. She also looked for run-ons and fragments. She made her changes with proofreading marks.

Celia's comparison after proofreading

¶ *On both science and social studies, you learn about the world and how parts of it work together.*

~~Science~~ In science, you learn about the natu-

ral world. You study the makeup of things

like chemical el*e*ments, cells, and orga-

nizms*;* you learn how they group together to

form plants, animals, and minerals. In

social studies, you learn *that people also* ~~how people work~~

form groups. They interact to form ~~together.~~

families, communities, and countries.

Think and Discuss
- Which words did Celia correct for spelling?
- What letter did she capitalize? Why?
- What punctuation mark did she change? Why?

On Your Own

1. **Proofreading Practice** Proofread this paragraph, and then copy it correctly. There is one run-on sentence that should be corrected. One noun should be capitalized. There is an incorrect plural ending and one incorrect possessive. Two commas are missing.

    Two kinds of dogs the golden retriever and
    the Irish setter have many similaritys, but
    they are not identical. The easiest way to tell
    them apart is by color. The fur of irish set-
    ters is reddish, a golden retrievers' fur is a
    rich gold.

2. **Proofreading Application** Proofread your paper, using the Proofreading Checklist and the Grammar and Spelling Hints below. If you wish, mark your corrections with a colored pencil. Check your spellings in a dictionary.

Proofreading Checklist	Proofreading Marks
Did I	⌒ Indent
☑ 1. indent?	∧ Add
☑ 2. capitalize correctly?	⩝ Add a comma
☑ 3. use possessive and plural nouns correctly?	ⱽⱽ Add quotation marks
	⊙ Add a period
	ℓ Take out
☑ 4. use proper punctuation?	≡ Capitalize
	/ Make a small letter
☑ 5. spell all words correctly?	⌒ Reverse the order

The Grammar/Spelling Connection

Grammar Hints
Remember these rules from Unit 3 when using nouns.

- An appositive should be set off with commas when it is *not* needed to identify the noun. (*My brother, Michael, is away at college.* This means that Michael is the speaker's *only* brother.)
- An appositive should *not* be set off with commas when it *is* needed to identify the noun. (*My brother Michael is away at college.* This means that the speaker has more than one brother.)
- To form the possessive of a singular noun, add an apostrophe and *s*. (*Gail–Gail's; woman–woman's*)

Spelling Hints
Remember these principles when writing nouns.

- Check a dictionary to find out whether a compound noun is written as one word or two or if it is hyphenated. (*boardwalk, check list, forget-me-not*)
- When a noun ends in a consonant and *y*, form its plural by changing the *y* to *i* and adding *es*. (*activity–activities; quality–qualities*)

Step 5: Publish

Celia decorated a folder with an attractive design made up of science and social studies terms. She enclosed her paper and shared it with her science and social studies teachers.

On Your Own

Follow the steps below to make a finished copy, and you will be ready to share your paper.

1. **Copy** Make a neat handwritten or typed copy of your proofread paper.
2. **Give it a title** Your title should tell what you are comparing and contrasting and catch your readers' interest.
3. **Check** Read your paper again to make certain you have left nothing out and have made no mistakes.
4. **Share** Think of a way to share your paper.

Ideas for Sharing

- With your classmates, bind your essays into a reference book on comparisons and contrasts. Illustrate the book, and add a table of contents and an index.
- Make a pamphlet of your paper, adding headings, artwork, and captions where appropriate.
- Make a poster, illustrating the two things you compared or contrasted. Attach your paper, and display the poster.

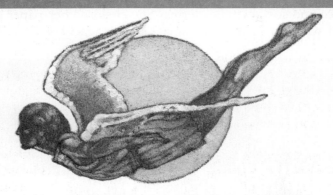

Literature and Creative Writing

In the myth of Icarus and Daedalus on pages 114–116, Daedalus makes wings with which he and his son escape their prison. Daedalus flies safely to freedom, but Icarus flies too close to the sun. The wax on his wings melts, and he falls to the sea.

Now use what you have learned about writing comparisons and contrasts to complete one or more of these activities.

1. **Contrast father and son.** What differences between Daedalus and Icarus help to explain their different fates? Write a paragraph contrasting father and son.

2. **A man or a bird?** Imagine that a bird glides by Daedalus in the sky. As soon as it gets close, the bird realizes that this is no relative of his. How does the bird know? Write a paragraph about the ways in which Daedalus differs from a bird, even with his wings on. Write as if you were the bird.

3. **Compare and contrast sea and sky.** Imagine yourself on a clear day flying like a bird between the sea and sky. What would the sky look like? What would the sea look like? Write two brief paragraphs, one comparing the sea and sky, the other contrasting them.

Remember these things ☑
- Write a paragraph for each main idea.
- Write a topic sentence that states the main idea.
- Write sentences that support the main idea. Organize them in a way that makes sense.

Writing Across the Curriculum
Mathematics

Mathematics involves comparing and contrasting numbers and quantities. The method of comparison and contrast is also used to evaluate business systems that use mathematics.

Do one or more of the following activities.

1. **Compare and contrast the methods.** Is there any difference between using a calculator for math and figuring on paper? How are these methods alike and different? Share your comparison with your math teacher.

| calculate |
| estimate |
| operation |
| method |
| process |
| procedure |
| malfunction |
| batteries |

2. **Compare and contrast the systems.** Students in your age group are among the first in the nation to have been taught two systems of measurement all through school. Compare the benefits and drawbacks of the International Metric System with those of the U.S. Customary System.

3. **Compare and contrast the programs.** Software development companies must compare their products with others on the market. Imagine that you work for the company that developed your favorite program. Compare this program with another that you have used. You may want to submit this comparison to your school newspaper for a column.

Scott had so enjoyed reading "Icarus and Daedalus" that he decided to read *Myths and Legends of the Greeks* by Nicola Ann Sissons. Scott liked the humans in these stories much better than the gods, who were often cruel and disagreeable. He especially liked the story of two friends—Damon and Pythias. He decided to share the story with his classmates by making up an interview with Damon. Scott took the part of Damon and asked a friend to be the interviewer. This is the interview.

INTERVIEWER: Good evening. I am talking with Damon here in the king's prison. Damon, why are <u>you</u> here? I thought that Pythias was the one arrested.

DAMON: He was, but he asked me to change places with him while he made a visit home. If he didn't make some arrangements, his family would starve!

INTERVIEWER: You took his place in prison, and you really expect him to return?

DAMON: Of course Pythias will come back! Our friendship is strong and he is a man of honor. I would do the same for him.

INTERVIEWER: Well, I hope you're right. Why was he arrested, anyhow?

DAMON: Pythias spoke out against our cruel king. Pythias told him what a wicked tyrant he is!

INTERVIEWER: But that means a death sentence! Damon, Pythias will never come back! You will be executed instead!

DAMON: No, Pythias will return for me.

INTERVIEWER: <u>Will</u> Pythias return? Read "Damon and Pythias" in <u>Myths and Legends of the Greeks</u> by Nicola Ann Sissons.

Think and Discuss
- Who are the characters in the story?
- What did you find out about the characters?
- Why is this a good way to share a story?

Share Your Book

Interview a Book Character

1. Decide which character to interview. It can be a major character or a minor character who knows the story.
2. Decide which parts of the book you will tell about. Choose exciting incidents that will interest your classmates. Ask your character questions about these incidents. Try to ask questions that will give background information.
3. Write down the lines you are giving to the interviewer and to the character. Ask a classmate to read the part of the interviewer while you take the part of the book character. Be careful not to tell too much of the plot. Leave your audience wondering how the story ends.
4. Start your interview by having the interviewer introduce the character and give the title and author of your book.

Other Activities

- Write an interview in which a character in your book asks the author questions. For example, the character might want to know what happens to him or her after the story ends.
- Ask two classmates to take the parts of their book characters. Plan an interview in which you introduce the two to each other and ask questions to help them compare their stories. Present the interview to the class as though it were a radio or television program.
- Create a large picture of the setting for your interview. It might be a landscape, a room, or perhaps a map of the area where the story takes place. Use this as the background if you present the interview as a television program. If you choose radio, create some good sound effects.

 # The Book Nook

The Heroes: Greek Fairy Tales *by Charles Kingsley* The adventures of Perseus, the Argonauts, and Theseus are retold by a master storyteller.	Greek Myths *by Olivia Coolidge* This collection of famous myths includes a table of the chief gods of ancient Greece.

Language and Usage

The splendor falls on castle walls
And snowy summits old in story;
The long light shakes across the lakes—
And the wild cataract leaps in glory.
Blow, bugle, blow, set the wild echoes flying,
Blow, bugle; answer, echoes, dying, dying, dying.

Alfred, Lord Tennyson
from "The Princess"

Verbs

Getting Ready We speak and write about the past, the present, and the future. We tell of action and of being. None of this would be possible without verbs! In this unit you will learn more about verbs and how to use them correctly.

ACTIVITIES

Listening Listen as your teacher reads the verse that goes with the photograph. List the verbs that you hear. Do they tell of the past, present, or future?

Speaking Look at the picture. What can you see in this picture that is described in the poem? Notice that the poem says light *shakes;* try to think of unusual, strong, and surprising verbs. Have someone list them on the board.

Writing In your journal, write about what you think might have happened at this castle.

1 | Kinds of Verbs

Action and Being Verbs

You know that every sentence has a verb. The verb tells what the subject *has, does, is,* or *feels.*

Ed and Iris raise vegetables.   They feel happy.

Verbs express action or being. An **action verb** tells what the subject *has* or *does.* An action verb can express **physical** or **mental action**. Verbs like *run* and *look* express physical action. Verbs like *think* and *dream* express mental action.

PHYSICAL: Farmers plow fields. Gardeners plant seeds.
MENTAL: Farmers fear drought. They hope for rain.

A **being verb** does not refer to action but describes a state of being. It tells what the subject *is* or *feels.* Verbs such as *be, feel, appear, become,* and *seem* show being.

The crop is ready for harvest.   The beans look healthy.
The tomatoes feel soft.   The onions smell.

Guided Practice Find each verb. Does it express mental action, physical action, or being?

Example: Ed and Iris planted pumpkin seeds.
          planted   **physical action**

1. Ed fed the seedlings.
2. The plants became bushy.
3. The pumpkins looked ripe.
4. Ed picked a pumpkin.
5. Iris dreamed of pumpkins.
6. Ed hoped for more pumpkins.
7. The squash was ripe too.
8. They put it into their basket.

Linking Verbs

A verb that expresses being is called a **linking verb** when it links the subject with a word in the predicate. The word in the predicate describes or identifies the subject.

Dill is an herb.   It looks feathery.

You can think of linking verbs as equal signs.

Pepper is a spice. (Pepper = a spice)

Pepper tastes spicy. (Pepper = spicy)

Here are some common linking verbs.

appear	feel	remain	smell
be	grow	seem	sound
become	look	stay	taste

Some linking verbs can also be used as action verbs. If you can substitute a form of *be* for the verb, it is a linking verb.

LINKING	ACTION
The tomato grew moldy.	Jim grows tomatoes.
(The tomato was moldy.)	(Jim is *not* tomatoes.)
The beans taste salty.	The cook tasted the beans.
(The beans are salty.)	(The cook is *not* the beans.)

Guided Practice Find the verbs. Which ones are linking?

Example: Raymond grew thoughtful. *grew* **linking**

9. He looked at the recipe.
10. It looked difficult.
11. Chicken tastes delicious.
12. It was his favorite food.
13. Raymond became brave.
14. He plunged ahead.
15. He followed the recipe.
16. He smelled the garlic.
17. It smelled so good.
18. His task was successful.

Summing up

▸ A **verb** expresses *action*—physical or mental—or *being*. Being verbs are sometimes linking verbs.
▸ A **linking verb** expresses *being*. It links the subject with a word in the predicate that describes or identifies the subject.

Independent Practice Label each verb *action* or *linking*.

Example: Fred cooks delicious meals. *cooks* **action**

19. He enjoys tacos.
20. Tacos are a Mexican food.
21. Taco sauce is hot.
22. Tortillas feel soft.
23. Fred fries each tortilla.
24. The tortillas smell delicious.
25. Fred browns beef in a pan.
26. He chops vegetables.
27. The ingredients look colorful.
28. Fred fills each tortilla.

Writing Application: A Description Write a paragraph describing how a favorite holiday meal or food looks, tastes, and smells. Use linking verbs and underline them.

For Extra Practice, see p. 186.   Kinds of verbs **147**

2 | Verb Phrases

You often use more than one word to make up a verb.

> Iris has gone to the meet.
>
> She might not return until late, but we will wait

A **main verb** expresses action or being. A **helping verb** helps complete the meaning of the main verb. One or more helping verbs and a main verb together form a **verb phrase**.

HELPING VERB	MAIN VERB
Iris is	running well today.
Soon she will have been	running for an hour.
Maybe she will	be a winner.

Common Helping Verbs

be, am, is, are	have, has, had	can, could	will, would
was, were, been	do, does, did	shall, should	may, might

You can use forms of *be, have,* and *do* as both main verbs and helping verbs.

MAIN: Iris is not tired. She has an athlete's strength.

HELPING: She is running now. She has run eight miles.

Sometimes a helping verb is hidden in a contraction.

> She's running well today. (She's = She is)
>
> Soon she'll be ready for the race. (she'll = she will)

Sometimes other words interrupt a verb phrase. These words are never part of the verb phrase.

Do you see any signs?   I can't find the map.

I cannot learn this route.   I shall never learn it.

Guided Practice What is the verb phrase in each sentence? Which is the main verb, and which is the helping verb or verbs?

Example: Iris is reaching the finish line of the marathon.
> **verb phrase:** *is reaching*   **main verb:** *reaching*
> **helping verb:** *is*

1. Iris has trained for the race for months.

2. She's paced herself well throughout the race.

3. This marathon has always been twenty-six miles long.

4. Iris is now winning marathons.

5. She will fly across this finish line.

6. Iris has finally been rewarded for her months of hard work.

7. Will she compete in the next marathon?

8. She's already thinking about her preparations for it.

Summing up

> ▶ A **verb phrase** includes a main verb and one or more helping verbs.
> ▶ The **main verb** expresses the action or being.
> ▶ The **helping verb** or verbs help complete the meaning of the main verb.

Independent Practice
Write each verb phrase. Underline the main verb in each verb phrase.

Example: People have held athletic competitions since the days of the ancient Greeks. *have held*

9. Since those days athletes have been competing in many sports.

10. Track and field events have been very popular for a long time.

11. In one type of track event, an athlete must leap over hurdles.

12. A good hurdler should have speed, rhythm, and balance.

13. A successful hurdler should also move with long strides.

14. Of course a hurdler will have practiced for many hours before an important race.

15. A hurdler must jump over several low obstacles during a race.

16. Great athletes may have trained for years before an event.

17. Sprints, or short races, can be very difficult to train for.

18. The greatest sprinter may have been Jesse Owens.

19. Didn't Owens run much after that?

20. No, he did not run, but he did remain active in young people's sports programs.

21. Cross-country races are run over the countryside.

22. These races may start on a regular track, however.

23. Professional walkers can walk a mile in seven minutes or less.

24. Their feet must never lose contact with the ground.

Writing Application: A Paragraph
Write a paragraph telling about a sports event you have watched or a team sport you enjoy. Use main verbs and helping verbs in your sentences. Underline every verb and verb phrase.

For Extra Practice, see p. 187.   Verb Phrases   **149**

3 | Tenses

Time is shown by the **tense** of a verb. You use different tenses of verbs to express different times.

PAST TENSE: Last week we rehearsed all day every day.
PRESENT TENSE: Now we rehearse in the afternoons.
FUTURE TENSE: Next week we will rehearse in the mornings.

Principal Parts

To form tenses of verbs, you use **principal parts**. The principal parts of regular verbs follow a pattern.

The first principal part is the **base form** of the verb, for example, *jump*. The second principal part is the **present participle**. To form the present participle, add *-ing* to the base form of the verb: *jumping*. Use a form of the helping verb *be* with the present participle: *is jumping*.

The other principal parts are the **past** and the **past participle**. To form these principal parts of regular verbs, add *-ed* or *-d* to the verb: *jumped*. Use a form of the helping verb *have* with the past participle: *has jumped*.

Here are spelling rules for forming regular verb parts.

1. For a one-syllable verb ending with a single consonant, double the final consonant before adding *-ing* or *-ed*.

   chop—chopping—chopped

2. For verbs ending with *e*, drop the *e* before adding *-ed* or *-ing*.

   type—typing—typed

3. For verbs ending with a consonant + *y*, change *y* to *i* before adding *-ed*.

   cry—crying—cried

Guided Practice What are the principal parts of each verb? How do you spell them?

Example: wish   *wish   (is) wishing   wished   (has) wished*

1. close   **2.** try   **3.** expect   **4.** compare   **5.** plan

Simple Tenses

Verbs have three **simple tenses** in English.

Tense	Use	Example
Present walk(s)	For situations that exist now; for repeated actions.	She walks daily. They walk daily.
Past walked	For situations that occurred in the past.	Yesterday she walked. Yesterday they walked.
Future will walk	For situations that will occur in the future.	Later she will walk. Later they will walk.

Guided Practice What are the forms for the three simple tenses of each verb with *she* and with *they*?

Example: open   *She opens.   She opened.   She will open.*
They open.   They opened.   They will open.

6. mix   **7.** turn   **8.** step   **9.** survive   **10.** worry

Perfect Tenses

The three **perfect tenses** are the **present perfect,** the **past perfect,** and the **future perfect.**

Tense	Use
Present Perfect has, have rehearsed	For something that took place in the past and may still be going on.
Past Perfect had rehearsed	For something that took place before something else in the past.
Future Perfect will have rehearsed	For something that will take place before something else in the future.

PRESENT PERFECT: He has rehearsed every day this week.
PAST PERFECT: He had practiced before we came.
FUTURE PERFECT: He will have finished when the bell rings.

Guided Practice What are the forms for the three perfect tenses of each verb with *he* and with *they*?

Example: ask   *he has asked   he had asked   he will have asked*
they have asked   they had asked   they will have asked

11. cry   **12.** wash   **13.** scrape   **14.** clean   **15.** drop

▸ Every verb has four **principal parts**.
▸ Verbs have different **tenses** to express different times.
▸ Use the principal parts of a verb to form its tenses.

Independent Practice

A. Write the four principal parts of each verb.

Example: skip *skip skipping skipped (has) skipped*

16. hop   **18.** pry   **20.** receive   **22.** wipe
17. look   **19.** walk   **21.** paint   **23.** spell

B. Write each sentence, using the correct form of the verb and tense in parentheses.

Example: A producer _____ money. (raise—present)
A producer raises money.

24. Then the producer _____ on a director. (decide—present)
25. The director _____ the best cast for a play and plans the set with the stage designer. (select—present)
26. Last month our producer _____ Emily as director. (name—past)
27. Emily _____ on many fine productions before then. (work—past perfect)
28. In preparation for this new assignment, she _____ over the play very carefully. (look—past)
29. Then she _____ the position of director. (accept—past)
30. In another two weeks, she _____ an important task. (complete—past perfect)
31. She _____ outstanding actors and actresses to the tryouts and had picked the cast. (invite—past perfect)
32. She _____ the costume designer. (advise—past perfect)
33. Over the past few weeks, she _____ the cast in countless re-hearsals. (direct—present perfect)
34. She _____ out many difficulties. (iron—present perfect)
35. Tomorrow we _____ for the last time. (rehearse—future)
36. The director _____ if we get a good round of applause. (succeed—future perfect)

Writing Application: A Description Write a paragraph about a performance that you have attended or watched on TV. Use all of the six tenses.

4 | Forms of *be, have,* and *do*

Be, have, and *do* are verbs that you use very often. You can use them as main verbs and as helping verbs.

MAIN VERB	HELPING VERB
Beets are delicious.	We are growing beets this year.
Beets have edible roots.	We have grown them every year.
Beets do well in loamy soil.	Do you like beets? I really do.

All three verbs can form contractions with *not*: for example, *isn't, aren't, hasn't, haven't, doesn't, don't.*

Dana doesn't like beets.   Shaun isn't a gardener.

Be, have, and *do* have different forms for different subjects and for different tenses. The chart below shows present and past tense forms of *be, have,* and *do.*

Subject	be	have	do
Singular Subjects			
I	am, was	have, had	do, did
you	are, were	have, had	do, did
he, she, it	is, was	has, had	does, did
(or singular noun)			
Plural Subjects			
we	are, were	have, had	do, did
you	are, were	have, had	do, did
they	are, were	have, had	do, did
(or plural noun)			

Guided Practice Which verb form in parentheses completes each sentence correctly?

Example: The Dunns (is, are) good farmers. *are*

1. The weather (is, are) very dry this year.
2. The Dunns (does, do) not know what they will do if it (does, do) not rain soon.
3. The crops (do, did) well last year.
4. Animals (have, has) problems when the weather (is, are) dry.
5. Last year the Dunns (have, had) a healthy harvest.

6. This year their neighbor (has, have) a new irrigation system.
7. (Do, Does) wheat require a lot of water?
8. When (did, do) Mr. Cato plant his crops?
9. I (am, are) interested in farming.
10. How much rain (do, does) the crops need?
11. We (haven't, hasn't) had rain for weeks.
12. According to the radio, a storm (is, are) coming soon.

Summing up

> ▶ You can use *be, have,* and *do* as main verbs and as helping verbs.
> ▶ *Be, have,* and *do* have different forms for different subjects and for different tenses.

Independent Practice Write each sentence, using the correct form of the verb.

Example: The crops (have, had) no rain for weeks. *had*

13. The vegetable crops (has, have) wilted.
14. The Dunns (do, did) everything they possibly could do.
15. (Does, Do) the sky look dark?
16. (Am, Is) I imagining it, or are those rain clouds?
17. I (does, do) believe I see raindrops.
18. (Do, Does) you see them too?
19. (Are, Be) the crops going to be all right?
20. We will (have, has) a healthy harvest after all.
21. I (am, are) looking forward to eating fresh vegetables.
22. My favorite vegetable (is, are) the eggplant.
23. Where (do, did) it get its name?
24. (Does, Do) eggplants resemble eggs?
25. You (has, have) never seen white eggplant, (has, have) you?
26. White eggplants (is, are) smaller than purple ones.
27. They (is, are) sweeter and thinner too.
28. They really (does, do) look like white radishes.
29. (Didn't, Don't) Mr. Cato grow them?
30. I (had, has) some in an Italian restaurant recently.

Writing Application: A Description Write a paragraph describing weather conditions. You could tell how certain weather conditions affect you. Use *be* as a helping verb and *be* as a main verb. Do the same using *have* and *do.*

For Extra Practice, see p. 189.

5 | Irregular Verbs

To form the past and past participles of regular verbs, you follow a certain rule: you add *-d* or *-ed* to the base form of the verb. **Irregular verbs** do not follow any rules. You must learn the principal parts of each one. It may help you to use the verb forms in short sentences such as these.

Today I speak.   Yesterday I spoke.
Now I am speaking.   Often I have spoken.

You have just learned some forms of the verbs *be, have,* and *do.* Here are their principal parts.

Verb	Present Participle	Past	Past Participle
be	(is) being	was, were	(has) been
have	(is) having	had	(has) had
do	(is) doing	did	(has) done

The following irregular verbs are arranged in related groups.

Some irregular verbs have the same form for the verb, the past, and the past participle.

Verb	Present Participle	Past	Past Participle
burst	(is) bursting	burst	(has) burst
cast	(is) casting	cast	(has) cast
cost	(is) costing	cost	(has) cost
cut	(is) cutting	cut	(has) cut
hit	(is) hitting	hit	(has) hit
hurt	(is) hurting	hurt	(has) hurt
let	(is) letting	let	(has) let
put	(is) putting	put	(has) put
set	(is) setting	set	(has) set

Some irregular verbs have the same form for the verb and the past participle.

Verb	Present Participle	Past	Past Participle
become	(is) becoming	became	(has) become
come	(is) coming	came	(has) come
run	(is) running	ran	(has) run

Some irregular verbs have the same form for the past and the past participle.

Verb	Present Participle	Past	Past Participle
bend	(is) bending	bent	(has) bent
bring	(is) bringing	brought	(has) brought
buy	(is) buying	bought	(has) bought
catch	(is) catching	caught	(has) caught
feel	(is) feeling	felt	(has) felt
find	(is) finding	found	(has) found
hold	(is) holding	held	(has) held
lay	(is) laying	laid	(has) laid
lead	(is) leading	led	(has) led
leave	(is) leaving	left	(has) left
lend	(is) lending	lent	(has) lent
lose	(is) losing	lost	(has) lost
make	(is) making	made	(has) made
pay	(is) paying	paid	(has) paid
read	(is) reading	read	(has) read
say	(is) saying	said	(has) said
seek	(is) seeking	sought	(has) sought
sell	(is) selling	sold	(has) sold
shine	(is) shining	shone	(has) shone
sit	(is) sitting	sat	(has) sat
sleep	(is) sleeping	slept	(has) slept
stand	(is) standing	stood	(has) stood
sting	(is) stinging	stung	(has) stung
swing	(is) swinging	swung	(has) swung
teach	(is) teaching	taught	(has) taught
tell	(is) telling	told	(has) told
think	(is) thinking	thought	(has) thought
win	(is) winning	won	(has) won

Guided Practice What are the four principal parts of these irregular verbs?

Example: bring *bring is bringing brought has brought*

1. burst
2. have
3. swing
4. buy
5. lose
6. run
7. set
8. become
9. say
10. be
11. hit
12. come
13. cut
14. do
15. shine
16. hold

▶ **Irregular verbs** do not follow rules for forming the past and past participles. You must learn the principal parts of irregular verbs.

Independent Practice

A. Write each sentence, using the correct form of the verb in parentheses.

Example: I had _____ a few books about a great new sport.
(buy—*past participle*) *bought*

17. My father _____ me a rod, line, hooks, and bait. (lend—past)

18. Then he _____ me some basic skills. (teach—past)

19. Finally, the day had _____. (come—past participle)

20. I was _____ at the edge of the dock. (stand—present participle)

21. I _____ the rod back in a wide arc. (swing—past)

22. Then I _____ the line into the water. (cast—past)

23. The hook _____ the water lightly. (hit—past)

24. In a few seconds, I _____ a nibble on the line. (feel—past)

25. Dad and I were _____ the fish in with a net when I realized something. (bring—present participle)

26. I had _____ my first rainbow trout. (catch—past participle)

B. Write each sentence, adding the correct past or past participle of the verb in parentheses. Do not add helping verbs.

Example: Suki _____ a contest with a fish. (win) *won*

27. She had _____ the perfect spot in the stream. (seek)

28. She had also _____ a special, expensive fly. (bring)

29. Suki _____ her line into the stream. (cast)

30. The fish _____ off with the line. (run)

31. Finally, the line _____ on something. (catch)

32. Suki had _____ the fish and the expensive fly. (lose)

33. Later she _____ the huge fish in a bush. (find)

34. She _____ it loose and took it home. (cut)

Writing Application: A Paragraph Write a paragraph about an outdoor experience that you have had or read about. Use past or past participles of verbs from this lesson.

For Extra Practice, see p. 190.

6 | More Irregular Verbs

Here are two more groups of irregular verbs to learn.

The vowel in some irregular verbs changes from *i* in the verb and present participle to *a* in the past and *u* in the past participle.

Verb	Present Participle	Past	Past Participle
begin	(is) beginning	began	(has) begun
drink	(is) drinking	drank	(has) drunk
ring	(is) ringing	rang	(has) rung
sing	(is) singing	sang	(has) sung
sink	(is) sinking	sank	(has) sunk
spring	(is) springing	sprang	(has) sprung
swim	(is) swimming	swam	(has) swum

Other irregular verbs have past forms that follow no pattern and past participle forms that end with *n, en,* or *ne.*

Verb	Present Participle	Past	Past Participle
blow	blowing	blew	blown
break	breaking	broke	broken
choose	choosing	chose	chosen
drive	driving	drove	driven
eat	eating	ate	eaten
fall	falling	fell	fallen
fly	flying	flew	flown
forget	forgetting	forgot	forgotten
freeze	freezing	froze	frozen
give	giving	gave	given
go	going	went	gone
grow	growing	grew	grown
know	knowing	knew	known
lie	lying	lay	lain
ride	riding	rode	ridden
rise	rising	rose	risen
see	seeing	saw	seen
speak	speaking	spoke	spoken
take	taking	took	taken
throw	throwing	threw	thrown
wear	wearing	wore	worn
write	writing	wrote	written

Guided Practice What are the four principal parts of each of these irregular verbs?

Example: begin *begin (is) beginning began (has) begun*

1. eat   **3.** ring   **5.** write   **7.** choose
2. go   **4.** take   **6.** swim   **8.** know

Summing up

▶ You must learn the principal parts of irregular verbs.

Independent Practice

A. Write the principal parts of each verb.

Example: blow *blow blowing blew blown*

9. drive   **11.** give   **13.** ride   **15.** see
10. fall   **12.** sink   **14.** freeze   **16.** drink

B. Write each sentence, adding the past or the past participle of the verb in parentheses. Do not add helping verbs.

Example: Our class _____ on a nature hike last week.   (go)
Our class went on a nature hike last week.

17. Our teacher, Mr. Elias, had _____ to the area several times and _____ the trails.   (drive, know)
18. He had _____ us careful instructions.   (give)
19. Everyone _____ a lunch and _____ sturdy shoes.   (take, wear)
20. Amazingly, no one _____ lunch or anything else.   (forget)
21. When the group _____ some footprints, Mr. Elias _____ to us about the wildlife in the area.   (see, speak)
22. Several days earlier, a storm had _____ down several trees and had _____ many large limbs.   (blow, break)
23. We found a squirrel's nest that had _____ out of a tree.   (fall)
24. Beautiful flowers _____ wild.   (grow)
25. Too soon Mr. Elias _____ the bad news to us.   (break)
26. It was departure time, and we _____ on the way back.   (sing)
27. We _____ reports about what we had _____.   (write, see)
28. The trip had _____ and ended wonderfully.   (begin)

Writing Application: A Personal Narrative Write a paragraph about a school outing that you have participated in. Use the past tense or the past participle of verbs from the lists in this lesson.

For Extra Practice, see p. 191.   More Irregular Verbs

7 | Progressive Forms

The progressive form of a verb shows that the action is continuing. Study the verbs in the following sentences. When is the action taking place?

Tillie collects seashells.   Tillie is collecting seashells.

The sentence on the left tells you that Tillie collects seashells often or regularly. The sentence on the right tells you that Tillie is collecting them right now. The action is *in progress*. The verb *is collecting* shows a progressive or continuing action. The progressive form of a verb is the present participle combined with a form of *be*. Each of the six verb tenses has a progressive form. Forms of the helping verb *be* show the tense.

PRESENT PROGRESSIVE: The dolphin is performing now.

PAST PROGRESSIVE: It was performing yesterday.

FUTURE PROGRESSIVE: It will be performing tomorrow.

PRESENT PERFECT PROGRESSIVE: It has been performing all day.

PAST PERFECT PROGRESSIVE: It had been performing for an hour when we arrived.

FUTURE PERFECT PROGRESSIVE: It will have been performing for four hours when we leave.

Guided Practice What is the form of each of the verbs in parentheses?

Example: This summer a skin diver _____ a course at our community center.   (teach—present progressive)   *is teaching*

1. Brad and I _____ the course together.   (take—present perfect progressive)
2. We _____ about such a course last summer.   (think—past perfect progressive)
3. We _____ about special equipment for the sport.   (learn—present perfect progressive)
4. One day we _____ a slide show when a real diver came in. (watch—past progressive)
5. The diver _____ a face mask and breathing through a snorkel. (wear—past progressive)
6. While he was instructing us, we _____ strokes and discussing safety.   (practice—past progressive)

7. One day next week we _____ for the first time. (dive—future progressive)

8. By the time we go on vacation, we _____ about this sport for a month. (learn—future perfect progressive)

Summing up

▶ Each tense has a **progressive form** to express continuing action.
▶ Form the progressive with an appropriate tense of *be* plus the present participle.

Independent Practice Write each sentence, using the verb and the progressive form given in parentheses.

Example: Divers _____ all the time for treasures aboard ships that have sunk. (look—present progressive)
are looking

9. These divers _____ a different world under the surface of the sea. (find—present progressive)

10. Did you know that people _____ underwater for centuries? (dive—present perfect progressive)

11. Scientists _____ underwater equipment already in the eighteenth century. (test—past progressive)

12. Before that, divers _____ no special equipment. (use—past perfect progressive)

13. Since 1900, inventors _____ many technical problems. (solve—present perfect progressive)

14. In 1915 a large number of divers _____ ordinary air. (use—past progressive)

15. By 1939 they _____ mixtures of helium and oxygen. (try—past progressive)

16. Future divers _____ the sea floor at greater depths. (explore—future progressive)

17. They _____ underwater longer than ever before. (stay—future progressive)

18. Did you know that by the year 2000, divers _____ the deep for six thousand years? (explore—future perfect progressive)

Writing Application: Creative Writing Imagine that you are a deep-sea diver. You are searching for a treasure that is buried in the wreckage of a ship that sank fifty years ago. Write a paragraph describing your treasure hunt. Use at least five progressive forms.

For Extra Practice, see p. 192.   Progressive Forms   **161**

8 | Transitive and Intransitive Verbs

Most verbs express action. Often that action is directed toward another word in the predicate. A verb that directs action toward something or someone named in the predicate is called a **transitive verb**.

TRANSITIVE: The mechanic had repaired the truck.
The owner paid the mechanic.

The word in the predicate to which the action of the verb is directed is the **object**. A transitive verb always has at least one object. If you can answer the question *what?* or *whom?* after an action verb, then you know that the verb is transitive.

TRANSITIVE: The mechanic watched the *driver*.
(Watched *whom?* The driver.)

The driver unlocked the *cab*.
(Unlocked *what?* The cab.)

An **intransitive verb** does not have an object. There is no "receiver" of the action.

INTRANSITIVE: The truck was running well.
The driver turned left quickly.

Often words following an intransitive verb answer the questions *how?*, *when?*, or *where?*.

The driver drove away. (Drove *where?* Away.)
The truck ran smoothly. (Ran *how?* Smoothly.)

Sometimes, though, an intransitive verb is the only word in the predicate.

The driver continued.

Some verbs can be used either transitively or intransitively.

TRANSITIVE: He opened the window.
INTRANSITIVE: The window opened easily.

Linking verbs are always intransitive. They do not express action and they cannot, therefore, have objects.

LINKING VERBS: The driver looked comfortable.
The trip became a pleasure.

Guided Practice Find each main verb. Is the verb transitive or intransitive?

Example: Kyle very carefully hung the picture on the wall.
> *hung* **transitive**

1. First, he put some tape on the wall.
2. He gently hammered a nail into the tape.
3. The picture felt heavy to Kyle.
4. He attached strong wire to the back of the picture frame.
5. Finally, he lowered the picture over the nail.
6. Kyle stepped back from the picture.
7. It looked a little crooked to him.

Summing up

- ► A **transitive verb** expresses action that is directed toward a word in the predicate.
- ► The word to which the action is directed is the **object** of the verb.
- ► An **intransitive verb** does not have an object.
- ► Linking verbs are always intransitive.

Independent Practice List each main verb. Label it *transitive* or *intransitive*.

Example: The heavy rains had destroyed part of the road.
> *destroyed* **transitive**

8. After a few weeks, a road crew arrived at the spot.
9. First, trucks dumped several loads of dirt and rocks.
10. The workers shoveled dirt into the uneven places.
11. At lunchtime the workers ate their sandwiches on nearby rocks.
12. Several hours of work remained for the workers.
13. Next, the leveling machine came to the site.
14. It pushed piles of dirt into the washed-out area.
15. The machine moved back and forth several times.
16. The roller then flattened the dirt.
17. The workers left the area in the afternoon.
18. Lightly at first, the rain began again.

Writing Application: A Paragraph Have you ever watched anything being repaired—a road, a bicycle, a watch, a torn hem? Write a paragraph about it. Label each main verb *transitive* or *intransitive*.

For Extra Practice, see p. 193.

9 | Direct and Indirect Objects

Direct Objects

You know that transitive verbs are action verbs. Transitive verbs have objects.

Arlene has the ball.   The umpire annoyed the catcher.

The **direct object** is a noun or a pronoun in the predicate to which the action of the verb is directed or done. The direct object answers the question *whom?* or *what?*

TRANSITIVE: The pitcher noticed me. (Noticed *whom?* Me.)

The pitcher threw the ball. (Threw *what?* The ball.)

As you know, intransitive verbs do not take objects. Do not be confused by words in the predicate that tell how, when, or where an action happens.

INTRANSITIVE: The ball swerved suddenly. *(how?)*

We will play again tomorrow. *(when?)*

Direct objects may be compound.

The catcher wanted his mask but not his mitt.

Did the manager ask the umpire or the third-base coach?

The bat boy dropped the ball and the bat.

Guided Practice Find the verbs. What are the direct objects of the verbs?

Example: Ezra's new uniform had grease on it.
    verb: *had*   **direct object:** *grease*

1. He had not washed the dust, dirt, and grime from it in ages.
2. The uniform ruined his performance.
3. Plain soap and water did not remove the dirt.
4. Finally, Ezra tried a commercial cleaner.
5. The local dry cleaner had recommended the product highly.
6. The cleaner dissolved the filth instantly.
7. He just sprayed the liquid onto the uniform.
8. Ezra wrote a letter to the manufacturer.
9. Could he do a commercial about his dazzling uniform?

Indirect Objects

A sentence may have more than one kind of object.

Ezra <u>wrote</u> the manufacturer a letter.

An **indirect object** tells *to* or *for whom* or *what* the action of the verb is done. The indirect object comes between the verb and the direct object. The indirect object is always a noun or a pronoun.

          IO   DO   IO   DO

Jay's homer <u>gave</u> the team a lead.   The team <u>awarded</u> him a trophy.

When *to* or *for* appears before a noun or a pronoun, the noun or pronoun is not an indirect object.

                                          IO   DO

INDIRECT OBJECT: The manufacturer <u>sent</u> him a letter.

                                  DO

NO INDIRECT OBJECT: He <u>sent</u> a letter to him.

Like a direct object, an indirect object may be compound.

           IO   IO   DO

The coach <u>gave</u> the pitcher and the batter some advice.

    IO   IO   DO

He <u>told</u> Sam and Jim a joke.

Guided Practice Find each verb and its object or objects. Is each object a direct or an indirect object?

Example: The catcher gave Johnson the signal for a curve ball.
        verb: *gave* **indirect object:** *Johnson* **direct object:** *signal*

10. The shortstop sent the outfielder the sign.
11. Johnson threw the batter the ball.
12. The batter delivered a fly ball to the left fielder.
13. The fielder caught it, and the batter was out.
14. The bat boy handed the next player a bat.
15. Johnson threw the batter his most famous pitch.
16. The knuckle ball caught the air currents and danced wildly.
17. The batter held the bat out and tapped the ball forward.
18. He sent the pitcher a bunt.

> ▶ The **direct object** of a sentence is a noun or a pronoun in the predicate on which the action of the verb is done.
> ▶ The **indirect object** is a noun or a pronoun in the predicate that tells *to* or *for whom* or *what* the action is done. The indirect object comes between the verb and the direct object.

Independent Practice Write each verb or verb phrase. If it is transitive, write its object. Label each object *direct object* or *indirect object*.

Example: The radio announcer is giving the audience a play-by-play report.
  verb phrase: *is giving*
  indirect object: *audience*   **direct object:** *report*

19. The umpire has just handed the players his decision.
20. Certainly this will teach the visitors a lesson.
21. Browning's play probably gave this boisterous crowd the thrill of a lifetime.
22. Now the spectators are giving this great player a loud cheer.
23. Will this move bring Browning a new contract next season?
24. The coach must have shown him some new strategies.
25. The umpire's call should give this team an edge.
26. Stratton just slammed his bat onto the ground.
27. He's rejecting the bat for another one.
28. Smith hits the ball into left field.
29. Gilmore misses the catch but recovers the ball!
30. This slugger surely gives fielders a scare.
31. Stratton reaches first base and is safe!
32. Evans is coming to the plate.
33. The catcher tosses the pitcher the ball.
34. Browning throws to the plate.
35. Evans hits a high fly ball!
36. Fox has it, and the game is over!
37. The two teams will meet again in Toronto tomorrow night.
38. Jack Torres should pitch an exciting game.

Writing Application: A Paragraph Imagine that you are a sportscaster or a news reporter. Write a paragraph reporting a sports or news event. Use at least five objects. Underline each direct object once and each indirect object twice.

 For Extra Practice, see p. 194.

10 | Predicate Nouns and Predicate Adjectives

A linking verb links or connects the subject to a word in the predicate. This word in the predicate always refers to the subject.

Cheese is good for you.   Edam is a cheese.

Sometimes the word that is linked to the subject is a noun that renames the subject. It is called a **predicate noun**.

Cheese is a dairy product.   Cheddar remains my favorite cheese.

Sometimes the word that is linked to the subject is an adjective that describes the subject. This word is called a **predicate adjective**.

Cheese tastes delicious.   Some cheeses smell strong.

Be sure that you do not confuse the linking verb *be* with the helping verb *be*.

HELPING VERB: Daniel is making blueberry yogurt.
(*Yogurt* is a direct object.)

LINKING VERB: Yogurt is a tasty, healthful food.
(*Food* is a predicate noun.)

Like other parts of a sentence, predicate nouns and predicate adjectives may be compound.

Blue cheese is moldy but healthful.
Roquefort is a village in France and a cheese.

Guided Practice What are the subjects and the linking verbs in these sentences? Is the underlined word a predicate noun or a predicate adjective?

Example: Cheese is an important underlined food.
  subject: Cheese   linking verb: is   predicate noun: food

1. Cow's milk is the base for most of our cheeses, yogurts, and ice creams.
2. Cheeses from the milk of goats are not only available but also delicious.

3. In Asia, buffalo milk remains the major <u>ingredient</u> of some cheeses.
4. Cheese from reindeer's milk seems <u>similar</u> to Swiss cheese.
5. Cheese from camel's milk is <u>popular</u> in certain areas of central Asia.
6. Sheep's milk has long been <u>common</u> in the Middle East.
7. Cheeses from these animals may be <u>mild</u> or <u>strong</u>.
8. Cheese is the favorite <u>food</u> of many people.

Summing up

▶ Predicate nouns and predicate adjectives follow linking verbs.
▶ A **predicate noun** identifies or renames the subject.
▶ A **predicate adjective** describes the subject.

Independent Practice Write each verb. If it is a linking verb, write and label the predicate noun or the predicate adjective.

Example: About four hundred cheeses are available.
linking verb: are **predicate adjective:** *available*

9. The manufacturing processes are alike for all cheeses.
10. The curd is the solid part of the milk.
11. The liquid part is the whey.
12. The cheesemaker separates the curd from the whey.

13. Milk thickens with the addition of rennet and certain bacteria.
14. Rennet is a substance in the lining of a cow's fourth stomach.
15. The thickened mass eventually becomes cheese.
16. Cheesemakers drain off the whey.
17. The curd is pressed together, and it becomes more solid.
18. Finally, the curd must be dried in curing rooms.
19. To most people, the result of this procedure tastes delicious.
20. I eat cheese once a week.

Writing Application: A Description Imagine that you are a restaurant critic for a newspaper or for a food magazine. You have just eaten a magnificent meal at a new restaurant that served exquisite and exotic food. Write one or more paragraphs about the meal, describing how the food looked, smelled, and tasted. Include predicate nouns and predicate adjectives in your description.

For Extra Practice, see p. 195.

11 | Active and Passive Voices

In most sentences the subject performs the action, and the verbs are in the **active voice**. In the **passive voice**, the subject receives the action.

ACTIVE: Electric motors run high-speed trains.
PASSIVE: High-speed trains are run by electric motors.

The object of the verb in the active voice becomes the subject of the verb in the passive voice.

                                verb   DO

ACTIVE: Magnets in the motor and the track create a <u>force</u>.

           subject   verb

PASSIVE: A <u>force</u> is created by magnets in the motor and the track.

To change a verb from the active voice to the passive voice, use the corresponding tense of the verb *be* and change the main verb to its past participle.

> The magnetic force moves vehicles. (present tense of *move*)
> Vehicles are moved forward by the magnetic force.
> (present tense of *be* + past participle of *move*)

The performer of the action does not always appear with a verb in the passive voice.

> The original model has been perfected.

Only transitive verbs—verbs that have objects—can be in the passive voice. If there is no object of a verb in the active voice, then there is nothing to become the subject of the verb in the passive voice.

INTRANSITIVE: Dr. Sato <u>travels</u> by train often. *(no object)*

                                  DO

TRANSITIVE: Dr. Sato <u>developed</u> a train. *(active)*

              subj.

          A train was developed by Dr. Sato. *(passive)*

The passive voice in general is weaker and more awkward than the active voice. Use the passive voice when the doer of the action is unknown or unimportant. Use the active voice when you want direct, forceful sentences.

PASSIVE: This train was tested. (Sentence emphasizes the fact that these trains have been tested.)
ACTIVE: Engineers tested this train. (Sentence emphasizes who tested the train.)

Guided Practice

A. Which verbs are in the active voice? Which are in the passive voice?

Example: Automobiles have changed the world. *have changed* active

1. Cars are used by nearly everyone.
2. Future drivers are given safety tips.
3. Fuel conservation is important for everyone.
4. Air quality has been improving recently.

B. How would you change the active to the passive voice? How would you change the passive to the active?

Example: These problems are solved by people.
   People solve these problems.

5. Government programs promote safety on the highways.
6. Safety features are put into new cars by manufacturers.
7. Cars now need less gas than before.
8. Less noisy engines are developed by engineers.

Summing up

> ▸ The subject of a verb in the **active voice** performs the action.
> ▸ The subject of a verb in the **passive voice** receives the action.
> ▸ Use the passive voice when the doer of an action is unimportant.
> ▸ Use the active voice for direct, forceful sentences.

Independent Practice

Rewrite each sentence, changing the active to the passive voice and the passive to the active voice.

Example: The train was replaced by the automobile.
   The automobile replaced the train.

9. Today people seek other methods of transportation.
10. Trains are used by people more often.
11. Some action was taken by railroad officials.
12. One railroad company improved tracks.
13. Cars are driven less by people.
14. Bicycles are seen more frequently by everyone.

Writing Application: A Paragraph

Imagine that you are trying to sell a car. Write a paragraph to explain how the car has been improved. Use verbs in both the active and the passive voice.

 For Extra Practice, see p. 196.

12 || Subject-Verb Agreement

Singular and Plural Subjects

In every sentence you write, the verb must agree with its subject in number. Use a singular verb with a singular subject and a plural verb with a plural subject.

SINGULAR: The <u>kitten</u> plays.   PLURAL: The <u>kittens</u> play.

Singular	Plural	Singular	Plural
I run	we run	I see	we see
you run	you run	you see	you see
he, she, it runs	they run	he, she, it sees	they see

Guided Practice Which verb agrees with each subject?

Example: Foxes (roam, roams) throughout North America.   *roam*

1. The red fox (live, lives) alone most of the year.
2. In the spring, however, pairs (make, makes) dens in burrows that other animals have left.
3. In this lair three to nine cubs (is, are) born.
4. After sunset a fox (hunt, hunts) rabbits and rodents in woodland areas.
5. In folk tales the fox (has, have) a reputation for cleverness.
6. In fact, foxes (avoid, avoids) capture in very clever ways.

Compound Subjects

A compound subject may have a singular or a plural verb, depending on the conjunction you use. If you use *and* to join the parts of a compound subject, use a plural verb.

Shrews, moles, <u>and</u> hedgehogs eat insects.

A mole <u>and</u> a hedgehog were in my garden last night.

If you use *or, nor, either . . . or,* or *neither . . . nor* to join the parts of a compound subject, the verb agrees with the nearer subject.

PLURAL: <u>Neither</u> pandas <u>nor</u> koalas are in our zoo.

PLURAL: <u>Either</u> a panda <u>or</u> two koalas live in that zoo.

SINGULAR: Two koalas <u>or</u> a panda is coming later.

Guided Practice Which verb agrees with each subject?

Example: Both koalas and pandas (resembles, resemble) bears.
   resemble

7. Like a true bear, the koala and the panda (has, have) stout bodies, short legs, round heads, and big paws.
8. Actually, neither the koala nor its relatives (is, are) bears.
9. The koala and the kangaroo (belongs, belong) to the same family.
10. Neither bears nor koalas (is, are) related to the panda.
11. The panda and the raccoon (is, are) closely related.

Summing up

> ▶ A subject and its verb must agree in number.
> ▶ Use a plural verb with a compound subject joined by *and*.
> ▶ Use a verb that agrees with the nearer of two subjects joined by *or*.

Independent Practice Write each sentence, using the correct verb.

Example: Otters, skunks, minks, and badgers (is, are) in the weasel family. *are*

12. A black badge, or mark, (give, gives) the badger its name.
13. Intruders often (provoke, provokes) a surprised skunk to spray.
14. Minks, weasels, and badgers also (discharge, discharges) a smelly liquid.
15. Neither a river otter nor a sea otter (spray, sprays).
16. Minks and otters (have, has) lustrous fur.
17. Neither skunks nor badgers (are, is) such beautiful animals.
18. In cold climates, some weasels (turn, turns) white.
19. This kind of weasel (are, is) called an ermine.
20. Some weasels and the skunk (has, have) black and white fur.
21. Both the river otter and the sea otter (swim, swims) well.
22. The killer whale and human beings (is, are) the sea otter's enemies.

Writing Application: A Comparison Write a paragraph comparing and contrasting two animals or pets you are familiar with. Use four compound subjects joined with *and* and two compound subjects joined with *or*. Make sure that your verbs agree with your subjects.

  For Extra Practice, see p. 197.

13 | More About Subject-Verb Agreement

Titles, Names, and Nouns Ending with *s*

A title or a name takes a singular verb form, even though it may look plural. A noun ending with *s* or nouns joined by *and* can actually refer to one person or thing.

> *Antony and Cleopatra* [a play] was written by Shakespeare.
> The United States [a country] is over two hundred years old.
> Davis, Wu, and Lee [a store] sells quality clothing.

Certain nouns ending with *s* always take a singular verb.

SINGULAR: Mumps is no longer common.
The news was encouraging today.

Other nouns ending with *s* always take a plural verb.

PLURAL: These scissors cut well.
Those pants are in the washing machine.

Guided Practice What is the correct verb in each sentence?

Example: Dramatics (is, are) the art of acting and stagecraft. *is*

1. *The Two Gentlemen of Verona* (is, are) a play by Shakespeare.
2. Shorts (was, were) worn in Shakespeare's day.
3. The Blackfriars theater (was, were) where plays were performed.
4. *The Merry Wives of Windsor* (is, are) also by Shakespeare.
5. News of a performance (spreads, spread) quickly even today.

Collective Nouns and Nouns of Amount

A **collective noun** names a group acting as a single unit.

Common Collective Nouns			
team	collection	clan	group
herd	Congress	committee	student body
flock	Senate	orchestra	crew
family	legislature	club	jury

Usually you use a singular verb with a collective noun. You must use a plural verb with a collective noun that refers to the individuals in the group.

SINGULAR: The <u>team</u> is playing well tonight.
(*Whole team together.*)

PLURAL: The <u>team</u> are putting on their helmets.
(*Each team member.*)

SINGULAR: My <u>family</u> is going to the seashore for the summer.

PLURAL: My <u>family</u> are all going to different places this summer.

Terms that refer to amounts—such as money, time, weight, measurements, or fractions—are usually singular when thought of as a single unit. When terms that refer to amounts are thought of as separate items or units, they are plural, and they require a plural verb.

SINGULAR: <u>Ten dollars</u> is too much for that hat. (*One amount.*)

PLURAL: <u>Ten quarters</u> are in each cup. (*Ten separate coins.*)

SINGULAR: <u>Twelve years</u> seems like a long time.
(*One time period.*)

PLURAL: Those <u>twelve years</u> are important ones.
(*Twelve separate years.*)

Guided Practice What is the correct verb in each sentence?

Example: The theater company (is, are) presenting a play.
The theater company is presenting a play.

6. For weeks the cast (has, have) been rehearsing their lines with one another.
7. The group (has, have) been working together productively.
8. Eight weeks (is, are) usually enough time to rehearse a play.
9. Those eight weeks (is, are) usually scheduled one by one.
10. After all the expenses of this production, only two quarters (is, are) left in the cash box.
11. Five dollars (is, are) a reasonable price for a ticket.
12. The stage crew (has, have) completed the scenery.
13. During dress rehearsal, the cast (was, were) performing well.
14. The orchestra (is, are) tuning up one by one.
15. The audience (was, were) whispering to one another during the opening scene tonight.
16. As the curtain opens for the second act, the whole audience (seem, seems) attentive.

> ▶ Use a singular verb with a title or a name of a single thing, with a collective noun referring to a whole group, and with a noun of amount.
> ▶ Use a plural verb with a collective noun referring to the individual members of a group and with a noun of amount when the individual units are referred to.

Independent Practice
If the underlined verb is correct, write *correct*. If it is not correct, rewrite the sentence correctly.

Example: Shakespeare's *Romeo and Juliet* <u>was</u> written over three hundred years ago.   *correct*

17. Three hundred years <u>are</u> a long period of time.
18. Those three hundred years <u>has</u> included countless productions of Shakespeare's plays.
19. In the play Romeo's family <u>has</u> hated Juliet's family for years.
20. Juliet's family <u>have</u> a deep hatred of Romeo's family.
21. The cast of *Romeo and Juliet* <u>speak</u> to one another in verse.
22. Even today the audience <u>are</u> moved by the timeless story.
23. The Royal Shakespeare Company <u>performs</u> Shakespeare's plays.
24. *Antony and Cleopatra* <u>are</u> one of its recent productions.
25. Beginning in 1603 the King's Men <u>was</u> Shakespeare's theater company in the court of King James.
26. Politics <u>were</u> an influence on plays of those times.
27. Because it offended the king, a rival company <u>were</u> forced to leave Blackfriars, a theater.
28. For this reason, Blackfriars <u>were</u> made available to Shakespeare and his company.
29. His acting troupe <u>was</u> recognized for outstanding performances.
30. Twelve pennies <u>were</u> the highest cost of a theater seat.
31. News of Shakespeare's successes <u>was</u> widespread in his day.
32. Three centuries of popularity <u>is</u> a great tribute to an author.

Writing Application: An Interview Think of a current author whose books or stories you have read and enjoyed. Then write questions you might ask this author about the books or stories and the times and the customs in them. Use at least one title, a collective noun, and a noun of amount. Make sure that your subjects and verbs agree with each other.

14 | Agreement in Inverted and Interrupted Order

Inverted Order

A sentence in **natural order** begins with the subject.

subj. verb
Four ducks live by the pond.

A sentence that begins with all or part of the predicate is in **inverted order.**

verb subj.
By the pond live four ducks.

No matter where the subject is in a sentence, the subject and the verb must agree. Pay particular attention to subject-verb agreement when the subject does not appear first in a sentence. First, find the subject. Then make the verb agree with it.

verb subj.
In the zoo live deer.
There are two roads to the zoo.
Where is the fox?

subj. verb
Among the trees a deer eats quietly.

verb subj. verb
Have you ever seen a red fox?

You determine the form of the verb by the number and the person of the subject. Make sure that the subject and the verb agree with each other in sentences in inverted order.

Guided Practice What is the subject of each sentence? Which verb form agrees with it?

Example: In oceans and rivers (swim, swims) wild dolphins.
                subject: *dolphins*   **verb:** *swim*

1. In the New England Aquarium (is, are) some dolphins.
2. (Have, Has) you ever studied their behavior?
3. There (is, are) many theories about their communication.
4. Through their speech dolphins (show, shows) feelings.
5. How (do, does) researchers study dolphin behavior in the wild?

Interrupted Order

The verb does not always agree with the nearest noun. This noun may be part of a phrase between the subject and the verb. A sentence is in **interrupted order** when a word or a phrase interrupts the subject and the verb in a sentence. First, find the subject, and then make the verb agree with it.

The mice in that cage are growing very fast.
Bebo, one of the smallest mice, is the oldest.

Guided Practice What is the subject of each sentence? Which verb form agrees with it?

Example: The group of toothed whales (include, includes) many
species. **subject: *group*   verb: *includes***

6. The whales of this group (has, have) blowholes and teeth.
7. The narwhal whale, one of these, (has, have) a long tusk.
8. The tusk of this species (is, are) actually a sensitive tooth.
9. Usually only male adults of this group (has, have) tusks.
10. No expert on whales (knows, know) the function of the tusk.

Summing up

▶ The subject of a sentence in **inverted** order follows all or part of the predicate.
▶ First, find the subject. Then make the verb agree with it.

Independent Practice Write the subject of each sentence and the verb form that agrees with it.

Example: There (is, are) two groups in the whale family.
subject: *groups*   verb: *are*

11. Among the whalebone whales (is, are) the blue whale.
12. The length of some blue whales (reaches, reach) ninety feet.
13. (Has, Have) photographs of this creature ever been taken?
14. Where in the world (is, are) blue whales found?
15. Here (is, are) a fact about the blue whale.
16. A blue whale (consumes, consume) two tons of food a day.

Writing Application: An Interview You are about to meet Jacques Cousteau, the undersea explorer. Write six questions about whales and dolphins. Use inverted order to vary your style. Make sure that subjects and verbs agree.

For Extra Practice, see p. 199.   Inverted and Interrupted Order

15 | *lie, lay; rise, raise*

The verb *lie* means "to rest or to remain." It is intransitive: it never takes a direct object. The verb *lay* means "to put or to place." It is transitive: it takes a direct object. *Rise* means "to get up or to move upward." It is intransitive. *Raise* means "to lift or to grow." It is transitive.

Susan will lie down.   First, she will lay her <u>book</u> down.

Soon she will rise.   She will raise her <u>hands</u>.

See Lessons 5 and 6 for the principal parts of *lie, lay,* and *rise*.

Guided Practice Which verb correctly completes each of these sentences?

Example: Ms. Chu (lay, laid) her pen down.   *laid*

1. She said to the class, "Please (rise, raise)."
2. "(Lie, Lay) the mats on the floor for warm-up exercises."
3. Gina had (raised, risen) early that morning.
4. Ms. Jonas continued, "Now (lie, lay) down for leg-raises."
5. The gymnasts (lay, laid) down and (rose, raised) their legs.

Summing up

- ▸ Use *lie* for "to rest or to remain." *Lie* is intransitive.
- ▸ Use *lay* for "to put or to place." *Lay* is transitive.
- ▸ Use *rise* for "to get up." *Rise* is intransitive.
- ▸ Use *raise* for "to lift or to grow." *Raise* is transitive.

Independent Practice Write the verb form that correctly completes each sentence. Label it *transitive* or *intransitive*.

Example: The team (raised, rose) early.   *rose*   **intransitive**

6. The equipment had been (raised, risen) to regulation height.
7. Mats had been (lain, laid) everywhere.
8. The gymnasts (lay, laid) on the floor for warm-ups.
9. The teams (raised, rose) and rotated for each event.
10. They (lay, laid) their sweatsuits on the benches.

Writing Application: A Description Write about an exercise class. Use the verbs *lie, lay, rise,* and *raise* correctly.

    For Extra Practice, see p. 200.

16 | *affect, effect; accept, except*

Other words may be confusing. The verb *affect* means "to influence." *Effect* as a noun means "result of action." As a verb *effect* means "to cause to happen."

The new law will affect many people.
The effect should be felt in several months.
Congress will effect the law next month.

Accept is a verb meaning "to receive willingly." *Except* is usually a preposition meaning "excluding, other than."

Congress accepted the proposal.   All except the last item passed.

Guided Practice Which word is correct in each sentence?

Example: Park rangers (accepted, excepted) a new plan.   *accepted*

1. Their work should (affect, effect) the condition of our parks.
2. The new plan will have an (affect, effect) on all of us.
3. The major (affect, effect) will be more beautiful parks.
4. Park visitors must now (accept, except) the new rules.
5. All visitors (accept, except) park employees must register.

Summing up

> ▶ The verb *affect* means "to influence."
> ▶ The verb *effect* means "to cause to happen."
> ▶ The noun *effect* means "result."
> ▶ The verb *accept* means "to receive."
> ▶ The preposition *except* means "excluding."

Independent Practice Write the correct words.

Example: A zoning change will (affect, effect) the town.   *affect*

6. The height of new buildings will be (affected, effected).
7. Developers will have to (accept, except) limits or not build.
8. All (accept, except) the fire chief have voiced dismay.
9. Most people, however, (accept, except) the law.
10. Careful planning will be the (affect, effect) of this law.

Writing Application: A Paragraph Recommend some rules. Use *affect, effect, accept,* and *except* at least once.

Grammar-Writing Connection

Using Tenses Correctly

The tense of a verb shows the time of an event. When you write, choose each tense carefully. Remember these points.

1. Use verbs in the same tense to talk about events occurring at the same time.

   INCORRECT: Jeannette Rankin ran for Congress and wins.
   CORRECT: Jeannette Rankin ran for Congress and won.

   INCORRECT: She was elected in 1916. She serves for two years.
   CORRECT: She was elected in 1916. She served for two years.

2. Use verbs in different tenses for events occurring at different times.

   Women in Congress were rare then but are common now.

   Women have been in Congress since 1917, and they continue to serve in many branches of government today.

   After Rankin had served one term, she lost her next election.

   By the time we can vote, many women will have served in Congress.

Revising Sentences

Rewrite the sentences, using each verb in the correct tense.

1. Years ago women who become lawyers faced many obstacles. A few succeed anyway.
2. Many women practice law today, but few women practice law or have careers of any kind outside the home in the past.
3. There are no women lawyers until 1869. Then Arabella Babb Mansfield became a lawyer.
4. She had passed her exam with high scores, but the state of Iowa refuses her application.
5. Finally, after a judge rules against the state, she was accepted by the Iowa legal community.
6. She then won another victory. The following year Iowa removes the words "white male" from a lawyer's qualifications.
7. By the time this year is over, my sister will become a lawyer.
8. My cousin Sarah is a lawyer for three years, and she practices law in San Francisco now.

Creative Writing

Pablo Picasso, *Mandolin and Guitar*
Guggenheim Museum, N.Y.

This painting by Pablo Picasso may seem like a meaningless jumble of shapes, patterns, and colors. However, if you focus more closely, you will realize that it is actually a still life with musical instruments. Picasso creates objects from an interplay of simple shapes and colors.

- What objects can you recognize? In what ways are they *not* realistic-looking?
- How does this picture remind you of a collage?

Activities

1. **Make up an explanation.** Picasso often included musical instruments in his paintings. Why do you think he did this—for instance, did he actually want to be a singer instead of an artist? Write an inventive explanation of why Picasso's art often contains references to music.
2. **Write a humorous narrative.** Imagine that your room at home is transformed into a room like the one in this painting. What do you look like when you step inside the room? How do you manage to sit on the furniture? Write a humorous narrative about your experience in the "Picasso room."

Check-up: Unit 5

Kinds of Verbs, Verb Phrases *(pp. 146, 148)* Write each verb phrase. Underline the main verb once and the helping verb or verbs twice. Then label each verb phrase *action* or *linking*.

1. Have you seen the newspaper yet?
2. It does look especially fat today.
3. I must pay special attention to the news about my town.
4. We shall have finished the paper before noon.
5. I couldn't have understood those articles without your help.

Tenses, Forms of *be, have,* **and** *do* *(pp. 150, 153)* Rewrite each item, using the verb and tense in parentheses.

6. they (have—past perfect)
7. we (do—future perfect)
8. I (have—present perfect)
9. she (do—future)
10. he (be—past)
11. we (rely—past perfect)
12. you (regret—present perfect)
13. they (state—future)
14. we (hail—present)
15. you (annoy—past perfect)

Irregular Verbs *(pp. 155, 158)* Rewrite each sentence, adding the verb and tense in parentheses.

16. Election time _____ up on us again. (creep—present perfect)
17. I _____ to you this year seeking the office of president. (come—present perfect)
18. I _____ much praise for the job that I did as treasurer last year. (get—past)
19. I assure you that by the end of next year, I _____ equal praise for my work as president. (get—future perfect)
20. My support _____. (grow—present perfect)
21. I _____ costs and saved money for the class. (cut—past)
22. At times I _____ myself out. (wear—past)
23. I _____ my best effort. (give—present perfect)

Progressive Forms *(p. 160)* Write the progressive form of each verb and tense in parentheses.

24. The rehearsal _____ well. (go—past perfect)
25. Julio _____ tired. (grow—past)
26. He _____ for hours. (rehearse—present perfect)
27. He _____ soon. (stop—future)
28. By this coming Monday, Julio _____ with us for a month. (work—future perfect)

Transitive and Intransitive Verbs, Direct and Indirect Objects, Predicate Nouns and Predicate Adjectives *(pp. 162, 164, 167)* Write each verb and label it *transitive* or *intransitive*. Then write each object and label it *direct object* or *indirect object*. Write each predicate noun and predicate adjective, and label it *predicate noun* or *predicate adjective*.

29. Hand me that atlas!
30. Many country music stars record their songs in Nashville.
31. This area has not always been Tennessee.
32. Its name was Franklin in the eighteenth century.
33. Cotton is king in the city of Memphis.
34. Farmland has now become urban.
35. Tennessee produces an enormous amount of marble.

Active and Passive Voices *(p. 169)* Rewrite each sentence, changing the active voice to the passive voice or the passive voice to the active voice.

36. A gifted guitarist accompanied the singer.
37. The audience applauded both performers.
38. Their concerts are attended by thousands of Europeans.
39. Their records are played by Jasper often.
40. Students around the world know all their songs.

Subject-Verb Agreement *(pp. 171, 173, 176)* Write each sentence, using the correct verb.

41. A group at my school (is, are) showing a movie today.
42. The movie, three hours long, (tell, tells) of a prince.
43. Either the janitors or Mr. Wu (has, have) the projector.
44. Seated in their chairs, the audience (quiet, quiets) down.
45. Both the students and their teacher (seem, seems) fascinated.
46. In the audience (is, are) two stars of the movie.

lie, lay; rise, raise; affect, effect; accept, except *(pp. 178, 179)* Write the verbs that correctly complete these sentences.

47. (Lay, Lie) everything down, and (lay, lie) on the floor.
48. (Raise, Rise) your legs as high as possible.
49. This exercise (affects, effects) your muscles.
50. You may feel the (affects, effects) tomorrow.
51. Now please (raise, rise), (accept, except) those in front.
52. Come forward to (accept, except) the award.
53. This is the (affect, effect) of your hard work.
54. (Lay, Lie) the award down near the trophy case.

Enrichment

Planets Galore

Make a planet fact sheet. List or make a diagram of the nine planets in order of their distance from the sun. Look up the planets and gather two or three interesting facts about each. Write these facts in complete sentences. Use direct objects, predicate nouns, and predicate adjectives.

> Mars is a rugged planet. It has volcanoes, canyons, and water. Its atmosphere is cold and thin.

Extra! Include a drawing of each planet. Use color.

Crisscross Verbs

Write a sentence on paper, using a regular past tense verb in the active voice. Then rewrite the sentence in the passive voice, running it down the page so that the main verb is in both sentences. Do the same with three more verbs.

> Dinner
> was
> Hans cooked dinner.
> by
> Hans.

The Best Test

What if you could give a test instead of taking one? Imagine that you are to write a test on the words *lie/lay, rise/raise, affect/effect,* and *accept/except.* Write ten fill-in-the-blank test items in complete sentences. Use the lessons on pages 178–179 for ideas. Then make an answer key. How many points will you give for each answer? If you wish, let a classmate take your test. Then correct it.

Get a Job!

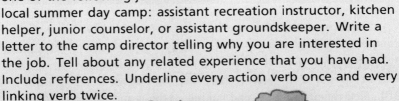

Imagine that you would like one of the following jobs at a local summer day camp: assistant recreation instructor, kitchen helper, junior counselor, or assistant groundskeeper. Write a letter to the camp director telling why you are interested in the job. Tell about any related experience that you have had. Include references. Underline every action verb once and every linking verb twice.

Principal Parts Play

Players—2–4. **You need**—1 manila folder (for gameboard); 7 index cards, a pencil, and a gamepiece (such as a button) for each player. **How to play**—Each player writes *1, 2, 3,* and *4* on 4 cards and places the cards face down in a central pile. Each player then writes *present participle, past,* and *past participle* on the last 3 cards and places them face down in another pile. Together make a gameboard such as the one below, with an irregular verb from page 155 or 156 in each space.

Taking turns, draw a number card and move the gamepiece the number of spaces shown. Then draw a principal parts card and say that principal part for the verb on the gameboard where the marker landed. If the verb form is correct, stay there. If the verb is incorrect, move back to where you were before your turn.

Scoring—The first player to reach the *END* space wins.

grow	take	wear	think	sing	ride	E N D
have	numbers					
know	sit	speak	swim	fly	go
past			principal parts		do
START	begin	break	bring	catch	choose

Extra Practice: Unit 5

● Write each underlined verb. Label it *action* or *linking*.
  Example: Thanksgiving dinner <u>is</u> my favorite meal. *is* **linking**
  1. The turkey <u>looks</u> delicious.
  2. You <u>carve</u> it easily with a sharp carving knife.
  3. I <u>smell</u> the aroma of bread baking in the wood-burning stove.
  4. It <u>smells</u> absolutely wonderful to me.
  5. I <u>baked</u> some butternut squash as a vegetable side dish.
  6. This <u>was</u> my contribution to the meal.
  7. Todd <u>prepared</u> potatoes, peas, and cauliflower.
  8. I <u>like</u> this joyous holiday so much!
  9. The food <u>becomes</u> better and better every year.

▲ Write each verb. Label it *action* or *linking*.
  Example: Herbs are important to a good cook. *are* **linking**
  10. People use different herbs in different countries.
  11. Some herbs smell wonderful, like mint and parsley.
  12. I smell garlic in this tasty chicken dish.
  13. I tasted herbs in the lettuce and tomato salad.
  14. I added some more spices to the spaghetti sauce.
  15. The onions and spices changed the flavor of the sauce.
  16. The taste of the onions remains strong even in the sauce.
  17. I know the names of many different herbs and spices.
  18. Hungarian paprika can be sweet, or hot and spicy.

■ Write sentences, using the given subjects and adding the kind
  of verb in parentheses.
  Example: On the stove the spaghetti sauce _____. (action)
           On the stove the spaghetti sauce bubbled.
  19. Some spices such as cinnamon and nutmeg _____. (linking)
  20. Too many spices in the sauce _____. (action)
  21. The smell of the clam chowder _____. (action)
  22. Alexandra and her cousin Jennifer _____. (action)
  23. An excellent cook _____. (linking)
  24. The golden whole-wheat bread in the oven _____. (linking)
  25. The addition of wheat germ, bran flakes, or oatmeal _____.
      (action)
  26. The taste of slow-rising yeast bread _____. (linking)

2 ‖ Verb Phrases (p. 148)

● Write the underlined verb phrase. Underline the main verb once and the helping verb or verbs twice.

Example: Scientists have been studying earthquakes for years.

have been studying

1. Today we are still learning about the causes of earthquakes.
2. Winds, waves, cars, and volcanos can all cause vibrations.
3. Real earthquakes are caused by other conditions.
4. Rock may seem quite hard.
5. It may even snap under a great deal of pressure.
6. This will produce vibrations or waves for miles around.
7. Cracks in the ground may become the paths for these waves.
8. Scientists haven't known this until recently.

▲ Write each verb phrase. Underline the main verb once and the helping verb twice.

Example: For many, earthquakes are connected with the West.

are connected

9. Actually, earthquakes have occurred in many different places.
10. In 1775 Boston was struck by a strong quake.
11. Northern New York may suffer frequent quakes.
12. Even rockbound Manhattan has trembled on several occasions.
13. The South has not remained free of earthquakes either.
14. Charleston, South Carolina, did have an earthquake once.
15. When will the next earthquake be?
16. Scientists are looking for the answer to that question now.

■ Write each sentence, adding a verb phrase to complete it. Underline all main verbs once and all helping verbs twice.

Example: _____ you _____ the cause of earthquakes?

Do you know the cause of earthquakes?

17. Earthquakes _____ *tectonic or volcanic.*
18. A tectonic quake _____ by a flaw in the earth's crust.
19. A volcanic quake _____ the result of sudden movement of lava below the earth's surface.
20. An earthquake _____ one thousand miles from its source.
21. _____ you _____ earthquakes in geography class?
22. One of the worst earthquakes _____ in 1906 in San Francisco.
23. The damage _____ at $520,000,000.
24. The damage of a recent earthquake _____ quite high.

3 | Tenses (p. 150)

● Write the tense of the verb phrase in each sentence.
  Example: They had not started out yet. *past perfect*

1. They live nearby.
2. Nothing will happen.
3. You carried the bags.
4. We had ordered tickets.
5. We had hopped on a jet.
6. He will know the time.
7. You have opened the door.
8. He will have waited.
9. They had closed the door.
10. We have answered the call.
11. She will have played ball.
12. You have not started.
13. I have remained at home.
14. They had checked the roof.
15. They will have repaired it.
16. We had hoped for sun.

▲ Write each sentence, using the correct form of the verb and tense in parentheses.
  Example: Lana _____ of stardom. (dream—past perfect)
            Lana had dreamed of stardom.

17. This night _____ the result of much hard work. (be—present)
18. Lana _____ all her energy for the performance. (need—future)
19. She _____ hard for this part. (practice—past perfect)
20. The members of the cast _____ long hours for months.
    (work—present perfect)
21. They _____ until midnight last night. (rehearse—past)
22. The critics _____ the play by tomorrow morning.
    (review—future perfect)
23. Everyone _____ for good reviews. (hope—present)
24. Broadway audiences _____ fresh talent. (recognize—future)

■ Write each sentence, using an appropriate tense of the verb in parentheses. Label the verb tense.
  Example: Popcorn _____ for a long time. (exist)
            Popcorn has existed for a long time. **present perfect**

25. Native Americans _____ corn thousands of years ago. (pop)
26. People _____ popcorn earlier, however. (use)
27. In a cave in New Mexico recently, scientists _____ popcorn that
    was 5600 years old. (discover)
28. Popcorn already _____ in 3600 B.C. (exist)
29. By 1900 Mr. Cretors _____ the popping machine. (invent)
30. Today Americans _____ over 500,000,000 pounds of popcorn
    each year. (consume)
31. Midwesterners _____ the greatest amount. (use)
32. Next year Americans _____ over 600,000,000 pounds of un-
    popped corn. (purchase)

4 | Forms of *be, have,* and *do* (p. 153)

● Write each sentence, using the correct verb form in parentheses.

Example: What (do, does) you know about corn?

What do you know about corn?

1. We (is, are) learning about corn in social studies class.
2. Corn (is, are) a very important crop in the United States.
3. It (has, have) always grown in North and South America.
4. Farmers (has, have) developed bigger and better corn.
5. Today they (has, have) big machines and large fields.
6. The plants (has, have) been growing stronger and healthier.
7. Corn (do, does) grow well in many states.
8. (Do, Does) it grow well in California?
9. I (have, has) started my report on corn products already.

▲ Write each sentence, using the correct verb form in parentheses. Then label that verb *main* or *helping.*

Example: People (has, have) grown corn for thousands of years.

People have grown corn for thousands of years. **helping**

10. It (was, were) around before Columbus sailed.
11. Corn always has (been, be) an important crop.
12. Corn production (is, are) second only to wheat production.
13. In fact, corn (does, do) have uses other than as food.
14. Manufacturers (has, have) hundreds of uses for corn.
15. (Does, Do) you know some of them?
16. I (has, have) no idea.
17. Some paper (is, are) made from corn.
18. Corn products (is, are) used in glue, starch, and fabrics.

■ Write each sentence, using the form of *be, have,* or *do* that best completes it. Then label that verb *main* or *helping.*

Example: In Great Britain corn _____ called maize.

In Great Britain corn is called maize. **helping**

19. Grains like wheat and oats _____ called corn.
20. Corn has always _____ a favorite vegetable in both North America and South America.
21. For centuries people _____ enjoyed corn in different ways.
22. How many ways _____ you know?
23. I _____ two ears of corn in my refrigerator right now.
24. Latin Americans probably _____ the greatest number of uses for corn as food.
25. They _____ many wonderful things with corn.
26. How many ears of corn have you _____ today?

5 | Irregular Verbs (p. 155)

● Write each sentence, using the principal part of the verb in parentheses.

Example: The Tylers _____ an interesting thing.   (do—past)
The Tylers did an interesting thing.

   1. They _____ some large pots to the roof.   (bring—past)
   2. Then they _____ soil and seeds in the pots.   (put—past)
   3. After a week, tiny green shoots _____ through.   (come—past)
   4. They _____ into blossoms.   (burst—past)
   5. The blossoms _____ beautiful strawberries.   (become—past)
   6. Last week the Tylers had _____ out a bucket of strawberries.
      (leave—past participle)
   7. Some birds _____ the berries that same day.   (find—past)
   8. They _____ no berries for the Tylers!   (leave—past)
   9. The Tylers _____ out more plants.   (set—past)
   10. Again they _____ their berries.   (lose—past)
   11. They are not _____ out plants now.   (put—present participle)

▲ Write the present participle, the past, and the past participle forms of the verbs. Include helping verbs.

Example: pay   *is paying   paid   has paid*

12. make	**16.** find	**20.** have
13. read	**17.** become	**21.** win
14. stand	**18.** be	**22.** hold
15. set	**19.** run	**23.** do

■ Write each sentence, using the correct past or past participle of the verb in parentheses.

Example: Many birds _____ overhead.   (be)
Many birds were overhead.

   24. Jeff and Randy _____ under a huge, old oak tree.   (sit)
   25. Had the two men really _____ their way?   (lose)
   26. They had _____ to the lake with some other friends.   (come)
   27. They all had _____ the cottage an hour ago.   (leave)
   28. Jeff and Randy _____ that the woods were familiar by now.
      (think)
   29. They _____ the way back to the cottage.   (seek)
   30. The sun had already _____ an hour before.   (set)
   31. Shortly, they _____ their compass.   (find)
   32. Jeff _____ the compass steadily on the way back.   (hold)
   33. Finally, the men _____ to the cottage.   (come)
   34. They had never _____ so happy in their lives.   (be)

6 | More Irregular Verbs (p. 158)

● Write each sentence, using the principal part of the verb in parentheses.
Example: Sam had _____ the juice. (drink—past participle)
　　　　　Sam had drunk the juice.
1. The *Titanic,* a ship, _____. (sink—past)
2. The parade is _____. (begin—present participle)
3. Marcy had _____ across the lake. (swim—past participle)
4. The ice is _____. (freeze—present participle)
5. The telephone has _____ five times. (ring—past participle)
6. Kim _____ the red balloon. (choose—past)
7. Brad _____ down for a rest. (lie—past)
8. Donna is _____ the snowmobile. (drive—present participle)
9. She has _____ the window. (break—past participle)

▲ Write each sentence, choosing the correct principal part. Use your dictionary if you need help.
Example: A scientist (spoke, spoken) to us about the desert.
　　　　　A scientist spoke to us about the desert.
10. He had (took, taken) many trips to deserts around the world.
11. Many colorful flowers (grew, grown) after a rainfall.
12. Wind had (blew, blown) sand into many shapes and patterns.
13. People (rode, ridden) camels in the hot deserts.
14. These people (wore, worn) scarfs over their faces for protection against the sand.
15. The barrel cactus (drank, drunk) its fill of rainwater.
16. Its sharp spines (gave, given) it a dangerous appearance.
17. I had not (knew, known) that deserts grow cold at night.
18. Water in a canteen had (froze, frozen) one night.

■ Write each sentence, using the past or past participle form of the verb in parentheses. Then label it *past* or *past participle*.
Example: My family _____ a trip through the Grand Canyon. (take)
　　　　　My family took a trip through the Grand Canyon. **past**
19. I had never _____ a mule before this trip. (ride)
20. The mules _____ a trail along the edge of the river. (choose)
21. Many travelers had _____ the same trail for years. (take)
22. We _____ while on a raft on the Colorado River. (sing)
23. Our raft _____ it through the white water. (make)
24. The mules _____ down the south side of the canyon walls. (go)
25. Large boulders had _____ on the trail. (fall)
26. We had _____ all our meals by a small fire. (eat)

7 | Progressive Forms (p. 160)

● Write the progressive form from each sentence.

Example: Harry had been watching birds.   *had been watching*

1. Grace is watching seagulls at the beach.
2. She will be watching them all day long.
3. She was watching them all last week too.
4. Grace has been looking for unusual gulls for two weeks.
5. She had been listening to the radio for reports first.
6. She is discovering new facts about gulls daily.
7. She has been identifying different gulls with her friend.

▲ Write each sentence, using the correct progressive form of the verb and tense in parentheses.

Example: Jacques Cousteau _____ sea life for many years.
        (study—present perfect progressive)
        Jacques Cousteau has been studying sea life for years.

8. He and his crew _____ more and more about the sea all the time. (learn—present progressive)
9. His ship, the *Calypso*, _____ the sea since 1951.   (explore—present perfect progressive)
10. His expedition _____ the Red Sea when it discovered a ship from the third century B.C.   (study—past progressive)
11. Cousteau _____ the need for conservation of the ocean. (explain—present perfect progressive)
12. People _____ to protect the sea.   (work—present perfect progressive)
13. Our conservation efforts _____ marine life for future generations. (preserve—future progressive)

■ Write each sentence, replacing each underlined verb with its progressive form.

Example: The storm had brewed for several hours.
        The storm had been brewing for several hours.

14. The waves crash onto the rocks.
15. Thunder and lightning will come soon.
16. The temperature has dropped several degrees.
17. Storm clouds had gathered in the sky since 6 A.M.
18. All small boats returned to the safety of the harbor.
19. The radio will broadcast reports about the storm all day.
20. By the end of the day, the forecaster will have forecast the path of the storm for twenty-four hours.

8 | Trans. and Intrans. Verbs (p. 162)

● Write each underlined verb. Label it *transitive* or *intransitive*.
Example: People <u>need</u> shelter.   *need*   **transitive**
1. Early humans <u>lived</u> in caves or in the open air.
2. Later people <u>built</u> huts out of sticks or mud.
3. Today many people <u>construct</u> large houses.
4. People <u>use</u> different kinds of materials for their houses.
5. Builders on a construction site <u>work</u> quickly.
6. First, workers <u>dig</u> a foundation for support of the building.
7. They usually <u>raise</u> beams or columns next.
8. The beams or columns <u>form</u> the skeleton of the house.
9. The final structure <u>looks</u> quite different from the skeleton.

▲ Write each verb. Label it *transitive* or *intransitive*.
Example: Water wells draw water from the ground.
          draw   **transitive**
10. Ground water from rain flows into the wells.
11. The water is sometimes hundreds of feet down.
12. In these cases, power-driven pumps draw the water.
13. Many people depend on wells for their water supply.
14. Scientists locate wells with modern equipment.
15. In earlier times, people found water with a forked branch.
16. The main stem pointed down to a water supply.
17. People were seldom successful with this method.
18. This method is not really very accurate.

■ (19–34)   Write each main verb. Label it *transitive* or *intransitive*.
Example: A modern skyscraper can spring up within one year.
          spring   **intransitive**
First, an architect must design the building. Next, the construction company plans carefully. Before the construction starts, engineers test the soil. Clay, rock, and sand are different kinds of soil. Each requires a different kind of foundation. Finally, large cranes appear on the site. They dig the foundation. Work begins on the skeleton of the building. Usually someone already has cut the steel to the necessary size. A number is on each piece. Workers place the steel according to the number on each piece. Workers bolt the pieces of steel together. Then they weld the steel permanently. At last the builders apply the outside walls. They do this work quickly, and interior decoration begins next. The skyscraper looks grand.

9 | Direct and Indirect Objects (p. 164)

● Write each underlined object. Label it *direct object* or *indirect object*.

Example: All mystery writers offer readers the same basic plot.

   readers **indirect object**   *plot* **direct object**

1. Writers use different details and characters, of course.
2. All mystery stories solve the same problem.
3. The hero or heroine discovers the guilty person.
4. Edgar Allan Poe presented the problem in 1841.
5. He gave the world its first mystery story.
6. Sir Arthur Conan Doyle followed Poe by forty years.
7. Sir Arthur gave us our best-known detective.
8. He gave mystery fans everywhere the famous Sherlock Holmes.

▲ Write the verbs and their objects. Label each object *direct object* or *indirect object*.

Example: The criminal left Detective Green an important clue.

   verb: *left*   **indirect object:** *Detective Green*
   direct object: *clue*

9. The detective searched the room for a clue.
10. The maid brought Detective Green one gold earring.
11. The maid's friend Margo had lent the victim the earrings.
12. Margo had owed the victim some money.
13. The single missing earring offered Green a hint.
14. Margo told the detective a suspicious story.
15. Her story had too many contradictions.
16. Green offered her the chance to confess.

■ Write the sentences, adding objects as shown in parentheses. Use articles where you need them. Remember to place your objects correctly.

Example: The phone awakened _____.   (direct)
   The phone awakened the detective.

17. She grabbed her _____ and listened to the message.   (direct)
18. "Thanks, I owe _____."   (direct and indirect)
19. Who had so abruptly sent _____?   (direct and indirect)
20. Suddenly she remembered _____.   (direct)
21. She dressed without any to-do and left _____.   (direct)
22. Would she find _____ in time to prevent disaster?   (direct)
23. Had someone given _____?   (direct and indirect)
24. In a short while, she would know _____.   (direct)

10 | Pred. Nouns and Pred. Adjectives (p. 167)

● Write each underlined word. Label it *predicate noun* or *predicate adjective*.

Example: Milk is the first <u>food</u> for many babies.

　　　　　food   **predicate noun**

1. With milk, children will grow <u>strong</u>.
2. Cows are the main <u>source</u> of milk in this country.
3. Goat milk and sheep milk are <u>common</u> elsewhere.
4. The milk from these animals tastes <u>different</u> from cow milk.
5. Milk must remain very <u>clean</u>.
6. Otherwise, milk drinkers can become <u>ill</u>.
7. In colonial days the family cow was the main <u>supplier</u> of milk.
8. Now most people are the <u>customers</u> of dairy farmers.
9. Dairy farming is an important <u>industry</u>.

▲ Write each linking verb. Then write each predicate noun and predicate adjective. Label it *predicate noun* or *predicate adjective*.

Example: Milk directly from the cow is warm.

　　　　　linking verb: *is*   **predicate adjective:** *warm*

10. It becomes a home for germs if not refrigerated.
11. Dairy farmers are careful about cleanliness.
12. The barns, the cows, and the equipment are very clean.
13. Milk drinkers in the United States feel safe and secure.
14. Milk is a product of many areas of the United States.
15. Cows are important farm animals.
16. Northeastern Europe was the original home of our dairy cows.

■ Write each sentence. Underline the linking verb. Add a predicate noun or a predicate adjective and label it.

Example: Cows were a _____ of milk five thousand years ago.

　　　　　Cows <u>were</u> a source of milk five thousand years ago.

　　　　　predicate noun

17. About 10,270 pounds of milk can be the yearly _____ of a cow.
18. Only half of the milk from dairy farms remains _____.
19. The other half becomes other dairy _____.
20. Examples of such products are _____ and _____.
21. Milk from different cows doesn't look _____.
22. The traditional containers for milk were _____ or bottles.
23. These appeared in the 1880s and became quite _____.
24. Now, coated paper containers have grown more _____.

11 | Active and Passive Voices (p. 169)

● Write each underlined verb. Then label it *active* or *passive*.
Example: Cars and airplanes <u>are steered</u> by their drivers.

> *are steered*   **passive**

1. Railroad trains <u>are pulled</u> by locomotives.
2. Passenger trains still <u>run</u> along many routes.
3. Many railroads still <u>run</u> passenger trains.
4. Most trains in the United States today <u>carry</u> products.
5. Still, thousands of people <u>are carried</u> by trains.
6. Many cities in Europe <u>are served</u> by high-speed trains.
7. Japanese trains <u>exceed</u> the speed of European trains.
8. Special services <u>are offered</u> on some Japanese trains.

▲ Rewrite each sentence, changing the passive voice to the active voice or the active voice to the passive voice.
Example: The earliest trains were pulled by men or horses.

> *Men or horses pulled the earliest trains.*

9. Wagons full of coal were pulled up from mines by miners.
10. These wagons were guided along by two wooden rails.
11. Later the rails were covered with iron for more strength.
12. Meanwhile the steam engine was being developed by inventors.
13. The English constructed the earliest engines.
14. The first public railroad was built by English engineers.
15. Railroad officials opened it in 1825.
16. The railroad carried freight for twenty miles.

■ Rewrite each sentence, changing the passive voice to the active voice or the active voice to the passive voice. Label the new sentence *active* or *passive* to describe the verb.
Example: A horse and a locomotive ran a race.

> *A race was run by a horse and a locomotive.*   **passive**

17. The locomotive had been built by Peter Cooper of New York.
18. Cooper had given it the name of a character in a fairy tale.
19. A new railroad was using horses to pull trains.
20. The operators were being urged by Cooper to use locomotives.
21. In 1830 a race between a horse and the locomotive *Tom Thumb* was proposed by a stagecoach owner.
22. The race was almost won by the little locomotive.
23. Then an engine belt was dropped by *Tom Thumb*.
24. Still, a horse and a locomotive had made history.
25. Trains were called "iron horses" by many people.

12 | Subject-Verb Agreement (p. 171)

● Write each sentence, using the correct verb in parentheses.
  Example: The walrus (lives, live) in northern oceans.
            The walrus lives in northern oceans.
  1. Only killer whales (is, are) the natural enemies of walruses.
  2. Its four flippers (makes, make) the walrus a good swimmer.
  3. Its long, ivory tusks (grows, grow) forty inches and (weighs, weigh) nine pounds.
  4. Both the male walrus and the female walrus (has, have) tusks.
  5. Neither seals nor sea lions (has, have) tusks like walruses.
  6. Cows, bulls, and calves (likes, like) to lie in the sun.
  7. Several walruses and their young (is, are) resting on ice.
  8. Neither an old walrus nor a calf (likes, like) to be disturbed when asleep.

▲ Write each sentence, using the correct verb in parentheses.
  Example: A wallaby (is, are) a small kangaroo.
            A wallaby is a small kangaroo.
  9. Wallabies (lives, live) on the continent of Australia.
  10. This animal also (lives, live) in New Zealand.
  11. Both the kangaroo and the wallaby (leaps, leap) high into the air.
  12. A baby wallaby (is, are) called a *joey.*
  13. A newborn joey (measures, measure) only about one inch.
  14. Wallabies (carries, carry) their young in pouches.
  15. A joey (leaves, leave) the pouch after six months but (returns, return) at any sign of danger.
  16. Neither a wallaby nor male gray kangaroos (grows, grow) over six feet tall.

■ Write each sentence, using the present tense of the verb in parentheses.
  Example: Kenya _____ famous for its wildlife. (be)
            Kenya is famous for its wildlife.
  17. Elephants, giraffes, and zebras _____ freely in game reserves. (roam)
  18. Many tourists _____ each year to these game reserves. (come)
  19. Neither a giraffe nor a zebra _____ a meat-eater. (be)
  20. Both giraffes and zebras _____ plants. (eat)
  21. This movie _____ many colorful animals of Africa. (show)
  22. Both a leopard and a lion _____ running fast. (be)
  23. A hippo or a crocodile _____ in the river. (be)
  24. A lion or two cheetahs _____ behind the tree. (be)

13 | More About Subj.-Verb Agreement (p. 173)

● Write each sentence, using the correct verb in parentheses.
Example: The store Jones and Bailey (sells, sell) plays.
>*The store Jones and Bailey sells plays.*

1. Shakespeare's *Antony and Cleopatra* (is, are) still read after three hundred years.
2. *Romeo and Juliet* (is, are) another play by Shakespeare.
3. The Neighborhood Players (is, are) performing it tonight.
4. Five dollars (does, do) not seem too much to pay for a play by Shakespeare.
5. Romeo and Juliet (is, are) two young people in love.
6. Romeo's family (has, have) quarreled with Juliet's family.
7. The couple (faces, face) difficulties throughout the play.
8. The audience usually (expresses, express) their feelings.
9. The drama club often (performs, perform) Shakespeare's plays.
10. Two dollars (is, are) the price of a student ticket.

▲ If the underlined verb form is correct, write *correct*. If it is not correct, rewrite the sentence, using the correct form. *make correct*
Example: The panel has chosen a play for next season. *correct*

11. *The Boys from Syracuse* is based on a play by Shakespeare.
12. Jim said that $154 was spent on one costume alone.
13. Tights are worn by the men.
14. The chorus sing different parts.
15. Six dollars are the cost of each ticket.
16. The crowd make their escapes one by one.
17. Holinshed's *Chronicles* were the source book for many of Shakespeare's plays.
18. The National Theatre in London perform Shakespeare's plays.
19. The news are that their plays are terrific.
20. Dramatics is exciting to take part in.

■ Write each sentence, using a verb in the present tense. Label each verb *singular* or *plural.*
Example: In any play scenery _____.
>*In any play scenery is important.* **singular**

21. The audience always _____.
22. Twelve years _____.
23. The Drama Club _____.
24. Dressmakers' shears _____.
25. *Mutt and Jeff* _____.
26. The cast _____.
27. The group _____.
28. Trousers _____.
29. Thousands _____.
30. Pliers _____.

14 | Inverted and Interrupted Order (p. 176)

● Write each sentence, using the verb form in parentheses that agrees with the underlined subject.

Example: People of the world (shares, share) information.

People of the world share information.

1. How (does, do) people communicate with each other?
2. There (is, are) many different ways of communicating.
3. Here (is, are) some examples.
4. On your lips (is, are) a smile.
5. The expressions on your face (sends, send) messages to others.
6. A movement of your hand also (says, say) something.
7. The ring of telephones (means, mean) someone is calling.
8. Notes of music (expresses, express) emotions.

▲ If the underlined verb form is correct, write *correct*. If it is incorrect, rewrite the sentence, using the correct form.

Example: Smoke signals is a kind of language.

Smoke signals are a kind of language.

9. Pictures on a cave wall communicate.
10. What is the beginnings of written language?
11. Long ago a string of pictures were used to tell a story.
12. In one story was many pictures.
13. The details in the pictures was hard to draw.
14. Soon one group of lines were used for one idea.
15. Here was an important step toward written words.
16. Was simple pictures or symbols the first written language?

■ Write each sentence. Underline the subject and use the past tense form of *be* that agrees with it.

Example: The invention of alphabets _____ a great step forward.

The invention of alphabets was a great step forward.

17. In the Middle East _____ people who first used an alphabet.
18. The sounds in their speech _____ written with pictures.
19. A combination of pictures _____ used for a word.
20. What _____ these drawings similar to?
21. An important development for human beings _____ the more recent letter alphabet.
22. There _____ no longer a different symbol for each word.
23. There _____ only a short list of symbols.
24. _____ there many more people able to read and write?

15 | *lie, lay; rise, raise* (p. 178)

● Write each sentence, using the correct verb in parentheses.
   Example: The principal (raises, rises) the flag each morning.
            The principal raises the flag each morning.
   1. John (raised, rose) to ask a question.
   2. In our meeting, Ann has (raised, risen) an interesting issue.
   3. We will (lie, lay) the question before the Student Council.
   4. A dictionary was (lying, laying) in Ann's lap.
   5. Carl nervously (raised, rose) his hand.
   6. He (lay, laid) his glasses down for a moment and looked up.
   7. Carl has just (lain, laid) down backstage.
   8. The audience is (raising, rising) to applaud the council.
   9. Will the Student Council (raise, rise) the issue again?

▲ Write each sentence, using the correct verb in parentheses.
   Example: The curtain (rises, raises) on a cabin in the woods.
            The curtain rises on a cabin in the woods.
   10. Then the lights are (raised, rose) to show early morning.
   11. Smoke is (raising, rising) slowly up the chimney.
   12. A hunting dog is (lying, laying) near the kitchen stove.
   13. The mother (raises, rises) the window to call Jesse to eat.
   14. Only a few of the family members have (raised, risen).
   15. Several small children are still (lying, laying) in bed.
   16. A red and white tablecloth (lay, laid) on top of the table.
   17. Plates of food had been (lain, laid) on the table.
   18. Jesse enters the cabin and (lies, lays) down his cap.

■ Write each sentence, choosing first the correct verb and then
   its correct form in the tense in parentheses.
   Example: I _____ early for the rehearsal.   (raise/rise—past)
            I rose early for the rehearsal.
   19. The backstage crew _____ a couch in the center of the stage.
        (lay/lie—past)
   20. The crew _____ on the couch.   (lay/lie—past progressive)
   21. Four people _____ the lights above the stage.   (raise/rise—
        present progressive)
   22. The lights _____ six feet.   (raise/rise—present)
   23. We _____ a carpet down for the first act.   (lay/lie—future)
   24. The stagehands _____ for the applause.   (raise/rise—past)
   25. I _____ a warm sweater across my shoulders.   (lay/lie—past)
   26. Some helium balloons for decoration had _____ to the ceiling.
        (raise/rise—past perfect)

16 | *affect, effect; accept, except* (p. 179)

● Write the sentence, choosing the correct word.

Example: The use of computers has (affected, effected) students' grades.

The use of computers has affected students' grades.

1. National test scores are certainly (affected, effected) by student use of computers.
2. The greatest (affect, effect) was on math scores.
3. All classes (accept, except) social studies are using computers.
4. We completed all the programs (accept, except) the last one.
5. The best (affect, effect) of computer use has been an improvement in student attitude.
6. The school will (accept, except) the gift of new computers.
7. The teachers will (accept, except) late computer homework.

▲ Write each sentence, choosing the correct word.

Example: The debate team (accepted, excepted) a challenge.

The debate team accepted a challenge.

8. (Accept, Except) for Sharon, all members will participate.
9. Sharon was not (accepted, excepted) for the debate because of lack of experience.
10. The debate will be on the (affect, effect) of computers on student learning.
11. We (accepted, excepted) the argument in favor of computers.
12. John said that computers don't (affect, effect) education.
13. He will argue that computers have a bad (affect, effect).
14. Our arguments should (affect, effect) the judges' decision.

■ Write each sentence, using *accept, except, affect,* or *effect* correctly.

Example: I corrected all my mistakes _____ one.

I corrected all my mistakes except one.

15. Computers have _____ business and office practices.
16. A major _____ has been the processing of greater amounts of information.
17. Word processors have an _____ on office skills.
18. Word processors have _____ greater requirements for speed and accuracy in typing.
19. Typists' skills, _____ for proofreading, have been _____.
20. Office workers have _____ computers as an improvement.
21. Most workers' skills have been _____ by using computers.
22. The minicomputer has _____ the way people prepare a budget.

Literature and Writing

What we least expected generally happens.

Benjamin Disraeli
from *Henrietta Temple*

Story

Getting Ready A good short story needs a good beginning. Without that, it would have fewer readers. It also needs a good ending. It may be a totally unexpected ending, but it must be a believable one if the story is to work. In this unit you will read short stories and you will try writing your own. Start looking for ideas. The best ideas are those that are familiar to you.

ACTIVITIES

Listening Listen to the quotation on the facing page. Do you agree? Think of an incident in which something totally unexpected happened to you. Was it a beginning or an ending? Could you use it in a story?

Speaking Look at the picture. Could this be the beginning or the ending of a story? Perhaps it is the middle! Share your ideas. Who are the two boys? What are they like? Whose window is this? Share your ideas with your class.

Writing Imagine what the two boys in this photograph will do next. Write about it in your journal.

LITERATURE

*If two journeys lead to the same end, does it matter
what happens along the way?*

The Two Brothers

By Leo Tolstoy

Two brothers set out on a journey together. At noon
they lay down in a forest to rest. When they woke
up they saw a stone lying next to them. There was something written on the stone, and they tried to make out
what it was.

"Whoever finds this stone," they read, "let him go
straight into the forest at sunrise. In the forest a river will
appear; let him swim across the river to the other side.
There he will find a she-bear and her cubs. Let him take
the cubs from her and run up the mountain with them,
without once looking back. On the top of the mountain he will see a house, and in that house will he find
happiness."

When they had read what was written on the stone,
the younger brother said:

"Let us go together. We can swim across the river,
carry off the bear cubs, take them to the house on the
mountain, and together find happiness."

"I am not going into the forest after bear cubs," said
the elder brother, "and I advise you not to go. In the first
place, no one can know whether what is written on this
stone is the truth—perhaps it was written in jest. It is
even possible that we have not read it correctly. In the
second place, even if what is written here is the truth—
suppose we go into the forest and night comes, and we
cannot find the river. We shall be lost. And if we do find
the river, how are we going to swim across it? It may be
broad and swift. In the third place, even if we swim
across the river, do you think it is an easy thing to take
her cubs away from a she-bear? She will seize us, and,

instead of finding happiness, we shall perish, and all for nothing. In the fourth place, even if we succeeded in carrying off the bear cubs, we could not run up a mountain without stopping to rest. And, most important of all, the stone does not tell us what kind of happiness we should find in that house. It may be that the happiness awaiting us there is not at all the sort of happiness we would want."

"In my opinion," said the younger brother, "you are wrong. What is written on the stone could not have been put there without reason. And it is all perfectly clear. In the first place, no harm will come to us if we try. In the second place, if we do not go, someone else will read the inscription on the stone and find happiness, and we shall have lost it all. In the third place: if you do not make an effort and try hard, nothing in the world will succeed. In the fourth place: I should not want it thought that I was afraid of anything."

The elder brother answered him by saying: "The proverb says: 'In seeking great happiness small pleasures may be lost.' And also: 'A bird in the hand is worth two in the bush.' "

The younger brother replied: "I have heard: 'He who is afraid of the leaves must not go into the forest.' And also: 'Beneath a stone no water flows.' "

Then the younger brother set off, and the elder remained behind.

No sooner had the younger brother gone into the forest than he found the river, swam across it, and there on the other side was the she-bear, fast asleep. He took her cubs, and ran up the mountain without looking back.

When he reached the top of the mountain the people came out to meet him with a carriage to take him into the city, where they made him their king.

He ruled for five years. In the sixth year, another king, who was stronger than he, waged war against him. The city was conquered, and he was driven out.

Again the younger brother became a wanderer, and he arrived one day at the house of the elder brother. The elder brother was living in a village and had grown neither rich nor poor. The two brothers rejoiced at seeing each other, and at once began telling of all that had happened to them.

"You see," said the elder brother, "I was right. Here I have lived quietly and well, while you, though you may have been a king, have seen a great deal of trouble."

"I do not regret having gone into the forest and up the mountain," replied the younger brother. "I may have nothing now, but I shall always have something to remember, while you have no memories at all."

Think and Discuss

1. The two brothers' journeys led them to the same end. Yet the younger brother claimed that his journey had been more worthwhile. What were his reasons?
2. The two brothers made different decisions about the message on the stone. Each brother explained his decision by quoting two proverbs. What does each pair of proverbs mean?
3. This story is a **parable,** a simple tale that answers a question or teaches a lesson. The lesson, however, is left to the reader to figure out. What lesson do you think this parable teaches? Explain why you agree or disagree with the lesson.

Who shows the most self-control in this story?

The Dinner Party

By Mona Gardner

The country is India. A colonial official and his wife are giving a large dinner party. They are seated with their guests—army officers and government attachés and their wives, and a visiting American naturalist—in their spacious dining room, which has a bare marble floor, open rafters, and wide glass doors opening onto a veranda.

A spirited discussion springs up between a young girl who insists that women have outgrown the jumping-on-a-chair-at-the-sight-of-a-mouse era and a colonel who says that they haven't.

"A woman's unfailing reaction in any crisis," the colonel says, "is to scream. And while a man may feel like it, he has that ounce more of nerve control than a woman has. And that last ounce is what counts."

The American does not join in the argument but watches the other guests. As he looks, he sees a strange expression come over the face of the hostess. She is staring straight ahead, her muscles contracting slightly. With a slight gesture she summons the servant standing behind her chair and whispers to him. The servant's eyes widen, and he quickly leaves the room.

Of the guests, none except the American notices this or sees the servant place a bowl of milk on the veranda just outside the open doors.

The American comes to with a start. In India, milk in a bowl means only one thing—bait for a snake. He realizes there must be a cobra in the room. He looks up at the rafters—the likeliest place—but they are bare. Three corners of the room are empty, and in the fourth the servants are waiting to serve the next course. There is only one place left—under the table.

His first impulse is to jump back and warn the others, but he knows the commotion would frighten the cobra into striking. He speaks quickly, the tone of his voice so arresting that it sobers everyone.

"I want to know just what control everyone at this table has. I will count three hundred—that's five minutes—and not one of you is to move a muscle. Those who move will forfeit fifty rupees. Ready!"

The twenty people sit like stone images while he counts. He is saying ". . . two hundred and eighty . . ." when, out of the corner of his eye, he sees the cobra emerge and make for the bowl of milk. Screams ring out as he jumps to slam the veranda doors safely shut.

"You were right, Colonel!" the host exclaims. "A man has just shown us an example of perfect control."

"Just a minute," the American says, turning to his hostess. "Mrs. Wynnes, how did you know that cobra was in the room?"

A faint smile lights up the woman's face as she replies: "Because it was crawling across my foot."

Think and Discuss

1. Who do you think shows greater self-control—the American guest or the hostess? Explain why.
2. How does the American figure out that there is a cobra under the table?
3. The series of events in a story is called the **plot.** Not every series of events can be called a plot, however. A plot needs a **conflict** or problem of some kind that reaches a **climax,** a high point. After the climax, the problem is resolved in some way, good or bad. Look at the events in "The Dinner Party." What is the conflict? When does it reach its climax?
4. The colonel believes that women behave very differently from men in a crisis. What do you think of the colonel's statement?

RESPONDING TO LITERATURE

The Reading and Writing Connection

Personal response In "The Dinner Party," the colonel made a generalization about women, and he was proved wrong. Have you ever changed your mind about an idea you believed? Did your thinking change little by little or all at once? Write about how your thinking changed.

Creative writing Near the end of "The Two Brothers," Tolstoy wrote that the brothers "began telling of all that had happened to them." Turn this statement into a dialogue. Have the brothers tell each other just what *did* happen. Use your imagination.

Creative Writing

Cast a play Imagine that you are looking for actors for a modern TV version of "The Two Brothers." How could the different personalities of the brothers be brought out in their looks? their voices? their mannerisms? Make a list of features for each brother to help the casting director find the right actors.

Act out Act out the plot of "The Dinner Party." You will need at least six people. Use the dialogue in the story, but add gestures and expressions that help to build suspense and show what the characters are like.

Vocabulary

A *bungalow* is a common type of house in India. It usually includes a *veranda*. Using a dictionary, describe a bungalow and a veranda. Why do you think these styles became popular in India?

Looking Ahead

A story Later in this unit you will learn how to write a story. In each story you have just read, the **setting**—where and when the story takes place—helps the plot come alive. Where will your own story take place? on an island? in an old, dusty attic? on another planet? Begin to think about an interesting setting.

VOCABULARY CONNECTION
Borrowed Words

English has a rich assortment of words from almost every place on earth.

> In India, milk in a bowl means only one thing—bait for a snake. He realizes there must be a **cobra** in the room.
> *from "The Dinner Party" by Mona Gardner*

Cobra is borrowed from the Portuguese word *cobra de capello* meaning "snake with a hood."

When Modern English began to develop, the great age of European exploration and discovery also began. The English sailed the world and brought back not only material wealth and new experiences, but also new words to describe them.

Here are some more borrowed words.

avalanche (French)	boss (Dutch)
piranha (Portuguese)	opera (Italian)
waltz (German)	taco (Spanish)
episode (Greek)	fjord (Norwegian)
goulash (Hungarian)	parka (Aleutian)

Many Native American words have also been added to the English vocabulary:

avocado	totem
moccasin	tomato

New words are being added to our language all the time. Many of them come from new discoveries and inventions in science and technology.

Vocabulary Practice

A. For each of these words from the literature in this unit, write the meaning and the language from which the word was borrowed. Use a dictionary.

1. attachés   **2.** veranda   **3.** colonel   **4.** proverb

B. The word *rupees* is the name of the official currency of India. Use an encyclopedia to list five other currencies and the lands where they are used. Compare information with a classmate.

Prewriting Story

Listening: Predicting Outcomes

Good storytellers keep you actively engaged by using the technique of **foreshadowing** to hint at future events. When you predict a story's outcome, you interpret that foreshadowing to guess what might happen next. Read the passage below.

> As he looks, he sees a strange expression come over the face of the hostess. She is staring straight ahead, her muscles contracting slightly. With a slight gesture she summons the servant standing behind her chair and whispers to him. The servant's eyes widen, and he quickly leaves the room.
>
> *from "The Dinner Party" by Mona Gardner*

- What clues tell you that something is wrong?
- What outcome might the passage lead you to predict?

Now read the next two paragraphs of the story.

> Of the guests, none except the American notices or sees the servant place a bowl of milk on the veranda just outside the doors.
>
> The American comes to with a start. In India, milk in a bowl means only one thing—bait for a snake. . . .
>
> *from "The Dinner Party" by Mona Gardner*

- What new information made you change your prediction?

Guidelines for Predicting Outcomes

1. Concentrate. Pay attention to potential clues.
2. Make predictions about what will happen, based on the clues and on your own knowledge and experience.
3. Change your predictions as new clues and events demand.

Prewriting Practice

Listen as your teacher reads a selection. At each pause, write a prediction of what might happen next.

Thinking: Solving Problems

A story usually revolves around a problem that requires a solution. In "The Dinner Party," for example, the American's quick thinking solves a problem: how to keep the other guests from harm as a poisonous snake glides out from under their feet. Not all problems are resolved in such a sudden and dramatic way, however.

Suppose you come home after school and realize that you left your key on the kitchen table. What do you do? Here is a good way to go about solving this or any other problem.

Guidelines for Solving Problems

1. **Define the problem.** You want to get into your house or apartment, but you do not have your key.

2. **Explore the problem.** Is there any other way to get in? No, the back door uses the same key. Is there a window you could open? No, all the windows are locked from the inside, and you don't want to break one. Could you go to a friend's house until someone comes home? You could go to Mark's, but you need to study for a geography test, and your notes are at home. Does a neighbor have a key? No. Who does have a key? Your parents, your grandparents, and your younger sister all do.

3. **Narrow the problem.** You need to find some way to get the key from one of the people who has one.

4. **List the possible solutions.** You could call your father, who works in the next town. You could go to your mother's office or ask her to come home. You could call your grandparents, or you could find your sister.

5. **Examine each solution.** Your father is out of town on business. It would take you an hour each way to get to and from your mother's office. Your grandparents live too far away. You are not sure where your sister is, but you think she has basketball practice today.

6. **Decide on the solution.** You will walk back to the school and see if your sister is at basketball practice. If she isn't, you will call her best friend, Louisa, who will almost certainly know where she is.

If the missing key were really your problem, you would probably think through the steps in less time than it takes to read them. However, suppose you were faced with a problem such as finding a summer job, figuring out how to improve your grades, or settling a misunderstanding with a friend. You can use exactly the same steps, no matter how difficult the problem is.

A group can also follow these six steps to solve a problem. Because there are more people, there will be more ideas suggested. If the discussion is well-organized and keeps to the point, a group may come up with a more interesting solution than one person alone could find.

Prewriting Practice

A. Think of a problem that would make a good basis for a story. Then plan how the story's main character will solve the problem. Work through the six problem-solving steps as if you were your main character. Write each step, creating a list like the one on page 212.

B. Work with five or six other students. Imagine that your group is the planning committee for the school fair. You just found out that the park where the fair has always been held is already reserved for that day by another school. Using the six steps given above, write your solution for the problem and discuss it with your group.

C. Using the six steps for solving problems, write a solution for two of these problems. Compare your solutions with those of a partner.

1. You want to try out for the football team, but practice is at the same time as your baby-sitting job.

2. One of your closest friends seems to be behaving strangely but has not told you why.

3. You are having a math test tomorrow. You have studied hard, but there is one topic you do not understand at all.

4. You and three friends have formed a band, and you need to find a place to practice.

Composition Skills
Story

Plot ☑

When people ask, "What is that story about?" they are usually wondering about the story's **plot**. The plot is the series of events that take place in a story.

Suppose you were to list, in order, the main things you did on a particular day. Your list would be a series of events, but it would not be a plot. Why not? A plot has a definite shape, or form.

The form of a story usually follows this pattern.

1. One or more characters have a **conflict**, or problem.
2. The conflict builds to a **climax**, or high point.
3. The climax is followed by a **resolution**. In the resolution, you find out how the conflict was solved.

This diagram of "The Dinner Party" can help you understand the form of a plot.

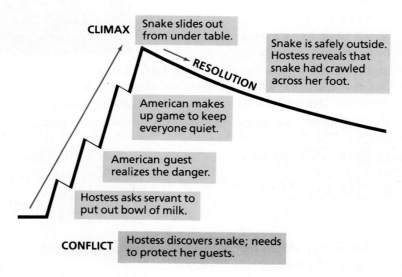

CLIMAX Snake slides out from under table.

Snake is safely outside. Hostess reveals that snake had crawled across her foot.

RESOLUTION

American makes up game to keep everyone quiet.

American guest realizes the danger.

Hostess asks servant to put out bowl of milk.

CONFLICT Hostess discovers snake; needs to protect her guests.

A plot does not have to be as dramatic as in "The Dinner Party," and the ending does not have to be a happy one. You can write a story with a more ordinary conflict, like trying to make the basketball team, and with a sad resolution, like not making it.

Prewriting Practice

A. Read the following plot summary. Decide what is the conflict, the climax, and the resolution. Then make a diagram of the plot, following the model on page 214.

> A **young** boy always challenges his father to wrestle. As the boy gets older, the wrestling matches become rarer. One night, when he is in high school, he challenges his father again. Does the boy really want to win? The two have a long, fairly even struggle, and the boy finally pins his father to the floor. The father laughingly tells the boy to wait till next time. They both know there won't be one. Tears run down the boy's cheeks.
>
> *based on "The Cub" by Lois Dykeman Kleihauer*

B. Make up a story plot, or think of one you know from a book, movie, or TV show. Make a diagram of the plot, showing all the key events. Label the conflict, the climax, and the resolution. Use the diagram on page 214.

Setting ☑

The events of "The Dinner Party" unfold in a dining room. "The Two Brothers" opens in a forest. The particular place and time are the **setting** of a story. In some stories, you may barely be aware of the setting. In others, the setting is so clear and so important that it stays in your mind as you read.

Read this opening paragraph.

> The country is India. A colonial official and his wife are giving a large dinner party. They are seated with their guests . . . in their spacious dining room, which has a bare marble floor, open rafters, and wide glass doors opening onto a veranda.
>
> *from "The Dinner Party" by Mona Gardner*

These details not only paint a clear picture for you but are important to the events, as shown below:

DETAIL OF SETTING	ROLE IN PLOT
India	India has cobras.
Dining room	Gives cobras only one good place to hide.
Open rafters	Give American a place to look for snake.
Doors to veranda	Give the snake a way to escape.

A story's setting can also help to create the **mood** of the story. The mood is the general feeling or atmosphere surrounding the events. When writers describe a setting, they choose words and details that bring out the right mood. The time of year or the time of day, the weather, and particular objects in the setting can all help to convey a mood that is somber or joyful, peaceful or excited, quiet or mysterious.

The following settings create two very different moods.

> If you kept walking you finally came to the most beautiful forest, with tall trees that mirrored themselves in deep lakes. The forest stretched all the way to the sea, which was blue and so deep that even large boats could sail so close to the shore that they were shaded by the trees.
>
> *from "The Nightingale" by Hans Christian Andersen*

> During the whole of a dull, dark, and soundless day in the autumn of the year, when the clouds hung oppressively low in the heavens, I had been passing alone, on horseback, through a singularly dreary tract of country . . .
>
> *from "The Fall of the House of Usher" by Edgar Allan Poe*

- What is the mood of the first story? the second?
- What words and details help to create each mood?

Prewriting Practice

A. In "The Dinner Party," the setting was a home in India. Suppose you were to write a similar story but with a different setting. Your story might take place in an American household, at a school, or around a campfire. Using the first paragraph of "The Dinner Party" as a model, write a paragraph that gives the details of the new setting.

B. List four or five words or details that would create a mood for a particular setting. Make up a setting, or choose one of these.

1. An amusement park at night
2. The bottom of the ocean
3. A record store on a Saturday afternoon
4. A lake in autumn

Characters ☑

Any person or animal that takes part in the action of a story is a **character**. Even an object can be a character if the author brings it to life.

A story can have few characters, as in "The Two Brothers," or it can have many. The most important or main character is usually the one who faces the conflict. In "The Dinner Party," the American and the hostess are the main characters.

When you write a story, help your readers get to know your characters. You have five main ways of showing your readers what your characters are like.

1. Tell directly about the character's personality.
2. Describe the character's appearance.
3. Have the character speak.
4. Have one character talk about another character.
5. Show what the character does.

As you read the following passage, notice what methods the writer used to show what the character Mary is like. Keep in mind that another character is narrating the story.

Two weeks we had been moving when we picked up Mary, who had run away from somewhere that she wouldn't tell. Pa didn't want her along, but she stood up to him with no fear in her voice.

"I'd rather go with a family and look after kids," she said, "but I ain't going back. If you won't take me, I'll travel with any wagon that will."

Pa scowled at her, and wide blue eyes stared back.

"How old are you?" he demanded.

"Twenty," she said.

from "The Day the Sun Came Out"
by Dorothy M. Johnson

The above passage tells you a great deal about Mary's background and personality. This chart shows you the methods the writer used.

WHAT YOU KNOW	HOW YOU KNOW IT
Mary has run away; she is strong-willed, brave, blue-eyed.	From the character narrating the story
She is twenty and very determined.	From Mary's words

As much as we learn about Mary, we know almost nothing about her appearance. The author concentrates on her words and actions, as described by one of the other characters.

In the following passage, on the other hand, the author focuses on a character's appearance as a clue to his personality. The author gives a clear picture of what the real Johnny Appleseed looked like.

> In personal appearance Chapman was a small, wiry man, full of restless activity; he had long dark hair, a scanty beard that was never shaved, and keen black eyes that sparkled with a peculiar brightness.
>
> *from "Johnny Appleseed, A Pioneer Hero" by*
> *W.D. Haley*

- What does this description suggest to you about Johnny Appleseed's personality?
- Which words give you that impression?

Prewriting Practice

A. Make up a character of your own. Will your character be outgoing, shy, mysterious, or adventurous? Choose one of the five methods on page 217 to show what your character is like. Write four sentences using the method you have chosen.

B. Imagine that you are in a restaurant. At the next table, two people are eating and talking. One seems pleasant and likeable; the other does not. Write a few sentences that show what each character is like. Use two of the methods on page 217 for each character.

Point of View ☑

Suppose you were writing about a party that everyone you know and like had attended. Chances are you would describe the party enthusiastically. Now suppose a new girl in town had also come to the same party. Her description might be quite different from yours, because she would have experienced the party from a very different **point of view**.

When you write a story, you need to choose a point of view from which to tell it. You have two main choices. Your choice will determine what the reader will see through the narrator's eyes.

1. **Limited point of view** You can tell a story from a character's point of view. A character's point of view is called *limited* because the writer is limited to what that character sees, hears, feels, and thinks. "The Dinner Party" is told from a limited point of view.

> The American does not join in the argument but watches the other guests. As he looks, he sees a strange expression come over the face of the hostess.
>
> *from "The Dinner Party" by Mona Gardner*

It is through the eyes of the American that you know what is happening. Because third-person pronouns are used to tell the story, this is called a **third-person** point of view.

The American does not tell the story himself. If he did, the point of view would be different, as in this excerpt.

> I was restless, and I went up into the hills in midafternoon. I ranged the woods for miles, thinking all the time of Colin.
>
> *from "Last Cover" by Paul Annixter*

Here an "I," not a "he," is telling the story. Because first-person pronouns are used, it is a **first-person** point of view. The story is told by one of the characters in the story.

The first-person point of view is personal. The reader usually sides with the narrator. As in the third-person point of view, the information presented is limited because the narrator can only tell what happens to him or her or what he or she sees happening to the other characters.

2. Omniscient point of view Sometimes a writer prefers to let you look into the minds of all the characters. The word *omniscient* means "knowing everything." When a writer uses the omniscient point of view, the narrator of the story knows everything. You, the reader, can then be told everything that *all* the characters think, feel, see, and do. A story with an omniscient point of view is almost always told in the third person.

This passage is from a story that has an omniscient point of view.

> He was afraid for the minute; but it is impossible for a mongoose to stay frightened for any length of time, and though Rikki-tikki had never met a live cobra before, his mother had fed him on dead ones, and he knew that all a grown mongoose's business in life was to fight and eat snakes. Nag knew that too, and at the bottom of his cold heart he was afraid.
>
> *from "Rikki-Tikki-Tavi" by Rudyard Kipling*

• What makes this point of view omniscient?

Prewriting Practice

A. Read this passage from a story. Decide whether the point of view is first person or third person, and whether it is limited or omniscient. Explain how you can tell.

I had called upon my friend, Mr. Sherlock Holmes, one day in the autumn of last year, and found him in deep conversation with a very stout, florid-faced, elderly gentleman with fiery red hair. With an apology for my intrusion, I was about to withdraw when Holmes pulled me abruptly into the room and closed the door behind me.

from "The Red-Headed League" by Sir Arthur Conan Doyle

B. Think of something you were involved in—such as a contest, an accident, a misunderstanding, or a narrow escape—that also involved one or more other persons. Pick one very small part of it—a one- to five-minute period. Write four or five sentences in the first person describing this incident from your own point of view. Then write about the incident using an omniscient point of view. Tell what at least two different characters are thinking.

C. Rewrite the fourth paragraph of "The Dinner Party" from the point of view of the hostess. Use a third-person limited point of view.

The Grammar Connection

The Right Verb

When you are writing a story, choose your verbs carefully. Verbs are the "action" in your sentences. Choose the ones with the most life—the ones that make the reader see just what is happening.

The following three sentences are identical except for the verbs.

a. The four children came through the kitchen and went down to the basement.

b. The four children stampeded through the kitchen and clattered down to the basement.

c. The four children crept through the kitchen and tiptoed down to the basement.

How are the three sentences alike? Which sentence gives the *least* information? What does each of the other two sentences suggest about the children's activities?

Practice Change the verbs in each sentence to fit the mood given in parentheses.

1. Melissa took the box and removed the wrapping paper. (excitement)
2. Abby walked to her room and closed the door. (anger)
3. Beneath his feet a stream flowed; above his head birds called. (happiness)
4. Roberto sat on the couch and talked about everything that had gone wrong that day. (discouragement)

The Writing Process
How to Write a Story

Step 1: Prewriting—Choose a Topic

Hiroshi had been keeping a notebook of story ideas. He chose three ideas and made some notes on each one.

A school's top runner loses a race and learns that you can't always win.

This would be quite a serious story, and Hiroshi decided he would rather write something lighter.

A space traveler goes to Earth to locate his only living relative.

He had a great plot in mind for this idea, and he could already imagine the setting and characters.

A scientist visits an active volcano. He returns with startling news.

This would require too much research, and Hiroshi was unsure about how to end it.

Hiroshi circled the space story idea on his paper.

On Your Own

1. **Think and discuss** Using pictures, headlines, overheard conversations, your memory, and the Ideas page, make a list of story ideas. Discuss your list with a partner.
2. **Choose** Ask these questions about each idea on your list.
   Who are the characters? What are they like?
   Can I picture the setting and describe it?
   What will happen in the conflict? climax? resolution?
   Which characters, plot, and setting can I best imagine?
   Circle the story idea you decide to write about.
3. **Explore** What will you write? Do one of the activities under "Exploring Your Story" on the Ideas page.

Ideas for Getting Started

Choosing a Story Idea

Story Ideas

In a parable, a wandering storyteller raises this question: When is it *not* wise to plan ahead?

The guests at a dinner party slowly realize that one of them is a stranger to everyone there—including the host.

Three teenagers are rescued from a sinking ship by dolphins.

An eighth grader dreams that she has been made principal of her school.

Story Plans

Make story plans like this to help you choose a story idea.

setting: far in the future, on a spacecraft, and in a city on Earth

character: a young space pilot, who has been planet-hopping most of his life

plot: The pilot locates his only relative, who is in a dangerous situation. The pilot accidentally saves both of their lives.

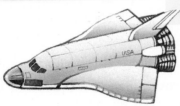

Exploring Your Story

Plan Your Story

Use the plan above as a model. Make a more detailed plan of your chosen story idea. Write every detail you can to help make your characters and setting come alive. Think about your plot, and plan the events and their order carefully.

Talk About It

With a partner, discuss your story idea. Then role-play an interview with your main character. Play the part of your character, and have a partner ask you questions. As you answer, try to get inside your character to imagine how he or she feels and thinks.

Step 2: Write a First Draft

Hiroshi decided to write his story for the school's literary magazine. He wanted other students to enjoy it.

Hiroshi wrote his first draft without worrying about mistakes. He knew he would have time to make changes and corrections later.

The beginning of Hiroshi's first draft

~~We were~~ A spaceship was heading toward a space station. Steven Ozlo, a pilot-in-training, felt as though he had been cooped up forever. Commander Wilson was explaining something to him, but Steven wasn't paying attention. He asked to be dismissed, saying he didn't feel well. It wasn't a lie. Steven has never felt well since the day the terible news came.

Think and Discuss ☑
- What point of view did Hiroshi finally choose for his story?
- Who is the main character? What do you learn about him?
- How could Hiroshi make the characters and the setting seem more real?

On Your Own

1. **Think about purpose and audience** Answer these questions.
   For what audience am I writing?
   What point of view is best for this plot and for these characters?
2. **Write** Write your first draft. Use details, dialogue, and actions to show, not just tell about, your characters and plot. Use your senses to include details that help readers see your setting. Do not worry about mistakes, but write on every other line to leave room for changes.

Step 3: Revise

As Hiroshi read his first draft, he realized he had told rather than shown what was happening. He added dialogue and details to make his readers feel as if they were right there on the spaceship.

Hiroshi wanted to know if he had really brought the setting and characters to life. He read his story to Peter.

Reading and responding

Peter: It's a really exciting story. I enjoyed it.

Hiroshi: Thanks a lot. Did you really feel as though you were on a spaceship?

Peter: Yes, and I got quite interested in Steven. You know so much about science fiction, though, that I expected more details on the setting.

Hiroshi: Good idea. I could easily add more. Thanks again.

Hiroshi made some notes on their discussion and then went over his story. He found several places where he could add details to make the setting clearer.

The beginning of Hiroshi's revision

> As the spaceship made its long journey
>
> ∧ ~~We were~~ A spaceship was heading toward a (toward Molenium X at light speed)
> ~~space station.~~ Steven Ozlo, a pilot-in-
> (listened to the engine's endless humming. ¶ "If only)
> training, ~~felt as though he had been cooped up~~ (it would stop for just five minutes," he thought☉)
> ~~forever.~~ Commander Wilson was explaining
> (about the wall of screens and dials)
> something to him, but Steven wasn't paying
> (¶ "May I be dismissed, sir?" he said.)
> attention. ~~He asked to be dismissed, saying~~
> ("I don't feel well." ¶)
> ~~he didn't feel well.~~ It wasn't a lie. Steven
>
> has never felt well since the day the terible
>
> news came.

Think and Discuss ☑

- Compare Hiroshi's old beginning with the revised one.
- What details did he add to make the setting seem real?
- How did he bring his main character to life?

On Your Own

Revising checklist

☑ Does the plot have a conflict? a climax? a resolution?

☑ Do the characters seem real? Where could I add dialogue, details, or actions to show them more clearly?

☑ Have I used details effectively to show this setting?

☑ Have I used the same point of view throughout?

1. **Revise** Make changes in your first draft. Cross out any sections you can improve, and write changes between the lines and in the margins. You may wish to use the thesaurus below or the one at the back of this book.

2. **Have a conference** Read your story to your teacher or a classmate and note their comments on your paper.

WRITING CONFERENCE

Ask your listener:	As you listen:
"Can you follow the plot?" "Can you imagine the setting?" "Do the characters seem real?"	I must listen carefully. Can I imagine the characters and setting? Is the plot clear? Where could details and dialogue be added?

3. **Revise** After considering your partner's suggestions and any other ideas you have, make changes on your paper.

Thesaurus

angry *adj.* furious, irritated, seething, inflamed

move *v.* leap, jump, hop, bolt

rich *adj.* wealthy, affluent, well-to-do

run *v.* gallop, dart, shoot

see *v.* spot, notice, perceive

small *adj.* little, tiny, petite, paltry, meager, minute

Step 4: Proofread

Hiroshi proofread his story for spelling, capitalization, and punctuation errors. He also checked his verb forms. He checked his spellings in a dictionary and used proofreading marks to make corrections.

This is the way the beginning of Hiroshi's story looked after proofreading.

Part of Hiroshi's story after proofreading

toward Molenium X at light speed.
space station. Steven Ozlo, a pilot—in—
listened to the engine's endless humming. ¶ "If only
training, ~~felt as though he had been cooped up~~
it would stop for just five minutes," he thought⊙
~~forever.~~ Commander Wilson was explaining
about the wall of screens and dials
something to him, but Steven wasn't paying
¶ "May I be dismissed, sir?" he said.
attention. ~~He asked to be dismissed, saying~~
"I don't feel well." ¶
~~he didn't feel well.~~ It wasn't a lie. Steven
ha~~s~~ᵈ never felt well since the day the terᴿible

news came.

Think and Discuss
- Which spelling did Hiroshi correct?
- Which verb did he correct? Why?
- What punctuation did he add? Why?

On Your Own

1. **Proofreading Practice** Proofread this paragraph. Correct the mistakes, and write the paragraph correctly. There are two spelling errors, two capitalization errors, one wrong punctuation mark, one mistake in paragraph format, and two incorrectly formed verbs.

   The first lap I had drove at monaco I had took
   at a quick 91 mph. I would need another 3
   mph to qualafy up front. It was my last
   chance, I gunned my bright red ferrari around
   the last turn at 135 mph and finally exhailed.

2. **Proofreading Application** Proofread your story, using the Proofreading Checklist and the Grammar and Spelling Hints below. Check your spellings in a dictionary. If you like, mark your changes with a colored pencil.

Proofreading Checklist	Proofreading Marks
Did I ☑ **1.** indent? ☑ **2.** capitalize and punctuate correctly? ☑ **3.** use the right verbs and verb forms? ☑ **4.** spell all words correctly?	¶ Indent ∧ Add ∧ Add a comma “” Add quotation marks ⊙ Add a period ℓ Take out ≡ Capitalize / Make a small letter ∽ Reverse the order

The Grammar/Spelling Connection

Grammar Hints

Remember these rules from Unit 5 when you use verbs.

- Verbs must agree with their subjects. *(I go. He goes.)*
- Do not shift tense unnecessarily. (Wrong: *I was tired, so I sleep.* Right: *I was tired, so I slept.*)

Spelling Hints

Remember these spelling principles.

- Some words sound alike but are spelled differently. *(reign, rain; gate, gait; sole, soul)*
- The plural of some words that end in *o* is formed by adding *s*. For others, the plural is formed by adding *es*. *(patios, memos, vetoes, potatoes)*

Step 5: Publish

Hiroshi made a neat finished copy of his story. He chose two of the story's most exciting parts and drew illustrations of them. Using his illustrations as a front and back cover, he made his story into a booklet. After his teacher had checked it, Hiroshi submitted his booklet to the school literary magazine.

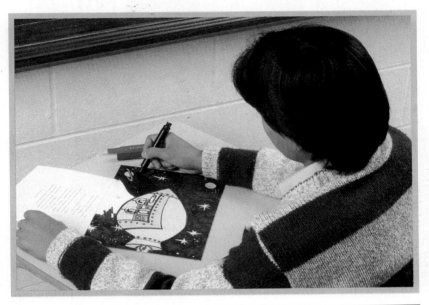

On Your Own

1. **Copy** Carefully copy or type your story.
2. **Give it a title** Your title should describe your story and capture your readers' attention.
3. **Check** Read your story again to be sure you have not omitted anything or made any errors.
4. **Share** Decide on a way to share your story.

Ideas for Sharing

- Write a brief, interesting summary of your story for a book review magazine. Don't give away the ending!
- Read your story to your class. Practice first to give each part the right tone and expression.
- Make a comic strip of a scene from your story that uses dialogue.

Applying Story Writing

Literature and Creative Writing

In the parable "The Two Brothers," on pages 204–206, the younger of two brothers takes a risk that leads him to adventure. In the story "The Dinner Party," on pages 207–208, guests at a dinner party are saved from a deadly cobra.

Keeping these stories in mind, use what you have learned about writing stories to complete one or more of the following activities.

1. **Take the throne.** How would you feel if you suddenly became a king, like the younger brother in Tolstoy's story? What might you do? Use your imagination to write a story about the younger brother's life as king.

2. **Throw a party.** Use a dinner party as the setting for a mystery or a comedy. Be mysterious or be hilarious, but make the plot, characters, and details of the setting fit your mood.

3. **Tell the snake's story.** Events do not have to be seen through human eyes. Imagine that you are the snake in "The Dinner Party." Rewrite the story from your point of view.

Remember these things ☑
- Write a plot with a conflict, a climax, and a resolution.
- Make your setting and characters real for your readers.
- Tell your story from a single point of view.

Writing Across the Curriculum
Environmental Issues

As people have learned to control nature through technology, they have also gained a greater responsibility to protect the environment. Many writers have chosen environmental issues as themes for their stories. Through their stories, they remind people to value the natural world, and they warn of the possible consequences of carelessness.

Choose one or more of the following activities. Develop the plot. Decide on your point of view.

1. **Write about an endangered species.** Endangered species are plants and animals that will soon become extinct if they, and the land they live on, are not protected. Do some research on the grizzly bear, the California condor, the sandhill crane, or any other endangered species. Then write a story in which the main character is a member of that species. Although your story will be fiction, weave into it some of the real reasons why the species is in danger.

Word Bank
species
extinct
pollution
recycle
habitat

2. **Write about a solution.** Write a science-fiction story in which the main character invents an ingenious solution to an environmental problem.

After reading "The Dinner Party" and "The Two Brothers," Suki read a book of short stories. She decided to share one of the stories with her class by rewriting part of it as a play. Suki chose a story called "The Necklace," by Guy de Maupassant. This is how she presented one scene.

<u>Place</u>: Paris, France   <u>Time</u>: Sometime in the 1800s

<u>Characters</u>: Mathilde Loisel, wife of a government
                    clerk
                Jeanne Forestier, a very wealthy
                    woman and an old school friend of
                    Mathilde's

<u>Scene</u>: Jeanne's parlor. The two women are seated.

JEANNE: Mathilde, you seem nervous. What is the
    matter?
MATHILDE: (looks unhappy) Well, my husband and I
    are invited to a big reception. We've never
    been to one.
JEANNE: That's wonderful! Aren't you pleased?
MATHILDE: I should be, and we have to go! My hus-
    band was told at work that it was required.
    Of course, I had no suitable dress, but we
    agreed I must use our savings and buy one.
JEANNE: Then what is the trouble?
MATHILDE: I have no jewelry. Everyone else will
    be richly dressed, and I'll feel odd. I won-
    dered if I could borrow a necklace from you?
JEANNE: Of course! What are friends for? (gets
    jewelry box)
MATHILDE: (looks in) Oh, this is beautiful! May I
    borrow it? I'll return it right away!
JEANNE: Of course! Borrow it and enjoy it!

Think and Discuss
• Who are the characters? What do you learn about them?
• What do the words in parentheses tell you?
• Why do you think she chose this part of the story?

Share Your Book

Write a Play

1. Choose a part of your book that would make a good play. List the characters that will appear. Describe the setting, or the time and place of the play.
2. Write dialogue for your characters. If you wish, use what the characters actually say in the book or story. However, you will probably have to add more dialogue in order to make certain parts clear. Be sure the dialogue that you add fits the character.
3. Write your play. Use stage directions in parentheses to help explain the action. Make a copy for each character that appears in the play.
4. Ask classmates to help you present the play.

Other Activities

- Make an attractive program for your play. Include the title, author, setting, and a brief summary of what happens in each scene. List the characters in order of their appearance on stage. Across from each character, write the name of the actor who plays that role. Below the list of characters, list the names and jobs of anyone else involved.
- Try acting out a few lines of each character in your play. What kind of voice should the character have? How old is each character? How can you bring out the character's personality?
- Tape-record a part of your play that will stir up interest without giving away the plot. Present it to the class as a "coming attraction."

 # The Book Nook

A Day's Wait *by Ernest Hemingway* A very short story about a father and son who live through one important day in their lives together.	**The Day the Sun Came Out** *by Dorothy M. Johnson* A short story about a girl who joins a motherless family traveling across the prairie.

Pushing up their heads
Proudly

Like
Golden nuggets
On green velvet

But
Lawn owners don't love them

Carlos Cortez, "May Song"

Modifiers

Getting Ready Modifiers can change a noun or a verb so much you would hardly recognize it! They can change the words *cat stalking* from a *small gray cat quietly stalking* to a *huge jungle cat fiercely stalking.* Modifiers make all the difference! In this unit you will learn new ways to make modifiers work for you as you try to make your own writing vivid and interesting for your readers.

ACTIVITIES

Listening Listen as the poem that goes with the picture is read. If you could not see the picture, would you know what the poet is describing? What modifiers do you hear? (Listen for words that tell *how* and *what kind*.) What other adjectives and adverbs could you use to describe dandelions? With what does the poet compare them?

Speaking Look at the picture. With what else could you compare these flowers? What modifiers could you use to make that comparison? Write your ideas on the board.

Writing If dandelions in the grass are "Like / Golden nuggets / On green velvet," what might clouds in a sunset be like? In your journal, write some comparisons of your own.

1 | Adjectives

You can use **modifiers**, or words that describe, to make your language clear and colorful. One kind of modifier is an adjective. An **adjective** modifies a noun or a pronoun.

A dancer performed on the bare revolving stage.

He was slender and graceful.

Adjectives tell different kinds of details about the words they modify.

WHICH: the, that, those, other, my, which, Jeb's
WHAT KIND: young, happy, deserted, yellow, aging, uneven, famous
HOW MANY: three, some, several, few, little, half, many, much

Possessive nouns function as adjectives.

Mr. Gerry's son is an actor.   The boy's love is theater.

Other kinds of words can work as adjectives in sentences.

That director is famous.   The book is his script.

The grinning actress fell.   The completed script arrived.

We entered the movie theater.   They used a cardboard prop.

The words *a, an,* and *the* are special adjectives called **articles.** *A* and *an* are called **indefinite articles** because they refer to any person, place, or thing. Use *a* with a noun or a pronoun beginning with a consonant. Use *an* with a noun or a pronoun beginning with a vowel.

A dancer can be tall or short. (any dancer)

An actress came to see the tryouts. (any actress)

The is called a **definite** article because it points out a specific noun or pronoun.

The dancer on stage is tall. (a specific dancer)

The actresses from *Annie* arrived. (particular actresses)

You can form **proper adjectives** from many proper nouns. Capitalize proper adjectives.

French drama   Mexican art   Russian ballerina

Most often you use adjectives before the noun or the pronoun that they modify.

that long, dark alley   an exciting new play

Sometimes you may want to place adjectives after a noun or a pronoun for special emphasis. Use commas to set off such adjectives.

The dancers, hot and flushed, rested in the wings.

Adjectives used in this way can also come before a noun.

Hot and flushed, the dancers rested in the wings.

A **predicate adjective** follows a linking verb. As you know, a predicate adjective always describes the subject.

The dancers were hot and flushed from their efforts.

Guided Practice Which words are used as adjectives? Include articles in your answers. Which words do they modify?

Example: A serious young actor waited.
   A serious young—actor

1. Black and white photographs of this actor are in our local movie theater.
2. Kind and generous, he has sponsored many acting scholarships.
3. He is calm and patient with all children.
4. This new movie theater runs our favorite French films.
5. Several Spanish tourists took pictures of the movie set.
6. The comedian, funny but unsmiling, amused every member of the receptive audience.
7. Each performance at this modern theater was fresh, alive, and entertaining.
8. The six players discussed their next few roles.
9. The mirrored wall reflected their dancing silhouettes.
10. The acting troupe rehearsed for a radio play.
11. Eager and smiling, the lead spoke the first words.
12. The audience grew still as he uttered his hushed speech.
13. Crashing noises came from the stage wings.
14. A figure, enormous and shadowy, appeared on stage.
15. Was this an unexpected visitor or a surprise twist in plot?

An **adjective** describes, or modifies, a noun or a pronoun.
An adjective formed from a proper noun is a **proper adjective**.
Capitalize proper adjectives.
A **predicate adjective** follows a linking verb and describes the subject.

Independent Practice Write each word used as an adjective, including articles. Then write the word it modifies.

Example: Handwritten manuscripts were the main records of human history until the fifteenth century.

Handwritten—manuscripts   the   main—records
human—history   the   fifteenth—century

16. In ancient times many manuscripts were written on papyrus.
17. Papyrus was made from a tall, needlelike Egyptian plant.
18. Connected papyrus sheets were formed into long rolls.
19. Most rolls were six meters in length.
20. Parchment, another ancient writing material, was an improvement over papyrus.
21. Parchment was stronger, smoother, and cheaper than papyrus.
22. Vellum, smooth and precious, is parchment of high quality.
23. The invention of modern paper was a Chinese contribution to the craft of bookmaking.
24. The Chinese carved each page from a wooden block and spread ink over the raised surface.
25. In the fifteenth century in Germany, Gutenberg invented a printing press that used movable metal type.
26. Soon the northern Italian city of Venice became a book center.
27. Early printers converted household cheese presses into printing presses.
28. The first printed English book appeared in 1474.
29. Paris became an important bookmaking center in the 1500s.
30. Shakespeare's plays were published in quarto form.
31. Large printed sheets were folded into four quarters.
32. By the 1700s printers produced portable and inexpensive books.
33. Paperback books became popular in the 1800s.
34. Book publishing has become mechanized and computerized.

Writing Application: A Description Write a paragraph describing a scene from a book or from a play. Use different kinds of adjectives in your description.

2 Comparing with Adjectives

Degrees of Comparison

You can use adjectives to compare two or more persons, places, or things. To do this, you use different forms, or **degrees**, depending upon how many things you are comparing.

Degree	Example
Positive (basic form): Makes no comparison.	The Empire State Building is a tall structure.
Comparative: Compares 2.	The World Trade Center is taller than the Empire State Building.
Superlative: Compares 3 or more.	The Sears Tower is tallest of the three.

Guided Practice What is the correct form of each adjective in parentheses? Is it positive, comparative, or superlative?

Example: Sullivan was _____, but Wright was _____.   (great, great)
     great **positive**   *greater* **comparative**

1. Frank Lloyd Wright is considered the _____ architect of the twentieth century.   (great)
2. Wright was _____ than Louis Sullivan, who was his employer and teacher.   (young)
3. Wright had a _____ interest in nature than Sullivan.   (strong)
4. None of Wright's _____ skyscrapers was ever built.   (proposed)
5. His "Fallingwater" may be the _____ house ever built.   (fine)

Forms of Comparison

You can make comparisons by adding *-er* and *-est* or *more* and *most* to adjectives. The chart shows you how.

Adjective	Positive	Comparative	Superlative
One syllable	warm	warmer	warmest
Two syllables	pretty famous	prettier more famous	prettiest most famous
Three or more syllables	reliable	more reliable	most reliable

Check your dictionary about whether to use *-er* and *-est* or *more* and *most* with an adjective of two syllables.

When you want to show less rather than more, use *less* to form the comparative and *least* to form the superlative.

POSITIVE: Sullivan was enthusiastic about skyscrapers.
COMPARATIVE: His partner, Adler, was less enthusiastic than he was.
SUPERLATIVE: Wright was least enthusiastic of the three.

A few spelling changes can occur when you add *-er* and *-est* to adjectives.

Spelling Rules

1. **One-syllable adjectives ending with one vowel and a consonant:**
   Double the final consonant. Then add *-er* or *-est*.
   thin—thinner—thinnest
2. **Adjectives ending with a consonant and *y*:**
   Change the *y* to *i*. Then add *-er* or *-est*.
   happy—happier—happiest
3. **Adjectives ending with a consonant and *e*:**
   Drop the *e*. Then add *-er* or *-est*.
   cute—cuter—cutest

You must learn the irregular forms of a few adjectives.

POSITIVE	COMPARATIVE	SUPERLATIVE
good	better	best
bad	worse	worst
many, much	more	most
little (quantity)	less	least
far	farther	farthest

Use *little, less,* and *least* with things that cannot be counted. Use *few, fewer,* and *fewest* with countable things.

UNCOUNTABLE: Is there less interest in Sullivan than in Wright?
COUNTABLE: Are fewer skyscrapers being built now?

Use *much* with uncountable things. Use *many* with countable things.

UNCOUNTABLE: Wright's work created much excitement.
COUNTABLE: Many architects follow his example.

Avoid using *more* or *most* with *-er* or *-est*.

INCORRECT: Wright was more greater. Was he most happiest?
CORRECT: Wright was greater. Was he happiest?

Guided Practice What is the correct comparative or superlative form of the adjective in parentheses?

Example: Is the Sears Tower _____ than the Hancock Building? (tall)
Is the Sears Tower taller than the Hancock Building?

6. Who is the _____ of all modern architects? (prominent)
7. Is Philip Johnson a _____ architect than Louis Kahn? (good)
8. Johnson designed _____ glass buildings than brick ones. (many)
9. Perhaps Johnson's _____ work of all was his design for the new wing of the Boston Public Library. (good)
10. Of all his designs, the "Glass House" is not his _____. (bad)

Summing up

▸ Use the **comparative degree** of an adjective to compare two things.
▸ Use the **superlative degree** to compare three or more things.
▸ Form the comparative degree with -*er* or *more*.
▸ Form the superlative degree with -*est* or *most*.

Independent Practice

A. Write the sentence, using the correct comparative or superlative form of the adjective in parentheses.

Example: The _____ cities of all were in the Near East. (old)
The oldest cities of all were in the Near East.

11. Architecture was a _____ field than many. (honorable)
12. Were the Greeks _____ builders than the Romans? (good)
13. Is a Greek temple _____ than a Roman one? (fine)
14. The interior was _____ than the exterior. (impressive)

B. Rewrite each sentence correctly.

Example: The Greeks built the beautifulest temples.
The Greeks built the most beautiful temples.

15. The lovelyest Greek temple ever built is the Parthenon.
16. The Roman Empire was one of the bigest in the world.
17. Romans spent their most greatest efforts building cities.
18. They built less temples and more apartment buildings.

Writing Application: A Comparison Write a paragraph comparing three buildings. Use the comparative and superlative forms of different adjectives.

For Extra Practice, see p. 263.   Comparing with Adjectives **241**

3 | Adverbs

Identifying Adverbs

Adverbs modify verbs, adjectives, or other adverbs.

MODIFIES VERB: Jules Verne wrote clearly and colorfully.

MODIFIES ADJECTIVE: He is quite popular with many readers.

MODIFIES ADVERB: He handled his subjects remarkably well.

Adverbs tell *how, when, where,* and *to what extent.*

HOW: Sam read the novel carefully.
WHEN: We read that story yesterday.
WHERE: Verne's books are read everywhere.
TO WHAT EXTENT: I am very interested in science fiction.

Many adverbs that tell *to what extent* are **intensifiers**—they add to the meaning of the words they modify.

almost	least	most	really	terribly
awfully	less	quite	slightly	too
extremely	more	rather	so	very

Verne's style is quite realistic. He writes extremely well.

The words *how, when, where,* and *why* are adverbs.

How did he write? Where did he live?

Some adverbs are formed by adding *-ly* to adjectives.

ADJECTIVE:	wise	slow	kind	awful
ADVERB:	wisely	slowly	kindly	awfully

However, not all words that end with *-ly* are adverbs.

ADJECTIVES: Phileas Fogg seems lonely and friendly, not ugly.

Guided Practice Identify the adverbs, and tell which words they modify. Which adverbs are intensifiers?

Example: The day was terribly gloomy.
intensifier: terribly **word modified:** *gloomy*

1. How could I pass the time indoors?
2. I looked very hard for a really good book.

3. I read almost steadily for a few hours.

4. I exercised rather vigorously here and there.

5. I ran up and down repeatedly and rested afterward.

6. I finally became hungry and made a very large pot of soup.

Position of Adverbs

You can place most adverbs that modify verbs in different positions in a sentence. Use a comma after most adverbs that begin a sentence.

> Thoughtfully, Jan read the book.
> Jan thoughtfully read the book.
> Jan read the book thoughtfully.

Moving some adverbs may change their function and the meaning of a sentence.

> Only Verne worked in France. (*Only* describes *Verne* and is an adjective. No one else worked there.)
> Verne only worked in France. (He lived elsewhere.)
> Verne worked only in France. (He did not work elsewhere.)

Be careful to place words like these as close as possible to the words they modify.

almost	hardly	nearly	only
even	just	merely	scarcely

You should place most adverbs that modify adjectives and adverbs close to the words they modify. Misplaced modifiers may confuse your readers.

MISPLACED: Deeply Phileas Fogg was grateful. (*Deeply* seems to modify Phileas Fogg.)

CORRECTED: Phileas Fogg was deeply grateful.

Guided Practice Which adverbs should not be shifted? Which adverbs can be shifted? Shift those adverbs to another part of the sentence. (There may be more than one correct way to change some sentences.)

Example: Actually, science fiction can be traced back to myths.
Science fiction can actually be traced back to myths.

7. A Greek writer merely rewrote myths as science fiction.

8. In the 1600s, modern science was just developing.

9. Modern science fiction developed also at this time.

10. Some early scientists wrote about science fiction accurately.

11. Probably Jonathan Swift produced the first science fiction master-piece, *Gulliver's Travels*, in 1726.

Summing up

▸ **Adverbs** modify verbs, adjectives, or other adverbs. Adverbs usually tell *how, when, where,* and *to what extent.*

▸ **Intensifiers** are adverbs that tell *to what extent.*

▸ Some adverbs should be placed as close as possible to the modified words.

Independent Practice

A. Write the adverbs and the words that they modify. Label the intensifiers.

Example: H. G. Wells wrote science fiction brilliantly and intelligently.
brilliantly   intelligently—wrote

12. Why did his books sell so well?

13. First, Wells mainly wrote fiction.

14. He then developed rather naturally into a bold forecaster.

15. Later, Wells became quite deeply involved in world events.

16. He went everywhere and spoke often against certain political beliefs.

17. He firmly believed that these beliefs were driving humanity downward.

18. Many people still read Wells's works enthusiastically.

B. If an adverb can be shifted without changing its function, rewrite the sentence with the adverb in a different position. If it cannot be shifted, write *no change.* (There may be more than one correct way to change some sentences.)

Example: H. G. Wells wrote repeatedly about science fiction.
H. G. Wells wrote about science fiction repeatedly.

19. Imaginatively, he described trips to the future.

20. In 1909 he even described airplanes and submarines.

21. Such trips seemed highly improbable then.

22. Wells did not only write science fiction.

Writing Application: A Persuasive Letter Write a letter to convince a friend to read your favorite kind of book. Use some adverbs, including intensifiers.

4 | Comparing with Adverbs

Degrees of Comparison

You can use adverbs to compare the actions of two people or things. Like adjectives, adverbs have three **degrees**.

Positive (basic form): Makes no comparison.	Cars travel fast.
Comparative: Compares 2.	Trains travel faster than cars.
Superlative: Compares 3 or more.	Planes travel fastest of all.

Guided Practice What form of the adverb completes each sentence correctly? What is its degree?

Example: Modern bicycles travel _____ than older ones.   (fast)
         faster   **comparative**

1. Years ago cyclists pedaled _____ on their wooden bikes than cyclists do today.   (hard)
2. You needn't push so _____ on lightweight bikes.   (hard)
3. What kind of bike lasts _____ of all?   (long)
4. Obviously, metal bikes last _____ than wooden ones.   (long)
5. A six-day bicycle race will be held here _____.   (soon)

Forms of Comparison

Adverbs change form to show comparison.

Adverb	Positive	Comparative	Superlative
One syllable	soon	soon er	soon est
Two or more syllables	early clearly	earli er more clearly	earli est most clearly

Most adverbs of two or more syllables form comparisons with *more* and *most*. Check your dictionary if you are not sure.
    Use *less* and *least* to show less rather than more.

POSITIVE: The pilot flew skillfully.
COMPARATIVE: The trainee flew less skillfully than the pilot.
SUPERLATIVE: The beginner flew least skillfully of all.

You must follow certain spelling rules when you add *-er* or *-est* to adverbs.

Spelling Rules

1. Adverbs ending with a consonant and *y*:
Change the *y* to *i*. Then add *-er* or *-est*.
early—earlier—earliest

2. Adverbs ending with a consonant and *e*:
Drop the *e*. Then add *-er* or *-est*.
late—later—latest

Some adverbs have irregular forms.

POSITIVE	COMPARATIVE	SUPERLATIVE
well	better	best
badly	worse	worst
much	more	most
far	farther	farthest
far	further	furthest
little	less	least

Use *farther* and *farthest* when you talk about physical distance. Use *further* and *furthest* in all other cases.

A jet travels farther than a glider.
Let's look into this problem further.

As with adjectives, you should also avoid using *more* or *most* with adverbs ending in *-er* or *-est*.

INCORRECT: This train travels more faster than that one.
CORRECT: This train travels faster than that one.

Guided Practice
What comparative or superlative form of the adverb in parentheses completes each sentence correctly?

Example: The bicycle has changed _____ than other forms of transportation. (little)
The bicycle has changed less than other forms of transportation.

6. A wooden bicycle without pedals came _____ of all. (early)
7. Pedals were added about twenty years _____. (late)
8. Today's bicycles do perform _____ than older ones. (good)
9. You can certainly travel _____ in comfort than before. (far)
10. People now ride bicycles _____ than they used to. (much)
11. Of all sports, many people enjoy bicycling _____. (much)

Independent Practice

A. Write each sentence, using the correct comparative or superlative form of the adverb in parentheses.

> Example: In 1897 people rode bicycles _____ than they did before.   (frequently)
> *In 1897 people rode bicycles more frequently than they did before.*

12. Then people began to drive cars _____ than they rode bicycles.   (often)
13. They could go _____ in a car than on a bicycle.   (fast)
14. They could also go _____ than on a bike.   (far)
15. Today the bicycle is again one of the _____ used vehicles of all.   (commonly)
16. Bikes move _____ in traffic jams than cars do.   (well)
17. In city traffic a bike may arrive _____ than a car.   (early)
18. A cyclist who obeys traffic laws _____ than another will be safer in the long run.   (carefully)
19. Of the different kinds of bicycles, some young people like high-risers _____.   (much)
20. Most older people like high-risers _____ of all.   (less)

B. Rewrite each sentence correctly.

> Example: A bicycle can travel further than a car.
> *A bicycle can travel farther than a car.*

21. What is the most economicalest means of transportation?
22. Certainly bicycle travel costs littlest of all.
23. The supersonic jet flies speedilyest.
24. I'll try to research the question farther.
25. Is it worser to travel by bus than by train?

Writing Application: A Comparison Write a paragraph to compare the movements or actions of three kinds of transportation. Use some comparative and superlative forms of adverbs in your paragraph.

For Extra Practice, see p. 265.

5 || Negatives

A **negative** is a word that means "no" or "not." The word *not* is often used as an adverb. You often join *not*, or its contraction *n't*, with a verb. *Not* or *n't* makes a verb negative.

> Shirley has not spotted an oriole yet.
> I cannot find the birds.
> They can't have flown away.

Other words are also negatives.

> I have never seen such a mess as this one.
> I can hardly move around in this room.
> There's nowhere I can go from here.
> No one seems to hear me.
> Nothing is happening in this house.

A **double negative** is the use of two negative words to express one negative idea. Be careful to avoid double negatives. Most negative words have positive forms. You can usually use positive forms to correct double negatives.

Negative	Positive	Negative	Positive
neither	either	none	any
never	ever	no one	anyone
no	any, a	nothing	anything
nobody	anybody	nowhere	anywhere

INCORRECT: Won't nobody help me clean up?
 CORRECT: Won't anybody help me clean up?
          Will nobody help me clean up?

INCORRECT: I can't find the soap nowhere.
 CORRECT: I can't find the soap anywhere.
          I can find the soap nowhere.

The words *hardly*, *scarcely*, and *barely* are negatives. Do not use them with another negative to express a negative idea.

INCORRECT: I can't hardly see the floor.
 CORRECT: I can hardly see the floor.

INCORRECT: There's barely no light in here.
 CORRECT: There's barely any light in here.

INCORRECT: There is scarcely nobody around.
 CORRECT: There is scarcely anybody around.

Guided Practice Change the sentences to avoid double negatives. (There may be more than one correct answer.)

Example: I didn't see nothing I liked in the store.
I saw nothing I liked in the store.

1. There weren't no sweaters in the closet.
2. Isn't there an Irish knit sweater nowhere in this room?
3. I couldn't find hardly any shirts in the drawer.
4. My brother couldn't find nothing either.
5. Doesn't nobody know where we can find a simple white shirt?
6. Brenda hasn't scarcely begun to look for me.

Summing up

▶ A **negative** means "no" or "not."
▶ A **double negative** is the use of two negatives to express one negative idea. Avoid double negatives.

Independent Practice Rewrite each sentence correctly. (There may be more than one correct way to change a sentence.)

Example: There isn't scarcely any firewood left.
There is scarcely any firewood left.

7. Didn't nobody bring some into the house?
8. We can't cook nothing unless we get some wood.
9. We can't keep warm neither.
10. I've never gone nowhere that's colder than this.
11. You can't hardly expect any heat in the mountains.
12. There isn't nothing we can do unless we have help.
13. Won't nobody go out and get some wood?
14. There isn't none in the shed behind this cottage.
15. You can't barely see at night in there.
16. I can't see in this cottage neither.
17. Won't nobody come with me to look?
18. No one said nothing about wood this morning.
19. Haven't you never heard of electricity?
20. We don't have no electricity in this cottage.

Writing Application: A Paragraph Write a paragraph about something you forgot to do or about something that didn't turn out quite right. Include some negatives in your paragraph. Be sure to use them correctly.

For Extra Practice, see p. 266.

6 || Adjective or Adverb?

You have learned about adjectives and adverbs and how to make comparisons with them. You must be careful not to confuse adjectives and adverbs.

INCORRECT: Albert Schweitzer played the organ good.

CORRECT: Albert Schweitzer played the organ well.

INCORRECT: Schweitzer felt badly about the underprivileged.

CORRECT: Schweitzer felt bad about the underprivileged.

Remember what adjectives and adverbs do.

Adjectives: Modify nouns and pronouns.	Which one What kind How many	that person red hat five men
Adverbs: Modify action verbs, adjectives, and other adverbs.	How When Where To what extent	played well came yesterday lived upstairs really well

ADJECTIVE: Schweitzer had a quick wit. His wit was quick.

ADVERB: Albert Schweitzer thought quickly.

Use *good, bad, sure,* and *real* as adjectives. Remember that adjectives (not adverbs) follow linking verbs.

Schweitzer felt bad.   He was sure.

His intentions were good.   His concerns were real.

Use *well, badly, surely,* and *really* as adverbs.

Schweitzer knew music well. (*not* good)

He didn't play badly. (*not* bad)

He surely was kind. (*not* sure)

He was really charitable. (*not* real)

Well is an adjective when it refers to health.

Many of Schweitzer's patients became well under his care.

Guided Practice Which words in parentheses correctly complete the sentences?

Example: It's (real, really) strange that Einstein didn't do (good, well) in school as a boy. *really   well*

1. He did (bad, badly) in history and languages.
2. Mathematics and science came (easy, easily) to him.
3. By his teens he was (sure, surely) of his abilities.
4. He (sure, surely) developed into a brilliant scientist.
5. His scientific contributions are (real, really) important.

Summing up

> ► Use *good, bad, sure,* and *real* as adjectives to modify nouns or pronouns and after linking verbs.
> ► Use *well, badly, surely,* and *really* as adverbs to modify verbs, adjectives, or other adverbs.
> ► Use *well* as an adjective when you mean "healthy."

Independent Practice Rewrite each sentence, using adjectives and adverbs correctly.

Example: To some people math comes easy.
To some people math comes easily.

6. Other people become real nervous when they are faced with math problems.
7. They would do good if they relaxed.
8. Math anxiety is not a real uncommon feeling.
9. It has been discussed good in many books.
10. Many people are not real sure of themselves with numbers.
11. They feel so uncomfortably before a math test.
12. Something sure can be done about math anxiety.
13. Not everyone does bad in math.
14. Good coaching will sure help anyone with this problem.
15. Teachers are becoming real good at recognizing the problem.
16. More confidence and less nervousness sure are the answers.
17. People must become real sure of their natural abilities.
18. Many people can do good in math if they relax.

Writing Application: A Personal Narrative Write a paragraph about your ability in math, English, or history. Use adjectives and adverbs, such as *good, well,* and *badly.*

Grammar-Writing Connection

Using Modifiers for Variety

You have learned that modifiers describe nouns and pronouns. When you use modifiers in your writing, you give your reader a clear picture. You have also learned that some modifiers can occur in various positions. You can use modifiers, then, to vary your sentences. Remember these ways of using modifiers to help you write better.

1. Use modifiers that are exact.

    UNCLEAR: Some nights last week were bad .

      EXACT: Two nights last week were cloudy , hot , and humid .

Not all modifiers describe exactly. Avoid general adjectives like *some, bad, good,* and *nice.* Decide exactly what you want to say, and then choose the modifier that says it best.

2. Use modifiers to combine short, choppy sentences.

    TWO SENTENCES: Stars shone above. They were bright and clear .

    ONE SENTENCE: Bright and clear , stars shone above.

    TWO SENTENCES: Stars move across the sky. They move slowly .

    ONE SENTENCE: Stars move slowly across the sky.

3. Vary your sentences by shifting the position of modifiers.

    ADJECTIVES: Stars, bright and clear , shone above.

              The bright , clear stars shone above.

      ADVERBS: Slowly stars move across the sky.

              Stars slowly move across the sky.

              Stars move across the sky slowly .

Revising Sentences

Rewrite the sentences. Change the position of modifiers, replace general modifiers with more exact modifiers, or use modifiers to combine sentences.

1. Tony wrote a good report on some stars for some class.
2. Some stars are nice to look at.
3. Stars are made up of gases. These gases are hot.
4. We see stars on some nights. The nights are dark and clear.
5. Shining stars are usually colorful and bright.
6. Meteors are rocks or metal that fall rapidly from the sky.

Creative Writing

Rembrandt, *The Polish Rider*
The Frick Collection, N.Y.

Who is this dashing young horseman? What adventure has taken him into this dark, lonely land? By filling the canvas with deep, rich colors and a warm, glowing light, Rembrandt created a sense of mystery and danger. Perhaps he wanted us to weave our own story.

- How does Rembrandt focus your attention on the horseman?
- Does the horse look strong and proud, or thin and tired? Why do you think Rembrandt painted the horse this way?

Activities

1. **Write the horseman's story.** Imagine that Rembrandt showed you this painting and asked you to tell the story of the horseman's journey. How would you explain where the horseman is from and where he is going? Write the story you would tell.
2. **Write a poem.** Imagine that this horseman is a hero who has done a brave deed for the people of his country. Write a poem that praises the horseman's courage.

Adjectives *(p. 236)* Write the adjectives, including the articles, and the words that they modify.

1. The long, narrow canoe glided along the smooth waters.
2. Two men, quiet and serious, concentrated on their actions.
3. They dipped their paddles in a slow, steady rhythm.
4. The shore, wooded, dark, and unfriendly, appeared at last.
5. The men beached the canoe beneath a large willow tree.

Comparing with Adjectives *(p. 239)* Write each sentence, using the correct form of the adjective in parentheses.

6. Deserts may be the _____ places in the world to live. (hard)
7. The Sahara is _____ than the Mojave desert. (dry)
8. The Empty Quarter in Saudi Arabia may be _____ of all. (arid)
9. Death Valley, California, is the _____ place in America. (hot)
10. Azizia, Libya, though, is _____ than Death Valley. (hot)
11. Not all deserts are _____. (hot)
12. The Gobi desert in central Asia is _____ than most. (cold)
13. Sometimes it is one of the _____ places on earth. (cold)
14. Some deserts are _____ than others. (pretty)
15. A few are among the _____ regions of all. (spectacular)

Adverbs *(p. 242)* Write the adverbs and the words that they modify. Underline the intensifiers.

16. The day had begun quite satisfactorily.
17. In only one hour, Ted had nearly finished his chores.
18. Now the smells of breakfast floated outdoors invitingly.
19. He sniffed appreciatively, and he walked homeward.
20. He suddenly felt quite hungry, and he rushed into the house.
21. On the table was a very small glass of orange juice.
22. Ted was greatly disappointed by this.
23. Shortly his mother appeared with a plate of warm bread.
24. "So that's what smelled so good," he said.
25. She said, "You've been working so hard every morning that to-day I decided to bake you some bread."
26. Ted could not have been more pleased, and he thanked her.
27. Soon Mrs. Rizzo brought a puffy cheese omelet into the room.
28. Ted ate quickly and enthusiastically.
29. "The white part is the plate," said Mrs. Rizzo jokingly.
30. Then Ted gratefully thanked his mother and left briskly.

Comparing with Adverbs *(p. 245)* Write each sentence, using the correct positive, comparative, or superlative form of the adverb in parentheses.

31. Computers solve problems _____ than people do.   (accurately)
32. Programmers once worked _____ than they do now.   (slowly)
33. Programmers worked _____ of all on program development. (hard)
34. These programmers learned _____ that routine computer tasks could be stored in the machine's memory.   (quickly)
35. Programming was done _____ after this than before.   (easily)
36. Programs are now stored _____ in the computer's memory than on magnetic tape.   (often)
37. Programming languages have been written that resemble English _____ than machine languages.   (closely)
38. A list of these languages would _____ than not include BASIC, FORTRAN, COBOL, and Pascal.   (likely)
39. Recently, programmers have developed computer languages even _____ than before.   (far)
40. Pascal can produce new programs _____ of all.   (easily)
41. We must work _____ than before to make computing easier. (much)

Negatives *(p. 248)* Rewrite each sentence correctly.

42. We had hardly never seen such a storm.
43. By afternoon we didn't have no power.
44. Nobody on the whole street had no light or heat.
45. There isn't no warm place anywhere in the house.
46. I couldn't hardly stand the freezing cold weather.
47. There didn't seem to be no blankets anywhere.
48. Neither of my sweaters was not warm enough.

Adjective or Adverb? *(p. 250)* Rewrite each sentence correctly.

49. Tim looks especially well today in that suit.
50. His new blue suit is real smart looking.
51. He sure shows excellent taste in all his clothing.
52. Does he feel badly about getting ketchup on his jacket?
53. He certainly doesn't feel well about it.
54. Wasn't Sue feeling good yesterday?
55. I've never had salmon near this good.
56. Those old records sound well for their age.
57. Maeve and Herb surely dance good.
58. They can do some real lively dances.

Cumulative Review

Unit 1: The Sentence

Subjects and Predicates *(pp. 16, 18)* Write each sentence. Draw a line between the complete subject and the complete predicate. Underline the simple subject once and the simple predicate twice.

1. The ginkgo has survived for millions of years.
2. Many people refer to this tree as a living fossil.
3. A ginkgo can grow to a height of 130 feet.
4. Its different types of flowers do not grow on the same tree.
5. The roasted nut of the ginkgo is a delicacy in the Far East.

Combining Sentences: Compound Sentences *(p. 24)* Combine each pair of simple sentences into a compound sentence.

6. Sailboats were once simple. They could sail great distances.
7. Most people buy boats. Some people make their own.
8. Parts come in a kit. A builder can fit them together.
9. Aluminum is a common material. People still use wood.
10. Some people take sailing lessons. They learn on their own.

Conjunctions, Complex Sentences *(pp. 26, 28)* Write and label the coordinating, correlative, and subordinating conjunctions.

11. When you visit New York, you should see either the Empire State Building or the World Trade Center towers.
12. Actually, a visit to both the Empire State Building and the World Trade Center is nice if you have enough time.
13. Be sure to go to the tops because the views are magnificent.
14. Don't bother going if the day is overcast.
15. Although these two buildings are tall, the Sears Tower in Chicago is taller.

Correcting Fragments and Run-ons *(p. 31)* Rewrite each item, correcting the fragments and run-ons.

16. The Library of Congress in Washington.
17. Because it is the biggest library in the United States.
18. The library collects materials from all over the world the materials are in 468 languages.
19. And papers of twenty-three Presidents are housed there.
20. It is a huge place, it is located in several buildings.
21. Millions of maps, recordings, and photographs in the library.

Unit 3: Nouns

Kinds of Nouns *(pp. 88, 90)* Write the nouns. Label each one either *concrete* or *abstract* and either *common* or *proper*. Label the compound and collective nouns.

22. Afghanistan is a mountainous nation with valleys and deserts.
23. This country in Central Asia is slightly smaller than Texas.
24. The people are known for their bravery.
25. They have often fought against invaders to keep their freedom.
26. The landscape shows snow in winter and dust in summer.
27. Spring is beautiful, with colorful flowers all over the land.
28. Snow panthers and mountain goats are found there.

Singular, Plural, and Possessive Nouns *(pp. 92, 95)* For each singular noun, write the singular possessive, the plural, and the plural possessive forms. Use your dictionary if you need help.

29. Diaz
30. pony
31. doe
32. tuna
33. butterfly
34. Roy
35. chickadee
36. Vietnamese
37. son-in-law
38. octopus
39. Dailey
40. buffalo

Combining Sentences: Appositives *(p. 97)* Combine each pair of sentences by changing the second sentence into an appositive. Write the new sentences. Add commas where necessary.

41. Lemurs live in Madagascar. They are mammals with huge eyes.
42. Madagascar lies off the coast of Africa. Madagascar is the fourth largest island in the world.
43. Gentleness and timidity are characteristics of the lemur. Gentleness and timidity are two endearing traits.
44. A Latin word gave this animal its name. The word is *lemures*.
45. The largest lemur can weigh more than twenty pounds. The largest lemur is the indri.
46. One kind of lemur looks like a raccoon. It is the aye-aye.
47. At least one species of lemur is strictly vegetarian. The greater dwarf lemur is strictly vegetarian.
48. Many lemurs are nocturnal animals. Nocturnal animals are creatures that move only at night.
49. The face of the lemur somewhat resembles that of another animal. The other animal is the fox.
50. The body and tail, however, are more like those of another animal. The body and the tail are like those of the monkey.
51. Fat-tailed dwarf lemurs are inactive during the drier months. The drier months are April through October.

Cumulative Review, *continued*

Unit 5: Verbs

Verbs, Verb Phrases, Tenses *(pp. 146, 148, 150)* Write the verbs. Label them *action* or *linking*. Then label tense.

52. Newton was born in 1642, the same year that Galileo had died.
53. Before Newton died eighty-five years later, he had changed the way that people thought about the universe.
54. Newton's works are masterpieces of scientific writing.
55. Sir Isaac also invented a new kind of mathematical analysis.
56. Explanations of the natural world had been imprecise before.

Irregular Verbs *(pp. 155, 158)* Write the principal parts for each verb.

57. teach	60. become	63. put	66. sink	69. lie
58. write	61. think	64. lay	67. bring	70. rise
59. read	62. speak	65. be	68. freeze	71. do

Direct and Indirect Objects, Predicate Nouns and Adjectives *(pp. 164, 167)* Write each sentence. Label the direct and indirect objects, the predicate nouns, and the predicate adjectives.

72. I have just finished a book by Ved Mehta.
73. The book taught me an important lesson.
74. The struggle against a handicap is not impossible.
75. Mehta was blind from the age of three.
76. Nevertheless, he overcame his handicap.
77. He attended college, and he also became a writer.
78. He did numerous surprising things.
79. He hitchhiked across America, played chess, and rode a bike.
80. He is really a wonderful writer too.
81. Blind people can sometimes sense the presence of objects.
82. Vicente gave me a book about blindness.

Subject-Verb Agreement *(pp. 171, 173, 176)* Write each sentence. Underline the subject. Use the correct form of the verb.

83. That pile of baseballs (is, are) for us.
84. That is fine, but there (is, are) no bats.
85. Behind the dugout there (is, are) two of them.
86. The other team, the Bobcats, always (use, uses) our equipment!
87. My trousers (is, are) quite dirty from the mud on the mound.

Unit 7: Modifiers

Adjectives, Adverbs *(pp. 236, 242)* Write the adjectives and the adverbs. Do not list any articles. Then write the words that the adjectives and the adverbs modify.

88. The Sumerians created the first civilization.

89. In ancient times, they settled in a land between two rivers.

90. This rich land, which was called Mesopotamia by the Greeks, was ideally suited for agricultural cultivation.

91. The Sumerians probably first used irrigation successfully.

92. They built impressive cities from natural, bricklike materials.

93. They made very effective bronze tools and weapons.

94. Most significantly, they created one of the finest legal codes ever.

Comparing with Adjectives and Adverbs *(pp. 239, 245)* Write each sentence, using the form of the word in parentheses.

95. In addition to water and oxygen, food is one of man's _____ daily needs. (important—superlative)

96. People must satisfy this need as _____ as possible. (nutritiously—positive)

97. A balanced diet is _____ than one lacking in essential nutrients. (beneficial—comparative)

98. A sandwich can sometimes provide good energy, but a balanced meal provides _____ nutrition. (good—comparative)

99. Proteins, carbohydrates, fats, vitamins, and minerals are the _____ building blocks for the body. (necessary—positive)

100. For a long time, people thought that animal protein was the _____ kind of protein. (good—superlative)

101. Soybeans are now a _____ source of protein than they used to be. (popular—comparative)

Adjective or Adverb? *(p. 250)* Write each sentence, choosing the correct modifier.

102. Oh, Marlene, aren't you feeling (good, well) today?

103. You look (terrible, terribly)!

104. Didn't you sleep (good, well) last night?

105. I hope you won't do (poor, poorly) on the exam.

106. I (hard, hardly) worry about Mr. Alberti's tests.

107. His tests (sure, surely) are fair.

108. I always do (real, really) well on them.

Enrichment

Poster Politics

Choose a past presidential election. Make a campaign poster for each major candidate. Use adjectives on each poster to give voters the most precise information about each candidate. Also try to select adjectives to persuade people to vote for the candidate. Make each poster eye-catching and convincing.

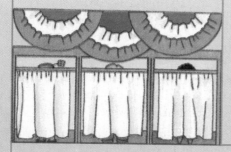

Missing Modifiers

Find a favorite descriptive paragraph from a story in your reading book or in a library book. Copy the paragraph onto a piece of paper. As you do so, leave out all the adjectives and adverbs, drawing a fill-in line for each missing modifier. Exchange your paragraph with a classmate. Have your partner write in adjectives and adverbs that make sense. Then compare the new paragraph with the one in the book. How is the new paragraph like the original? How is it different?

TV Awards

Assume that you are announcing this year's TV awards. Select winners for the best TV drama series and the best TV comedy series. Also select a runner-up in each category. Then prepare a statement to read at the awards ceremony, comparing the best show in each category with its runner-up. Concentrate on using descriptive language, and be sure to use comparative and superlative forms of modifiers correctly.

Brave the Caves!

The world has many fascinating caves and caverns. Look up one of these: the Blue Grotto, Carlsbad Caverns, Luray Caverns, or the Wind Cave. Write one paragraph for a travel folder. Describe this place, making it sound attractive and inviting to a tourist.

Extra! Make a travel leaflet using your paragraph, colorful lettering, and pictures.

Scrambled Modifiers

Players—2. **You need**—paper and pencils.
How to play—Each person writes a list of 20 common adjectives and adverbs and then on another piece of paper scrambles the letters of each word.
Exchange your lists. Unscramble each word and write it in a complete sentence. Then label each word *adjective* or *adverb.* Exchange again and correct each other's work. **Scoring**—1 point for each unscrambled word; 2 points for each sentence; 2 points for each correct label.

Example: *mtoals = almost*

adverb
The game was <u>almost</u> canceled because of the weather.

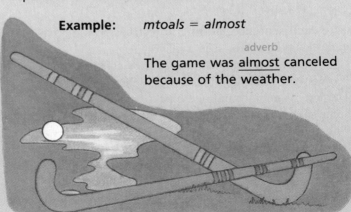

1 | Adjectives (p. 236)

● Write the adjectives, including the articles.

Example: Most summer theaters are small. *Most summer small*

1. The final rehearsal for the show is next Tuesday.
2. Every performer seems nervous.
3. The graceful dancers stand on the empty stage.
4. Which person will be successful in ten years?
5. That tall and attractive actor is dreaming about fame.
6. Those singers are resting for the next song.
7. A happy director enters and announces the wonderful news.
8. A famous Broadway director will see the first performance.
9. Everyone becomes cheerful, eager, and talkative.

▲ Write each adjective and the word it modifies. Include articles.

Example: In summer theater many performers are young and eager.

summer—theater   many   young   eager—performers

10. The cast members perform many different tasks.
11. Everyone does almost every job.
12. One day a bright, talented actor will sweep the stage floor.
13. The previous day that person may have painted some scenery.
14. A strong, slim dancer helps a hesitant actress with her lines.
15. On opening night, the audience is large and enthusiastic.
16. Pleased and smiling, it applauds this funny French play.
17. Some audience members shout "Bravo!" to joyful performers.
18. For the weary but satisfied actors, the work was worthwhile.

■ Rewrite each sentence, adding adjectives.

Example: Has the visitor seen a play?

Has the Italian visitor seen a Broadway play?

19. People were waiting in line to buy tickets.
20. The line wound around one block.
21. Some sailors from a country were talking to a man.
22. One group of children made everyone else in the crowd smile.
23. Boys sat on the curb while a teacher waited.
24. A car came around the corner and pulled up to the door.
25. The crowd watched as the actor entered the theater.
26. The box office in front of the theater opened, and the crowd bought tickets to the play.

2 | Comparing with Adjectives (p. 239)

● Write the titles for three columns: *Positive, Comparative,* and *Superlative.* Copy the adjectives below into the *Positive* column. Then write each comparative and superlative form.
  Example: cold   *comparative: colder*   *superlative: coldest*
  1. red   **3.** bad   **5.** large
  2. comfortable   **4.** noisy   **6.** terrible

▲ Write each sentence, using the correct positive, comparative, or superlative form of the adjective in parentheses.
  Example: A building must withstand the _____ climate of all.   (bad)
           A building must withstand the worst climate of all.
  7. Builders of the past had _____ technical know-how than we have today.   (little)
  8. Their _____ structure of all used vertical posts and horizontal beams.   (common)
  9. The _____ builders of all used timber, stone, or mud.   (early)
  10. They used _____ materials.   (available)
  11. Wood and stone were _____ in some areas than in others.   (scarce)
  12. Therefore, the _____ material of all was mud.   (popular)
  13. Mud bricks were _____ than wood.   (heavy)

■ Write each sentence, using the correct positive, comparative, or superlative form of the adjective in parentheses. Then label the adjective *positive, comparative,* or *superlative.*
  Example: The Romans were _____ users of the arch.   (creative)
           The Romans were creative users of the arch. **positive**
  14. The arch spanned _____ distances than posts and beams had spanned.   (great)
  15. It also required _____ stones or bricks than posts and beams.   (few)
  16. Therefore, the Romans could build _____ structures with _____ material than ever before.   (big, little)
  17. In a _____ period than this, the Middle Eastern arch was brought to Europe.   (late)
  18. This arch was _____ than the Roman arch.   (pointed)
  19. Pointed arches were used in the _____ structures of all in the Middle Ages, the cathedrals.   (wonderful)
  20. Their structure made it possible to have _____ walls than other buildings had had before.   (thin)

3 | Adverbs (p. 242)

● Write the adverbs in these sentences.

Example: Jules Verne looked ahead to certain inventions clearly.

ahead   clearly

1. He predicted airplanes and guided missiles accurately.
2. Surprisingly, his books remain popular today.
3. Verne cleverly used realistic details in his fantastic tales.
4. Verne wrote only one book and then became famous.
5. Verne's books were very successful.
6. People were quite interested in science in the 1800s.
7. That most certainly added to the popularity of Verne's books.
8. He almost entered law school, but fortunately he changed his mind early.
9. The world really would have missed his interesting tales.

▲ Write the adverbs and the words that they modify. Underline the adverbs that are intensifiers.

Example: Jules Verne took his readers almost everywhere.

<u>almost</u>—everywhere   everywhere—took

10. *Twenty Thousand Leagues Under the Sea* is very famous.
11. A rather mad sea captain travels happily under the ocean.
12. *Around the World in Eighty Days* takes readers farther away.
13. Phileas Fogg travels around the earth in only eighty days.
14. Then eighty days seemed like an extremely short time.
15. Why did Fogg foolishly attempt this rather remarkable task?
16. Actually, he just wanted to win a bet.
17. Verne's readers can travel quite safely to the center of the earth and afterward to the moon.

■ Rewrite each sentence, adding two or more adverbs.

Example: Science fiction is popular.

Science fiction is currently very popular.

18. The interesting plots involve space travel or time travel.
19. Marvelous inventions are another frequent theme.
20. Many science fiction stories are set in the future.
21. They may be set in the present or in the past.
22. Science fiction is different from fantasy.
23. Fantasy relates impossible events.
24. In science fiction the events could occur.
25. Science fiction writers have a solid background in science.
26. In the space age, science fiction stories have become complicated.

4 | Comparing with Adverbs (p. 245)

● Write the titles for three columns: *Positive, Comparative,* and *Superlative.* Copy the adjectives below into the *Positive* column. Then write each comparative and superlative form.
Example: soon   *comparative: sooner*   **superlative:** *soonest*

1. early   4. late   7. speedily
2. quickly   5. well   8. little
3. frequently   6. far   9. badly

▲ Write each sentence, using the form of the adverb in parentheses that best completes it.
Example: In the 1780s ships sailed _____ than before.   (far)
          In the 1780s ships sailed farther than before.

10. The *Columbia* sailed around the world _____ than any other American ship.   (early)
11. Every merchant wanted a ship that went _____ than other ships. (fast)
12. For years, first schooners and then clippers sailed _____ of all the different kinds of ships.   (fast)
13. The British worked _____ on steamships than on clipper ships. (much)
14. Steamships crossed the ocean _____ than clippers.   (speedily)
15. Of all the sailing countries, England built the luxury passenger liner the _____.   (early)
16. Passengers were treated _____ than ever before.   (well)
17. Of all ways to travel at that time, people enjoyed these ocean liners the _____.   (much)

■ Write each sentence, using the form of the adverb in parentheses that best completes it. Use the *comparative* or *superlative* forms and label each one.
Example: People always want to move _____ than usual.   (fast)
          People always want to move faster than usual.   **comparative**

18. Does moving the _____ mean moving the _____?   (fast, well)
19. Let us examine the matter _____ than this.   (far)
20. Most people try to advance _____ than other people.   (quick)
21. Sometimes we do _____ if we go _____.   (well, slow)
22. We need time to think _____ than we do now.   (much)
23. Furthermore, people often behave _____ when they are tired than when they are rested.   (bad)
24. Those who do _____ of all are those who can relax.   (well)

5 | Negatives (p. 248)

● Write each sentence, choosing the correct adverb.
   Example: I don't (never, ever) remember a hotter day.
             I don't ever remember a hotter day.
   1. Nobody wants to do (nothing, anything) in this heat.
   2. Even the mosquitoes (can, can't) scarcely move.
   3. There's no breeze (anywhere, nowhere).
   4. The fan doesn't do (no, any) good.
   5. It (can, can't) barely push the heavy air around.
   6. Doesn't (anybody, nobody) have air conditioning in this old
        building?
   7. Usually we don't need (none, any) here.
   8. We can't sit on the hot porch (neither, either).
   9. Doesn't (anyone, no one) want to go to the beach?

▲ Rewrite each sentence to correct the double negative. (There
   may be more than one way to correct each sentence.)
   Example: There isn't scarcely anyone here yet.
             There is scarcely anyone here yet.
   10. Didn't no one put the juice in the refrigerator?
   11. There won't be nothing cold to drink.
   12. I can't find my record albums nowhere.
   13. Eva can't find her cassette tapes neither.
   14. You can't hardly hear the music in the other room.
   15. Isn't Chris bringing no records for us to listen to?
   16. He didn't bring none with him last evening.
   17. Hasn't nobody answered the front door yet?
   18. I didn't hear no one ring the doorbell.

■ Rewrite each sentence that has a double negative. (There may
   be more than one way to correct a sentence.) If there is no
   double negative, write *correct*.
   Example: They haven't done nothing about fixing the bike.
             They haven't done anything about fixing the bike.
   19. I can't go nowhere until they do fix it.
   20. Wasn't anybody at the repair shop?
   21. Nobody never answers the telephone there.
   22. No one can drive to the repair shop this afternoon.
   23. We don't have no spare time right now.
   24. You shouldn't never leave your bike in the driveway again.
   25. Hardly no one could see it lying there.
   26. There's not enough light on the street.

6 | Adjective or Adverb? (p. 250)

● Write each sentence, using the word in parentheses that correctly completes it.

Example: Chester is (real, really) happy about his summer job.
Chester is really happy about his summer job.

1. He was not (sure, surely) that he would get it.
2. Chester is normally a very (good, well) swimmer.
3. He did not swim (good, well) for his lifesaving test, however.
4. All week he had had a (badly, bad) cold.
5. When he took his test, he was not feeling (good, well).
6. He was certain that he had done (bad, badly) on the test.
7. Fortunately his fears were not (real, really).
8. Otherwise he (really, real) would not have gotten the job.
9. He feels (really, real) better today.

▲ Rewrite each sentence correctly.

Example: The dancer did not look well in her costume.
The dancer did not look good in her costume.

10. She looked real good in strong colors.
11. Pale pink made her look ill even when she felt good.
12. She was not surely what to do about the costume.
13. The director knew that the problem was real serious.
14. He sure wanted her to look good on stage.
15. If she felt uncomfortable, she might dance bad.
16. He felt surely that he could think of something.
17. His idea sounded well to the dancer.
18. She would dance good in bright-colored ribbons, and she would feel real good too.

■ Rewrite each incorrect sentence correctly. Label each corrected word *adjective* or *adverb*. If a sentence is already correct, write *correct*.

Example: The new restaurant seems to be doing good.
The new restaurant seems to be doing well.   well   **adverb**

19. Everything smells and tastes well.
20. The meal we had last night sure was delicious.
21. The table looked really good too.
22. The flowers were real, and the colors matched well.
23. Unfortunately, Tom was not feeling well last night.
24. He skated bad at the hockey game and then went home.
25. He felt badly about missing such a good meal.
26. I feel sure that we will go to this restaurant again.

Literature and Writing

Roll on, thou deep and dark blue ocean—roll!
Ten thousand fleets sweep over thee in vain.

George Gordon, Lord Byron
from "Childe Harold's Pilgrimage"

Description

Getting Ready What kind of an observer are you? What did you pass by on the way to school this morning? Did you notice only the obvious—the person who bumped into you, the smell of exhaust, how bright the sun was? Did you hear other voices? smell the flowers you passed? see how the sun glittered on the windows? In this unit you will read descriptions written by people who have learned to use their senses and to use descriptive language. Then you will write your own.

ACTIVITIES

Listening Listen as the selection on the opposite page is read. Which words appeal to the senses?

Speaking Look at the picture. As a class, make a list of words and phrases that describe the ocean in this picture.

Writing Imagine what it would feel like to be in the curl of this wave. Write your thoughts in your journal.

LITERATURE

What is it like to be a teen-aged sailor at sea for the first time?

First Time Aloft

By Herman Melville

These excerpts are from a chapter in Melville's novel *Redburn*, which is based on his experiences at sea.

The second day out of port, the decks being washed down and breakfast over, the watch was called, and the mate set us to work.

It was a very bright day. The sky and water were both of the same deep hue; and the air felt warm and sunny; so that we threw off our jackets. I could hardly imagine that this was the same ocean, now so beautiful and blue, that during part of the night-watch had rolled along so black and forbidding.

There were little traces of sunny clouds all over the heavens; and little fleeces of foam all over the sea; and the ship made a strange, musical noise under her bows, as she glided along, with her sails all still. It seemed a pity to go to work at such a time; and if we could only have sat in the windlass[1] again; or if they would have let me go out on the bowsprit[2] and lay down between the *man-ropes*[3] there, and look over at the fish in the water, and think of home, I should have been almost happy for a time.

I had now completely got over my seasickness, and felt very well; so that I could now look around me, and make observations.

---

[1]**windlass** (wǐnd′ləs): A device for raising or lowering objects by winding or unwinding rope around a cylinder.
[2]**bowsprit** (bou′sprǐt′): A pole projecting from the bow.
[3]**man-ropes**: Ropes used as guardrails or supports.

And truly, though we were at sea, there was much to behold and wonder at to me, who was on my first voyage. What most amazed me was the sight of the great ocean itself, for we were out of sight of land. All round us, on both sides of the ship, ahead and astern, nothing was to be seen but water—water—water; not a single glimpse of green shore, not the smallest island, or speck of moss anywhere. Never did I realise till now what the ocean was: how grand and majestic, how solitary, and boundless, and beautiful and blue; for that day it gave no tokens of squalls or hurricanes, such as I had heard my father tell of; nor could I imagine how anything that seemed so playful and placid, could be lashed into rage, and troubled into rolling avalanches of foam, and great cascades of waves, such as I saw in the end.

I must now tell of my first going aloft at sea.

It happened on the second night out of port, during the middle watch, when the sea was quite calm, and the breeze was mild.

The order was given to loose the *main-skysail*, which is the fifth and highest sail from deck. It was a very small sail, and from the forecastle[4] looked no bigger than a cambric pocket-handkerchief.

---

[4]**forecastle** (fōk′səl): The deck area at the bow.

. . . But I have heard that some ships carry still smaller sails, above the skysail; called *moon-sails,* and *sky-scrapers,* and *cloud-rakers.* But I shall not believe in them till I see them; a *skysail* seems high enough in all conscience; and the idea of anything higher than that seems preposterous. Besides, it looks almost like tempting heaven, to brush the very firmament so, and almost put the eyes of the stars out; when a flaw[5] of wind, too, might very soon take the conceit out of these cloud-defying *cloud-rakers.*

Now, when the order was passed to loose the skysail, an old Dutch sailor came up to me, and said, "Buttons, my boy, it's high time you be doing something; and it's boy's business, Buttons, to loose de royals,[6] and not old men's business, like me. Now, d'ye see dat leetle fellow way up dare? *dare,* just behind dem stars dare: well, tumble up, now, Buttons, I zay, and looze him; way you go, Buttons."

All the rest joining in, and seeming unanimous in the opinion, that it was high time for me to be stirring myself, and doing *boy's business,* as they called it, I made no more ado, but jumped into the rigging. Up I went, not daring to look down, but keeping my eyes glued, as it were; to the shrouds,[7] as I ascended.

It was a long road up those stairs, and I began to pant and breathe hard, before I was half way. But I kept at it

---

[5]**flaw:** A sudden gust.
[6]**royals:** The sails just below the skysails.
[7]**shrouds:** The ropes steadying the tops of the masts.

till I got to the *Jacob's Ladder,*[8] and they may well call it so, for it took me almost into the clouds; and at last, to my own amazement, I found myself hanging on the skysail-yard, holding on might and main to the mast; and curling my feet round the rigging, as if they were another pair of hands.

For a few moments I stood awestricken and mute. I could not see far out upon the ocean, owing to the darkness of the night; and from my lofty perch, the sea looked like a great, black gulf, hemmed in, all round, by beetling[9] black cliffs. I seemed all alone, treading the midnight clouds, and every second, expected to find myself falling—falling—falling, as I have felt when the nightmare has been on me.

I could but just perceive the ship below me, like a long narrow plank in the water; and it did not seem to belong at all to the yard, over which I was hanging. A gull, or some sort of sea-fowl, was flying round the truck[10] over my head, within a few yards of my face; and it almost frightened me to hear it, it seemed so much like a spirit, at such lofty and solitary height.

Though there was a pretty smooth sea, and little wind; yet, at this extreme elevation, the ship's motion was very

---

[8]**Jacob's Ladder:** A ladder named for the ladder to heaven that Jacob saw in a dream (Gen. 28:12).
[9]**beetling:** Overhanging.
[10]**truck:** The round tip of a mast.

great; so that when the ship rolled one way, I felt something as a fly must feel, walking the ceiling; and when it rolled the other way, I felt as if I was hanging along a slanting pine tree.

But presently I heard a distant, hoarse noise from below; and though I could not make out anything intelligible, I knew it was the mate hurrying me. So in a nervous, trembling desperation, I went to casting off the *gaskets,* or lines tying up the sail; and when all was ready, sung out as I had been told, to "*hoist away!*" And hoist they did, and me too along with the yard and sail; for I had no time to get off, they were so unexpectedly quick about it. It seemed like magic; there I was going up higher and higher; the yard rising under me, as if it were alive, and no soul in sight. Without knowing it at the time, I was in a good deal of danger, but it was so dark that I could not see well enough to feel afraid—at least on that account; though I felt frightened enough in a promiscuous[11] way. I only held on hard, and made good the saying of old sailors, that the last person to fall overboard from the rigging is a landsman, because he grips the ropes so fiercely; whereas old tars are less careful, and sometimes pay the penalty.

Think and Discuss

1. How did Buttons feel about his first time at sea? How might you guess this was his first sea voyage even if he didn't tell you so?
2. What is the skysail? How high did it seem to Buttons?
3. The **mood** of a story is its general feeling or atmosphere. A mood can be eerie, solemn, joyful, or whatever suits the writer's purpose. Look again at the first five paragraphs of "First Time Aloft." What is the mood? Describe it in a word or two. Then list four or five words and phrases from the story that help to create that mood.
4. Tell what the "saying of old sailors" in the last sentence means. Do you think the saying might hold true for people other than sailors? Explain your answer.

[11]promiscuous: Confused.

The River Took My Sister

By Shirley Crawford

Up on the green bank of the
river I stand waiting for
the sister I once called mine.

She left me years ago. The
day was bright, warm. We raced
to the clear blue water.

We raced back to shore. I
found myself alone. The blue
water kept my sister.

He loved her too.

Think and Discuss
1. Tell what happened to the speaker's sister. What parts
   of the poem give you this information?
2. Describe the setting of the poem on the day the speaker
   is remembering.
3. Crawford uses only a few simple details in this poem.
   Most of them paint a bright, pleasant scene. Do you
   think she chose her details well? Tell why or why not.

Sky Diver

By Adrien Stoutenberg

Grotesque, jumping out
like a clothed frog, helmet and glasses,
arms and legs wading the sky,
feet flapping before the cloth flower opens;
then suspended, poised,
an exclamation point upside-down,
and going down, swaying over corn and creeks
and highways scribbled
over the bones of fish and eagles.

There is the interim between air and earth,
time to study steeples
and the underwings of birds going over,
before the unseen chasm,
the sudden jaw open and hissing.

Lying here after the last jump
I see how fanatic roots are,
how moles breathe through darkness,
how deep the earth can be.

Think and Discuss

1. Where is the sky diver in the first stanza? in the second? What does he or she see?
2. In the last stanza, what do the words "the last jump" suggest has happened? What lines in the middle stanza prepare you for this?
3. A **simile** compares things that are not usually thought of as similar: the sky diver is "like a clothed frog." A simile always includes the word *like* or *as*. A **metaphor**, on the other hand, suggests that one thing *is* something else: the sky diver is "an exclamation point upside-down." No *like* or *as* appears in a metaphor. Is "cloth flower" in the poem a simile or a metaphor? Tell what it describes.
4. How would you change this poem to give it a different ending? Rewrite the last stanza.

RESPONDING TO LITERATURE

The Reading and Writing Connection

Personal response In "First Time Aloft," the first days at sea turned out to be beautiful and exciting. Write about the first time you were in a particular place or situation. Were you excited? disappointed? surprised? Try to capture that mood in your writing. Use specific details.

Creative writing Buttons began his voyage with fine weather, an exciting setting, and a challenge that he met with success. Write a story about someone who begins a trip under the opposite conditions. At first everything goes wrong. Then what happens?

Creative Activities

Illustrate The poet paints word pictures that show the sky diver and the view at three stages of the jump. Draw or paint the sky diver and the scene in one of the first two stages. Use the details that the poet gives. You may add some of your own as long as they fit the scene.

Read aloud Practice reading aloud either "Sky Diver" or "The River Took My Sister." Think about the feelings you want to convey. Change your tone at the appropriate point in the poem. Be prepared to read the poem to the class.

Vocabulary

The word *hissing* in "Sky Diver" is an example of **onomatopoeia**—the use of words that imitate the sounds they represent. What sounds do ducks make? water? food frying? List some onomatopoeic words.

Looking Ahead

Description Later in this unit, you will be learning to use your five senses—touch, sight, hearing, taste, and smell—to write a description. Look again at the descriptions in "First Time Aloft." Which senses does Melville use? Which doesn't he use?

VOCABULARY CONNECTION
Noun Suffixes and Adjective Suffixes

A **prefix** is a word part that is added to the beginning of a word. A **suffix** is a word part that is added to the end of a word.

> But I kept at it . . . and at last, to my own **amazement**, I found myself hanging on the skysail-yard, holding on. . . .
> *from "First Time Aloft" by Herman Melville*

Notice how the suffix -*ment* changes the verb *amaze* to the noun *amazement*. Here are some examples of **noun suffixes**.

Suffix	Meaning	Example
-er, -or	one who does	governor
-hood	condition or quality of	neighborhood
-ment	act of	amusement
-ness	quality of, state of	kindness
-tion, -ion	act of	champion

Many adjectives are formed by adding certain suffixes to words. Here are some common **adjective suffixes**.

Suffix	Adjective	Suffix	Adjective
-able	agreeable	-ish	childish
-al	comical	-less	worthless
-en	wooden	-ly	lonely
-ful	helpful	-ous	ridiculous
-ic	heroic	-y	hairy

Vocabulary Practice

A. Add an adjective suffix to each of these words from "First Time Aloft." Use your dictionary to check the new words.

1. foam   3. danger   5. account   7. watch   9. flaw
2. end   4. green   6. magic   8. work   10. might

B. Add a noun suffix to each of these words from "First Time Aloft." Then use each new noun in a sentence.

11. sail   12. mild   13. wonder   14. great   15. good

Speaking: Adapting to Purpose and Audience

When you describe something, you usually have a purpose in mind—to convey an impression, to inform, or to amuse. You also choose topics that will appeal to your specific audience, children or adults, people you know or people you don't know. You adapt your language and content to suit your purpose and audience. Read these passages.

> . . . from my lofty perch, the sea looked like a great, black gulf, hemmed in, all around, by beetling black cliffs.
>
> *from "First Time Aloft" by Herman Melville*

> Hey, this place is something else! The water is so clear, you can see ten feet below.

- Who is Melville's audience? What is his purpose?

- Who is the audience for the second passage? the purpose?

Guidelines for Adapting to Purpose and Audience

1. Determine your purpose. Is your description meant to amuse? to convey an impression? to instruct? to persuade? Use language that suits your purpose.
2. Consider the age and experience of your audience. Use **informal**, everyday language with friends and relatives. Use **formal** language with all others.
3. Fit the content to your purpose and audience. Choose a subject that will interest your audience.
4. Choose your tone, vocabulary, and sentence length. Be humorous if you want to amuse. Be direct if you wish to instruct.

Prewriting Practice

Think of a place you enjoy visiting. List details to describe it to (1) a child whom you want to amuse and (2) an adult from another country, who is unfamiliar with the place.

Thinking: Making Generalizations

Suppose you are on a whale-watching excursion. After being at sea for an hour, you notice seagulls circling overhead and a large school of fish skimming the water's surface. Suddenly, a huge whale rises out of the sea. When you notice the same thing happening again later, you describe the behavior of whales as follows:

> Sometimes whales come to the surface of the water when seagulls and large schools of fish are in the area.

You have just made a **generalization,** a broad statement or conclusion about some events or facts that appear to be related. You make a generalization when you notice that your observations share a common element. Making generalizations helps you to understand information as a whole and to describe that information concisely to others.

Because generalizations are not facts, they may or may not be true. Be careful to avoid making **hasty generalizations** or **overgeneralizations**. These are made without sufficient data; they go beyond the available facts. Read this example.

> Whales always come to the surface of the water when seagulls and large schools of fish are in the area.

As you know, you observed only two instances in which a whale surfaced when seagulls and large schools of fish were in the area. These two observations do not give you enough information to make the absolute statement that whales *always* surface when seagulls and schools of fish are in the area. You can avoid hasty generalizations and overgeneralizations by using limiting words such as "some," "sometimes," or "many," and by avoiding absolute words such as "always" or "never."

Read this generalization. Do you think it is sound?

> I only held on hard, and made good the saying of old sailors, that the last person to fall overboard from the rigging is a landsman, because he grips the ropes so fiercely; whereas old tars are less careful, and sometimes pay the penalty.
>
> *from "First Time Aloft" by Herman Melville*

The "old sailors" mentioned above had spent years observing people on the rigging, so there will probably be enough evidence to support the generalization. Also, the generalization is limited. It does not state that a landsman *never* falls overboard, but only that he is "the last person" to do so. It does not state that experienced sailors *always* fall overboard, but only that they "sometimes" do.

Suppose Buttons made the following generalization, based only on his first day at sea, in a letter to his family.

> The ocean always remains beautiful, blue, and calm. Its waves rock you gently and are never threatening.

- Did Buttons gather enough facts? Why or why not?

Now consider these observations and generalizations.

OBSERVATIONS Only a few sunbathers rested on the beach.
All along the beach people flew kites.
Brightly colored kites decorated the sky.

GENERALIZATIONS Most people go to the beach to fly kites.
Some people go to the beach to fly kites.
People always fly kites at the beach.

- Which is the most valid generalization? Why?

Guidelines for Making Generalizations

1. Make some observations or note some facts.
2. Determine whether your observations or facts have something in common. Do they suggest anything to you?
3. Make a broad, general statement about your observations.
4. Verify that you have enough data or examples to make your generalization valid.
5. Be prepared to modify your generalization if new information becomes available.

Prewriting Practice

Write a generalization about each set of facts below.

1. There was no moon, no stars. Sky and water formed a solid black mass, relieved only by the foamy white streaks whipped up by the wet wind. The ocean played with the ship, tossing it back and forth at will. On my first night at sea, I lay wide awake.
2. The two gentlest, sweetest dogs I know are mixed breeds from the animal shelter. The two others are pure-bred dogs. One is very nervous, and the other is unfriendly.

Choosing Details ☑

Compare the two stanzas below.

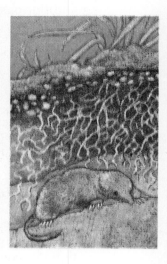

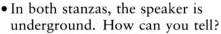

> Lying here after the last jump
> I see how fanatic roots are,
> how moles breathe through darkness,
> how deep the earth can be.
> *from "Sky diver" by Adrien Stoutenberg*
>
> Lying here after the last jump
> I feel how embracing the soil is,
> how soft and fragrant the darkness is,
> how warm the earth can be.

- In both stanzas, the speaker is underground. How can you tell?
- What words have been changed or added in the second stanza? How do they change the feeling of Stoutenberg's poem?

The setting in both versions is the same, but each writer describes it from a different attitude. The attitude is called **point of view.**

When you describe something, you should first choose a point of view. Then decide how the place or thing you are describing would appear from that point of view. If the subject is your room, through whose eyes are you seeing it? your own? your mother's? your friend's? a stranger's? Would that person see your room as messy? cozy? strange? colorful? Once you know your point of view and the overall impression you want to give, choose only the details that help to create that impression. If you decided, for example, that your room has more objects per square foot than most rooms, that would be your point of view. Then you would choose only the details that show how crowded your room is.

Here are two descriptions of the same scene. Notice what different impressions they give.

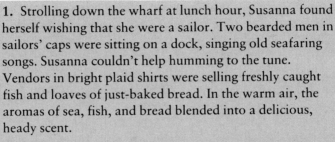

1. Strolling down the wharf at lunch hour, Susanna found herself wishing that she were a sailor. Two bearded men in sailors' caps were sitting on a dock, singing old seafaring songs. Susanna couldn't help humming to the tune. Vendors in bright plaid shirts were selling freshly caught fish and loaves of just-baked bread. In the warm air, the aromas of sea, fish, and bread blended into a delicious, heady scent.

2. Susanna walked as quickly as she could past the dilapidated wharf buildings. Two scruffy men sprawled on a dock, bellowing old sailing songs. Susanna cupped her hands over her ears to drown out the racket. When she passed some fish and bread vendors, Susanna thought she would faint from the stale odors that wafted toward her on the stifling air.

- What is Susanna's point of view in the first paragraph? in the second?
- What details does the writer use to support each point of view?

When you write a description, remember these points.

1. Have a clear purpose and point of view in mind.
2. Choose only those details that will support your purpose and point of view.

Prewriting Practice

A. Look around the school lunchroom at mealtime. What can you see? hear? taste? touch? smell? Jot down as many details as you can for each sense. Then group the details into these two lists.

1. Details that would describe the lunchroom from the point of view of a student who likes it
2. Details that describe the lunchroom from the point of view of a student who dislikes it

B. Think of something you can describe in detail—a person, place, object, animal—anything that interests you. Choose a point of view or an attitude toward your subject. Decide what overall impression you want to create in your description. Then list five or six details that support your point of view and purpose.

C. Imagine that the creator of the painting below was a writer rather than a painter. Instead of painting this scene, he described it in words.

  1. What was his point of view? Write a sentence describing his feelings or attitude toward the scene.

  2. List four details in the picture that support the point of view that the artist portrays.

Using Descriptive Language ☑

Shakespeare, the great sixteenth-century English writer, called the imagination the "mind's eye." When you read, you use your mind's eye to "see" what the writer describes. To help you, a writer often uses **imagery**—language that appeals to your senses. Imagery paints pictures for your mind's eye. How clear would your picture of Buttons's second day at sea have been if the author had described it this way?

> It was a nice day. The sky and water were both of the same hue; and the air felt good.

Can you picture the day? You know it was pleasant, but was it warm? cold? What color were the sky and water? There are no images for your mind's eye to see.

Exact adjectives *Nice, good,* and *same* are adjectives, but they do little to help you imagine the setting. When you write, use adjectives that paint a clear, lively picture, as Melville did.

> It was a very *bright* day. The sky and water were both of the same *deep* hue; and the air felt *warm* and *sunny*.
> *from "First Time Aloft" by Herman Melville*

Exact nouns, verbs, and adverbs Not only your adjectives but other words as well should be exact when you write a description. Here are some examples of the difference between general and exact nouns, verbs, and adverbs.

	GENERAL	EXACT
VERBS	go	leave, disappear, dash, creep, slide
	do	perform, achieve, create, solve, complete
	walk	stroll, amble, saunter, hike, tramp, pace, stride, swagger
NOUNS	person	teen-ager, mechanic, Joshua
	scenery	valley, Rocky Mountains, Lake Michigan
	trip	vacation, excursion, outing, junket, jaunt, flight, cruise
ADVERBS	well, nicely	powerfully, efficiently, smoothly, politely, smilingly, brightly
	quickly	briefly, hastily, speedily, nimbly, hurriedly, animatedly

Figurative language   Along with using exact words, writers also create clear pictures by making comparisons. They describe something by showing how it is like something else. For example, Melville said "the sea looked like a great, black gulf." By comparing it to something else, he was helping you picture what Buttons saw. Melville used the word *like* to make the connection between the sea and the gulf. Comparisons that use the words *like* or *as* are called **similes**. Here are four more similes from Melville's "First Time Aloft."

> [the sails] overhang the wide water, like the wings of a great bird
>
> I felt something as a fly must feel, walking the ceiling
>
> [the gull] seemed so much like a spirit
>
> the ship below me, like a long narrow plank in the water

• What two things are being compared in each simile?

Another kind of comparison is called a **metaphor**. A metaphor does not say that one thing is *like* another. It says that one thing *is* another. If you describe a traffic jam by saying, "The highway was a parking lot," you are using a metaphor. Here are some other examples of metaphors.

> Elizabeth's life was one endless soap opera.
>
> The telephone wires were thin pencil lines across the sky.
>
> The flowers were bright flags signaling the return of spring.
>
> To the astronauts, Planet Earth was a friendly, familiar, and beautiful face.

• What two things are being compared in each metaphor?
• How would you change these metaphors to make them similes?

Descriptive language that uses comparisons, such as similes and metaphors, is known as **figurative language**.

Prewriting Practice

A. Rewrite each of the following descriptions twice. Use a different point of view for each version, and add details that support that point of view. Use exact words to give your reader a clear picture.

1. The view from the building was nice.
2. A person went down the street fast.
3. Although the day was bad, the celebration went well.
4. The band of musicians began to play.
5. A good time was had by all.

B. Rewrite each description twice, first using a simile, then a metaphor.

1. The smell of roasting turkey greeted us.
2. The old jalopy came bouncing down the street.
3. Agatha's scream broke the silence.
4. Bright yellow dandelions dotted the grass.
5. Waves crashed against the jagged rocks.

The Grammar Connection

Using Adjectives

Because adjectives describe nouns, writers use them to help create a clear picture in your mind. You could say that an adjective takes over where a noun leaves off.

Read this sentence that contains no adjectives.

A bird landed on the deck of the ship.

What kind of bird did you picture? What kind of ship? Now read the sentence with adjectives.

A tiny red bird landed on the teak deck of the clipper ship.

In the second sentence, the adjectives make you see just what the writer wants you to see.

Practice Turn each of the following nouns into a vivid picture by adding two adjectives.

1. car	5. rain	9. bread	13. voice
2. shirt	6. dog	10. perfume	14. light
3. ring	7. music	11. hand	15. smile
4. boy	8. floor	12. chair	16. tree

Organizing Your Description ☑

Once you have decided what details you want to include in a description, you need to decide in what order to put them.

Spatial order If you are describing a place, one way to organize the details is by using **spatial order.** Spatial order is based on the *location* of things. Read this description.

> I could but just perceive the ship below me, like a long narrow plank in the water; and it did not seem to belong at all to the yard, over which I was hanging. A gull, or some sort of sea-fowl, was flying round the truck over my head, within a few yards of my face. . . .
>
> *from "First Time Aloft" by Herman Melville*

Melville arranged the details in this description from those that were farthest from Buttons to those that were nearest. However, when you use spatial order, you can also take your reader from nearest to farthest, left to right, lowest to highest, or use whatever arrangement creates the most vivid picture.

What kind of spatial order is used in this description?

> In the gutters stood enormous heaps of snow, pale and dark in the shadows, stretching away from him like a string of mountains. He moved out of the shadows, between two piles of snow, and into the center of the street; where he stood for a moment gazing down the white road that gradually grew darker until it melted into the gloom at the far end.
>
> *from "Sled" by Thomas E. Adams*

In the description above, the spatial order moves from nearest to farthest. The writer uses words such as *away, out, between,* and *down* to make the order clear.

Here are some other words and phrases that help to show spatial order.

next to	near	in the distance	adjoining
left	on	close by	across
behind	above	not far	farther
south	beyond	beside	below

Order of importance You might also arrange your details in order of importance. You can go from most to least important, or from least to most important.

> The cave was nearly dark. The walls glistened with dampness, and there was a sound like rain in a barrel. It was water dripping off a small ledge into a shallow pool. There, by the pool, lying on its side and dented as if it had been dropped, was the silver urn.

- Are the details above organized from most to least or from least to most important?

Order in which details strike you There are other ways to arrange a description. You might begin with the detail that struck you first, as this writer did.

> When I open the door to Dom's Pizzeria, the smell rushes out and flows around me. It is a heady mixture of dough, cheese, and garlic, surrounded by the sweet odor of olive oil. Only after I digest the smell do I walk inside to greet the rush of people and noise.

Remember that when you write a description, you should decide on the best way to organize your details. Here are some possible ways.

1. Use spatial order.
2. Use order of importance (most to least important).
3. Use order of importance (least to most important).
4. Put the details in the order in which they strike you.

Prewriting Practice

Look out the window and take notes on what you see. Arrange the details in the four different ways listed above. Each list you prepare may help you see additional details. Compare your lists and see if you can add more details to each.

Step 1: Prewriting—Choose a Topic

Amy made a list of things she could describe. She crossed off a few and then thought about the rest.

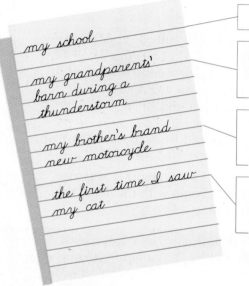

my school — This topic was too broad.

my grandparents' barn during a thunderstorm — She remembered how she had felt about this, but she couldn't remember enough details.

my brother's brand new motorcycle — Though she could describe it in detail, Amy didn't find this interesting enough.

the first time I saw my cat — Amy could recall exactly how the cat had looked and how she had felt about it.

Amy circled the last topic.

On Your Own

1. **Think and discuss** Make a list of things you might describe. Use the Ideas page for help. Talk about your ideas with a partner.

2. **Choose** Answer these questions about each of the topics on your list.

   Which one can I look at before I write, or which one can I remember most clearly?

   Which topic is narrow enough to be described completely?

   Which topic would I most enjoy describing?

3. **Explore** To help you plan your description, do one of the activities under "Exploring Your Topic" on the Ideas page.

Ideas for Getting Started

Choosing a Topic

Topic Ideas

My first view of . . .
A view from up high
An unusual building
The tree outside my
  window
The view from my window
My sister or brother
My favorite piece of
  clothing
My favorite singer's
  costume
A musical instrument
A thunderstorm

Description Starters

Read these starters for
ideas.

Hers was a comfortable
  face, worn and lived in.
The stairwell was dark and
  empty. It made me feel
  three years old and lost.
The shoes had the kind of
  sole that sticks to the
  floor in movie theaters.
The trees march up the
  mountainside like soldiers.

Exploring Your Topic

Cluster

Write your topic in the
center of a page. Circle it,
and in other circles around
it, write the different parts
of the thing you are de-
scribing. Off each of these
circles, write words to
describe that part. Here is
the cluster Amy made.

Talk About It

Turn your description into
a riddle. Describe your
topic in detail to a partner,
and have your partner
guess what it is. What details do you need to add?

Step 2: Write a First Draft

Since her class often shared their writing with the elementary school, Amy chose the fifth graders as her audience. She wanted them to see the cat as she had seen it.

As she wrote her first draft, Amy did not worry about making mistakes at this time. She knew she would correct her paper later.

The first part of Amy's first draft

~~The poor cat looked miserable.~~ It was dark out, and the wether was terrible. I didn't see the cat right away, but then I saw two green, shining eyes by the steps of my building. As I nelt down to pet him, I thought he was the worse-looking cat I had ever seen. He looked really miserable. Then I looked again. No, although he sure was a mess, this cat had style. His fur was short and sleek, and his

Think and Discuss ☑
- Why did Amy start over, changing her first sentence?
- What details help you see the cat the way Amy did?
- Where could she have used more exact words or details?

On Your Own

1. **Think about purpose and audience** Answer these questions.
   For what audience shall I write?
   What is my purpose? How do I want my readers to see this topic? Do I want to show how I feel about it?
2. **Write** Write the first draft of your description, using all the details that fit your purpose. Do not worry about mistakes in this draft. To leave room for changes, write on every other line.

Step 3: Revise

Amy read her first draft. She noticed that she had not described the weather very vividly. She added some exact words to show how it looked and felt.

Amy read her description to Lin to see if a reader would be able to picture her cat.

Reading and responding

Lin: I don't usually like cats, but you convinced me I'd like yours.

Amy: Oh, good! Was there anything I said about him that you couldn't picture?

Lin: I wasn't really sure why he looked so bad to you at first.

Amy: I guess I was pretty general about that. I'll add some details. Thanks for the idea!

Amy thought back and remembered exactly what she had first noticed about her cat. She added these details to her description.

The first part of Amy's revision

~~The poor cat looked miserable.~~ It was dark out, and the wether was ~~terrible~~ *drizzly and raw*. I didn't see the cat right away, but then I saw two green, shining eyes by the steps of my building. As I nelt down to pet him, I thought he was the worse-looking cat I had ever seen. ~~He looked~~

His bones stuck out, and his face was as thin and pointy as a rat's.

Think and Discuss ☑
- What details did Amy add to help you feel the weather?
- What details did she add about her cat? Why?
- What two things does Amy compare?

On Your Own

Revising checklist

☑ Have I selected details that support my purpose and point of view?

☑ Have I organized my details? What organization did I use?

☑ Have I given my reader a clear picture of what I am talking about?

☑ Where might I add more figurative language or exact words?

1. **Revise** Cross out any words, sentences, or sections that need improving. Between the lines or in the margins, add figurative language and sensory details. Use the thesaurus below or the one at the back of this book.

2. **Have a conference** Read your description to someone else—your teacher or a classmate. Discuss your description and take notes about any new ideas you get from reading aloud or from the discussion.

Ask your listener:	As you listen:
"Can you picture what I am describing?" "Which parts help you see it most clearly?" "Is any part unclear?" "What could I add?"	Listening carefully, can I picture this clearly? Is any part unclear or confusing to me? What would I like to know more about?

3. **Revise** Think about your listener's suggestions. Can you add any other improvements? Make changes on your paper.

Thesaurus

bright *adj.* shining, brilliant, dazzling
colorless *adj.* faint, faded, dull, indistinct
damp *adj.* humid, moist, muggy, soggy, dewy
dark *adj.* shaded, dim, shadowy, dusky

quickly *adv.* swiftly, instantaneously, rapidly
smooth *adj.* polished, satiny, sleek, slick
tall *adj.* colossal, rangy, towering
very *adv.* exceedingly, exceptionally, heartily

Step 4: Proofread

Amy proofread her description for mistakes in grammar, spelling, and punctuation. She checked her spellings in a dictionary and used proofreading marks to make changes.

This is how the beginning of Amy's paper looked after she had proofread it.

The beginning of Amy's proofread description

> ~~The poor cat looked miserable.~~ It was dark
> out, and the we~~a~~ther was ~~terrible~~ *drizzly and raw*. I didn't see
> the cat right away, but then I saw two green,
> shining eyes by the steps of my building. As I
> *k*nelt down to pet him, I thought he was the
> wors~~e~~*t*-looking cat I had ever seen. ~~He looked~~
> ~~really miserable.~~ Then I looked again. No,
> although he sure*ly* was a mess, this cat had
> style. His fur was short and sleek, and his

Think and Discuss
- What two spellings did Amy correct?
- What comparative word did she change to a superlative? Why did she do this?
- Why did she change an adjective to an adverb?

On Your Own

1. **Proofreading Practice** Proofread this paragraph, and then copy it correctly. There are three incorrect modifiers, one spelling error, and one capitalization error.

   > At the Station, you should look for a man
   > with hair more redder than carrots, wearing a
   > plaid rain coat. He will be real tall, and he
   > will be carrying less bags than most of the
   > other passengers.

2. **Proofreading Application** Use the Proofreading Checklist
and the Grammar and Spelling Hints below to proofread
your paper. Check your spellings in a dictionary. If you
wish, use a colored pencil to make corrections.

Proofreading Checklist	Proofreading Marks
Did I	⌥ Indent
☑ 1. indent where needed?	∧ Add
☑ 2. use capitals correctly?	⋏ Add a comma
	ᵛᵛ Add quotation marks
☑ 3. punctuate correctly?	⊙ Add a period
	ℓ Take out
☑ 4. use adjectives and adverbs correctly?	≡ Capitalize
	/ Make a small letter
☑ 5. spell all words correctly?	↻ Reverse the order

The Grammar/Spelling Connection

Grammar Hints

Remember these rules from Unit 7 when using the comparative and superlative forms of modifiers.

- Use -er to compare two things and -est to compare three or more things. (the old er of the two boys; the old est of the three boys)
- Use -er and -est with short adverbs and adjectives; use more and most with long adverbs and adjectives. (Short adjective: the smallest dot; long adjective: the most minuscule dot)
- Do not use more or most with adjectives or adverbs ending in -er or -est. (Incorrect: the most shortest route; correct: the shortest route)

Spelling Hints

Remember these spelling principles.

- Adding the suffixes -ious and -able may affect the spelling of the base word. (myster y, myster ious; inflat e, inflat able)
- Some nouns ending in f or fe form the plural by changing the f to v before adding s or es. (hal f, hal ves; wi fe, wi ves)

Step 5: Publish

Amy drew pictures of her cat eating, sleeping, cleaning himself, and exploring. She attached the pictures and her description to a poster titled "A Day in the Life . . ." Then she took it to the fifth graders and read it to them.

On Your Own

1. **Copy** Neatly copy or type your description.
2. **Title** Give your description a title that will get your readers' interest.
3. **Check** Check your description again to be sure you have included everything and made no mistakes.
4. **Share** Choose a way to share your description.

Ideas for Sharing

- Read your description aloud to a small group. Then ask your listeners to draw what they saw.
- With your class, make a bulletin board display of your descriptions. Group them under general categories such as people, places, the weather, and animals. Use illustrations instead of words to label the categories.
- With your classmates, make a list of all the similes and metaphors you used in your descriptions. Provide a copy of the list for everyone in the class.

Applying Description

Literature and Creative Writing

In "First Time Aloft" on pages 270–274, excited young Buttons is at sea for the first time. An old sailor orders him to climb the tallest mast and "loose the main-skysail." Although scared by the height, he passes his first test.

Use what you have learned about writing descriptions to complete one or more of these activities.

1. **Describe your surroundings.** Buttons was awed by the vast sea. Think of a place that seemed awesome or fascinating to you. Write a description that will help someone else see what you saw.

2. **Describe harsh weather.** Buttons describes a perfect day at sea, but he hints that rougher days lie ahead. Describe a tornado, a heat wave, a blizzard, or any other kind of extreme weather, either at sea or elsewhere.

3. **Describe an unearthly sea voyage.** Pictures of Mars show reddish deserts, craters, canyons, polar caps, and mysterious canals. The canals contain no water, but imagine that they do. Describe a voyage down the canals of Mars.

Remember these things ☑
- Choose details that support your purpose and your point of view.
- Use exact words and figurative language.
- Put your details in order.

Writing Across the Curriculum
History

A historian often gathers information from descriptions written by people long ago about life in their own times. The historian may then write his or her own description of that period from a modern point of view.

Choose one or more of the activities below.

1. **Describe historical fashions.** In a history book or encyclopedia, find pictures showing the way people dressed in another era. Write a description of one of the outfits.

Word Bank

yoke
bodice
tunic
hoop skirt
ruff
bloomer
spat

2. **Write about local history.** Has any part of your community changed in the past ten years? Write a description of it.
3. **Write for future readers.** Just as everyday objects from the past are interesting to us, our own everyday objects will be strange and interesting to future generations. Describe something ordinary and familiar in a way that will help people living hundreds of years from now to picture it.

Gabriel really enjoyed "First Time Aloft." He loved stories of travel and adventure, especially the descriptions of what places looked like and how people felt seeing them for the first time. Gabriel liked maps, too. When he read *The Cruise of the Arctic Star* by Scott O'Dell, he decided to share the book by making a map of the voyage. He included pictures and brief descriptions on his map. Then he told his class about the book, using the map to point out some of the highlights. This is part of Gabriel's map.

<u>The Cruise of the Arctic Star</u> by Scott O'Dell

<u>Along the California Coast</u>

(Search for Gigi, gray whale from Sea World)

Sites in author's story about Kit Carson

Oceanside

Siege of Starvation Peak

(Swordfish gets away)

Del Mar

San Pasqual 1846

(cacti and no water!)

Scripps Institute

"the silver trees"

Arctic Star sails from San Diego (bay named by Vizcaíno, 1602)

Point Loma (Pea soup fog)

On Board are:
Scott O'Dell
Elizabeth O'Dell (navigator)
Rodney Lambert, Del Boyce (crew)

Think and Discuss

- What places did Gabriel show on the map? what events?
- What sights did he illustrate?
- What other information about the book does the map give?
- What kinds of books can you best share in this way?

Share Your Book

Make a Map

1. Decide what kind of map you can make and what shape it should be. If your book is about a journey, you will need a long piece of paper. If the action takes place in a single area, a large square will be better. Make the map as large as you can.

2. Sketch the map lightly with a pencil. You may measure carefully or make a freer drawing. Plan, so that everything will fit! Mark important places on the map.

3. When you are satisfied with your sketch, go over the pencil lines with a marker.

4. Add small illustrations and a few words describing key events at the points where they took place.

5. Label the map with the book title and author. List the main characters in one corner.

6. Show the map to your class as you tell about the book. Don't give away the ending!

Other Activities

- Choose a few words that best describe each character. Write them after the characters' names.
- Pretend you are a reporter for a local paper at one place in the story. Write a short news item about the characters.
- What was happening in the rest of the world at the time of this story? Research and list some major events.
- Make a time line of the events in the story.
- Make a travel brochure that would interest tourists in visiting one place in the story. Include illustrations and brief descriptions of the main attractions.

 # The Book Nook

The Incredible Journey *by Sheila Burnford* Three household pets left on their own make an incredible journey across Canada to find their owner.	**Julie of the Wolves** *by Jean C. George* An Eskimo girl leaves home to trek south to Seattle alone. She befriends wolves, which help her.

Mechanics

Diver on the board
lunges toward the edge;
hedges;
takes a deep breath;
hesitates;
　　　　plunges.

Eve Merriam
"Markings: The Semicolon"

Capitalization and Punctuation

Getting Ready Punctuation marks are like traffic signs and lights. Each one is there for a reason! If streets were sprinkled with extra lights, there would be massive traffic jams. If important highway signs were missing, people would get lost. In this unit you will learn more about making every mark count.

ACTIVITIES

Listening Listen as the poem on the opposite page is read. It is about one of the most misused and misunderstood of all the punctuation marks. Where is it used in the poem? Why?

Speaking Look at the picture. This diver is stranded in midair, waiting for you to get him down! Create a sentence that will let him complete his plunge into the water and will bring him safely to the surface again. Use at least one semicolon.

Writing Using this poem as a model, write your own short poem, using semicolons to show definite pauses. Use your journal to write the drafts of your poem.

1 | Sentences and Interjections

Every sentence begins with a **capital letter** and ends with a **period**, a **question mark**, or an **exclamation point**.

DECLARATIVE: I read a book.   IMPERATIVE: Read it.
INTERROGATIVE: Did you read it?   EXCLAMATORY: It's great!

As you know, an interjection is a word such as *oh, wow,* or *bravo.* When an interjection expresses strong feeling, follow it with an exclamation mark. When an interjection expresses milder feeling, punctuate it with a comma.

Wow! I just solved the mystery.   Oh, tell me about it.

Guided Practice How would you correct these sentences?

Example: when was the first modern detective story written
When was the first modern detective story written?

1. the story appeared in 1841
2. who wrote it
3. Edgar Allan Poe wrote it
4. what a creative writer he was
5. don't tell me the ending
6. oh I wouldn't do that

Summing up

> ▶ Every sentence begins with a **capital letter.**
> ▶ Use a **period** after declarative and imperative sentences.
> ▶ Use a **question mark** at the end of interrogative sentences.
> ▶ Use an **exclamation point** at the end of exclamatory sentences and after an interjection expressing strong feeling.
> ▶ Use a **comma** after an interjection expressing milder feeling.

Independent Practice Write each sentence, adding the appropriate capitalization and punctuation.

Example: great I guessed the ending   *Great! I guessed the ending.*

7. Dickens wrote detective stories
8. wow what a surprise that is
9. wasn't his last book a mystery
10. he never finished it
11. tell me more about it
12. what a good tale it is

Writing Application: A Book Review Write a paragraph about a book that you like. Include one sentence of each type and one interjection.

2 | Proper Nouns and Proper Adjectives

Geographical Names

You know that a **proper noun** names a particular person, place, or thing and that a proper noun always begins with a capital letter. Therefore, you must capitalize proper nouns from geography. Do not capitalize small words like *the* and *of*.

1. Capitalize cities, states, countries, and continents.

   Chicago   Texas   Austria   South America

2. Capitalize bodies of water and geographical features.

   Ohio River   White Mountains   the Gulf of Mexico

3. Capitalize the names of areas. Do not capitalize directions.

   the Southwest   the Middle East   Central Asia
   We traveled south along the coast, then east.

4. Capitalize streets and highways.

   Route 66   Wall Street   Avenue of the Stars

5. Capitalize buildings, bridges, and monuments.

   Fort Knox   World Trade Center   Brooklyn Bridge

You can form a **proper adjective** from a proper noun. Capitalize proper adjectives.

PROPER NOUNS	PROPER ADJECTIVES
Mexico	Mexican art
North America	North American birds
Paris	Parisian fashion
Jefferson	Jeffersonian democracy

Guided Practice Which words should be capitalized?

Example: The nile river flows from south to north in africa.
The Nile River flows from south to north in Africa.

1. The egyptian museum in cairo has many treasures.
2. Egypt and the suez canal are part of the middle east.
3. Aswan is a city in the nile valley in southern egypt.
4. I visited the institute of africa on elm road.
5. An exhibition of african art included carved masks.

Titles, Organizations, Dates, and Subjects

Other proper nouns that you should capitalize include titles, names of organizations, historical events and periods, certain dates, and certain subjects.

1. Capitalize titles for people. Do not capitalize titles if they are used alone as common nouns.

   Captain Ahab   Dr. Kaplan   Father
   The doctor will see you now.   My uncle is the president.

2. Capitalize organizations, institutions, and businesses.

   United League   Dallas Symphony   Hirsch Institute
   Tampa High School   Ted's Garage   Branford Company

3. Capitalize languages and specific school subjects followed by a number. Do not capitalize general school subjects.

   English   Biology I   Algebra 2
   social studies   science   math

4. Capitalize historical events, periods of time, and documents.

   Boston Tea Party   Revolutionary War   Age of Reason
   Roaring Twenties   Gettysburg Address   Constitution

5. Capitalize days, months, and holidays, but not seasons.

   Monday   November   Fourth of July
   spring   autumn   winter

Guided Practice What words should be capitalized?

Example: My brother and aunt ingrid teach at adams academy.
         My brother and Aunt Ingrid teach at Adams Academy.

1. In social studies and history I, we are studying the civil war.
2. The gettysburg address was delivered by president lincoln.
3. Jefferson davis was the president of the confederacy.
4. General lee appeared at appomattox court house in april 1865.
5. Lee became president of washington college after the war.

Summing up

▶ A proper noun begins with a capital letter.
▶ You can form proper adjectives from proper nouns.
▶ Capitalize proper adjectives.

Independent Practice

A. Write the incorrect sentences, adding capital letters where needed. If a sentence is already correct, write *correct*.

Example: The museum of science on barberry road has a new and exciting exhibit.
The Museum of Science on Barberry Road has a new and exciting exhibit.

6. The exhibit runs from thursday, september 4, through tuesday, december 30.
7. The museum of science will remain open on memorial day.
8. Every fall and spring, the museum has a special exhibit.
9. It is held by the world ocean society on clinton avenue.
10. The current exhibit is on the world's natural waterways.
11. Research by the national science foundation is included.
12. Interest in science increased in the middle ages.
13. Today professor wyman is taking the geography 101 class of bentley university to the exhibit.
14. Other geography classes will visit during the spring break.
15. The atlantic ocean is half the size of the pacific ocean.
16. The atlantic was named for the atlas mountains in africa.
17. There are mountain ranges under the ocean.
18. The tallest mountains on land are the himalayas.
19. The george washington bridge spans the hudson river.
20. From the bridge, you can see the world trade center.

B. Write each sentence. Make the proper noun in parentheses a proper adjective. Use your dictionary if you need help.

Example: Norway and Sweden are _____ countries. (Scandinavia)
Norway and Sweden are Scandinavian countries.

21. The _____ summer is unusual. (Norway)
22. The sun shines all night in the northern part of this _____ country. (Europe)
23. Many people admire _____ furniture. (Denmark)
24. Strindberg was a well-known _____ playwright. (Sweden)
25. Norway and Sweden touch the _____ border. (Finland)
26. Finland extends eastward to the _____ border. (Russia)

Writing Application: A Paragraph Write a paragraph describing the town or the city where you live. Include its location, and name some important buildings or landmarks. Use a proper noun or a proper adjective in each sentence.

For Extra Practice, see p. 334. Proper Nouns and Adjectives

3 | Uses for Commas

You often use commas to separate items in a series. A **series** is three or more related words, phrases, or clauses.

WORDS: Leon photographed cities, people, and parks. (nouns)
He aimed, focused, and took the picture. (verbs)
The tree was old, twisted, and leafless. (adjectives)

PHRASES: He worked in the morning, at dusk, and in the evening.

CLAUSES: Leon developed the photos, I enlarged the best ones, and Tim put them in frames.

Use a comma between two or more adjectives that come before a noun.

Leon photographed the dilapidated, rusty jalopy.

Do not use a comma with two or more adjectives if the adjectives are used together to express a single idea. To decide whether to use a comma, try reading the adjectives with *and* or reverse the adjectives. If the sentence sounds awkward, do not use a comma.

AWKWARD: Leon uses an expensive and Japanese camera.
AWKWARD: Leon uses a Japanese expensive camera.
CORRECT: Leon uses an expensive Japanese camera.

You know that a compound sentence is made up of two or more independent clauses. Use a comma to separate these clauses. You may omit the comma if the clauses are short.

I brought a camera, Leo brought film, and Inez brought a flash. We wanted a picture of the sunrise, but it rained that day. The rain stopped and the sun came out.

Guided Practice Where should commas be used in these sentences? Which sentences do not need commas?

Example: People take photographs of people places and things.
People take photographs of people, places, and things.

1. Photographers view the scene set the camera and shoot.
2. Modern cameras are complicated but many of them are automatic.
3. Some impressive American cameras develop pictures instantly.
4. Cameras are useful entertaining and relatively inexpensive.
5. You can take pictures anywhere with sensitive color film.
6. Inexpensive cameras can take clear lifelike pictures.

Summing up

▶ Use a comma to separate items in a series.
▶ Use a comma between two or more adjectives that come before a noun. Do not use a comma if they express a single idea.
▶ Use a comma to separate the simple sentences in a compound sentence.

Independent Practice Write the incorrectly punctuated sentences, adding commas where needed. If a sentence needs no commas, write *correct*.

Example: Large bulky cameras have just about disappeared.
Large, bulky cameras have just about disappeared.

7. Modern cameras are small light and convenient.
8. Good amateur photographers are becoming more common.
9. A camera some film a good eye and an interesting subject are the basic requirements for photography.
10. Photography may seem like a recent invention but people have been taking photographs for almost 150 years.
11. A practical French inventor produced the first sharp photograph in 1839.
12. His impressive exciting achievement caused a sensation.
13. Pictures of people buildings and landmarks were now possible.
14. Photography did not stand still and inventors made new discoveries in the 1850s.
15. A piece of metal was coated with varnish a chemical was poured over the metal and the metal was exposed to light.
16. The resulting tintypes were inexpensive useful and popular.
17. Tintypes were used to decorate rings tie tacks and cuff links.
18. Professional photographers took pictures at crowded places and the pictures were sold to their subjects.

Writing Application: Creative Writing Imagine that you are a famous photographer. Write a paragraph about one or more pictures that you have taken. Include items in a series and adjectives that come before a noun. Be sure that you use commas correctly.

For Extra Practice, see p. 335.   Uses for Commas   **309**

4 || More Uses for Commas

Use commas after words, phrases, and clauses that come at the beginning of a sentence.

INTRODUCTORY WORDS: Oh, I need a sharper pencil.
Yes, they are in the supply cabinet.

INTRODUCTORY PHRASES: Arriving late, Walt sat near the door.
During the long meeting, he fell asleep.

INTRODUCTORY CLAUSES: After the session ended, I spoke to Hal.
While I waited, I made some phone calls.

Interrupters are words that break up a sentence and add emphasis. Use commas to separate interrupters from the rest of the sentence.

INTERRUPTERS: You know, of course, the purpose of this meeting.
We will meet again next week, by the way.

A **noun of direct address** is the name of a person or persons spoken to directly. It can come anywhere in the sentence. Use commas to separate nouns of direct address from the rest of the sentence.

DIRECT ADDRESS: John, I will need your help with this.
Come into my office, Janice, for a few minutes.
Staple these pages together, James.

As you know, an **appositive** adds information about the noun that directly precedes it. Use commas to separate an appositive only if it is not necessary to identify the noun.

APPOSITIVE: The president, Harold White, will present the award.

If the appositive is necessary to explain or identify the noun, do not use commas.

The documentary *Space Exploration* won an award.

Guided Practice Where are commas needed in these sentences? Which sentence does not need any commas?

Example: Yes my friend the business office has a new look.
Yes, my friend, the business office has a new look.

1. If the office is modern you will see few typewriters or pens.
2. Wooden desks and bookcases Flora are things of the past.

3. Looking around you notice that everything is steel or plastic.
4. Of course John the photocopy machine is always in use.
5. The most important office tool the computer commands people's attention.
6. In a small room the noisy printer rolls out page after page.
7. The pamphlet "Your Friendly Computer" sits on everyone's desk.

Summing up

▸ Use commas after words, phrases, and clauses that come at the beginning of sentences.
▸ Use commas to separate interrupters, nouns of direct address, and unnecessary appositives in a sentence.

Independent Practice Write each incorrectly punctuated sentence, adding commas where needed. If a sentence does not need commas, write *correct*.

Example: ENIAC the first electronic computer was built in 1946.
ENIAC, *the first electronic computer, was built in 1946.*

8. Yes everyone is affected by a computer in some way.
9. When you dial the phone a computer connects your call.
10. At the local supermarket a computer speeds your check-out.
11. Regulating electricity the computer supplies constant power.
12. Weather forecasters you know rely on computer information.
13. Although computers are changing our lives they are only tools.
14. No my friend they are not smarter than humans.
15. They were in fact created by humans.
16. Like any other tool the computer helps you do things Peter.
17. ENIAC the Electronic Numerical Integrator and Computer is huge.
18. Now Susan compare the giant ENIAC to the desk-top computer.
19. ENIAC as a matter of fact covered 1500 square feet.
20. The book *Computers in Your Life* will give you some history.
21. In the early sixties the electronic transistor appeared.
22. Today's computers marvels of speed and compactness use tiny silicon chips an invention of the 1970s.

Writing Application: A Letter Write a letter to an imaginary foreign pen pal. Describe either your classroom or the computer center at your school. Include sentences with introductory words, introductory phrases, introductory clauses, and interrupters. Be sure to use commas correctly.

For Extra Practice, see p. 336.   More Uses for Commas

5 || Dates, Addresses, and Letters

Without commas, these items would be difficult to read.

July 4 1776   Philadelphia Pennsylvania

With dates, use commas to separate the month and the day from the year, and the year from the rest of the sentence. Do not use commas if you do not include a specific day.

> July 4, 1776, is the day our nation was born.
> July 1776 was an important time in history.

In an address, use a comma between the names of the city and the state. If the address is within the sentence, also use a comma after the name of the state.

> Philadelphia, Pennsylvania, is our nation's birthplace.

When an address appears within a sentence, use a comma to separate each item in the address except the ZIP Code.

> Send the bill to 4 Hall Street, Miami, Florida 33142.

You probably already know the parts of a friendly letter. In addition to the writer's address and the date, a friendly letter includes a greeting and a closing. Use a comma after the greeting in a friendly letter and after the closing in both a friendly letter and a business letter.

Dear Betty,   Your friend,   Sincerely yours,

Guided Practice (1–11)   Where are commas needed?

Example: She lives at 370 Grand Street Akron Ohio 44309.
She lives at 370 Grand Street, Akron, Ohio 44309.

> 48 Kent Drive
> Lexington KY 40511
> January 29 1990

Dear Alissa

  Your letter of May 30 1989 just got here! Since you didn't write the ZIP, it went to Lexington Massachusetts 02173. Anyway, I'll see you at 12 Lee Road Atlanta Georgia on February 14 1990.

> Your friend
> Olivia

Summing up

▶Use a comma to separate the month and the day from the year.
▶Use a comma between the city and the state. Use a comma after the state if the address is within the sentence. Use a comma to separate each item except the ZIP Code.
▶Use a comma after the greeting in friendly letters and after the closing in both friendly and business letters.

Independent Practice (12–30) Write the letter, adding commas where needed.

Example: September 13 1620 is when the Pilgrims left England.
September 13, 1620, is when the Pilgrims left England.

> 1320 Adams Road
> Stillwater Oklahoma 74074
> March 27 1990

Dear Aunt Jessie

    April 7 1990 is when I will finally be in Boston! I can't wait to see you and Uncle Raymond. Except for visits to Tulsa Oklahoma in November 1986 and to Houston Texas in January 1987, I've never been away from Stillwater. It certainly will be exciting to see a place as different from Stillwater as Boston Massachusetts.

    I've been studying some history. April 19 1775 was the first battle of the American Revolution. I will be there this April to celebrate. Isn't the battle acted out every year in Concord Massachusetts?

    Can we also visit the site of the Boston Tea Party, which occurred on December 16 1773 in Boston Harbor? My Boston tour book lists addresses of other historical sites, like the home of Paul Revere at 19 North Square Boston Massachusetts 02107. Is that far from the Computer Museum, which is at 300 Congress Street Boston? I would also like to see Harvard University in Cambridge. It all sounds wonderful!

> Your nephew
> Leo

Writing Application: A Persuasive Letter Write a letter to convince a real or imaginary out-of-town friend to visit you soon. Include in your letter your return address, the date, a greeting, and a closing. Tell your friend about some events that you would like to attend together. Give the complete dates and addresses of these events.

6 | Quotation Marks

Direct Quotations

When you write a **direct quotation**, you write a speaker's exact words. Use quotation marks to set apart a speaker's words from the rest of the sentence.

> "Please open your books now," said Mr. Emory.
> Then he said, "We're ready to begin."

Notice that you begin a direct quotation with a capital letter. You use a comma to separate the quotation from the rest of the sentence.

Place question marks and exclamation points that belong to the quotation inside the quotation marks. Place question marks and exclamation points that do not belong to the quotation outside the quotation marks. Always place periods and commas inside the quotation marks.

> "Where is Tasmania?" asked the teacher.
> Ralph said, "I don't know where it is."
> Did Denise say, "It is near Australia"?

The example below shows how to punctuate a divided quotation that is all one sentence. Notice, however, that when a divided quotation is two separate sentences, you must capitalize the first word of the second part.

> "Here," Kim replied, "is Tasmania."
> "Here is Tasmania," she said. "It is off the southeastern coast of Australia."

An **indirect quotation** tells what someone said without using the speaker's exact words. Do not use quotation marks around indirect quotations.

> Kim said that Tasmania is off the coast of Australia.

Guided Practice Where are commas, quotation marks, and capital letters needed? Which sentences are already correct?

Example: Mr. Romero asked is Australia a country?
Mr. Romero asked, "Is Australia a country?"

1. Yes replied Lauren.
2. Mr. Romero asked is Australia a continent?
3. Howard answered I'm not sure.

4. Please reply said Mr. Romero if you know the answer.
5. Anna said that Australia was a continent.
6. That's right said Mr. Romero. It is a country and a continent.
7. Did Mr. Romero say tell me more about Australia?
8. He told us that the test will be tomorrow.

Titles of Short Works

You also use quotation marks around titles of short works. The first, last, and all important words in a title are capitalized. Do not capitalize any unimportant word such as *the, a, and, of, for,* or *to* unless it is the first or last word in the title.

SHORT STORY:	"Jug of Silver"
POEM:	"Jabberwocky"
CHAPTER OF A BOOK:	"Writing Business Reports"
MAGAZINE ARTICLE:	"How to Ask for a Raise"
SONG:	"The Star-Spangled Banner"

Guided Practice How would you capitalize and punctuate these items?

Example: the kangaroo and the koala   (book chapter)
"The Kangaroo and the Koala"

9. looking for the kiwi   (short story)
10. the extraordinary animals of australia (magazine article)
11. waiting for the boat to take me there (song)
12. in the station   (poem)
13. the raising of sheep in australia (book chapter)
14. all about new zealand   (magazine article)
15. coming of age in the outback   (book chapter)
16. australia and tasmania   (poem)

Independent Practice
Write each sentence. Capitalize and punctuate it. If a sentence is already correct, label it *correct*.

Example: The name of the Australian national anthem is advance australia fair.

The name of the Australian national anthem is "Advance Australia Fair."

17. Name some Australian animals said Mr. Romero.
18. Judy answered the kangaroo and the koala are Australian.
19. Did Howard say I think that the platypus is an Australian animal?
20. Mr. Romero held up an article called the animals of Australia.
21. Here he said is a picture of two birds, the emu of Australia and the cassowary of New Guinea.
22. Neither of these birds flies he added. The emu looks very much like an ostrich.

23. Lauren said that she had once read a poem that was called the emu and you in the zoo.
24. The kookaburra is another Australian bird that is known for its harsh call read Mr. Romero.
25. Jeffrey exclaimed what a strange name that is!
26. Lauren asked Mr. Romero what a wombat is.
27. It's a marsupial, along with kangaroos, koalas, and wallabies piped in Joshua.
28. Who asked what a marsupial is?
29. Don't marsupials carry their young in pouches asked Elizabeth.
30. That's right answered Mr. Romero. Australia has about 150 species of marsupials.
31. Why asked Mr. Romero are the animals of Australia so unusual?
32. Lauren said that she did not know the answer.
33. She asked the class if anyone had ever read the poem be wary of the cassowary.
34. Mr. Romero repeated why are Australian animals so unusual?
35. I have an idea said Howard. Here it is.
36. Australia he continued is separated from the other continents.
37. Mr. Romero exclaimed that's absolutely right!
38. For homework that night, he assigned the chapter that is called kangaroos and koalas.

Writing Application: A Dialogue Using direct quotations, write a short dialogue between two people talking about unusual animals or faraway places. Be sure to use correct capitalization and punctuation.

7 | Titles of Long Works

You know that the titles of short works are enclosed in quotation marks. In print, the titles of long works like books, magazines, newspapers, movies, TV series, and musical works appear in italics. **Italics** is a special kind of slanted print that looks like this: *italics*. When you write or type, you underline the titles of long works to represent italics.

BOOK:	*A Summer to Remember*
MAGAZINE:	*Sports Illustrated*
NEWSPAPER:	*Denver Post*, *The New York Times*
PLAY:	*The Butler Did It*
MOVIE:	*Black Stallion*
TV SERIES:	*Happy Days*
PAINTING:	*Sunflowers*
MUSICAL WORKS:	*Symphony No. 5*, *The Marriage of Figaro*

Notice that the first word, the last word, and all important words in each title begin with a capital letter. Do not capitalize a word like *a*, *the*, *of*, *for*, *to*, or *and* unless it is the first or last word in the title. Do not underline *the* with newspapers unless *the* is part of the title.

Guided Practice What words in each of these titles should be capitalized?

Example: *leave it to beaver*   *Leave It to Beaver*

1. *the sound of music*
2. *alice in wonderland*
3. *the barber of seville*
4. *minneapolis star tribune*
5. *my three sons*
6. *road and track*
7. *los angeles times*
8. *seventeenth summer*
9. *for whom the bell tolls*
10. *saturday evening post*
11. *symphony no. 9*
12. *singing in the wilderness*
13. *a bell for adano*
14. *a night at the opera*
15. *a street in tahiti*
16. *as you like it*
17. *the diary of anne frank*
18. *riders to the sea*

> **Summing up**
>
> ▶ Underline the titles of major works like books, magazines, newspapers, plays, movies, paintings, and long musical works.

Independent Practice

A. Rewrite the titles, capitalizing them where necessary.

Example: *on a clear day you can see forever*
On a Clear Day You Can See Forever

19. *a bridge too far*
20. *a day of triumph*
21. *the dallas weekly*
22. *father knows best*
23. *the taming of the shrew*

24. *the big valley*
25. *san francisco chronicle*
26. *out of the blue*
27. *museums of the world*
28. *portrait of a woman*

B. Write each sentence. Underline the titles of long works, and put quotation marks around the titles of short works. Capitalize the titles correctly.

Example: Rachel took out the book a treasury of music.
Rachel took out the book A Treasury of Music.

29. The opera the magic flute was to be televised.
30. Rachel found it in the book stories of operas.
31. Rachel had seen the show west side story.
32. It was based on Shakespeare's play romeo and juliet.
33. Rachel wrote a poem about it called a place for everyone.
34. One of Rachel's favorite songs is I feel pretty.
35. While waiting, Rachel read the magazine home and garden.
36. An article entitled building a rack for your records interested her.
37. Then she watched an episode of nova on TV.
38. Today's issue of flash arrived.
39. It contained a story called a painting for my father.
40. Birds, bees, and flowers was the name of the painting.
41. The movie called summer music was on TV.
42. Rachel read part of the book the old man and the sea.
43. She heard the opera porgy and bess on the radio.
44. The song summertime was her father's favorite.
45. Rachel played the album mozart's prague symphony.

Writing Application: A Description Write a paragraph telling your favorite short story, book, movie, song, and TV series. Include their titles, and be sure to capitalize and punctuate each title correctly.

8 || Colons and Semicolons

You know that you use a comma after the greeting in a friendly letter. Use a colon after the greeting in a business letter.

Dear Mrs. Tomasello: Dear Sir:

When you write the time, you use a colon to separate the hour from the minute.

8:40 A.M.   6:30 P.M.

Use a colon before a list of items in a sentence. Words like *the following* or *these* often signal the use of a colon.

> In music we study these composers: Copland, Ives, and Barber.
> Bring the following: your book, a notebook, and a harmonica.

However, you should not use a colon after a verb or after a preposition.

> Bring a music book, a harmonica, and a notebook to class.
> The program consists of a solo, a duet, and a trio.

You know that a compound sentence is made up of two related complete thoughts that are joined by *and, but, or, nor, for,* or *yet.*

> I practiced for three hours, and now I'm ready.

You can use a semicolon in place of the conjunction when the relation between the two clauses is very clear.

> I practiced for three hours; now I'm ready.
> This music is very difficult; it is for an advanced student.

Also use a semicolon to join two independent clauses when the second clause begins with an adverb such as *however, therefore, consequently, besides, moreover, furthermore,* or *nevertheless.*

> I played my best; however, I still need more practice.
> The piano needed tuning; therefore, I couldn't play it today.

Use a semicolon to separate two independent clauses that have commas within one or both of them. The semicolon shows your reader where the complete thoughts begin and end, thus avoiding confusion.

> Tom plays the clarinet, the saxophone, and the piccolo; and his brother plays the piano and the flute.

Guided Practice Where are colons and semicolons needed?

Example: The concert is at 830 therefore, let's meet at 745.
The concert is at 8:30; therefore, let's meet at 7:45.

1. Dear Ms. Delaney
2. The West Indian concert will be held at 730 P.M. on Friday.
3. The following school groups will participate the Glee Club, the Folk Singers, and the Steel Band.
4. You study music therefore, we recommend this concert.
5. The guests of honor are Jim Evans, Elena Cruz, and Carlos Fores and additional groups are Star, Flash, and Fire.

Summing up

> ▶ Use a **colon** after a greeting in a business letter, between the hour and the minute in time, and before a list.
> ▶ Use a **semicolon** to connect independent clauses that are closely related in thought or that have commas within them.

Independent Practice Write these parts of a letter, adding semicolons and colons where necessary.

Example: The concert starts at 1030 it will last for an hour.
The concert starts at 10:30; it will last for an hour.

6. Dear Mr. Marley
7. You have requested information about steel bands consequently, I am sending you several pamphlets.
8. They include the following "The Steel Band," "Beating the Drum," and "West Indian Music."
9. The pamphlets will not arrive for two weeks therefore, I shall describe steel bands briefly in this letter.
10. In the 1940s steel bands first became popular in Trinidad they quickly spread to other parts of the Caribbean.
11. The main types of drums are the ping pong, the guitar, and the bass they are tuned to different notes.
12. The Jamaica Steel Band concerts are Monday, Tuesday, and Wednesday and the time is 815 P.M.

Writing Application: An Announcement Write an announcement of a school band rehearsal that includes the date and the time, the place, and a list of items that the members should bring. Punctuate your announcement correctly.

Abbreviations

You have already learned that a title used with a person's name is capitalized. Titles that are shortened forms of words are called **abbreviations.** Initials are another form of abbreviation. Most abbreviations begin with a capital letter and end with a period.

NAMES:	Mr.—Mister	Sr.—Senior
	Mrs.—married woman	Jr.—Junior
	Ms.—any woman	James K. Polk—Knox
	Dr.—Doctor	Gen.—General
ADDRESSES:	St.—Street	P.O.—Post Office
	Rd.—Road	H.S.—High School
	Ave.—Avenue	Apt.—Apartment
BUSINESSES:	Co.—Company	Corp.—Corporation
	Inc.—Incorporated	Ltd.—Limited
ORGANIZATIONS:	NATO—North Atlantic Treaty Organization	
	SBA—Small Business Administration	
STATE NAMES:	ME—Maine	IL—Illinois
DAYS:	Mon.—Monday	Thurs.—Thursday
MONTHS:	Jan.—January	Aug.—August
UNITS OF	mph—miles per hour	hp—horsepower
MEASURE:	l—liter	in.—inch or inches
TIME:	A.M.—midnight to noon	P.M.—noon to midnight

Note these additional facts about abbreviations.

1. To save space in addresses and names of businesses, you use abbreviations for some words.
2. Periods do not usually appear after abbreviations for organizations, and all the letters are capitals.
3. The United States Postal Service uses a capitalized two-letter abbreviation with no period for each state. See the list of abbreviations in the Capitalization, Punctuation, and Usage guide at the end of this book.
4. You cannot abbreviate the months of May, June, and July.
5. Do not capitalize or use periods after abbreviations for units of measure. The only exception is the abbreviation for *inch,* which is followed by a period.
6. If you use the abbreviation for a unit of measure, then you must use a numeral with it.

Guided Practice How would you use abbreviations in each item?

Example: Captain Ramirez   *Capt. Ramirez*

1. High School 89
2. Thursday
3. April 9
4. Mister Logan
5. Route 189
6. Data, Incorporated
7. February 14

8. John Ray Jenks, Senior
9. 8 feet
10. Grand Boulevard
11. Arlington, Texas
12. 9 inches
13. Doctor Peter J. Shea
14. Mount McKinley

Numbers

In writing you should always spell out numbers under one hundred. Use numerals for numbers over one hundred except for even hundreds.

> There are eighty-two students present.
> There are 182 students in my school.
> There were two hundred students last year.

Always spell out a number that begins a sentence.

> One hundred thirty-five students attended the meeting.

You should also spell out expressions of time when you use the word *o'clock*. Use numerals, however, when the time is followed by A.M. or P.M. or is used alone as an exact time.

Let's meet at seven o'clock.   The taxi came at 6 P.M.
We took the 2:15 train.   It arrives at 2:45.

Use numerals to refer to sections of writing.

Chapter 6   Unit 10   line 13

Guided Practice Which numbers in these sentences should be spelled out? Which should be written as numerals?

Example: 42 people met at 3 o'clock.
   Forty-two people met at three o'clock.

15. Aren't there more than 45 people in the group?
16. Everyone must catch the bus at 3 o'clock exactly.
17. We leave in 25 minutes, according to page two of the schedule.
18. 7 minutes later, 12 additional people had arrived.
19. All 61 were there by 3:23 P.M., 2 minutes before the bus left.

▸ Most abbreviations begin with a capital letter and end with a period.
▸ Spell out numbers under one hundred and numbers at the beginning of a sentence. Use numerals for numbers over one hundred and for sections of writing.

Independent Practice

A. Write these items, using correct abbreviations.

Example: 60 miles per hour   *60 mph*

20. Mister Chan
21. Barstow, California
22. Wednesday
23. Apartment 4B
24. Jenkins Company
25. Rand High School
26. Mister Jon Ross, Senior
27. December 30
28. thirteen inches

29. 8 feet
30. Saturday, January 14
31. Central Intelligence Agency
32. Riverside Drive
33. Ray Michael Barnes, Junior
34. Doctor Shirley Jane Belle
35. Department of Public Works
36. Dallas, Texas
37. Post Office Box 109

B. Rewrite each incorrect sentence, using numerals or words for the numbers. If a sentence is already correct, write *correct*.

Example: At seven-ten there were only fourteen people in the theater.
At 7:10 there were only fourteen people in the theater.

38. The performance was supposed to start at seven-thirty P.M.
39. The ushers had studied Section One of the instructions.
40. 5 minutes later, twenty-two ticket holders were waiting.
41. Two hundred twenty-five tickets had been sold.
42. We were missing one hundred eighty-nine people at 7:15.
43. At exactly seven-eighteen, a crowd of 55 people arrived.
44. Three or four minutes later, the auditorium was full.
45. Before 7 o'clock, only 2 or 3 people had been there.
46. By curtain time at 7:30, more than 225 were seated.

Writing Application: An Advertisement Write a newspaper ad to sell a household item. Use as many abbreviations as possible, giving the following information: street address with state, the size of the item, and the day and the time the seller is available to show the item.

For Extra Practice, see p. 341.   Abbreviations and Numbers   **323**

10 | Apostrophes

You have already learned to use an apostrophe to show possession and to replace letters that you drop in contractions. Remember that to form a possessive noun, you add an apostrophe and s to most singular nouns and plural nouns not ending in s.

girl—girl's   children—children's

You add only an apostrophe to most plural nouns ending in s to make them possessive.

girls—girls'   Roys—Roys'

Remember that possessive pronouns, such as *its, hers,* and *theirs,* never contain apostrophes.

To form contractions with verbs, you use an apostrophe to replace the missing letters.

does not—doesn't   have not—haven't   would not—wouldn't

To form contractions with pronouns and verbs, you also use an apostrophe to replace dropped letters.

you are—you're   they would—they'd   she will—she'll

Use an apostrophe and s to form the plural of letters, numerals, and symbols.

i's   *p*'s and *q*'s   7's   4's   +'s   #'s

Follow the same rule to form the plural of words that refer to themselves as names of words.

The judge would not listen to any *if*'s, *and*'s, or *but*'s.

Guided Practice Where are apostrophes needed in each sentence?

Example: Elenas *i*s werent dotted.   *Elena's i's weren't dotted.*

1. The classs assignment isnt difficult.
2. Theyre studying my geography teachers map.
3. The *'s on their map indicate capitals.
4. Guss error in the spelling of *Mississippi* is understandable.
5. Dont forget that there are four *s*s, four *i*s, and two *p*s.
6. Youre remembering your *s*s in *Tennessee,* arent you?
7. Rays problem is remembering the Canadian prime ministers name.

> ▶ Add an apostrophe and *s* to singular nouns and to plural nouns not ending in *s* to show possession. Add an apostrophe to plural nouns ending in *s* to show possession.
> ▶ Add an apostrophe and *s* to form the plural of letters, numerals, symbols, and words that refer to themselves. Use an apostrophe in contractions to replace missing letters.

Independent Practice Write the sentences, adding apostrophes where necessary.

Example: The childrens drawings arent very accurate.
The children's drawings aren't very accurate.

8. Theyre drawing maps of South American countries.
9. What do the #s mean on Nicholass map?
10. Arent they the Andes Mountain boundaries?
11. Carlas mountains have +s all around them.
12. Dont you know that the Andes are the longest mountain range?
13. Two students maps have different colors.
14. Youre using a lot of red in your map, arent you?
15. Andreas name hasnt been spelled correctly on this list.
16. Hectors map is finished, isnt it?
17. Why are there so many *Souths* on Harrys map?
18. *Chile* doesn't have two *l*s, Miranda.
19. Use *s to mark the capital of each country.
20. Peoples understanding of geography is strange.
21. Argentina isnt on Lionels map.
22. Jennys map doesnt show the capital of Brazil.
23. Didnt Beas map show all of South America?
24. The list of symbols on the map shows some %s.
25. The cities on this map are marked with †s.
26. Can you abbreviate all the *and*s and the *but*s?
27. Theres a globe on the corner of Susans desk.
28. Its brand new and hasnt been used yet.
29. The classs next assignment will be a map of Europe.
30. Wont Mr. Rosss map be a model for the assignment?

Writing Application: A Description Write a paragraph about the geography of a place that you have visited or would like to visit. Include some contractions, possessive nouns, and plurals of symbols or numerals. Be sure to use apostrophes correctly.

For Extra Practice, see p. 342.
Apostrophes 325

11 | Hyphens, Dashes, and Parentheses

Use a **hyphen** to divide a word at the end of a line. Only words with more than one syllable can be divided. Do not leave a single letter at the end or at the beginning of a line.

INCORRECT: e-lection   librar-y   CORRECT: elec-tion   li-brary

Use a hyphen in compound numbers from twenty-one to ninety-nine and in fractions used as adjectives.

thirty-two   a two-thirds majority   one-half teaspoon

You have seen hyphens in some compound nouns. When two or more words expressing one thought act as an adjective before a noun, use a hyphen to connect them.

long-range plans   up-to-the-minute report   well-known man

Use a **dash** to set off a sudden change of thought or an afterthought, or to mean *namely* or *in other words*.

Tom and Alex are very close—most brothers are.
The game—it went into overtime—was really exciting.

Parentheses indicate another type of interruption. They enclose information that isn't necessary to the meaning of a sentence or information that some readers may already know.

Charles Lindbergh (1902–1974) was a pioneer in aviation.
The president (Cooper Smith) presented the award.

Guided Practice

A. Use hyphens and dashes correctly in these sentences.

Example: Has Lu thought about furniture its history and uses?
Has Lu thought about furniture—its history and uses?

1. One of the best known pieces of furniture is the bed.
2. A king size bed the largest size is wider than a double bed.
3. How do you divide *furniture, fur niture* or *furni ture*?

B. Where are parentheses needed in these sentences?

Example: Furniture originally a French word includes beds.
Furniture (originally a French word) includes beds.

4. A double bed is four and a half feet 1.37 meters wide.
5. French beds of the Empire period early 1800s were large.

Summing up

> ► Use a **hyphen** to divide a word at the end of a line, to join the parts of compound numbers, and to join two or more words that work together as one adjective before a noun.
> ► Use **dashes** to show a sudden change of thought.
> ► Use **parentheses** to enclose unnecessary information.

Independent Practice

A. Write each sentence, adding hyphens and dashes where needed.

> Example: Primitive people hardy souls slept on leaves.
> *Primitive people—hardy souls—slept on leaves.*

6. A very rough bed is often called a bunk from Middle Dutch *banc* meaning "shelf" or "bench."
7. Colonists usually stuffed their beds with whatever was plentiful corn husks, wood chips, or straw.
8. Could a bed be one third husks and two thirds straw?
9. The bedroom rarely a separate room could be in a corner.
10. Privacy a sought after condition was almost impossible.
11. Children slept with their parents or in a trundle bed a bed pushed under the parents' bed during the day.
12. How is *centimeter* divided *centi meter* or *cen timeter*?
13. Outside, many people use sleeping bags most campers do.
14. Two thirds activity and one third sleep a very common division of time describe my day.

B. Write each sentence adding parentheses where necessary.

> Example: Some people the Japanese and the Eskimos did not always sleep on beds.
> *Some people (the Japanese and the Eskimos) did not always sleep on beds.*

15. The invention of bedsprings 1831 made beds comfortable.
16. By then 1830s some houses were two stories high.
17. A double bed is just over six feet 1.88 meters long.
18. The largest bed California king is nearly nine feet close to three meters long.

Writing Application: A Description Write a paragraph describing your bedroom or another room at home. Use a hyphen, a dash, and a pair of parentheses correctly in your paragraph.

For Extra Practice, see p. 343.   Hyphens, Dashes, and Parentheses   **327**

Grammar-Writing Connection

Writing Dialogue

Dialogue is written conversation. Writers use it to make characters and plots more vivid. Compare these passages.

> Alex and his father enjoyed walking over the Brooklyn Bridge while in New York. The view of the city was lovely.

> "Look at New York! It's fabulous!" exclaimed Alex.
> "I'm really glad Pete told us to walk across the Brooklyn Bridge," said his father. "I never would have thought of it."

Since dialogue is such an important writing tool, you should know how to write it correctly. Study these rules.

1. Use quotation marks only with the speaker's actual words. Do not use quotation marks with indirect quotations.

   > "Bridges," said Mr. Beck, "have always interested me."
   > Mr. Beck said that bridges have always interested him.

2. Capitalize the first word of a quotation and the first word of each new sentence within a quotation.

   > Mr. Beck continued, "The number of bridges in New York City is surprising. There must be over a thousand!"

3. Begin a new paragraph each time the speaker changes.

   > "Does any other city have as many bridges as New York has?" asked Alex.
   > "Sydney, Australia," said Mr. Beck, "almost does."

Revising Sentences

Rewrite the paragraph, using dialogue wherever possible.

Lily told Roy that she was writing a report on bridges for social studies. Roy asked whether she had picked up any unusual facts. Lily replied that she had learned a lot. She said that, for example, the first toll bridge in the United States was built in Massachusetts in 1654. What Lily thought was funny was that the toll was charged for animals. People crossed free. Roy exclaimed that that was pretty funny! Actually, he noted that it wasn't so different from today's bridges and asked Lily if she knew that cars had to pay tolls on some bridges while pedestrians could walk across without paying. Lily said that he was right and that she had forgotten about that.

Creative Writing

Jacob Lawrence, *Parade*
Hirschhorn Museum and Sculpture Garden
Smithsonian Institution

Is it possible to paint a moving line of colors and sounds? Jacob Lawrence's picture of a parade in Harlem, New York City, captures this fleeting sight. Through a repetition of colors and shapes, Lawrence conveys the parade's rhythmic march.

- Does the picture seem soft or sharp? Explain.
- How do the spectators add to the mood of the painting?

Activities

1. **Write a feature story.** Imagine that you are a reporter for the newspaper, the *Harlem Herald*. Write a feature story describing the parade.
2. **Write a letter.** Suppose a critic named Art S. Puzling says that this painting is just a confusion of colors and shapes. Imagine that you are the artist, Jacob Lawrence. Write a letter to Puzling explaining what you tried to convey in your painting.
3. **Describe your perceptions.** Remember how amazing parades seemed when you were very young? Describe your childhood perceptions of a parade and how they have since changed.

Check-up: Unit 9

A **Sentences and Interjections** *(p. 304)* Write each sentence, adding the correct capitalization and punctuation.

1. am I going to fall
2. signal when you're ready
3. wow I'm standing up
4. oh no I'm losing my balance
5. it was certainly fun
6. do you like skiing

B **Proper Nouns and Proper Adjectives** *(p. 305)* Rewrite each sentence, capitalizing all proper nouns and proper adjectives.

7. The doctor that I go to for my eyes is dr. lessell.
8. His office is at the patrick t. wellington hospital.
9. That hospital is located on charles street.
10. I see him each spring and autumn, usually in may and november.
11. I ordered some new french eyeglass frames after my last visit.

C **Uses for Commas** *(pp. 308, 310)* Write these sentences, adding commas where needed.

12. One Portuguese prince Henry the Navigator started the era of global exploration in the fifteenth century.
13. Prince Henry himself of course never sailed on such a voyage.
14. At Sagres Portugal Prince Henry founded a naval observatory.
15. This center drew scholars astronomers and sailors people who knew the Atlantic well.
16. Yes Portugal led the way for later discoveries.

D **Dates, Addresses, and Letters** *(p. 312)* Rewrite each item, adding the correct punctuation.

17. Please call me on Tuesday March 22 1994 before noon.
18. Myra's address is 12 Rancho Road Las Vegas Nevada 89107.
19. Why dont we meet in Cleveland Ohio tomorrow?
20. Dear Maxine   Your brother
21. The correct address is St. Croix Falls WI 54024.

E **Quotation Marks** *(p. 314)* Rewrite each sentence. Capitalize and punctuate it correctly. Use quotation marks where necessary.

22. What asked Miss Valdez is our national anthem?
23. The Star-Spangled Banner is by Francis Scott Key.
24. Frieda inquired when was it written?
25. The words were written in 1814 Joe answered when the British attacked Fort McHenry in Baltimore.
26. Jerry added the music, however, was an old English tune.

Titles *(pp. 315, 317)* Write the sentences. Underline the titles of long works. Put quotation marks around the titles of short works. Capitalize the titles correctly.

27. Did you read the article records take new forms?
28. I read in Time about a new recording of the Eroica Symphony.
29. For more information about the symphony read the book called recorded music.
30. That TV show called national nightly news isn't very good.
31. One national newspaper is entitled the wall street journal.

Colons and Semicolons *(p. 319)* Write these items, adding semicolons and colons where needed.

32. Dear Ms. Floyd-Smythe
33. The beginning sewing classes will meet at 1030 A.M.
34. You may take the following Tailoring, Embroidery, or Cutting.
35. Bring these items scissors, thread, and material.
36. Sewing machines are available for all students in addition, needles and thimbles will be supplied for handwork.

Abbreviations and Numbers *(p. 321)* Write the sentences, using abbreviations where possible and the correct form for numbers.

37. Pick up your packages after 3 o'clock on Monday, November 10.
38. They are being stored in Cheesequake, New Jersey.
39. Ask for Mister Malfitano, who can locate them for you.
40. Coast Storage Incorporated closes at five-thirty.
41. You will be billed for two hundred fifty cubic feet of space.

Apostrophes *(p. 324)* Write the sentences, adding apostrophes where needed.

42. Teen-agers volunteer to teach children their *abc*s.
43. Two girls tables are here, and the childrens books are there.
44. Use the materials on your tables; don't use theirs.
45. Tracy no longer confuses *b*s and *d*s.
46. Jesss spelling should continue to improve in the future.

Hyphens and Parentheses *(p. 326)* Write the sentences, adding hyphens and parentheses where needed.

47. Bernardo O'Higgins 1776–1842 was a remarkable Chilean hero.
48. He was a well respected liberator.
49. O'Higgins an Irish name worked hard to free Chile.
50. He died in exile at the age of sixty six.

Enrichment

Using Capitalization and Punctuation

▦ Quips and Quotes

"Four score and seven years ago," began Abraham Lincoln.

Players—2. **You need**—paper, pencils, scissors, a history book. **How to play**—Each player copies 5 famous quotations from a history book. For each quotation, think of a word that means "said." Write the word with the author's name. Decide whether the word and the author's name should be before or after the quotation.

On paper strips, write full sentences, using each quotation, its author's name, and the word for *said*. Punctuate your sentences correctly. Cut off each quotation from the rest of the sentence to make a puzzle. Exchange puzzles with your partner and solve them. **Scoring**—2 points for each correctly matched puzzle. The player with the most points or who completes all 5 puzzles first wins.

Dear Author

Write a letter to an author. Tell why you like a certain book or character.

Address the letter to the author in care of the publisher. (Look for the name and address on the title page.) Include your return address and use abbreviations. Revise and proofread your letter, and make a final copy. Address an envelope, stamp it, and mail the letter.

Space Journeys

Many space missions have carried people. These include Mercury, Gemini, Apollo, and Skylab. Choose one of these flights and make a chart about it, listing in complete sentences (1) its destination, (2) astronauts who flew on it, (3) its purpose and accomplishments, and (4) its date. Capitalize and punctuate your sentences correctly. Abbreviate dates and the astronauts' titles.

Extra Practice: Unit 9

1 | Sentences and Interjections (p. 304)

● Write the kind of sentence shown in parentheses. Begin it with a capital letter, and add the correct punctuation.

Example: wow what a great story that was   (exclamatory)
Wow, what a great story that was!

1. many detective stories are not about detectives   (declarative)
2. give me an example   (imperative)
3. have you ever heard of Miss Marple   (interrogative)
4. she solved mysteries in Agatha Christie's books   (declarative)
5. how simple and innocent Miss Marple was   (exclamatory)
6. was she ever wrong about a crime   (interrogative)
7. well that would have been a surprise   (exclamatory)
8. lend me your book by Agatha Christie, please   (imperative)

▲ Write the sentences. Capitalize and punctuate them correctly.

Example: aha what a surprise that ending was
Aha! What a surprise that ending was!

9. mysteries became very popular in the 1900s
10. were the mysteries always solved by detectives
11. no many of the crimes were solved by amateurs
12. give me some examples
13. didn't one series of detective stories feature a doctor
14. wow what a clever idea that was
15. don't forget Nancy Drew
16. oh I would never forget the famous teen-age investigator

■ Rewrite each sentence as the type of sentence shown in parentheses. Change, add, or omit words if necessary. Add the correct capitalization and punctuation.

Example: are there women detectives   (declarative, exclamatory)
There are women detectives. There are women detectives!

17. how typical is the female detective   (declarative, exclamatory)
18. you find her in older stories   (interrogative, imperative)
19. women detectives appeared in fiction over a hundred years ago (exclamatory, interrogative)
20. you did tell me about the first female writer of detective stories (interrogative, imperative)
21. did Alan say that she was Anna Green   (imperative, declarative)
22. is that a surprise   (declarative, exclamatory)

2 | Proper Nouns and Adjectives (p. 305)

● Write these sentences, capitalizing the underlined words if necessary. If a sentence is already correct, label it *correct*.

Example: What countries are on the continent of <u>south america</u>?
What countries are on the continent of South America?

1. Mexico was a <u>spanish</u> colony for three hundred years.
2. Mexicans celebrate their <u>independence day</u> on September 16.
3. The capital of this country is <u>mexico city</u>.
4. Wasn't <u>grandfather</u> born in <u>mexico</u>?
5. Yes, he and <u>uncle</u> Pedro were both born there.
6. They have lived in <u>pasadena</u> now for twenty years.
7. I visit them in <u>california</u> every <u>winter</u>.
8. We saw the <u>rose parade</u> there on <u>new year's day</u> last <u>january</u>.

▲ Write each sentence, using capital letters where necessary.

Example: The month of july has some interesting days.
The month of July has some interesting days.

9. On july 4, 1776, the declaration of independence was signed.
10. It was signed in philadelphia, pennsylvania, by the continental congress.
11. A hero of the american revolution, captain john paul jones, was born in july.
12. David farragut and emma lazarus were also born in july.
13. farragut was the first admiral of the united states navy.
14. Emma lazarus wrote the poem that is on the statue of liberty.
15. A copy of the statue stands on the seine river in paris.
16. The parisian people love to stroll along the riverbanks.

■ Write each sentence, using capital letters only where needed. If the sentence is already correct, label it *correct*.

Example: Which Continent is larger, Europe or north america?
Which continent is larger, Europe or North America?

17. The North american continent is larger than the european.
18. In both size and population, asia is the largest continent.
19. This land includes tiny singapore and huge china and india.
20. The japanese ruler Hirohito became emperor in 1926.
21. A past ruler of India was Prime Minister Indira Gandhi.
22. The greatest holiday of the japanese year is new year's day.
23. Yasunari Kawabata was the first japanese to win the Nobel Prize for literature.
24. The Taj Mahal is a famous monument in northern India.

3 | Uses for Commas (p. 308)

● Write these sentences, adding commas where needed to the underlined parts.

Example: Mathew B. Brady was a <u>famous successful</u> photographer.

Mathew B. Brady was a famous, successful photographer.

1. Photographs became a <u>common popular</u> feature of American life.
2. Brady was a good <u>photographer and</u> he was also a businessman.
3. Brady was <u>talented ambitious and industrious</u>.
4. Before he was <u>twenty-one he</u> already had his own studio.
5. <u>Senators Presidents and famous people</u> came to his studio.
6. Then the Civil War <u>began and</u> Brady wanted to photograph it.
7. His <u>dramatic clear</u> photographs have become pieces of history.

▲ Write each sentence, adding one or more commas where needed. If the sentence needs no commas, write *correct*.

Example: Wet-plate photography was messy limited and crude.

Wet-plate photography was messy, limited, and crude.

8. Early photographers dealt with messy chemicals handled wet plates and developed the plates immediately.
9. Some important new photographic discoveries began in 1871.
10. A dry-plate process was invented and it changed the photographer's job.
11. Exposure time was faster and cameras could be hand-held.
12. The new plates were dry clean and effective.
13. Photographers previously had made their own plates and developed them.
14. Now companies perform these complicated burdensome tasks.
15. By the 1880s, experiments in photography had led to smaller cameras faster shutters and shorter exposure times.

■ Add a word, a phrase, or a clause, as shown in ( ), so that the sentence requires one or more commas. Write the new sentence.

Example: Today's cameras are small and light.   (word)

Today's cameras are small, light, and convenient.

16. The camera was a practical invention.   (word)
17. You can take a camera to the beach or to a party.   (phrase)
18. Just pick up your camera and position your subject.   (clause)
19. Some photographers take pictures of people.   (clause)
20. Photographs are exhibited in studios and homes.   (word)
21. Cameras track storms and photographers film them.   (clause)
22. A photograph can change our way of seeing its subject.   (clause)

4 | More Uses for Commas (p. 310)

● Write the sentences, adding commas to the underlined parts where necessary.

Example: <u>Lisa</u> do you ever make long-distance calls?

Lisa, do you ever make long-distance calls?

1. <u>If you use a pay phone</u> you may be surprised.
2. <u>After a few clicks</u> you will hear a voice.
3. <u>Sounding a bit strange</u> the voice will tell you the cost.
4. Do not <u>however</u> talk to the voice.
5. There is not a real person on the other end <u>my friend</u>.
6. <u>Although it sounds like a person</u> the voice is from a computer.
7. This program <u>the Automatic Coin Telephone Service</u> is common.
8. The computer <u>by the way</u> has a vocabulary of seventy words.
9. Each word and number was first recorded by a person <u>of course</u>.

▲ Write each sentence, adding commas where needed. If no commas are needed, label the sentence *correct*.

Example: How does a computer work Mrs. Chun?

How does a computer work, Mrs. Chun?

10. A computer Dennis can be programmed.
11. Yes it can be given instructions.
12. Because it is programmable we can tell it what to do.
13. The program specific instructions tells the computer what to do.
14. With each new program the computer can do a different job.
15. A home computer for example can help you budget your money.
16. You can use another program a word-processing program to write your history essay.
17. Insert still another program and play the game "Mystery."

■ Write each sentence, adding an interrupter or an introductory word, phrase, or clause as shown. Use commas correctly.

Example: Describe the future factory.   (noun of direct address)

Describe the future factory, Janet.

18. Future factories may be run by one person.   (interrupter)
19. Labor will be done by robots.   (noun of direct address)
20. This may eventually happen.   (clause)
21. Robots are taking over many tasks.   (phrase)
22. Robots lift parts onto conveyor belts.   (phrase)
23. Most robots are not shiny metal people.   (word)
24. They are industrial machines.   (interrupter)
25. A student wrote a story about a robot.   (appositive)

5 | Dates, Addresses, and Letters (p. 312)

● Rewrite the items. Add commas where needed in the under-lined places. If an item is already correct, label it *correct*.
Example: My best friend lives in Redding California.
  My best friend lives in Redding, California.

1. 781 Fourth Avenue
2. Santa Fe New Mexico 87501
3. August 15 1990
4. Dear Marissa
5. I'm really looking forward to my visit to Redding California.
6. I learned that on September 9 1850 California became a state.
7. On September 9 1990 I'll be arriving in California.
8. Your cousin

▲ Rewrite the items, adding commas where necessary.
Example: The San Francisco California quake was in April 1906.
  The San Francisco, California, quake was in April 1906.

9. 1190 Grand Boulevard
10. Springdale Arkansas 72764
11. May 23 1990
12. Dear Uncle Lyle
13. I wrote to the *World Almanac* 200 Park Avenue New York NY 10017 for the answers to your questions.
14. The fire in Chicago Illinois took place on October 8 1871.
15. The worst forest fire ever also occurred on October 8 1871.
16. That happened in Peshtigo Wisconsin.

■ You and your friend Desmond have been quizzing each other on little-known facts, and you have the answers to his ques-tions. Write the information in a letter to him. Use commas correctly.
Example: February 16 1948—first daily TV news show
  February 16, 1948, was the date of the first daily TV news show.

17. Your address, including the town, state, and ZIP Code
18. Today's date
19. Greeting
20. First United States telephone book—New Haven Connecticut February 21 1878
21. First parking meter—Oklahoma City Oklahoma July 16 1935
22. Closing

6 | Quotation Marks (p. 314)

● Write each sentence. Add quotation marks where needed.
   Example: Anna asked, What do you know about Australia?
            Anna asked, "What do you know about Australia?"
   1. Josh said, Here's a book about Australia.
   2. Josh went to the chapter called Strange and Surprising Facts.
   3. What are some of the facts? asked Anna.
   4. Well, said Josh, here's something interesting.
   5. Listen, he said. Australia has more sheep than people.
   6. He asked Anna about the chapter called In the Outback.
   7. Had she read the poem entitled Walking in the Outback?
   8. Anna asked, What is the outback?
   9. The outback, answered Josh, is the middle of Australia.
   10. Few people live there, he said. Most live on the coast.

▲ Write the sentences. Capitalize and punctuate them where necessary. If a sentence is already correct, label it *correct*.
   Example: Many nations are crowded Josh said but not ours.
            "Many nations are crowded," Josh said, "but not ours."
   11. Josh was reading an article called the tourist in Australia.
   12. The Australian song waltzing matilda was playing.
   13. Anna asked have you learned anything new from that article?
   14. Yes Josh replied there are a few new facts in here.
   15. He continued do you know where most Australians live?
   16. No, I don't said Anna. where do they live?
   17. Josh said that over half the people live in six cities.
   18. Anna exclaimed that's really surprising!
   19. Had Anna read her poem called a pouch for a kangaroo?
   20. Please begged Josh let me read it.

■ (21–28) Rewrite the passage. Capitalize and punctuate it.
   Example: Who wrote the Australian national anthem asked Anna.
            "Who wrote the Australian national anthem?" asked Anna.
       Josh told Anna that he had become very interested in Australia.
   He had just finished an article called the people of australia.
       What sorts of people are Australians? asked Anna.
       Well, the first settlers of Australia Josh replied were British prisoners who arrived in 1788.
       Anna asked were they the first people there?
       No answered Josh they weren't. People called *aborigines* had been living there for thousands of years. Then he showed Anna the story he had written called Australian newcomers.

7 | Titles of Long Works (p. 317)

● Write the titles, underlining them and using capital letters where necessary.

Example: david and lisa   (movie)   *David and Lisa*

1. green mansions   (book)
2. car and driver   (magazine)
3. star wars   (movie)
4. the company   (TV series)
5. into the dark   (play)
6. the daily news   (newspaper)
7. maids of honor   (painting)
8. the firebird   (musical work)
9. raisin in the sun   (play)
10. homework made easy   (book)

▲ Write each sentence. Capitalize the titles and add quotation marks or underlining where necessary.

Example: Is the play the importance of being earnest by Wilde?
   Is the play The Importance of Being Earnest by Wilde?

11. Jake had been reading the magazine young people's digest.
12. It contained an article called remember your favorite things.
13. He decided to write a poem and name it our favorite things.
14. A tale of two cities was one of his favorite books.
15. Oklahoma! was his mother's favorite song.
16. It was in the play and the movie oklahoma!
17. His father's favorite piece of music was carmen, by Bizet.
18. In his clinton herald, Jake saw a beautiful painting reproduced.
19. It was called the rehearsal of the ballet on stage.
20. It reminded him of the painting mandolin and guitar.
21. His favorite painting by Renoir was picnic on the grass.

■ Complete each sentence with a correctly written title of your own.

Example: Have you read the book _____?
   Have you read the book A Wrinkle in Time?

22. Yesterday I read an interesting article called _____.
23. It was in the _____, a newspaper that I often read.
24. The last movie I saw was _____.
25. The TV series _____ is one of my favorites.
26. _____ is a poem I have memorized because I wanted to.
27. _____ is a song I like to sing frequently.
28. I would like to name my best painting _____.
29. _____ is the book I have read most often.
30. I would like to write a story called _____ and publish it in the magazine _____.
31. If I could see a play right now, it would be _____.
32. For homework we must read the chapter called _____.

8 | Colons and Semicolons (p. 319)

● Write the items. Add the needed colons and semicolons to the underlined parts.

Example: I enjoy silent <u>films therefore</u>, I have seen many.
I enjoy silent films; therefore, I have seen many.

1. Dear Mr. <u>Greenberg</u>
2. *City Lights* is playing at the <u>following theaters the Strand</u>, Cinema 9, and Newtown Plaza.
3. The movie is shown at <u>445, 630, 815, and 1000</u> P.M.
4. No one talked in silent <u>films however</u>, there was music.
5. The presentation of *City Lights* will be accompanied by <u>these musicians two</u> violinists, a cellist, and a bass player.
6. Charlie Chaplin became <u>famous his</u> name is still known.

▲ Write the items. Add the needed colons and semicolons.

Example: I heard my favorite song it was on at 335 P.M.
I heard my favorite song; it was on at 3:35 P.M.

7. Dear Mrs. Ruiz
8. I enjoyed your article on popular music furthermore, I can add some facts about its history.
9. Hit songs are nothing new they have existed for centuries.
10. The song "Greensleeves" was a hit in the sixteenth century moreover, many people still know it today.
11. Some hits of the eighteenth century were the following "All Through the Night," "Yankee Doodle," and "Rule, Britannia."
12. You can turn to station WYRO at 720 A.M., 1220 P.M., or 920 P.M., and you will hear a program called *Hits of the Past.*

■ Rewrite each item to include a colon or a semicolon. Change the wording, the capitalization, and the punctuation where necessary.

Example: We sang "Yesterdays," "Swanee," and "Ida."
We sang the following songs: "Yesterdays," "Swanee," and "Ida."

13. Dear Mr. Singer,
14. Early movies were very emotional, silent, and black and white. They were very popular anyway.
15. The first "talkie" was *The Jazz Singer*. It starred Al Jolson.
16. A song came from the screen. The voice sounded like Jolson's.
17. Viewers were suspicious. They looked behind the screen.
18. *The Jazz Singer* is at ten-thirty A.M. and eight-thirty P.M.

9 | Abbreviations and Numbers (p. 321)

● Rewrite each item, using abbreviations for the underlined words.

Example: Carl Raymond Smith, Senior   C. R. Smith, Sr.

1. August 22
2. Sentix, Incorporated
3. Doctor Miller
4. Senator Russell
5. Mister Baxter
6. 17 feet
7. 12 liters
8. Portland, Maine
9. Fifth Avenue
10. Paul Robert Cahill
11. American Medical Association
12. 16 inches
13. Friday
14. Apartment 2
15. Chapter 9
16. Wednesday, February 9
17. United Nations
18. Route 192
19. James Roger Perl, Junior
20. High School 179

▲ Write each item using correct abbreviations where possible. For the items containing numbers, keep them as numerals if they are correct. Otherwise, write them out.

Example: Finally, 6 o'clock arrived.   *Finally, six o'clock arrived.*

21. Doctor Carla Fay Jones
22. Better Business Bureau
23. Sunday, June 22
24. 12 pounds, 4 ounces
25. Winston John Remo, Senior
26. Witfield, Limited
27. Whittier High School
28. Science Department
29. six centimeters
30. 65 plants were sold.
31. Is it 8 o'clock yet?
32. It's only 7:33 P.M.
33. Read Chapter 19.
34. Take the 4:30 bus.
35. Are there 57 books?
36. No, there are 157.
37. Meet me in 12 minutes.
38. 10 liters

■ If an item contains an incorrect abbreviation, rewrite it correctly. If it is already correct, write *correct.*

Example: Novem. third at 6 o'clock   *Nov. 3 at six o'clock*

39. Sat. at four-eighteen P.M.
40. Doc. J. M. Reilly
41. the 5:29 o'clock train
42. Mar. 14 at nine o'clock
43. Unicef meeting
44. M. F. Bidwell
45. 250 ft. 4 in.
46. 99 students
47. 5 m
48. Jun. 11
49. Apart. A
50. Seattle, WASH
51. Sun., Dec. 8, at 10 AM
52. Unit Twelve
53. I.B.M. in WY.
54. Presdt. James J Boardman
55. 187 sheets of paper
56. Sen. John J. Hocks

10 || Apostrophes (p. 324)

● Write each sentence. Add an apostrophe to each underlined word.

Example: We heard Mr. <u>Gosss</u> lecture on Europe.
We heard Mr. Goss's lecture on Europe.

1. <u>Ronas</u> report on the Industrial Revolution was interesting.
2. Other countries followed <u>Englands</u> lead in industry.
3. <u>Peoples</u> interest in freedom increased after 1700.
4. <u>Youre</u> going to report on that, <u>arent</u> you?
5. Please remember to write *and*<u>s</u> rather than <u>&s</u> in your report.
6. <u>Its</u> easier to read when you <u>dont</u> use symbols.
7. <u>Theyll</u> listen to two <u>students</u> reports each day.
8. <u>Didnt</u> you know that there are two <u>ss</u> in Russia?
9. In <u>Nicholass</u> report, he used <u>xs</u> to cross out words.

▲ Write each sentence, adding apostrophes where needed.

Example: Its true that our history is connected with Europes.
It's true that our history is connected with Europe's.

10. Youre going to write on the beginnings of the university.
11. Im writing my report on Europes languages.
12. Isnt it true that some countries have four or five languages?
13. Rosss report is on the history of Germany from 1930 to 1945.
14. Russias alphabet is Larrys subject.
15. Its different from ours, and hes including examples.
16. The Russians *r*s look like *p*s, and their *s*s look like *c*s.
17. Youll use **s for your footnotes, wont you?
18. All *and*s and *with*s should be spelled out, shouldnt they?

■ Write each sentence, adding apostrophes where needed.

Example: Thats an interesting fact about the worlds languages.
That's an interesting fact about the world's languages.

19. Spains main language and Italys are different, of course, but theyre related.
20. Youre writing a report on the subject, arent you?
21. Use *and*s instead of *&*s or +s in your report, please.
22. There are too many *I*s, *my*s, and *me*s in Boriss report.
23. Spaniards have *ñ*s and *ch*s in their alphabet, dont they?
24. Spanish also uses *el*s and *la*s where we use *the*s.
25. Hasnt our art been influenced by the Europeans art?
26. Italys great contribution began in 1300, and its art spread throughout Europe between 1400 and 1600.

11 | Hyphens, Dashes, and Parentheses (p. 326)

● Write the sentences, adding the punctuation in parentheses to the underlined parts.

Example: Chippendale <u>1718–1779</u> was a furniture designer.   (parentheses)

Chippendale *(1718–1779) was a furniture designer.*

1. Chippendale's <u>well designed</u> pieces are prized.   (hyphen)
2. Furniture <u>chairs, tables</u> can be works of art.   (dashes)
3. The golden age of English furniture <u>1714–1820</u> had other masters.   (parentheses)
4. Chippendale <u>probably the most famous</u> wrote a book.   (dashes)
5. His book gave <u>up to date</u> information on design.   (hyphens)
6. The word *information* is divided <u>in for ma tion.</u>   (hyphens)

▲ Write each sentence, adding the punctuation in parentheses.

Example: Tudor furniture 1500–1600 features large scale pieces.   (parentheses, hyphen)

Tudor furniture (1500–1600) features large-scale pieces.

7. Even the earliest furniture no one knows exactly when that was probably had decorations.   (dashes)
8. Ancient Egypt's New Kingdom 1570–1090 B.C. has given us examples of well designed furniture.   (parentheses, hyphen)
9. Symbols of strength and power lions' paws or oxen's hooves were often carved on furniture legs.   (parentheses)
10. A fifty page article in *Today* features furniture.   (hyphen)
11. Ten pages a significant amount show ancient Rome.   (dashes)
12. *Significant* is divided *sig nif i cant.*   (hyphens)

■ If a sentence has an error, rewrite it correctly. If a sentence is already correct, write *correct*.

Example: A well thought of furniture maker was Duncan Phyfe.

A well-thought-of furniture maker was Duncan Phyfe.

13. Duncan Phyfe 1768–1854 was a Scotland born colonial.
14. He brought his talents they were great to the New World.
15. Can there really be twenty eight pieces by Duncan Phyfe in that well presented furniture exhibit, the Governor Museum?
16. Machine made furniture became fashionable earlier than you might think as early as 1820, in fact.
17. How is *fashionable* divided, *fa-shion-able* or *fash-ion-able*?
18. The first real furniture factory was built in Michigan Grand Rapids and was the start of an important American industry.

Literature and Writing

A word is dead
When it is said,
　　Some say.
I say it just
Begins to live
　　That day.

Emily Dickinson

Persuasive Letter

Getting Ready How many letters do you write? We have grown used to picking up the telephone just to say hello. Letter-writing is not dead, however! With a letter no one can say, "But that's not what you said!" There they are, your written words! In this unit you will read a letter—a firm, persuasive letter— and write one of your own.

ACTIVITIES

Listening Listen while the poem on the opposite page is read. Do you think the poet is talking about the spoken word? the written word? both? When might words be considered dead? When might words take on a life of their own?

Speaking Look at the picture. Do you think the letter is one she just received or one that she is rereading? Have you ever received letters that you have kept and reread later? Have you ever read old letters—perhaps from someone you never knew? Share your experiences.

Writing Think of a problem that you have a solution for. In your journal, make notes about how you would persuade someone to use your solution.

LITERATURE

O Captain! My Captain!

By Walt Whitman

O Captain! my Captain! our fearful trip is done,
The ship has weathered every rack,* the prize we sought
   is won,
The port is near, the bells I hear, the people all exulting,
While follow eyes the steady keel, the vessel grim and
   daring;
   But O heart! heart! heart!
   O the bleeding drops of red,
      Where on the deck my Captain lies,
         Fallen cold and dead.

---

*rack: Here, the stress of a storm.

O Captain! my Captain! rise up and hear the bells;
Rise up—for you the flag is flung—for you the bugle trills,
For you bouquets and ribboned wreaths—for you the
    shores a-crowding,
For you they call, the swaying mass, their eager faces
    turning;
  Here Captain! dear father!
    This arm beneath your head!
      It is some dream that on the deck
        You've fallen cold and dead.

My Captain does not answer, his lips are pale and still,
My father does not feel my arm, he has no pulse nor will,
The ship is anchored safe and sound, its voyage closed and
    done,
From fearful trip the victor ship comes in with object
    won;
  Exult O shores! and ring O bells!
    But I with mournful tread
      Walk the deck my Captain lies,
        Fallen cold and dead.

Think and Discuss

1. A **symbol** is something that stands for something else.
   The captain, the ship, and the voyage in this poem are
   all symbols for real persons, things, and events. The
   poem was written at a dramatic time in American history. The terrible Civil War was ending, and President
   Lincoln had just been assassinated. Who, then, might
   the captain be? What does his ship represent? What
   was the voyage that was "closed and done"?

2. The **repetition** of sounds and words emphasizes certain
   words and feelings and adds to the musical quality of a
   poem. In this poem, words are repeated
   a. within the same line
   b. from one line to the next
   c. from one stanza to the next
   Find an example of each kind of repetition.

3. Notice that each stanza expresses both happiness and
   sadness. Find the words that show these emotions. How
   does this contrast fit the events of the time?

347

What does Abraham Lincoln propose to his stepbrother?

Lincoln's Reply

By Abraham Lincoln

Abraham Lincoln's stepbrother wrote to Lincoln asking for a loan. This was Lincoln's reply.

[Dec. 24, 1848]

Dear Johnston:

Your request for eighty dollars, I do not think it best to comply with now. At the various times when I have helped you a little, you have said to me, "We can get along very well now," but in a very short time I find you in the same difficulty again. Now this can only happen by some defect in your conduct. What that defect is, I think I know. You are not *lazy,* and still you *are* an *idler.* I doubt whether since I saw you, you have done a good whole day's work, in any one day. You do not very much dislike to work, and still you do not work much, merely because it does not seem to you that you could get much for it.

This habit of uselessly wasting time, is the whole difficulty; it is vastly important to you, and still more so to your children, that you should break this habit. It is more important to them, because they have longer to live, and can keep out of an idle habit before they are in it, easier than they can get out after they are in.

You are now in need of some ready money; and what I propose is, that you shall go to work, "tooth and nail," for somebody who will give you money for it.

Let father and your boys take charge of your things at home—prepare for a crop, and make the crop, and you go to work for the best money wages, or in discharge of any debt you owe, that you can get. And to secure you a fair reward for your labor, I now promise you that for every dollar you will, between this and the first of May, get for your own labor either in money or in your own indebtedness, I will then give you one other dollar.

By this, if you hire yourself at ten dollars a month, from me you will get ten more, making twenty dollars a month for your work. In this, I do not mean you shall go off to St. Louis, or the lead mines, or the gold mines, in California, but I mean for you to go at it for the best wages you can get close to home—in Coles County.

Now if you will do this, you will soon be out of debt, and what is better, you will have a habit that will keep you from getting in debt again. But if I should now clear you out, next year you will be just as deep in as ever. You say you would almost give your place in Heaven for $70 or $80. Then you value your place in Heaven very cheaply, for I am sure you can with the offer I make you get the seventy or eighty dollars for four or five months' work. You say if I furnish you the money you will deed me the land, and if you don't pay the money back, you will deliver possession——

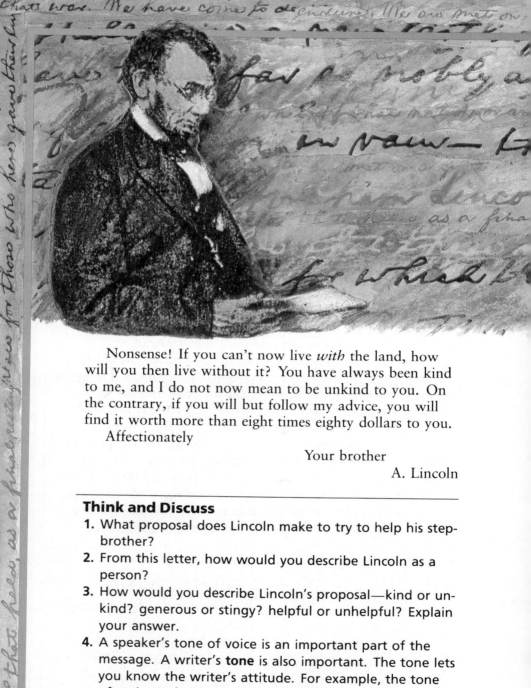

Nonsense! If you can't now live *with* the land, how will you then live without it? You have always been kind to me, and I do not now mean to be unkind to you. On the contrary, if you will but follow my advice, you will find it worth more than eight times eighty dollars to you.

Affectionately

Your brother

A. Lincoln

Think and Discuss

1. What proposal does Lincoln make to try to help his step-brother?

2. From this letter, how would you describe Lincoln as a person?

3. How would you describe Lincoln's proposal—kind or unkind? generous or stingy? helpful or unhelpful? Explain your answer.

4. A speaker's tone of voice is an important part of the message. A writer's **tone** is also important. The tone lets you know the writer's attitude. For example, the tone of a piece of writing can be angry or sympathetic, humorous or serious, admiring or resentful, formal or informal. How would you describe Lincoln's tone in this letter? Explain your answer.

RESPONDING TO LITERATURE

The Reading and Writing Connection

Personal response The poet Walt Whitman was deeply moved by Lincoln's assassination. When have you felt strongly about something that happened in the nation or in the world? Write about the event and your feelings.

Creative writing Imagine that you are Lincoln's stepbrother, and you are making your daily entry in your diary. You have just received Lincoln's letter. How do you feel about his proposal? Does it seem fair? Will you accept it? Write your reaction to the letter in your diary entry.

Creative Activities

Illustrate Imagine that you are one of the artists contributing to the book *Impressions of Poems.* You choose to illustrate "O Captain! My Captain!" In a drawing, a painting, or a collage, show an impression of the poem—express its feeling rather than the actual events.

Read aloud Work with two or three classmates. Experiment with dividing "O Captain! My Captain!" into parts for each of you to read aloud. Decide on the best division and then practice your parts. Emphasize the repeated words. Be prepared to read the poem to the class.

Vocabulary

Lincoln calls Johnston an idler. The dictionary meaning of *idle* is "doing nothing." An idle afternoon could be a slow, pleasant one. Lincoln, however, uses *idle* in a negative way, to mean "wasting time." Write sentences using these words first in a negative and then in a positive way: *habit, lazy, nonsense.*

Looking Ahead

A persuasive letter Later in this unit, you will write a persuasive letter. Look again at Lincoln's letter. What arguments did Lincoln use in it to persuade his stepbrother to accept his proposal?

VOCABULARY CONNECTION
Prefixes, Suffixes, Base Words, Word Roots

Many words are made up of different parts. A **prefix** is a word part added to the beginning of a base word or word root. A **suffix** is a word part added to the end of a **base word** or **word root**.

> . . . I now promise you that for every dollar you will . . . get for your own labor either in money or in your own **in**debted**ness**, I will then give you one other dollar.
>
> *from "Lincoln's Reply" by Abraham Lincoln*

When the prefix *in-* (in) and the suffix *-ness* (state of) are added to the base word *debted*, the new word means "in a debted state."

A **word root** has meaning, but it is always combined with at least one other word part.

Word	Prefix	Word Root	Suffix
dismissal	dis- "apart"	-mis-, (-mit-) "to send"	-al "action"
emotion	e- (ex-) "out"	-mot- "to move"	-ion "state, action"
composer	com- (con-) "together"	-pos- (-pon-) "to place"	-er (-or) "a doer"
resonance	re- "back, again"	-son- "to sound"	-ance (-ence) "condition"

If you know what the parts of a word mean, you can figure out the meanings of many unfamiliar words.

Vocabulary Practice

A. Find the meaning of each word by combining the meanings of its parts from the chart in this lesson. Write the meaning and check it in your dictionary.

1. commotion **2.** mission **3.** remittance **4.** expose

B. Choose four words that contain word roots from anywhere in this lesson. Write a sentence for each word.

Listening: Distinguishing Fact from Opinion

In his letter, Lincoln tried to persuade his brother to get a job. People often try to persuade you to do or to believe something. Sometimes they give you facts; other times they just offer their opinions. In order to make judgments about what you hear or read, you need to know the difference between fact and opinion.

Fact A **fact** is a statement that can be proved. You can prove it yourself, or you can use a reliable authority. Here are some examples of facts and how they can be proved.

STATEMENTS OF FACT	SOURCES OF PROOF
Abraham Lincoln was assassinated.	History book
Mr. Guthrie teaches math.	Experience
Jeff won the election.	Number of votes
Your table is fifty inches long.	Measurement

Laws and **observations** are also forms of fact. A law may be based on science (the law of gravity) or an established government authority (the speed limit). You can prove an observation, such as "Some stars are brighter than others," by pointing it out yourself or by testing it scientifically.

Opinion An **opinion** cannot be proved. It is based only on someone's thoughts, feelings, or judgment.

OPINIONS: Abraham Lincoln was a great man.
Mr. Guthrie works his students too hard.
Jeff is the better candidate.
You should have a larger table.

Some people may think that these statements are true; others may disagree. Listen for words like *good, nice, bad, wonderful,* and *should*. They can help you identify opinions.

Some opinions, however, are sounder than others. While they cannot be proved, they can be backed up with facts. Someone who tells you that Jeff is the better candidate can support this opinion by giving facts about Jeff's experience and past actions. Historians who believe Lincoln was great can support their opinion with facts about his achievements.

A **hypothesis** is a form of opinion. It is a reasonable guess made to explain an observation. Each hypothesis must be tested to make sure it is a good guess.

HYPOTHESES: Objects move only when they are pushed
            or pulled.
            The car stopped because it ran out of gas.
            Green food makes me sneeze.

You can test the last hypothesis by seeing if you really do sneeze whenever you eat something green. If you also sneeze when you eat something yellow, you may have to change your hypothesis.

A **theory** is also an opinion, but it is not a guess. A theory is an accepted explanation of a set of observations. A theory often includes several hypotheses that belong together and have been tested successfully. If a theory is good, it can be used to explain other things.

THEORIES: Heat results from the movement of tiny particles.
          All the forces of nature are interrelated.

Here are examples of some other kinds of opinions.

SPECULATIVE STATEMENT: Alison Packer is going to win the
                        seat in the state legislature.
VALUE JUDGMENT: She is the best candidate.
EXAGGERATION: Alison Packer will get billions of votes.
BELIEF: She will change the government as she
         has promised.

When you listen to someone—in a lecture, a commercial, an election campaign, or even just conversation—be aware of the difference between a fact and an opinion. Do not be persuaded by an opinion unless the speaker supports it with facts.

Prewriting Practice

A. Number your paper from 1–5. Listen carefully as your teacher reads a group of statements. Write *fact* or *opinion* next to the number of each statement. Circle the number of the statement that is a hypothesis.

B. Listen carefully to a radio or TV commercial and write down as many statements as you can remember. Read the statements to a small group of classmates. Discuss whether each is a fact or an opinion.

Thinking: Critical Thinking

In his letter, Lincoln denied his stepbrother's request for money and instead tried to persuade him to find work. Lincoln offered various arguments for his stepbrother to consider.

You too probably encounter many situations in which people or advertisements are trying to persuade you to do or to think something. How do you deal with those attempts? You learn to judge whether the information they offer is accurate and sound. In other words, you learn to **think critically**.

When you distinguished fact from opinion, you were practicing critical thinking. You will also have to think critically when you evaluate persuasion or plan a persuasive argument.

Guidelines for Critical Thinking

1. **Consider the accuracy and reliability of the information.**
   a. Has all of the information been presented? Is it accurate? Be sure to verify each fact.
   b. Does the information come from a qualified and reliable source? For example, a known Lincoln scholar is a better source of information about Lincoln than a reporter is. Beware of statements that begin with the words "the experts say" or "they say."

2. **Recognize contradictions.** Look for statements that do not agree with each other and cannot both be true.

   Poets spend all of their time observing and daydreaming. Walt Whitman was a printer, journalist, and hospital aide.

3. **Be alert for hasty generalizations and overgeneralizations.** These are general statements that are not backed up by sufficient facts. Watch for absolute words such as *all* or *always.*

   The poets in this book are romantic. Therefore, all poets are romantic.

4. **Recognize exaggeration.** Watch for statements that stretch the truth, that say something is more than it is.

   Walt Whitman is the world's greatest poet.

5. **Question assumptions.** Question statements that you are expected to accept without evidence.

   It is difficult to write poetry.

Think critically as you read this editorial. Each sentence after the topic sentence is flawed in its thinking.

> **(1)** Next week the town council votes on whether to erect a statue in honor of Abraham Lincoln in Lincoln Park.   **(2)** Let us be the first town in this region to commemorate an American president.   **(3)** Lincoln was not only the finest leader our country has ever known, but also as perfect a human being as the world can produce.   **(4)** All Americans admire his beliefs and his deeds.   **(5)** Council member Jay Daniels assures us that the sculptor selected for the job does fine work.   **(6)** The cost is reasonable for such a statue and can be funded comfortably from tax income.   **(7)** Furthermore, money to construct a park statue is money well spent.   **(8)** Do not let our fair town be outdone by Eastport, which three years ago erected a statue of John F. Kennedy.

- Which two statements are contradictory?
- Which statement is an exaggeration?
- Why is statement 4 not persuasive?
- How would you evaluate statement 7?
- Is Jay Daniels a qualified authority? Why or why not?
- Which statement needs facts to support its accuracy?

Prewriting Practice

A. Read the letter part below. Each statement is unsound in at least one respect. With a partner, use the guidelines to think critically about each statement. Jot down your thoughts.

   (1) Fourteen-year-olds are too immature to handle their own money. **(2)** You have wasted every cent you have earned, **(3)** just as all young teen-agers do. **(4)** You have created a sensible budget and stuck to it, and I am very proud of you. **(5)** In a recent editorial, the editor of the city paper declared that parents should take charge of their teen-agers' funds. **(6)** Indeed, figures show that more is saved when parents manage the money.

B. Read a newspaper editorial, and take notes on any unsound statements.
   Then discuss the editorial with a group of your classmates.

Composition Skills
Persuasive Letter

Writing Business Letters ☑

Abraham Lincoln's persuasive letter to his stepbrother discussed business, but it was not a **business letter.** It was written to someone Lincoln knew well, and the language and tone were informal. A business letter is often sent to someone the writer does not know personally. The language is formal, the tone polite, and the style direct.

HEADING	15 Walnut Street Decatur, IL 62521 September 8, 1990
	2 spaces
INSIDE ADDRESS	Poetry Society in America 15 Gramercy Park New York, NY 10003
	2 spaces
SALUTATION	Dear Sir or Madam: *colon*
BODY	*2 spaces* The enclosed poem, "Abe in Illinois," is my entry for your poetry contest.
	I understand that contestants must be between fourteen and sixteen. I won't turn fourteen for another month, but that fact alone should not prohibit my entering. I will probably be fourteen when the final judging takes place.
	2 spaces
	Thank you.
CLOSING	Yours truly,
SIGNATURE	*4 spaces→*Lucas Mutch Lucas Mutch
	2 spaces
	Enclosure

A business letter usually has at least one of these purposes: to order something, to ask for information, to complain about a product or service, to apply for a job, or to persuade someone to do something. Here are some rules for writing business letters.

Guidelines for Writing Business Letters

Content
1. Be formal and courteous.
2. Make your point briefly and directly.
3. Include all the information that the person receiving the letter will need.

Form
1. **Heading** The heading contains your address and the date. The placement of the heading varies, depending upon which letter style you use. In modified block style, you line up the heading at the center of the page. In block style you line up the heading at the left margin. (See the illustration on the next page.)
2. **Inside Address** Skip a line or leave space between the heading and the inside address. If you know the name and title of the person to whom you are writing, write this at the left margin. Then write the name of the company, if there is one, and the address to which the letter is being sent. (This is the same address that you will use on the envelope.)
3. **Salutation** Skip a line after the inside address. Use a colon after the salutation. If you do not know the name of the person to write to, use *Dear Sir or Madam* or use the company's name after *Dear.*
4. **Body** Skip a line and write your message. Indent each paragraph unless you are using block style.
5. **Complimentary Close** Skip a line after the body of the letter and line up the closing with the heading. Use a formal closing such as *Yours truly* or *Sincerely yours.* Capitalize only the first word and use a comma after it.
6. **Signature** Write your full name below the closing. Then print or type your name below the signature.
7. Write *Enclosure* or *Enc.* at the bottom left if you have enclosed something with the letter.

Compare these outlines of a letter written in modified block style and a letter written in block style.

Modified Block Style   **Block Style**

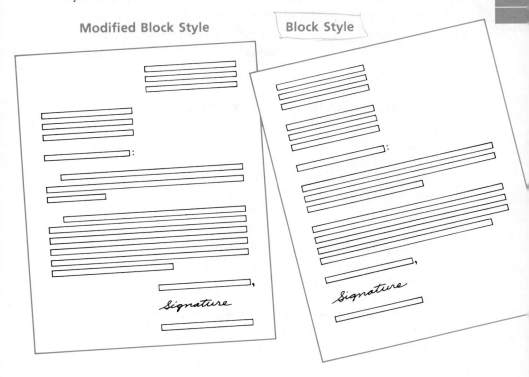

Prewriting Practice

Write a business letter for one situation below. Use your own name and address. Follow the guidelines given in this lesson. Choose either the block or modified block style.

1. Write to Ms. Edith Perkins, Editor of *Young Art* magazine, 354 Rainbow Circle, Topeka, KS 66607. Ask Ms. Perkins to consider your illustration to accompany the poem "O Captain! My Captain!" for publication in the magazine. Give two reasons why she should accept your drawing.

2. Write to Writewell Pens, Inc., 1945 Main Street, Portland, OR 97231. Persuade the company to send you a refund for a pen, model #224, that you bought at Jason's Bookstore a week ago for $5.50. The pen has been leaking.

3. Write to the National Singing Contest at 103 Central Avenue, Cincinnati, OH 45205. Request information on how to enter the contest.

The Grammar Connection

Capitalization and Punctuation: Envelopes

If you do not address envelopes for your letters correctly, your letters will never arrive. Both business letters and friendly letters have two addresses on the envelope. You write the return address—your own name and the address from the heading of your letter—in the upper left-hand corner. You write the mailing address—the same as the inside address of a business letter—in the center. Refer to Unit 9 for the correct capitalization, punctuation, and abbreviations of names and addresses.

Perhaps you have seen the word *Attention* with a name on a business envelope. If you are writing to a business in general but want to bring the letter to the attention of a particular person at the same time, you may wish to use this word. Here is a sample business envelope.

RETURN ADDRESS

Ms. Loretta Mutch
153 Guild St.
Dallas, TX 75074

Commonwealth Publishing
Attention Ms. Lynn Ostuni
832 Revere Ave.
Dallas, TX 75230

MAILING ADDRESS

Practice Using your own return address, address business envelopes to these places. Use abbreviations where possible. Capitalize and punctuate correctly.

1. Churchill laboratories, incorporated, post office box 663, charleston, south carolina 29402. Address the envelope to the attention of doctor david churchill, junior.

2. Ms. beth brink, the brink company, 1 lloyd street, room 12, little rock, arkansas 72207.

Stating and Supporting an Opinion ☑

When was the last time you tried to persuade someone of something? Did you succeed? If you did, then you probably supported your opinion well.

In his letter, Lincoln began by stating his opinion clearly.

> Your request for eighty dollars, I do not think it best to comply with now.
>
> *from "Lincoln's Reply" by Abraham Lincoln*

Lincoln gave the following reasons to support his opinion.

1. Though he had helped him before, his stepbrother had fallen into debt again quickly.
2. If he lent him money, his stepbrother would soon be in debt again.
3. If his stepbrother got a job and if Lincoln matched the wages, the stepbrother would soon be out of debt.
4. Doubled wages might help the stepbrother develop a good habit and keep out of debt.

When you write to persuade, first state your opinion clearly. Then support it with reasons and factual examples.

The following opinion is addressed to teen-agers.

OPINION: A good way for a teen to earn money is baby-sitting.

REASONS	EXAMPLES
Jobs are easy to get.	We get calls every weekend.
The work can be enjoyable.	Children say hilarious things.
You can study when the baby is asleep.	Dana baby-sits in the evenings and gets all her homework done.
You can choose the people you work for.	Marcos baby-sits only for neighbors he knows.
There are few other jobs for someone under sixteen.	Lisa tried to find a job for six months without luck.

After you have a list of supporting reasons and examples, ask yourself these questions about each reason.

1. **Is the reason suited to the audience?** *Young teen-agers often charge less* would make an impression on a parent, but it would not be a good reason to offer to a teen-ager.
2. **Is the reason directly related to the opinion?** *Some children are hard to care for* has to do with baby-sitting, but it does not support the opinion above.

3. **Is the reason provable?** Is it a fact rather than another opinion? *Teens are better baby sitters than adults* is not a fact. Do not use opinions to support opinions.

4. **Is the reason expressed in strong, clear language?** *The people can be nice* is a weak statement. Avoid words like *nice*, *bad*, *good*, and *sort of*. Use precise, exact words instead: *You will meet new people when you baby-sit.*

- Read again the reasons given in support of the opinion on page 361. Ask the four questions about each reason. Are the reasons all good ones?

Prewriting Practice

A. Work with a partner. Imagine that you are trying to persuade your school principal that your school should have a debating team. Test each reason below against the four guideline questions in this lesson. Write the number of each reason that would persuade your principal. Then suggest how to change the weak reasons into stronger arguments.

1. Debating is fun.
2. We are the only middle school in the state with more than 500 students that does not have a debating team.
3. A lot of students here want a debating team.
4. Many great debaters have turned their public speaking abilities into personal gold mines.
5. All sixty-two students in speech classes have signed a petition requesting a team.
6. Debating is as good as football or basketball.
7. Debating is an intellectual activity that requires quick thinking and an accurate grasp of the facts of an issue.
8. With four prize-winning debaters in the school, we already have the makings of a team.

B. Choose two of the opinions below. For each opinion name the audience you will try to persuade, such as a friend, parent, or teacher. Give reasons that support each opinion. Then give one example to support each reason.

1. Young people should start to earn money as early as possible.
2. The school day should end an hour earlier.
3. I should be allowed to do my homework after dinner instead of right after school.
4. All TV ads should appear only at the beginning or at the end of programs, not in the middle.

Using Persuasive Strategies ☑

Once you have an opinion and reasons that support it, how can you be really persuasive? You should become familiar with some **persuasive strategies**—techniques that people use to try to convince someone of something.

Here are some basic persuasive strategies.

1. **Offer a precedent** A *precedent* is a situation that may be used as an example in dealing with a similar situation later. Has someone you know behaved in a way that you might offer as an example? Then, to persuade your neighbor to let you baby-sit, you might say this.

   > My brother Andy baby-sat for the Cohens when he was my age, and they were very pleased with him.

2. **Appeal to fairness** You can try to appeal to your audience's sense of what is fair or not fair. Be sure, however, that you have a solid example to back up this reason. It is not enough simply to state that something is unfair. To persuade your neighbor that you are not too young to baby-sit, you might give this reason.

   > It is not fair to judge me on my age alone. I've had experience baby-sitting in my own family, and my parents agree that I am responsible and capable.

3. **Overcome objections** Think about likely objections when you plan your argument, and answer them before they are raised. If you think that your neighbor might object to your lack of formal baby-sitting experience, you might present this argument.

   > While it is true that I have never had a baby-sitting job outside my home before, I have often taken care of my two younger sisters.

4. **Explore consequences** What could happen if you succeed in persuading your audience? What are some of the possible results of your argument? List the favorable ones and overcome the unfavorable ones. Here is what you might tell your neighbor.

   > If I do a good job, then you will have found a reliable sitter who can work every afternoon. If I do not do a good job, then you can simply look for someone else.

Prewriting Practice

A. List the persuasive strategy being used in each argument.

OPINION: The Harris homestead should become a landmark and be preserved.

1. By making it a landmark, we can attract tourists.
2. Although it will be expensive to fix up this building, the increase in visitors will repay some of the cost.
3. The Gould mansion in the next town was fixed up two years ago, and it has become an important and popular site.
4. The Harris homestead is older and more important in history than the Gould mansion. The Gould mansion is already a landmark. Doesn't the Harris homestead have even more of a right to be a landmark?

B. Work with one or two classmates. Write four reasons that support each opinion—one reason for each of the four strategies described on page 363.

1. Young people should be allowed to work at age fourteen.
2. TV programs should be rated.

Shaping Your Argument ☑

How should you order your reasons and strategies? In a persuasive paragraph, arrange your reasons and examples in the order that will be most convincing to your audience, in their order of importance—from most to least important or from least to most important. You may find the least-to-most-important order most useful. This organization builds interest and leaves the reader with the strongest argument. The last reason read is the one most likely to be remembered.

The following paragraph is addressed to a teen-ager.

If you are a young teen-ager who wants to earn money, try baby-sitting. First of all, you can choose the people you work for. You can even decide to work only for people you know. Furthermore, taking care of a child is a serious responsibility, but you can have a good time doing it. Then, after the child is asleep, you can get your homework done. Most important, baby-sitting is one of the few ways someone under sixteen can earn money.

- What is the most important reason? Why is it most important? Where is it located in the paragraph?

A concluding statement that emphasizes or restates your opinion will also give your paragraph a strong ending. Read the next paragraph, which is addressed to a parent. Look for the order of reasons and the concluding statement.

> Hire a young teen-ager as a baby sitter, and both you and your child will be happy. Young teens are often available because there are few other things they can do to earn money. They also have more time than older teens because high-school pressures have not yet begun. Since they are just starting out, they often charge less. Furthermore, the children like them. According to all but one family in the Weston area, children take to young teens immediately. Most important, these teen-agers are young enough to enjoy children but old enough to be responsible. Next time you look for a baby sitter, look for a young teen.

- What order is followed in this paragraph? Why?
- How does the paragraph end? Why does it end this way?

Remember these points for organizing your persuasive paragraph.

1. Begin with a clear topic sentence that states your opinion.
2. Support it with reasons and examples appropriate to your audience.
3. Order your reasons from most to least important or from least to most important.
4. Add a summary statement to restate or emphasize your argument. Leave your reader with a strong impression.

Prewriting Practice

A. With a partner list reasons and examples to support the opinions below. Give the most important reason last.

1. The school should (should not) have a dress code.
2. Boys make better (worse) baby sitters than girls.

B. Look for a newspaper editorial or other piece of persuasive writing. List the supporting reasons that the writer used. In a small group, discuss the order used and what order you would use.

The Writing Process
How to Write a Persuasive Letter

Step 1: Prewriting—Choose a Topic

Kristen thought about some things she might persuade others to do. Then she made a list and considered each topic.

get Mr. Cox to extend lunchtime

convince class to hold cleanup party

write Sen. Bly to support endangered species bill

get Transit Authority to refund the fare for that awful bus ride

Kristen thought of some good arguments for this topic.

Her class was a difficult audience; they would probably object.

This would involve research. Kristen decided to write this at a later time.

She felt strongly about this and thought of specific arguments.

Kristen circled the last topic because she cared more about it than the first topic.

On Your Own

1. **Think and discuss** Make a list of things you would like to persuade someone to do. Use the Ideas page to help you. Discuss your ideas with a partner or small group.
2. **Choose** Ask yourself these questions about each topic.
   Does this issue really matter to me?
   Do I know or can I easily find out enough about this?
   Can I think of factual reasons and examples, not just feelings, to support my opinion?
   Circle the topic you decide to write about.
3. **Explore** To plan your argument, do one activity under "Exploring Your Topic" on the Ideas page.

Ideas for Getting Started

Choosing a Topic

Topic Ideas

Persuade someone that what he or she is asking you to do is not a good idea right now.

Persuade a friend or relative to take over your home chores while you work elsewhere for wages.

Convince your parents to let you see a particular movie.

Write to a company and request a refund on a faulty product.

Get an official to correct a safety hazard in your park or neighborhood.

Test Your Topics

Which topic should you choose? Chart your best bets. Follow this example.

Who: Mom and Dad

What: To raise my allowance $1.00.

Why: Costs have risen (give examples), and I have two new expenses (give amounts).

Possible Objections: Amount of my labor has not increased.

Argument: The value of my labor *has* increased because of inflation.

Exploring Your Topic

Chart It

Make a chart like the one in Test Your Topics, but more detailed. First brainstorm. Write *everything* you can think of about your argument. Don't stop to judge; just write. Then cross out reasons that are not relevant or specific. Order your reasons. Finally, choose persuasive strategies.

Talk About It

Have a partner take the role of the person who will receive your letter. Present your opinion and then your supporting reasons. Your partner should present possible objections, and you should present counter-arguments to those objections. Keep track of your new ideas.

Step 2: Write a First Draft

Kristen wrote her letter to the Transit Authority's public relations manager. She wanted her to refund her fare.

After she had organized her argument, she wrote her first draft. She did not worry about mistakes. She knew she would correct them later.

Kristen's first draft

> Dear Ms. Chung:
>
> Your billboards say, "Get your money's worth. Get their on time. Take the bus." I believed them. I took the bus ~~and~~ which cost me a dollar and was a bad experience.
>
> None of your claims were true. ~~It~~ The bus was dirty. The ads were tacky. The bus was crowded. I did not get their on time I did not get my money's worth.
>
> In all fareness you owe me a dollar.

Think and Discuss ☑
- Who is Kristen's audience? Is her language appropriate?
- What is Kristen's purpose? Is her opinion clear?
- What is the topic sentence of each paragraph?
- Which supporting reasons are not relevant? not specific?

On Your Own

1. **Think about purpose and audience** Answer these questions.
   To whom am I writing?
   What do I want my reader to do?
2. **Write** Write your first draft. Be sure to write clear topic sentences supported by relevant, specific reasons. Do not worry about errors, but write on every other line, leaving room for changes.

Step 3: Revise

Kristen read her first draft and decided she needed more specific reasons in the second paragraph. She took out one, changed one, and added one.

To test her argument, Kristen read Doug her letter.

Reading and responding

Doug: You give good reasons, but would it be clearer to tell her right off that you want a refund?

Kristen: I don't know. I'll have to think about it.

Doug: Do you think she'll bother with only a dollar?

Kristen: That is an objection she might make. Thanks for pointing that out to me.

Kristen decided to ask for her refund in her first paragraph. In the last paragraph, she dealt with the possible objection. Then she used a thesaurus to change a few vague words to more precise words.

The last part of Kristen's revision

> None of your claims were true. ~~It~~ The bus was dirty. *littered with trash. We could not get a seat because* ~~The ads were tacky.~~ The bus was *so* ˰crowded. I did not get their on time I did not
>
> get my money's worth.
> ¶ *You may not think a dollar is so much money,* ˰In all fareness you owe me a dollar.
> *but my allowance is only 5 dollars.*

Think and Discuss ☑

- How did Kristen improve her paragraph?
- What details did she add? Why?
- Which detail did she take out? Why?
- What persuasive strategies did Kristen use?

Revising checklist

☑ Have I stated my opinion clearly? Have I supported it?
☑ Does each paragraph have a topic sentence?
☑ What other reasons or examples could I add?
☑ Have I arranged my reasons in a convincing order?
☑ Have I made clear what I want the reader to do?
☐ What other persuasive strategies could I use?

1. Revise Make changes in your draft. Write between the lines. If you need to find exact words, use the thesaurus below or the one at the back of this book.

2. Have a conference Read your letter to a teacher or to a classmate.

WRITING
CONFERENCE

Ask your listener:	As you listen:
"Is my opinion clear?" "Which reasons are strongest?" "What details should be more specific? taken out?" "Is my request clear?" "Are you convinced?"	I must listen as if I were receiving the letter. Do I understand the request? Are the reasons clear? Am I convinced? How could the argument be improved?

3. Revise Consider your partner's suggestions. What else needs improving? Make revisions on your paper.

Thesaurus

argument *n.* case, position, stand, issue
conclusion *n.* end, close, termination, upshot, finish
consequence *n.* effect, result, outcome, solution
detail *n.* fact, evidence, reason, information, proof
example *n.* case, instance, illustration

objection *n.* opposition, doubt, misgiving
opinion *n.* belief, point of view, attitude, feeling, judgment
persuade *v.* convince, win over, influence
reason *n.* cause, grounds, basis, motive
therefore *adv.* thus, hence

Step 4: Proofread

Kristen added the heading, inside address, closing, and signature to her letter. Then she proofread her letter. She used a dictionary to check spellings, and she used proofreading marks to make changes.

The last part of Kristen's proofread letter

None of your claims were ~~were~~ *was* true. ~~It~~ The bus *littered with trash. We could not get a seat because* was ~~dirty. The ads were tacky.~~ The bus was *so* ~~crowded.~~ crowded. I did not get their *re* on time, I did not get my money's worth. ¶ *You may not think a dollar is so much money,* In all fareness you owe me a dollar. *but my allowance is only 5 dollars.* *five*

sincerely,

Kristen R. Gray

Kristen R. Gray

Think and Discuss

- What words and number did Kristen change? Why?
- What punctuation and capitalization did she add? Why?

On Your Own

1. Proofreading Practice Proofread this partial letter. Copy it over correctly. There are three spelling errors, three capitalization errors, two missing commas, two incorrectly written numbers, and two incorrect punctuation marks.

Dear sir or madam,

    I am writing to complane about your Television ads that show glamerous men driving cars recklessly. You brag that your cars go from zero to seventy mph in seconds a speed over the legal limit.

    Do your ads temp young people to drive dangerously and break the law. Yes they do.

2. **Proofreading Application** Use the Proofreading Checklist and the Grammar and Spelling Hints below to proofread your letter. Check your spellings in a dictionary. If you wish, use a colored pencil to make your corrections.

Proofreading Checklist	Proofreading Marks
Did I	⌐┬ Indent
☑ **1.** follow proper business letter form?	∧ Add
	⋏ Add a comma
☑ **2.** capitalize correctly?	⌄⌄ Add quotation marks
☑ **3.** punctuate properly?	⊙ Add a period
☑ **4.** use abbreviations and numbers correctly?	ℓ Take out
	≡ Capitalize
	/ Make a small letter
☑ **5.** spell all words correctly?	∿ Reverse the order

The Grammar/Spelling Connection

Grammar Hints
Remember these rules from Unit 9 when writing a letter.

- Use commas to separate the day from the year and the city from the state in a heading. *(April 4, 1987; Minneapolis, MN)*
- Use a comma after the greeting in a friendly letter and a colon after the greeting in a business letter. *(Dear Joan, Dear Dr. Little:)*
- Use a comma after the closing in both business and friendly letters. *(Sincerely, Love,)*

Spelling Hints
Remember these spelling principles.

- Capitalize proper nouns and proper adjectives. *(Sweden, Swedish; Olympia, Olympic)*
- Use periods in most abbreviations to show that letters have been left out. Do not use periods in acronyms (words that have been invented by using the first letters of words). *(C.O.D., P.O.; IOU, NASA, scuba)*
- Spell out numbers used with words. Use numerals for words used with symbols or abbreviations. *(five o'clock, two dollars; $10, 5 A.M.)*

Step 5: Publish

Kristen typed her letter, being careful to follow correct business letter form. She checked it to be sure she had made no mistakes and had put on the correct address. Then, on a business-sized envelope, Kristen typed Ms. Chung's address and her return address. She put her letter into the envelope, along with her bus ticket stub, and mailed it.

On Your Own

1. **Copy** Type or copy your letter very neatly.
2. **Check** Read your letter again to check for mistakes and omissions. Recheck the form of the letter.
3. **Share** Decide how you will share your letter. If you choose to mail it, have your teacher check it over first.

Ideas for Sharing

- Exchange letters with a classmate. Write answers to each other's letters, pretending you are the person to whom the letter was written.
- Make a file of sample business letters to be used as references for your class.
- Present your argument orally to the class. Let your classmates decide how the person receiving the letter would respond.
- Hold a debate, with one team taking the part of the letter writer and the other team taking the part of the recipient.

Literature and Creative Writing

In 1848 Lincoln's stepbrother wrote Lincoln for a loan of eighty dollars—a lot of money when ten dollars was a fair month's wage. Instead, the future President tried to persuade Johnston to seek a job, offering to match his wages.

You have already written a persuasive letter. Now use what you have learned about writing a persuasive letter to complete one or more of these activities.

1. **Ask for the moon.** Imagine that you could ask a favor of some important and powerful person. What favor would you ask? Would you want a crater on the moon named for you? Would you like to be an ambassador to an interesting country? Write to the person you choose, persuading him or her to grant you a favor.

2. **Consider me.** Is there something that you've always wanted to do if only you had the money? Would you like to study music? travel? open a special kind of hospital? Pretend you are writing to a committee who is choosing someone to receive a large amount of money. Persuade the committee that you should be chosen. Use a persuasive strategy.

3. **Save a place.** Think of a place that has some importance for you. Imagine that the place is now in danger of being destroyed. Write a letter asking that it be preserved. Be funny or serious, but above all be persuasive!

Remember these things ☑
- Use the correct form for your letter.
- Give reasons and examples to support your opinion.
- Use persuasive strategies.
- Arrange your reasons from least to most important.

Writing Across the Curriculum
Careers

What do you want to do when you leave school? Do you plan to go to college? enroll in a training program? get a job immediately? Whatever you do, you will probably have to write a letter of application. You will need to persuade someone to consider you because of your qualifications and interests.

Choose one or more of the following activities. Follow the business letter guidelines that you learned in this unit. Use persuasive strategies. Support your opinions with reasons and examples.

1. **Convince the personnel manager.** Imagine that you have found an ad for the perfect job, but the ad asks for someone with experience. You haven't had a real job in this area, but you know that you would be an excellent employee. Write a letter to persuade the manager. Be sure to include related experience, responsibilities, and interests.

Word Bank

applicant
responsibilities
training
references
interview
experience

2. **Persuade the admissions director.** Think of some further training you would like to have to get a job you want. Write a letter of application. Convince the director of the program to admit you.

3. **Apply for membership in a group.** Find a group, such as Future Teachers of America or 4-H, that does work related to your career interest. Write a letter to the leader of one of these groups, requesting membership. Persuade the person that you would be a good addition to the group. Talk about your belief in the group's ideals and work.

Anne enjoyed reading Lincoln's letter to his stepbrother. She had never thought about Lincoln as a person writing letters to family members. She had only thought about him as a President. She wanted to read letters by some of the other Presidents. At the library, she found *Theodore Roosevelt's Letters to His Children*. She decided to share this book by writing a letter about it to a friend. This is the letter Anne wrote.

1132 Oak Street
Dayton, Ohio 45449
Feb. 18, 1990

Dear Aaron,

    I have just read <u>Theodore Roosevelt's Letters to His Children</u>. You might think a whole book of letters from a father would be boring, but these are really interesting!

    In the book, there are letters to Ted, Archie, Quentin, Edith, Ethel, and Kermit. Their father seemed to know what each one was doing and what each one liked the most. When they were children, he wrote them letters with lots of little pictures in them. As they grew up, he wrote more adult letters. He wrote about everything from meeting royalty to rescuing kittens. He sounds great! Did you ever think of a President climbing trees with his kids?

    If you read this book, you might even decide to write a letter to a friend. I know it's given me some good ideas!

Your friend,

Anne

Think and Discuss
- What did you learn about the book from this letter?
- What did you learn about the people in the book?
- Who is the author of the book?

Share Your Book

Write a Persuasive Letter About a Book

1. Choose a book that you really like. Whom could you write to that would really enjoy the book? What would this person particularly like about it? Do you want to write about the illustrations in this book? Decide which parts of the book you will highlight for your audience.

2. Write your letter in correct friendly letter form. Be sure to include the name of the book and the author. Try to persuade your friend that this is a book that should not be missed!

3. Share your letter with your classmates. Then mail the letter to your friend. Find out if your enthusiasm is catching!

Other Activities

- Write a letter to a young child that you know. Describe a book that you used to like when you were the same age. You might draw pictures or paste pictures about the story in the margins of the letter. Mail the letter.

- Write to the author or illustrator of your book. Tell what you think about some part of the book or the artwork. If you have any criticism, offer it tactfully. If you really liked the book, you might urge the author or illustrator to write or illustrate more.

- Start a collection of interesting letters and postcards. They may be from family or friends, copies of old family letters, letters written by famous people, or letters by book characters that you find as you read. Use all or some of these letters and postcards along with photographs or drawings to make an eye-catching collage.

 # The Book Nook

Abe Lincoln Grows Up	Dear Bess
by Carl Sandburg	*by Harry Truman*
An account of Lincoln as a boy that helps you see the real man behind the statues and speeches.	Letters from President Truman to his wife, both before and after their marriage.

Who would succeed in the world should be wise in the use of pronouns. Utter the *you* twenty times, where you once utter the *I*.

John Milton Hay
"Distichs, no. 13"

Pronouns

Getting Ready Pronouns are useful little words. It would be tiresome to constantly repeat people's names every time you spoke of them. It would be even sillier to have to call yourself by name rather than say *I* or *me*. Of course, it is important to be perfectly clear about just which *he, she,* or *it* you are talking about! In this unit you will learn more about how to use pronouns precisely.

ACTIVITIES

Listening Listen while the words of wisdom on the facing page are read. What exactly does the writer mean? Try to put this message into your own words.

Speaking Look at the picture. What might the woman in the picture be saying to the man? What sort of tone do you think she is using?

Writing In your journal, make up a dialogue between the two people in this picture.

1 || Personal and Possessive Pronouns

Personal Pronouns

You can replace nouns with **pronouns** to make your speaking and writing flow more smoothly.

NOUNS: Don and *Don's* brother like books. *The brothers* read whenever *the brothers'* schedules leave *the brothers* some time.

PRONOUNS: Don and his brother like books. They read whenever their schedules leave them some time.

Pronouns such as *they* and *them* are called **personal pronouns**. Personal pronouns have different forms to show person, number, and gender.

Personal pronouns show **person**. A pronoun in the **first person** shows who is speaking. A pronoun in the **second person** shows who is being spoken to. A pronoun in the **third person** shows who or what is being spoken about.

FIRST PERSON: I want to go to the library tomorrow.

SECOND PERSON: Do you have any books to return?

THIRD PERSON: She returned them yesterday.

Personal pronouns also show **number**. **Singular** pronouns refer to one person or thing. **Plural** pronouns refer to more than one.

SINGULAR: He chose three books.

PLURAL: They worked on the class report.

Third person singular pronouns show **gender**. *She* and *her* are **feminine**. *He* and *him* are **masculine**. *It* is **neuter**.

FEMININE: Ask Annie what she thinks about that topic.

MASCULINE: Rob says he found a useful book.

NEUTER: The book has two chapters about it.

Personal Pronouns		
Person	**Singular**	**Plural**
First	I, me	we, us
Second	you	you
Third	he, him, she, her, it	they, them

Guided Practice What are the person and number of each underlined pronoun? Is each third person singular pronoun masculine, feminine, or neuter?

Example: <u>He</u> has a part-time job. *third singular masculine*

1. Sharon and <u>I</u> work with <u>him</u>.
2. <u>We</u> collect used paper on Saturdays.
3. Do all of <u>you</u> know that paper is a valuable product?
4. When <u>it</u> is recycled, energy and trees are saved.
5. If people knew that, <u>they</u> wouldn't throw paper away.

Possessive Pronouns

You have learned that possessive nouns show ownership. You can use **possessive pronouns** to replace possessive nouns.

<u>Ben's</u> book is a biography.   His book is a biography.

Possessive Pronouns		
Person	**Singular**	**Plural**
First	my, mine	our, ours
Second	your, yours	your, yours
Third	his, her, hers, its	their, theirs

Most possessive pronouns have two forms for each person. One form describes a noun, as an adjective does. Use *my*, *your*, *his*, *her*, *its*, *our*, and *their* before nouns. The other form replaces a noun. The pronouns *mine*, *yours*, *his*, *hers*, *ours*, and *theirs* are used alone.

USED BEFORE A NOUN

That book is not my book.

That was her magazine.

USED ALONE

That book is not mine.

The magazine was hers.

Do not confuse possessive pronouns and contractions. A possessive pronoun never has an apostrophe.

The book has lost its cover.

Your book is broken.

It's coming apart.

You're going to repair it.

POSSESSIVE PRONOUNS

your

its

their

theirs

CONTRACTIONS

you're (you are)

it's (it is)

they're (they are)

there's (there is)

Guided Practice

A. What possessive pronoun completes each sentence pair?

Example: She and he read the bestseller. It is _____ book. *their*

6. She and he bought a new book. It is _____.
7. That poem is by Emily Dickinson. It is _____ poem.
8. That poem is by Emily Dickinson. The poem is _____.
9. This one is by Robert Frost. The poem is _____.

B. What is the correct form to complete each sentence?

Example: (They're, Their) letters are lengthy. *Their*

10. Can this possibly be (you're, your) signature?
11. The envelope is missing (it's, its) contents.
12. Have they picked up (they're, their) mail yet?

Summing up

▶ A **pronoun** is used to replace a noun.
▶ **Personal pronouns** have different forms to show person, number, and gender.
▶ A **possessive pronoun** can replace a possessive noun.

Independent Practice

A. Write the correct pronoun for each sentence pair.

Example: The Library of Congress belongs to us. It is _____. *ours*

13. At first the Library of Congress was only for lawmakers. It was _____.
14. In 1812 we lost the library. _____ nation's library burned.
15. Thomas Jefferson helped. He sold _____ books.
16. There were seven thousand items. _____ filled the library.

B. Write the form that correctly completes each sentence.

Example: The library hall is famous. (It's, Its) marble. *It's*

17. (You're, Your) library is the largest in the West.
18. (It's, Its) collections grow by a million a year.
19. Three Presidents have given it (their, they're) names.
20. (They're, Their) Jefferson, Adams, and Madison.

Writing Application: A Persuasive Letter Write a letter in which you try to convince a friend that recycling is important and fun. Use at least five pronouns from this lesson.

 For Extra Practice, see p. 408.

2 | Pronoun Antecedents

Agreement with Antecedents

You know that a pronoun takes the place of a noun.

<u>Don</u> spoke to the audience. He read the news.

The noun that the pronoun replaces is called its antecedent. The prefix *ante-* means "before," and the root *-ced-* means "go." An **antecedent** usually *goes before* a pronoun and names the person, place, or thing to which the pronoun refers. Sometimes the antecedent is in an earlier sentence.

The radio is old, but it works well.

Lucas listened to his radio.

The speakers should be on the shelf. Are they there?

The records were left uncovered. Are they dusty?

The antecedent does not always go before the pronoun. Sometimes the antecedent comes after the pronoun.

Although she was late, the announcer walked slowly.

The antecedent of one pronoun may be another pronoun.

By seven o'clock, I had turned off my radio.

A pronoun must always agree with its antecedent in number and in person. A pronoun that is third person singular must agree with its antecedent in gender as well.

THIRD PERSON SINGULAR

MASCULINE: Keith finished his work.

FEMININE: Evelyn completed her assignment too.

NEUTER: The report is in its folder.

When the antecedent is two or more nouns joined by *and,* use a plural pronoun.

James and Clark will give their report next week.

When the antecedent is two or more nouns joined by *or,* use a pronoun that agrees with the noun nearest the pronoun.

SINGULAR: Did Leon or Roy forget his cue?

PLURAL: The sportscaster or the reviewers will give their reports on the game.

Guided Practice What is the correct pronoun in each sentence? What is its antecedent?

Example: In (his, her) report, Sharon told about funny errors.
her   Sharon

1. She or Mary is writing about William Spooner in (her, their) report for class this week.
2. We owe Spooner a debt. He gave (our, their) vocabulary a word.
3. Escorting a lady to her seat, Spooner said, "Let me sew you to (her, your) sheet."
4. This was (his, her) most famous "spoonerism."
5. Don't laugh! A tongue-twister may play (its, their) tricks on you some day!
6. Lucy or the twins will give (her, their) report on language in English class next week.

Clear Antecedents

You can use pronouns to make your writing more interesting and smooth. However, you must make sure that the pronouns you use have clear antecedents.

UNCLEAR: They say that trash can be a source of energy.
They present a lot of ads on radio.
It says that liftoff will be at dawn tomorrow.
You can learn from some TV shows.

The sentences above contain pronouns with unclear antecedents. Who are *they, it,* and *you?* Try to avoid writing or saying sentences like these. Use nouns or different wording instead.

CLEAR: Experts say that trash can be used as a source of energy.
Sponsors present a lot of ads on radio.
The newspaper says that liftoff will be at dawn tomorrow.
People can learn from some TV shows.

Be sure also that there is only one clear antecedent for each pronoun that you use.

UNCLEAR: Dan interviewed Greg when he was in town.
(Was Dan or Greg in town?)
CLEAR: Dan interviewed Greg when Dan was in town.
Dan interviewed Greg when Greg was in town.
When Dan was in town, he interviewed Greg.

Guided Practice How would you correct the unclear pronoun antecedents in these sentences?

Example: They say good headlines are hard to write.
Reporters say good headlines are hard to write.

7. They say that there is really only one main rule.
8. They must tell a story accurately.
9. It should not, however, tell the whole story.
10. You should want to read past the headline.
11. If a story has too long a headline, it spoils it.

Summing up

▶ An **antecedent** is a noun or pronoun to which a pronoun refers.
▶ A pronoun must agree with its antecedent in person, number, and gender.

Independent Practice

A. Write each sentence, using the correct pronoun. Underline its antecedent.

Example: A newspaper rarely raises (its, their) price.
A newspaper rarely raises its price.

12. How do newspapers get (their, its) money?
13. (They, You) get money from ads and daily sales.
14. My brother and I enjoy reading the daily paper. (He, We) would like to be reporters.
15. In (his, their) dreams, my brother writes about world events.
16. I think (our, my) specialty would be sports.

B. Rewrite the following sentences correctly and clearly.

Example: You can see a variety of stories in the papers.
Newspapers have a variety of stories.

17. Beat reporters cover your everyday news stories.
18. They can be very exciting or humdrum.
19. They interview famous people when they are in town.
20. It may take an investigative reporter weeks for one story.

Writing Application: A Newspaper Article Imagine that you are a reporter or a reviewer for a newspaper. Write a paragraph about a news event, a concert, or a movie. Use pronouns and be sure that they have clear antecedents.

For Extra Practice, see p. 409.   Pronoun Antecedents **385**

3 | Pronoun Case

Subject and Object Pronouns

You have learned that pronouns replace nouns and that nouns can be used as subjects or objects in a sentence. Pronouns have different forms, called **cases**, that show whether they are being used as subjects or as objects.

Pronouns used as subjects or as predicate pronouns, which replace predicate nouns, are called **subject pronouns**. They are in the **nominative case**.

> I love art.

Pronouns used as direct or indirect objects are called **object pronouns**. They are in the **objective case**.

> Art fascinates me.

Nominative case		
I	we	We admired Cara's artwork.
you	you	The artist was she.
he, she, it	they	
Objective case		
me	us	Cara called us.
you	you	She showed us her work.
him, her, it	them	

Notice that the pronouns *you* and *it* are the same in the nominative and objective cases.

Guided Practice Is each underlined word or phrase used as a subject, a predicate noun, a direct object, or an indirect object? What pronoun can replace each word or phrase?

Example: Yesterday <u>the class and I</u> studied a painting.   *subject   we*

1. The <u>painting</u> was called *Children's Games.*
2. Mr. Santoro gave <u>the class and me</u> an assignment.
3. Find ten familiar games. Will someone list <u>the games</u>?
4. Tell <u>Janice</u> the games one at a time, please.
5. <u>Janice</u> will write as fast as possible. Go!
6. The painter's initials are P. B. Can you name <u>the man</u>?
7. Was it Pieter Brueghel? Yes, it was <u>Pieter Brueghel.</u>

Pronouns in Compounds

Many sentences have compound subjects or objects.

Tracy and I will be at the museum.   Will you join Tracy and me?

When a pronoun is part of a compound subject or a compound object, be sure to use a pronoun in the correct case.

Pronouns in Compound Sentence Parts	
Nominative Case	
Compound subject	Tom and she design the sets.
	He and she design the sets.
Compound predicate noun	The designers are Tom and she.
or predicate pronoun	The designers are he and she.
Objective Case	
Compound direct object	The artist drew Len and her.
	The artist drew him and her.
Compound indirect	We gave Sue and him a sketch.
object	We gave her and him a sketch.

If you are not sure which case to use in these compounds, say the sentence with the pronoun alone.

William and (she, her) painted in New York.
She painted in New York.
William and she painted in New York.

(He, Him) and (she, her) lived there.
He lived there. She lived there.
He and she lived there.

Please show (he, him) and (I, me) the art.
Please show him the art. Please show me the art.
Please show him and me the art.

Guided Practice What is the correct pronoun form?

Example: Sue and (I, me) liked the Brueghel painting.   *I*

8. (He, Him) and his relatives were artists.
9. Five Brueghels created important artworks. Their admirers include you and (I, me).
10. We studied Pieter the Elder. (He, Him) and two of his sons are the most famous.
11. Still popular are Jan the Elder, Pieter the Younger, and (he, him).
12. Mr. Santoro assigned Sue and (I, me) to write another report on this famous family next week.

> ▶ Subject pronouns are in the **nominative case**.
> ▶ Use the nominative case for pronouns used as subjects and predicate pronouns.
> ▶ Object pronouns are in the **objective case**.
> ▶ Use the objective case for pronouns used as direct objects and indirect objects.

Independent Practice Write the pronoun form that correctly completes each sentence. Label it *nominative* or *objective*.

Example: Tell me again about Brueghel. Who was (he, him)?
    he **nominative**

13. By "Brueghel" I mean Pieter the Elder. The class liked (he, him) best.

14. The Brueghel born in 1525 was (he, him).

15. His sons, grandsons, and (he, him) all became well-known artists.

16. Didn't Mr. Santoro describe (they, them) to the class?

17. Yes, but wasn't (he, him) kidding?

18. No, (they, them) were real people who painted in Europe in the 1500s and the 1600s.

19. Believe (I, me). There were two Pieters, two Jans, and an Ambrose.

20. How will (we, us) remember which Brueghel is which?

21. You and (I, me) can use the titles "Elder" and "Younger" as a way to remember.

22. Can't you give (we, us) more information than that?

23. Ask Sue and Tim. (She, Her) and (he, him) made a chart.

24. (They, Them) have really worked hard on this project.

25. The subject interests (they, them).

26. I hope the topic you and (I, me) receive will interest (we, us)!

Writing Application: A Description Write a paragraph that describes the people in a painting or other picture from this book. Use at least five pronouns in the nominative and objective cases in your description. Label the pronouns *nominative* or *objective*.

 For Extra Practice, see p. 410.

4 || Interrogative Pronouns

When you ask questions, you use another kind of pronoun.

Who said that?   What did he say?   Which is it?

A pronoun that is used to form a question is called an **interrogative pronoun.** The antecedents of interrogative pronouns are the words that answer the questions.

Who said that? Holmes said that.

What did he say? He said "Aha!"

Which do you mean? I mean the mystery.

If the words *which* and *what* come directly before nouns, they act as adjectives, not as pronouns. If *which* and *what* stand alone, they act as pronouns.

ADJECTIVES: Which picture do you like? What plan will you follow?
PRONOUNS: Which do you like? What is your plan?

The interrogative pronoun *who* has different forms to reflect case depending on how you use it in a sentence.

NOMINATIVE CASE: who   *(subject pronoun)*
OBJECTIVE CASE: whom   *(object pronoun)*

Who knows the story? He knows.

To whom did you give a book? I gave a book to her.

To help you decide whether to use *who* or *whom*, turn the question into a statement. Substitute *he* or *she* for *who*, and use *him* or *her* in place of *whom* to see which case is correct.

QUESTION: (Who, Whom) will we pick?
STATEMENT: We will pick (who, whom). We will pick (he, him).

The objective case is correct here, so *whom* should be used.

When the interrogative pronoun shows possession, use *whose*, the possessive form of *who*. Do not confuse the pronoun *whose* and the contraction *who's*, which sound alike. *Who's* means "who is."

POSSESSIVE PRONOUN: Whose are these glasses?
CONTRACTION: Who's at the door?

Guided Practice Which pronoun or contraction is correct?

Example: (Who, Whom) was Franklin W. Dixon?   *Who*

1. (Who, Whom) did Carolyn Keene create?
2. (Who, Whom) is her most important character?
3. (What, Who's) is the most popular mystery series?
4. (Which, Whom) is it—the one about Nancy Drew or the one with the Hardy boys?
5. (Who, Whom) is the best teen-age investigator?
6. (Who, Which) do you prefer?
7. (Who, Whom) does Paul like the best?
8. (Who's, Whose) going to solve the mystery first?
9. (Whose, Who's) are these books?
10. (Who, Whom) should we ask?

Summing up

- Interrogative pronouns like *who, which, what, whom,* and *whose* ask questions.
- Use *who* as a subject, *whom* as an object, and *whose* as a possessive.
- Do not confuse the pronoun *whose* with the contraction *who's.*

Independent Practice Write the form of the pronoun in parentheses that correctly completes each sentence.

Example: (Who's, Whose) your favorite mystery character?   *Who's*

11. (Who, Whom) decided to put on this play?
12. (Who, Whom) did he meet at the theater?
13. (Who's, Whose) trying out for the female lead?
14. (Who, Whom) recommended her for this part?
15. (Who, Whom) had you nominated?
16. (Who, Whom) did the director choose?
17. (Who's, Whose) going to put up the posters?
18. (Who, Whom) will make the costumes?
19. (Who, Whom) will be the next star of the show?
20. (Who's, Whose) name will be in the newspaper article?

Writing Application: An Interview Write at least five questions to use in interviewing your classmates about their favorite mysteries. Use interrogative pronouns.

   For Extra Practice, see p. 411.

5 | Demonstrative Pronouns

You can use another kind of pronoun to point out persons, places, things, or ideas.

This is a weasel.   Those are its babies.

A pronoun that points out something is called a **demonstrative pronoun.**

A demonstrative pronoun must agree in number with the noun it points out or with its antecedent.

SINGULAR: This is a mink.

That is a polecat.

PLURAL: These are minks.

Those are polecats.

Use *this* and *these* to point to things nearby. Use *that* and *those* to point to things farther away.

This is a white weasel.
These are weasels with long tails.
That looks like a weasel over there.
Those are probably weasels with short tails.

Like *which* and *what,* the words *this, that, these,* and *those* may function as adjectives or as pronouns in a sentence. When they come directly before a noun, they are demonstrative adjectives. When they stand alone, they are demonstrative pronouns.

DEMONSTRATIVE ADJECTIVE

I don't like this animal.   These animals are small.

DEMONSTRATIVE PRONOUN

I don't like this.   These are small.

You should avoid expressions like *this here* and *that there.* *This* already means "the one here," and *that* already means "the one there."

This is a beaver.   (*not* This here)
That is a cute animal.   (*not* That there)
These are not mice.   (*not* These here)
Those must be moles.   (*not* Those there)

Guided Practice Which words are correct in the following sentences? Which nouns do the words refer to?

Example: (This, These) is a giraffe with a sleek, long neck.
This   giraffe

1. (These, These here) are my favorite animals.
2. (That, Those) are the zebras we saw yesterday.
3. (That, That there) is a beautiful old camel.
4. (This, That) must be a water buffalo down there.
5. (These, Those) are lions over there.

Summing up

▶ A **demonstrative pronoun** points out something.
▶ *This* and *that* refer to singular nouns or pronouns.
▶ *These* and *those* refer to plural nouns or pronouns.
▶ *This* and *these* point out things that are close.
▶ *That* and *those* point out things that are farther away.

Independent Practice

A. Write each sentence, using the correct demonstrative pronoun. Underline the noun it points out.

Example: (This, That) is a monkey in the far corner.
That is a <u>monkey</u> in the far corner.

6. Is (this, that) its baby right here?
7. (This, These) could be chimps.
8. (This, These) must be the mother chimpanzee.
9. (That, Those) cannot be real gorillas.
10. (These, Those) must be baboons in the next room.

B. Rewrite each sentence correctly. Underline the demonstrative pronoun.

Example: I prefer that there.   *I prefer <u>that</u>.*

11. This must be your favorite animals.
12. Do you like this here or that?
13. These here are the animals I like best.
14. That is my favorite birds in the tree over there.

Writing Application: A Photo Essay Imagine that you are a photojournalist on assignment in a zoo. Write captions for four or more pictures, using demonstrative pronouns.

 For Extra Practice, see p. 412.

USAGE

6 || Indefinite Pronouns

Kinds of Indefinite Pronouns

Words like *someone* and *something* refer to a person or thing that is not identified. Such pronouns are called **indefinite pronouns**.

Someone is arriving.   Something delayed the flight.

An indefinite pronoun that refers to only one person or thing is singular. An indefinite pronoun that refers to more than one is plural.

sing.   pl.
Everyone enjoys travel.   Many of us love to fly.

Some indefinite pronouns can be either singular or plural, depending on what they refer to in a sentence.

sing.   pl.
All of the fuel is used.   All of the flights are canceled.

Singular			Plural	Either
another	everybody	nothing	both	all
anybody	everyone	other	few	any
anyone	everything	one	many	most
anything	neither	somebody	ones	none
each	nobody	someone	others	some
either	no one	something	several	

Some words that can function as indefinite pronouns can also act as adjectives modifying nouns.

ADJECTIVE: Each plane is ready.
INDEFINITE PRONOUN: Each of the planes is ready.

Guided Practice Identify each indefinite pronoun. Is it singular or plural? Not every sentence has an indefinite pronoun.

Example: Many of us want to travel, but not everyone can.
        Many **plural**   *everyone* **singular**

1. Last year some of the boys and girls in Mrs. Leyden's class traveled with her to the Netherlands.
2. Not everyone, however, took all of the tours that were planned for each day.
3. Naturally, no one wanted to miss the trip to a chocolate factory.

4. Many of us spent hours traveling up and down the narrow canals of Amsterdam.
5. The trip had something to offer for everyone.
6. One day several of us visited the pottery factory at Delft, where we saw several of the crafts workers hand-painting some vases.
7. Did you know that all of western Holland is below sea level and that *nether* means "low"?
8. Both Mrs. Leyden and her daughter were born in The Hague, but neither of them had much time to visit relatives.
9. Some of the most magnificent flowers anybody had ever seen appeared in the flower exhibit in Dam Square in Amsterdam.
10. None of us will ever forget the Anne Frank House, where Anne's family and several friends hid for two years.

Agreement with Indefinite Pronouns

You know that verbs must agree with their subjects in number. When an indefinite pronoun is the subject, the verb must agree with it.

SINGULAR: Someone is traveling to China.

PLURAL: Several in this row have tickets to London.

The chart on the preceding page will help you remember whether an indefinite pronoun is singular or plural. Some pronouns, however, can be either singular or plural. The meaning of the pronoun in the sentence determines its number. The words that follow the pronoun will tell you whether the meaning is singular or plural. If the pronoun refers to something that cannot be counted, it is singular.

SINGULAR: Most of the food has been eaten.

PLURAL: Most of the passengers have finished their meals.

In the first sentence, *most* refers to a single, uncountable amount of food. Therefore, *most* has a singular meaning here. In the second sentence, *most* refers to several passengers. In this case, then, *most* has a plural meaning.

You have also learned that pronouns and their antecedents must agree in number. When an indefinite pronoun is the antecedent of a personal pronoun, the personal pronoun must agree with it.

SINGULAR: Everything has been put in its place.

PLURAL: Both have been put in their places.

Most singular indefinite pronouns can refer to either males or females. There is no agreement problem, however, if the gender is made clear by other words in the sentence.

> Each of the two women raised <u>her</u> hand.
> Neither of the brothers has packed <u>his</u> bags.

When the gender is not clear, try to avoid awkward constructions. Whenever possible, use plural pronouns instead.

> AWKWARD: Everyone on the plane had his or her luggage.
> BETTER: All on the plane had their luggage.

Remember that the words *everyone* and *everybody* are singular indefinite pronouns. Do not use the personal pronoun *their* with *everyone*.

Guided Practice Which word in parentheses is correct?

Example: All of the work (is, are) completed. *is*

11. None of us (has, have) been to the museum, so some of us (is, are) going one day while others (is, are) going the next.
12. Everybody (want, wants) to pack (his or her, their) suitcases before the last day of the trip.
13. All of our luggage (has, have) grown smaller since we arrived!
14. Each of the men (is, are) stopping in Frankfurt, Germany, on the way to (his, their) destination.
15. Both of the customs officials (has, have) finished checking most of the passengers.
16. (Has, have) all of them brought (his or her, their) passports?
17. All of the jobs (is, are) done.
18. None of the tickets (has, have) been picked up yet.
19. Everybody on the overseas flight (was, were) delayed.
20. Few in the last hour (was, were) able to land.
21. Many in the room could not find (his, their) bags.

Summing up

- An **indefinite pronoun** does not refer to a specific person or thing.
- Verbs must agree in number with indefinite pronouns used as subjects. Pronouns must agree with indefinite pronouns used as antecedents.

Independent Practice

A. Write each sentence. Underline each indefinite pronoun and label it *singular* or *plural*.

Example: Everyone reported on several of the books.
everyone **singular**   *several* **plural**

22. Have all of you read *Hans Brinker, or The Silver Skates*, which is one of my favorite books?
23. Neither of us remembered to bring some refreshments for the book report party.
24. Everyone did some research, but no one had spent a lot of time on it.
25. Nevertheless, most of us participated in the discussion and several shared original artwork.

B. Write the sentences, using the correct form of the words in parentheses.

Example: Each of the men has picked up (his, their) luggage.
Each of the men has picked up his luggage.

26. All of the suitcases (has, have) been claimed.
27. None of the trunks (was, were) damaged.
28. One of the girls left (her, their) skis behind.
29. Most of the children (is, are) on the bus.
30. Many of their parents (is, are) ready too.
31. Neither of the girls has found (her, their) hat.
32. (Do, Does) both of the bats belong to you?
33. Some of the suitcases have stains on (it, them).
34. All of the oil (has, have) been removed now.
35. Some of the boys have lost (his, their) skates.
36. Has either of the men used (his, their) ticket?
37. Few in the crowd have received (his, their) passports.
38. Everyone (want, wants) to return to Europe, but few (has, have) the money to do that soon.
39. On the next trip, some (plan, plans) to visit other countries.
40. (Has, Have) either of you told all the boys (his, their) seat assignments?

Writing Application: A Survey Ask several friends to give you their opinions about air travel. You might ask how often they have flown, what they like or dislike about airports, whether they plan to fly again soon, and so on. Write a paragraph that compares their opinions, using at least five indefinite pronouns from the chart.

For Extra Practice, see p. 413.

7 | Reflexive and Intensive Pronouns

You often use pronouns that end in *-self* or *-selves*. These forms are either reflexive pronouns or intensive pronouns. Although their spellings are the same, their uses in sentences are different.

REFLEXIVE: Harry splashed himself with water.
INTENSIVE: The children made that rug themselves.

A **reflexive pronoun** has as its antecedent the subject of the sentence. It completes the meaning of a sentence and generally cannot be left out.

Burton knows himself very well.   Did you teach yourself music?

An **intensive pronoun** is used to emphasize another word, its antecedent. An intensive pronoun may or may not refer to the subject of the sentence. It can usually be left out without destroying the meaning of the sentence.

Sid himself hung the picture on the wall.

The landscape was painted by Sid himself.

Both reflexive and intensive pronouns must agree with their antecedents in person, number, and gender.

I will fix myself lunch in a while.   Jack can fix a sandwich himself.

Reflexive and Intensive Pronouns	
Singular	**Plural**
myself	ourselves
yourself	yourselves
himself, herself, itself	themselves

Do not use reflexive or intensive pronoun forms in place of personal pronouns.

Ron and I repaired the lamp.   (*not* Ron and myself)
This is between you and me.   (*not* between you and myself)

Never use such incorrect forms as *hisself* or *theirselves*.

Mr. Gilman built the house himself.   (*not* hisself)
His family lived there themselves.   (*not* theirselves)

Guided Practice

A. Find the antecedent of each underlined pronoun. Is the pronoun reflexive or intensive?

Example: Mr. Chapman <u>himself</u> told us how to redo the kitchen.
Mr. Chapman **intensive**

1. Hubert found <u>himself</u> in the middle of a flood.
2. We met the plumber <u>herself</u>.
3. The oven cleaned <u>itself</u>.
4. Let's try to fix the sink <u>ourselves</u>.
5. I will call the painters <u>myself</u>.
6. Don't slip and hurt <u>yourselves</u>.

B. How would you correct each of the following sentences?

Example: Why don't you go with Jim and myself?
Why don't you go with Jim and me?

7. The painters protected theirselves from fumes.
8. Mrs. Sullivan and myself found the source of the leak under the sink.
9. Her son can repair pipes hisself now.
10. Herself and Russell will fix the sink tomorrow.

C. Complete each sentence with an appropriate pronoun. Is it reflexive or intensive?

Example: Eleanor _____ told me the news.
Eleanor herself told me the news. **intensive**

11. Her brother has taught _____ a lot about house repair and maintenance.
12. The painters should see _____ in those funny hats.
13. We _____ aren't sure of the color we should use.
14. You should learn to repair things _____.
15. The work _____ is not difficult.

Summing up

> ▶ A **reflexive pronoun** ends in *-self* or *-selves* and refers to the subject of the sentence. It generally cannot be left out of the sentence.
> ▶ An **intensive pronoun** ends in *-self* or *-selves* and emphasizes another word in the sentence.
> ▶ Avoid using pronouns with *-self* or *-selves* as personal pronouns.

Independent Practice

A. Write the reflexive or intensive pronoun in each sentence. Label it *reflexive* or *intensive*.

Example: The painters saw themselves in the mirror.
        themselves **reflexive**

16. They themselves knew they looked funny.
17. One had painted himself green.
18. Another had decorated herself with blue spots.
19. The paint itself was splattered all over the floor.
20. The painters thought themselves very comical.
21. I myself had to try hard not to laugh.

B. Rewrite each sentence correctly. Underline the corrected word.

Example: Many people like to fix things theirselves.
        Many people like to fix things <u>*themselves*</u>.

22. My brother and myself tried something once.
23. My brother fooled hisself that time.
24. Himself and I tried to fix a clock.
25. Between you and myself, we ruined the job.

C. Rewrite each sentence, adding an appropriate reflexive or intensive pronoun.

Example: You should prepare _____ properly for repair jobs.
        You should prepare yourself properly for repair jobs.

26. First, you should read the directions _____.
27. A repair person _____ gave me that advice.
28. Manuals _____ give excellent safety tips.
29. I _____ found out about manuals the hard way.
30. Dad and Mom had given _____ an evening out.
31. Meanwhile, I tried to fix the alarm clock _____.
32. My brother Pat said, "You can't do that _____."
33. He decided to help me _____.
34. We could have saved _____ all that trouble.
35. The clock _____ needed only a new battery!

Writing Application: An Interview Imagine that you are interviewing yourself about something that you have made or fixed. Write several questions and answers about your accomplishment. Use both reflexive and intensive pronouns in your interview.

For Extra Practice, see p. 414.   Reflexive and Intensive Pronouns   **399**

8 | Choosing the Right Pronoun

Using *we* and *us* with Nouns

Occasionally you may need to use the pronouns *we* and *us* with nouns for identification or special emphasis.

> The dancers want music, but we readers want silence.
> The dancers won't let us readers have peace.

If you are using *we* or *us* with a noun, use the pronoun case you would use if the noun were not there. With a subject or a predicate pronoun, use the nominative case. With a direct or indirect object, use the objective case.

NOMINATIVE: We girls will sing soon.

OBJECTIVE: You should join us altos in the back row.

Guided Practice Which sentences are correct? If a sentence is incorrect, how should it be corrected?

Example: Us violinists will attend a workshop. *We violinists*

1. The bus will pick up us violinists near here.
2. We students will listen to professionals.
3. Us amateurs will certainly benefit from the experience.
4. The conductor directed we violinists to our places.
5. Us lucky ones will never forget the workshop.

Pronouns in Comparisons

You often use pronouns when you make comparisons.

I like the viola better than she.   Suki plays as well as he.

These comparisons are incomplete. If you are not sure which pronoun to use, add words to complete the comparison.

I like the viola better than she likes it.   Suki plays as well as he plays.

The pronoun used in a comparison may change, depending on the meaning that you have in mind.

> He likes music as much as her. (He likes music as much as he likes her.)
> He likes music as much as she.   (He likes music as much as she likes music.)

Guided Practice Choose the correct pronoun. If a sentence has two possible answers, explain your choice.

Example: Rose is a better violinist than (I, me).   *I*

6. Why is she a better musician than (I, me)?
7. Brad and I practice more than (she, her).
8. We know our music as well as (she, her).
9. People listen to Rose more than (we, us).
10. Brad gives me more advice than (she, her).
11. I should listen to her more than (he, him).

Summing up

▶ If you use *we* or *us* with a noun, use the pronoun case that you would use if the noun were not there.
▶ To decide which pronoun form to use in an incomplete comparison, add words to complete the comparison.

Independent Practice Rewrite each sentence correctly.

Example: Us students talked about talent today.
         We students talked about talent today.

12. Genius fascinates we less talented people.
13. Us amateurs practice long hours with small results.
14. Why did Bach or Mozart have more talent than you or me?
15. Why is another student a better musician than you or me?
16. These questions annoy we music students.
17. Do us jealous pupils really want the answers?
18. Why are some better than us? Talent may run in certain lucky families.
19. Mozart's sister may have been as talented as him.
20. Us curious readers also know about the Mendelssohns.
21. Felix's sister composed music as easily as him.
22. However, Fanny was not as famous as him.
23. People admire him more than she.
24. Why was Felix more famous than her?

Writing Application: Comparison and Contrast Compare your likes or dislikes in music with a classmate's taste in music. Write a paragraph using *than* or *as* in at least five statements of comparison. Use *we* or *us* correctly with a noun as a subject or object in at least one sentence.

For Extra Practice, see p. 415.   Choosing the Right Pronoun   **401**

Grammar-Writing Connection

Writing with Clear Antecedents

The meaning of a pronoun comes from its antecedent, the noun that it replaces. In your writing, you must give each pronoun a clear antecedent. Otherwise, the meaning of the pronoun will not be clear. Remember these points when you write.

1. Do not use *it, they,* or *you* without a definite antecedent. To correct vague pronoun references, use a noun or else omit the pronoun.

   UNCLEAR: They tried to teach apes sign language.
   It says in the article that researchers studied apes.
   They say that gorillas are usually rather shy.
   In some experiments you get surprising results.

   CLEAR: Researchers tried to teach apes sign language.
   The article says that researchers studied apes.
   Gorillas are usually rather shy.
   In some experiments scientists get surprising results.

2. Make sure that the antecedent of each pronoun is clear. Be especially careful when more than one noun precedes the pronoun. If the antecedent of a pronoun can be misunderstood, use a noun instead of the pronoun.

   UNCLEAR: A trainer brought the chimp to her husband.
   CLEAR: A trainer brought the chimp to the trainer's husband.

   UNCLEAR: As she spoke to the chimp, she fell asleep.
   CLEAR: As she spoke to the chimp, the chimp fell asleep.

Revising Sentences

Rewrite each sentence, correcting the unclear pronoun.

1. They say that dogs can be trained to understand certain words.
2. In obedience class they teach dogs to follow spoken commands.
3. People can teach dogs to obey, but they cannot talk back.
4. In this article, it tells about work with apes and language.
5. They say that the chimp learned to use hundreds of signs.
6. Dr. Gardner raised the chimp as if she were human.
7. Through their experiments with chimps, researchers realized that they played jokes, expressed emotions, and even lied.
8. You can teach animals to answer questions and to use words.

Creative Writing

M. C. Escher, *Relativity*
© M. C. Escher Heirs c/o Cordan Art
Baarn, Holland, Photo courtesy Collection
Haags Gemeentemuseum, The Hague

In this print M. C. Escher very cleverly uses tricks of perspective to shift our point of view.

- Turn the picture around and look at it from different angles. Which parts make sense at each turn?
- How do the people react to one another? Do people on one plane see or react to people from another?

Activities

1. **Imagine an interview.** Pretend that you are a reporter. Interview people from each plane. Ask them these questions: Are they all happy? Do they see this place as a vacation spot or as a prison? Write your report.
2. **Make a verbal maze.** Write a poem that shifts images as Escher's pictures do. Use metaphors and similes that contradict the thing being described. Try to make the poem end where it started.

Personal and Possessive Pronouns *(p. 380)* Write the pronouns in each sentence. Identify the person and number of each one, and write the gender of all third person singular pronouns.

1. I have found many clamshells on the beach near my house.
2. Did you know that they can dissolve in water?
3. They are made of calcium carbonate.
4. It is carried by the water and can harden into calcite.
5. Calcite can mix with particles and cement them together.
6. We tried an experiment with clamshells in science class.
7. She brought hers, and I brought mine.
8. The teacher carefully dissolved them for us.

Pronoun Antecedents *(p. 383)* Rewrite the sentences, using pronouns and antecedents correctly and clearly.

9. A supermarket must pay attention to how they display goods.
10. People with pets, for example, want to find everything for it in the same aisle.
11. The market should have their detergent and bleach together.
12. They should also be an attractive place to shop.
13. Let's go into this market and see what they have.

Pronoun Case *(p. 386)* Write the pronoun that correctly completes each sentence.

14. Both you and (I, me) think Jenny Lind was a great singer.
15. Many people would agree that it was (she, her).
16. P. T. Barnum managed (she, her) in the United States.
17. (He and she, Him and her) worked together for two years.
18. Don't you think that you and (I, me) could choose (she, her) as the subject of a report for Mr. Munro's class?
19. I'm sure the students and (he, him) would be interested.

Interrogative Pronouns *(p. 389)* Write the pronoun that correctly completes each sentence.

20. (Who's, Whose) is this bicycle?
21. (Who, Whom) left this racing bike here?
22. (Who's, Whose) going to enter the race?
23. (Who, Whom) won the grand prize last year?
24. (Who, Whom) did the winner have to beat?
25. (Who, Whom) did the spectators cheer most enthusiastically?

Demonstrative Pronouns *(p. 391)* Rewrite each sentence, using demonstrative pronouns correctly.

26. (This, These) are geodes, hollow rocks with crystals inside.
27. (These here, These) are purple, but (those there, those) are green.
28. (That, Those) are quartz crystals.
29. (These, These here) are square, but (those, those there) are hexagonal in shape.
30. Could (this, these) be geodes?
31. We'll have to crack (this here, this) open to find out.

Indefinite Pronouns *(p. 393)* Write each sentence. Underline each indefinite pronoun and the verb or pronoun that agrees with it.

32. Everybody in Westwood schools (has, have) to study history.
33. All in the eighth grade (studies, study) European history.
34. Each of the teachers, Mr. Rose and Mr. Nakamura, has (his, their) specialty.
35. Both of them (teach, teaches) modern history.
36. Neither of them (teach, teaches) ancient history.
37. Each of these two teachers is famous in (his, their) field.
38. Everybody here (has, have) read one of (his, their) books.

Reflexive and Intensive Pronouns *(p. 397)* Rewrite each sentence, using reflexive and intensive pronouns correctly.

39. My brother and I considered us excellent cooks.
40. The other members of the family convinced theirselves to let us cook Thanksgiving dinner.
41. My brother hisself admits that the dinner was not a success.
42. He and myself burned the turkey.
43. We had forgotten about it while we busied us trying to get the lumps out of the mashed potatoes.
44. If all of you find you craving an unusual dinner, just give us Townsends a call.

Choosing the Right Pronoun *(p. 400)* Rewrite each sentence, correcting pronoun errors.

45. Clarkson does better than us in swimming.
46. Our teams competed last week, and us juniors won.
47. Us Rangers might be able to win the meet this year.
48. Corky Bancroft swims with us, and no one is better than him.
49. I suppose us swimmers can never hope to be as fast as he.
50. He amazed all we swimmers with a new freestyle record.

Enrichment

Using Pronouns

News Survey

Interview ten people. Ask what their main source of news is—television, radio, magazines, or newspapers. Also find out how much time they spend each day learning about the news. Then write a paragraph to summarize your findings. Include subject and object pronouns. Tell what percentage of the group uses each source and the average amount of time the group spends on the news.

▦ Pronoun Word Search

Players—2. **You need**—graph paper, red and blue pencils. **How to play**—First, write 5 interrogative and 4 demonstrative pronouns randomly across and down a piece of graph paper, one letter per square. Then hide these pronouns by filling in the remaining squares with other letters.

Exchange your word search with a classmate. Working independently, circle the interrogative pronouns in red and the demonstrative pronouns in blue. Then write a sentence using each pronoun correctly. **Scoring**—1 point for each interrogative or demonstrative pronoun circled, 1 point for each correct identification, 2 points for each correct sentence. The player with the most points wins.

What is the shortest distance between two points? This is a great book.

To the Editor

Read some letters to the editor in your school or local newspaper. Clip one letter that you especially like. Underline all the pronouns. Then write a letter to the editor, giving your views on the same topic. (You may also choose a different topic. Consider writing about what you think could be done to improve something in your school or community.) Use pronouns correctly. Mail the letter and watch for it to be published.

Pronoun Ticktacktoe

Players—2. **You need**—24 index cards, 2 pencils, paper for a ticktacktoe board.
How to play—Each of you writes on the cards *I, me, she, her, he, him, you, it, we, us, they,* and *them*, one pronoun per card. Shuffle all the cards and place them face down in a pile. Draw a ticktacktoe board.

Pick 2 cards, use the 2 pronouns in a simple sentence, and tell if the pronouns are being used as subjects or objects. If you both agree that you are correct, put an X in a space on your ticktacktoe board. Then have your partner do the same, making an O on the board if correct.
Scoring—The first one to get 3 X's or 3 O's in a row, or ticktacktoe, wins.

Undersea World

Many extraordinary creatures live in the sea. Choose one that interests you, such as the octopus, the sea horse, or the hammerhead shark. Look up information about it in a reference book. Using complete sentences, write at least five interesting facts about what the creature eats, what it looks like, and what its habits are. Use at least three pronouns. One should be intensive and one reflexive. Add an illustration.

Extra! Make a booklet of information about several sea creatures. Include a table of contents.

1 | Personal, Possessive Pronouns (p. 380)

● Write *personal* or *possessive* for each underlined pronoun.

Example: <u>We</u> have newspapers in every room of <u>our</u> house.

We—personal   our—possessive

1. My brother and <u>I</u> work in a newspaper office.
2. <u>We</u> have worked there for three months now.
3. <u>He</u> wants to become a reporter.
4. News reporting is also a goal of <u>mine</u>.
5. What are <u>your</u> plans for a career?
6. Is anyone in <u>your</u> family in the news business?
7. How did <u>he</u> or <u>she</u> become interested in it?
8. Billy got <u>his</u> job through an ad in the newspaper.

▲ Write each pronoun. Label it *personal* or *possessive*.

Example: He has finally made up his mind about the news job.

He—personal   his—possessive

9. She told us about it last week, and then we told him.
10. Three other students work at the newspaper, but you do not know them.
11. They bring their lunch with them every day.
12. If I had my choice, I would have a job like yours.
13. If your office is near ours, why not visit us someday soon?
14. We can take our lunches to the park.
15. Would you recommend the work for all people?
16. No, news work has its advantages, but it is very hard.

■ Rewrite the incorrect sentences. Write *correct* if a sentence has no errors.

Example: Its always busy in a newsroom.

It's always busy in a newsroom.

17. Your always racing against time.
18. The work gets done, but theirs never enough time.
19. The editor and Mr. Carey told us how they're computers help.
20. You're daily paper, for example, may be in color.
21. A few years ago, your paper was in black and white.
22. Now theirs a satellite that can give us news instantly.
23. When we get the news, it's truly new.
24. Your right; its an amazing world we live in.

2 | Pronoun Antecedents (p. 383)

● Rewrite each sentence, choosing the personal or possessive pronoun that agrees with the underlined antecedent.

Example: TV is popular, but <u>radio</u> still has (its, their) fans.

TV is popular, but radio still has its fans.

1. Many <u>people</u> listen to (his, their) radios during the day.
2. <u>Anna</u> has a clock radio next to (her, their) bed.
3. Anna's <u>parents</u> listen to the news as (it, he, they) dress for work in the morning.
4. <u>They</u> have a small radio in (her, its, their) room.
5. With (his, its) own money, Anna's <u>brother</u> bought a radio.
6. <u>We</u> have a radio with a headset at (our, its, their) house.
7. Does <u>Anna</u> or her <u>mother</u> use a headset with (her, their) radio?

▲ Rewrite each sentence, choosing the correct personal or possessive pronoun. Underline its antecedent.

Example: I prefer radio to TV, for I can use (my, its) imagination.

I prefer radio to TV, for I can use my imagination.

8. My sister is graduating from college next year, and (she, he) plans to work in radio.
9. Although (it, she) has a nice speaking voice, my sister does not want to be an announcer.
10. She and a friend have (her, their) hearts set on being producers for public radio.
11. Even though (he, they) are not heard, producers are important.
12. A producer lines up guests and prepares (it, them) for the show.
13. Has your sister or her friend gotten (her, their) first job yet?

■ Rewrite each incorrect sentence, correcting pronouns and antecedents as necessary so that each sentence can stand alone. If a sentence has no errors, write *correct*.

Example: They say, "No news is good news."

Someone said, "No news is good news."

14. The reporters returned to her radio newsroom quickly.
15. In the newsroom they were sending in messages.
16. Their evening news stories were being prepared by the writers.
17. The news editor and the producer were reviewing her notes for that evening's broadcast.
18. Would Eva's story or Joe's story ever be on the air?
19. Joe interviewed the President when he visited recently.
20. Soon the red light was blinking their signal.

3 | Pronoun Case (p. 386)

● Write *subject* or *object* to describe each underlined pronoun.
  Example: Who are Georgia O'Keeffe and Alfred Stieglitz?
            They are artists.   *subject*

1. She and he worked in different fields.
2. O'Keeffe admired him greatly.
3. Eventually, her teacher was he.
4. Stieglitz encouraged her in her art career.
5. O'Keeffe's work was big and bold. It startled people.
6. Tell us something about this kind of art.
7. Do you and Kim understand it?
8. I think so.
9. More important, these works please her and me.

▲ Write the correct pronouns to complete these sentences. Label each pronoun *subject, predicate pronoun, direct object*, or *indirect object*.
  Example: Todd and (I, me) are working on a photography project.
            I *subject*

10. (He, Him) and Jennie used to work together.
11. (He, Him) and (I, me) are developing black and white prints.
12. The only ones in the class are (we, us).
13. Mr. Chan gave Todd and (I, me) some instructions.
14. (He, Him) and an associate visited (we, us).
15. (We, Us) told (they, them) the procedures in steps.
16. Todd and (I, me) also showed slides.
17. Mr. Chan offered (we, us) good suggestions.

■ Rewrite any incorrect sentences. If a sentence has no errors, write *correct*.
  Example: Leah and me are making a statue.
            Leah and I are making a statue.

18. The process has interested her and me for a long time.
19. Our teachers gave her and I some directions.
20. First, Leah and I prepared a clay model.
21. Her and me let the model harden.
22. Then the teachers asked us to prepare a mold.
23. When unmolding time came, them and us held our breath.
24. Unfortunately, we had not prepared for air bubbles.
25. The most surprised were her and I!
26. We named our project Bubbles.

4 | Interrogative Pronouns (p. 389)

● Write the interrogative pronoun in each sentence.
   Example: Who is writing a story?   *Who*
   1. Who likes mystery stories?
   2. Whose is that story?
   3. Whom did the witness see clearly?
   4. Who stole the diamond necklace?
   5. Who's hiding something under a newspaper?
   6. Whose was the emerald necklace?
   7. Whom did the police arrest?
   8. What happens next?
   9. Which of the two possible endings do you prefer?
   10. Who's the real villain?

▲ Rewrite each sentence, using the correct interrogative pronoun
   or contraction.
   Example: (Who, Whom) knows the answer to this question?
            Who knows the answer to this question?
   11. (Who, Whom) wrote the first story?
   12. (Who, Whom) in the story did you suspect?
   13. (Who, Whom) did you like?
   14. (Whose, Who's) was the better ending?
   15. (Who, Whom) guessed the ending?
   16. (Who's, Whose) going to write the next mystery story?
   17. (Who, Whom) will be the victim?
   18. (Who, Whom) will you make the guilty person?
   19. (Who's, Whose) going to figure it out?

■ Rewrite each incorrect sentence. If a sentence has no errors,
   write *correct*.
   Example: Whose your favorite mystery writer?
            Who's your favorite mystery writer?
   20. Whom has heard of the writer Agatha Christie?
   21. Who knew that Agatha Christie was a skilled and inventive
       British mystery writer?
   22. Whom has been able to guess any of the endings?
   23. Whose is that copy of *The Mousetrap*?
   24. Whom has read the whole book?
   25. Who thought it was exciting and surprising?
   26. Whose going to see the play made from that book?
   27. Who does the play have as its star?
   28. Who is in the supporting cast?

5 | Demonstrative Pronouns (p. 391)

● Write the demonstrative pronoun in each sentence.
  Example: This is an interesting museum.   *This*
  1. That is a beaver.
  2. Those are large front teeth!
  3. These are its kits over here.
  4. That is a waterproof coat it has.
  5. This is its den right here, with its underwater entrance.
  6. This is its favorite food, bark and wood.
  7. Is that the dam it built of twigs, mud, and rocks?
  8. These are the logs it cut with its strong teeth.
  9. Those are busy little animals!

▲ Write each sentence, using the correct demonstrative pronoun.
  Underline the word that it points out.
  Example: (Those, Those there) are striped tree squirrels.
          Those are striped tree <u>squirrels</u>.
  10. (This here, This) is a very young squirrel.
  11. (This, These) are very industrious animals.
  12. (This, These) is a picture of flying squirrels.
  13. One kind of squirrel is (that, that there).
  14. (Those, That) in the other picture are white squirrels from Asia.
  15. (Those, These) are certainly very large eyes on that squirrel over there.
  16. Isn't (that, that there) a very bushy tail on that squirrel?
  17. Is (this, that) its nest in the elm tree over there?
  18. (This, That) is its pile of nuts and seeds right here.

■ Write each sentence, using a correct demonstrative pronoun.
  Underline the word that it points out.
  Example: Is _____ a molehill over there?
          Is that a <u>molehill</u> over there?
  19. _____ is a strange-looking creature in the far corner.
  20. _____ are very tiny eyes it has.
  21. _____ is a very impressive tunnel down here.
  22. Is _____ the place where the mole lives over there?
  23. _____ are earthworms, beetles, and slugs here!
  24. _____ is the diet of the well-fed mole.
  25. Are _____ some more molehills right here?
  26. Can _____ be the claws of the mole breaking through the ground over there?

6 | Indefinite Pronouns (p. 393)

● Write each sentence. Use the word in parentheses that agrees with the underlined indefinite pronoun.
Example: Somebody in our family (is, are) flying to England today.
Somebody in our family is flying to England today.

1. Everybody (is, are) happy for Terry.
2. Many of us (is, are) going to the airport with him.
3. Nobody in the family (has, have) been to England before.
4. Several (has, have) relatives in the city of London.
5. Most of us would like to visit (his, our) London relatives.
6. Most of Terry's clothing (is, are) already packed.
7. Neither of the aunts has said (her, their) good-bys yet.
8. All of the trip (has, have) been carefully planned.

▲ Write each sentence correctly. Underline each indefinite pronoun and the form that agrees with it.
Example: Everybody in London (seems, seem) to be in a hurry.
Everybody in London seems to be in a hurry.

9. Everyone in the tour group (has, have) boarded a special bus.
10. Has someone dropped (his, their) camera?
11. Most of the passengers (has, have) never been to London before.
12. Does everybody have (his, their) camera ready?
13. Most of the city (is, are) filled with traffic.
14. Few of the streets of the city (is, are) empty.
15. None of the people on the bus (seems, seem) to mind, however.
16. Most of London (is, are) right outside their bus windows.

■ Rewrite each incorrect sentence. If a sentence has no errors, write *correct*.
Example: Most of the passengers have fastened his seat belts.
Most of the passengers have fastened their seat belts.

17. Everybody in the aisles are being directed toward a seat.
18. Several of the passengers are tucking their hand luggage away.
19. Others still hasn't finished reading the instructions.
20. Is all of the hand luggage out of the way now?
21. Some of the seats is leaning back and must be straightened.
22. Most of the work have now been done.
23. Are everything in the cabins ready for takeoff?
24. None of the passengers aboard has forgotten their passports, I hope.

7 | Reflexive and Intensive Pronouns (p. 397)

● Write each sentence, using the correct pronoun.

Example: Should David paint his room (hisself, himself)?

Should David paint his room himself?

1. He asked (hisself, himself) whether he could do it.
2. Then he asked if I could help (him, himself).
3. We bought (us, ourselves) paint and rollers.
4. His parents covered the furniture (themselves, theirselves).
5. David and (I, myself) just had to mix the paint.
6. David wanted to do the ceilings (himself, hisself).
7. I found (me, myself) just watching David and waiting.
8. He finished and handed (myself, me) the roller.

▲ Write each sentence, using the correct pronoun. Underline its antecedent.

Example: Mr. Best taught (hisself, himself) to braid rugs.

<u>Mr. Best</u> *taught himself to braid rugs.*

 9. Mr. and Mrs. Best made (theirselves, themselves) two rugs.
10. Jim and I had planned to buy (us, ourselves) a rug.
11. Mr. Best taught Jim and (me, myself) to make one instead.
12. I found (me, myself) surrounded by strips of fabric.
13. I divided the strips (theirselves, themselves) into groups of three.
14. Jim began to braid the strips (hisself, himself).
15. Mrs. Best (she, herself) helped me sew the strips together.
16. In a few weeks, Jim and I had made (us, ourselves) a rug.

■ Write each sentence, using a reflexive or intensive pronoun. Label the pronouns *reflexive* or *intensive,* and underline their antecedents.

Example: Pam and Jack were cooking dinner _____.

<u>Pam</u> and <u>Jack</u> *were cooking dinner themselves.*   *intensive*

17. First they decided to make _____ a big salad.
18. Jack found _____ with a sharp knife, two carrots, and a large head of lettuce.
19. Pam cut the cucumbers and green peppers _____.
20. Then they cooked _____ some delicious lasagna.
21. When they told me about the luscious meal they had prepared, I invited _____ for dinner.
22. We helped _____ to seconds on everything.
23. Since they were tired, I washed the dishes _____.
24. Have you ever prepared an entire meal _____?

8 | Choosing the Right Pronoun (p. 400)

● Write each sentence with the correct pronoun.
Example: Mrs. Davis showed (we, us) students an old viola.
   Mrs. Davis showed us students an old viola.

1. (We, Us) pupils all asked the age of the instrument.
2. The answer surprised (we, us) eighth graders.
3. It was over two hundred years older than (we, us) pupils.
4. (We, Us) students were almost afraid to touch it.
5. Mrs. Davis told (we, us) curious students to think of an Italian name.
6. The maker's name should be familiar to (we, us) musicians in the class.
7. Brad came up with an answer sooner than (I, me).
8. "The name begins with *S*," Brad told (we, us) slowpokes.

▲ Rewrite each sentence, correcting pronoun errors.
Example: Us students tried to guess who made the viola.
   We students tried to guess who made the viola.

9. Brad gave we pupils a good clue.
10. "His nickname rhymes with mine, but he is more famous than me," he said.
11. Brad certainly knows more about music than us.
12. Brad gave we classmates another clue.
13. He told we slowpokes that the name ends in *i*.
14. Us brave students named Stradivari.
15. However, this time us slowpokes and Brad were even.
16. We were all wrong. The maker was younger than him.

■ Write each sentence with the correct pronoun.
Example: _____ students had not heard of Lorenzo Storione.
   We students had not heard of Lorenzo Storione.

17. An Italian like Stradivari, Storione was born a century later than _____.
18. Then Mrs. Davis showed _____ musicians her own viola.
19. _____ pupils compared it with the Storione.
20. Brad and she played. He plays as well as _____.
21. Then Mrs. Davis asked _____ students to guess the age of her own viola.
22. We guessed that it was older than _____.
23. Again, the answer surprised _____ eighth graders.
24. It was younger than _____ and it was American-made.

Literature and Writing

A t every moment of our lives we are somewhere in space and somewhere in time. The ratio between a change of our position in space and the time it takes to happen is our speed.

Elizabeth A. Wood
from *Science for the Airplane Passenger*

When the jet reached ten thousand feet,
it was clear why the country
had cities where rivers ran
and why the valleys were populated.
The logic of geography—
that land and water attracted man—
was clearly delineated*
when the jet reached ten thousand feet.

When the jet rose six miles high,
it was clear that the earth was round
and that it had more sea than land.
But it was difficult to understand
that the men on the earth found
causes to hate each other, to build
walls across cities and to kill.
From that height, it was not clear why.

Think and Discuss
1. What parts of the earth could the poet see at first? at ten thousand feet? at six miles?
2. What does the poet mean by "the logic of geography"? Why does it become clear when seen from above?
3. Most pieces of literature have a **theme,** a central idea. The theme is rarely stated directly. "Geography Lesson" seems to be about the changing view from a jet plane. The actual theme, however, is revealed at the end. What is the real geography lesson of the poem? Why, do you think, did the poet include the first two stanzas?

*delineated: Outlined, spelled out.

The Eagle

By Alfred, Lord Tennyson

He clasps the crag with crooked hands;
Close to the sun in lonely lands,
Ringed with the azure* world, he stands.

The wrinkled sea beneath him crawls;
He watches from his mountain walls,
And like a thunderbolt he falls.

Think and Discuss

1. Poets often repeat words or sounds to achieve certain effects. **Alliteration** is the repetition of sounds at the beginning of words. Read the first line of "The Eagle" aloud. What three words begin with the same sound? Is the sound soft or strong? Why does that kind of sound fit the subject?
2. To create a vivid picture, poets sometimes talk about an object, an idea, or an animal as if it were human. This is called **personification**. What "human" word is used for the eagle's claws?
3. The eagle is often used as a symbol for strength and majesty. Is this how Tennyson sees the eagle? Give examples from the poem. Do you share Tennyson's view of the eagle? Explain why or why not.

---

*azure: Sky-blue.

How did people first try to conquer the air?

Early Theories of Flight

By Beril Becker

This article is part of a chapter from Beril Becker's book *Dreams and Realities of the Conquest of the Skies*.

In the ancient world flying belonged to the gods. The sun god of Egypt, Ra, flew with falcon wings. Mercury had winged sandals. Apollo in a chariot pulled the sun across the sky.

But men, too, entered the legends of speculation. We hear of Daedalus, a Cretan engineer, who learned to fly. Is there an unknown history behind Daedalus and his son, Icarus? Daedalus was skillful enough to build one of the great engineering works of the ancient world, the famous Labyrinth of King Minos of Crete.

It is interesting to speculate that there might be a connection between the sudden collapse of Cretan civilization in 1400 B.C. and the mysterious flight of Daedalus and Icarus. Did they seek to escape in gliders from the violent earthquake and inundation that overwhelmed Crete? Icarus was supposed to have lost his life because the wax that held his wings was melted by the sun. Could it have been instead his glider that collapsed?

By 400 B.C. Greek technology had advanced to the point where intricate mechanical clocks and calendars were built. In that period of history we hear of another flying wonder—the mechanical bird of Archytas of Tarantum, a Greek general and engineer. The records are lost, and we do not know whether this mechanical bird was sent flying by a clockwork mechanism or by use of jets of steam.

The history of flight begins again with a new civilization in the year 1256 A.D., when Roger Bacon published his *Mirror of Alchemy*. His scientific insights and predictions, like scattered seeds, grew and multiplied. Bacon suggested that the surface of the atmosphere must be a kind of "liquid fire" or "ethereal[1] air." This first prophet of mechanical inventions projected two methods by which man would be able to fly through the air. If "ethereal air" were obtainable, it could be enclosed in thin copper spheres, making it possible to carry a man aloft as a cork rises in water. Or else it might be worthwhile for man to invent a flying instrument that could be made to flap wings, to reach in this way the treasure of "liquid fire." Thus, at the very dawn of the history of flight, we have lighter-than-air and heavier-than-air competing with each other in the scientific imagination of one man.

Leonardo Da Vinci, two centuries later, concentrated on a heavier-than-air machine. He wrote, "A bird is an instrument working in accordance with mathematical law; which instrument it is in the capacity of man to produce." He failed to get his ornithopter, a self-propelled device, to work with the muscle power of arms and legs. Had he persisted he might have created an aerodynamic[2] glider, because he grasped the principles of air resistance and balanced flight. He seemed to see that when air flowed fast enough above and below a proper surface, lift occurred. This lift could keep a properly shaped object in the air for as long a time as the lift was present.

---

[1]**ethereal:** Like *ether*, the ancients' name for the atmosphere in space. They believed ether was a purer form of air or fire.
[2]**aerodynamic:** Using scientific principles of air motion.

However, this supremely gifted genius did go on to design a parachute—a starched linen dome eighteen feet square. Following his pattern, such a square parachute was built by a Venetian architect in 1618. Gripping the strings that dangled from each corner of his frame of rods, he managed to float down from high buildings, the first reported successful step in man's conquest of the air.

Since parachutes suggested the idea that air offered resistance, Galileo felt that air might be a substance that could be weighed. He blew extra air into a sealed vessel and found that the weight of the vessel increased. The fact that air could be contracted and expanded excited scientists in all the advanced countries. Inventors, taking their clue from water pumps, created various kinds of air pumps to study the weights and pressures of air.

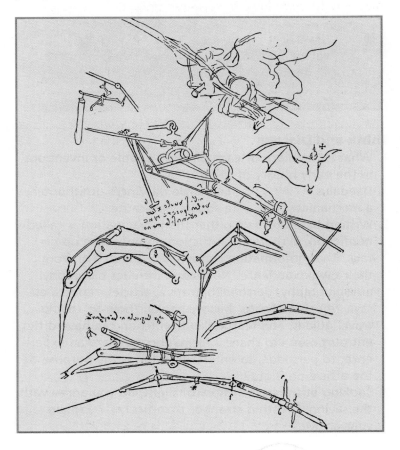

These investigations intrigued the head of a German principality, Otto von Guericke, and he created a pump capable of leaving a more perfect vacuum within a sphere. Then came a historic demonstration. Von Guericke made a brass sphere with two hemispheres, whose flanged edges fitted exactly, and from which all the air had been pumped out. Not even twenty horses tugging at either end, could pull the hemispheres apart. It became clear that man was living at the bottom of a heavy gas that pressed down on everything. The invisible air had become a palpable ocean that might be navigated by vessels as were the seven seas.

Think and Discuss

1. What is the place of each of these people or inventions in the early history of flight?
   Daedalus   Leonardo da Vinci's ornithopter
   a mechanical bird   a square parachute
2. Writing based on fact rather than imagination is called **nonfiction**. Writers of nonfiction do not make up details. Their information comes from research or from their own experience. Nonfiction includes biography, autobiography, personal narrative, articles, reports, essays, reference books, history books, "how-to" books, travel guides, and textbooks. Nonfiction can have different purposes—to share information, to share an experience, to persuade, to entertain. What is the purpose of the article on flight?
3. Looking at the early history of flight, do you agree with the saying, "Truth is stranger than fiction"? Explain your answer.

RESPONDING TO LITERATURE

The Reading and Writing Connection

Personal response What is the geography like where you live? Is there water nearby? Are there plains, mountains, woodlands, valleys? Why did people settle in your area? Write a description of the geography of your area.

Creative writing Imagine that you are a newspaper reporter in Venice in 1618. Your assignment is to report on a parachute drop by Faust Veranzio, an architect whose parachute is based on Leonardo da Vinci's design. Write your article.

Creative Activities

Be interviewed Imagine that you are the inventor of the mechanical bird that has just completed its first flight. A classmate is a TV reporter who interviews you. What does your bird look like? How does it fly? How long did you work on it? Is your invention a success? Think of imaginative answers to these and other questions.

Make a poster Make a poster about the history of flight. Draw or find pictures of various attempts to fly. Label each picture. You may want to look in an encyclopedia for more ideas. Choose a theme, such as *amusing aviators, fantastic failures, jazzy jets,* or *soaring successes.*

Vocabulary

The literature in this unit contains many terms for flying equipment and flying machines. What other such terms can you think of? Make a dictionary of flying terms that could be used in a report on air or space travel.

Looking Ahead

Research report Later in this unit, you will be writing a research report. Before you write, you will organize your ideas. Look at the article on flight. What is the main idea of each paragraph? Does every paragraph have a topic sentence?

VOCABULARY CONNECTION
Synonyms and Antonyms

Words that have nearly the same meaning are called **synonyms**. Note how the author of "Early Theories of Flight" used two different synonyms for *developed*.

> These investigations intrigued the head of a German principality, Otto von Guericke, and he **created** a pump capable of leaving a more perfect vacuum within a sphere. Then came a historic demonstration. Von Guericke **made** a brass sphere with two hemispheres. . . .
>
> *from "Early Theories of Flight" by Beril Becker*

Here are some other synonyms for *developed*.

formed	conceived
fashioned	formulated
built	

Using synonyms can help you avoid repeating the same word. You can use a thesaurus to look up synonyms.

Words that have opposite meanings are called **antonyms**.

wet–dry   above–below   night–day

Often you can change a word into its antonym simply by adding the prefix *un-* or *non-*.

WORD:	known	resident	flammable
ANTONYM:	unknown	nonresident	nonflammable

Vocabulary Practice

A. Write a synonym and an antonym for each of these words from "Early Theories of Flight."

1. heavy
2. sudden
3. clear
4. persist
5. contracted
6. ancient
7. violent
8. rises
9. increased

B. Choose two words from the Practice above. Write sentences using the two words, their synonyms, and their antonyms.

Prewriting
Research Report

Listening and Speaking: Interviewing

If Beril Becker had lived at the same time as some of the inventors he mentioned in "Early Theories of Flight," he might have interviewed them to obtain some of his information. When you interview people, you talk to them to find out what they know, think, and have experienced.

Interviewing is one way to obtain information for a research report. When planning an interview, first decide what you want to find out. Then write the questions that will allow you to get the information you need. Before the interview, telephone or write the person you want to interview. Explain your purpose and how long the interview might take. Make an appointment. For a successful interview, plan carefully, ask thoughtful questions, and take good notes.

Guidelines for Interviewing

Planning the Interview

1. Write down the specific purpose of the interview. Do you want the person to share an opinion? feelings? an experience? information?
2. Do some research before the interview so that you will ask knowledgeable questions and understand the answers.
3. Write down the questions you will ask in an order that makes sense. Use questions beginning with *who, what, when, where, why,* and *how* to encourage your subject to give full answers, not *yes* or *no* answers.

Conducting the Interview

1. Be on time. Be courteous at all times.
2. Bring your questions on a note pad, and a pen or pencil.
3. Introduce yourself and thank the person for seeing you.
4. Ask your questions clearly. Remember your purpose, and keep the interview on the topic. Ask additional questions that come to mind during the interview.
5. Listen carefully to the answers. Take notes, using short cuts. If you hear something striking that you may quote later, take down the exact words of the person.
6. End the interview on time, and thank the person again.

Read this partial interview carefully.

> HAL: How long have you been a pilot for Silverwings Airlines?
>
> MS. GERRISH: Twenty years.
>
> HAL: What did you do before you went to work for Silverwings?
>
> MS. GERRISH: I came here straight out of college. Silverwings was a great place to start because it was such a small airline.
>
> HAL: What are some of the different types of aircraft you've flown?
>
> MS. GERRISH: Well, to name a few, I've taken up big cargo planes, helicopters, and gliders.
>
> HAL: What's a glider?
>
> MS. GERRISH: A glider looks like a plane, but it has no engine. It flies in air currents, without making a sound. It reminds me of a bird, and I love its silent grace. I think it's my favorite kind of aircraft.
>
> HAL: How did you actually become a commercial pilot?
>
> MS. GERRISH: Well, first I got a private pilot's license. Then I got an instrument rating, which allowed me to fly in all kinds of weather. Finally, I logged in enough flying hours and got enough additional training to become a commercial pilot.
>
> HAL: What are your plans for the future?
>
> MS. GERRISH: I plan to keep flying for Silverwings for as long as I can. It's the greatest job in the world!

- What was Hal's specific purpose?
- Which question probably came up during the interview?
- What other question might Hal have asked?

During the interview, write a brief note for each answer given by the person you interview. Take just enough notes to help you remember each point but not so much that you prevent yourself from being a good listener. As soon as possible after the interview, review your notes. Complete any missing parts, making sure that you will be able to understand your notes later and that you have recorded all the important information while it is still fresh in your mind.

On the next page are some of the notes that Sara took during an interview with a balloonist. She later used these notes for an article in the school newspaper.

Q. When did you first become interested in ballooning?
   --watched cousin when "knee-high to a grasshopper"
   --cousin worked for National Weather Service, sent up balloons with weather-forecasting instruments
Q. When did you first go up in a balloon?
   --6 yrs. ago--at age 16
Q. What must one do to become a balloonist?
   --get license from FAA
   --be 16
   --have 10 hours flight experience w. qualified teacher
   --pass written exam
Q. What sorts of organized ballooning events are there?
   --races, rallies
   --international sport

- Did Sara write too much, too little, or just enough? Will she be able to understand her notes later?
- What abbreviation might she expand later?

Prewriting Practice

A. Take notes on the interview shown on page 428.

B. Pick two of the subjects below or two of your own. Write six interview questions for each.

   1. Someone who works in an airport control tower
   2. Someone who is an aircraft mechanic
   3. Someone who took a course in parachuting
   4. Someone who runs a flight school
   5. Someone who works as a flight attendant
   6. Someone who makes model airplanes

C. Interview a subject from Exercise B, using one of your sets of questions from the exercise. Plan the interview by determining your purpose and preparing questions, and then conduct the interview. Take notes.

D. In front of a small group, interview a classmate about a special interest. The group should take notes on the interview. Then with the group discuss how the interview went by having members compare their notes.

Thinking: Identifying Causes and Effects

> He [Galileo] blew extra air into a sealed vessel and found
> that the weight of the vessel increased.
> *from "Early Theories of Flight" by Beril Becker*

In this passage an event—blowing air into a vessel—
brought about a result—a weight increase. An event or condition that produces a result is a **cause.** The result is the **effect.**

The ability to identify causes and effects is especially valuable when you are conducting research for a report. You need
to understand the causes and effects stated in your source materials so that you can explain them to your readers.

In the example above, the cause was stated before the effect. Where are the cause and effect stated below?

> Had he [Leonardo da Vinci] persisted he might have
> created an aerodynamic glider, because he grasped the
> principles of air resistance and balanced flight.
> *from "Early Theories of Flight" by Beril Becker*

Here the effect—da Vinci's possible creation of an aerodynamic glider—is stated before the cause—his grasp of the principles of air resistance and balanced flight. Effect statements
may precede or follow cause statements.

Notice how the word *because* in the da Vinci passage helps
you distinguish cause from effect. Words such as *as a result*
and *therefore* also can signal a cause-effect relationship.

There may be more than one cause for an effect, and more
than one effect for a cause. Look at these examples.

EFFECT: The country has cities near rivers.
CAUSES: Rivers provide means of transportation.
           Rivers provide natural beauty.
           Rivers provide power to generate electricity.

CAUSE: Galileo discovered that air has weight.
EFFECTS: Inventors created air pumps to study weights and
           pressures of air.
           Scientists found that contracting air produces a vacuum.

Chains of causes and effects are also possible. You may remember that da Vinci noticed lift occurring when air flowed
fast enough above and below a surface. A chain of causes and
effects is involved here, as shown on the next page.

The top of a bird's or an airplane's wing is curved.
Because the wing moves forward, air travels around it.
Because the top is curved, the air has farther to go.
Because it has farther to go, the air moves faster.
Because the air moves faster over the top, the pressure drops.
Because air pressure drops above the wing, the pressure below the wing is higher.
Because the air pressure is higher below the wing, it pushes the wing up, and the bird or plane flies.

Not every cause or effect is equally direct. For example, a violent gust of wind might cause serious damage to an airplane because of some fault in the plane's structure. What caused the damage, then—the wind or the fault? The wind was the direct cause, while the fault was the underlying cause.

Do not confuse a sequence of events with a cause-effect relationship. Study this example.

SEQUENCE OF EVENTS: He watches from his mountain walls,
And like a thunderbolt he falls.
from "The Eagle" by Tennyson
CAUSE-EFFECT: Galileo blew air into the container,
and the container's weight increased.

Guidelines for Identifying Causes and Effects

1. Ask what event or condition produced what result. The event or condition is the cause; the result is the effect.
2. Be alert for more than one cause or effect.
3. Remember that effects may be stated before causes.
4. Consider underlying causes as well as direct ones.
5. Be alert for chains of causes and effects.
6. Distinguish a sequence of events from a cause-effect relationship.
7. Look for words that signal a cause-effect relationship.

Prewriting Practice

List three possible causes and three possible effects of the first two items. Create a cause-effect chain for the last.

1. the collapse of a civilization
2. the crash of a glider
3. a plane flies into some turbulence

Finding and Narrowing a Topic ☑

When you write a research report for school, your first task will be to think of a topic. The world is huge and fascinating, and the possibilities are unlimited. Where, then, should you look for a topic? Look first into your own mind. What are you interested in? What do you want to know more about? Think of a research report as a chance to find out more about a topic that interests you.

You might start by completing these sentence beginnings.

I wonder why . . .   I wonder what . . .
I wonder who . . .   I wonder where . . .

What thoughts occur to you? Think of your favorite school subjects, natural events you are curious about, places you would like to visit, or people you would like to meet.

You might also look through magazines, an encyclopedia, or the library card catalog. Ask friends and relatives what they wonder about. Keep writing down topics until you have a list of about ten possibilities.

Now ask these questions about each item on your list.

1. Does the topic really interest me?
2. Will the topic interest my readers?
3. Can I find information about it easily?
4. Is the topic narrow enough for a short report?

If you answer *no* to any of the first three questions, cross out the topic. If you answer *no* only to question 4, then you may need to narrow the topic.

Remember that the purpose of a report is to share information. If the topic is too general you cannot cover it properly in a short report, and you will not succeed in your purpose.

Compare these sets of topics. Notice how each general topic is narrowed and then narrowed again.

GENERAL	NARROWER	STILL NARROWER
famous fliers	famous women fliers	Jacqueline Cochran
outdoor life	camping	buying the right tent
good health	eating right	importance of fiber

How do you get your topic narrow enough? One good way is to ask questions about the topic, answer them, and then ask questions about the answers. Here is an example.

GENERAL TOPIC: pilot training
    QUESTION: What basic courses do pilot trainees take?
     ANSWERS: ground school
              flight school
    QUESTION: What do pilot trainees learn in flight school?
     ANSWERS: take-offs and landings
              rules of cross-country navigation
              how to operate radio devices and instruments
              how to perform emergency maneuvers
    QUESTION: What kinds of emergency maneuvers do pilot trainees
              learn?
     ANSWERS: what to do if an engine fails
              how to recover from stalls

Notice how each set of answers raises another question. Each question narrows the topic further.

Another way to narrow your topic is to ask yourself whether you could tell about a single aspect of it—just one part, one person, one example, one period of time, one event, or one place. Whatever method you use, be sure that you can cover your topic in the amount of space that you have.

Prewriting Practice

A. Work with a partner. Choose three of the general topics from the list below. Using the methods suggested in this lesson, list four narrowed topics for each of your three general topics.

1. Flight	**5.** Dancing	**9.** Insects
2. Dogs	**6.** The great outdoors	**10.** Immigration
3. Soccer	**7.** Conservation	**11.** The United States
4. Diet	**8.** Famous athletes	**12.** Agriculture

B. Read your topics from Exercise A to a small group of classmates. Find out which topics they would be most interested in knowing more about. Discuss why some topics might be more interesting than others. Also discuss which topics would be easier to research than others. Finally, circle the two or three best topics for a report.

Planning and Researching a Report ☑️

If you do not plan your report first, you may waste time finding unnecessary facts. Ask yourself what you want to know about your topic. Here is an example.

TOPIC: the bald eagle
QUESTIONS: Where is the bald eagle found?
What does it look like?
Why is it called the bald eagle?
What is its diet?

Your questions can serve as your rough outline. You can make changes in this plan as you go along.

Your next step is to look for the answers to your questions. In the library you will find these reference books to help you.

Encyclopedias An encyclopedia is a volume or a set of volumes that contains articles on many subjects arranged alphabetically. The encyclopedia is a good place to start when you are gathering information for a report. Some encyclopedias include a bibliography at the end of important articles. This list of sources may be useful to you for further research on your topic.

To use an encyclopedia efficiently, follow these steps.

1. Look up your subject in the index, using a key word.
2. Use the guide letters or words and numbers on the spines of the volumes to find each article.
3. Look at the headings and subheadings to see if the article has information you want.
4. Use the cross-references to find additional information.

These are some well-known encyclopedias.

The Encyclopedia Americana
The Encyclopaedia Britannica
The World Book Encyclopedia

Atlases An atlas is a book of detailed maps and tables that shows weather patterns, population, industries, natural resources, geographical features, historical information, and points of interest. Indexes tell you where on a table or map you can find the information you want.

These are two popular atlases.

National Geographic Atlas of the World
Rand McNally Cosmopolitan World Atlas

Almanacs Almanacs are published every year. They contain up-to-date information on many subjects, such as weather, sports, world events, government, entertainment, and awards. The information is brief and is often presented in the form of lists, tables, and charts. For information, look in the index.

The following are frequently used almanacs.

> *The Information Please Almanac*
> *The World Almanac and Book of Facts*
> *The Guinness Book of World Records*

Dictionary A dictionary contains not only words but also brief biographical and geographical entries, pictures, a variety of alphabets, such as Braille or the Morse code, and tables or charts, such as of the metric system.

Biographical Reference Books Biographical reference books give you more information about a person than do encyclopedias, especially if the person is alive. *Current Biography* gives detailed, up-to-date information about people in the news. Its monthly issues are bound into an annual volume called the *Current Biography Yearbook*.

Here are some other biographical reference books.

> *Who's Who in America*
> *Who's Who in the World*
> *Who's Who of American Women*
> *Who's Who Among Black Americans*
> *Dictionary of American Biography*
> *Webster's New Biographical Dictionary*

Nonfiction Books Nonfiction books are factual books. Use the card catalog to find nonfiction books on your topic. The card catalog is a set of file drawers containing cards for all the books in a library. The cards are filed alphabetically. Each book has a title, author, and subject card.

Newspapers Newspapers contain news stories on current topics. You will find, in addition, information on business and finance, sports, and entertainment.

Readers' Guide to Periodical Literature The *Readers' Guide* lists articles published in magazines and other periodicals. Articles are listed alphabetically by subject and by author's name. Every few months a small volume appears that lists the articles published during that period. The small volumes are then collected in an annual issue.

Here is a sample from the *Readers' Guide*.

SUBJECT ENTRY	**Eagles**
ARTICLE TITLE	Comeback for a national symbol [bald-eagle] S. Begley. il *Newsweek* 104:64–5 Jl 9 '84
	Eagles [bald eagles in Montana]
MAGAZINE TITLE	*New Yorker* 60:39–40 D 3 '84
	Lead shot takes its toll [bald eagles fall
AUTHOR	victim to lead shot] S. Iker. il *Natl Wildl* 22:46–7 O/N '84
AUTHOR ENTRY	**Early, Patricia**
ILLUSTRATION	The French prize [story] il *Teen* 28:32† N '84
	Earth scientists
CROSS REFERENCE	*See also*
	Geologists
	Petroleum engineers
	Earth sheltered houses *See* Houses, Earth sheltered
	Earthquakes
SUBTITLE	Measurement
"SEE" REFERENCE	*See* Seismometers and seismometry
	Prediction
	See Earthquake prediction
	California
	California's 'no fault' fault [San Andreas fault] S. Begley. il *Newsweek*
VOLUME, PAGE NUMBERS, MONTH, DAY, YEAR	104:111 O 15 '84

Prewriting Practice

A. Number from 1–5 on a piece of paper. Write the name of the source you would use to find the answer to each question—encyclopedia, atlas, almanac, biographical reference, or *Readers' Guide*.

1. When did Leonardo da Vinci die?

2. What is the latest information on the moons of Jupiter?

3. What countries border Switzerland?

4. What are the chief agricultural products of Guatemala?

5. What movies has Meryl Streep starred in?

B. Work with a partner. Using the appropriate sources, find the answers to the first five questions above.

Taking Notes ☑

When you are ready to do your research, go to the library with your list of questions, a pencil or pen, and some note cards. Then follow the steps below.

1. Look at one or more encyclopedias and other reference books for a general view of your subject.
2. Use the card catalog to find nonfiction books.
3. Prepare a source or bibliography card. List each source you might use, including all the publishing information about the source. Number the sources.

Here is an example of a source or bibliography card for a report on eagles. Notice how each source is numbered, written, and punctuated. You will use your source card later when you write your bibliography page.

> 1. Drury, William H. "Eagle." *The World Book Encyclopedia.* 1988 ed.
> 2. Attenborough, David. *The Living Planet.* Boston: Little, Brown and Company, 1986.
> 3. Wallis, M. "Into the Air, Little Baldies." *Life,* May 1988, pp. 52–56.

- Where are punctuation marks and abbreviations used?
- What kind of source is the first entry?
- What kind of source is the second entry? What information is given?
- What kind of source is the third entry?

When you are ready to start taking notes, review your questions so that you will remember what information you are looking for. Look first in an encyclopedia for an overview of your topic. Here is part of the article "Eagle" from the first source listed on the above bibliography card.

The bald eagle is not really bald. It looks bald because its head is covered with white feathers. Its tail also is white. A young bald eagle is dark brown and has scattered light markings.

from The World Book Encyclopedia

Here is a sample note card. It includes only the information that answers the question. The number identifies the source from the bibliography card.

> *Why called bald eagle ?*
> *— only looks bald*
> *— white feathers on head*
> *① p. 2*

Follow these points when you take notes.

1. Skim each source. In articles and parts of books, look at the headings and the important words. If the source is an entire book, look at the table of contents and the index. If you find relevant material, read it carefully.
2. Write your notes on index cards. At the top, write the question you want to answer, abbreviating it if you like. Answer the question briefly in your own words, using separate cards for different facts.
3. Copy direct quotations exactly, using quotation marks.
4. Write the number of the source from your bibliography card at the bottom left of your note card and circle it. Write the page number of the source.

Prewriting Practice

Take notes on the following article to answer the question, *How do bald eagles and golden eagles differ?* Then exchange notes with a partner. Do your notes answer the question?

Bald and golden eagles can be found in North America, although golden eagles also live in Europe, Asia, and northern Africa. Both species are 30 to 35 inches long, weigh 8 to 13 pounds, and have a 7-foot wingspan. The bald eagle, a shy hunter, usually eats only fish or dead animals. Although its beak is smaller than the bald eagle's, the golden eagle is a stronger hunter. It lives mainly on rabbits, hares, squirrels, and birds. To make their hunting easier, golden eagles build their *eyries,* or nests, on high mountain cliffs. Bald eagles usually nest in tall treetops near water.

Making an Outline ☑

An outline will help you to organize your notes before you begin writing your report. If your outline is carefully planned, it will provide a clear map for you to follow as you make your way through your report.

An outline has main topics, subtopics, and details. **Main topics** are the main ideas and are placed after Roman numerals. **Subtopics** are the facts that support the main topics. They are placed after capital letters. **Details** give specific facts about the subtopics. They are placed after numbers.

To write an outline from notes, sort your note cards into groups by the question they answer. Then turn each question on your note cards into a main topic. Arrange the main topics in a sensible order. Decide which facts on each card support the main topic, and write them as subtopics. Write the facts or examples that tell about these subtopics as details.

Compare these notes with the section of outline below.

What does weightlessness do to the body?
—eliminates wrinkles   —1–2 inches taller
—slight crouch when standing   —reduces foot size
—backward lean when sitting

TITLE	Life in Space
MAIN TOPIC	I. Effects of weightlessness
SUBTOPIC	A. Changes in body features
DETAILS	1. Wrinkles eliminated
	2. Foot size reduced
	3. One or two inches taller
	B. Changes in posture
	1. Slight crouch when standing
	2. Backward lean when sitting

- How are main topics, subtopics, and details set off?
- How did the writer choose appropriate subtopics?

Notice that the titles for the subtopics do not actually appear in the notes. To find subtopics, you often have to group similar details together and write a subheading that describes them. There must be at least two subtopics and two details under each heading.

Prewriting Practice

Write an outline section for the notes given below. Your outline should have a main topic, subtopics, and details.

```
What is the bald eagle's diet?
--eats fish
--flies over water
--picks fish out of water
--follows other fish-eating birds to find fish
--eats water birds
```

Writing Introductions and Conclusions ☑

All reports should begin with an introduction and end with a conclusion.

Introductions The introduction for a short report is usually one paragraph long.

1. Begin your introduction in a way that immediately captures the reader's interest. A brief story or anecdote related to the topic is one way to begin.
2. Include a sentence that tells exactly what the report is about. This sentence usually comes at the end of the introduction. If appropriate, it can be in the form of a question.

Here is the introduction to a report about an interesting model of a dinosaur.

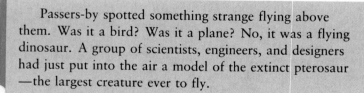

Passers-by spotted something strange flying above them. Was it a bird? Was it a plane? No, it was a flying dinosaur. A group of scientists, engineers, and designers had just put into the air a model of the extinct pterosaur —the largest creature ever to fly.

- How did the writer get your attention?
- What sentence tells you what the report is about?
- Does the introduction succeed in attracting your attention immediately? Why or why not?

Conclusions The conclusion sums up the main ideas and finishes the report. In a short report, the conclusion is usually one paragraph.

1. Your conclusion should restate the main idea of the report.
2. You may also want to review the main points.

Read the conclusion to the report on the dinosaur model.

Thanks to a team of dedicated and imaginative model builders, the extinct pterosaur is flying again. Using an extraordinary combination of fossil records, computers, electric motors, and anything else that worked, the team put together a flying dinosaur that should tell us a lot about how things fly.

Prewriting Practice

A. Read these three introductions to a report on the topic *Important events that occurred on my birthday.* Answer the questions after you read the introductions.

1. Every day people are born, and being born is the most important thing for those people. At that moment, they have no idea of the other things that may be happening around them.

2. Just 156 years and six days after Francis Scott Key wrote the words to "The Star-Spangled Banner," I was born "by the dawn's early light." Every day something important happens somewhere. What important events in United States history have happened on September 20?

3. I was born on September 20, 1975. I will tell about things that have happened on that date.

   a. Which introduction does not state the topic?
   b. Which introduction states the topic but is boring?
   c. Which introduction is the best? Why?

B. Rewrite the following introductory and concluding paragraphs. Use the facts in the outline on page 439. Read your paragraphs to a small group of classmates. Do they think your paragraphs are good? Why or why not?

1. My report is about life in a space capsule. I will write about what happens to people's bodies out there.

2. Life in a space capsule is really interesting. Many things happen to a person's body.

Making Transitions ☑

The body of your report will consist of a number of paragraphs. There will be one or more paragraphs for each main topic, depending on the amount of information the topic covers. As you write, try to connect sentences and paragraphs with **transitional words and phrases**. Transitional words and phrases build bridges between sentences and between paragraphs so that the writing flows more smoothly and clearly.

Different transitional words and phrases serve different purposes. In the sentences below, the transitional word and phrases are underlined. Notice that these words and phrases are usually followed by a comma. You can use transitions in the following ways.

1. To introduce examples

Several of the eagle's features have given it the image of a fierce bird. For example, eagles have large, slightly hooded eyes and strong beaks tipped with sharp hooks. They also have long, curved talons to carry their prey.

2. To add another point

Saturn is the sixth closest planet to the sun and second largest planet in the solar system. Its temperature is much colder than the Earth's. Saturn has seven rings around it. This planet is best known for these colorful rings. In addition to its rings, Saturn has twenty-three satellites.

3. To show time relationships

Gold was discovered in California in 1849. Before long, thousands of gold seekers were surging west.

4. To signal results or effects

Charles Lindbergh's wife, Anne, served as his copilot and navigator on many trail-blazing flights. As a result, she received many aviation awards.

5. To show comparison or contrast

The Rocky Mountains, on the other hand, have high, jagged peaks. Unlike the Appalachian Mountains, they are not worn down by erosion.

6. To connect ideas

Most people know the importance of eating properly. Many, however, do not follow up on what they know.

The following chart lists transitional words and phrases that can help you connect the ideas between your sentences and between your paragraphs.

TO INTRODUCE EXAMPLES

for example	in one instance
for instance	in one case
to illustrate	in fact
in one example	as proof
to begin with	

TO ADD ANOTHER POINT

in addition (to)	furthermore
also	moreover
another	a second (third, fourth, etc.)
besides	a further

TO SHOW TIME RELATIONSHIPS

before	since	in the meantime
after	meanwhile	to begin with
next	eventually	at the same time
then	at last	not long after
finally	afterward	as time passed
soon	at this point	first, second, third, etc.

TO SIGNAL RESULTS OR EFFECTS

as a result	due to
because (of)	for this reason
therefore	in response to
thus	in conclusion
consequently	

TO SHOW COMPARISON OR CONTRAST

similarly	different from
like	in contrast
unlike	on the other hand
just as	on the contrary
the same as	equally important
as well (as)	

TO CONNECT IDEAS

yet	so
however	nevertheless
though	moreover

Another way to make transitions between paragraphs is to use the topic sentence of a paragraph to refer to a thought in the preceding paragraph. Read the following paragraphs. Pay special attention to the underlined words and phrases.

> A squirrel spends a busy summer gathering nuts and hoarding them. When winter comes, the squirrel has enough to eat.
>
> Is <u>this animal</u> acting intelligently? Is it deliberately planning ahead, as a person plans ahead when he puts money in the bank?
>
> Scientists have performed experiments to try to answer <u>these questions</u>. They have raised squirrels in warm, comfortable laboratories, where they never experience winter and never know a hungry day. Yet when these squirrels are given nuts for the first time, they immediately look for a place to bury them.
>
> *from* How Animals Learn *by R. Freedman and J. E. Morris*

- To what does *this* in the second paragraph refer?
- What word is used instead of *squirrel* to avoid repeating the word?
- To what does the phrase *these questions* in the third paragraph refer?
- In which other two sentences are the ideas connected by repeating part of the first sentence in the second?

You can use these same techniques to make transitions between sentences.

Prewriting Practice

A. Add an appropriate transitional word or phrase to make the relationship between each pair of sentences clearer.

1. The national parks of the United States preserve many beautiful and unusual features. _____ the Grand Canyon and Yosemite contain extraordinary formations.
2. The climate of Chicago has extremes of hot and cold. _____ San Francisco has a mild climate all year round.
3. Many people try to jog every morning. _____ not all achieve their goal, especially when bad weather arrives.
4. For centuries humans dreamed of traveling to the moon. _____ the dream came true.

B. Look in newspapers and magazines to find at least ten examples of transitional words and phrases. With a partner, identify the purpose of each one.

C. Work with a partner. Write five pairs of sentences. Use a transitional word or phrase to join each pair.

The Grammar Connection

Demonstrative Adjectives and Pronouns

You have learned that you can use *this, that, these,* and *those* as transitional words to connect ideas between sentences and between paragraphs.

> Some squirrels appear to have wings. These animals do not really fly.

This, that, these, and *those* may be used as demonstrative adjectives or as demonstrative pronouns. However you use them, remember that demonstratives must agree in number with the words they refer to.

SINGULAR: A flying machine that finally succeeded astounded the world. This was the Wright brothers' airplane.
Orville Wright piloted the aircraft. This plane was a heavier-than-air machine.

PLURAL: Flying machines have changed. Those of the twentieth century would amaze early inventors.
The *Concorde* is an SST. These letters stand for supersonic transport.

Practice Write each sentence, completing it with a correct demonstrative adjective or pronoun.

1. The zeppelin was named after its inventor. _____ airship was a lighter-than-air vehicle.
2. The United States operates several space shuttles. _____ are reusable space vehicles.
3. Neil Armstrong took the first step on the moon in 1969. _____ was on the Apollo 11 mission.
4. Space stations are currently in orbit. _____ experiments make the study of other planets possible.
5. Plants and animals grow differently in space. Gravity does not affect _____ living things there.

Step 1: Prewriting—Choose a Topic

Eduardo made a list of topics he was curious about. Then he shortened his list by eliminating some topics that were too broad. He reread his list to be sure all the topics were narrow enough to cover in a short report.

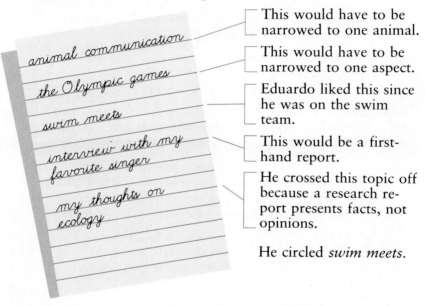

animal communication — This would have to be narrowed to one animal.

the Olympic games — This would have to be narrowed to one aspect.

swim meets — Eduardo liked this since he was on the swim team.

interview with my favorite singer — This would be a first-hand report.

my thoughts on ecology — He crossed this topic off because a research report presents facts, not opinions.

He circled *swim meets*.

On Your Own

1. **Think and discuss** Using the Ideas page, make a list of five topics that interest you, and narrow your topics. Discuss your ideas with a small group of classmates.
2. **Choose** Answer these questions about each of the topics on your list.
   Is information readily available on this topic?
   How can I narrow it to a more specific, workable topic?
   Which topic do I most want to learn about?
   Circle the topic you chose.
3. **Explore** What will you cover in your report? Do one of the activities under "Exploring Your Topic" on the Ideas page.

Ideas for Getting Started

Choosing a Topic

Topic Ideas

The zeppelin
The history of balloons
A day in space
How dolphins communi-
cate with each other
The origins of the electric
guitar
The basic laser
Use of special effects in a
science fiction film
Emily Brontë's early years
Ballet: the first twenty-five
years
How books are printed

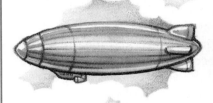

Sample Narrowed Topics

Read these topics to see
how to narrow a broad
topic.

Symbolic animals: the dove

The life of John Lennon:
John Lennon's school
years

Careers in art: careers in
graphic design

Computers: how the first
computer worked

The history of sports: the
history of basketball

The recording industry:
how records are promoted

Sleep: REM sleep

Movies: the twenties

Exploring Your Topic

Writing Questions

List at least five questions
to answer when you re-
search your topic. Answer
any you can, but remem-
ber to check these answers
when doing your research.
These questions will guide
your research and become
the rough outline for organizing your report.

Talk About It

How much do you know
about your subject? What
should you find out? Have
a classmate interview you
about your topic. Become
an expert. Use the ques-
tions you cannot answer as
information to look for
when you research your
topic.

Step 2: Plan Your Report

Here is the list of questions Eduardo wrote about his topic.

What is a swim meet?
When and where was the first swim meet held?
What events take place at a meet?
—how are races timed?
Where are swim meets held?
Who participates?

Eduardo used the questions as a working outline to begin his research. Later he could add items, cross off questions, and rearrange the order. For now, at least, he had a rough plan.

In the library, whenever Eduardo found facts that answered one of his questions, he wrote the source information, including author, title, place of publication, publisher, date, and page numbers, on his bibliography card. He would use this card for his bibliography page later.

Eduardo wrote the facts on separate note cards. At the top of each card, he put the question the facts answered. At the bottom, he wrote a number and circled it. That number matched a number on the bibliography card and identified the source. Next to the circled number on the note card, he wrote the page number where he found the fact. Below is one of Eduardo's note cards and a partial bibliography card.

Where are swim meets held?

Olympic-size pools 25 or 50 meters long
pools can be inside or outside

① p. 632

1. "Swimming." National Encyclopedia. 1980
ed., p. 632.
2. Wein, Janet C. Competitive Swimming.
Boston: Butler Books, 1986, pp. 2, 4.
3. "Olympic Swimming." News Today,
June 2, 1985, p. 32.

After gathering his information, Eduardo sorted his note cards into piles, one pile for each main question in his rough outline. As he had not been able to find any facts about the very first swim meet, Eduardo omitted this question.

Eduardo organized his notes into a final outline. His main questions from his working outline became his main topics, but he rearranged the order. Using his note cards, he filled in the subtopics and details. Here is part of his outline.

```
II. Seven events at a swim meet
    A. Five events require swimmers to use
       specific strokes
       1. Butterfly, backstroke,
          breaststroke, freestyle
       2. Individual medley, or I.M.,
          uses all of the above
    B. Two events are relays
       1. Freestyle relay
       2. Medley relay
```

Think and Discuss ☑

- What main question does this part of the outline answer?
- What are the subtopics? the details?

On Your Own

1. **Plan your research** After you have chosen your topic, make a list of questions about it. Use your questions to make a rough outline to direct your research.
2. **Take notes** From reference materials, books, magazines, and newspapers, take notes to answer your questions. Make a bibliography card and note cards, following Eduardo's example.
3. **Organize your facts** Sort your note cards, making a pile for each main question in your working outline. In each pile, group the cards for each subtopic. Remove any cards you think are unrelated or unimportant.
4. **Make a final outline** Write a final outline, arranging your main topics, subtopics, and details logically. Write a title at the top of your outline.

Step 3: Write a First Draft

As he began to write a first draft, Eduardo kept in mind that his audience included his class as well as his teacher. He wrote an introduction first. Then, following his outline, Eduardo wrote a paragraph for each of his main topics. Next, he wrote a conclusion. Last, using his bibliography card, he wrote his bibliography page, alphabetizing his sources.

Eduardo did not worry about mistakes. He just tried to write logically. He knew he would polish his report later.

The beginning of Eduardo's first draft

> Swim meets are a series of races in which they compete for the fastest time.
>
> ~~These~~ Each event begins with the swimmers standing on starting blocks, which are poolside plateforms. When the starter says, "take your mark" they bend over to dive. This is my favorite part. Then, by shooting a gun or beeping a beeper, she starts the race and the electrionic timer connected to touch pads in the pool.

Think and Discuss ☑
- Can you think of a way to improve Eduardo's introduction?
- Which sentence does not belong in a research report?

On Your Own

1. **Think about purpose and audience** Answer these questions.
   Who is my audience? How can I interest them?
   What is my purpose? How can I present my facts clearly?
2. **Write** Write your first draft, following your final outline. Do not worry about mistakes.
3. **Write** Write a bibliography, alphabetizing your sources.

Step 4: Revise

Eduardo read his first draft. Noticing that some transitions between paragraphs were not smooth, he added some transitional words and rewrote several sentences.

To see if his report was clear, Eduardo read it to Emma.

Reading and responding

Emma: Your report was clear, except for one thing. Are all starters women?

Eduardo: No. I'd better check all my pronouns.

Emma: Could you make the introduction as exciting as the description of how swim meets begin?

Eduardo: Maybe. Thanks for the suggestions.

After jotting down Emma's comments, Eduardo rewrote the introduction. Next, he revised to correct any confusing pronouns.

Part of Eduardo's revision

Golfers golf in tournaments. Tennis players play in matches. Swimmers, however, swim in called events.

Swim meets are a series of races in which

they compete for the fastest time.

~~These~~ Each event begins with the swimmers

standing on starting blocks, which are

poolside plateforms. When the starter says,

the swimmers

"take your mark" ~~they~~ bend over to dive. ~~This~~

~~is my favorite part~~. Then, by shooting a gun

the starter

or beeping a beeper, ~~she~~ starts the race and

the electrionic timer connected to touch pads

in the pool.

Think and Discuss ☑

- Why did Eduardo add *called events* to the introduction?
- Why did he take out *This is my favorite part*?
- Which pronouns did he change? Why?

On Your Own

Revising checklist

☑ Have I introduced my topic in an interesting way?
☑ Is the information complete and clearly presented?
☑ Does each paragraph focus on one main idea?
☑ Does each paragraph lead logically to the next?
☑ Does the conclusion summarize the main ideas?

1. **Revise** Make changes in your first draft. Cross out any un-clear words, phrases, or sentences, and write your changes above them or in the margins. Add transitions where needed. Use the thesaurus below or the one at the back of this book to find exact or precise words.

2. **Have a conference** Read your report to your teacher or a classmate. Write down the comments and suggestions.

WRITING CONFERENCE

Ask your listener:	**As you listen:**
"Can you follow the main idea easily?" "Are any parts unclear?" "Where do I need to add information?" "What would make it more interesting?"	Can I follow the main ideas? Is the report clear? Do I need any further information? What have I learned about this topic?

3. **Revise** Think about your partner's suggestions, and decide which ones to take. Do you have any other ideas for revisions? Make these changes on your paper.

Thesaurus

after *adv.* subsequently, later, once, thereafter, then

because of *prep.* on account of, as a result of

before *prep., adv.* prior to, previously, in the past

confusing *adj.* unclear, murky, puzzling, enigmatic

exciting *adj.* thrilling, spellbinding, exhilarating

expert *n.* source, leading figure, noted author, researcher, spokesperson, authority, scientist

interesting *adj.* entertaining, intriguing, amusing, fascinating

Step 5: Proofread

Using a dictionary to check spellings and proofreading marks to make changes, Eduardo proofread his report for punctuation, capitalization, and spelling errors. He also proofread his bibliography page to be sure he had alphabetized and punctuated it correctly and indented it properly. He checked that he had underlined or put quotation marks around all titles.

Part of Eduardo's report after proofreading

~~These~~ Each event begins with the swimmers standing on starting blocks, which are poolside plateforms. When the starter says, "take your mark" ~~they~~ *(the swimmers)* bend over to dive. ~~This is my favorite part~~. Then, by shooting a gun or beeping a beeper, *(the starter)* ~~she~~ starts the race and the electrionic timer connected to touch pads in the pool.

Think and Discuss
- Which words did Eduardo correct for spelling?
- What letter did he capitalize? Why?
- Why did he add a comma?

On Your Own

1. **Proofreading Practice** Proofread this paragraph. After correcting the mistakes, write the paragraph correctly. There are two misspelled words, three incorrect pronouns, one capitalization error, and two missing commas.

   To learn how lasers work, I interveiwed two Scientists. Obviously, they're language was more technical than us eighth graders understand. Keeping you and I in mind they promised simple explainations. Therefore they began with the basic laser.

2. Proofreading Application

A. Now proofread your report. Use the Proofreading Checklist and the Grammar and Spelling Hints below. Use a dictionary to check spellings. You may wish to use a colored pencil to mark your corrections.

B. Proofread your bibliography page to make sure you have used the correct form, capitalization, punctuation, and spelling. Refer to the model in the Capitalization, Punctuation, and Usage Guide.

Proofreading Checklist	Proofreading Marks
Did I	⌧ Indent
☑ **1.** indent paragraphs and sources?	∧ Add
	⋏ Add a comma
☑ **2.** spell all words correctly?	⌄⌄ Add quotation marks
	⊙ Add a period
☑ **3.** capitalize and punctuate correctly?	ℓ Take out
	≡ Capitalize
☑ **4.** use commas correctly?	/ Make a small letter
	∽ Reverse the order
☑ **5.** use the correct forms of nouns and pronouns?	

The Grammar/Spelling Connection

Grammar Hints

Remember these rules from Unit 11 when you use pronouns in your writing.

- Each pronoun must have a clear antecedent. (Unclear: *They say flying is fun.* Corrected: *Balloonists say flying is fun.*)
- Pronouns must agree with their antecedents in number and gender. *(Alan should be here by now. Hasn't he arrived yet?)*

Spelling Hints

Remember these spelling principles.

- A possessive pronoun never has an apostrophe. *(its, your, their)*
- A pronoun with an apostrophe is a contraction. *(it's, you're, they're)*

Step 6: Publish

Eduardo made a final copy of his report. He checked it one last time and then attached his bibliography page and added a title page. He titled his report "Swimming to Win."

Eduardo's class had chosen to present their reports orally in small groups. Eduardo decided to make a visual aid to use in his presentation. He used poster paper and snapshots of a recent meet to make a photo essay about the meet. When he presented his report, he used the photo essay to illustrate some of his points.

On Your Own

1. **Copy** Carefully copy or type your report.
2. **Give it a title** Your title should tell what your report is about and catch your readers' interest.
3. **Check** Read your paper again to be sure it is error free.
4. **Share** Decide on a way to share your report.

Ideas for Sharing

- Have a classmate read your report and prepare questions. In front of the class or a small group, your partner can interview you as the resident expert on your topic.
- You and some classmates may want to collect and put together your reports to make a classroom encyclopedia.

Literature and Creative Writing

"The Eagle" described the majestic bird standing over the world. "Geography Lesson" took you higher and higher in a jet plane as you watched the world become smaller and smaller. "Early Theories of Flight" reported on ways people first tried to get themselves into the air.

You have already practiced writing a research report. Now use what you have learned to do one or more of the following activities.

1. **Report on the early theories of . . . .** You read about some of people's first attempts to fly. Now find out about the first attempts to do something else, such as heating homes, keeping food cold, recording music, or performing surgery. Write a research report about it.

2. **Report on something that flies.** What are some of the things that fly? There are birds, bats, insects, gliders, and model planes, for example. Write a research report about something that flies. Be sure to tell how it flies.

3. **Report on a symbolic animal.** The eagle is a symbol for strength and majesty. Other animals, such as the lion and the dove, have become symbols for other qualities. Write a research report on one of these animals to tell why it symbolizes what it does.

Remember these things ☑

- Be sure your topic is narrow enough.
- Plan and organize your report.
- Present your ideas clearly.
- Use transitional words and phrases.

Writing Across the Curriculum
Space Exploration

Few fields of study have developed as rapidly as astronautics, the science and technology of space flight. Scientists hope that their research in space may have many useful applications to life on Earth.

Choose one or more of the following activities.

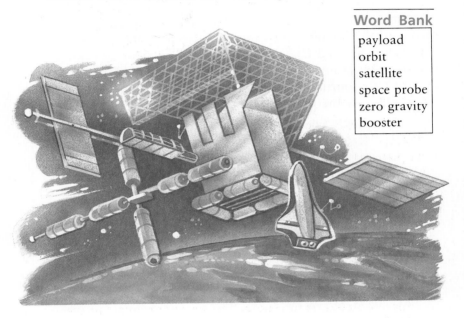

Word Bank

| |
| payload |
| orbit |
| satellite |
| space probe |
| zero gravity |
| booster |

1. **Research space stations.** In the future, space stations (manned satellites that orbit Earth) will become more common. Research to find out what the major purposes of space stations are and will be. What effect will these space stations have on life on Earth? Illustrate your report.

2. **Travel with Voyager 2.** In 1977 Voyager 2 was launched to probe and study the distant planets. During its travels it made numerous discoveries. Research these discoveries. You might want to include a map of Voyager 2's journey through the solar system.

3. **Research the spin-offs.** Many space-related inventions have been modified for use on Earth through NASA's Technology Utilization Program. Research to find at least five of these technological spin-offs. Find out how they are being used. What has been their effect on our lives on Earth?

Benito enjoyed reading "Early Theories of Flight" and learning about how humans had tried to fly before actually succeeding.

Benito thought about another frontier, too. Exploring the secrets of the ocean seemed just as exciting as exploring the sky. When he read *Undersea Explorer: The Story of Captain Cousteau* by James Dugan, Benito decided to share the book by writing a journal entry for Dumas, one of Cousteau's divers. Here is the journal entry.

Summer 1952

Ever since I was thirteen years old and uncovered a two-thousand-year-old grave on the seashore, I have been interested in how people lived long ago. Now, with Jacques Cousteau, I am looking for a ship that sank a thousand years ago! Professor Benoit, who has studied ancient Greek ruins, is here to help us.

Today I dived where an earlier diver had seen great clay pots on the ocean floor—the kind of pots used to carry cargo on ancient Greek and Roman ships. By the time I had to come up, I had found nothing. Professor Benoit wanted to move the ship on to the next site, but Captain Cousteau decided to keep the Calypso here. He himself dived to the place where I had come up. I trust his hunches! As I sit here writing, Cousteau is still below. He has stayed down to the end of his safety limit. When will he surface? What, if anything, has he found?

Our ship's recorder, James Dugan, is writing Undersea Explorer: The Story of Captain Cousteau. He is waiting too.

Think and Discuss
- What did you learn about the people in the book?
- What did Benito not tell you that you would like to know?
- Why is this a good way to share a book?

Share Your Book

Write a Journal Entry

1. Decide which book character you will pretend to be. You may choose to be the main character or another character who will give a different view.
2. Choose a particular day to write about. It should be the day of some exciting event in the story.
3. Write the journal entry from the point of view of the character you have chosen. Try to use words that this person would use. Describe the action, but stop at an exciting place. Keep your readers in suspense.
4. Read the entry to the class. You may want to post your work on the bulletin board.

Other Activities

- Draw a map or a diagram of the setting to illustrate your journal entry. Add pictures of the event. Do not show the outcome of the incident.
- Write a journal entry for the same day from the point of view of another character in the story.
- Make a collage or a bulletin board display of what was happening elsewhere in the world on the same date as your journal entry. Find out what was happening by reading newspapers and magazines from that day or week. Look at an almanac from that year. Illustrate your display with your own drawings and photocopies of news stories and magazine pictures. Share your display.
- Choose one character from your book. Write a set of questions that you as a newspaper reporter could use in an interview with this person.

The Book Nook

Flying to the Moon and Other Strange Places	Twenty Thousand Leagues Under the Sea
by Michael Collins	*by Jules Verne*
Early dreamers of flight would thrill to this account of the flight of Apollo 11 to the moon.	A science fiction story written in 1870 foretells of undersea explorations like those of Jacques Cousteau.

Language and Usage

. . . and the government of the people, by the people,
and for the people shall not perish from the earth.

Abraham Lincoln
from The Gettysburg Address

Phrases

Getting Ready We have been told and retold that our sentences should be well-constructed, clear, and easy to understand. Why should we clutter them up with phrases? A good phrase that explains your subject just a little bit more can make that light bulb of understanding turn on inside your reader's head. In this unit, you will learn more about the use of phrases.

ACTIVITIES

Listening Listen while some words are read that should be very familiar to you. What are the three familiar phrases? Read the words without those phrases. Why are the phrases important?

Speaking Look at the picture. It is perhaps our most famous national monument, and it honors a man known for a very short speech, The Gettysburg Address. He made every word count. Read the quotation twice. First, emphasize each preposition. Next, emphasize the nouns. What effect does that have on the meaning?

Writing What does Lincoln mean by "government . . . for the people"? Write your thoughts in your journal.

1 | Prepositions and Prepositional Phrases

A **preposition** is a word that shows a relationship between a noun or a pronoun and another word in the sentence. Different prepositions convey different meanings.

My friend Irene sings in the opera house.
My friend Irene sings near the opera house.
My friend Irene sings outside the opera house.
My friend Irene sings behind the opera house.

Here is a list of common prepositions.

about	beneath	in place of	over
above	beside	in spite of	past
according to	besides	inside	since
across	between	instead of	through
after	beyond	into	throughout
against	but	like	to
along	by	near	toward
among	despite	next to	under
around	down	of	underneath
aside from	during	off	until
as	except	on	unto
at	for	on account of	up
because of	from	onto	upon
before	in	out	with
behind	in back of	out of	within
below	in front of	outside	without

In a sentence a preposition is always followed by a word called the **object of a preposition**. The object may have one or more modifiers.

The opera will be performed on a large stage.

A preposition followed by more than one object has a **compound object of a preposition**.

Between City Hall and the library is the opera house.

A preposition, its object or objects, and any modifiers form a **prepositional phrase**. A phrase is a group of words that functions as a single word.

Irene sang the high note with ease.

Many sentences have more than one prepositional phrase. Each phrase includes a preposition and its objects along with any other accompanying words.

> At the end of the opera, people in the audience cheered.

When the object of a preposition is a pronoun, you must be careful always to use the objective case.

> Sheila attended the opera with them and me.

You may have noticed that many prepositions are words that can also function as adverbs. Remember that a preposition always has an object. An adverb does not have an object.

PREPOSITION: We went inside the opera house.

ADVERB: We went inside.

Guided Practice

A. What are the prepositional phrases in these sentences? Identify each preposition and each object.

> Example: Myths and legends often provide a basis for music, art, and literature.
> *for music, art, and literature*   **prep.:** *for*
> **objects:** *music   art   literature*

1. One opera by Wagner is based on legends from earlier centuries.
2. The name of this famous opera is *Lohengrin*.
3. The events of the complicated plot take place in the tenth century.
4. During the first act, a boat drawn by a swan comes into view.
5. According to legend, a marriage takes place between a knight and a princess.
6. The famous melody of the "Wedding March" from this opera is often played at weddings.

B. Choose the correct pronoun to complete each sentence.

> Example: Have you sent the tickets to him or (I, me)?
> *Have you sent the tickets to him or me?*

7. That hit play was written by (she, her).
8. Between you and (I, me), I found the plot confusing.
9. Alan Ellis played the lead instead of (he, him).
10. Without the efforts of you and (they, them), this play would not have been so successful.

Summing up

▸ A **preposition** is a word that shows a relationship between a noun or a pronoun and another word in the sentence.
▸ A **prepositional phrase** includes a preposition, its object or objects, and all of the modifiers of the object.
▸ When a pronoun is the object of a preposition, use the objective case.

Independent Practice

A. Write each prepositional phrase. Underline the preposition once and its object or objects twice.

Example: Igor Stravinsky was known as a composer of great ballet music.

> <u>as</u> a <u>composer</u>   <u>of</u> great ballet <u>music</u>

11. Stravinsky was born in Russia but left before the beginning of World War I.
12. He lived in France for many years, and then he moved to the United States in 1939.
13. Some of his scores were based on Russian legends.
14. He first gained fame with his music for *The Firebird*.
15. It tells about the rescue of a fantastic bird by a prince.
16. After this kind act, the prince gets a special feather from the firebird.
17. Because of the feather and the firebird, the prince wins a battle and gains the love of a princess.
18. Stravinsky depended on Russian musical folklore in his early music.
19. Later he was known as a composer of very modern music.
20. Stravinsky died in 1971, but his influence on music goes on.

B. Write each sentence, using the correct pronoun.

Example: A talk on myths was given by (she, her).
> *A talk on myths was given by her.*

21. According to (she, her), legends are often fantasy.
22. It is known to (we, us) that legends may be partly true.
23. Lara read about King Arthur to Carlos and (I, me).
24. Just between you and (I, me), I like Greek myths best.

Writing Application: A Story Write a brief story, retelling a legend or myth that you know. Use at least five prepositional phrases, and underline them.

For Extra Practice, see p. 490.

2 | Prepositional Phrases as Modifiers

You know that a phrase is a group of words used as a single word. Prepositional phrases always act as modifiers.

A prepositional phrase that modifies a noun or pronoun is an **adjective phrase**. It tells *which, what kind,* or *how many.*

Go to the beach near the road.

One of the lifeguards from the town will be there.

A prepositional phrase that modifies a verb, an adjective, or an adverb is an **adverb phrase**. An adverb phrase tells *how, when, where,* or *to what extent.*

We went on the ferry. They met us later in the afternoon.

You may use prepositional phrases either before or after the words they modify as long as the meaning of the sentence is clear. Sometimes another word or phrase comes between the modified word and the prepositional phrase.

The lone runner jogged steadily along the deserted beach.

For years people worked hard on fishing boats.

To be clear, you should always place an adjective phrase next to the word it modifies. Place an adverb phrase as close as possible to the word or words it modifies, or place it at the beginning or end of the sentence.

UNCLEAR: A man rescued a dog in a hat. (Who wore the hat?)

CLEAR: A man in a hat rescued a dog.

Guided Practice

A. Find each adjective phrase. What does it modify?

> Example: A friend of mine read a book about Cape Cod.
> *of mine—friend   about Cape Cod—book*

1. A cape is a point of land.
2. Cape Cod in Massachusetts has the shape of a hook.
3. Beaches for swimmers and sunbathers attract visitors.
4. The cape got its name from the cod in local waters.

B. Find each adverb phrase. What does it modify?

Example: On Cape Cod visitors can gather cranberries.
On Cape Cod—can gather

5. By the early summer, Cape Cod is full of visitors.
6. Tourists come to Cape Cod from many countries.
7. In early times, Norsemen may have fished near Cape Cod.
8. An Englishman first sailed around Cape Cod in 1602.

Summing up

▸ Prepositional phrases always function as modifiers.
▸ **Adjective phrases** modify nouns or pronouns.
▸ **Adverb phrases** modify verbs, adjectives, or adverbs.

Independent Practice

A. Write each adjective phrase and the word it modifies.

Example: Martha's Vineyard is an island off Cape Cod.
off Cape Cod—island

9. It is an area with beautiful views of sand and sea.
10. Many visitors to the Vineyard rent beach cottages.
11. Residents of the island make preparations for winter.
12. The long months of winter can be a time of isolation.
13. Islanders then enjoy the calm of the island without tourists.
14. All of the beaches are empty during the winter.

B. Write each adverb phrase and the word or words it modifies.

Example: Martha's Vineyard is not far from Cape Cod.
from Cape Cod—far

15. The island was discovered in 1602 and claimed by New York.
16. After some years it was given to Massachusetts.
17. Famous authors come to the island for peace and quiet.
18. Many people travel from the mainland in the summer.
19. Because of the weather, few people visit in winter.
20. You can reach the island only by boat or plane.

Writing Application: A Description Most people enjoy traveling because they see interesting or beautiful sights and they learn something new. Write a paragraph describing the most beautiful or interesting place you have ever visited. Use at least five prepositional phrases. Underline each adjective phrase once and each adverb phrase twice.

 For Extra Practice, see p. 491.

3 || Choosing the Right Preposition

Choosing *between* or *among*

Many people confuse the prepositions *between* and *among*. When the object of the preposition refers to two people, things, or groups, use *between*. When it refers to more than two, use *among*.

> The lines were divided between the actor and the actress.
> The lines were divided among the six cast members.

> Relations between the actors and the producers were good.
> Relations among the entire crew were good.

Guided Practice Which preposition correctly completes each sentence?

Example: The director chose (among, between) Clara and Sue.
The director chose between Clara and Sue.

1. The school Drama Club decided on one musical (among, between) many different shows.
2. The final choice was (among, between) the two most popular shows, *Oklahoma!* and *Carousel.*
3. Similarities exist (among, between) the two musicals; both were written by Rodgers and Hammerstein.
4. An agreement about the show was reached (among, between) the club members.
5. The plans from now on will be made (among, between) the director and the stage manager.

Using *beside* and *besides*

The prepositions *beside* and *besides* also have different meanings. *Beside* means "next to."

> Please come sit beside me.
> I always keep a book beside my pillow.

Besides means "in addition to."

> Is anyone besides Jeff going skating?
> Besides my sisters, I've invited three friends.

Guided Practice Which preposition correctly completes each sentence?

Example: Who (beside, besides) Hammerstein worked with Rodgers?
Who besides Hammerstein worked with Rodgers?

6. A book on their musicals lies (beside, besides) my desk.
7. (Beside, Besides) this book I have read nothing today.
8. Few popular composers deserve a place (beside, besides) them.
9. They wrote many musicals (beside, besides) *Carousel*.
10. (Beside, Besides) musicals, Rodgers wrote music for a TV show.

Summing up

▶ Use **between** with two persons, things, or groups.
▶ Use **among** with more than two persons, things, or groups.
▶ Use **beside** to mean "next to."
▶ Use **besides** to mean "in addition to."

Independent Practice Write each sentence, using the correct preposition. Underline the preposition.

Example: The score for *Gigi* lies (beside, besides) the piano.
The score for Gigi lies beside the piano.

11. Do you have a preference (between, among) musicals and opera?
12. Does anyone (beside, besides) Dina prefer musical comedy?
13. (Beside, Besides) musicals, Dina also enjoys jazz.
14. Other writing teams (beside, besides) Rodgers and Hammerstein have created musicals together.
15. (Between, Among) them are Lerner and Loewe, who wrote *Camelot*.
16. The relationship (between, among) the composer and the writer of the lyrics must be a very special one.
17. Cooperation (between, among) producers, directors, scriptwriters, and designers is also important.
18. *Oklahoma!* was the first musical to place dancers right (beside, besides) singers on the stage.

Writing Application: A Paragraph Write a paragraph about the preferences you would have if you were an actor. Would you work on stage or in films and TV? Would you like to do comedy or drama? Use *among, beside, besides,* and *between* at least once in your paragraph.

 For Extra Practice, see p. 492.

4 | Verbals: Participles

You know that verbs tell what the subject of a sentence does or is. You can use certain forms of verbs in another way, too, as verbals. A **verbal** is a word that is formed from a verb but is used as a noun, an adjective, or an adverb.

There are three kinds of verbals: participles, gerunds, and infinitives. Notice how forms of the verb *climb* are used as verbals in these sentences.

PARTICIPLE: Pat's climbing friends get together regularly.

GERUND: Climbing is Pat's hobby.

INFINITIVE: She hopes to climb a lot this summer.

A **participle** is a verb form used as an adjective. You have learned about the principal parts of verbs. You can use the present participle and the past participle forms as verbals.

Verb	Present participle	Past participle
climb	climbing	climbed
burst	bursting	burst
pay	paying	paid
think	thinking	thought
spring	springing	sprung
break	breaking	broken
know	knowing	known
take	taking	taken

Since participles act as adjectives, they modify nouns or pronouns.

The blinding storm kept the climbers indoors for several more days.

The trained guide went out into the snow.

His forgotten pick lay on the table.

A participle can come either before or after the noun or pronoun that it modifies.

Chilled and exhausted, most of the climbers returned home after an hour.

Those remaining left shortly afterwards.

Guided Practice What is the participle in each sentence? Which word does it modify?

Example: Trained mountain climbers always plan carefully.
trained   climbers

1. A challenging mountain offers excitement to a climber.
2. Experienced climbers look for new mountains to climb.
3. Spiked boots are one necessary piece of equipment.
4. Climbers also use ropes, axes, and specialized tools.
5. Good climbers, tiring, will rest where they can.
6. Those resting will check their equipment and their route.

Summing up

▶ A **verbal** is a word that is formed from a verb but used as a noun, an adjective, or an adverb.
▶ A **participle** is a verbal that is used as an adjective. You can use the present or past participle form of a verb as a verbal.

Independent Practice Write the participles and the words they modify.

Example: Some mountains challenge even skilled climbers.
skilled   climbers

7. Most mountain climbers follow carefully mapped routes.
8. Still, climbers must anticipate unexpected events.
9. Mountaineers must watch out for loose or falling rocks.
10. Surprised climbers sometimes find blocked paths.
11. Those climbing may rope themselves together.
12. Spiked shoes help climbers move securely on rock and ice.
13. Loaded backpacks are carried by most climbers.
14. Inside the backpack are dried food and other needed supplies.
15. One piece of equipment, forgotten or broken, can bring a climb to a sudden halt.
16. Among the leading areas for climbs in the United States are Mount Rainier and the Rocky Mountains.

Writing Application: A Journal Entry Imagine that you have climbed a mountain with a group of friends. Write in your journal about the experience. Write as though everything were happening right now, in the present tense. Describe the climb in detail, using at least five participles.

 For Extra Practice, see p. 493.

5 | Participial Phrases

Sometimes a participle is accompanied by other words that complete its meaning.

> Amazed by his success, the scientist continued.

A participle and its accompanying words make up a **participial phrase**. A participial phrase, like a participle alone, modifies a noun or a pronoun.

> Sitting in his office, he reread the instructions.

The words that complete a participial phrase may be one or more prepositional phrases.

> Edison, experimenting with different materials in his laboratory, improved the light bulb.

A participial phrase may contain a direct object, and it may be modified by an adverb.

>   participle DO
> Fearing failure, the scientist almost abandoned his work.
>   adverb participle   DO
> Then, steadily gaining confidence, he succeeded.

You will not confuse the main verb of a sentence with a participial phrase as long as you first identify the subject and the simple predicate of the sentence.

>   subject   simple pred.   DO   participial phrase
> The crowd was watching the inventor testing his new creation.

A participial phrase may come before or after the word it modifies. If too many words come between the participle and the word it modifies, however, the meaning becomes unclear.

MISPLACED: John created a robot experimenting in his lab. (Who was experimenting, the robot or John?)

To be clear, place a participial phrase next to the word it modifies.

CORRECT: Experimenting in his lab, John created a robot.

Use a comma after a participial phrase that introduces a sentence. Also use commas to set off a participial phrase following the subject if the phrase is not necessary to the meaning of the sentence.

Struck by joy, Dee laughed.   Jon, waving good-by, drove away.

Guided Practice Identify each participial phrase. What word does it modify?

Example: Early films were still pictures projected onto a wall.
    projected onto a wall   pictures

1. How could someone photograph objects moving rapidly?
2. In the 1870s, this was a serious question facing inventors.
3. Meeting the challenge, one photographer found a solution.
4. He worked with twenty-four cameras neatly arranged in a row.
5. A horse ran past, causing each camera to shoot.
6. For the first time, people saw something moving in a picture.

Summing up

▶ A **participial phrase** is made up of a participle and its accompanying words.
▶ Participial phrases may contain direct objects, prepositional phrases, and adverbs.

Independent Practice Write each sentence. Underline each participial phrase and the word it modifies. Add commas as needed.

Example: The tin can invented in 1812 kept food from spoilage.
    The tin <u>can</u>, <u>invented in 1812</u>, kept food from spoilage.

7. In the Civil War, food sealed in cans was given to soldiers.
8. Troops in the hot South could now eat totally unspoiled food.
9. Pork and beans canned in tomato sauce became popular.
10. Soldiers returning from the war asked for canned food.
11. Canning everything from milk to cherries canners were selling thirty million cans a year by 1870.
12. Inventors noting the success of cans turned to frozen food.
13. Actually, history shows one inventor experimenting with frozen meat as early as 1626.
14. He died from exposure suffered during his experiments.
15. Quickly frozen food did not become practical until 1917.
16. Clarence Birdseye had watched Eskimos freezing food.
17. Adapting their methods he developed packaged frozen food.
18. In 1951 frozen meals appeared causing a minor food revolution.

Writing Application: A Report Write a paragraph reporting on a science experiment. Include some participial phrases.

6 | Verbals: Gerunds

You have learned that a participle is one kind of verbal. Another kind of verbal is a gerund.

> Bowling is a very old sport.
> Gardening is a satisfying hobby.

A **gerund** is the present participle of a verb (the *-ing* form) used as a noun. In a sentence a gerund can function in all of the ways that a noun does. Here are some examples.

> SUBJECT: Reading is my favorite activity.
> DIRECT OBJECT: I enjoy reading.
> OBJECT OF PREPOSITION: Today is a good day for reading.
> PREDICATE NOUN: My favorite activity is reading.

You know that a word ending with *-ing* might be either a verb, a participle, or a gerund. To determine which it is, you must see how it is used in the sentence. First, find the simple subject and the simple predicate. That will help you to know whether a word is a gerund.

> Cora and Andy are running. (*Running* is part of the verb phrase *are running*.)
> The running water overflowed. (*Running* is a participle here, modifying the subject *water*.)
> Running is good exercise. (*Running* is the subject of this sentence. It is a gerund.)

Guided Practice Find each gerund in these sentences. Is it used as a subject, a direct object, an object of a preposition, or a predicate noun? Some sentences have no gerund.

Example: Do you like fishing? *fishing* **direct object**

1. Sketching is fun for me.
2. Marya exercises every day by swimming.
3. Her other leisure activity is painting.
4. She and I are singing in the chorus tonight.
5. Of all my interests, I care most about reading.
6. Traveling comes second or third on my list of favorites.
7. What is the most interesting hobby for you?

▶ A **gerund** is the present participle of a verb used as a noun.
▶ A gerund functions in all of the ways that a noun does.

Independent Practice Write each sentence. Underline the gerund. Then write *subject, direct object, object of a preposition,* or *predicate noun* to tell how each gerund is used. Write *none* if a sentence does not have a gerund.

Example: Walking and running are Harris's favorite outdoor activities.
  Walking and *running* are Harris's favorite outdoor activities. **subjects**

8. A hobby can be anything from fishing to painting.
9. Few things are better for relaxing than a satisfying hobby.
10. Some people enjoy gardening while others prefer reading.
11. Gardening gloves protect the hands of those who do yard work.
12. Many people find pleasure in painting, sculpting, or carving.
13. Practical hobbies include sewing, building, and cooking.
14. Skating, skiing, and swimming are some healthful hobbies.
15. Winston Churchill, a former Prime Minister of Great Britain, liked painting.
16. Collecting was President Franklin D. Roosevelt's hobby, and he acquired an amazing stamp collection.
17. President Eisenhower's favorite kind of exercise was golfing.
18. Relaxing in the White House, he also tried painting.
19. A great number of people relax by jogging.
20. In fact, jogging is becoming a hobby as well as an exercise.
21. Jogging shoes and clothes are sold in many stores.
22. After jogging, a person might enjoy relaxing by reading.
23. Reading about faraway places is satisfying to many people.
24. For others, only traveling itself can fulfill their longing for a change of scene.
25. Often, though, simply visiting an unfamiliar place near home can be as refreshing as a long trip spanning the globe.

Writing Application: A Paragraph Write a paragraph about your favorite activities or hobbies. Do you enjoy outdoor or indoor activities? Do your activities change with the seasons or the weather? Use at least five gerunds in your paragraph, underlining each one.

For Extra Practice, see p. 495.

7 || Gerund Phrases

Gerund Phrases in Sentences

Like a participle, a gerund can sometimes be accompanied by other words that complete its meaning. A **gerund phrase** consists of a gerund accompanied by an adjective, an adverb, a direct object, or a prepositional phrase.

Wearing tight shoes hurts.   (gerund + direct object)
Long-distance running is fun.   (adjective + gerund)
I like dancing on ice.   (gerund + prepositional phrase)
Performing alone is his dream.   (gerund + adverb)

Gerund phrases, like gerunds alone, function as nouns in sentences. Like a noun, a gerund phrase can be a subject, a direct object, an object of a preposition, or a predicate noun.

SUBJECT: Preparing for a concert takes time.
DIRECT OBJECT: Lane began practicing his flute.
OBJECT OF PREPOSITION: Before playing the music, he studied it.
PREDICATE NOUN: His big challenge was walking onstage.

Be careful not to confuse a gerund phrase with a participial phrase. If the phrase functions as a subject or an object in the sentence, it is a gerund phrase. If it serves as an adjective, it is a participial phrase.

GERUND PHRASE: Singing softly was difficult. (subject)

PARTICIPIAL PHRASE: Singing softly, he calmed the baby.

GERUND PHRASE: We began singing the song. (direct object)

PARTICIPIAL PHRASE: The girl singing the song is Pat.

Guided Practice Identify each gerund phrase and participial phrase. Does each gerund phrase act as a subject, a direct object, an object of a preposition, or a predicate noun?

Example: Singing opera requires special skills.
          Singing opera   **subject**

1. Singing opera, they use their voices in special ways.
2. Bart received the prize for being the best tenor.
3. Being the best tenor, Bart had many solo parts.

4. You should try singing high C.

5. Humming in the background, the chorus set a mood.

6. Kristen's dream was appearing with a professional cast.

7. Facing the audience can be the hardest part.

Possessives in Gerund Phrases

Sometimes a noun or a pronoun comes before a gerund.

> Michael's leaving is a disappointment.
>
> I can't imagine his going away.

You should always use a possessive noun or a possessive pronoun before a gerund.

> Because of Roger's being the director, our class play was very successful.
>
> His directing is unequaled.

When you are in doubt about which form to use before a gerund, substitute another noun for the gerund. You know that you need to use a possessive form before a noun. Because a gerund functions as a noun, only a possessive form is correct before a gerund, as well.

> Because of Roger's skill, our class play was very successful.
>
> His talent is unequaled.

Guided Practice Which word correctly precedes the gerund phrase in each sentence?

Example: We were delighted by (Joe, Joe's) fine acting.
   We were delighted by Joe's fine acting.

8. I warned Gino about (them, their) being late.

9. I don't appreciate (him, his) talking back to me.

10. (Fran, Fran's) leaving will solve the problem.

11. (Me, My) being there was a help.

12. That ended (Martha, Martha's) disrupting the rehearsals.

Summing up

> ▶ A **gerund phrase** can be a subject, a direct object, an object of a preposition, or a predicate noun.
>
> ▶ Use a possessive noun or a possessive pronoun before a gerund.

Independent Practice

A. Write each gerund phrase and underline the gerund. Then write how the gerund is used in the sentence: *subject, direct object, object of a preposition,* or *predicate noun.*

Example: A program for helping young artists has begun.
helping young artists   object of a preposition

13. Its goal is providing students with artistic opportunity.
14. Few question the benefits of encouraging talent.
15. The problem is obtaining the necessary money.
16. People find different ways of raising funds.
17. Asking for funds is an important activity.
18. Supporters must continue advertising the program.
19. Now the group will try campaigning on a large scale.
20. Starting such a campaign is a challenging task.
21. Requesting funds from large corporations will be the first strategy.
22. Contacting firms is the director's role.
23. Companies find different ways of being helpful.
24. Helping young artists is a worthwhile cause.

B. Write each sentence, using the correct word before each gerund phrase.

Example: (Sam, Sam's) playing the oboe raised concern.
Sam's playing the oboe raised concern.

25. We all discussed the problem of (him, his) practicing at home in the evening.
26. Sam patiently listened to (us, our) discussing the problem at length.
27. Everyone cheered at the (landlord, landlord's) suggesting a compromise.
28. (Mr. Cole, Mr. Cole's) speaking up that way surprised us.
29. (Sam, Sam's) practicing in the afternoon was the best idea.
30. (Us, Our) working out a solution was not so difficult.

Writing Application: A Report You are planning to write a report about a type of music that you enjoy listening to or performing. Write a paragraph, mentioning points that you might include in your report. Use some gerund phrases in your sentences. Include a possessive noun or a possessive pronoun before the gerund in some sentences.

8 || Verbals: Infinitives

You have learned about participles and gerunds. The third kind of verbal is the infinitive. An **infinitive** is made up of the word *to* and the base form of the verb.

> Paul wants to leave. It is necessary to go.

You can use infinitives as nouns, adjectives, or adverbs.

Uses for an Infinitive	
As a noun:	
subject	To leave would be rude.
direct object	I want to leave.
predicate noun	His decision is to leave.
object of a preposition	I want nothing except to leave.
As an adjective:	
modifies a noun	Now is the time to leave.
modifies a pronoun	She is someone to follow.
As an adverb:	
modifies a verb	To leave, use the back door.
modifies an adjective	We are ready to leave.
modifies an adverb	He is well enough to travel.

Be careful not to confuse infinitives with prepositional phrases that begin with *to*.

> **INFINITIVE:** Is this the road to take?
> **PREPOSITIONAL PHRASE:** Is this the road to the store?

Guided Practice Find each infinitive. Is it used as a noun, an adjective, or an adverb?

Example: To study, you may go to a quiet library.
> *To study—adverb*

1. Do you want to study?
2. When you need to concentrate, look for peace and quiet.
3. Many people go to some quiet corner of their home.
4. Soft music may make it easier to concentrate.
5. The best time to study is before you become tired.
6. To learn, you should organize the information.
7. To summarize is helpful to most people.

▶ An **infinitive** is formed with the word *to* and the base form of the verb.
▶ An infinitive can be used as a noun, an adjective, or an adverb.

Independent Practice Write each infinitive. Then label it *noun, adjective,* or *adverb* to tell how it is used in the sentence. Write *none* if a sentence has no infinitive.

Example: To learn, you must find a good way to study.
　　　　*To learn—**adverb**　to study—**adjective***

8. To study, you must apply your mind to a subject.
9. To question and to think are important parts of studying any subject.
10. One way to study is to memorize.
11. You may not find most things difficult to memorize.
12. To understand, however, is much harder.
13. Knowledge of some kind is important to everyone.
14. For that knowledge, you usually need to study.
15. Not everyone knows the best way to learn.
16. To read, you should have good light.
17. Go to a quiet place without distractions.
18. Important materials to have include pencil and paper.
19. As you study, you will usually want to write.
20. Sometimes you may want anything except to work.
21. The thing to do is to persist.
22. You need to plan and to organize.
23. Make notes to yourself and write an outline.
24. Look in your notes for main ideas to underline.
25. Make a list of important information to review.
26. A good thing to do is to ask yourself questions.
27. A call to a friend or to the library can sometimes help you to find information.
28. To succeed, study only when you feel alert.

Writing Application: A Letter to Yourself Do you ever write resolutions—firm vows to achieve certain goals? Think of five goals you want to accomplish within the next year, and write them down. Then write a letter to yourself about these goals. Use infinitives to tell what you want to do and how you plan to accomplish these goals.

For Extra Practice, see p. 497.

9 | Infinitive Phrases

An **infinitive phrase** is made up of an infinitive and the words that complete its meaning. The phrase may include direct objects, predicate nouns, predicate adjectives, prepositional phrases, or modifiers.

```
       infin.        DO                   infin. prep. phrase
    To invent a machine is not easy to do in a hurry.
    infin.            PN                      infin.   PA
    To be a good inventor, it is important to be calm and
         infin.       adverb
    to concentrate carefully.
```

Infinitive phrases, like infinitives alone, can be used as nouns, as adjectives, or as adverbs.

Uses for an Infinitive Phrase

As a noun:	
subject	To discover a new continent must have been exciting for Columbus.
direct object	About 2500 B.C. the Egyptians started to use metal rings as money.
predicate noun	Edison's goal was to improve the electric light bulb.
object of a preposition	Some people want nothing except to have a long, healthy life.
As an adjective:	
modifies a noun	It is time to try your invention.
modifies a pronoun	I need someone to help me.
As an adverb:	
modifies a verb	The teacher wrote to the patent office to register his invention.
modifies an adjective	His students were all eager to hear about his project.
modifies an adverb	Russ is well enough to continue work now that he is using crutches.

Remember that an infinitive phrase is different from a prepositional phrase.

```
                    infin. phrase
    Columbus tried to discover China.   (to + a verb)
                    prep. phrase
    Columbus sailed to America.   (to + an object)
```

Guided Practice Identify each infinitive phrase. Is it used as a noun, as an adjective, or as an adverb?

Example: The watt is used to measure power.

             *to measure power—**adverb***

1. People most often relate this measurement to electric power.
2. Have you ever stopped to look at the number on a light bulb?
3. The number is meant to show the power requirement in watts.
4. I am going to the store to buy a two-hundred-watt bulb.
5. I plan to use it in the floor lamp.
6. To read more comfortably, I need a stronger light.

Summing up

▶ An **infinitive phrase** is made up of an infinitive and the words that complete its meaning.
▶ Infinitive phrases act as nouns, adjectives, or adverbs.

Independent Practice Write each infinitive phrase. Label it *noun, adjective,* or *adverb* to tell how it is used in the sentence. Write *none* if a sentence does not have an infinitive phrase.

Example: We turn to a clock or watch to find out the time.

             *to find out the time—**adverb***

7. People have always wanted to know the time.
8. To tell time, people once depended on the sun.
9. Early clocks were hard to read accurately.
10. Later, clocks were able to keep more accurate time.
11. Until the nineteenth century, only the wealthy owned clocks.
12. A person might go to an inn to check the time.
13. Clocks on buildings were easy to see clearly.
14. In the 1780s cuckoo clocks were brought to this country.
15. In the 1800s many companies began to make clocks.
16. Now everyone had a way to know the exact time.
17. To get somewhere on time became easier to do.
18. Some used their clocks only to get to work on time.
19. The next step was to develop an alarm clock.
20. By the 1870s people used alarm clocks to wake up on time.

Writing Application: A Paragraph What would you like to invent? Write a paragraph about a gadget to perform some special task. Use at least five infinitive phrases.

For Extra Practice, see p. 498.   Infinitive Phrases   **481**

A series of short, choppy sentences, all beginning with a subject, can be boring to read.

> I read a book. Willa Cather wrote it. It was called *My Ántonia*. The book was fine.

You can create a more interesting effect in your writing by balancing short sentences with longer ones. One way to create longer sentences is to combine shorter sentences with phrases. The sentences above can be rewritten as one.

> I read a fine book by Willa Cather called *My Ántonia*.

You can combine sentences by using prepositional phrases, gerund phrases, and infinitive phrases.

TWO SENTENCES:	I saw Elise. She was at the library.
PREPOSITIONAL PHRASE:	I saw Elise at the library.
TWO SENTENCES:	I saw Ivan. He was writing a book report for our history class.
PARTICIPIAL PHRASE:	I saw Ivan writing a book report for our history class.
TWO SENTENCES:	I write poetry. That's my hobby.
GERUND PHRASE:	Writing poetry is my hobby.
TWO SENTENCES:	I may write a novel. That's my dream.
INFINITIVE PHRASE:	My dream is to write a novel.

You can combine sentences in different ways to emphasize different words or ideas.

TWO SENTENCES:	Write more often. You will improve your skills.
PARTICIPIAL PHRASE:	Writing more often, you will improve your skills.
GERUND PHRASE:	Writing more often will improve your skills.
INFINITIVE PHRASE:	To improve your skills, write more often.

You can also combine more than two sentences into one, using different kinds of phrases.

> I saw a famous poet. She read some of her works. She was at the public library.
> I saw a famous poet reading some of her works at the public library.

Guided Practice Use the kind of phrase named in parentheses to combine each pair of sentences.

Example: I use the library. I enjoy it.   (gerund)
  I enjoy using the library.

1. People go to the library. They read books.   (infinitive)
2. They borrow books. That's not their only purpose.   (gerund)
3. They sit at tables. They use reference books.   (participial)
4. Readers find books. The books cover all topics.   (prepositional)
5. You want to fly a plane. You can find out how.   (infinitive)

Summing up

> ▶ You can combine short sentences into longer, more interesting ones by using prepositional phrases, participial phrases, gerund phrases, and infinitive phrases.

Independent Practice Rewrite each pair of sentences as one sentence, using the kind of phrase named in parentheses.

Example: Willa Cather wrote novels about frontier life. She is known for that.   (gerund)
  Willa Cather is known for writing novels about frontier life.

6. Willa Cather was born in 1873. The place was Virginia.   (prepositional)
7. She grew up in Nebraska. She lived among hard-working farmers.   (participial)
8. At the University of Nebraska, Cather showed great talent. She wrote well.   (gerund)
9. She worked on a magazine. She became the managing editor.   (participial)
10. She left. She devoted herself to writing.   (infinitive)
11. Willa Cather wrote the novel *O Pioneers!* She told of the spirit of frontier women.   (infinitive)
12. She described the hardships and beauty of prairie life. That became her specialty.   (gerund)

Writing Application: A Report Write a short report about an author whom you know about or whose work you have read. Use the kinds of phrases that you have studied in this unit to vary your sentences and to make them interesting.

Grammar-Writing Connection

Modifying Clearly with Phrases

When you combine sentences, remember that the relationship between the combined sentences must remain clear. When you combine sentences with phrases, each phrase must clearly refer to the word you want it to modify. Remember these points when you combine sentences with phrases.

1. Be sure that the phrase does not dangle. There must be a word that the phrase modifies.

    DANGLING: Waiting for the published book, Ann's hands trembled. (Were Ann's hands waiting?)

    CORRECT: Waiting for the published book, Ann noticed that her hands trembled.

    DANGLING: Hoping for success, her manuscript had been sent in.

    CORRECT: Hoping for success, Ann had sent her manuscript in.

2. Place each modifying phrase so that it refers clearly to the word it modifies. The modifying phrase should be as close as possible to the noun or the pronoun that it modifies.

    MISPLACED: Ann writes stories for journals about her family. (Are the journals about her family?)

    CORRECT: Ann writes stories about her family for journals.

    MISPLACED: Ann answered the telephone rising from her desk. (Was the telephone rising from her desk?)

    CORRECT: Rising from her desk, Ann answered the telephone.

Revising Sentences

Rewrite the sentences, correcting the dangling or misplaced modifiers.

1. Ann wrote a book about her family called *Fun and Games*.
2. Sitting down to write, a fire alarm sounded.
3. After working all day, a restful evening was needed.
4. Ann greeted fans eating her dinner.
5. Ribs were served to the guests covered with sauce.
6. Ann interviewed many people writing her book.

Creative Writing

Pieter Bruegel the Elder, *The Fall of Icarus*
Musées Royaux des Beaux-Arts de Belgique, Brussels

Bruegel has focused his painting on Icarus, a figure from Greek mythology. Icarus and his father, Daedalus, were imprisoned on an island. To escape, Daedalus made wings of feathers and wax for them. Though warned by Daedalus, Icarus flew too close to the sun. His wings melted, he fell into the sea, and he was drowned.

- Can you find Icarus? Look at the bottom right of the painting. Are the other people interested in Icarus?
- What might Bruegel have been saying about the relationship between the people of the time and the old legends and traditions?

Activities

1. **Write a new ending.** Pretend that Icarus did not crash but continued his flight and accomplished many great deeds. Make up an adventure for him and write the story.
2. **Put yourself in the picture.** If you lived in this painting, where would you like to be? What would you be doing? Would you live in the city? work in the fields? sail away on a ship? tend sheep? Write a description of your day.

Prepositions and Prepositional Phrases *(p. 462)* Write each prepositional phrase, underlining the preposition once and each object twice.

1. *Xerography* refers to a process of duplication.
2. This process was invented by Chester Carlson in 1938.
3. *Xerography* comes from the Greek words for "dry" and "write."
4. The process was crude at first, but the first copier was sold for office use around 1960.
5. With xerographic copiers we can make copies of anything from printed matter to color photographs.

Prepositional Phrases as Modifiers *(p. 465)* Write the prepositional phrases and the words that they modify.

6. The Big Badlands of South Dakota is famous for its fossils.
7. Badlands are formed in dry areas with nonabsorbent soil on top of rock.
8. The ground is unprotected by plants.
9. Water from rain or snow cuts into it.
10. The land is quite useless for farming or development.
11. The beauty of the landscape attracts many to the area.

Choosing the Right Preposition *(p. 467)* Write each sentence, using the correct preposition.

12. (Between, Among) baseball's best sluggers was Josh Gibson.
13. In a 1930 game (among, between) two black teams, Gibson's home run won the championship for Pittsburgh.
14. No other American player (beside, besides) Gibson has ever averaged as many home runs per times at bat.
15. Gibson's performance can be ranked (beside, besides) Aaron's.
16. Few minor leaguers (beside, besides) Gibson are in the baseball Hall of Fame.

Participles and Participial Phrases *(pp. 469, 471)* Write each sentence. Underline each participial phrase once and the word or words it modifies twice.

17. Atlantis was a fabulous, legendary continent located in the Atlantic Ocean and inhabited by a perfect society.
18. Setting out to conquer neighboring lands, the inhabitants of Atlantis lost to the Athenians ten thousand years ago.

19. Atlantis, sunk by earthquakes and floods sent by the legendary Athenian gods, has aroused the interest of many.
20. Exploring a Greek island, scientists in 1967 discovered a buried city.
21. Is this city a civilization lost centuries ago?

Gerunds and Gerund Phrases *(pp. 473, 475)* Write each gerund or gerund phrase. Then write *subject, direct object, object of a preposition,* or *predicate noun* to show how it is used.

22. Gesturing is visual signaling with the body.
23. Much gesturing is the same around the world, and origins date back thousands of years.
24. Wagging an index finger from side to side can tell a small child not to do something.
25. You may say "Okay" by forming a circle with two fingers.
26. Waving with the palm upward and outward usually means good-by.
27. Your style of walking may even show how you feel.

Infinitives and Infinitive Phrases *(pp. 478, 480)* Write each infinitive or infinitive phrase. Then write *noun, adjective,* or *adverb* to show how it is used.

28. In 1970 Dave Kunst's goal was to walk around the world.
29. Walking so far, Dave, of course, had obstacles to overcome.
30. He returned home midway to recuperate from an attack.
31. When he was forbidden to cross China, he sailed to Australia.
32. To cross Australia takes as many steps as to cross China.
33. Eager to get home, Dave completed his trek in 1974.
34. Was he the first one to walk around the world?

Combining Sentences: Phrases *(p. 482)* Rewrite each group of sentences as one sentence, using one or more phrases.

35. I will describe avalanches. That is my purpose.
36. Some avalanches consist of dry, powdery snow. The avalanche moves up to two hundred miles an hour.
37. The very fine snow crystals travel down a mountain slope. They destroy everything in their path.
38. A great shock wave comes before this type of avalanche. The wave has tremendous force.
39. Another kind of avalanche is called a slab avalanche. It is the most dangerous.
40. The snow cover on the mountain slope breaks up. It swallows anything in its way.

Enrichment

Using Phrases

Weather Watcher Words

Think of ten words used to predict or describe the weather. Make a weather glossary. Include in it weather terms that you hear frequently, as well as more unusual terms such as *cyclone*, *gale warning*, and *tidal wave*. List the terms in alphabetical order. Use prepositional phrases in your definitions.

flash flood—a sudden forceful flood after a heavy rain

Bulletin Board

Imagine that your dentist has hired you to make a colorful bulletin board for the small children who come to the dentist's office. You have completed the entire design except for a list of advice to children on brushing, flossing, and healthy eating. Write ten statements about good dental habits. Use gerunds and gerund phrases in as many items as possible.

Geometric Shapes

Draw five different geometric shapes. Use a ruler, a compass, and a protractor; be exact. On another piece of paper, write instructions for drawing each shape. Assume that someone who has no idea what the shapes are will be following these instructions. Use prepositional, participial, gerund, and infinitive phrases. Then give your instructions to a classmate. Do not tell what the shapes are. If your classmate cannot draw all five shapes, revise your directions to make them clearer.

Mottoes for Motors

Create mottoes for three bumper stickers, using one or more of these prepositions correctly: *between, among, beside, besides.* Write each motto on a piece of paper cut to the size of a bumper sticker. Use neat, colorful lettering. You may wish to illustrate your bumper sticker.

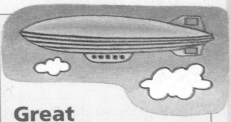

Great Disasters

The sinking of the *Titanic* in 1912 and the explosion of the *Hindenburg* in 1937 are two of the most famous disasters in history. Why? Imagine that you are a reporter going back in time to the scene of one of these disasters. In the library, find out as many details as you can about what happened. Then write a newspaper account of the incident for readers of that time. Include people's reactions to the disaster by using quotes from imaginary interviews. Use at least one participial phrase and one gerund phrase.

◫ To Be or Not To Be?

Players—2–4. **You need**—pencils, paper, 7 index cards for each player. **How to play**— Each player writes an infinitive on each of 4 cards and a label—*noun, adjective,* and *adverb*—on each of the other 3 cards. Shuffle each pile of cards separately and place them face down in separate piles. Taking turns, draw one card from each pile and write a sentence using the infinitive in an infinitive phrase. Shuffle each pile of cards after it is used up.

Scoring—1 point for every sentence that uses the infinitive correctly. The first player to score 10 points wins.

Extra Practice: Unit 13

● Copy the underlined prepositional phrase. Underline the preposition once and each object twice.

Example: You may think of operas as <u>very serious music</u>.

as very serious <u>music</u>

1. Some operas are based <u>on legends</u>.
2. Do you know the story <u>of Hansel and Gretel</u>?
3. <u>According to the tale</u>, they are brother and sister.
4. They save themselves and others <u>from a terrible fate</u>.
5. There is an opera <u>about these two young people</u>.
6. The opera was written <u>by a German composer and his sister</u>.
7. It was first performed <u>toward the end</u> of the last century.
8. <u>Because of its lively music</u>, the opera is quite popular.

▲ Write each prepositional phrase. Underline the preposition once and each object twice.

Example: Opera was born in the Italian city of Florence.

in the Italian <u>city</u>   of <u>Florence</u>

9. Opera was first performed in the late sixteenth century.
10. An opera is a combination of a story and music.
11. The story is sometimes ignored on account of the music.
12. You may be pleased with an opera despite its silly plot.
13. In many good operas, the drama is heightened by the music.
14. For many years most operas were based on myths and legends.
15. During the nineteenth century, operas about more realistic subjects appeared in Italy and other countries.

■ Write each sentence, supplying a pronoun as the object of the preposition. Underline the prepositional phrase.

Example: Tickets for the opera were sent to Jane and _____.

Tickets for the opera were sent <u>to Jane and him</u>.

16. Are the opera tickets for you and _____?
17. *The Magic Flute* was seen by Ronald and _____ last week.
18. According to Evan and _____, the opera was by Mozart.
19. The man next to Evan and _____ said it was written in 1791.
20. Everyone except Maria and _____ enjoyed the opera very much.
21. Did you walk past _____ and her sister in the lobby?
22. I just heard something about their father and _____.

2 | Prep. Phrases as Modifers (p. 465)

● Write the adjective phrase or the adverb phrase that modifies the underlined word in each sentence.

Example: Another <u>word</u> for a cape is a point.   *for a cape*

1. Cape Fear is a <u>point</u> in North Carolina.
2. Cape Fear <u>extends</u> into the Atlantic Ocean.
3. It is an interesting <u>part</u> of the state.
4. It <u>got</u> its name for a very good reason.
5. During September, fierce storms often <u>hit</u> the area.
6. The <u>ocean</u> around Cape Fear becomes quite rough.
7. <u>Ships</u> with excellent radar watch the weather carefully.
8. People <u>watch</u> with fear the approach of a powerful hurricane.

▲ Write the adjective phrases or the adverb phrases in each sentence. The word in parentheses tells you which kind to look for. Then write the words that the phrases modify.

Example: A cape near the tip of Africa is quite famous.   (adjective)
          near the tip—cape   of Africa—tip

9. The Cape of Good Hope is a place of great interest.   (adjective)
10. Because of its location and history, it is famous. (adverb)
11. It was discovered in 1488 by a Portuguese explorer. (adverb)
12. The weather around the cape was stormy. (adjective)
13. The explorer from Portugal named it the Cape of Storms. (adjective)
14. Soon after that, its name was changed by a king.   (adverb)
15. The Portuguese hoped for a new trade route. (adverb)
16. In 1497 their ship sailed around the cape to India. (adverb)

■ Write each prepositional phrase. Label it *adjective* or *adverb*. Then write the word or words that it modifies.

Example: Cape Horn lies at the southern tip of South America.
          *at the southern tip—**adverb**—lies*
          *of South America—**adjective**—tip*

17. The cape is on Horn Island in Chile.
18. The cape and the island were named by a Dutch sailor in 1616.
19. They were named after the city of Hoorn in Holland.
20. The cape extends from the island into the sea.
21. Ships went around Cape Horn from the Atlantic to the Pacific.
22. The slow trip around the cape was filled with many dangers.
23. Then the Panama Canal was built as a link between the oceans.
24. Today many ships pass through the Panama Canal.

3 | Choosing the Right Preposition (p.467)

● Write each sentence, adding the preposition in parentheses that correctly completes it.

Example: Who (beside, besides) Dora is trying out for *Carousel?*
    Who besides Dora is trying out for Carousel?

1. The director must choose (between, among) four people for the part of Billy Bigelow in *Carousel.*
2. (Beside, Besides) Billy, there are other important male roles.
3. The director must also decide (between, among) Nancy, Sarah, and Pam for the part of Julie Jordan.
4. The play is about the love (between, among) Billy and Julie.
5. They stand (beside, besides) each other and sing a duet.
6. (Beside, Besides) "If I Loved You," the most famous song from *Carousel* is "You'll Never Walk Alone."

▲ If a preposition is incorrect, rewrite the sentence correctly. If the sentence is correct, write *correct.*

Example: The club is choosing among *South Pacific* and *42nd Street.*
    The club is choosing between South Pacific and 42nd Street.

7. The people sitting right besides Gino want *42nd Street.*
8. Between the other six members of the cast, *South Pacific* is the favorite.
9. Does *42nd Street* have any big numbers besides the title tune?
10. Isn't there a dance routine among the male lead and female lead?
11. Beside Rose and Gino, who can dance well enough for the show?
12. Ted and Charlotte have worked out a routine among themselves.
13. The teacher will make the final decision among the two plays.
14. Either would definitely be among the best shows we have ever done at Broadmoor School.

■ If a preposition is incorrect, rewrite the sentence correctly. If the sentence is correct, write *correct.*

Example: Respect between all members of the cast is essential.
    Respect among all members of the cast is essential.

15. The link between the music, the story, and the dancing is very important.
16. When I stood besides Kim to sing our duet, I was thrilled.
17. Beside a change of pace, the music can add drama.
18. A duet makes the ties between two characters clearer.
19. Performers should have musical talent beside acting ability.
20. The people in this play are among the most talented that I know.

4 | Verbals: Participles (p. 469)

● Write the underlined noun or pronoun. Then write the participle that modifies it.

Example: Many people enjoy organized <u>hikes</u>.   *hikes   organized*

1. A challenging <u>hike</u> is good exercise.
2. Years ago, a traveling <u>person</u> would usually walk or ride.
3. Sitting in a moving <u>car</u> provides no exercise.
4. Many recreation departments offer planned <u>hikes</u>.
5. <u>Those</u> leading are usually expert guides.
6. An experienced <u>guide</u> will point out features along the trail.
7. Attentive <u>hikers</u>, listening, can learn about nature.
8. Hikers should not go alone into deserted <u>areas</u>.

▲ Rewrite each sentence, adding a participle formed from the verb in parentheses to modify each underlined noun or pronoun.

Example: Can we enjoy a <u>walk</u> in the woods?   (relax)
    Can we enjoy a relaxing walk in the woods?

9. <u>Forests</u> are becoming more common.   (damage)
10. There is a <u>decrease</u> in the number of forests.   (alarm)
11. <u>Those</u> are declining in size.   (remain)
12. <u>Hikers</u> are finding fewer places worth exploring.   (dedicate)
13. Forests are being replaced by <u>areas</u>.   (develop)
14. Many problems can arise from <u>forests</u>.   (disappear)
15. <u>Trees</u> produce oxygen and help to clean the air.   (grow)
16. The <u>number</u> of forests threatens our world.   (decline)
17. <u>People</u> can do much to improve this situation.   (interest)

■ Rewrite each sentence, adding a participle to modify at least one noun or pronoun.

Example: Forest fires are a cause of forest damage.
    Forest fires are a leading cause of forest damage.

18. Flames kill not only trees but other things in the forest.
19. Ashes on streams can kill fish and pollute the water.
20. After a fire, a forest is a wasteland.
21. Hikers and campers must be careful with matches and campfires.
22. As a result of a forest fire, floods can occur.
23. The plants and trees that absorb rainwater are destroyed.
24. Everything in the forest is in danger when a forest fire rages.
25. Schools can teach fire prevention to students.
26. Firefighters are happy to share their knowledge with others.

5 | Participial Phrases (p. 471)

● Each participle is underlined. Write each sentence, and underline all the words that make up the participial phrase.

Example: <u>Standing</u> on the corner, Dan waited for a green light.
    <u>Standing on the corner</u>, Dan waited for a green light.

1. Traffic lights, <u>developed</u> a century ago, are now widespread.
2. The first lights directed the flow of carriages <u>pulled</u> by horses.
3. Boats <u>floating</u> on the canals of Venice obey traffic lights.
4. <u>Installed</u> in London in 1868, a very early signal had mechanical arms for daytime and a gaslight for nighttime.
5. <u>Seeing</u> a need for improvement, cities developed better lights.
6. The first electric traffic light, <u>blinking</u> red and green, appeared in Cleveland, Ohio, in 1914.
7. Early lights <u>operated</u> by hand required an attendant.
8. Automatic lights <u>controlling</u> busy streets appeared in 1926.

▲ Write each sentence. Underline each participial phrase once and the word or words it modifies twice.

Example: Wanting some milk, I reached for a glass.
    <u>Wanting some milk</u>, I reached for a glass.

9. The first glass was a material formed by volcanoes.
10. Using this material, primitive people made knives.
11. The first glass made by people appeared about 3500 years ago.
12. People using fire may have discovered glass by accident.
13. Sand, soda, and lime melted together form glass.
14. With a tube dipped in molten glass, glassblowers made bottles.
15. Using great skill, glassblowers make fragile works of art.

■ Write each sentence, adding commas where necessary. Underline each participial phrase once and the word modified twice.

Example: Used first only in China the umbrella is now common.
    <u>Used first only in China</u>, the <u>umbrella</u> is now common.

16. An umbrella decorated with jewels showed wealth and power.
17. A person holding an elaborately decorated one may well have been royalty.
18. Becoming fashionable in England in the late 1700s the umbrella developed opposition.
19. Drivers of horse-drawn cabs fearing a loss of business wanted to dispose of umbrellas.
20. Staying dry with umbrellas people would not need cabs so often.

6 | Verbals: Gerunds (p. 473)

● Write each underlined gerund. Then label it *subject, direct object, object of a preposition,* or *predicate noun* to tell how it is used in the sentence.

Example: Some people, like squirrels, enjoy <u>collecting</u>.

        collecting **direct object**

1. Have you ever tried <u>drawing</u>?
2. One restful activity is <u>reading</u> books and magazines.
3. <u>Relaxing</u> is important for everyone.
4. Some people relax by <u>dancing</u>.
5. You might like <u>singing</u> in a large chorus.
6. Another possibility is <u>acting</u> in school plays.
7. Many prefer athletic hobbies like <u>skating</u>.
8. <u>Running</u> has become an increasingly popular activity recently.
9. Everyone needs some rest from <u>working</u>.
10. <u>Doing</u> nothing on occasion is not a bad thing.

▲ Write each gerund. Then label it *subject, direct object, object of a preposition,* or *predicate noun* to tell how it is used.

Example: Singing is one kind of performing.

      *Singing—***subject** *performing—***object of a prep.**

11. Many people enjoy performing.
12. Two very popular hobbies are singing and acting.
13. Dancing can be an entertaining activity too.
14. More and more people are enjoying dancing.
15. Looking for a new activity, you might investigate juggling.
16. Activities like juggling can be demanding, however.
17. Practicing and performing can take a lot of time.
18. Some people seeking a hobby might do well in acting.
19. Usually someone finds something interesting about performing.
20. When you start working full-time, you will have less free time.

■ Write a sentence, using each of the following gerunds as the part of the sentence named in parentheses.

Example: hiking   (predicate noun)

      My favorite activity is hiking in Wyoming.

21. swimming   (obj. of prep.)
22. traveling   (direct object)
23. sculpting   (obj. of prep.)
24. conversing   (subject)
25. farming   (predicate noun)
26. using   (obj. of prep.)
27. cleaning   (subject)
28. training   (direct object)
29. working   (predicate noun)
30. thinking   (obj. of prep.)

7 | Gerund Phrases (p. 475)

● Copy each underlined gerund phrase. Then label it *subject, direct object, object of a preposition,* or *predicate noun.*
   Example: The decorator loved visiting the museum.
                    visiting the museum   direct object
   1. Looking at the prints was her favorite activity.
   2. After walking through those rooms, she always had new ideas.
   3. The Cooper-Hewitt Museum had a show on brushing your teeth.
   4. Its aim was reviewing the history of the toothbrush.
   5. Visitors would finish by rushing out for a new toothbrush.
   6. I have tried finding something dull at this museum.
   7. Showing objects of daily life is the museum's purpose.
   8. Visitors enjoy discovering the beauty of these objects.

▲ Write each gerund phrase. Label it *subject, direct object, object of a preposition,* or *predicate noun* to tell how it is used.
   Example: Visiting a museum can be an exciting experience.
                    Visiting a museum   subject
   9. Your goal should be finding the right museum for you.
   10. Some museums prefer concentrating on one type of collection.
   11. Mary's favorite activity is visiting the Museum of Modern Art.
   12. Daniel enjoys dividing his time between the Detroit Institute of Arts and the Dossin Great Lakes Museum.
   13. The Smithsonian aims at attracting all sorts of people.
   14. Finding your way around that gigantic institution is not easy.
   15. Are you searching for a historic airplane, or would you prefer looking at the dresses of Presidents' wives?

■ Write a sentence, using each gerund phrase in the way indicated in parentheses.
   Example: designing houses   (subject)
                    Designing houses is an architect's job.
   16. looking at artwork   (predicate noun)
   17. producing a new style   (object of a preposition)
   18. painting a realistic portrait   (direct object)
   19. being artistic   (predicate noun)
   20. sketching with charcoal   (direct object)
   21. framing a photograph   (subject)
   22. painting in a new way   (object of a preposition)
   23. studying the history of art   (object of a preposition)
   24. often confusing one style with another   (predicate noun)

8 | Verbals: Infinitives (p.478)

● Write the infinitive in each sentence.

Example: To learn is not usually easy.   *To learn*

1. What would you like to know?
2. Some things are difficult to understand.
3. To practice is often important.
4. Good athletes always find time to practice.
5. Your greatest ambition may be to act.
6. Lines may not be easy to memorize.
7. Have you always wanted to skate?
8. To skate requires a lot of practice.
9. For some, an important goal is to teach.
10. For others, to learn is the most important challenge.
11. To succeed, you usually must work long and hard.

▲ Write each infinitive. Then label it *noun, adjective,* or *adverb* to tell how it is used in the sentence.

Example: Both you and I have always liked to swim.

        to swim   **noun**

12. Swimming is not terribly difficult to learn.
13. It is necessary to practice, however.
14. To begin, you may go to a pool or to a lake.
15. The ocean is not a good place to start.
16. The ability to swim does not come naturally to people.
17. I know several people who are not even willing to learn.
18. The first thing to do is to float.
19. To move, you kick your way to the other side of the pool.
20. For every new stroke you learn, you will need to concentrate and to practice.
21. At the end of each lap, remember to turn.
22. Win or lose, the most important thing is to participate.

■ Write a sentence, using each infinitive as the part of the sentence or the part of speech named in parentheses.

Example: to learn   (direct object)

       All her life my grandmother has loved to learn.

23. to fly   (subject)
24. to go   (adverb)
25. to drive   (obj. of prep.)
26. to write   (predicate noun)
27. to start   (adjective)
28. to stop   (predicate noun)
29. to ask   (obj. of prep.)
30. to decide   (subject)
31. to sail   (adverb)
32. to expect   (adjective)
33. to relax   (adverb)
34. to enjoy   (direct object)

9 | Infinitive Phrases (p. 480)

● One sentence in each pair has an infinitive phrase. Write the sentence with the infinitive phrase.

Example: Jill is not going to summer camp this year. She plans to get a job. *She plans to get a job.*

1. Do you want to save money? You can take it to a bank.
2. Walk up to any window. The person to see is a teller.
3. To put money into your account, first fill out a slip. Then give your money and the slip to the teller.
4. Here is another reason for going to a teller. Tellers help you to take money out too.
5. Remember to check your statement. A statement comes to you regularly.
6. It is unsafe to keep much cash at home. Deposit it in an account at the bank.
7. Banking is safer to do. Have you spoken to your banker?

▲ Write each infinitive phrase. If a sentence does not have an infinitive phrase, write *none*.

Example: In ancient times, some people liked to keep money in safes.
to keep money in safes

8. Others held on to their money for safekeeping.
9. Often you do not want to spend all your money immediately.
10. You may still use a bank to keep your money safe.
11. A bank is usually a good place to put your money.
12. A bank account makes it easier to pay bills.
13. When you give money to a bank, the bank uses it.
14. It lends your money to someone else for a good purpose.
15. The bank's purpose is to make money for itself.

■ Write each infinitive phrase. Then write *noun, adjective,* or *adverb* to tell how it is used. If it is used as a noun, label it *subject, direct object, object of a preposition,* or *predicate noun.*

Example: This summer Ernesto wants to buy a new bicycle.
to buy a new bicycle **noun   direct object**

16. To earn some money, he found a good job.
17. To carry his money around might be dangerous.
18. He might find a reason to spend it instead of saving it.
19. Yesterday he went to the bank to open an account there.
20. He plans to deposit money in his account every week.
21. The bank must be able to return his money when he needs it.
22. In the meantime, it will use his money to make loans.

10 | Combining Sentences: Phrases (p. 482)

● Rewrite each pair of sentences as one sentence. Use the underlined phrase in the new sentence. Use commas as needed.

Example: Books were written 5500 years ago. They were made of
         clay.   *Books made of clay were written 5500 years ago.*

1. Ancient people wrote symbols. They wrote on wet clay.
2. They wanted to make the clay hard. They baked it.
3. Clay books can be seen today. They are in museums.
4. The messages are readable. They were baked into clay.
5. Later, people began using brushes or reeds. People wrote books on lamb skin or other materials.
6. Someone wanted to write a book. It took weeks or months.
7. People were copying books. That took a long time too.
8. The solution was this. It was printing books mechanically.

▲ Rewrite each pair of sentences as one sentence, using the kind of phrase named in parentheses.

Example: Someone would write a book by hand. That took months.
         (gerund)   *Writing a book by hand took months.*

9. Books were written by hand. This was true for thousands of years.   (prepositional)
10. Few people needed them. They didn't use books.   (infinitive)
11. Later, people liked books. They read them.   (gerund)
12. Books were scarce. They were written by hand.   (participial)
13. People were making books. A faster way was needed.   (gerund)
14. A new machine was invented. It changed the world.   (participial)

■ **(15–34)**   Rewrite the following paragraph. Using prepositional, participial, gerund, and infinitive phrases, combine some sentences to make the paragraph more interesting and varied.

Abraham Lincoln was born in Kentucky. That was in 1809. Later he moved with his family to Indiana. Young Abe grew up on the Indiana frontier. He received almost no formal education. Still, he loved one thing. That was to read. Abe had to walk a great distance for a book. He was willing. Books and paper were scarce. He made his own arithmetic book from boards. That was like other young people of his time. He did his work on the boards. After that, he would shave them clean with a knife. Abe Lincoln wanted to be educated. That was his dream. Finally, he borrowed law books from a friend. He became a lawyer. Books remained important to Lincoln. That was true all his life.

Language and Usage

Y ou, whose day it is,
Make it beautiful.
Get out your rainbow colors,
So it will be beautiful.

Nootka

Clauses

Getting Ready Clauses can give a fuller, richer meaning to a simple sentence. If they are overused, however, they can turn your sentence into a swamp of words. If you have been afraid to use clauses or been uncertain just what one is, this unit is for you.

ACTIVITIES

Listening Listen while this brief poem is read. How many sentences do you hear? Each sentence has two clauses. Can you find them?

Speaking Look at the picture. What makes this picture a good illustration for the poem?

 **Writing** Imagine that this poem is addressed to you. In your journal, write a two- or three-sentence poem that answers the poet, using the pronoun "I." Tell what you will do with your day and how you will make it beautiful.

1 | Independent and Subordinate Clauses

When you studied sentences, you learned that a **clause** is a group of words with a subject and a predicate.

SUBJECT   PREDICATE

The air   grew cool.

There are two major kinds of clauses, main or independent, and dependent or subordinate. An **independent clause** expresses a complete thought. A simple sentence has one independent clause.

> The air grew cool.

A compound sentence has two or more independent clauses.

> The air grew cool, and it rained.

A **subordinate clause** has a subject and a predicate but does not express a complete thought. It cannot stand alone as a sentence. It depends on, or needs, an independent clause to complete its meaning. A **complex sentence** has one or more subordinate clauses and an independent clause.

>   subordinate   independent
> When the sun set, the clouds appeared.

A subordinate clause may come before or after an independent clause.

> Before spring comes, it will snow.   It will snow before spring comes.

Clauses can be introduced by the same words that introduce phrases, such as *before, after, until,* and *since.* A clause always has a subject and a predicate; a phrase never does.

CLAUSE: I'll see you before the sun sets.

PHRASE: I'll see you before sunset.

Guided Practice

A. Is each clause subordinate or independent?

> Example: when Cary arrives   *subordinate*

1. he will arrive
2. since you aren't going
3. I didn't like it
4. after he got here
5. soon Cary will leave
6. until he departs

B. Is the underlined group of words a phrase or a clause?

Example: You'll have to wait <u>until the rain stops</u>. *clause*

7. You'll need to stay here <u>until the end</u> of the storm.
8. <u>After the rain ended</u>, the traffic reporter watched the roads.
9. <u>From the helicopter</u> he could see everything.
10. He would continue his work <u>until another shift came on</u>.

Summing up

- ▸ A **clause** is a group of words that has a subject and a predicate.
- ▸ An **independent clause** expresses a complete thought.
- ▸ A **subordinate clause** does not express a complete thought and cannot stand alone as a sentence.

Independent Practice

A. Write each clause. Label it *subordinate* or *independent*.

Example: if a tornado develops
         if a tornado develops   **subordinate**

11. tornadoes do not last
12. before the wind blows
13. since they are strong
14. first you take cover
15. when a tornado hits

16. while the storm rages
17. you should stay low
18. it can be noisy
19. soon the storm ends
20. then all is peaceful

B. Write each underlined group of words. Label it *phrase* or *clause*.

Example: People are usually warned <u>before a bad storm</u>.
         before a bad storm   **phrase**

21. Storm warnings were issued <u>before modern forecasting methods existed</u>.
22. <u>During a storm</u> telegraph operators sent warnings.
23. In 1854 French ships suffered terrible losses <u>after being caught</u> in a storm.
24. The ships should have been warned <u>before the storm started</u>.
25. <u>After that occurred</u>, France started the first national storm-warning service.

Writing Application: A Personal Narrative Write a paragraph about an experience that you have had in a storm. Use phrases and clauses. Underline each subordinate clause.

For Extra Practice, see p. 529.   Independent, Subordinate Clauses   **503**

2 | Adjective Clauses

Subordinate clauses, like phrases, can be used in sentences as if they were single words.

ONE WORD: The loud dog followed us home.
PHRASE: The dog, barking loudly, chased us.
CLAUSE: The dog, which was barking loudly, followed us.

You know that a word that modifies a noun or a pronoun is an adjective. An **adjective clause** is a subordinate clause that modifies a noun or a pronoun. Like all other subordinate clauses, an adjective clause cannot stand by itself. It needs an independent clause along with it to complete its meaning.

        independent   subordinate
We need a dog that can guard.

An adjective clause usually follows the word that it modifies. Sometimes an adjective clause may interrupt the main clause.

There must be someone who can tell us more about dogs.
The dog that I like best is the Old English sheepdog.

Adjective clauses are often introduced by relative pronouns. A **relative pronoun** *relates* a clause to the word or words that it modifies. The most common relative pronouns are *who*, *which*, and *that*.

Relative Pronouns	
who refers to people	People who own dogs may exhibit them.
which refers to animals or things	Anyone could enter early dog shows, which were not regulated.
that refers to people, animals, or things	The group that regulates dog shows is the American Kennel Club.

You can also use the words *where* and *when* to introduce adjective clauses.

This is the kennel where we left our dog.
Friday is the day when we left it.

Guided Practice Identify each relative pronoun and adjective clause. Which noun or pronoun does the clause modify?

Example: A dog that does not bark is the basenji.
that—that does not bark—dog

1. A purebred dog is one that has parents of the same breed.
2. The American Kennel Club, which registers purebred dogs, is known as the AKC.
3. Those who own purebred dogs often receive pedigree papers from the club.
4. A dog that has a pedigree must have ancestors that are known and registered.
5. This dog looks like a beagle, which is a type of hound.

Summing up

▸ An **adjective clause** modifies a noun or a pronoun.
▸ A relative pronoun such as *who, which,* or *that* usually introduces an adjective clause.
▸ *Where* and *when* may also introduce adjective clauses.

Independent Practice Write the adjective clauses. Underline the relative pronouns. Write the words that they modify.

Example: Dog breeds that are recognized by the AKC are in six groups. *that are recognized by the AKC—breeds*

6. One group is made up of dogs that are bred as bird dogs.
7. Bird dogs form a group that includes setters and spaniels.
8. The nonsporting group, which is a mixed category, has dogs that are kept for show and companionship.
9. Herders, guard dogs, sled dogs, and farm dogs are among those that are classified as working dogs.
10. Anyone who likes small wire-haired dogs with bushy whiskers and eyebrows will like the terrier group.
11. People who like tiny dogs have a choice among fifteen kinds.
12. Someone who has a Saint Bernard must like big dogs.
13. Irish wolfhounds are the dogs that are the tallest.
14. There are wolfhounds that stand ninety-one centimeters high.

Writing Application: A Description Write a description of a pet dog. Include at least five adjective clauses.

For Extra Practice, see p. 530. Adjective Clauses **505**

3 | Adjective Clauses with *who, whom,* and *whose*

You have already studied adjective clauses introduced by the relative pronoun *who*.

> Emily Dickinson, who lived in the 1800s, was a poet.

The relative pronouns *whom* and *whose* are forms of *who* that you can use in an adjective clause describing a person.

> Dickinson was influenced by the English writer Emily Brontë, whom she admired.
>
> Ralph Waldo Emerson was another writer for whom Dickinson had great respect.
>
> Dickinson, whose life was spent alone, wrote with great intensity.

To decide whether to use the relative pronoun *who, whom,* or *whose* in an adjective clause, see how the pronoun is used *within* the clause.

Using *who, whom,* and *whose* as Relative Pronouns	
who Use as a subject in a clause.	Dickinson was a private person who did not travel far from home.
whom Use as a direct object or an object of a preposition in a clause.	She is a poet whom many admire. She had a small circle of friends to whom she was dedicated.
whose Use as a possessive pronoun in a clause.	Dickinson, whose poems were not published in her lifetime, is well known today.

Remember that the independent clause does not affect your choice of a relative pronoun. Decide how the relative pronoun functions in the adjective clause. If it is the subject, use *who*. If it is an object, use *whom*.

> subj.
> Emily Dickinson is the poet who wrote those lines.
>
> DO
> Emily Dickinson is the poet whom I admire most.

Guided Practice Complete each sentence with *who,* *whom,* or *whose.* What is the subordinate clause?

Example: Everyone _____ knows Mr. Arno enjoys his company.
   who   who knows Mr. Arno

1. Mr. Arno, _____ has five brothers, has only one sister.
2. He lives next door to his sister, _____ children he adores.
3. The children, for _____ he writes poems, adore him.
4. He has become a serious poet _____ work is published.
5. He is a creative person _____ everyone likes.

Summing up

► Use *who* when the relative pronoun is the subject of the adjective clause.
► Use *whom* when the relative pronoun is the direct object or an object of a preposition in the adjective clause.
► Use *whose* when the relative pronoun shows possession.

Independent Practice Write each sentence, using *who,* *whom,* or *whose.* Underline the adjective clause.

Example: Poe is a writer _____ tales are often dramatized.
   Poe is a writer whose tales are often dramatized.

6. There are many people to _____ his mystery stories appeal.
7. Poe, _____ was a fine writer, wrote many of these stories.
8. Those for _____ Poe wrote found meaning in his strange tales.
9. "The Fall of the House of Usher" is a story _____ main characters are twins.
10. Poe created some characters _____ provided models for future detectives in fiction.
11. Poe is a writer _____ people admire throughout the world.
12. He is also a person _____ life remains somewhat mysterious.
13. Poe, _____ is known for his short stories, is also famous for writing poems like "The Raven" and "The Bells."
14. Among scholars he is regarded as an important critic _____ views influenced other writers of his time.

Writing Application: A Description Imagine that you are writing a short story. What will your characters be like? Write a description of one or more characters for your story. Use *who, whom,* and *whose* in at least five adjective clauses.

For Extra Practice, see p. 531.

USAGE

4 | Essential and Nonessential Clauses

You may have noticed that some adjective clauses are set off with commas while others are not.

> The Eiffel Tower was named after the man who designed it.
> The tower, which was built between 1887–1889, still stands.

When an adjective clause is necessary to identify the word it modifies, you do not set it off with commas. This kind of clause is called an **essential clause** because it is essential to the meaning of the sentence. Essential clauses are also known as restrictive clauses.

ESSENTIAL: The Eiffel Tower is the building that defines the Paris skyline.

The man who designed this tower was an engineer.

When an adjective clause is not necessary to identify the word it modifies, you do use commas to set it off from the rest of the sentence. This kind of adjective clause is called a **nonessential clause**. Another name for a nonessential clause is nonrestrictive clause.

NONESSENTIAL: Big Ben, which is the symbol of London, is a clock on a tower.

Big Ben sits atop the Houses of Parliament, which are London's government buildings.

Your decision whether to use commas with an adjective clause may depend on what you want the sentence to mean. Notice how commas change the meaning of this sentence.

ESSENTIAL: People honored the architects who designed City Hall. (Only some architects were honored.)

NONESSENTIAL: People honored the architects, who designed City Hall. (All of the architects designed City Hall, and all of them were honored.)

Using Essential and Nonessential Clauses	
Essential (no commas)	Identifies the noun or pronoun it follows and is needed for the sentence to make sense
Nonessential (commas)	Adds optional information not necessary for the meaning of the sentence

Guided Practice Identify each adjective clause. Is it essential or nonessential? Where are commas needed?

Example: People who move from place to place build temporary homes.

who move from place to place—essential—no commas

1. Such shelters which are easily built are made of various materials.
2. Tents that are made of birch poles and bark are lightweight.
3. One shelter is the igloo which is made of ice, wood, or stone.
4. Igloos that are made of ice have long passageways for entrances.
5. The skins that cover the interior help keep in the heat.

Summing up

▶ An adjective clause is essential or nonessential.
▶ An **essential clause** identifies the noun or pronoun it modifies. It is not set off with commas.
▶ A **nonessential clause** gives extra information about the noun or pronoun it modifies. It is set off with commas.

Independent Practice Write each sentence, underlining the adjective clause. Add commas where they are needed. Label each clause *essential* or *nonessential*.

Example: In the Middle Ages, nobles who had territory to protect built castles.

In the Middle Ages, nobles who had territory to protect built castles. **essential**

6. Some castles that were built in the Middle Ages still stand.
7. The nobles who had them built used them as forts.
8. The castles which were for protection were strongly built.
9. Hundreds of workers who labored for years built the castles.
10. Massive walls which were made of stone, mortar, and iron chains surrounded the structures.
11. Temples that were built in ancient Egypt were made of stone.
12. Stone which was hard to handle was not used for homes.
13. Instead, homes were built of bricks which were easier to use.
14. Bricks that were made of water and clay were dried in the sun.

Writing Application: A Paragraph Write a paragraph about a building that you might design. Use at least two essential clauses and two nonessential clauses.

For Extra Practice, see p. 532.   Essential, Nonessential Clauses

5 | Adverb Clauses

You have been learning about subordinate clauses used as adjectives. An **adverb clause** is a subordinate clause used as an adverb.

> We visited New York after we had seen Washington.

Like an adverb, an adverb clause modifies a verb, an adjective, or another adverb.

> You should check your camera before you take the picture. (modifies the verb *check*)
> New York was still busy while other cities slept. (modifies the adjective *busy*)
> I walked faster in New York than I normally do. (modifies the adverb *faster*)

An adverb clause is introduced by a **subordinating conjunction**. The subordinating conjunction relates the adverb clause to an independent clause.

> adverb clause   independent clause
> When our visit ended, we returned home.

Common Subordinating Conjunctions

after	before	till
although	even though	unless
as	if	until
as if	in order that	when
as long as	provided (that)	whenever
as soon as	since	where
as though	so that	wherever
because	than	while

Different subordinating conjunctions express different relationships.

> WHEN: Whenever I see an airplane, I want to travel.
> WHERE: My little brother wants to go wherever I go.
> HOW: He acts as though I should take him everywhere.
> WHY: He cries because I do not always take him along.
> COMPARISON: My sister is more patient with him than I am.

When you use a subordinating conjunction, think about the meaning that you intend. Choose the conjunction that best expresses that meaning. Using a different conjunction can change the meaning of a sentence. Notice that a comma is used after an adverb clause that begins a sentence.

> Whenever I see a skyscraper, I am impressed.
> Before I see a skyscraper, I am impressed.
> After I see a skyscraper, I am impressed.
> Even though I see a skyscraper, I am impressed.

Guided Practice

A. What is the adverb clause in each of the following sentences? What word or words does each clause modify? Where should commas be used?

> Example: Since the Sears Tower was built I have visited it often.
> *Since the Sears Tower was built—have visited—comma after* <u>built</u>

1. From the top I can see for miles when the day is clear.
2. When I move around the deck I see different views.
3. The city view is spectacular after the sun goes down.
4. Before I go there again I'll buy a new camera.
5. I'd like to take a snapshot while the sun is setting.
6. Chicago is lively because there is always plenty to do.

B. Supply an appropriate subordinating conjunction from the chart on page 510 to complete each sentence.

> Example: _____ people visit Arizona, they think it is all desert. *Before*

7. Visitors may be surprised _____ half the state is high and cool.
8. _____ I visit Arizona, I see its desert scenery.
9. _____ I go, there are interesting things to do.
10. No state has more spectacular sights _____ Arizona does.
11. Millions of people go there _____ they can see the Painted Desert and the Petrified Forest.
12. Residents can live _____ winter did not exist.

Summing up

- An **adverb clause** is a subordinate clause used as an adverb.
- A **subordinating conjunction** introduces an adverb clause.
- Use a comma after an adverb clause that begins a sentence.

Independent Practice

A. Write each sentence, adding commas where they are needed. Underline each adverb clause once and each subordinating conjunction twice.

Example: As long as the weather is warm enough tourists flock to Maine.

As long as the weather is warm enough, tourists flock to Maine.

13. Maine becomes quieter when the weather turns cold.
14. However, Maine offers attractions whenever you go there.
15. Although winters are very cold they are also very beautiful.
16. Most people prefer to visit while the summer sun shines.
17. Few places are more beautiful than Maine's rocky coast is.
18. Wherever you go on the coast look for crashing surf and famous lighthouses.

B. Write each sentence, using an appropriate conjunction from the chart on page 510. Underline each adverb clause.

Example: _____ you go to Maine, try to visit its beautiful national park.

If you go to Maine, try to visit its beautiful national park.

19. _____ you visit Maine in season, you can take hikes in Acadia National Park.
20. Plan to enjoy a traditional clambake _____ you are on Maine's rugged coast.
21. _____ you travel away from the coast, you will find rivers, lakes, forests, and mountains.
22. Maine manufactures wood products _____ it is heavily forested.
23. Many amateur sailors flock to Maine in the summer _____ they may enjoy its beautiful waters.
24. _____ the ocean stays cold all summer, swimming is still fairly popular.

Writing Application: Comparison and Contrast Write a paragraph about two vacation spots that you know about. How are they alike and different? Use at least four adverb clauses.

For Extra Practice, see p. 533.

6 | Noun Clauses

Uses for Noun Clauses

You have studied adjective clauses and adverb clauses. Another kind of clause is the noun clause. A **noun clause** is a subordinate clause that functions as a noun. You can use noun clauses in all the ways that you can use nouns.

subject

NOUN: The message was clear.

subject

NOUN CLAUSE: What he said was clear.

direct object

NOUN: I don't know his telephone number.

direct object

NOUN CLAUSE: I don't know how he can be reached.

indirect object

NOUN: Give Claire Mahoney the message.

indirect object

NOUN CLAUSE: Give whoever answers the message.

obj. of prep.

NOUN: I sent the notice to Raymond Johnson.

obj. of prep.

NOUN CLAUSE: I sent the notice to whoever was interested.

pred. noun

NOUN: That is my intention.

pred. noun

NOUN CLAUSE: That is what I intend.

Words That Introduce Noun Clauses

how	what	where	which	whoever
if	whatever	wherever	whichever	whomever
that	when	whether	who, whom	why

Many words that introduce a noun clause can also introduce other kinds of subordinate clauses. To tell such clauses apart, determine how they are used in the sentence.

NOUN CLAUSE: Phil noticed that the phone was buzzing. (The clause serves as direct object.)

ADJECTIVE CLAUSE: The phone that was buzzing was off the hook. (The clause modifies *phone*.)

Guided Practice Identify each noun clause. Is it used as a subject, a direct object, an indirect object, an object of a preposition, or a predicate noun?

Example: Have you ever wondered how a telephone works?
how a telephone works **direct object**

1. You know that the telephone uses electricity.
2. What you say into a phone creates sound waves.
3. An electric current carries the sound to whoever is listening.
4. Basically this is how a telephone operates.
5. You can talk to whomever you like and say whatever you think.

Noun Clauses with *who* and *whom*

To decide whether to use *who* or *whom* in a noun clause, first decide how the relative pronoun functions within the clause. Use *who* or *whoever* as the subject of a verb within a noun clause.

Who is calling is not clear.   I know who is calling.
Whoever calls can talk to me.   Give the note to whoever answers.

Use *whom* or *whomever* as the object of a verb or the object of a preposition that is within a noun clause.

Whom you meant is not clear.   (You meant whom.)
I don't know whom you talked to.   (You talked to whom.)
Whomever you called didn't answer.   (You called whomever.)
I'll give the message to whomever it was meant for.   (It was meant for whomever.)

Look for how the relative pronoun is used in the clause, not how the clause is used in the sentence. The use of the pronoun tells you whether *who(ever)* or *whom(ever)* is correct.

Guided Practice Identify the noun clause in each sentence. Which relative pronoun is correct?

Example: (Who, Whom) we'll elect is unknown.   *Whom we'll elect*

6. (Whoever, Whomever) they choose will probably accept.
7. Tell me (who, whom) is likely to run for that office.
8. I will vote for (whoever, whomever) will do the best job.
9. The candidate chosen was exactly (who, whom) you predicted.
10. Give my congratulations to (whoever, whomever) chose her.

▸ A **noun clause** is a subordinate clause that acts as a noun.
▸ Use *who* and *whoever* as subjects in noun clauses.
▸ Use *whom* and *whomever* as objects in noun clauses.

Independent Practice

A. Write each noun clause. Label it *subject, direct object, indirect object, object of a preposition,* or *predicate noun.*

Example: Do you know that telephones are important
in elections?
that telephones are important in elections
direct object

11. Campaign workers use whatever helps them.
12. That telephones can be very helpful has been shown in many elections.
13. Who will win the election is what people want to know.
14. Through telephone calls, campaign workers can discover how their candidate is doing.
15. Telephoners ask whoever answers whom they are voting for in the upcoming election.
16. Whether a candidate is popular is a vital matter.
17. Another question may be what the major issues are.
18. Voters usually give whoever is calling an answer.
19. Such surveys can be valuable to whoever uses them.
20. Their real value depends on how the results are interpreted.

B. Write each sentence, using the correct relative pronoun. Underline the noun clause.

Example: (Whoever, Whomever) called will call back.
<u>Whoever called</u> will call back.

21. (Whoever, Whomever) was calling asked about the election.
22. Campaign workers call (whoever, whomever) voted last year.
23. They ask (who, whom) the voter prefers in this election.
24. The call is taken by (whoever, whomever) is home.
25. The answer depends on (who, whom) the caller speaks to.

Writing Application: A Persuasive Paragraph Write a paragraph urging students to vote for your candidate in a school election. Use noun clauses with *who, whom, whoever,* and *whomever.*

For Extra Practice, see p. 534.
Noun Clauses **515**

7 | Combining Sentences: Subordinate Clauses

You already know that one or more subordinate clauses joined to an independent clause form a complex sentence. You can use different kinds of subordinate clauses to join related ideas into a single complex sentence.

When the idea in one sentence is less important than the idea in another sentence, you can make the less important idea into a subordinate clause.

> Our neighbor visited Hawaii. He is a travel agent.
> → Our neighbor, who is a travel agent, visited Hawaii.

Sometimes you can use clauses to combine several sentences into a single sentence.

> We needed information about Hawaii. We called our neighbor. He had taken pictures there.
> → When we needed information about Hawaii, we called our neighbor, who had taken pictures there.

You can combine sentences by using the three kinds of subordinate clauses that you have studied in this unit.

TWO SENTENCES: He told us about Hawaii. That was interesting.
NOUN CLAUSE: What he told us about Hawaii was interesting.

TWO SENTENCES: We are ready for our trip. It will be soon.
ADJECTIVE CLAUSE: We are ready for our trip, which will be soon.

TWO SENTENCES: The weather will be warm. We'll take our suits.
ADVERB CLAUSE: Because the weather will be warm, we'll take our suits.

Guided Practice Combine each group of sentences, using subordinate clauses with the connecting words given. Where are commas needed?

Example: Hawaii is so beautiful. People visit. They hate to leave. (because, who)
Because Hawaii is so beautiful, people who visit hate to leave.

1. Hawaii is a state. It is not part of the mainland.   (that)
2. It is one state. It is a chain of 122 islands.   (although)

3. Many visit Hawaii. They love its scenery. Hawaii sits in the middle of the Pacific Ocean.   (who, even though)
4. I read about Hawaiian history. It was interesting.   (what)
5. Most of the world did not know of Hawaii. James Cook discovered it in 1778. He was a British sea captain.   (until, who)
6. Local chiefs ruled the islands until about 1800. Then the islands were united under a Hawaiian king.   (when)

Summing up

▶ You can use subordinate clauses to combine sentences with related ideas into a single complex sentence.

Independent Practice Combine each group of sentences by using one or more subordinate clauses and the word or words in parentheses. Use commas where needed.

Example: Alaska became a state in 1959. It is the largest state.
   (which)   *Alaska, which became a state in 1959, is the largest state.*

7. Alaska is the largest state. It has the fewest people.   (although)
8. It became a state in 1959. It was the forty-ninth.   (when)
9. The summer sun shines about twenty hours a day. Crops grow rapidly.   (because)
10. Russia offered Alaska to the United States in 1867. Secretary of State Seward bought it for $7,200,000.   (after)
11. The region was an icy wasteland. Many Americans thought this.   (that)
12. People thought Alaska was a waste of money. They called it "Seward's Folly."   (who)

13. Alaska is rich in natural resources. It has paid back its purchase price hundreds of times. (which)
14. Alaska has vast areas of wilderness. These areas attract people. They like the outdoors. (that, who)
15. Expert climbers go to Alaska. They can tackle its peaks. The peaks are the highest in North America.   (so that, which)

Writing Application: Creative Writing Imagine that you are on an unusual island. Write a paragraph about it, using five or more subordinate clauses in your sentences.

Grammar-Writing Connection

Writing Complex Sentences

You have now learned about three kinds of subordinate clauses. You also know how to combine short, choppy sentences into longer, more interesting ones by using subordinate clauses. Here are some hints to help you achieve variety and clarity when you write complex sentences.

1. Use a variety of kinds of clauses in complex sentences.

   ADVERB CLAUSE: Because the day was lovely, we took a walk.
   ADJECTIVE CLAUSE: The bees that buzzed around ignored us.
   NOUN CLAUSE: Suddenly we noticed that there was a beautiful butterfly on the bush.

2. Vary your sentences by changing the position of subordinate clauses.

   We stood very still when we saw the butterfly.
   When we saw the butterfly, we stood very still.

3. Place an adjective clause next to the word that it modifies so that the meaning of the sentence is clear.

   UNCLEAR: There was a picture of a butterfly in Hugo's book that had an orange and black design. (What had a black and orange design—the butterfly or the book?)
   CLEAR: In Hugo's book there was a picture of a butterfly that had an orange and black design.

Revising Sentences

Combine each group of sentences into one sentence that has one or more subordinate clauses. Make sure that the resulting sentences are clear and varied.

1. The monarch is a butterfly. It has orange and black coloring.
2. Scientists study butterflies. They know the monarch.
3. Monarchs taste bad to birds. Scientists know that.
4. These enemies spot the monarch's colors. They stay away.
5. Another butterfly benefits from this fact. It is the viceroy.
6. Its enemies stay away from it. It is quite edible.
7. Its colors are like the monarch's. Birds are fooled.
8. Birds avoid the viceroy. It might be a monarch. They think that.

Creative Writing

Frederick Evans admired medieval architecture and liked to take careful photographs of it. This photograph shows a detail of a fortress.

- Even though this photograph is black and white, Evans has created great depth. How has he done this?
- What lines are repeated in the photograph that give it rhythm and balance? Notice how the arch on the right and its shadow are balanced by the arch on the left and its shadow. These repeated diagonal lines unify the photograph.

Frederick Evans, *Mont St. Michel: Staircase in the Merveille.* Courtesy Museum of Fine Arts, Boston, Gift of David H. McAlpin

Activities

1. **Pretend you were there.** Imagine that you are a prisoner being taken from the dungeon up these stairs. What fate awaits you? What are your thoughts as you climb the stairs? What were you doing when you were taken prisoner?
2. **What happens next?** Imagine that two friends are touring this site when suddenly the wall they are leaning against gives way and they find themselves facing these stairs. They cannot get back to the tour group. Then they hear a harp playing and someone singing. What do they do?
3. **Write a shape poem.** As a very young child long ago, you lived in this castle. Write a poem describing your life and the people. See if you can write your poem in a shape representing some aspect of the photograph, such as the staircase or archway, to add meaning to the poem.

Check-up: Unit 14

Independent and Subordinate Clauses *(p. 502)* Write each underlined group of words. Label it *phrase* or *clause*. Then label each clause *subordinate* or *independent*.

1. The gnu, <u>known also as the wildebeest</u>, is an African antelope.
2. <u>With its massive shoulders and thick neck</u>, the gnu is large.
3. <u>Despite its size</u>, the gnu stands on thin legs.
4. <u>It can travel fast</u> since it takes long strides.
5. <u>When it is disturbed</u>, a herd of gnus performs certain actions.

Adjective Clauses *(p. 504)* Write each adjective clause and underline the relative pronoun. Then write the word or words that the clause modifies.

6. There are many cities that have popular nicknames.
7. Some are names that tell the city's most important industry.
8. Pittsburgh is a place that is called the Steel City.
9. Another major city is Detroit, which is known throughout the world as the Motor City.
10. The people of Dallas, who affectionately call their city Big D, express great pride in their hometown.

Adjective Clauses with *who, whom,* and *whose* *(p. 506)* Write each sentence, using *who, whom,* or *whose*.

11. There are many people _____ inventions improved our lives.
12. An inventor to _____ we are grateful is Alexander Graham Bell.
13. Bell, _____ invented the telephone, also designed devices to help deaf people.
14. This inventor, _____ was born in Scotland, lived in North America most of his life.
15. An inventor _____ many have praised, Bell also made discoveries about aircraft.

Essential and Nonessential Clauses *(p. 508)* Write each sentence, using the appropriate relative pronoun. Label each adjective clause *essential* or *nonessential*.

16. The Eskimos _____ live in the northernmost part of Canada use different dwellings _____ are called igloos.
17. In summer, many Eskimos live in tents _____ are made of canvas.
18. Their winter homes, _____ are sometimes made from blocks of snow, are dome-shaped.

19. The kayak, ＿＿＿ is a boat for one person, has a wooden frame.
20. The Eskimos call themselves *Inuit,* ＿＿＿ means "people."

Adverb Clauses *(p. 510)* Write each sentence, adding commas where needed. Underline each adverb clause.

21. Because they were considered great delicacies oranges have been cultivated since ancient times.
22. Orange cultivation spread as the Roman Empire grew.
23. Before Columbus sailed orange trees grew in the Canary Islands.
24. Sweet, sour, and mandarin are the three main categories of oranges although there are many hybrids.
25. Although sweet oranges grow in warm areas some mandarin oranges can grow in the colder Gulf Coast region.

Noun Clauses *(p. 513)* Write each noun clause. Label it *subject, direct object, indirect object, object of a preposition,* or *predicate noun* to show how it is used in the sentence.

26. Studies show that dreams include sensations of sight, touch, and hearing.
27. Why images of smell and taste are rare in dreams is not known.
28. No one really knows what the purpose of dreams is.
29. One theory is that dreams help solve problems.
30. Ask whomever you know about their dreams.

Combining Sentences: Subordinate Clauses *(p. 516)* Rewrite each pair of sentences as one sentence. Use a subordinate clause that begins with the word in parentheses.

31. A parachute is an umbrella-like device. It is used to slow a body falling through the air. (that)
32. Parachutes now have many uses. They were used only for escape during World War I. (although)
33. Parachutes were used for descents from balloons. They were used for escape from damaged planes. (before)
34. The war ended. Parachutes became standard airplane equipment in the United States and British armies. (after)
35. Many people think this. Parachutes are for recreation. (that)
36. Parachutes can be used to deliver cargo to locations. These places are difficult to reach. (that)
37. Did you know this? Artificial satellites and manned space craft can be slowed down with parachutes. (that)
38. Leonardo da Vinci first thought of a parachute in 1495. He was primarily an artist. (although)

Cumulative Review

Unit 1: The Sentence

Sentences, Subjects and Predicates *(pp. 6, 18, 22, 24, 28)* Write each sentence. Label it *simple, compound,* or *complex*. Draw a line between each complete subject and complete predicate. Underline simple subjects once and simple predicates twice.

1. People wrote on bones or clay before the development of paper.
2. Paper was first made from plants.
3. Plants and water were mixed, pounded, and squeezed into paper.
4. Paper was later made from wood.
5. Machines now produce paper, which people use extensively.

Combining Sentences, Conjunctions, Fragments and Run-ons *(pp. 24, 26, 31)* Rewrite each pair of sentences as one compound sentence, avoiding fragments and run-ons. Use appropriate conjunctions, and add commas where necessary.

6. Kris's grandparents live in Stockholm. He is visiting them.
7. His grandparents will show him around. He'll go sightseeing later.
8. Stockholm is built on islands. You can see it well from a boat.
9. The boat winds through the city. The guide points out sights.
10. Stockholm is a modern city. Its history goes back to the 1200s.
11. Kris has never been to Sweden. His grandparents haven't been to America either.

Unit 3: Nouns

Singular, Plural, and Possessive Nouns *(pp. 92, 95)* Copy each singular noun. Then write its singular possessive, its plural, and its plural possessive forms.

12. Morris   13. mouse   14. child   15. finch   16. fox

Combining Sentences: Appositives *(p. 97)* Rewrite each pair as one sentence with an appositive. Use commas correctly.

17. Cecilia Beaux was a portrait painter. She lived from 1855 to 1942.
18. She is compared to another artist. He is John Singer Sargent.
19. Beaux wrote an autobiography. *Background with Figures* was its title.
20. A friend praised Beaux's talent. The friend was Leila Mechlin.
21. Beaux had a purpose. That was the presentation of reality.

Unit 5: Verbs

Kinds of Verbs, Verb Phrases, Transitive and Intransitive Verbs, Direct and Indirect Objects, Predicate Nouns and Adjectives *(pp. 146, 148, 162, 164, 167)* Write each sentence. Then underline the verbs. Label each verb or verb phrase *action* or *linking* and *transitive* or *intransitive*. Then write *DO* (direct object), *IO* (indirect object), *PN* (predicate noun), and *PA* (predicate adjective) above the appropriate words.

22. How does a simple telescope work?
23. Some telescopes are reflective.
24. The lens gathers light from an object.
25. The light bends to a point, or focus.
26. At the focus, the original object becomes an image.
27. The eyepiece magnifies the image.
28. Then the human eye can see the enlarged image.
29. Willis gave his brother a telescope for graduation.

Tenses; *be, have, do* *(pp. 150, 153)* Write the four principal parts of each verb.

30. hop	32. aim	34. worry	36. be
31. bathe	33. play	35. do	37. have

Irregular Verbs, Progressives *(pp. 153–158, 160)* Write each sentence, using the correct verb. Underline the verb phrase. Label its tense and, when appropriate, its progressive form.

38. The human race (has, have) always studied the stars.
39. People (have, had) been gathering information about the heavens before anyone (make, made) telescopes.
40. Seventeen hundred years before Columbus, a person (shown, showed) that the earth (is, are) a globe.
41. In the 1600s, Galileo (can, could) see details of the planets.
42. After this, scientists (was, were) still searching for better ways to make telescopes.
43. Isaac Newton (make, made) the first telescope that (produce, produced) a really sharp image.
44. By the 1800s, Alvan Clark (was, were) making powerful lenses that astronomers are still (use, using).
45. What will scientists (have, has) found by the next century?
46. Scientists will be (look, looking) for glass that can be large but will not (crack, cracks) when cooled.
47. A large telescope will (show, showing) the disk of a star.

Cumulative Review, *continued*

Unit 7: Modifiers

Adjectives and Adverbs *(pp. 236, 242)* Write each modifier, labeling it *adjective* or *adverb*. Then write the word or words that it modifies. Do not list articles.

48. Certain North American pioneers built wooden cabins.
49. Swedish settlers probably built log cabins in the 1600s.
50. Logs were not cut carelessly, for their size was important.
51. Carefully the builder fit the split logs together.
52. Few people could afford costly glass panes in their windows.

Comparing with Adjectives and Adverbs *(pp. 239, 245)* Write each sentence, using the correct degree of each modifier.

53. One of the _____ castles in the world is in Bavaria.   (elaborate)
54. Of all the castles he has seen, Marc likes this one, built by King Ludwig II, _____.   (well)
55. Ludwig's Linderhof is _____ than his other castles.   (unusual)
56. Linderhof has the _____ opera stage ever built.   (strange)
57. Linderhof has _____ charm than Ludwig's other castles.   (much)

Unit 9: Capitalization and Punctuation

Sentences; Proper Nouns and Adjectives; Dates, Addresses, and Letters; Abbreviations; Commas; Colons and Semicolons *(pp. 304, 305, 308, 312, 319, 321)* Write the following letter, using capital letters and punctuation where necessary.

58.   15 ridge st
59.   orange ca 92667
60.   feb 18 1988
61. stamp masters inc
62. p o box 583
63. beaumont tx 77704
64. dear sir
65.   please send me the following items one stock book one pair of tweezers one stamp album and one box of hinges
66. these were advertised in your spring catalogue
67.   i understand that you are opening a store in encino
68. That will please us western customers
69.   sincerely yours
70.   kirk o'brien

Quotations, Titles *(pp. 314, 317)* Write each sentence, adding the correct punctuation and capitalization.

71. What does the word *philately* mean Kirby asked.
72. It is the collection Barney responded of postage stamps.
73. Kirby then asked what was the first American stamp magazine?
74. Barney said that it was called the stamp collector's review.
75. Todd asked to borrow Barney's book, famous stamps of europe.

Commas *(pp. 308, 310)* Write each sentence, adding commas where necessary.

76. Paris the City of Light is a favorite tourist spot.
77. My friends you should visit this city.
78. Some people like Paris in winter but most prefer it in spring.
79. Looking from the top of Notre Dame you can see the entire city spread out before you.
80. The Paris Opera which has ceilings by Chagall is a spectacularly beautiful building.

Unit 11: Pronouns

Pronoun Case, Choosing Pronouns *(pp. 386, 400)* Write each sentence correctly. Label the pronouns *subject* or *object*.

81. Mr. Cargill asked Ben and (I, me) to name a volcano in Italy.
82. Neither (he, him) nor (I, me) knew.
83. (We, Us) boys hadn't studied.
84. Lu and (she, her) mentioned Mt. Etna.
85. "Ask (she, her) and (I, me) the next question, please."

Indefinite Pronouns *(p. 393)* Write the form in parentheses that agrees with each indefinite pronoun.

86. All (has, have) completed (his or her, their) lists of state mottos.
87. Not everyone (has, have) defined *Eureka* as "I have found it."
88. Each of the teachers (has, have) checked the work.
89. Most of the students (has, have) remembered Nevada.
90. None of the answers on my test (was, were) wrong.

Antecedents, Kinds of Pronouns *(pp. 383, 389, 391, 397)* Rewrite each sentence, correcting any pronoun errors.

91. This here painting was done by Ron and myself.
92. Who's paintings are in the museum this month?
93. Sam told Dan that he visited the Brooklyn Museum.
94. Who did you take with you to the exhibit?
95. Who have you told about it besides herself?

Cumulative Review, continued

Unit 13: Phrases

Prepositional Phrases as Modifiers *(p. 465)* Write each prepositional phrase and the word it modifies.

  96. Periwinkles are a kind of sea snail.
  97. You can find them off the coasts of the Atlantic and the Pacific.
  98. Periwinkles depend on algae for food.
  99. Algae are sea plants without stems, roots, or leaves.

Participles and Participial Phrases *(pp. 469, 471)* Write the participial phrases and the words modified. Underline each participle.

  100. Letters sent to John Adams by his wife still exist.
  101. Married fifty-four years, John and Abigail were a close couple.
  102. The political advice given in Abigail's letters was usually sound.
  103. Telling much about her times, her letters express strong feelings about women's education and freedom.

Gerunds and Gerund Phrases *(pp. 473, 475)* Write each gerund phrase, underlining the gerund. Then label it *subject, direct object, object of a preposition,* or *predicate noun.*

  104. You can learn a lot by reading the newspaper.
  105. Scanning the headlines daily will help you be informed.
  106. Jason's favorite activity is doing the crossword puzzle.
  107. Myra likes reading about travel.

Infinitive Phrases *(p. 480)* Write each infinitive phrase. Label it *noun, adjective,* or *adverb* to tell how it is used.

  108. Now is the time to improve your diet.
  109. To eat wisely is important to your well-being.
  110. One way is to consume whole grains.
  111. To have a better diet, you should consume less fat.

Combining Sentences: Phrases *(p. 482)* Rewrite each pair of sentences as one, using the kind of phrase in parentheses.

  112. Bret Harte was born in Albany, New York, in 1836. He moved when he was eighteen. (participial)
  113. He was out West. He worked for a newspaper. (prepositional)
  114. He wanted something. He would gain recognition. (infinitive)
  115. He wrote a story. It brought him fame. (gerund)

Unit 14: Clauses

Adjective Clauses *(pp. 504, 506, 508)* Write each sentence. Underline the adjective clause once and the relative pronoun twice. Add commas if necessary.

116. *Madama Butterfly* which is an opera about Japan was written by a composer whose name was Puccini.
117. *The Girl of the Golden West* which is an opera about the Old West was written by the same composer.
118. Puccini also wrote an opera that takes place in Paris.
119. He never finished *Turandot* which is his finest work.

Adverb Clauses *(p. 510)* Write each sentence. Underline the adverb clause once and the subordinating conjunction twice.

120. Weather seems unpredictable because we have not yet learned enough about the forces affecting it.
121. Forecasters make use of sensitive equipment so that they can make accurate observations of the weather.
122. Although they are often correct in their predictions, sometimes the weather surprises forecasters.
123. Even though a storm stays at sea, its effect can extend hundreds of miles.
124. Strong winds can take control of a storm while other conditions are being measured.

Noun Clauses *(p. 513)* Write each noun clause. Label it *sub.*, *dir. obj.*, *indir. obj.*, *obj. of a prep.*, or *pred. noun.*

125. Whoever is interested in the sea may enjoy visiting an aquarium.
126. The aquarium near the waterfront is where I'd like to go.
127. Beth suggested that we go there next Saturday.
128. We will probably go to wherever there are dolphins.
129. Ask whoever has the guidebook where we should go.

Combining Sentences: Subordinate Clauses *(p. 516)* Rewrite each pair of sentences as one sentence, using the kind of clause and the introductory word given in parentheses.

130. William Carlos Williams carried on a successful career as a doctor. He wrote poetry. *(adverb, while)*
131. Wallace Stevens was a successful lawyer and businessman. His poetry is very symbolic. *(adjective, whose)*
132. The poet e. e. cummings was also a painter. Do you know? *(noun, that)*

Enrichment

Using Clauses

Clause Capers

Choose a subordinating conjunction from page 510. Write a subordinate clause starting with it. Make each following word begin with the next letter of the conjunction. Underline the first letter of each word. Then add an independent clause to form a sentence. How many sentences can you write?

UNLESS   Unless <u>N</u>ed Lehman <u>e</u>ats <u>s</u>ome <u>s</u>upper, he won't have energy for soccer.

Cartoon Clauses

Cut out of a newspaper five comic strips or editorial cartoons that have sentences with clauses, or write your own sentences with clauses for the cartoons.

Extra! Draw your own cartoon. Write a sentence with a clause to explain it.

Clause-Clues Crossword

Create a crossword puzzle. Choose ten words, with at least five that you can define by using clauses. Write the longest word on graph paper—down or across—one letter per square. Crisscross as many words as you can. Give each word a number.

Find the words in your dictionary. On separate paper, write clues or definitions. Write complete sentences, with clauses in at least five of them. Number them and put them into columns for *Across* and *Down*.

On clean graph paper, copy the outline of the puzzle, leaving out the letters but including the numbers. Give the puzzle and clues to a classmate to solve.

1 | Indep. and Subord. Clauses (p.502)

● Write each underlined clause. Label it *subord.* or *indep.*
  Example: <u>Because sea water is salty</u>, it is not drinkable.
       Because sea water is salty **subord.**
  1. <u>Since sea water contains salt</u>, the water tastes bitter.
  2. In general, <u>most sea water is about 3 percent salt</u>.
  3. <u>Although some seas are saltier</u>, that is the average.
  4. <u>The Dead Sea, for example, is twenty-five percent salt</u>.
  5. <u>While it is the saltiest sea on Earth</u>, it is small.
  6. Nothing lives in the Dead Sea <u>because the sea is so salty</u>.
  7. <u>Certainly salt water freezes</u>, as you may know.
  8. <u>Where the ocean is deep</u>, salt water can't freeze.

▲ Write each underlined word group. Label it *phrase* or *clause.*
  Example: <u>Before modern forecasting</u>, what did people know about
       the weather? *Before modern forecasting* **phrase**
  9. <u>Before people understood weather</u>, they observed and recorded it.
  10. Sailors were the best observers <u>until modern times</u>.
  11. <u>Since their lives depended on weather</u>, they watched it closely.
  12. Ships met tropical storms <u>after new sea routes were developed</u>.
  13. Europeans never knew such storms <u>before the fifteenth century</u>.
  14. *Hurricane* is a name <u>based on an Indian word</u>.
  15. <u>Until winds reach seventy-four miles per hour</u>, a storm is not considered a hurricane.

■ Write *phrase* or *clause* to identify each word group. Change each phrase into a subordinate clause, and then write a complex sentence using each subordinate clause.
  Example: before the end of the day
       phrase *Before the day ends, a major storm may strike.*
  16. before a hurricane occurs
  17. until weather predictions become accurate
  18. after a severe hurricane or other storm
  19. after spotting a tornado in the distance
  20. before the invention of the thermometer in the 1600s
  21. until actually experiencing a blizzard
  22. because of the severity of some storms

2 | Adjective Clauses (p. 504)

● Each adjective clause is underlined. Write the noun or pronoun that it modifies.

Example: The bloodhound, <u>which is used for tracking</u>, is a gentle dog.   *bloodhound*

1. The dog <u>that has the best sense of smell</u> is the bloodhound.
2. Bloodhounds came from England, <u>where they were well known</u>.
3. People <u>who are familiar with bloodhounds</u> know they are gentle.
4. These dogs are different from others <u>that are used by police</u>.
5. Bloodhounds, <u>which are calm and friendly</u>, offer no protection.
6. Instead, they are used for their amazing noses, <u>which help them to track criminals and lost persons</u>.
7. Someone <u>who is trailed by a bloodhound</u> will often be found.

▲ Write each adjective clause and the word or words that it modifies.

Example: The golden retriever, <u>which is an attractive dog</u>, is a breed <u>that originated in England in the 1800s</u>.

   which is an attractive dog—golden retriever
   that originated in England in the 1800s—breed

8. These dogs, which really are golden, are handsome.
9. It is one breed that is used for guiding people who are blind.
10. World War I was the time when dogs were first trained for this.
11. Morristown, New Jersey, is the place where many seeing-eye dogs are trained.
12. Dogs are trained there and given to people who need them.
13. The golden retriever, which is smart, even-tempered, and devoted, has a personality that is ideal for the job.

■ Add one or more adjective clauses to each independent clause to form a complex sentence.

Example: Some people prefer dogs.
   Some people who like pets prefer dogs that are good watchdogs.

14. People may want watchdogs.
15. Other people may prefer a different kind.
16. Anyone can find a good dog.
17. Animal shelters take in animals.
18. The shelters are usually full of animals.
19. Each of the animals will be right for someone.
20. An animal lover will probably go home with a new pet.

3 | Clauses: *who, whom, whose* (p. 506)

● The adjective clause in each sentence is underlined. Write the clause correctly using *who, whom,* or *whose* to complete it.

Example: Washington Irving was an author _____ wrote with humor.
        who wrote with humor

1. Washington Irving, _____ was born in 1783, was a New Yorker.
2. Irving was an American writer _____ Europeans admired.
3. He was an author _____ favorite topic was New York.
4. Those _____ have heard of Irving know "Rip Van Winkle."
5. Rip Van Winkle was a person _____ life took a strange turn.
6. He was the man _____ fell asleep for twenty years.
7. Washington Irving's last work was a life of George Washington, for _____ he had been named.

▲ Write each sentence, using *who, whom,* or *whose.* Underline the adjective clause.

Example: People for _____ poetry is fun like to read poems aloud.
        People for whom poetry is fun like to read poems aloud.

8. Those _____ write poems use language in a special way.
9. There are poets _____ work has been read for centuries.
10. The poet _____ people call the Bard of Avon is Shakespeare.
11. Readers to _____ words and their sounds appeal enjoy poetry.
12. A person _____ reads a poem aloud may appreciate it more.
13. Anyone _____ has something to say can say it in a poem.
14. There are poets _____ poems tell a story.
15. There are some for _____ a poem expresses feelings.

■ Add an adjective clause introduced by *who, whom,* or *whose* to each independent clause to form a complex sentence. Vary the pronouns.

Example: People usually like to read.
        People who like to write usually like to read.

16. Writers are people.
17. Shakespeare was a sixteenth-century writer.
18. Among writers are many women.
19. One American poet is Emily Dickinson.
20. Poe was a skilled writer.
21. Many people dream of creating great works of literature.
22. There are best-selling writers.
23. The most popular books are about people.
24. Writers have opportunities in the theater, movies, and TV.

4 | Essential and Nonessential Clauses (p. 508)

● Write *essential* if the underlined adjective clause is necessary to the meaning of the sentence. Write *nonessential* if the clause only adds information.

Example: People have always needed shelters that protect them.
        essential

1. At first people lived in caves that were in hills and cliffs.
2. The first people who moved out of the caves built huts.
3. The huts, which were very crude, did offer shelter.
4. These early builders, who used sticks, mud, or reeds, were the world's first architects.
5. Soon huts were built for animals, which also needed shelter.
6. Then came more shelters, which were used for storage.
7. Eventually, people built structures that were large and strong.

▲ Write each sentence. Underline the adjective clause. Label it *essential* or *nonessential*.

Example: The Egyptian climate, which is hot, requires cool homes.
      The Egyptian climate, which is hot, requires cool homes.
      nonessential

8. Ancient Egyptians built houses that were designed to be cool.
9. The windows, which were small and few, admitted little sunlight.
10. Doorways faced north to catch the breeze that came from there.
11. Outside walls, which were whitewashed, reflected the sun's heat.
12. Most houses had a lobby that led to a cool inner room.
13. The Egyptians, who liked decorations, often painted this room.
14. Even in the homes of people who were not wealthy, the inner walls were often decorated.

■ Rewrite each sentence as a complex sentence that includes an adjective clause. Label it *essential* or *nonessential*. Use commas correctly.

Example: Kent designed two buildings.
      The two buildings that Kent designed both won architectural awards. **essential**

15. The architect designed the house.
16. The house sits on a cliff above the beach.
17. The owners approved the design.
18. Visitors often admire the house.
19. The house next door is painted gray.
20. The Justins built that house themselves.

5 | Adverb Clauses (p. 510)

● The adverb clause in each sentence is underlined. Write each subordinating conjunction.

Example: <u>When city space became scarce</u>, people built skyscrapers.
When

1. <u>Because skyscrapers extend upward</u>, they take up little land.
2. Skyscrapers became common <u>as the price of steel went down</u>.
3. Skyscrapers are built with steel skeletons <u>because steel can support the weight of these buildings</u>.
4. <u>Before steel was used</u>, the walls had to support the weight.
5. Tall structures could not be built <u>unless walls were very thick</u>.
6. Skyscrapers can have glass walls <u>if the steel structure is solid</u>.
7. Some skyscrapers are taller <u>than the Empire State Building is</u>.
8. We visited the World Trade Center <u>when we were in New York</u>.

▲ Write each adverb clause, underlining the subordinating conjunction. Write the word or words that the clause modifies.

Example: Before a skyscraper is built, engineers check the soil.
<u>Before</u> a skyscraper is built—check

9. Before a proper foundation is designed, a soil test is done.
10. If the test results are approved, plans can continue.
11. After the building site is cleared, the digging begins.
12. When the digging is done, the base and superstructure are begun.
13. Each piece of steel is numbered so that workers know its place.
14. The pieces are bolted until welders join them permanently.
15. The construction seems to go faster than passers-by expect.
16. Unless something unexpected occurs, people can soon move in provided that everyone cooperates.

■ Write a complex sentence by adding an adverb clause to each independent clause. Use a subordinating conjunction.

Example: I want to travel.
Whenever I see a plane or train, I want to travel.

17. I would first like to tour the United States.
18. There will be interesting things to see.
19. I can plan the trip in my imagination.
20. I will visit the southern states.
21. I plan to remain there.
22. The cooler Northeast will beckon.
23. My next visit will be to the southwestern states.
24. I will travel to the Northwest and then to the Midwest.

6 | Noun Clauses (p. 513)

● Each noun clause has been underlined. Write *subject, direct object, indirect object, object of a preposition,* or *predicate noun* to tell how the clause is used in the sentence.
  Example: Did you ever wonder <u>how other people answer the phone?</u>
          direct object

  1. <u>How people answer the phone</u> varies around the world.
  2. In Israel you give <u>whoever telephones</u> a big "Shalom."
  3. "Bueno" is <u>what a Mexican says on the telephone.</u>
  4. In Italy, "Pronto" says <u>that you are ready to talk.</u>
  5. <u>Where you are speaking from</u> does make a difference.
  6. "Hello" is similar to <u>what natives say in France and Germany.</u>
  7. You may wonder <u>why people say "moshi-moshi" in Japan.</u>
  8. That is <u>how the Japanese say hello.</u>

▲ Write each noun clause. Label it *subject, direct object, indirect object, object of a preposition,* or *predicate noun.*
  Example: That telephones have changed is quite obvious.
          that telephones have changed   ***subject***

  9. Did you know that the first telephones were sold in pairs?
  10. A direct wire ran between wherever the two phones were placed.
  11. How to extend the use of telephones was solved by cables.
  12. Wires ran to a central office from wherever there was a phone.
  13. One person with a phone could talk to whoever else had one.
  14. By World War I, a telephone was what every American wanted.
  15. A telephone offered whoever used it a new way to communicate.
  16. Di said that coin-operated calls used to cost a nickel.

■ Write each sentence, using *who, whoever, whom,* or *whomever.* Then write *subject, direct object,* or *object of a preposition* to tell how the relative pronoun functions in the clause.
  Example: Give the information to _____ calls.
          Give the information to whoever calls.   ***subject***

  17. _____ uses the telephone should thank its inventor.
  18. Offer _____ invented the phone your appreciation.
  19. _____ you should thank is Alexander Graham Bell.
  20. Telephones are taken for granted by _____ uses them.
  21. What if Bell had not been _____ he was?
  22. How would you contact _____ you wanted to contact?
  23. You would speak directly only to _____ you saw.
  24. Appreciate the phone when you next reach _____ you try to call.

7 | Combining Sentences: Clauses (p. 516)

● Combine each pair of sentences using the word in parentheses. Write each new sentence.

Example: I want to visit many places. I travel.   (when)
I want to visit many places when I travel.

  1. Puerto Rico is an island. I would like to visit it.   (that)
  2. Many tourists go there. It has a fine climate and beautiful beaches.   (because)
  3. The island is a part of the United States. Columbus landed there. (where)
  4. Columbus claimed the island for Spain. He landed on the island in 1493.   (when)
  5. Spain originally named the major city Puerto Rico. Puerto Rico means "rich port."   (which)

▲ Write a sentence, combining each group of sentences by using a subordinate clause. Use the word or words in parentheses.

Example: San Juan is Puerto Rico's capital. It is on the sea.   (which)
San Juan, which is Puerto Rico's capital, is on the sea.

  6. San Juan has a pleasant climate, lovely beaches, and fine hotels. It is a popular resort.   (which)
  7. It is a fine place to visit. Most tourists know.   (that)
  8. Puerto Ricans are citizens of the United States. They can move to the mainland. They may want to.   (who, whenever)
  9. Many speak English there. Spanish is the main language. It is used socially and in business.   (although, that)
  10. Columbus landed there in 1493. He claimed Puerto Rico for Spain. Spain had sponsored his exploration.   (when, which)

■ Write a sentence, combining each group of sentences by using subordinate clauses.

Example: Colonists arrived from Spain. They settled in Puerto Rico.
Colonists who arrived from Spain settled in Puerto Rico.

  11. Columbus set out on his second voyage to the New World. He reached Puerto Rico in 1493.
  12. Columbus had already discovered the island. A group of Spaniards settled there in 1508. They were led by Ponce de León.
  13. Life for the settlers was difficult. The population slowly grew. The colony finally reached a significant size.
  14. In a 1967 election, Puerto Ricans decided something. They would remain a commonwealth rather than become a state or an independent nation.

Student's Handbook

STUDY STRATEGIES

Using the Dictionary

Your dictionary contains a lot of information. Learning to use it efficiently will help you to find facts quickly.

Guide words At the top of each page you will find the first and last words that are on the dictionary page. Guide words help you to locate the words you are looking for more quickly. Which pair of guide words below would you find at the top of a page listing the word *gape?*

gangway • garish   **garnet • gaslight**

The excerpt below includes typical features of a dictionary entry.

> **gar • gle** (gär′gəl) *v.* **gar • gled, gar • gling. 1.** To tilt the head back and exhale air through a liquid held in the back of the mouth in order to wash the mouth or throat. **2.** To produce the sound of gargling. —*n.* **1.** A solution, often medicated, used for gargling. **2.** A sound made by gargling. [Old French *gargouiller*, from *gargouille*, throat.]

Syllabication Entry words are divided into syllables, separated by dots.

Phonetic respelling To help you to pronounce the entry word, its phonetic respelling is given. Stress marks show where a word has primary (′) and secondary (′) accents. A **pronunciation key** at the foot of each or every other page explains the phonetic symbols. Check the pronunciation key for examples of the sounds shown in the respelling.

ă pat   ā pay   â care   ä father   ĕ pet   ē be   ĭ pit   ī ice   î near   ŏ pot
ō go   ô paw, for   oi oil   ŏŏ book   ōō boot   yōō cute   ou out   ŭ cut
û fur   th the   th thin   hw which   zh usual   ər butter
ə ago, item, pencil, atom, circus

Part-of-speech label Following the phonetic respelling is the part of speech of the entry word, often abbreviated *n., v., adj., adv., prep.* This label can be a clue to choosing the definition that you need. Notice how the word *groom* is used in the sentence *Mr. Apple wants to groom Brian to be a salesperson. Groom* is used as a verb. Now check the verb definitions in the entry below. Definition 3 fits the sentence above.

> **groom** (grōōm) *or* (grŏŏm) *n.* **1.** A person who takes care of horses. **2.** A bridegroom. —*v.* **1.** To make neat. **2.** To clean and brush (an animal). **3.** To train (a person), as for a certain job or position.

Definitions The meanings of a word form the main part of a dictionary entry. Definitions are numbered if there are more than one.

Etymology The history or origin of a word—its *etymology*—often appears in brackets at the end of a definition. From what languages does the word *gargoyle* come?

> **gar • goyle** (gär′goil′) *n.* A roof spout carved to represent a grotesque human or animal figure. [Middle English *gargoyl,* from Old French *gargouille,* throat, from Latin *gurgulio,* windpipe.]

Shown below is the entry for a word with an interesting etymology. Notice that *insulate* comes from *insula,* the Latin word for "island." Think about how the present meaning of *insulate* is related to the Latin word: (An island is land that is isolated or detached.)

> **in • su • late** (ĭn′sə lāt′) *or* (ins′yə-) *tr. v.* -lat • ed, -lat • ing. **1.** To detach; isolate. **2.** To prevent the passage of heat, electricity, or sound into or out of, especially by surrounding or lining with material that blocks such flow. [From Latin *īnsula,* island, isle.]

Homographs Some words have the same spellings but different meanings and origins. These words are listed as separate entries. In the homographs shown on the next page, you can see that *sash¹* and *sash²* have different origins. Notice that *sash¹* comes from Arabic, and *sash²* comes from French.

> **sash¹** (săsh) *n.* A band worn about the waist or
> over the shoulder. [Arabic *shāsh*, muslin.]
> **sash²** (săsh) *n.* A frame in which the panes of a
> window or door are set. [From French *châssis*,
> a frame.]

Usage labels The label *Informal* is used to identify words not suitable for formal writing but frequently used in conversation and ordinary writing. The label *Slang* identifies words appropriate only in casual speech.

> **sa • shay** (să shā′) *intr. v. Informal.* To strut or
> flounce. [Var. of French *chassé*, a dance step.]

Other information A dictionary also can serve as a reference aid. You may find information about the population and location of many places. Maps may be included. Entries for famous people may include dates of birth and death, nationalities, and important accomplishments. Significant events, such as holidays and wars, may be listed as well. Various tables may show an alphabet such as Braille, the metric system, Morse code, and proofreading marks. Check the table of contents to see what other information your dictionary offers.

Practice

A. Using the dictionary excerpts on pages 537 and 538, write answers to the following questions.

  1. Which syllable of *gargle* is pronounced with greater stress?
  2. What part of speech is *gargoyle*?
  3. From what language does the word *gargle* come?

B. Use the dictionary excerpt on page 537 to determine the meaning of *gargle* in each sentence below. Then write the part of speech and the number of the correct meaning.

  4. The doctor prescribed salt water as a *gargle*.
  5. Dad remembers to *gargle* every morning.
  6. His loud *gargle* often awakens my sister and me.

C. Using your dictionary, write answers to these questions.

  7. Who was John Marshall?
  8. What is the capital city of the nation of India?
  9. Where is Brittany?
  10. What is a kookaburra?

Using the Library

Most libraries have a systematic arrangement that makes it possible to locate any book. All of the books are organized into categories and are then arranged alphabetically within those categories. Fiction books are shelved by the last names of the authors. Nonfiction works are organized by the Dewey Decimal System or the Library of Congress System. Most libraries use the Dewey Decimal system.

Dewey Decimal System In this system, books are grouped into ten major categories, or subject areas. Each category includes a range of numbers, and every book in the category has its own number within that range. For example, books in the science category have numbers from 500 to 599. Decimals are used to indicate the smallest subdivisions. One science book might have the number 542.16, and another might be numbered 581.42. The number assigned to a particular book is its **call number**. The following table gives the numbers of the major categories in the Dewey Decimal System.

000–099	**General works** (encyclopedias and other reference materials)	400–499	**Language** (grammar books, dictionaries)
100–199	**Philosophy** (also includes psychology and ethics)	500–599	**Science** (astronomy, biology, chemistry, mathematics, physics)
200–299	**Religion** (includes mythology)	600–699	**Technology** (aviation, engineering, hygiene, medicine)
300–399	**Social sciences** (communication, economics, education, etiquette, folklore, government, law, sociology, statistics, transportation)	700–799	**The arts** (crafts, hobbies, music, painting, photography, sports)
		800–899	**Literature** (essays, plays, poetry)
		900–999	**History** (biography, geography, travel)

Card catalog To locate a nonfiction book easily, you need to find its call number in a library card catalog. The catalog is a set of file drawers containing three kinds of cards, all filed alphabetically for every book included in that library. Each card lists the call number of the book.

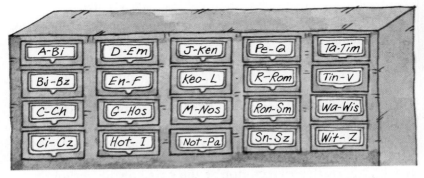

Title card Every book has a card filed according to the first word in its title, excluding the words *A, An,* and *The.*

Author card Every book has a separate author card filed according to the last name of the author of the book.

Subject card Many books have a card filed according to the subject of the book. If the subject you have in mind is not listed, think of a related subject. Some cards give cross-references like this one:

SEA ANIMALS. *See* MARINE LIFE.

You can locate a book in the library by finding any one of its three cards in the card catalog. Look at the sample cards below. Each one states the title and the author of the same book, the publisher, and the date of publication. Sometimes a brief summary is given. The call number is at the top left of each card.

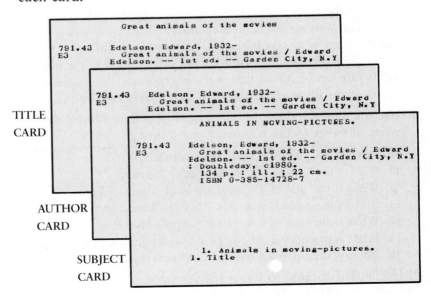

TITLE
CARD

AUTHOR
CARD

SUBJECT
CARD

Besides the call number of the book you want, you need to know how the library is arranged. Often, a sign at the end of each shelf shows the range of the call numbers of the books stored there.

All the fiction books in a library are usually placed in a separate section and arranged alphabetically by the authors' last names. Some libraries also group autobiographies and biographies in a separate section. Although biographies are non-fiction, each book is shelved alphabetically by the name of the person who is the subject, not by the name of the author.

A library also has a section of reference books, including atlases, encyclopedias, dictionaries, and almanacs. (See pages 434–435 for more information about reference books.) When you see R or Ref above the call number on a catalog card, it means that the book is a reference work. Although libraries let you borrow other kinds of books, most libraries do not allow you to check out reference materials.

Practice

A. Use the card catalog on page 541. Write the letters of the drawer that probably contains the card you would need to answer each question.

1. Does the library have books by Lawrence Yep?
2. Is *Summer of the Swans* in the library?
3. What books about insects does the library have?
4. Does the library have books about the Alvin Ailey dancers?
5. Is *The Westing Game* in the library?
6. Are there books by Barbara Corcoran in the library?
7. Is there a biography of Elizabeth Cady Stanton in the library?
8. Is *Life on the Mississippi* in the library?
9. Does the library have books by Nathanial Benchley?

B. Use the card catalog in your school or public library to write answers to the following questions.

10. What is the title of a book by Scott O'Dell?
11. Who is the author of *The Incredible Journey*?
12. What is the title of a nonfiction book about camping?
13. Who is the author of *A Day No Pigs Would Die*?
14. What is the title of a book by Virginia Hamilton?
15. What is the title of a book of stories by James Thurber?
16. What is the title of a book about home aquariums?

C. Use a card catalog to write answers to A above.

The Parts of a Book

If you are searching for information in a nonfiction book, it may not be necessary to read the entire book. There are several features that can help you to figure out what topics are covered and where to find them.

Book jacket Not only are the title and the author's name printed on the front of the jacket, but also there may be a summary of the book on the inside front jacket flap. A brief biography of the author may appear on the inside back jacket flap.

Title page The title, author, publisher, and place of publication are listed on the title page.

Copyright notice On the back of the title page, the copyright notice tells the year in which the book was first published and whether it has been revised since then. This date is important if you want the most up-to-date information.

Table of contents The contents page will give you a general overview of the subjects covered in the book. It may list only chapter headings, or it may list the main topics as units or parts and the subtopics as chapters. Notice the sections of the sample table of contents from a book entitled *Transportation in the United States.*

CONTENTS

STUDY STRATEGIES

You can see that the book is divided into three major parts, each labeled with a Roman numeral. Subtopics, or chapters, are labeled with Arabic numerals. Notice that page numbers are listed only for the chapters.

A quick look at this table of contents may tell you whether *Transportation in the United States* has the information you need. For instance, if you want to know about the early use of trains, you will probably want to read Chapter 3 of Part I, which is about railroads. It begins on page 65. Suppose you want information about submarines, however. The chapter headings will not tell you whether the book treats that topic.

Appendix Tables, charts, graphs, lists, or diagrams often appear at the end of a book in a special section called an appendix.

Bibliography The author, title, publisher, and publication date for other books used as references by an author are listed in a bibliography. Here is an example:

Wells, Jesse. *Wagons to the West.* Boston: Houghton Mifflin Company, 1982.

Check the bibliography if you want to read more about a topic covered in the book. A bibliography may be at the back of a book or at the end of a chapter.

Index An alphabetical list of topics covered in the book, the index, can help you to locate specific information. Using an index is a good way to find facts quickly. Shown below is part of the index for *Transportation in the United States.* Some main topics are followed by subtopics, as in the entry for the National Road. After each entry are the page numbers for that topic.

Mail car, 172	National Road, 51–58, 70–73
Minot, Charles, 121	construction, 51–53
Mississippi River, 102–103.	cost, 52
See also Steamboating.	repair and maintenance, 57
Missouri River, 89	New Orleans, 63–65, 64*m*
Morse code, 114*c*	Night coach, 211–213
Morse, Samuel, 112–113	Nunn, Robert, 316

A cross-reference is listed after some topics, as in the entries for the Mississippi River. It refers you to a related entry. Abbreviations such as *d, p, m, c,* and *t* may be used to indicate diagrams, pictures, maps, charts, and tables. Notice that a chart of Morse code appears on page 114.

Headings and subheadings The words and phrases used to set off chapters and sections of a chapter, or headings and subheadings, can help you to locate and understand information. Also look for key words that relate to your topic of interest.

Notes Authors sometimes write notes that may be helpful when you are reading the text. An asterisk (*) or a raised number (^{1}) indicates that there is a note. Read the paragraph below, which contains an asterisk.

> The Erie Canal was forty feet wide at the surface and twenty-eight feet wide at the bottom. The water was only four feet deep. The canal was carried above the rivers by means of viaducts.* It wound through cities, forests, and farmlands.

The asterisk after *viaducts* tells you that an explanatory note appears elsewhere. The note may be a footnote at the foot of the page, a note at the end of a chapter, or a marginal note beside the text. Notes may explain a term or give the source of a quotation, fact, or idea. Such notes are sometimes numbered and grouped at the end of a chapter or unit.

Practice

A. Write answers to the following questions.
  1. Where would you find a list of books that the author used as references?
  2. What part of a book gives you an overview of its contents?
  3. What part of a book tells the date of publication?
  4. What part of a book would help you quickly to locate a specific fact?
  5. Where might you find a brief biography of the author?

B. Refer to the table of contents on page 543 and the index on page 544 to write answers to these questions.
  6. In which unit and chapter can you read about canals?
  7. In which unit and chapter can you read about jets?
  8. On which page can you read about Charles Minot?
  9. On which page is there a map of New Orleans?
  10. On which pages can you read about the construction of the National Road?

Many articles and books include lists and drawings to present information in an easy-to-read form.

Tables, charts Facts and figures can be displayed in an organized way on tables and charts. The table below lists the largest U.S. national parks. The title tells you that only those parks with over one million acres are listed. The horizontal lines of information usually are called rows, and the vertical lines are referred to as columns. Notice that each of the four columns is labeled with a caption such as *Year Established*. Each row is labeled with the name of a national park. To find facts about Denali National Park, read down Column 1 until you find the name *Denali;* then read across Row 3 to get the information you need.

U.S. National Parks over 1 Million Acres

Name	State	Year Established	Number of Acres
Wrangell–St. Elias	Alaska	1980	8,945,000
Gates of the Arctic	Alaska	1980	7,500,000
Denali	Alaska	1917	4,700,000
Katmai	Alaska	1980	3,716,000
Glacier Bay	Alaska	1980	3,225,200
Lake Clark	Alaska	1980	2,874,000
Yellowstone	Wyoming-Idaho Montana	1872	2,219,823
Kobuk Valley	Alaska	1980	1,750,000
Everglades	Florida	1934	1,398,937
Grand Canyon	Arizona	1919	1,218,375
Glacier	Montana	1910	1,013,595

Notice that the parks are listed in order of their size, with the largest park first. Use the table to find the fifth largest park. Glacier Bay is fifth, with 3,225,200 acres. Find the state with the most national parks. How many does it have? Alaska has seven of the eleven parks listed in the table.

Graphs Numerical information often appears in graphs: picture graphs, bar graphs, line graphs, or circle graphs. On the next page is a circle graph. The sections of the circle represent percentages, or parts, of the total (100 percent).

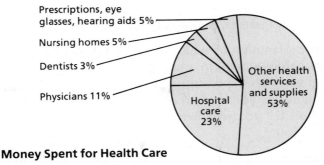

Prescriptions, eye
glasses, hearing aids 5%

Nursing homes 5%

Dentists 3%

Physicians 11%

Hospital
care
23%

Other health
services
and supplies
53%

Money Spent for Health Care

Notice that nearly one fourth of the circle (23 percent) is devoted to one type of expense. How is that money spent? Twenty-three percent of the total goes to hospitals. More than half of the total (53 percent) is labeled *other health services and supplies*. Does this percentage include money spent for physicians? No, another section shows the percentage spent for physicians' services.

Diagrams For showing how something is put together or how it works, diagrams can be useful. The two diagrams below are labeled Figure 1 and Figure 2, and each drawing is captioned with a brief description. Figure 1 shows an early elevator design. Figure 2 shows a modern design.

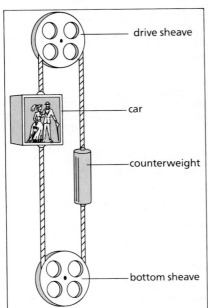

drive sheave

car

counterweight

bottom sheave

Figure 1. On an early elevator, a motor
turned the sheave, which moved the cables.

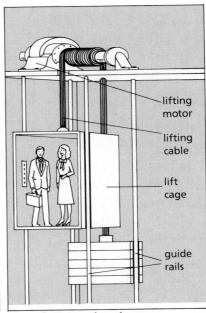

lifting
motor

lifting
cable

lift
cage

guide
rails

Figure 2. On a modern elevator,
an electric motor moves the cables.

Maps Shown below is a map of the city of Albuquerque, New Mexico. It shows streets, highways, and important places.

Legend An explanation of what various symbols represent often appears below a map, in a legend. You can see that the interstate highways are represented by thick, dark lines; all of the other highways and city streets are shown with thin lines. Other symbols tell you whether a highway is an interstate, federal, or state route.

Compass rose The directions *north*, *south*, *east*, and *west* are shown in the compass rose. Use the direction arrows to figure out how one place is related to another. For example, the Albuquerque Airport is in the southern part of the city.

Scale You can determine the distance from one place to another by using the scale of distance. Suppose you are traveling west on Route 40 and you want to know how far it is from Route 25 to Rio Grande Boulevard. To find out, place the edge of a sheet of paper so that it lines up with the

Albuquerque, New Mexico

Legend

Interstate
Federal
State

dots that show where Route 40 intersects Rio Grande and Route 25. Make marks on the paper to indicate where the two dots are. Then line up the marked sheet with the scale of distance. Read the number above the second mark to figure out the distance. Rio Grande Boulevard is about two miles from the intersection of Routes 25 and 40.

Now see if you can figure out how to get from one place to another by using the Albuquerque map. First, pretend that you are at the State Fairgrounds at the corner of Louisiana Boulevard and Route 352 (also called Lomas Boulevard). You want to go to the Albuquerque Academy, which is shown at the top of the map at the corner of Wyoming Boulevard and Academy Road. What is the most direct route from the State Fairgrounds to the Academy?

Using the map, notice that you would head east on Route 352 for two blocks. Then you would travel north on Wyoming Boulevard for several miles until you reached the Academy.

Practice

A. Refer to the table of national parks on page 546 to write answers to these questions.

1. How many acres make up Wrangell–St. Elias National Park?
2. Which Alaskan park was established before 1980?
3. Which two parks are in Montana?
4. Of the parks listed, which was established first?

B. Use the graph of health-care costs on page 547 to write answers to these questions.

5. How much of the total is paid to nursing homes?
6. How much of the total is paid to dentists and physicians?
7. Where might private-home nurses be included on the graph?

C. Use the diagrams on page 547 to answer these questions.

8. In the early elevator, which part turned the cables?
9. In the modern elevator, which part pulls the cable?
10. What keeps the modern elevator on track?
11. What are two names for the box in which people travel?

D. Use the map of Albuquerque to write answers to these questions.

12. Which interstate highway runs north and south?
13. How would you travel from the Rio Grande Nature Center to the airport?

Skimming and Scanning

You do not always need to read every word of a nonfiction article. Depending on your purpose for reading, you can skim or scan to find quickly the information you need.

Skimming When you want just an overview, or a general idea, skim a selection. Follow these steps to skim effectively.

Strategies for Skimming

1. Read the title and any headings.
2. Read all of the first paragraph or two.
3. Read the first sentence or two and the last sentence of the other paragraphs. Look for key words.
4. Look at any illustrations, and read the captions.
5. Read all of the last paragraph or two of the article. These may provide a summary.

Scanning When you need to find specific information, scan a selection. To scan quickly, follow these suggestions.

Strategies for Scanning

1. Look for a key word or words that will help you to find the facts you need. For example, to answer a question about marine life, look for related terms, such as *ocean*.
2. Next, look for typographic aids, such as numerals, capitalized words, and words in **bold** or *italic* type.
3. When you think you have found the facts you need, read that section slowly and carefully.

Remember these two ways of reading when you want to locate information quickly. Skim to get an overview or the main idea. Scan to get specific facts.

Practice

A. Skim the article "Early Theories of Flight" on pages 421–424. Then write the main idea in a complete sentence.

B. To write answers to the following questions, scan "An Introduction to Greek Mythology" on pages 117–120.

1. Where did Zeus live?
2. Who reigned before Zeus?
3. Which of the Greek gods were twins?
4. Who was the Greek goddess of wisdom?

STUDY STRATEGIES

Summarizing

A **summary** is a shortened form of a longer article or story. By writing a summary, you can better understand fiction and nonfiction that you read.

Summarizing fiction Below is a summary of "The Two Brothers," a tale on pages 204–206 of this book. Read, or reread the story. Then read this summary. Notice how the writer was able to retell the story briefly.

> Two brothers discovered a stone on which a list of directions was written. Whoever did what the stone directed was to find happiness at the top of a mountain. The younger brother decided to go; the elder brother did not. After following all the directions, the young man was met by a crowd of people who made him their king. After ruling for five years, he was driven out by another king. One day he arrived at the house of the elder brother, who "had grown neither rich nor poor." After they shared their stories, the elder brother said that he had been right to ignore the stone. The younger brother replied, "I may have nothing now, but I shall always have something to remember, while you have no memories at all."

Read a story carefully before you write a summary. Follow these guidelines for summarizing a fictional work.

Strategies for Summarizing Fiction

1. Identify the major characters and events. Decide what aspects of the story to emphasize. In "The Two Brothers," the plot is very important. For another story you might stress the development of the characters.
2. Write clearly and briefly, but be certain that you tell enough about the plot to make the story easy for your reader to understand.
3. Include important names, dates, and places. The setting may be especially important in historical stories.
4. If possible, include information that captures the tone or the mood of the story. You may wish to quote a sentence or a phrase from the story, as was done in the summary of "The Two Brothers." If you do decide to use any of the author's exact words or phrases, you must use quotation marks around them in order to set them apart from your own words.

Summarizing nonfiction Below is a summary of a thousand-word article about the Sahara Desert. Notice how details are condensed into general statements.

> The Sahara, the largest desert in the world, covers much of northern Africa. It extends from the Atlantic Ocean on the west to the Red Sea on the east, from the Mediterranean Sea on the north to the Sudan on the south. Sahara land forms include mountains, plateaus, plains, and sand dunes. Water is present in occasional oases. Some people of the Sahara live in cities and some are farmers, but many are nomads who herd sheep, goats, and cattle. Plant growth is sparse because temperatures can be high and rainfall is rare in many areas. Rich in minerals, the Sahara is a source of oil, iron ore, and natural gas.

Before you summarize nonfiction, be sure that you understand the major points. Then follow these guidelines.

Strategies for Summarizing Nonfiction

1. Begin with a clear, brief statement of the main idea of the essay or article.
2. In the other sentences, give details that support and expand the main idea. It may help you to jot down the sentences that state the main idea of each paragraph in the article. Then you can combine and restate those sentences in shortened form.
3. Include important names, dates, numbers, and places.
4. If you are explaining events or steps, be sure to list them in the proper order.
5. Use as few words as possible. Try to put the facts into your own words, being careful not to change their meaning. Occasionally you may want to quote directly from the article, using quotation marks to identify the words of the article.

Practice

A. Read "Icarus and Daedalus" on pages 114–116. Then write a summary of the story. Try to use no more than ten sentences.

B. Read "Early Theories of Flight" on pages 421–424. Then write a summary of the article. Try to use no more than eight sentences.

Test-taking Strategies

Many tests give you a choice of answers for each item. If you understand the subject matter, follow directions, and read each question carefully, you should do well on such tests. However, there are some additional strategies that can help you to take tests successfully.

Analogies An analogy item is designed to test your reasoning ability. It requires you to figure out the relationships between words.

Choose the word that correctly completes the analogy.

ELM : TREE :: POTATO : ——

A. ground   B. meat   C. vegetable   D. oak

Strategies for Completing Analogies

1. Figure out the relationship between the first two words. Some common types of relationships are part to whole, category to member, object to characteristic, object to use, worker to tool, worker to product, synonyms, and antonyms. (Some relationships may be reversed, for example, whole to part.)
2. Look at the first word in the second pair. Then try each of the five answers in the blank. Each answer choice is probably related in some way to one or more words in the analogy. You must determine, however, which *one* word creates the same relationship in the second pair as the relationship you identified in the first pair.
3. Double-check your answer. Say the completed analogy to yourself, substituting for the colons the words that explain the relationship.

Now look at the example again. The relationship between elm and tree is member to category—an elm is a type of tree. What answer choice names a category of which potato is a member? Answer A, *ground,* is not a category. Answer B, *meat,* is another category. Answer D, *oak,* is another member of the tree category. The correct answer is C, *vegetable,* the category of which potato is a member.

Usage Often used on English tests, usage questions measure your ability to use language correctly.

> Read the sentences below. Choose the line that has no error in usage.
>
> A. Skating across the ice, my nose became frostbitten.
> B. My nose became frostbitten, skating across the ice.
> C. My nose, skating across the ice, became frostbitten.
> D. As I skated across the ice, my nose became frostbitten.

Strategies for Answering Usage Items

1. Read the item through once to become familiar with it.
2. Read it slowly again, looking for usage errors such as incorrect forms of verbs, adjectives, adverbs, and pronouns; fragments and run-ons; and dangling modifiers.
3. Check your solution by figuring out how to correct it.
4. If you think there is no error, check again for all the types of usage errors above.

Sentence A is unclear—your nose couldn't skate across the ice! B and C have misplaced modifiers. D is correct.

Proofreading Some items test your knowledge of mechanics.

> Read the sentence and look at the items that follow. Decide which items best correct the underlined words. If the underlined words are correct as is, choose C.
>
> The <u>ship *Marine beauty*</u> will dock in <u>Wellfleet, Maine.</u>
>   1   2
>
> 1. A. Ship *Marine beauty*   2. A. Wellfleet, Maine
>   B. ship *Marine Beauty*   B. Wellfleet Maine.
>   C. No change   C. No change

Strategies for Answering Proofreading Items

1. Read the group of words. Is any punctuation missing?
2. Should any word be capitalized or not capitalized?
3. Before you choose C, double check that none of the other answers could be used in the group of words.

Now look at the example again. For item 1, B is correct because *Beauty* must be capitalized. For item 2, C is the correct answer because there are no errors in item 2.

Reading comprehension Some tests check your understanding of what you have read.

The early settlers on the Great American Plains led difficult, exhausting lives. In a land of few trees and little surface water, they had to struggle to overcome their surroundings. They built houses from blocks of sod, tangled grass and earth cut from the ground. They broke the sod to plant crops, and they dug down to find water for wells and irrigation. They had to survive drought, prairie fires, attacks by wild animals, and illness. The settlers who stayed on the plains were brave, sturdy people.

1. Which sentence best states the main idea of the paragraph?
   A. Plains settlers had to survive drought, prairie fires, attacks by wild animals, and illness.
   B. Plains settlers lacked trees and surface water.
   C. Life was very hard for settlers of the plains.
2. What was sod?
   A. dirt   B. grass and soil   C. blocks for building
3. Why did the settlers build houses of sod?
   A. There were few trees.
   B. Sod kept the houses well insulated.
   C. The settlers had dug up extra sod while planting.

Strategies for Answering Reading Comprehension Items

1. If you are asked to give the main idea, choose the answer that is broad enough to cover most of the passage.
2. If you are asked about a detail, scan the passage for that fact.
3. If you are asked to draw conclusions or give cause-and-effect relationships, base your answer on what is stated directly or indirectly.

Practice

Write the word that correctly completes each sentence.

1. When doing an analogy, figure out the _____ between words.
2. Proofreading items often ask you to identify correct capitalization and _____ in underlined portions of sentences.
3. Some reading-comprehension items require you to draw _____ from information given in the passage.

S
T
U
D
Y

S
T
R
A
T
E
G
I
E
S

How to Listen

Ancient myths were not written down at first. Someone would tell a story, travelers would listen to it, and then they would repeat the story in the next town. To pass a good story along, a person had to listen well and remember it.

Are you a good listener? You may hear well, but do you listen well? Careful listening is a skill. The following rules will help you keep TRACK of what you hear.

Strategies for Keeping Track

T = think
Think about the speaker's ideas and message. Do you understand them? If you don't, ask questions.

R = review
Review the speaker's main points. Are they clear? Have you forgotten anything? Ask questions about points you do not understand. Fill in information you have forgotten.

A = attention
Pay careful attention. Listen actively. As you listen, ask yourself questions about what you are hearing.

C = concentrate
Do not let your mind wander. Think about the topic. Always concentrate on the speaker's words.

K = keep up
Keep pace with the speaker. Follow the speaker's points. Do not let yourself get lost.

Practice

Listen as your teacher reads a myth to you. Imagine that you are an ancient Greek traveler listening to a tale at an inn. Keep TRACK as you listen. When you arrive in the next town, retell the myth in your own words to a partner. Then listen to the tale again. How well did you preserve the myth?

How to Follow and Give Instructions

Have you ever gotten lost because you did not listen carefully to instructions, or directions? Have you ever lost a game or answered a test question incorrectly for the same reason? Careful listening is always important, but it becomes vital when you listen to instructions.

Good instructions are given in a series of steps, each of which can be fairly complicated. Think about the steps involved in these instructions for batik—a way of making colored designs on fabric.

> You make batik by waxing parts of a fabric and dyeing the unwaxed parts. First, you prepare the fabric, wax, and dye. Tack the fabric to a picture frame. Heat the wax in a double boiler. Prepare the dye according to the directions on the package. You may use more than one dye.
>
> Now you are ready to dye. First, sketch a design on the fabric. Next, brush melted wax on the parts you do not want dyed. Then untack the fabric, soak it in the dye, rinse, and let it dry.
>
> Finally, you must remove the wax. Put the dyed fabric between layers of paper toweling. Next, cover an ironing board with newspaper. Then iron the parts of the fabric from which you want to remove the wax.
>
> Repeat the dyeing and wax-removal steps for each color.

- What are the three main steps in making batik?
- What parts does the second step have?

The guidelines below can help you listen to and follow even complicated instructions.

Guidelines for Following Instructions

1. Pay attention to the number and order of steps. Listen for order words such as *first, next, then,* and *finally.*
2. Try to picture each step. If the step has more than one part, be sure that you can picture every part.
3. Understand each step and how it leads to the next one.
4. Review the steps in your mind. Can you carry them out?
5. Ask questions about anything you do not understand.
6. Take notes if the instructions are long or complicated.

LISTENING AND SPEAKING STRATEGIES

When you follow instructions, you want to understand each step. When you give instructions, you want to help your listener understand each step. Use these guidelines.

Guidelines for Giving Instructions

1. Put yourself in your listener's place. Adapt your instructions to your purpose and audience.
2. Plan your instructions, step by step, before you start.
3. Give the steps in the order in which they should be done. Use order words such as *first, then,* and *next.*
4. Be sure to include every step the listener needs.
5. Include all information needed to carry out each step.
6. Speak slowly and clearly. Sound helpful and polite.

Suppose you want to tell someone how to make mashed potatoes. Which set of instructions should you give?

> 1. You want the potatoes to stay hot, so you must mash them quickly after they are cooked. First, cook them until they are soft but not falling apart. Let the water come to a boil before you put the potatoes in the pot. You can add butter and also a little milk to the mashed potatoes.
>
> 2. To make mashed potatoes, first wash the potatoes and cut them into small pieces. Then boil enough water in a pot to cover the potatoes. Put them in and let them boil until they are soft but not falling apart—about fifteen minutes. Next, remove the potatoes from the water and mash them with a fork or masher. Work quickly so they stay hot. Finally, mix in a dab of butter and some milk.

- Which set of instructions is easier to follow? Why?
- Would you give the same instructions to an experienced cook? Why or why not?

Practice

A. Listen, using the Guidelines for Following Instructions. Then try to follow the instructions as a partner watches.
B. Using the guidelines on this page, create instructions for an exercise routine for (1) adult athletes and (2) young children. Present each set of instructions to a partner. Can your partner follow your instructions?

LISTENING AND SPEAKING STRATEGIES

How to Speak Expressively

When you speak, you can express yourself in ways that are not possible in writing. Read this sentence to yourself.

The dog just barked again.

Now read it aloud, several times. Each time, try to convey one of the following attitudes.

anger, surprise, fear, statement of fact, humor, hopelessness, delight, concern, haste, sleepiness

What appeared to be a straightforward sentence now takes on many different meanings, without a word being changed.

Learn to take full advantage of the tools available to you when you speak—your voice, your facial expressions, your body. They will help make you an effective speaker.

Study these guidelines and learn to use them.

Guidelines for Speaking Expressively

1. **Consider your purpose.** How you say something varies with your purpose for saying it. Is your goal to amuse? inform? persuade? stir some emotion? Adjust your tone, volume, and pace accordingly. Practice saying each statement below with the purpose shown in parentheses.

   Now! Not later! We must act now! (persuade to take action)
   As he walked away, his eyes filled with tears. (sadden)

2. **Consider your audience.** Also suit your tone, volume, and pace to your audience. Practice saying these sentences to the two audiences indicated. Note the differences.

   Are wolves really mean and dangerous? No, they are not. (a kindergarten class, a Science Club meeting)

3. **Consider your meaning.** Be aware of the meaning you want to convey, and use your voice to help convey it. Say the sentence below several times. Each time, communicate one of the feelings shown in parentheses.

   The science report is due on Monday. (pleasure, regret, worry, anger, sympathy, determination, surprise)

LISTENING AND SPEAKING STRATEGIES

4. **Vary your volume and pace.** To alert your audience to a special point, speak more loudly or softly, or speed up or slow down. Such changes can keep your audience attentive.

5. **Vary your pitch.** Say the sentences below. Note how the rise and fall of your voice changes the meaning.

   Seth voted last year. (statement)
   Seth voted last year! (exclamation)
   Seth voted last year? (question)

6. **Put stress on words you want to emphasize.** Say the sentences below. Note how the meaning changes as you stress different words.

   My *brother* turned fifteen this year. (not someone else)
   My brother turned *fifteen* this year. (not any other age)
   My brother turned fifteen *this* year. (not any other year)

7. **Pause to separate ideas.** A *juncture,* or pause, is like a spoken punctuation mark. Pause at the commas below.

   Lisa, Mike and Chico voted. (Two people voted.)
   Lisa, Mike, and Chico voted. (Three people voted.)

8. **Use gestures and movements.** Your hands, arms, face, and body can "speak" too. Use them as you say these sentences.

   In four years, *you* will be voters! (point to the audience)
   Will you know how to vote? (lean toward the audience)
   Should you start educating yourself now? Yes! (nod your head)

Make use of these important speaking tools but do not rely on them alone. No matter how expressively you speak, if your words are dull, your speech will be too. Choose your words carefully. In particular, avoid **clichés** and **trite expressions**—phrases that have been used so often that they have lost their freshness. Here are examples.

She rose at the crack of dawn, full of good cheer.
Stay busy as a bee, and you'll live to a ripe old age.

Practice

Read a story part or editorial aloud to a small group, using the guidelines above. Ask for comments and suggestions.

How to Give a Speech

When you give a speech, you need to think about your audience, your speech, and yourself. Follow these guidelines.

Guidelines for Giving a Speech

Your Audience

1. Think about your **audience**. What will interest them?
2. Decide what sort of language to use. **Informal** speech is fine for friends or relatives. **Formal** speech is appropriate for a group or for teachers, employers, or other adults.

   INFORMAL: I got a real charge out of that show.

   FORMAL: I very much enjoyed the performance.

Your Speech

1. Choose a topic that interests both you and your audience.
2. Know your **purpose**. Plan your tone and language to suit that purpose. To share information, sound serious and direct. To persuade, be urgent and descriptive.

   TO SHARE INFORMATION: *Families* takes place during the Civil War. Jeb Warren is the star.

   TO PERSUADE: Go see *Families*! The fine acting and moving story are superb.

3. Plan. Think of a beginning that grabs your audience and tells them your topic. Plan an ending that leaves them with something to think about.
4. Prepare. Write key words on note cards. Use them as cues.
5. Practice. Rehearse until you know your speech. Practice in front of a mirror. Give the speech to friends or family.

Yourself

1. Stand straight but comfortably. Don't move around.
2. Make eye contact with your audience. Smile.
3. Speak slowly, clearly, and loudly enough to be heard.

Practice

Give a speech about a book that you like. Suit your tone and language to one of these purposes and audiences.

1. Persuade a group of English teachers to use the book.
2. Share information about it with the Media Club.

Making Introductions and Announcements

You have probably been introduced to adults many times in your life. Perhaps you were meeting a teacher or a new neighbor for the first time. Which would be the correct way for a mother to introduce her young son to an adult?

> 1. Kurt, I'd like you to meet Mr. Kline. Mr. Kline, Kurt.
>
> 2. Mr. Kline, I'd like you to meet my son, Kurt. Kurt, this is Mr. Kline, our new neighbor.

The second introduction is the proper one. When introducing a young person to an adult, you should always address the adult first.

Making introductions can be easy if you follow a few simple guidelines.

Guidelines for Making Introductions

1. When you introduce yourself, look at the person and say your full name. Then tell something appropriate about yourself.

   "Hello, my name is Victor Stein. I'm a friend of your brother Toby."

2. When you introduce two people to each other, say their full names clearly.

   "Ellen, this is Peter Chang. Peter, this is Ellen Smith."

3. Add some pleasant and helpful information about the person.

   "Peter just moved to Elkins, Ellen. He will probably be in some of your classes."

4. When you introduce a young person to an adult, speak to the adult first.

   "Dad, this is Maria Rosso. Maria, meet my father, Mr. Stein."

5. When you introduce someone to a group, address the group first.

   "Everyone, I'd like you to meet Rita Thomas. She's our newest member."

You hear announcements constantly—in class, in assembly, over intercom systems. A good announcement gives you clear and complete information.

How do you make good announcements? Follow these guidelines.

Guidelines for Making Announcements

1. Write down all the important information and memorize it. Then practice giving it aloud.
2. Give all the necessary information. Your announcement should answer the questions *who* or *what, when, where,* and *how* or *how much.* For a program or event, for example, you should give the name, date, time, place, and admission fee, if any.
3. Give details—such as special activities or famous names—that will make the program or event sound interesting.
4. Get everyone's attention before you begin.
5. Check to make sure that everyone can hear you.
6. Speak loudly, slowly, and clearly.

Now read this announcement.

> May I have your attention please. On Saturday, April 18, from 8:00 to 11:00 A.M., the eighth grade will be holding a book sale here in the gym. Door prizes will be given, and admission is free. I hope to see you all there.

- What information tells who? what? when? where?
- Which guidelines does this announcement follow?

Practice

A. Form a group with two other students. Take turns making the following introductions.

1. Introduce a friend from camp to your uncle.
2. Introduce a parent to your French teacher.
3. Introduce a new member to your chess club.

B. Prepare to give one of these announcements to your class.

1. A class trip next week to a museum
2. The results of a student election
3. Auditions for the drama club's play

LISTENING AND SPEAKING STRATEGIES

How to Explain a Process

How are reports written? How does water freeze? How are pencils made? When you answer such a question, you are explaining a **process**. A process is the series of steps involved in producing or carrying out something.

Read this explanation.

> The first step in creating a lead pencil is making the lead. This "lead" actually contains no lead at all. Instead, graphite, clay, and water are mixed together. The mixture is then squeezed through a small opening, and the resulting string of lead is cut into lengths of about 7¼ inches.
>
> Next, the wood is prepared. Logs are sawed into strips, or slats, and nine grooves are cut into each slat.
>
> To construct the pencils, a piece of lead is placed in each of the nine grooves. Next, another grooved slat is glued on top of the first one. This "sandwich" is then cut into nine pieces to form nine pencils.
>
> The erasers are added last. A *shoulder* is cut into one end of the pencil, a brass ring is placed on the shoulder, and an eraser is placed in the ring. The pencil is complete.

- Why are the steps explained in this order?
- Would this explanation be appropriate for a group of small children? Why or why not?

Guidelines for Explaining A Process

1. Suit your explanation to your purpose and audience. Should it be general or technical? simple or complicated?
2. Explain all the necessary steps, in order. Be sure it is obvious how each step follows from the preceding step.
3. Provide information that will make each step clear.
4. Use exact words and explain any technical terms.
5. Encourage your audience to ask questions.

Practice

Select a process that interests you. Do any needed research. Then use the guidelines above to explain the process to a partner. Was the explanation clear to your partner?

LISTENING AND SPEAKING STRATEGIES

How to Participate in Discussions

Conversation is often the main activity at a social gathering. People talk casually to each other, moving quickly from one subject to another. Sometimes at a social gathering the guests will have a discussion. A **discussion** is more focused than a conversation. It centers around one subject, and it has a definite purpose. Here are some types of discussions.

PURPOSE: To solve a problem or plan a course of action
EXAMPLES: Friends discuss whom to invite to a party.
         Glee Club committee discusses how to organize a concert.
         Executives discuss how to promote a new cereal.

PURPOSE: To give or exchange information
EXAMPLES: Biology class members discuss report on different plants.
         French Club members listen to and question speaker from France.
         Panel of scientists discusses hazards of space travel.

In order for people to discuss a topic thoroughly without wasting time, they need to organize their discussion. Here are two well-organized kinds of discussions.

1. In a **committee meeting**, the discussion is run by a chairperson. The chairperson keeps the discussion moving and makes sure it stays focused on the subject.
2. A **panel discussion** is also led by a chairperson, but it is more formal than a committee meeting. In a panel discussion, the chairperson introduces each panelist, who then presents certain information. After each panelist speaks, the other panelists and the audience make comments and ask questions.

These guidelines will help you lead and take part in a well-organized discussion.

Guidelines for Participating in Discussions

For the participants
1. Be prepared. Understand the topic and the purpose of the discussion. Read about the topic if necessary.
2. Take an active part. Add your facts, questions, or ideas.
3. Keep your statements brief and to the point.
4. Listen carefully when someone is speaking. Keep TRACK.
5. Always be polite, even when you disagree with someone.
6. Cooperate with the leader or chairperson.
7. If the group needs to reach a decision, try to help.

For the leader
1. Be prepared. Bring any information you might need.
2. Begin by stating the topic or purpose of the discussion.
3. Introduce the people in the group if necessary.
4. Keep the discussion focused on the topic.
5. Keep the discussion moving. Summarize the points made, ask questions, and bring up other points.
6. Don't give your opinion unless it is needed. Stay neutral.
7. Help participants settle any differences. Be polite.
8. Encourage everyone to participate. Don't let any one person take over the discussion.
9. Keep an eye on the time.
10. Summarize the results of the discussion.

Practice

A. With five or six classmates, take part in a committee discussion. Make up a topic or use one of these.

   1. How to raise money for team uniforms
   2. How to organize a poster contest
   3. How to design a school banner

B. With a partner, observe another group's discussion.

   1. Did the participants focus the discussion on the topic?
   2. Was a conclusion reached?
   3. Did the participants all agree with the conclusion?
   4. How might the discussion have been improved?

   Share your notes with the group.

How to Follow Parliamentary Procedure

Groups that meet on a regular basis often follow **parliamentary procedure,** a set of rules for discussion. Parliamentary procedure keeps a meeting orderly and efficient. A list of topics to discuss is usually prepared before the meeting. This **agenda** helps keep the meeting on track.

These are the basic guidelines for following parliamentary procedure.

Guidelines for Following Parliamentary Procedure

The meeting follows these steps.
1. The leader calls the meeting to order.
2. The secretary reads the **minutes** from the last meeting—a report of what took place.
3. The treasurer reports on any money made or spent, and the **balance,** or the money remaining.
4. Unfinished business from the last meeting is discussed.
5. New business is discussed.
6. The program (guest speaker, movies, music, etc.), if any, is presented.
7. The meeting is **adjourned,** or ended.

When parliamentary procedure is used, a discussion follows this pattern.
1. Someone raises his or her hand, waits to be recognized by the chairperson, and then makes a **motion,** or suggestion. The suggestion is stated by saying, "I move that . . ."
2. Someone who agrees with the suggestion says, "I **second** the motion." Then the suggestion is discussed. If no one seconds the motion, the suggestion is dropped.
3. The group votes on the motion. If there is a tie, the chairperson votes.

The Spanish Club used parliamentary procedure at this meeting.

CARMEN: The meeting will please come to order. The secretary will read the minutes of the last meeting. *(The minutes are read.)* Are there any corrections or additions?

PETER: *(rising)* Carmen?

CARMEN: Peter.

PETER: You left out my name as the new member of the Program Committee.

CARMEN: Thank you. The secretary will please make the correction. If there are no other corrections, the minutes are approved as corrected. Is there a treasurer's report?

ANDREW: *(rising)* The balance at our last meeting was $8.25. We collected $3.50 in dues and spent $2.75 for refreshments. We now have a balance of $9.00.

CARMEN: Is there any unfinished business?

MARC: The Program Committee reports that the Mexican consul has accepted our invitation to speak at an assembly on May 4.

CARMEN: Good. Is there any new business? Peter.

PETER: There's a movie from Spain at the New Cinema next week. I think we should see it for our April outing.

RONA: Great idea. I move that we see the Friday afternoon show.

PETER: I second the motion.

CARMEN: Is there any discussion? *(silence)* Then all in favor say "Aye." *(many ayes)* All opposed say "No." *(one no)* Motion is carried. We will now turn the meeting over to our program chairperson, Marc.

MARC: Rona will sing some songs from Spain. *(program follows)*

CARMEN: That was great, Rona. Our thanks to you and the committee.

JULIA: *(rising)* Carmen?

CARMEN: Julia.

JULIA: I move that we adjourn for refreshments.

DAVID: I second the motion.

CARMEN: All in favor say "Aye." *(many ayes)* All opposed say "No." *(silence)* The meeting is adjourned.

- How did the leader keep the meeting moving?
- When votes were taken, how did the group members show their approval? disapproval?
- How was the meeting adjourned?

Practice

Form a group of seven or eight classmates, and imagine that your group is a club, such as a hiking, service, or photography club. Choose a chairperson, a secretary, a treasurer, a program chairperson, and a program committee. Act out a ten-minute meeting of your club in which you plan an event, following parliamentary procedure.

How to Classify

What do newspapers, stores, dictionaries, biologists, and high schools have in common? They all depend on **classifying** —grouping things according to certain shared features. Newspapers classify information, stores classify merchandise, dictionaries classify words, biologists classify living things, and high schools classify students and courses.

Anything can be classified as long as common features are found. **Categories** are groupings made according to certain shared features. Without categories, it would become extremely difficult to locate, learn about, or even understand anything.

If you were organizing a high school curriculum, how would you classify the courses? You might begin as follows.

SCIENCE	Algebra I, Chemistry II, Basic Physics, . . .
ARTS	Art History, Music Theory, Modern Dance, . . .
POLITICAL SCIENCE	Chinese History I, Government I, Politics, . . .
LANGUAGE ARTS	Modern Literature, Journalism, Grammar I, . . .

If your purpose is to help students choose courses, you might use the grouping below.

REQUIRED	Algebra I, Basic Physics, Government I, Modern Literature, Grammar I, . . .
ELECTIVE	Chemistry II, Art History, Music Theory, Modern Dance, Chinese History I, Politics, Journalism, . . .

- In what other way might you classify the courses?
- What purpose might you have for such a classification?

Guidelines for Classifying

1. What is your purpose for classifying?
2. What features fit your purpose? They will determine the categories.
3. Which items share each feature? They will fit into the categories.

Practice

With a partner, brainstorm a list of clubs you would like to see at your school. Think of two purposes for classifying them and group them into two sets of categories.

How to Recognize Propaganda

A TV star assures you that Jill's Gel will make your hair look like his. A radio voice asks you to aid earthquake victims. You are bombarded with appeals like these every day. How do you decide what is reasonable and what is not? One way is to become aware of some **propaganda techniques**—methods that people use to try to influence you. Although a cause may be worthwhile, people's methods of persuasion may not be based on facts or solid arguments. When you recognize these techniques, ask yourself questions about how the propaganda relates to you.

1. **Testimonial** An expert or a famous person supports a product, an idea, or a person.

   > Basketball player Will Lang says, "I never go anywhere without my Jiffy compact hair dryer!"

   Ask yourself: What do I have in common with this person? Why should I buy this product?

2. **Transfer** A famous or glamorous person and a product are associated in order to persuade you to transfer your positive image of the person to the product. Unlike testimonial, transfer does not quote the person.

   > An ad shows Alison Graves, a famous actress, washing her face with Silky. The ad says, "Look like a movie star. Use Silky Soap."

   Ask yourself: Would I look like Alison Graves if I used Silky? Can Silky make anyone look different? What can Silky do for me?

3. **Bandwagon** You are urged to do something just because everyone else supposedly is doing it.

   > Everyone's talking about *Charge!* Read it now!

   Ask yourself: Do I in fact want to be like everyone else? Should *I* read *Charge!* just because others do?

4. **Name calling** The speaker criticizes a person or a product with little or no reason or evidence.

   > Gina Sheraton would make a terrible senator. How could anyone with that ridiculous hairstyle be trusted?

   Ask yourself: What are the facts? *Why* would she make a bad senator? How can a hairstyle affect qualifications?

5. Overgeneralization and Hasty generalization A statement about someone or something is too broad or based on very little evidence.

> When the Feline was compared with two other cars, it came out the winner in economy, traction, and general performance. Drive the best car of all. Drive the Feline!

Ask yourself: What are the facts? What cars was the Feline compared with and how were they all tested? Why is the Feline the best car of all?

6. Faulty cause and effect You are led to believe that one event caused another just because it happened first.

> Since Jim Bennett has been mayor, traffic accidents have increased by five percent. We need a new mayor—one who is concerned about our safety.

Ask yourself: Did the mayor cause the accidents? What is the real cause for the increase in traffic accidents? What does the mayor have to do with this? Is the present mayor really not interested in traffic safety?

7. Either-or You are told that there are only two extreme possibilities when actually there are many choices in between.

> If you are not in favor of a new teen center, then you must dislike young people.

Ask yourself: What are the reasons not to be in favor of a new teen center? What are the real issues?

8. Reasoning in a circle You are told something is so just because it is so. The reason is simply another way of saying the same thing.

> Nutribread is nourishing because it provides nutrients.

Ask yourself: What makes Nutribread nutritious? What nutrients does it contain? How can it be tested?

9. Emotional words Words are chosen to appeal to your emotions rather than to your common sense. Notice the emotional words underlined below.

> Don't settle for tired old outfits. Look and play like a professional athlete in elegant, stylish Jessama sports attire.

Ask yourself: To what emotions is this ad trying to appeal? Does my clothing affect my playing? How can Jessama clothes make me look and play any better than I do now?

THINKING STRATEGIES

These techniques try to prevent you from thinking clearly for yourself. When someone tries to persuade you about something, remember to think. Check the evidence and examine the reasoning.

Practice

A. Write the name of the propaganda technique used in each of the numbered examples.

testimonial   faulty cause and effect
transfer   either-or
bandwagon   reasoning in a circle
name calling   emotional words
hasty generalization

1. We asked cold sufferers to try our new medicine, Sniffle-free. All ten felt better quickly. Use Sniffle-free to be free of all cold symptoms.
2. Florence Farr, noted scientist, says, "I brush my hair with Bonnie Brushes because they're better for my hair."
3. Sweet foods are not good for you because they are so sweet.
4. Don't just sit there while everyone else talks about the exciting news in *Gossip!* Get the latest issue and join in the fun now!
5. Anyone who is not in favor of the new sports center is against progress.
6. Be good to yourself. Feel like a millionaire. Zip along the road grandly in the streamlined luxury of a Panther.
7. I used to watch TV for two hours before I went to bed, and I couldn't fall asleep. Now that I've stopped watching TV, I fall asleep immediately.
8. An ad for cars shows famous racing car driver Ernesto Spedetti getting into a new Speedo. The announcer says, "Buy a Speedo and race to the finish line."
9. Greeneze will let those old weeds feel right at home on your new lawn. Why keep on using it when you can have a weed-free lawn with new Fertilawn?

B. Work with a partner. Write examples of five different kinds of propaganda techniques. Read your examples to your class and see if your classmates can label them.

C. Bring in newspaper or magazine ads. Discuss the ads with a classmate and identify the different propaganda techniques used in them.

How to Make Inferences and Draw Conclusions

Suppose you are waiting to cross the street. You see a car approaching quickly, so you wait until the car passes. You have just made an **inference**. To make an inference, you combine a new observation with what you already know and then make a judgment about it. Making such a judgment is called drawing a **conclusion**. In the case above, you observed the approaching car. You knew from experience that cars can be fast and dangerous. You concluded that you should wait to cross.

You make inferences and draw conclusions all the time. When you ring a doorbell and no one answers, you conclude that no one is home. When someone laughs at your joke, you conclude that it was funny. Not all inferences are sound, however, and not all conclusions are valid. Here are some questions that will help you reach reasonable conclusions.

Guides: Making Inferences and Drawing Conclusions

1. **Do you have sufficient evidence or examples?** One silly TV program does not mean that all TV programs are silly.
2. **Do you have all the facts you need?** A growling dog is not necessarily a vicious dog. Has it ever bitten anyone?
3. **Is all the evidence relevant?** A shampoo may be packaged nicely, but that says nothing about how it washes hair.
4. **Is your conclusion the most likely one?** If you fall asleep reading a book, is the book necessarily boring?
5. **Does your conclusion follow from the facts?** You fall off your bike after a black cat crosses your path. Seeing a black cat did not necessarily cause you to fall.

Practice

With a partner, discuss why each conclusion is or is not sound.

1. You made lunch for four friends. Half the salad and one sandwich was left. You conclude that the lunch was not good.
2. Donna had more punctuation and spelling errors on her paper that you did, but she got a higher grade. You conclude that your grade was unfair.

How to Complete Analogies

An important part of thinking involves seeing the relationship between things. You can sharpen your thinking skills by doing exercises with **verbal analogies.** A verbal analogy is made up of two pairs of words. The words in the first pair have a certain relationship to each other. For example, if the words are *hot* and *cold,* the relationship is that they are opposites, or antonyms. The words in the second pair—for example, *up* and *down*—must then have the same relationship.

That verbal analogy would be written like this:

> hot : cold : : up : down

If you were to state that analogy in words, you would say it like this:

> *Hot* is to *cold* as *up* is to *down.*

Here are several kinds of verbal analogies. The first one is the kind you have just read about, using opposites. The others involve different kinds of relationships.

KIND OF ANALOGY	EXAMPLE
Word : Antonym	good : bad : : high : low
Word : Synonym	sad : unhappy : : sick : ill
Whole : Part	book : page : : piano : key
Category : Member	dog : poodle : : furniture : desk
Object : Use	knife : cut : : pencil : write
Worker : Tool	chef : pan : : dentist : drill
Worker : Product	baker : bread : : singer : song

Practice

A. Think of a word to complete each verbal analogy.

1. hot : cold : : big : __
2. small : tiny : : scared : __
3. chef : meal : : poet : __
4. knob : door : : leaf : __
5. tailor : needle : : farmer : __
6. wheel : turn : : airplane : __

B. With a partner, write an example of each kind of analogy.

1. word : antonym
2. worker : product
3. whole : part
4. word : synonym
5. worker : tool
6. category : member

Prefixes, Suffixes, and Word Roots

Many words are made up of different parts, such as pre-fixes, suffixes, or word roots. If you know what these parts mean, you can figure out the meanings of many unfamiliar words.

Suppose that the word *complicate* is unfamiliar to you. You can divide it into parts, like this.

Prefix	Word Root	Suffix
com-	-plic-	-ate
"together"	"fold"	"to make"

If you put together the meanings of the parts, you will find that *complicate* roughly means "to fold together." The diction-ary definition of *complicate* is "to make complex."

Study this chart of word parts. The meaning of each part is given. Notice that combining word parts can cause spelling changes.

Word Parts

Word	Prefix	Root	Suffix
propellant	pro- "forward"	-pel- "to push"	-ant (-ent) "a doer"
incredible	in- (im-) "not"	-cred- "to believe"	-ible "capable of"
duplexity	du- "two"	-plex- (-plic-) "fold"	-ity "condition"
interpose	inter- (intra-) "across"	-pos- (-pon-) "to place"	

Practice

Write the meaning of each word by combining the meanings of its parts. Check your answers in a dictionary.

1. duplicate   **2.** propose   **3.** proponent   **4.** compose   **5.** compel

Etymologies

Our language is always changing. Often we borrow words from other languages. We make up new words from old words and word parts. We give new meanings to old words. Therefore, languages and their individual words have histories. The history of a word is called its **etymology.**

Etymology can tell us many interesting and surprising facts about words and language. The word *eleven,* for example, originally meant "one left over after counting to ten." *Cow* and *beef,* oddly enough, both developed from the same word root. *Catch* and *chase* were once synonyms meaning "to chase."

Many dictionaries give complete or partial etymologies. There are also special dictionaries of etymologies. Knowing the history of language can give you a fuller understanding of English vocabulary.

Practice

Below are parts of six etymologies. Write a word from the box to match each etymology. You may use your dictionary.

meat	thunder	hibernate
anniversary	porcupine	tangerine

1. This word comes from a Latin word meaning "winter."
2. This word comes from a French phrase meaning "spiny pig."
3. Long ago, this word meant "any food in general."
4. This word was named after the city of Tangier, Morocco.
5. This word and *Thursday* are both related to Thor, a god in Old Norse mythology.
6. This word comes from the same word root as *annual.*

Homophones

At the beach, do you walk in the sand with *bear* feet, or with *bare* feet? **Homophones,** such as *bear* and *bare,* have the same sound but different meanings.

Homophones can be confusing. For example, if you write *pale* (lacking in color) instead of *pail* (bucket), you will mislead your reader. Be careful of troublesome homophones that you use every day—*it's* and *its, your* and *you're, they're, there,* and *their.* Here are some other homophones.

Word	Meaning
pair	a set of two things
pear	a fruit
pare	to peel
principal	most important; head of a school
principle	belief; rule of conduct
scent	a smell; to smell
sent	past tense of *send*
cent	a coin

Practice

Write the word in parentheses that correctly completes each sentence. Use your dictionary if you need help.

1. Ms. Konya is the (principal, principle) of our school.
2. The (sight, site, cite) of the new school is a block away.
3. Bloodhounds can follow a (cent, sent, scent).
4. Cleo tried not to (stair, stare) out the window.
5. The message was quite (plain, plane).
6. These old pipes are made out of (led, lead).

Homographs

Some words look alike but have different meanings. **Homographs,** like *present* (not absent) and *present* (a gift), have the same spelling but different meanings and histories.

Be careful not to confuse homographs. In a dictionary, homographs are listed separately because they come from different word roots or different languages. Notice that some homographs have different pronunciations.

Word	Meaning
bow (bou)	to bend forward
bow (bō)	a decorative knot
seal	to close tightly; a design or mark
seal	an animal
object (**ob'** jekt')	something seen and touched
object (əb **jekt'**)	to oppose
pound	to hit
pound	a place for stray animals
pound	a unit of weight or currency

Practice

Write a meaning for each underlined homograph. Use your dictionary if you need help.

1. The mason <u>ground</u> the rocks that she pulled from the <u>ground</u>.
2. The baseball <u>pitcher</u> gave a <u>pitcher</u> of water to the coach.
3. The <u>stern</u> captain stood at the <u>stern</u> of the boat.
4. I <u>long</u> to have very <u>long</u> hair.
5. Did the soldier <u>desert</u> his company in the hot, dry <u>desert</u>?
6. The tall, <u>lean</u> actor pretended to <u>lean</u> against the pole.
7. Ferdinand <u>left</u> the building and turned <u>left</u> at the corner.
8. The <u>page</u> took a <u>page</u> of the report to the senator.

Old English

The history of English as a distinct language begins around A.D. 450. Members of several Germanic tribes invaded the island of Britain. They conquered the Celts, the people in Britain, and settled there. They called themselves Saxons. We now call them Anglo-Saxons, and their language Old English.

Old English is the earliest form of our language. It looked and sounded very different from modern English. Compare this line of Old English with its modern translation.

When	I	then	this	all	remembered
ðā	ic	þā	ðis	eall	gemunde

The Anglo-Saxons had contact with other Europeans. The Danes and the Norwegians invaded Britain several times and settled in the areas that they conquered. Many Danish and Norwegian words were adopted by the Anglo-Saxons. Here are some examples of English words that come from Danish or Norwegian.

anger	husband	scrape	thrive	window
birth	calf	fellow	gate	leg
odd	skin	skirt	sky	take

Practice

Read the Old English words and their meanings. Then write the modern translation of each word. Use your dictionary to check your answers.

1. The word *utlaga* meant "someone living outside the law."
2. The word *eorthe* meant "the land."
3. The word *foeder* named a male parent.
4. The word *heafod* named the uppermost part of the body.
5. The word *botm* meant "the opposite of *top*."

Idioms

Imagine that you are new in the United States and do not know English very well. You go into a grocery store and ask for some pears. The clerk gives you this reply.

> I'm sorry, but we've run out of pears and oranges. Can you make do with apples? If you hold on a minute, I'll see how many I can come up with.

To understand fully the clerk's reply, you would have to understand idioms. An **idiom** is an expression that has a different meaning from the meanings of its separate words.

Here is the grocery clerk's reply without idioms.

> I'm sorry, but we've no more pears. Can you use apples instead? If you wait a minute, I'll see how many I can find.

Practice

Rewrite each sentence, using a word or a phrase for the underlined idiom. Make sure that the word or phrase means the same as the idiom. Use your dictionary if you need help.

Example: Our team won <u>hands down</u>.   *Our team won easily.*

1. Everyone on the team feels <u>at home</u> on a bicycle.
2. How do you <u>go about</u> fixing a hand brake during a race?
3. The referee told the noisy crowd to <u>pipe down</u>.
4. My parents said that a new racing bike was <u>out of the question</u>.
5. I don't know how our coach <u>puts up with</u> all our nonsense.
6. I suppose that he knows that we will never <u>let him down</u>.
7. When a race comes, he <u>puts his foot down</u> and trains us hard.
8. In training we can't <u>get away with</u> anything!
9. The coach knows all the <u>ins and outs</u> of increasing endurance.
10. I wouldn't <u>turn up my nose at</u> a chance to compete nationally.

When you diagram a sentence, you show the relationships among all its different parts. These lessons are designed to lead you through the diagraming process. In the first lessons, you will diagram only the basic parts of the sentence. In these first lessons, you will find certain structures that you do not yet know how to diagram. Do not be concerned. Diagram only those words for which you have directions. As you progress, you will eventually learn to diagram all the given constructions.

Subjects and Predicates (pp. 16–19)

The two main parts of the sentence are the subject and the predicate. In a diagram the simple subject and the simple predicate are placed on a horizontal line called the **base line**. The simple subject is separated from the simple predicate by a vertical line that cuts through the base line.

Each child wore a different costume.

child	wore

In an imperative sentence, a sentence that gives a command, the subject is understood to be "you." Notice how the simple subject and the simple predicate are diagramed.

Look at the knight's armor.

(you)	Look

Practice Diagram each simple subject and simple predicate.

1. Mr. Antonavich designed the gorilla suit.
2. Gus fanned his peacock feathers proudly.
3. Listen to the guitar music.
4. First prize went to the child inside the papier-mâché guitar.
5. Many costumes imitated the movie stars' clothes.

Compound Subjects and Predicates (pp. 22–23)

The parts of a compound subject or compound predicate are written on separate horizontal lines. The conjunction is written on a vertical dotted line joining the horizontal lines. Study the example at the top of the next page.

Charlie Chaplin, Ike, and Napoleon chatted and laughed together.

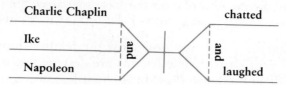

Practice Diagram the simple or compound subject and the simple or compound predicate in each sentence.

1. Masks, make-up, and hats were popular disguises.
2. Babe Ruth and Eleanor Roosevelt wore authentic costumes.
3. Parents and teachers watched and enjoyed each child's act.
4. A clown, a giraffe, and a helicopter led the costume parade.
5. The prizes and costumes pleased and delighted everyone.

Predicate Nouns *(pp. 167–168)*

Diagram predicate nouns by writing them on the base line after the verb. Between the verb and the predicate noun, draw a line slanting toward the subject to show that the subject and the predicate noun refer to the same thing. Study this example.

The automobile is a modern invention.

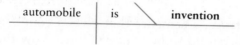

Notice how you diagram a sentence with a compound predicate noun.

The windshield is a protective barrier and a window.

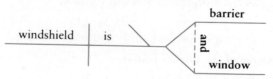

Practice Diagram the subjects, the verbs, and the predicate nouns in the following sentences.

1. Oliver Evans was an inventor and a steam engine designer.
2. Steam automobiles became the closest rival of the railroad.
3. Gottlieb Daimler and Karl Benz were the developers of the gasoline engine.
4. The trunk of a car was a large, metal box originally.
5. Two pedals are the brake and the accelerator.

Predicate Adjectives *(pp. 167–168)*

Diagram a predicate adjective on the base line after the verb. Draw a line slanting back toward the subject to show that the predicate adjective modifies the subject.

Study these diagrams of predicate adjectives.

In the late 1890s, the electric car was popular.

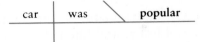

Steam cars had been impractical, noisy, and smelly.

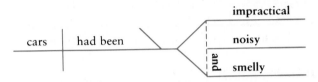

Practice Diagram the subjects, verbs, and predicate adjectives.

1. The world's first gasoline-powered vehicle was clumsy.
2. These carriages were horseless.
3. In the 1900s a muddy road could be messy and dangerous.
4. By 1908 the parts for cars of the same model were interchangeable.
5. Henry Ford's assembly line was fast, efficient, and inexpensive.

Direct Objects *(pp. 164–166)*

Diagram a direct object by writing it on the base line after the verb. Separate the direct object from the verb by a vertical line, but do not let the line cut through the base line.

Tom and Diane designed their new kitchen together.

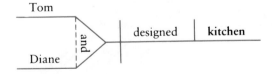

Study the diagram of a compound direct object.

They selected new appliances, cabinets, and fixtures.

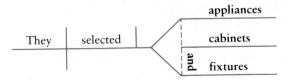

Practice Diagram each subject, verb, and direct object.

1. A carpenter and a plumber prepared the room for renovations.
2. Tom borrowed two ladders and some old canvas.
3. Tom, Diane, and her mother selected curtains for the windows.
4. Tom built shelves for the cookbooks.
5. Tom and Diane cleaned the woodwork, cabinets, and floors.

Indirect Objects *(pp. 164–166)*

Diagram an indirect object on a horizontal line below the base line. Draw a slanting line to connect it to the verb.

Mr. Talbot made us salads for lunch.

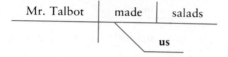

Practice Diagram the following sentences, showing the subjects, the verbs, the direct objects, and the indirect objects.

1. Catherine baked us a loaf of French bread.
2. I offered Dad a piece.
3. Justin handed Mr. Talbot a plate and a fork.
4. Dad told Justin a story about a Paris restaurant.
5. Mr. Talbot brought everyone cantaloupe for dessert.

Adjectives *(pp. 236–241)*

Diagram an adjective by placing it on a slanting line under the word it modifies. Join a series of adjectives with a dotted line parallel to the base line. Note where *and* is placed.

Most supermarkets carry fresh, frozen, and canned foods.

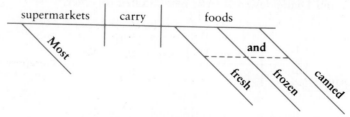

Practice Diagram all of the words in the following sentences.

1. The produce section contains fresh fruit.
2. Broccoli and peas are nutritious green foods.
3. Some groceries sell McIntosh, Cortland, and Delicious apples.
4. A tall, thin, blond man bought some green seedless grapes.
5. One employee was unpacking green, red, and yellow peppers.

SENTENCE MAPPING :: DIAGRAMING

Adverbs *(pp. 242–247)*

Diagram an adverb by placing it on a slanting line under the word that it modifies. Write the conjunction joining two or more adverbs on a dotted line between them.

The rather large wedding was planned quickly but carefully.

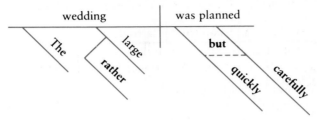

Practice Diagram all of the words in the following sentences.

1. Some very traditional music was chosen finally.
2. The bride and groom made a relatively long guest list.
3. They discussed their rather complex plans frequently and happily.
4. Fortunately they found an outstandingly creative caterer.
5. Two quite beautiful gold rings were selected carefully but excitedly.

Prepositional Phrases *(pp. 462–466)*

Diagram a prepositional phrase by writing it under the word it modifies. Place the preposition on a line slanting from the base line. Place the object of the preposition on a horizontal line. Diagram its modifiers in the usual way.

The fancy lettering was done by the hand of a calligrapher.

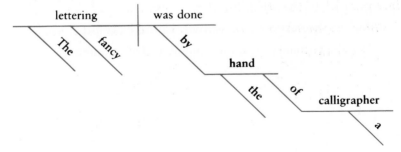

Practice Diagram all of the words in the following sentences.

1. Calligraphers hold their pens at a certain angle.
2. The tip of the pen is selected for its width.
3. This nib is attached to an ink pen.
4. Calligraphers paint decorations in the margins of their parchments.
5. Medieval examples of illumination are famous for their beauty.

Participles and Participial Phrases *(pp. 469–472)*

Diagram a participle on lines like those used for a prepositional phrase. In a participial phrase, the participle is followed by the word that completes the phrase.

Applauding the superstar wildly, they watched his hurried arrival.

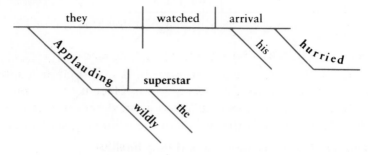

Practice Diagram all of the words in the following sentences.

1. Happily, they saw him descending the airplane steps.
2. Shouting his name repeatedly, the crowd followed his every move.
3. The smiling film idol loved their totally unquestioning approval.
4. Basking in the warm welcome, he made an unexpected speech.
5. Quite moved by their affection, he thanked the devoted fans.

Gerunds and Gerund Phrases *(pp. 473–477)*

Both a gerund and a gerund phrase are diagramed on a standard. Before you diagram the gerund, first write the other parts of the sentence on the base line. Then add the standard for the gerund or the gerund phrase. Each gerund curves down "steps" in the standard, as shown in the example.

The key to managing Katie's puppy is daily training.

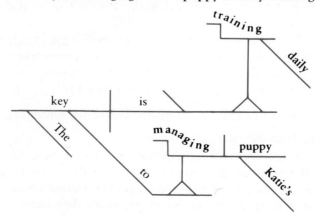

Practice Diagram all of the words in the following sentences.

1. Developing good habits in her puppy was Katie's goal.
2. By repeating Daffy's name with each command, Katie began her obedience training.
3. Another important factor in pet rearing is being consistent.
4. Placing the dog dish in the same spot at mealtime is one example of consistency.
5. Daffy loves earning an affectionate pat on the head from Katie.

Infinitives and Infinitive Phrases *(pp. 478–481)*

When an infinitive or an infinitive phrase is used as a subject, a direct object, or a predicate noun, place it on a standard. If an infinitive is used as a modifier, diagram it as you would a prepositional phrase.

To publish a cookbook was hard to accomplish.

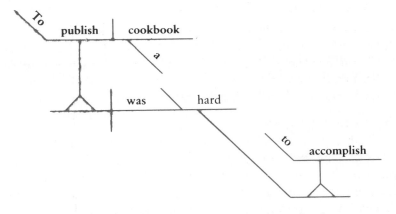

Practice Diagram the following sentences completely.

1. The management committee wanted to arrange the recipes in alphabetical order.
2. To organize the recipes into categories seemed more logical to others.
3. To find a chicken recipe meant looking in the poultry section.
4. The reader uses an alphabetical index to locate each recipe.
5. The cookbooks to be sold at the bazaar will raise funds for the needy.

Appositives *(pp. 97–99)*

Diagram an appositive by enclosing it in parentheses after the noun or the pronoun that it explains. Find the appositive in the sentence at the top of the next page. Then study how the appositive and its modifiers are diagramed.

Dr. Carl Cohen, my periodontist, specializes in gum diseases.

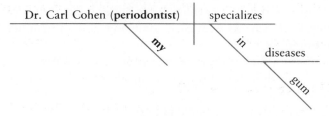

Practice Diagram all of the words in the following sentences.

1. Debbie Carleton, a dental hygienist, taught me to floss correctly.
2. Gingivitis, a common periodontal disease, inflames the gum tissue.
3. Gums can be irritated by plaque, a sticky form of bacteria.
4. Bacterial plaque hardens into calculus, another gum irritant.
5. Dr. Cohen performed a curettage, a surgical removal of plaque, calculus, and inflamed tissue.

Compound Sentences *(pp. 24–25)*

Diagram each clause of a compound sentence as if it were a separate sentence. Place the conjunction joining the clauses on a horizontal line to connect the verbs in the clauses.

William Shakespeare lived in Stratford, but Anne Hathaway, his wife, grew up in Shottery.

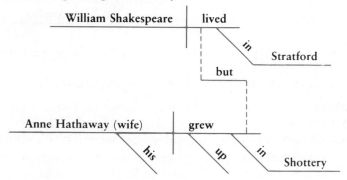

Practice Diagram the following sentences.

1. Shakespeare began his career as an actor, but he earned his fame as a playwright.
2. Shakespeare's birthplace is still standing on Henley Street, and many tourists visit it each day.
3. John Shakespeare, the writer's father, was a glovemaker, but he became mayor of Stratford in 1568.

4. Shakespeare's reputation was attacked in a pamphlet by Robert Greene in 1592, but Henry Chettle quickly published an apology for it.
5. Shakespeare earned some money from his plays, but his wealth probably came from stock in several theaters.

Adverb Clauses (pp. 510–512)

Place an adverb clause below the word that it modifies in the main clause, and diagram it as if it were a separate sentence. Place the subordinating conjunction on a dotted line to connect the verb in the clause with the word that the clause modifies. Study the example below.

If the bus fare increases, some commuters will form a car-pool.

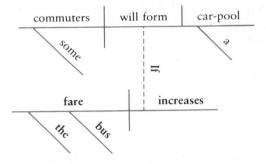

Practice Diagram the following sentences.

1. Because they travel to the office each weekday, they need five car-poolers.
2. Although the driving schedule is flexible, each person is responsible for one day every week.
3. After the car-pool was organized, Dave's day to drive was Thursdays.
4. While some car-poolers nap during the commute, others read.
5. When travel plans change unexpectedly, the driver must telephone the other car-poolers.

SENTENCE MAPPING :: DIAGRAMMING

■ COMPOSITION STRATEGIES ■

How to Write a Personal Narrative

A **personal narrative** is a story about a real experience you have had. A personal narrative allows the reader to share a part of your life.

Guidelines for Writing a Personal Narrative

1. Think about your purpose. Do you want to make your readers understand how you feel? Think about your audience. Whom do you want your story to interest?

2. Write a good beginning to catch your reader's attention. Start with an action, with details about the setting or characters, or with dialogue. You can also start with a general statement or in the middle or end of the plot.

3. Show, don't tell, what happens. Give details about people, places, things, and events. Supply enough details so readers can draw their own conclusions about actions and feelings.

4. Include dialogue to give information and to show how characters feel and think. Natural-sounding dialogue can bring characters to life and make actions seem real.

5. Write an ending that completes the action of the story, shows rather than tells, and fits the mood of the story. Leave your readers feeling that they have been told just enough—not too much or too little.

6. Write a catchy title that captures your reader's interest without revealing too much of the story.

Alligator Trouble

When our dog began barking at something, I hurried outside to see what was happening. I returned yelling, "Alligator! Alligator!"

"What do you mean, alligator?" asked my sister Lin.

"I mean there's an alligator in our back yard. It's by the canal," I screamed hysterically.

My frightened younger sister didn't know whether to believe me or not. She inched slowly toward the window, trying to look calm.

Writing Prompt

Directions: Think about the first time you met someone. The person might be a friend, a teacher, or a competitor in a sporting event. Where and why did you meet? What was your first impression of the person? Write a personal narrative so that other students in your class can read about your experience.

How to Write a Paragraph of Comparison and Contrast

When you **compare** two or more subjects, you show how they are alike. When you **contrast** subjects, you show how they are different. A paragraph of comparison and contrast shows similarities as well as differences.

Guidelines: Comparison and Contrast

1. Think about your purpose. What do you want your readers to learn from your paragraph? What do you want to learn? Think about your audience. For whom are you writing this paragraph?
2. Select a topic that has two things you can compare and contrast. List as many similarities and differences as you can about the two things.
3. Organize the details on your list in a logical order. Make each similarity and difference a separate point.
4. Write a topic sentence that clearly states the main idea. The topic sentence can appear at the beginning, middle, or end of your paragraph.
5. Use your list of details to write sentences that support the main idea of your paragraph. Include examples to make each point of comparison and contrast valid.
6. Use words such as *similarly, like, unlike, just as, as well as, the same as, different from, in contrast,* and *on the other hand* to help make your points of comparison and contrast clear.

Soccer and Field Hockey

Soccer and field hockey are team sports that have distinct similarities and differences. Both sports are played with a team of eleven players that include forwards, halfbacks, fullbacks, and a goalkeeper. Soccer players use their feet and heads to pass the ball to one another, unlike field hockey players who use sticks that are curved at one end to pass the ball. The object of both games is to score a point by getting the ball past the opposing team's goalkeeper and into the goal cage.

Writing Prompt

Directions: Look at the picture of the rowboat and the picture of the canoe. They are alike in some ways and different in others. Write a paragraph that compares and contrasts the rowboat and the canoe for a friend.

How to Write a Story

A **story** has a beginning, a middle, and an end. It can be an adventure, a mystery, or a true story. A story can take place in the past, the present, or the future.

Guidelines for Writing a Story

1. Think about your purpose. Do you want your story to be humorous? sad? exciting? Think about your audience. For whom are you writing?
2. Design your plot. First, decide on a conflict for your characters. Then create action events that build to a climax. Finally, solve the conflict in the resolution.
3. Create your characters. Show what your characters are like by giving details about their appearances. Bring your characters to life by revealing their words, thoughts, feelings, and actions.
4. Include a setting for your story. Show where and when your story takes place or let the reader try to figure out the setting. You can also create a mood in the setting.
5. Choose a point of view. Use a limited point of view if you want to tell your story from one character's point of view. Use an omniscient point of view if you want to reveal what all the characters think, feel, see, and do.
6. Write your story in the first person, using the pronoun *I* if you want a character to tell the story. Otherwise, write it in the third person, using the pronoun *he* or *she*.

The Secret of Lake Latonka

Detective Owen Shows sat in his paper-littered office, frowning at the telephone receiver dangling from his hand. "What's the trouble?" asked his assistant Marie. Owen shook his head. "I'm not sure," he said slowly. "According to a Mrs. Cohen, her son Robby and two other students from Selby High School went scuba diving last Friday at Lake Latonka. Her son returned home alone, mumbling something about a monster in the lake. The other divers never returned to their homes. It appears that they have just vanished!"

Writing Prompt

Directions: Look at this picture of four people in a cage. Why are these people in the cage? What circumstances got them there? What is the setting of the picture? Write a story about the picture for the other students in your class.

How to Write a Description

A **description** is a vivid word picture that relays your observations to other people.

Guidelines for Writing a Description

1. Think about your purpose. How do you want your readers to see your topic? How do you want your readers to feel about your topic? Think about your audience. For whom are you writing your description?
2. Choose a point of view. Keep in mind the overall impression you want to give. Use details that will support your point of view and purpose.
3. Use imagery—language that appeals to the senses—to show how something looks, sounds, feels, tastes, and smells.
4. Use exact adjectives, verbs, nouns, and adverbs in your description. Try to create a clear mental picture for your reader.
5. Create clear pictures by making comparisons. Include figurative language in your description. Use a simile to compare one thing to another, using *like* or *as*. Use a metaphor to say that one thing *is* another.
6. Organize your description by using spatial order, by beginning with the detail that strikes you first, or by arranging your details in their order of importance.

The Cave

I stood at the entrance of the cave where I had taken shelter from the heavy downpour. A river of rainwater rushed past my feet. The tall pines swayed and bent like graceful ballet dancers. Thunder boomed as lightning lit the dark sky. The storm frightened me. I shivered and retreated into the cave.

Inside, a crackling fire burned brightly. The reflections of its golden flames danced on the walls of the cave. The smell of burning wood mixed pleasantly with the musky aroma of the cave. I felt safe and warm inside the cave. I was no longer frightened. Soon I relaxed and forgot about the harsh storm that raged outside.

Writing Prompt

Directions: Imagine that you boarded your pet at a kennel. What did you see there? hear there? smell there? feel there? Write a paragraph, describing the kennel to a classmate.

How to Write a Persuasive Letter

When you write a **persuasive letter,** you are attempting to persuade someone to agree with and support your opinion.

Guidelines for Writing a Persuasive Letter

1. Think about your purpose and audience. What do you want to convince your reader to do? To whom are you writing?
2. Use correct letter form. Include a heading, a greeting, a body, a closing, and your signature. For a business letter, add an inside address and use the block style or the modified block style.
3. State your opinion in a topic sentence and support it with reasons and factual examples that are directly related to the opinion and are suited to your audience.
4. Use a persuasive strategy. You might offer a precedent, appeal to your audience's sense of fairness, and answer their possible objections. You might even explore the favorable and unfavorable consequences of persuading them.
5. Arrange your reasons and examples in their order of importance. Order them from most to least important or from least to most important.
6. Write a concluding statement to restate or emphasize your opinion.

Valley Middle School
Scottsdale, AR 85268
October 24, 1989

Dear Principal Stein,

    The Student Council would like you to approve a plan to bring senior citizens into our classrooms. We feel that the elderly can teach us some of the many valuable things they have learned over the years. Some might give us a new view of history. Others could teach us crafts and skills that are no longer taught. It would also give the elderly an opportunity to work with young people and to contribute to our school.
    Please support our plan!

Sincerely,

Mario Brando

Writing Prompt

Directions: Imagine your school is thinking about changing the school lunch program. The proposed plan will allow a fast-food chain restaurant to provide the school lunches every Friday. The cost of a lunch will be the same as the restaurant's regular prices.

Think about the proposal. Decide whether you are for or against it. Include several good reasons to support your opinion. Then write a letter to your principal.

How to Write a Research Report

A **research report** presents information about a particular subject that interests you.

Guidelines for Writing a Research Report

1. Think about your purpose and audience. How can you present facts clearly? Who will read your report?
2. Choose an interesting topic that is neither too broad nor too narrow. Make a list of questions that you would like to answer in your report.
3. Gather information. Use reference books, nonfiction books, and newspapers. Use the *Readers' Guide to Periodical Literature* to help you find magazine articles. Make a bibliography card for each source you use.
4. Write the questions you want to answer on separate index cards. Then take notes from more than one source. If you copy direct quotations, use quotation marks.
5. Write an outline from your notes. Turn your questions into main topics. Arrange the main topics in a sensible order. Write the facts that support the main topic as subtopics, and the facts that tell about these subtopics as details.
6. Expand your outline into paragraphs. Be sure each paragraph has a topic sentence that states one main idea. The other sentences should add details that develop the main idea.
7. Write an introduction and a title that captures your reader's interest and tells what your report is about.
8. Write a conclusion that restates the main ideas and finishes the report. Then alphabetize your sources and write a bibliography page.

Eleanor Roosevelt

Eleanor Roosevelt was the wife of President Franklin D. Roosevelt. She was one of the most active first ladies in the history of the United States.

Mrs. Roosevelt became politically active when her husband was crippled with polio in 1921. She traveled around the world, working with the underprivileged and fighting for the rights of minorities.

Mrs. Roosevelt was a member of the United Nations General Assembly from 1945–1951.

Writing Prompt

Directions: This picture shows an outline of Africa. Write a report about one of the countries. What is the climate like? What language is spoken? What things are manufactured and grown in this country? Use reference sources to find information. Then take notes and make an outline. Use your outline to write a report of several paragraphs to share with your classmates.

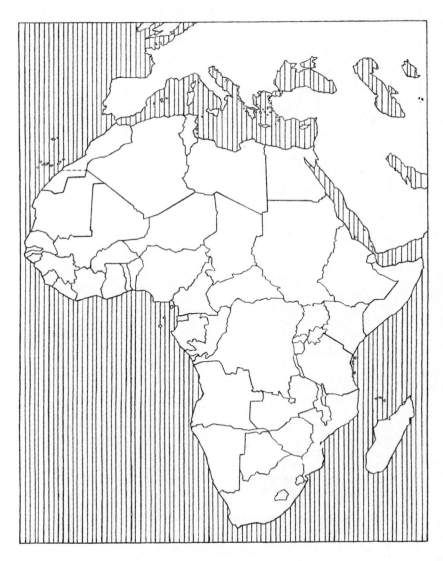

How to Write a Persuasive Argument

A **persuasive argument** is written in order to try to convince someone to share your opinion about an issue, a course of action, or a product.

Guidelines for Writing a Persuasive Argument

1. Carefully consider the topic of your argument. It should be something that is controversial or debatable.
2. Research your topic thoroughly in order to form a solid opinion about it. Explore all sides of the issue, all reasonable courses of action, or all features of the product. Find facts that will provide sound support for your opinion. Take notes.
3. Determine what reasons and examples will be most convincing to your audience.
4. Begin your argument with a topic sentence that strongly and clearly states your opinion. Then write supporting sentences that provide reasons and examples suitable for your audience. Organize them in order of importance. Use as many persuasive strategies as possible.
5. Conclude your argument with a strong summary statement.

An Opinion on Summer Work

Last week, the town council published a request to all young (13- to 14-year-old) teen-agers in our community. The council asked these teens to spend their summer working on local produce farms in order to boost our town's economy. I feel that these young teen-agers should not be asked to perform hard, manual labor.

In our area, most teen-agers begin working part-time and during summers by the time they are 16. To ask younger teens to give up their last few carefree summers is, I think, a harsh request. Soon enough, these young people will have to face the responsibilities of being adults.

Certainly, the opportunity to work and earn money is enticing. Farming, however, is hard work. Young farm employees must get up at 5:00 each morning and labor in the fields during the hottest part of the day. In our area, the summer heat and humidity can be grueling. Shouldn't these young people be entitled to their last few summers of lazy days?

Writing Prompt

Directions: Imagine that your town council will soon choose one of two plans for developing a parcel of town land. Under one plan, the land would become a park. Under the other plan, the land would be used for a shopping mall. Decide which plan you favor, and write an argument to persuade the council to vote your way.

How to Write Instructions

Instructions are directions that explain how to accomplish something. Complete and accurate instructions state all the materials and steps required to perform a task successfully.

Guidelines for Writing Instructions

1. Carefully consider your purpose and audience before beginning to write. Instructions that are appropriate for adults will not be suitable for young children. Adapt your language and details to suit your audience.
2. Mentally or actually perform the task you will be giving instructions for. Take notes on all the materials required and the steps involved.
3. Begin by stating your main idea and your purpose for writing. Make this part of an interesting introduction.
4. Include a complete list of the materials needed. Tell readers where they can obtain uncommon materials.
5. Clearly explain the entire series of steps to be performed, in the correct sequence. Sequencing words such as *before, while, next,* and *finally* can be helpful.
6. Write a brief conclusion that lets readers know the instructions are complete.

```
                      Mail—Order Magic
     Ordering products through the mail can save you
time and effort. If you follow a few simple steps, you
will avoid being disappointed with the mail—order
process.
     First, try to use the order form provided by the
mail—order company. Clearly print your name, com-
plete address, and telephone number (including your
area code) on the form. Then describe the goods you
are ordering. If you are ordering from a catalog, use
the product name exactly as it appears in the catalog
and note the stock or item number of the goods. State
the quantity you want, any color or size desired, and
the cost. If you are ordering more than one item, list
the cost for each and then figure the subtotal. Final-
ly, add in any sales tax and shipping costs and total
your order.
     Never send cash through the mail. Send a check or a
money order, or use a credit card to make your pur-
chase.
```

Writing Prompt

Directions: Imagine that you are teaching a student from another country how to play a board game. What is the game? What materials do you need to play it? How is the game scored? Write instructions that explain how to set up and play the game.

How to Write a Friendly Letter

A **friendly letter** is a thoughtful way of communicating with someone you know well. Its purpose is to share news or feelings or just to keep in touch.

Guidelines for Writing a Friendly Letter

1. Include the five basic parts of a letter: the heading, a salutation, the body, a complimentary close, and your signature. The heading contains your address and the date. You may use the Postal Service state abbreviation. Use a comma after the salutation and the closing.
2. Write neatly and legibly, or type your letter. If you type, sign in handwriting to add a personal touch.
3. Write your message (the body of the letter) in a cheerful and informal way. Indent each paragraph. Begin by showing some interest in your reader. Ask a question or refer to the last letter you received from the person. Then share some news or express your thoughts and feelings.
4. End your letter with questions or comments that will encourage your reader to write back promptly.

> 593 Middle Road
> Dallas, TX 75217
> February 11, 1990
>
> Dear Helen,
>
>   I thought of you last night because I knew you were giving your dance recital. How did it go? I wish I could have been there to cheer you on.
>
>   Ted Rucker and I are busy planning our presentation for drama class. I wish you hadn't moved away! We could use your help. Ted plans to write you this week.
>
>   Will you be coming back to visit soon? If so, I hope you can stay at my house for a few days.
>
>   Take care,
>
>   Marsha

Writing Prompt

Directions: Write a letter to a friend or relative who lives far away. Include news that brings the person up to date with the events in your life and share news about mutual friends.

How to Write a Narrative Poem

A **narrative poem** is a story told in verse form. It paints a vivid picture of an event, an experience, or a person.

Guidelines for Writing a Narrative Poem

1. Consider your purpose and audience. Do you want your poem to amuse, to intrigue, to excite, or to enchant your readers? Should your language be suitable for young children or for older readers?
2. Choose a subject. A good choice might be a thrilling experience or an especially memorable person.
3. Determine the poetic devices you will use. Will you divide your poem into stanzas? Will you use rhyme or a specific rhythm? Where will you use alliteration? onomatopoeia? personification? similes? metaphor?
4. Make a plot summary for your story. Jot down exact words and sense words that will make your setting and characters come alive for your readers.
5. Write your poem. Put the events in sequential order.
6. Give your poem a title that will capture your readers' interest.

A Tour of the Garden

With the pride of a man in charge of his world,
Sam guided me through his garden.
In row after row, so healthy and green,
Plants thrived as they followed Sam's plan.
Peas perfectly climbed to be warmed in the sun,
And carrot tops marched in a line.
Even the melons, those viney, fat fellows,
Did not dare to steal space from a squash.
Sam works in that garden each day for long hours,
Humming and feeding and weeding.
Like a wise, gentle father, he nurtures the young—
I'd like to be gardened by Sam.

Writing Prompt

Directions: Think of an experience that was powerful for you. It may have been a time when you succeeded at a task, felt an emotion for the first time, or learned something new and exciting. Write a narrative poem in which you share this experience and your feelings about it.

Words Often Misspelled

accept	busy	fourth	nickel	to
ache	buy	Friday	ninety	too
again	by	friend	ninety-nine	tried
all right	calendar	goes	ninth	tries
almost	cannot	going	often	truly
already	can't	grammar	once	two
although	careful	guard	other	tying
always	catch	guess	people	unknown
angel	caught	guide	principal	until
angle	chief	half	quiet	unusual

answer	children	haven't	quit	wasn't
argue	choose	hear	quite	wear
asked	chose	heard	really	weather
aunt	color	heavy	receive	Wednesday
author	cough	height	rhythm	weird
awful	cousin	here	right	we'll
babies	decide	hers	Saturday	we're
been	divide	hole	stretch	weren't
believe	does	hoping	surely	we've
bother	don't	hour	their	where

bought	early	its	theirs	which
break	enough	it's	there	whole
breakfast	every	January	they're	witch
breathe	exact	let's	they've	won't
broken	except	listen	those	wouldn't
brother	excite	loose	though	write
brought	expect	lose	thought	writing
bruise	February	minute	through	written
build	finally	muscle	tied	you're
business	forty	neighbor	tired	yours

Spelling Guidelines

1. Short and long vowel sounds in words of two or more syllables are usually spelled the same as in one-syllable words, but the **a, i, u,** and **ei** spellings of the /ā/, /ī/, /yo͞o/, and /ē/ sounds are not found in one-syllable words.

passion	raisin
meddle	legion
pennant	deceit
filter	climax
option	triumph
luster	donor
raven	unit

2. The /oi/, /ou/, /o͞o/, /o͝o/, /är/, /î/, /ôr/, and /ûr/ sounds in words of two or more syllables are usually spelled the same as in one-syllable words.

noisy	fully
flounder	wooden
neutral	frontier
booster	flourish
dilute	carton
bureau	cordial

3. Compound words may be spelled as one word, as a hyphenated word, or as two separate words.

newsstand	viewpoint
long-lived	all-around
dead end	cold front

4. Double-consonant spellings often occur when prefixes or suffixes are added to a word or word root and when two words are joined to make a compound word.

affectionate	aggravate
accompany	funny
starry	forbidden
controller	tonsillitis
overrate	unnatural
midday	irregular

5. Many words do not follow normal spelling rules. The spellings must be remembered.

mortgage	biscuit
pageant	beige
subtle	succumb
lieutenant	vehicle
massacre	cougar

6. Most plurals are formed by adding -s or es. A final **f** or **fe** often changes to **v** before -s or -es is added. The key word in hyphenated or separated compound words usually becomes plural. The original plural form is kept in some foreign nouns.

patios	by-products
cupfuls	phenomena
echoes	diagnoses
vetoes	analyses
shel**ves**	data
consu**ls** general	crises

7. Abbreviations are shortened words. Acronyms are made from the first letters of several words. Blends are parts of two words.

Corp.	Inc.
OPEC	UFO
motorcade	cablegram

8. The Latin prefixes **trans-** and **sub-** appear in many words. When **sub-** is added to a word or root beginning with **p**, the prefix becomes **sup-**.

transaction	**sub**urban
translate	**sup**plement
transfuse	**sup**posedly
submerge	**sup**ply
substance	**sup**press

9. The Greek suffix **-logy** means "study of." It is often used with Greek roots.

socio**logy**	geo**logy**
zoo**logy**	mytho**logy**
psycho**logy**	anthropo**logy**

10. Many Latin prefixes bring their meanings to words and word roots.

supersonic	**inter**pret
supervise	**counter**act
intravenous	**counter**attack

11. The suffixes **-ure, -age, -ion, -ment, -or,** and **-er** can affect the spelling of words or word roots.

text**ure**	ornam**ent**
bond**age**	moderat**or**
opin**ion**	lectur**er**

12. The prefixes **pre-, pro-, post-, anti-, ab-,** and **ad-** bring meaning to words and word roots. The prefix **ab-** is spelled **abs-** before a root that begins with **c** or **t**.	**pre**judge **pro**pel **post**pone	**anti**social **abs**cess **ad**journ
13. The suffixes **-ious, -ous, -able, -ible, -ile, -ial,** and **-al** form adjectives.	prec**ious** prob**able** frag**ile** artific**ial**	marvel**ous** tang**ible** fac**ial** man**ual**
14. Latin roots join with affixes to form new words. The meaning of the prefix is often added to the meaning of the root.	de**pose** in**fer** ex**tract** pro**ducer** **junc**tion **senti**ment **dic**tator	ex**pire** di**vert** re**plica** im**plore** **structure** in**voke** e**volve**
15. Words that are related in spelling and meaning are easier to remember in pairs.	severe excel assume	severity excellence assumption
16. Many English words originally came from ancient Greek, French, Spanish, and other languages. These words often have unusual spellings.	sphinx fillet lariat kayak	pharmacy brunette sierra ukulele
17. Some English words are formed from the names of people or places. Many of these words are no longer capitalized.	Braille sequoia cologne Cheddar	tuxedo pasteurize silhouette Olympic

Abbreviations

Abbreviations are shortened forms of words. Most abbreviations begin with a capital letter and end with a period.

Titles	Mr. *(Mister)*	Dr. *(Doctor)*
	Mrs. *(married woman)*	Sr. *(Senior)*
	Ms. *(any woman)*	Jr. *(Junior)*
	NOTE: *Miss* is not an abbreviation and does not end with a period.	
Initials	John F. Kennedy *(John Fitzgerald Kennedy)*	
	E. M. Forster *(Edward Morgan Forster)*	
Days of the week	Sat. *(Saturday)* Tues. *(Tuesday)*	
Months of the year	Feb. *(February)* Sept. *(September)*	
	NOTE: Do not abbreviate *May, June,* and *July.*	
Time	A.M. *(midnight to noon)* P.M. *(noon to midnight)*	
Words used in addresses	St. *(Street)*	Rte. *(Route)*
	Rd. *(Road)*	Apt. *(Apartment)*
	Ave. *(Avenue)*	Pkwy. *(Parkway)*
	Dr. *(Drive)*	Mt. *(Mount or Mountain)*
	Blvd. *(Boulevard)*	Expy. *(Expressway)*
Words used in business	Co. *(Company)*	Corp. *(Corporation)*
	Inc. *(Incorporated)*	Ltd. *(Limited)*
Other abbreviations	Some abbreviations are all capital letters, with a letter standing for each important word.	
	P.D. *(Police Department)* P.O. *(Post Office)*	
	R.N. *(Registered Nurse)* M.A. *(Master of Arts)*	
	Abbreviations for units of measure use neither capital letters nor periods. The only exception is the abbreviation for *inch.*	
	mph *(miles per hour)* in. *(inch)* l *(liter)*	
	Abbreviations of government agencies or national organizations do not usually have periods.	
	PBS *(Public Broadcasting Service)*	
	NATO *(North Atlantic Treaty Organization)*	

States

The United States Postal Service uses two capital letters and no period in each of its state abbreviations.

AL *(Alabama)*	MT *(Montana)*
AK *(Alaska)*	NE *(Nebraska)*
AZ *(Arizona)*	NV *(Nevada)*
AR *(Arkansas)*	NH *(New Hampshire)*
CA *(California)*	NJ *(New Jersey)*
CO *(Colorado)*	NM *(New Mexico)*
CT *(Connecticut)*	NY *(New York)*
DE *(Delaware)*	NC *(North Carolina)*
FL *(Florida)*	ND *(North Dakota)*
GA *(Georgia)*	OH *(Ohio)*
HI *(Hawaii)*	OK *(Oklahoma)*
ID *(Idaho)*	OR *(Oregon)*
IL *(Illinois)*	PA *(Pennsylvania)*
IN *(Indiana)*	RI *(Rhode Island)*
IA *(Iowa)*	SC *(South Carolina)*
KS *(Kansas)*	SD *(South Dakota)*
KY *(Kentucky)*	TN *(Tennessee)*
LA *(Louisiana)*	TX *(Texas)*
ME *(Maine)*	UT *(Utah)*
MD *(Maryland)*	VT *(Vermont)*
MA *(Massachusetts)*	VA *(Virginia)*
MI *(Michigan)*	WA *(Washington)*
MN *(Minnesota)*	WV *(West Virginia)*
MS *(Mississippi)*	WI *(Wisconsin)*
MO *(Missouri)*	WY *(Wyoming)*

Numbers

Spell out numbers under one hundred and numbers at the beginning of a sentence. Use numerals for numbers over one hundred.

My team has twenty-five players.

Two hundred sixty people were in the audience.

There are 147 apartments in my building.

Titles

Underlining

Titles of books, magazines, newspapers, long musical works, plays, works of art, movies, and TV series are underlined. The important words and the first and last words are capitalized.

In a Pickle *(book)*	As You Like It *(play)*
Miami Herald *(newspaper)*	Mona Lisa *(painting)*
Requiem *(musical work)*	Nature *(TV series)*

Titles continued

Quotation marks	Titles of short stories, articles, songs, poems, and book chapters are enclosed in quotation marks.

"The Party" *(short story)*   "If" *(poem)*
"Crewelwork" *(article)*   "Saxon Art" *(chapter)*
"America" *(song)*

Quotations

Quotation marks with commas and periods	Quotation marks are used to set a speaker's exact words apart from the rest of the sentence. The first word of a direct quotation begins with a capital letter. Question marks and exclamation points that belong to the quotation are placed inside the quotation marks. Question marks and exclamation points that do not belong to the quotation are placed outside the quotation marks. Commas separate a quotation from the rest of the sentence. Always place periods and commas inside quotation marks.

"Where," Saul asked, "did I leave my keys?"
Did Joe say, "I am going to Miami on my vacation"?
Linda replied, "I don't know what time it is."

Bibliography

	The basic organization of a bibliography is alphabetical. If the author's name is not given, list the title first, and alphabetize it by the first important word of the title.
Books	List the author's name (last name first), the book title, the city where the publisher is located, the publisher's name, and the year of publication. Note the punctuation.

Winkler, Connie. The Computer Careers Handbook. New York: Arco Publishing, 1983.

Encyclopedia article	List the author's name (last name first), then the title of the article (in quotation marks). Next, give the title of the encyclopedia (underlined), and the year of publication of the edition you are using. Note the punctuation.

Dertouzos, Michael. "Personal Computer." The World Book Encyclopedia. 1986 ed.

CAPITALIZATION, PUNCTUATION, USAGE

| Encyclopedia article (continued) | If the author of the article is not given, begin your listing with the title of the article. |
| | "Charles River." Collier's Encyclopedia. 1980 ed. |

Magazine or newspaper article	Study these examples carefully. Note the order and the punctuation.
	MAGAZINE: Horst, John. "Making a Sundial." Country Journal, March 1980, pp. 97–99.
	NEWSPAPER: Wren, Christopher S. "River Running in the Wilderness." The New York Times, August 31, 1986, Sec. 10, pp. 9, 16.
	NEWSPAPER: (no author) "Train Snarls Downtown Traffic." Somerville News, January 6, 1986, Sec. A, p. 5.

Here is another way that you can write these entries:

MAGAZINE: Horst, John. "Making a Sundial." Country Journal March 1980: 97–99.

NEWSPAPER: Wren, Christopher S. "River Running in the Wilderness." The New York Times 31 Aug. 1986, sec. 10: 9, 16.

Capitalization

| Rules for capitalization | Capitalize geographical names such as cities, states, countries, continents, bodies of water, geographical features, and geographical areas. Do not capitalize small words like *the* and *of*. |

Paris	Asia	Rock of Gibraltar
Vermont	Yangtze River	Eastern Europe
Brazil	Rio Grande	the Northeast

Do not capitalize directions.

We live ten miles east of Philadelphia.

Capitalize titles or their abbreviations when used with a person's name.

Governor Bradford   Senator Smith   Dr. Lin

Capitalize proper adjectives.

We ate at a Hungarian restaurant.

She is French.

Capitalize the names of months and days.

My birthday is on the last Monday in March.

Rules for capitalization (continued)

Capitalize the names of organizations, businesses, institutions, and agencies.

National Hockey League   The Status Company

Franklin Mint   Federal Aviation Agency

Capitalize names of holidays and other special events, streets, highways, buildings, bridges, monuments, historical events, periods of time, and documents.

Veterans Day	Lincoln Memorial
Route 9	French Revolution
World Trade Center	Jazz Age
Golden Gate Bridge	Bill of Rights

Capitalize the first and last words and all important words in the titles of books, newspapers, stories, songs, poems, reports, and outlines. (Articles, short conjunctions, and short prepositions are not capitalized unless they are the first or last word.)

Julie of the Wolves	"The Road Not Taken"
The New York Times	"Canadian National Parks"
"The Necklace"	"The Exports of Italy"
"Over the Rainbow"	

Capitalize the first word of each main topic and subtopic in an outline.

I. Types of libraries
     A. Large public library
     B. Bookmobile
     C. School library
II. Library services

Capitalize the first word in the greeting and closing of a letter.

Dear Marcia,	Your friend,
Dear Ms. Olsen:	Yours truly,

Capitalize nationalities, languages, religions, religious terms, and specific school subjects followed by a number.

Canadian	Menorah
Spanish	Koran
Old English	Geography 101
Buddhism	History I

CAPITALIZATION, PUNCTUATION, USAGE

Punctuation

End marks	A *period (.)* ends a declarative or imperative sentence. A *question mark (?)* follows an interrogative sentence. An *exclamation point (!)* is used after an exclamatory sentence and after an interjection that expresses strong feeling.

The scissors are on my desk. *(declarative)*
Look up the spelling of that word. *(imperative)*
How is the word spelled? *(interrogative)*
This is your best poem so far! *(exclamatory)*
Wow! We've just won the essay prize. *(interjection)*

Apostrophe

To form the possessive of a singular noun, add an apostrophe and *s*.
sister-in-law's   family's   Agnes's

To form the possessive of a plural noun that ends in *s*, add an apostrophe only.
sisters'   families'   Joneses'

For a plural noun that does not end in *s*, add an apostrophe and *s*.
women's   mice's   sisters-in-law's

Use an apostrophe and *s* to form the plural of letters, numerals, symbols, and words that are used as words.
s's   *i*'s   2's   *'s
Fill in the questionnaire with *yes*'s and *no*'s.

Use an apostrophe in contractions in place of dropped letters. Do not use contractions in formal writing.
isn't *(is not)*   they've *(they have)*   it's *(it is)*

Colon

Use a colon to separate the hour from the minute.
7:30 P.M.   8:15 A.M.

Use a colon after the greeting in a business letter.
Dear Mrs. Trimby: Dear Realty Homes:

Use a colon before a list introduced by words like *the following* or *these*. Do not use a colon after a verb or a preposition.
Call the following: Hester, Wanda, Doyle, and Carl.
Next year I am taking English, history, and math.
He arrived with a suitcase, a coat, and an umbrella.

Comma	**Use commas to separate words in a series.**
	Clyde asked if we had any apples, peaches, or grapes.

Use commas between two or more adjectives that come before a noun. Do not use a comma if the adjectives are used together to express a single idea.
Her shrill, urgent cry was alarming.
The tired British tourists decided to rest.

Use a comma to separate the simple sentences in a compound sentence.
Some students were at lunch, but others were studying.

Use commas after words, phrases, and clauses that come at the beginning of sentences.
No, you cannot avoid the deadline.
Following the applause, the speaker continued.
When you are in doubt, ask for advice.

Use commas to separate interrupters such as *of course, however,* **and** *by the way* **from the rest of the sentence.**
Maureen, of course, was late for the bus again.
The driver, however, had forgotten the directions.

Use commas to set off an appositive from the rest of the sentence when the appositive is not necessary to the meaning of the sentence.
The writer Charles Dickens created complex plots.
(The appositive is necessary to the meaning.)
Texas, the Lone Star State, borders Mexico.
(The appositive is extra, not needed for meaning.)

Use a comma to separate a noun in direct address.
Joe, help me fix this.   How was your trip, Pa?

Use a comma to separate the month and day from the year. Use a comma to separate the year from the rest of the sentence. Do not use commas if a specific day is not included.
January 12, 1987, is the date of the banquet.
Halley's Comet appeared last during April 1986.

Use a comma after an interjection that expresses mild emotion.
Gee, I hope the bus comes soon.

C A P I T A L I Z A T I O N , P U N C T U A T I O N , U S A G E

Comma (continued)	Use a comma between the names of a city and a state in an address. If the address is within a sentence, also use a comma after the name of the state. Do not use a comma before the ZIP Code. Does Chicago, Illinois, have the world's tallest building? Denise lives at 10 Palm Court, Lima, OH 45807.
	Use a comma after the greeting in a friendly letter and after the closing in all letters. Dear Deena, Sincerely yours,
	Use commas to set off a nonessential phrase or clause, which adds optional information not necessary to the meaning of the sentence. If a phrase or clause is essential, do not use commas. Emily Dickinson, who was born in 1830, was a poet. (The clause is not necessary to the meaning.) The man who read the poem is my father. (The clause is necessary to the meaning.)
Semicolon	Use a semicolon to connect independent clauses that are closely related in thought or that have commas within them. There were five movie tickets left; Ed needed six. He bought nuts, dates, and figs; we ate them all.
	Use a semicolon to join two independent clauses when the second clause begins with an adverb such as *however, therefore,* or *consequently*. It was growing dark; however, there were no clouds.
Hyphens, Dashes, Parentheses	Use a hyphen to join the parts of compound numbers, to join two or more words that work together as one adjective before a noun, or to divide a word at the end of a line. thirty-two long-range plans Raphael is known as one of Italy's many magnif-icent painters.
	Use dashes to show a sudden change of thought. The sky grew dark—it could mean snow.
	Use parentheses to enclose unnecessary information. Geraldine was re-elected (once more) as treasurer.

Problem Words

Words	Rules	Examples
a, an	The indefinite articles *a* and *an* refer to any person, place, or thing. Use *a* before a word that begins with a consonant sound. Use *an* before a word that begins with a vowel sound.	a banana an apple
the	The definite article *the* points out a specific noun or pronoun. Use *the* with both singular and plural nouns.	the apple the apples The books that I like are long.
accept	The verb *accept* means "to receive."	The club accepted her.
except	The preposition *except* means "excluding."	They all went except James.
affect	The verb *affect* means "to influence."	The rain affected my plans.
effect	The verb *effect* means "to cause to happen."	They effected many changes.
	The noun *effect* means "result."	What effect has Sara had?
bad	*Bad* is an adjective. It can be used after linking verbs like *look* and *feel.*	This was a bad day. I feel bad.
badly	*Badly* is an adverb.	I play badly.
beside	*Beside* means "next to."	He is sitting beside me.
besides	*Besides* means "in addition to."	Who, besides Al, is going?

Words	Rules	Examples
between	*Between* refers to two people or things.	I sat between Kyle and Pam.
among	*Among* refers to three or more people or things.	Talk among the four of you.
farther	Use *farther* to refer to physical distance.	Which town is farther away?
further	Use *further* in all other cases.	Please read further by tomorrow.
fewer	Use *fewer* or *fewest* with plural nouns.	Fewer boys are here today.
less	Use *less* or *least* with singular nouns.	I have the least money.
good	*Good* is an adjective.	The weather looks good.
well	*Well* is usually an adverb. It is used as an adjective only when it means "healthy."	She swims well. Do you feel well?
its	*Its* is a possessive pronoun.	The dog wagged its tail.
it's	*It's* is a contraction of *it is*.	It's cold today.
lie	*Lie* means "to rest, recline, or remain in one place."	The dog lies in its bed.
lay	*Lay* means "to put or place something."	Please lay the books here.
raise	*Raise* means "to move something up," "to increase something," or "to grow something."	Please raise the window. The store raised its prices. Maggie raises sunflowers.
rise	*Rise* means "to get up or go up."	This elevator rises slowly.
shall	*Shall* is used with *I* and *we* in formal English.	We shall be there today.
will	*Will* is used in all other cases.	He will go tomorrow.

Problem Words continued

Words	Rules	Examples
their	**Their** is a possessive pronoun.	Their coats are on the bed.
there	**There** is an adverb. It also begins sentences.	Is Carlos there? / There is my book.
they're	**They're** is a contraction of *they are*.	They're going to the store.
theirs	**Theirs** is a possessive pronoun.	This dog is theirs.
there's	**There's** is a contraction of *there is*.	There's his tag.
them	**Them** is *not* a demonstrative pronoun.	These (*not* Them) are mine.
whose	**Whose** is an interrogative pronoun.	Whose tickets are these?
	Whose is also a possessive pronoun.	Jan, whose book I borrowed, is here today.
who's	**Who's** is a contraction for *who is*.	Who's that woman?
your	**Your** is a possessive pronoun.	Are these your glasses?
you're	**You're** is a contraction for *you are*.	You're late again!

Adjective and Adverb Usage

Comparing	**To compare two things, add -*er* to one-syllable adjectives and adverbs or use the word *more*.**
	This lily is taller than that one. It grew more quickly.
	To compare three or more things, add -*est* or use the word *most*.
	This lily is the tallest of all. It grew most quickly.
	Add -*er* or -*est* to short adjectives or adverbs. Use *more* or *most* and *less* or *least* with most modifiers of two or more syllables.
	thinner fastest less colorful most easily
Double comparisons	**Avoid double comparisons.**
	She is a better (*not* more better) skier than he.
	This is the deepest (*not* most deepest) snow ever!

Irregular comparisons	**Some adjectives and adverbs have special forms for making comparisons.**

Adjectives

good	better	best
bad	worse	worst
many, much	more	most
little	less	least
far	farther	farthest

Adverbs

well	better	best
badly	worse	worst
far	further	furthest

Position of adverbs	**An adverb such as *almost, even, hardly, just, nearly, merely, only,* or *scarcely* should be placed as close as possible to the word that it modifies.**

Just Mark wants to come to the library. (Mark is the only person who wants to come.)

Mark wants to come just to the library. (Mark wants to come to the library and nowhere else.)

fewer, less, much, many	**Use *little, less,* and *least* with things that cannot be counted. Use *few, fewer,* and *fewest* with countable things. Use *much* with uncountable things. Use *many* with countable things.**

Is there less interest in Sullivan than in Wright?

Are fewer skyscrapers being built now?

The Hancock Building caused much trouble.

Many windows fell out onto the street.

real, really, sure, surely	***Real* and *sure* are adjectives. *Really* and *surely* are adverbs.**

This ring is made of real gold.

He is a really good skater.

Pat was sure of her answer.

He surely is an excellent cook!

Negatives

A double negative is the use of two negative words to express one negative idea. Avoid double negatives. *Barely, hardly,* and *scarcely* are considered negative words.

INCORRECT: I didn't hardly have enough time.

CORRECT: I hardly had enough time.

Pronoun Usage

Agreement	**A pronoun must agree with the antecedent to which it refers.** Kee bought a newspaper, but Mary read it first. Jeff and Cindy came to dinner. They enjoyed the meal.
Indefinite pronouns	**An *indefinite pronoun* does not refer to a specific person or thing. When you use an indefinite pronoun as a subject, the verb must agree with it.** Everyone is out. *(sing.)* Several were out. *(pl.)* Neither is here. *(sing.)* Many are here. *(pl.)* **Pronouns must agree with indefinite pronouns used as antecedents.** Each has its own name. Others forgot their books. Everyone should bring her own pencil.
Subject and object pronouns	**A pronoun used as a subject or as a predicate pronoun (after a linking verb) is called a *subject pronoun*. It is in the *nominative case*.** He composed many works for the piano. The writer was she. **A pronoun used as an object is called an *object pronoun*. It is in the *objective case*.** Clyde collected old coins and sold them. *(direct object)* Let's share these bananas with her. *(object of prep.)* She gave him a choice. *(indirect object)*
Compound subject and objects	**To choose the correct pronoun in a compound subject or a compound object, say the sentence with the pronoun alone.** Pedro and I went hiking. (I went hiking.) Sara is visiting Al and me. (Sara is visiting me.)
Incomplete comparisons	**To decide which pronoun form to use in an incomplete comparison, add the missing words.** Ben goes hiking more often than I (do). Lane gives him more help than (he gives) me.
Reflexive and intensive pronouns	**Do not use reflexive or intensive pronoun forms in place of personal pronouns.** INCORRECT: Ron and myself repaired the lamp. CORRECT: Ron and I repaired the lamp.

CAPITALIZATION, PUNCTUATION, USAGE

Reflexive and intensive pronouns (continued)	**Do not use** *hisself* **or** *theirselves*.
	INCORRECT: Adam will do that hisself.
	  CORRECT: Adam will do that <u>himself</u>.
	INCORRECT: They gave theirselves a head start.
	  CORRECT: They gave <u>themselves</u> a head start.

I, me	***I* is used as a subject. *Me* is used as an object.** Jan and <u>I</u> are going to the show. She is taking <u>me</u>. **When using *I* or *me* with other nouns or pronouns, name yourself last.** Beth and <u>I</u> will leave. Give the papers to <u>Ron and me</u>.
we, us	**To use the pronouns *we* or *us* correctly with a noun in a sentence, first look at the noun. If the noun is the subject of the sentence or if it follows a linking verb, use the pronoun *we* with it. If the noun is an object, use *us*.** <u>We</u> fans are proud. They saw <u>us</u> boys. It is <u>we</u> aunts again. He gave <u>us</u> girls a card.
who, whom	**Use the pronoun *who* as a subject. Use the pronoun *whom* as a direct object or object of a preposition.** <u>Who</u> was the surprise guest? *(subject)* <u>Whom</u> did you ask? (Did you ask <u>whom</u>?) *(direct object)* To <u>whom</u> did you speak? *(object of a preposition)*
who, whoever, whom, whomever	**The relative pronoun *who* or *whoever* can be used as the subject of a noun clause. The relative pronoun *whom* or *whomever* can be used as the object of a noun clause.** <u>Whoever</u> calls can talk to me. I know <u>who</u> is calling. <u>Whom</u> you meant is not clear. I'll give the message to <u>whomever</u> it was meant for.
who, whom, whose	**When the relative pronoun is the subject of an adjective clause, use *who*. When the relative pronoun is the object of a verb or a preposition in the relative clause, use *whom*. When the relative pronoun is possessive, use *whose*.** Jan is the student <u>who</u> has contributed the most. Jan is the writer <u>whom</u> we should all thank. Jan, <u>whose</u> stories are funny, will be our editor.

Pronoun Usage continued

this, that, these, those	**Do not use** *this here, that there, these here,* **or** *those there.* That (*not* That there) is a cute animal.

Verb Usage

Active and passive voice	**Use the passive voice when the doer of the action is unknown or unimportant. Use the active voice for direct, forceful sentences.** I baked the bread. (*not* The bread was baked by me.) The Erie Canal was completed in 1825.
Agreement: compound subjects	**A compound subject with *and* takes a plural verb.** Jason, Kelly, and Wanda have new dictionaries. **A compound subject with *or* or *nor* takes a verb that agrees with the nearer subject.** She or her cousins are ready to help. Her cousins or Paula is ready to help.
Agreement: titles, names, collective nouns, plural forms	**A title or name of a single thing takes a singular verb.** McNally, Doyle, and Hennessey is a law firm. *Journey Through Bookland* was Sophie's favorite book. **A collective noun takes a singular verb unless the group's *members* are referred to.** The committee is meeting at eight o'clock. The committee have different opinions about that issue. **A noun with a plural form that names a single amount or item takes a singular verb.** Ten dollars is too much to pay. (*the whole amount*)
Agreement: inverted and interrupted order	**Subject and verb must agree, no matter where the subject is.** In the pond were several frogs. The show of photographs is now open.
Possessives with gerunds	**Use a possessive noun or a possessive pronoun before a gerund.** David's traveling took place on weekends. Their singing made the choir remarkable.

CAPITALIZATION, PUNCTUATION, USAGE

Tenses	**Avoid unnecessary shifts in tense.**
	The sun came out, and we were (*not* are) surprised.

When a sentence describes actions that took place at two different times, use the past perfect for the earlier action and the past tense for the later action.

Bob had trained hard, but he lost the match anyway.

When a sentence describes two actions in the future, use the future perfect for the earlier action and the present for the later action.

I will have left for practice before the sun rises.

Use the present perfect for an action that occurred at an unspecified time in the past.

She has ridden a horse only once.

Irregular verbs	**Irregular verbs do not add -*ed* or -*d* to form the past participle. Their forms must be memorized. Use a form of *have* with the past participle.**

Verb	Past	Past Participle
be	was	been
begin	began	begun
buy	bought	bought
choose	chose	chosen
come	came	come
do	did	done
eat	ate	eaten
fly	flew	flown
go	went	gone
have	had	had
lay	laid	laid
lie	lay	lain
rise	rose	risen
shine	shone	shone
steal	stole	stolen
swim	swam	swum
take	took	taken
teach	taught	taught
tear	tore	torn
think	thought	thought
throw	threw	thrown
wear	wore	worn
write	wrote	written

■ THESAURUS PLUS ■

How to Use This Thesaurus

When do you use a thesaurus? You use one when you want to make your writing more exact or more interesting. Suppose you wrote the following sentence:

The night air felt cold.

Is *cold* the most exact word you can use? To find out, use your Thesaurus Plus.

Look up your word Turn to the index on pages 633–638. You will find

cold, adj.

Entry words are in blue type. Because *cold* is blue, you can look up *cold* in the Thesaurus Plus.

Use your thesaurus The main entries in the thesaurus are listed in alphabetical order. Turn to *cold.* You will find

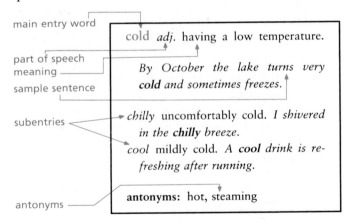

main entry word

part of speech
meaning

sample sentence

subentries

antonyms

> **cold** *adj.* having a low temperature.
>
> *By October the lake turns very **cold** and sometimes freezes.*
>
> **chilly** uncomfortably cold. *I shivered in the **chilly** breeze.*
> **cool** mildly cold. *A **cool** drink is refreshing after running.*
>
> **antonyms:** hot, steaming

Which word might better describe the tree in the sentence above? Perhaps you chose *chilly.*

Other index entries There are two other types of entries in your Thesaurus Plus Index.

1. The slanted type means you can find other words for *convey* if you look under *move.*

   convey move, *v.*
   convince persuade, *v.*

2. The regular type tells you that *corrupt* is the opposite of *good.*

   cool cold, *adj.*
   corrupt good, *adj.*

THESAURUS PLUS

Practice

A. Use your Thesaurus Index to answer these questions.

1. Is *trait* a main word or a subentry word?
2. What part of speech is *amble?*
3. What is the main entry word for *rough?*
4. Is *support* a subentry word or an antonym?

B. Use your Thesaurus Index and Thesaurus Plus to answer these questions.

5. What antonyms are listed for *dark?*
6. How many subentries are listed for *reason?*
7. What does *relocate* mean?
8. How many antonyms are listed for *rousing?*
9. What part of speech is *scrumptious?*
10. What does *undisturbed* mean?
11. What is another antonym for *rested?*
12. What color is *vermillion?*
13. What subentries are listed for *rely?*
14. What is an antonym for *sudden?*

C. Use your Thesaurus Index to find the main entry for each underlined word. Then use the Thesaurus Plus to rewrite each sentence, using a more exact or interesting word.

1. <u>Because of</u> the American Revolution, the United States is not a part of the British Empire.
2. The Boston Tea Party occurred <u>before</u> the Revolution.
3. <u>Angry</u> colonists boarded British ships and threw chests of tea into Boston Harbor.
4. They were expressing their <u>objections</u> to British rule.
5. The <u>argument</u> was about the British tax on tea.
6. It was the colonists' <u>belief</u> that the tax was unfair.
7. <u>Rapidly</u> they banded together to rebel.
8. Only a <u>small</u> quantity of colonists were pro-British.
9. The Declaration of Independence was an <u>effect</u> of the colonists' dissatisfaction with England.
10. On July 4, 1776, the Declaration of Independence <u>said</u> that the colonies should be self-governing.
11. The Treaty of Paris of 1783 brought an <u>end</u> to the war.
12. This was no <u>little</u> achievement for the colonists.
13. All had grown <u>tired</u> of the struggle.
14. Today many celebrate Independence Day by watching <u>exciting</u> parades.

THESAURUS PLUS

Thesaurus Plus Index

consider think, *v.*
continue persist, *v.*
contract, *v.*
contrast, *v.*
convey move, *v.*
convince persuade, *v.*
cool cold, *adj.*
corrupt good, *adj.*
crawl hurry, *v.*
creep hurry, *v.*
cried said, *v.*
crimson red, *adj.*
current ancient, *adj.*

D

damage fix, *v.*
damage harm, *v.*
damp, *adj.*
dark bright, *adj.*
dark, *adj.*
dash hurry, *v.*
dawdle hurry, *v.*
dazzling bright, *adj.*
dazzling exciting, *adj.*
decadent good, *adj.*
declared said, *v.*
decline reject, *v.*
delay hurry, *v.*
delectable good, *adj.*
delicious good, *adj.*
depart move, *v.*
depend rely, *v.*
depressed happy, *adj.*
deprived rich, *adj.*
detail, *n.*
dewy damp, *adj.*
dexterous good, *adj.*
difference likeness, *n.*
different alike, *adj.*
differentiate contrast, *v.*
dim bright, *adj.*
dim dark, *adj.*
diminish increase, *v.*
distinguish contrast, *v.*
doubt objection, *n.*
dry damp, *adj.*
dull colorless, *adj.*
dull exciting, *adj.*
dull interesting, *adj.*

dusky dark, *adj.*

E

earlier after, *adv.*
earlier before, *adv.*
earnest serious, *adj.*
effect consequence, *n.*
electrifying exciting, *adj.*
emerald green, *adj.*
enchanting exciting, *adj.*
end conclusion, *n.*
energetic tired, *adj.*
engrossing exciting, *adj.*
enigmatic confusing, *adj.*
enlarge increase, *v.*
entertaining interesting, *adj.*
enticing exciting, *adj.*
entreated said, *v.*
equivalent alike, *adj.*
ethical good, *adj.*
evacuate move, *v.*
even smooth, *adj.*
evidence detail, *n.*
evil good, *adj.*
examine, *v.*
example, *n.*
exceedingly very, *adv.*
exceptionally very, *adv.*
exciting, *adj.*
exclaimed said, *v.*
expand contract, *v.*
expedition trip, *n.*
experience, *v.*
expert good, *adj.*
expert, *n.*
expose, *v.*

F

fact detail, *n.*
faded colorless, *adj.*
faint colorless, *adj.*
fascinating exciting, *adj.*
fascinating interesting, *adj.*
feature characteristic, *n.*
feel experience, *v.*
feeling opinion, *n.*
finish conclusion, *n.*
fix, *v.*
flavorful good, *adj.*

fly hurry, *v.*
fooling serious, *adj.*
forget remember, *v.*
forlorn sad, *adj.*
formerly before, *adv.*
funny, *adj.*
furious angry, *adj.*

G

gallop run, *v.*
gifted good, *adj.*
glad sad, *adj.*
glassy smooth, *adj.*
glossy smooth, *adj.*
glum happy, *adj.*
go *through* experience, *v.*
good, *adj.*
gradual sudden, *adj.*
grainy smooth, *adj.*
grave serious, *adj.*
great small, *adj.*
green, *adj.*
griped said, *v.*
gripping exciting, *adj.*
groaned said, *v.*
grounds reason, *n.*
growled said, *v.*
grumbled said, *v.*
grunted said, *v.*
guide, *v.*

H

hair-raising exciting, *adj.*
happy sad, *adj.*
happy, *adj.*
harm, *v.*
haul move, *v.*
heavy, *adj.*
hence therefore, *adv.*
hilarious funny, *adj.*
hilly smooth, *adj.*
hissed said, *v.*
hollered said, *v.*
honorable good, *adj.*
hot cold, *adj.*
huge small, *adj.*
humdrum exciting, *adj.*
humid damp, *adj.*
hurl throw, *v.*

hurry, *v.*

I

illustration example, *n.*
imagine think, *v.*
immoral good, *adj.*
implored said, *v.*
impress move, *v.*
in the past before, *adv.*
increase, *v.*
indistinct colorless, *adj.*
inflamed angry, *adj.*
influence move, *v.*
influence persuade, *v.*
inform ask, *v.*
information detail, *n.*
inquire ask, *v.*
inquired said, *v.*
insipid exciting, *adj.*
inspect examine, *v.*
inspire move, *v.*
inspiring exciting, *adj.*
instance example, *n.*
instantaneously quickly, *adv.*
interesting, *adj.*
interrogate ask, *v.*
interrogated said, *v.*
intriguing exciting, *adj.*
intriguing interesting, *adj.*
irritated angry, *adj.*
issue argument, *n.*

J

joyful happy, *adj.*
joyful sad, *adj.*
judgment opinion, *n.*

L

large small, *adj.*
later after, *adv.*
later before, *adv.*
law-abiding good, *adj.*
lead guide, *v.*
leading figure expert, *n.*
level smooth, *adj.*
light dark, *adj.*
light heavy, *adj.*
liken contrast, *v.*
likeness, *n.*

THESAURUS PLUS

little small, *adj.*
long ago before, *adv.*
lug move, *v.*
lumpy smooth, *adj.*
luscious good, *adj.*

M

magenta red, *adj.*
main, *adj.*
mar harm, *v.*
maroon red, *adj.*
masterful good, *adj.*
meager small, *adj.*
melancholy sad, *adj.*
mend fix, *v.*
mesmerizing exciting, *adj.*
migrate move, *v.*
minute small, *adj.*
misgiving objection, *n.*
moaned said, *v.*
modest shy, *adj.*
moist damp, *adj.*
monotonous exciting, *adj.*
morose happy, *adj.*
motivate move, *v.*
motive reason, *n.*
mouth-watering good, *adj.*
move, *v.*
muggy damp, *adj.*
mumbled said, *v.*
murky confusing, *adj.*
murmured said, *v.*
muttered said, *v.*

N

needy rich, *adj.*
noble good, *adj.*
noted author expert, *n.*
notice see, *v.*
nubbly smooth, *adj.*

O

objection, *n.*
observe examine, *v.*
on account of because of, *prep.*
once after, *adv.*
once before, *adv.*

opaque clear, *adj.*
opinion, *n.*
opposite alike, *adj.*
opposition objection, *n.*
outcome consequence, *n.*
outgoing shy, *adj.*

P

paltry small, *adj.*
pass move, *v.*
patch fix, *v.*
peaceful smooth, *adj.*
pensive serious, *adj.*
perceive see, *v.*
persist, *v.*
persuade, *v.*
petite small, *adj.*
plod hurry, *v.*
point of view opinion, *n.*
polished good, *adj.*
polished smooth, *adj.*
poor rich, *adj.*
position argument, *n.*
previously after, *adv.*
previously before, *adv.*
primary main, *adj.*
primitive ancient, *adj.*
principal main, *adj.*
principled good, *adj.*
prior to after, *adv.*
prior to before, *adv.*
proclaimed said, *v.*
proficient good, *adj.*
pronounced said, *v.*
proof detail, *n.*
provocative exciting, *adj.*
pushiness spunk, *n.*
puzzling confusing, *adj.*

Q

qualified good, *adj.*
quality characteristic, *n.*
queried said, *v.*
query ask, *v.*
questioned said, *v.*
quickly, *adv.*
quit move, *v.*
quit persist, *v.*

R

radiant happy, *adj.*
rangy tall, *adj.*
rapidly quickly, *adv.*
reason detail, *n.*
reason think, *v.*
reason, *n.*
recall remember, *v.*
recollect remember, *v.*
red, *adj.*
reject, *v.*
relocate move, *v.*
rely, *v.*
remarked said, *v.*
remember, *v.*
repair fix, *v.*
replied said, *v.*
reply ask, *v.*
requested said, *v.*
researcher expert, *n.*
resemblance likeness, *n.*
respectable good, *adj.*
responded said, *v.*
rested tired, *adj.*
restore fix, *v.*
result consequence, *n.*
retorted said, *v.*
returned said, *v.*
reveal expose, *v.*
rich, *adj.*
righteous good, *adj.*
rise, *v.*
riveting exciting, *adj.*
roared said, *v.*
rose red, *adj.*
rough smooth, *adj.*
rousing exciting, *adj.*
ruby red, *adj.*
run, *v.*
rush hurry, *v.*

S

sad happy, *adj.*
sad, *adj.*
said, *v.*
satiny smooth, *adj.*
savory good, *adj.*
scarlet red, *adj.*

scientist expert, *n.*
scramble hurry, *v.*
screamed said, *v.*
scrumptious good, *adj.*
scrupulous good, *adj.*
see, *v.*
seething angry, *adj.*
sensational exciting, *adj.*
sense experience, *v.*
serene smooth, *adj.*
serious funny, *adj.*
serious, *adj.*
shaded dark, *adj.*
shadowy dark, *adj.*
shift move, *v.*
shining bright, *adj.*
shoot run, *v.*
short tall, *adj.*
shouted said, *v.*
show expose, *v.*
shrieked said, *v.*
shy, *adj.*
silky smooth, *adj.*
similar alike, *adj.*
similarity likeness, *n.*
sit rise, *v.*
skilled good, *adj.*
sleek smooth, *adj.*
slick smooth, *adj.*
slippery smooth, *adj.*
slowly quickly, *adv.*
small, *adj.*
smeared streaked, *adj.*
smooth, *adj.*
snapped said, *v.*
snarled said, *v.*
soggy damp, *adj.*
solemn funny, *adj.*
solution consequence, *n.*
some time back before, *adv.*
sorrowful happy, *adj.*
source expert, *n.*
speculate think, *v.*
spine-tingling exciting, *adj.*
spokesperson expert, *n.*
spot see, *v.*
spunk, *n.*
stammered said, *v.*
stand argument, *n.*
stand rise, *v.*

THESAURUS PLUS

THESAURUS PLUS

start conclusion, *n.*
stated said, *v.*
steaming cold, *adj.*
steer guide, *v.*
stirring exciting, *adj.*
streaked, *adj.*
striped streaked, *adj.*
study examine, *v.*
stuttered said, *v.*
subsequently after, *adv.*
subsequently before, *adv.*
sudden, *adj.*
support objection, *n.*
swiftly quickly, *adv.*

T

talented good, *adj.*
tall, *adj.*
teasing serious, *adj.*
tedious exciting, *adj.*
termination conclusion, *n.*
then after, *adv.*
thereafter after, *adv.*
therefore, *adv.*
think, *v.*
throw, *v.*
thus therefore, *adv.*
tiny small, *adj.*
tired, *adj.*
tiresome exciting, *adj.*
tiresome interesting, *adj.*
toss throw, *v.*
tote move, *v.*
touch move, *v.*
tour trip, *n.*
towering tall, *adj.*
trait characteristic, *n.*
tranquil smooth, *adj.*
transfer move, *v.*
transparent clear, *adj.*
transport move, *v.*
trip, *n.*
trust rely, *v.*
trustworthy good, *adj.*
turbulent smooth, *adj.*
turn down reject, *v.*

U

undisturbed smooth, *adj.*

unimportant main, *adj.*
unruffled angry, *adj.*
until now before, *adv.*
untroubled smooth, *adj.*
unwrinkled smooth, *adj.*
upright good, *adj.*
upshot conclusion, *n.*
upstanding good, *adj.*

V

vacate move, *v.*
vermillion red, *adj.*
very, *adv.*
virtuous good, *adj.*
vivid colorless, *adj.*

W

wealthy rich, *adj.*
weary tired, *adj.*
weighty heavy, *adj.*
well-to-do rich, *adj.*
whined said, *v.*
whispered said, *v.*
wicked good, *adj.*
win over persuade, *v.*
wretched sad, *adj.*

Y

yelled said, *v.*
yummy good, *adj.*

A

after *adv.* behind in place or order. *You go ahead, and we'll come along after.*

subsequently following in time. *Sue started out taking French but subsequently dropped it.*

later after a particular time or event. *Let's have dinner now and see the movie later.*

once immediately after. *Once Michelle arrives, we can begin.*

thereafter from then on. *Jill learned to sew and thereafter made all her own clothes.*

then afterward. *I went to Paris and then London.*

antonyms: before, earlier, previously, prior to

alike *adj.* exactly or almost exactly the same. *His twin sisters look very much alike.*

similar related in appearance or nature; somewhat alike but not the same. *Your new coat is similar to my coat.*

comparable capable of being compared; having like traits. *A parakeet and a canary are comparable in size.*

equivalent equal in amount, value, meaning, force, measure. *A dime is equivalent to ten pennies.*

antonyms: different, opposite

ancient *adj.* very old, aged. *The abandoned house on our street looks ancient.*

primitive of or in an early stage of development. *This museum has a collection of primitive South American sculpture.*

antonym: current

angry *adj.* feeling or showing ill temper. *The angry customer demanded a refund.*

furious full of extreme anger. *Lisa was furious when someone dented her new car.*

irritated annoyed; bothered. *Joel gets irritated when I call him Joe.*

seething violently agitated, disturbed, or annoyed. *Seething with anger, he stormed away.*

inflamed aroused by anger or other strong emotion. *The audience was inflamed by his unfair remarks.*

antonyms: calm, unruffled

argument *n.* a statement in support of a point of view; a reason. *The editorial listed several arguments against the proposed law.*

case a set of reasons offered in support of something. *She presented a strong case for buying a new bus.*

position a point of view or an attitude on a certain question. *The candidate's position on new taxes is well known.*

stand an opinion on an issue or question that one is prepared to defend. *The mayor took a strong stand against closing the school.*

issue a subject being discussed or disputed. *The new dress code is a hotly debated issue.*

ask, *v.* to seek an answer to. *Ask Mrs. Jurigian if she saw anyone unusual outside her house.*

interrogate to question closely. *The police interrogated a suspect.*

inquire to seek information from. *They inquired about her occupation.*

query to question. *Officer Gould queried them about their whereabouts on June 10.*

antonyms: answer, reply, inform

B

because of *prep.* being brought on or made possible by. *She succeeded because of her strong will.*

on account of due to. *The band concert had to be postponed on account of rain.*

as a result of being an outcome of. *As a result of the freezing weather, the pipes burst.*

Word Bank

before *adv*. at an earlier time.

at one time	earlier	in the past
back then	once	long ago
until now	formerly	some time
previously	prior to	back

antonyms: after, afterward, subsequently, later

---

bright *adj*. radiant with light or color. *Bright umbrellas make a rainy day more cheerful.*

shining giving off or reflecting a steady light. *A shining lantern lit the path.*

brilliant glittering; sparkling with light. *The costume was brilliant with sequins.*

dazzling so bright as to be blinding; blazing with light. *The lifeguard squinted in the dazzling sunlight.*

antonyms: dark, dim

C

characteristic *n*. something that makes one person, group, or thing different from others. *One characteristic of racing cars is a streamlined shape.*

trait a distinguishing aspect, as of a person or an animal. *Eye color is an inherited trait.*

quality a general tendency or effect. *Many folk songs have a sad quality to them.*

feature a noticeable part or aspect. *An important feature of this radio is its small size.*

clear *adj*. free from anything that dims, darkens, or obscures. *The clear ocean water was perfect for swimming.*

transparent of such texture that objects can be seen on the other side. *Her transparent plastic mask made everybody laugh.*

antonym: opaque

cold *adj*. having a low temperature. *By October the lake turns very cold and sometimes freezes.*

chilly uncomfortably cold. *I shivered in the chilly breeze.*

cool mildly cold. *A cool drink is refreshing after running.*

antonyms: hot, steaming

colorless *adj*. without a distinct hue. *The moon's landscape is colorless.*

faint not clearly seen; dim. *A faint light flickered in the distance.*

faded without brightness, owing to gradual changes. *The old curtains were faded from the sunlight.*

dull drab. *The desert's dull colors change with spring rains.*

indistinct not clear or well-defined; fuzzy. *The boat was indistinct in the fog.*

antonym: vivid

conclusion *n*. the last part of something. *The conclusion of her speech made us cheer.*

end the final part or limit of something. *Labor Day marks the end of summer.*

close an ending or finish. *Her home run brought the game to a close.*

termination a formal or official ending. *His failure to pay his dues led to the termination of his membership from the club.*

upshot the final result; outcome. *The upshot of her efforts was an increase in sales.*

finish a stopping point or end. *The race was thrilling from the start to the finish.*

antonyms: beginning, start

confusing *adj.* causing misunderstanding. *These **confusing** instructions won't help us learn how to wallpaper.*

murky vague; difficult to understand. *Her **murky** explanation was impossible to follow.*

puzzling hard to figure out. *The disappearance of the money is very **puzzling**.*

enigmatic not clear in meaning; mysterious. *We wondered how to interpret his **enigmatic** message.*

antonym: clear

consequence *n.* something that follows from an action or condition. *One **consequence** of the road construction was traffic delays.*

effect something that has happened in response or reaction to something else. *Sunshine and a cool breeze always has the **effect** of making me feel energetic.*

result the outgrowth of a particular action, operation, or cause. *He slept late and, as a **result**, missed the bus.*

outcome a final product. *To most people, the **outcome** of the election was no surprise.*

solution the successful outcome of a problem. *Moving to a dry climate was the **solution** to my cousin's health problems.*

antonym: cause

contract *v.* to draw together; make or become smaller in length. *She **contracted** her muscles to swing the baseball bat.*

compress to put pressure on something so as to reduce the space it takes up. *Everyone **compressed** their clothes to fit into their backpacks.*

antonym: expand

contrast *v.* to compare in order to reveal differences. *The reviewer **contrasted** two modern films with two silent movies.*

distinguish to recognize differences. *Some people cannot **distinguish** between red and green.*

differentiate to understand or show the differences between. *In her science report, Alison **differentiates** between spiders and true insects.*

antonym: liken

D

damp *adj.* slightly wet. *Our bathing suits are still **damp**.*

humid having a large amount of water vapor. *The rain shower made the air **humid**.*

moist slightly wet with water spread thinly over a surface. ***Moist** leaves clung to the windows.*

muggy unpleasantly warm and humid, with little or no breeze. *The **muggy** summer made us wish for a cool fall.*

soggy softened with moisture. *After the rain, our heels sank into the **soggy** earth.*

dewy slightly wet with water droplets. ***Dewy** spider webs glistened in the morning sun.*

antonym: dry

dark *adj.* without light or with very little light. *He felt his way across the **dark** cellar.*

shaded screened from light. *Most frogs like **shaded** places more than sunny ones.*

dim faintly lighted. *A **dim** shape appeared across the field.*

shadowy having scattered areas of shade. *A **shadowy** path led through the woods.*

dusky tending to darkness, as from the approach of night. *She lit a lamp in the **dusky** room.*

antonyms: bright, light

detail *n.* a part of a report or other composition that supports the main idea; an individual or specific item. *Adding a **detail** about the weather will help your story.*

detail continued

fact something real or known with certainty. *Pamela's idea was interesting, but she couldn't find the* **facts** *to back it up.*

evidence something that serves as proof. *In describing the author's life, Gordon presented little* **evidence** *of an unhappy childhood.*

reason a fact or cause that explains why something should or does exist. *The major stressed safety as a* **reason** *for widening the highway.*

proof demonstration of the truth of something. *Our success is* **proof** *that the plan works!*

information facts about a certain subject. *This textbook on intelligence contains much* **information** *about the brain.*

E

examine v. to look at carefully. *The child* **examined** *the strange new toy with interest.*

inspect to look at carefully in order to detect flaws. *You should* **inspect** *a used car before you buy it.*

study to look at closely in order to find out something. *He* **studied** *her face to see how she really felt.*

observe to watch with attention. *The two bird watchers* **observed** *a pair of nesting eagles.*

example n. one item that is typical of a whole class or category. *The Irish setter is an* **example** *of an excellent hunting dog.*

case a particular condition or occurrence. *Sometimes you get a busy signal, in which* **case** *you can phone again later.*

instance an action or occurrence that is representative of a general subject. *Interrupting the speaker was just one* **instance** *of her rudeness.*

illustration something that serves as an example or demonstration. *A falling rock is an* **illustration** *of the effect of gravity.*

Word Bank

exciting *adj.* arousing, stimulating.

stirring	spine-tingling
rousing	breathtaking
inspiring	electrifying
gripping	sensational
enticing	provocative
riveting	compelling
engrossing	hair-raising
absorbing	
dazzling	
alluring	
enchanting	
captivating	
fascinating	
intriguing	
mesmerizing	

antonyms: boring, bland, dull, tedious, tiresome, insipid, colorless, monotonous, humdrum

experience v. to take part in; live through. *Almost everyone* **experiences** *failure at times.*

feel to experience physically or emotionally. *He* **felt** *anxious alone in the house.*

sense to become aware of by instinct. *The animals* **sensed** *the approaching storm.*

go through to experience with pain or displeasure. *I hope you didn't* **go through** *much difficulty.*

expert n. a person with great knowledge in a particular field. *Dr. Lee is an* **expert** *on animal behavior.*

source a person who supplies information. *In describing the accident, the reporter used a witness as her* **source.**

leading figure a very important person in a certain field. *Her great talent made her a* **leading figure** *among painters.*

noted author a well-known writer. *A book by a noted author draws great interest.*

researcher a person who studies a subject in order to contribute new knowledge. *Medical researchers have developed cures for many different illnesses.*

spokesperson a person who speaks as a representative for others. *The spokesperson announced that the governor would hold a press conference tomorrow.*

authority an accepted source of knowledge or advice. *Her mother is an authority on gardening.*

scientist a person who studies the laws of nature. *Newton was the scientist who discovered the laws of gravity.*

antonym: amateur

expose *v.* to uncover; lay bare. *I exposed my back to the sun.*

show to make visible. *They showed us the way out of the jungle.*

reveal to make known; disclose. *The magician revealed her secrets.*

F

fix *v.* to set right. *This word processor fixes misspellings.*

repair to put back in useful condition after damage, injury, or wear. *My uncle repairs old lawnmowers.*

mend to repair by joining torn, frayed, or broken parts. *Can you mend this torn sleeve?*

patch to cover a hole, rip, or torn place with a small piece of material. *She patched the nail hole in the bicycle tire.*

restore to bring back to an original condition. *The owner is restoring this historic house.*

antonyms: break, damage

funny *adj.* arousing laughter or amusement. *Rosa thinks that her practical jokes are funny.*

hilarious causing a great deal of laughter. *The cartoon had a hilarious scene with a pig in the mud.*

comical humorous. *The monkey's comical tricks made us laugh.*

antonyms: serious, solemn

G

Shades of Meaning

good *adj.*

1. of high moral quality:
honorable
noble
upstanding
virtuous
trustworthy
respectable
scrupulous
ethical
law-abiding
conscientious
principled, upright
righteous

2. having much ability:
skilled
gifted
accomplished
talented
expert
masterful
proficient
qualified
adept
polished
dexterous

3. pleasant-tasting:
delicious, scrumptious, mouth-watering, delectable, appetizing, yummy, flavorful, savory, luscious

antonyms: wicked, evil, immoral, decadent, corrupt

green *adj.* having the color of most plant leaves and growing grass. *The fields turned green with the spring rains.*

chartreuse of a light yellowish green. *Most new fire engines are chartreuse instead of red.*

emerald of a dark yellowish green. *The cat's emerald eyes shone against its white fur.*

guide *v.* to direct the course of. *Our counselor guided us on our hike through the woods.*

lead to show the way by going ahead. *The captain always leads the team onto the field.*

steer to physically control the course of a vehicle, ship, or plane. *It is difficult to steer a truck on this winding road.*

H

happy *adj.* feeling satisfaction and pleasure. *She was very happy when the gift arrived.*

joyful feeling great happiness. *Their wedding anniversary was a joyful occasion.*

radiant glowing or beaming with happiness. *Her radiant face told us that she had won.*

blissful full of calm contentment. *He spent a blissful afternoon doing exactly as he pleased.*

antonyms: depressed, glum, morose, sad, sorrowful

harm *v.* to injure; hurt. *Looking directly at the sun can harm a person's eyes.*

damage to injure something so that it is less valuable or useful. *Frost damaged the orange crop.*

mar to spoil the surface or appearance of. *Those rough crates marred the table top.*

heavy *adj.* having relatively great weight. *The rocks by the river are very heavy.*

weighty having great weight. *This package is too weighty to carry all the way home.*

antonym: light

hurry *v.* to move or act with haste. *The students hurried back to their seats.*

dash to race with sudden speed. *He dashed through the closing elevator doors.*

rush to move or act with great haste. *The ambulance rushed to the accident scene.*

scramble to move quickly in a disorganized manner. *The players scrambled for the loose ball.*

fly to move swiftly. *The horses flew by in a cloud of dust.*

antonyms: amble, crawl, creep, plod, dawdle, delay

I

increase *v.* to make or become greater or larger. *The increase in pollution is dangerous to our planet.*

enlarge to make or become larger. *We had our favorite photographs enlarged.*

antonym: diminish

interesting *adj.* arousing and holding attention. *I read interesting books quickly.*

intriguing arousing one's curiosity. *The disappearance of the rake is an intriguing puzzle.*

entertaining pleasing and enjoyable. *His entertaining stories kept us amused.*

fascinating extremely interesting. *Visiting my foreign relatives is always fascinating.*

antonyms: boring, dull, tiresome

L

likeness *n.* a way in which things are the same. *I see a real likeness between the plots of those two mystery stories.*

similarity the quality of being alike but not identical. *The similarity between them was startling.*

resemblance a closeness in appearance. *There is a strong resemblance between twins.*

antonym: difference

M

main *adj.* most important; major. *The main ride is a water slide.*

principal first in rank or importance. *Willa is the principal soloist in the chorus.*

central having the most influence or control. *All orders come from the central headquarters.*

primary first or best; chief. *Her primary goal is to get into college.*

antonym: unimportant

Shades of Meaning

move *v.*

1. to take something from one place to another:
transport, carry, shift, transfer, convey, conduct, pass, bear, cart, haul, lug, tote

2. to leave one's location:
depart
relocate
quit
vacate
migrate
evacuate

3. to cause an emotion or change of feeling:
affect, arouse, touch, inspire, impress, motivate, influence

O

objection *n.* the expression of an opposing view or argument. *The committee explained their objection to the possibility of shortened library hours.*

opposition the act of resisting or being in conflict. *The mayor's decision met with angry opposition.*

doubt worry; concern. *Mai had serious doubts about most of our fundraising plans.*

misgiving uncertainty about the wisdom of an action. *Leon now has misgivings about buying that used compact disc player.*

antonyms: agreement, support

opinion *n.* a belief not based on positive knowledge. *I don't agree with the reviewer's opinion of that newly released movie.*

belief something thought to be true. *The coach has unshakable belief in the team.*

point of view the position from which something is considered. *From this point of view, the decision was unfair.*

attitude a state of mind regarding someone or something. *Jeff has a positive attitude toward his job.*

feeling a belief based on emotion or instinct. *She had a strong feeling that we would succeed.*

judgment a decision reached after careful weighing of evidence. *The skipper's judgment was that the seas were too rough to sail.*

P

persist *v.* to insist or repeat obstinately. *She persists in practicing her saxophone.*

continue to keep on. *Even in snow or sleet, the mailcarrier continues to work.*

antonym: quit

persuade *v.* to cause someone to do or believe something by arguing, pleading, or reasoning. *He **persuaded** us to wait another day.*

convince to cause someone to feel certain. *The lawyer had **convinced** the jury of her client's innocence.*

win over to appeal successfully to someone's emotions or sense of values. *His enthusiasm for the project **won over** the committee.*

influence to have an effect or impact on. *Our friendship did not **influence** my decision.*

Q

quickly *adv.* with speed; right away. *The teller **quickly** counted the coins accurately.*

swiftly with great speed and smoothness. *The runner **swiftly** passed the baton to his teammate.*

rapidly in very fast sequence. *A hummingbird's wings beat so **rapidly** that you see only a blur.*

instantaneously immediately. *We **instantaneously** recognized the man in the photograph.*

antonym: slowly

R

reason *n.* a statement or fact that explains why something exists or occurs. *Do you have a good **reason** for being late?*

cause a person, thing, condition, or action that makes something happen. *The **cause** of the fire was faulty wiring.*

grounds the foundation for a belief or an action. *They have no **grounds** for claiming that we are responsible for the mistake.*

basis an underlying cause, idea, or fact. *Belief in freedom is the **basis** of our Constitution.*

motive an emotion or desire that causes someone to act in a certain way. *His **motive** for working was to make money for camp.*

Shades of Red

red *adj.* the color of ripe strawberries.

- - - - - - - - - -

rose: a deep pinkish-red
scarlet: a bright orange-red
burgundy: a dark reddish-brown

vermillion: a bright red
cerise: a dark red
ruby: a very deep red

crimson: a vivid purplish-red
maroon: a dark purplish-red
carmine: a deep purplish-red
magenta: a strong reddish-purple

reject *v.* to refuse to accept, use, grant, consider. *My parents **rejected** my idea of a pet monkey.*

decline to refuse to accept or do. *He **declined** my offer to help him.*

turn down to reject. *The faculty **turned down** the principal's plan for a new gym.*

rely *v.* to count on the ability or willingness of someone or something. *I'll **rely** on you to do the job.*

depend to count on for support or help. *You can always **depend** on a good friend.*

trust to have confidence in the soundness or honesty of. *I **trust** you because you always tell me the truth.*

remember *v.* to think of again. *I just **remembered** that I was supposed to turn left.*

recollect to remember through deliberate effort. *I cannot **recollect** where I left my key.*

THESAURUS PLUS

bring to mind to cause to think of. *Your dog **brings to mind** one that I had years ago.*

recall to bring back to memory. *Can you **recall** the names of all the Great Lakes?*
antonym: forget

rich *adj.* having much money, goods, land, or other valuables. *If I were **rich**, I'd travel all over the world.*

wealthy having a great quantity of money, valuable possessions, or resources. *The United States is a **wealthy** nation.*

affluent having plenty of money. *Large, beautiful houses can be the mark of an **affluent** community.*

well-to-do well-off; enjoying wealth or profit. *Their successful business has made them **well-to-do**.*
antonyms: deprived, needy, poor

rise *v.* to go up; ascend. *The moon **rises** quickly.*

stand to take or maintain an upright position on the feet. *I don't like to **stand** in lines.*
antonym: sit

run *v.* to move on foot at a pace faster than a walk. *The hitter **ran** to first base.*

gallop to run at a fast, rhythmic pace. *We heard the mustangs **galloping** toward us.*

shoot to move swiftly and smoothly. *A meteor **shot** across the clear night sky.*

S

sad *adj.* showing, filled with, or expressing sorrow or regret. *The team members had **sad** faces after their loss.*

forlorn pitiful in appearance or condition. *The **forlorn** kitten cried for its mother.*

wretched full of misery or woe. *Brad felt **wretched** when he lost the club's money.*

melancholy gloomy; depressed. *Long periods of rain make many people feel **melancholy**.*
antonyms: glad, happy, joyful

Shades of Meaning

said *v.* spoke aloud.

1. said quietly or unclearly:
whispered, murmured, mumbled, muttered, grunted

2. said openly and clearly:
stated, announced, declared, articulated, pronounced, asserted, remarked, proclaimed

3. asked:
*questioned
queried
inquired
requested
interrogated*

4. answered:
replied, responded, retorted, returned

5. said in a complaining way:
whined, moaned, groaned, grumbled, griped

6. said in an angry way:
snarled, growled, snapped, hissed

7. said loudly:
*yelled
screamed
shrieked
bellowed
hollered
roared, shouted*

8. said in an excited or nervous way:
exclaimed, cried, stuttered, stammered

9. said in a pleading way:
begged, implored, entreated, beseeched

see *v.* to become aware of by sight. *In the distance, he saw clouds of black smoke.*

spot to detect; recognize; locate. *We spotted a fawn hidden under the huge bush.*

notice to become aware of casually or by chance. *On my way home, I noticed a hat on a park bench.*

perceive to recognize or understand information gathered through any of the senses. *He said that he was fine, but I perceived that he was very upset.*

serious *adj.* not joking or speaking casually. *Are you serious about moving to Chicago?*

earnest showing or expressing deep, sincere feeling. *The police chief made an earnest plea for help in solving the crime.*

grave extremely serious; solemn. *The doctor's face was grave as she gave them the bad news.*

pensive in a thoughtful mood. *Jan was not unhappy, but she was quite pensive.*

antonyms: fooling, teasing

shy *adj.* quiet and withdrawn in manner. *At first I was too shy to make friends.*

bashful timid and embarrassed. *Sam felt bashful when he suddenly became the center of attention.*

modest tending to play down one's own talents, abilities, or accomplishments. *Although she plays the piano well, she is modest about her talent.*

antonyms: bold, outgoing

small *adj.* slight in size, number, quantity, extent, volume, or importance. *Kate's room is too small for two people.*

little below average in size, quantity, or degree. *They have little faith in his promise.*

tiny extremely small. *The tiny ant looked like a speck.*

petite small and dainty. *One girl is tall, while the other is petite.*

paltry insignificant; small in power or value. *He was disappointed at the paltry sum that he had earned.*

meager lacking in quantity or richness; scanty. *We looked for wild strawberries, but the pickings were meager.*

minute exceptionally small. *Minute flecks of gold glittered among the stones.*

antonyms: big, great, huge, large vast

Shades of Meaning

smooth *adj.*

1. flat:
   even, level, unwrinkled

2. having a fine-textured surface:
   sleek, slick, satiny, silky, slippery, glossy, glassy, polished

3. calm:
   undisturbed, untroubled, peaceful, serene, tranquil

antonyms: hilly, coarse, bumpy, rough, grainy, nubbly, lumpy, turbulent

spunk *n.* spirit; courage. *My friend showed real spunk by calling an ambulance when I broke my arm.*

pushiness aggressiveness. *Your brother's pushiness is annoying.*

streaked *adj.* marked with irregular lines of color. *The sky was* **streaked** *with long, pink clouds.*

striped marked with straight, even lines of color. *His tie had a simple* **striped** *pattern.*

smeared marked with messy-looking streaks. *His apron was* **smeared** *with spaghetti sauce.*

sudden *adj.* happening without warning. *The rainstorm was surprisingly* **sudden.**

abrupt unexpected. *After the storm began, we made an* **abrupt** *change of plans.*

antonym: gradual

T

tall *adj.* of greater than average height. *The redwood is one of the* **tallest** *trees in the world.*

colossal extreme in size, extent, or degree; enormous; gigantic. *From a distance, the people climbing the* **colossal** *pyramid looked like ants.*

rangy long-legged and thin. *The* **rangy** *girl stepped over the fence with ease.*

towering of impressive height; very tall. **Towering** *skyscrapers hid the bright sun.*

antonym: short

therefore *adv.* for that reason. *He was sleepy and* **therefore** *took a long nap.*

thus consequently; as a result. *The home team scored a run to break the tie, and* **thus** *they won the baseball game.*

hence thereby. *This necklace is gold;* **hence,** *it is expensive.*

think *v.* to form an idea in one's mind. **Think** *about your purpose before you start writing.*

believe to suppose or to expect. *I* **believe** *that it will rain later today.*

consider to think over carefully. *Her family* **considered** *moving to Toronto, Canada.*

imagine to form a mental picture, idea, or impression of. *Can you* **imagine** *what the world would be like without colors?*

reason to think clearly and logically. *Let's look at the evidence and* **reason** *out what must have really happened.*

speculate to think deeply on a particular subject; to ponder. *Scientists have* **speculated** *for years about why dinosaurs died out.*

throw *v.* to send something through the air with a swift motion of the arm. *The catcher* **threw** *the ball back to the pitcher.*

hurl to throw with great force. *She* **hurled** *the javelin a record-breaking distance.*

toss to throw lightly. *He* **tossed** *the keys onto the desk.*

tired *adj.* having little physical or mental energy. *The* **tired** *dog paddled slowly to shore.*

weary feeling worn out. *We were* **weary** *after the long drive and needed a break.*

antonyms: energetic, rested

trip *n.* a journey from one place to another. *The Millers are taking a* **trip** *to Vancouver this summer.*

expedition a trip made by an organized group for a definite purpose. *The scientists made an* **expedition** *to photograph the eclipse.*

tour a trip to or through a place for the purpose of seeing it. *The factory provides guided* **tours** *for student groups.*

V

very *adv.* to a high degree. *A chimpanzee makes a* **very** *unusual pet.*

exceedingly to an extreme degree. *Computers can do mathematics* **exceedingly** *quickly.*

exceptionally to an unusual degree. *Saul is an* **exceptionally** *fine singer and musician.*

A

aerodynamic /âr′ ō dī **năm′** ĭk *adj.* Making use of scientific principles of air motion. *We studied the* **aerodynamic** *design of jet planes.*

allocate /**ăl′** ə kāt′/ *v.* allocated, allocating 1. To set aside for a special purpose. 2. To distribute according to a plan; to allot. *Our school* **allocated** *funds for computers.*

appraisal /ə **prā′** zəl/ *n.* The act of judging the quality of something. *The coach made an* **appraisal** *of her players' skills.*

astern /ə **stûrn′**/ *adv.* 1. Toward the rear of a ship. 2. Behind a ship. *We looked* **astern** *at the setting sun.*

attribute /ə **trĭb′** yoŏt/ *v.* To regard as belonging to. *We can* **attribute** *some air pollution to automobile fumes.*

awestricken /**ô′** strĭk′ ən/ *or* **awestruck** *adj.* Filled with dread and wonder. *I was* **awestricken** *by the size of the building.*

azure /**ăzh′** ər/ *adj.* Sky-blue in color. *She wore an* **azure** *blue gown.*

B

beetling /**bēt′** l ĭng/ *adj.* Overhanging. *The small cove was ringed by* **beetling** *hills.*

bowsprit /**bou′** sprĭt′/ *n.* A long pole sticking out from the bow of a sailing ship. *He wrapped the lines from the mast onto the* **bowsprit.**

C

cambric /**kām′** brĭk/ *n.* A finely woven white linen or cotton fabric. *The curtains were made of fine* **cambric.**

canvass /**kăn′** vəs/ *v.* canvassed, canvassing To go through a region, selling a product or seeking votes. *We* **canvassed** *our neighborhood, selling raffle tickets.*

capacity /kə **păs′** ĭ tē/ *n.* The ability to do something. *It is within your* **capacity** *to solve this math problem.*

cataract /**kăt′** ə răkt/ *n.* A waterfall or a floodgate. *The downpour from the* **cataract** *made a deafening sound.*

classify /**klăs′** ə fī/ *v.* classified, classifying To group or sort. *For me, baking cannot be* **classified** *as work.*

cleave /klēv/ *v.* To slice through. *A ship's hull can* **cleave** *the water.*

commuter /kə **myoo′** tər/ *adj.* A person who travels regularly from home, in one place, to work in another place. *She rode the* **commuter** *train to work.*

contract /kən′ **trăkt′**/ *v.* contracted, contracting To reduce in size by packing together; to compress. *Air may be* **contracted** *or compressed.*

D

deed /dēd/ *v.* To transfer property by means of a legal document showing ownership. *Father will* **deed** *me this ranch.*

delineate /dĭ **lĭn′** ē āt′/ *v.* delineated, delineating To draw or trace the outline of; to sketch out. *State boundaries were* **delineated** *on the map.*

despise /dĭ **spīz′**/ *v.* despised, despising To regard with great dislike. *My sister* **despised** *my gum-chewing habit.*

disastrous /dĭ **zăs′** trəs/ *adj.* Causing ruin. *The earthquake had* **disastrous** *effects.*

diverge /dĭ **vûrj′**/ *v.* diverged, diverging To go in different directions from a common point; to branch out. *The river **diverged** into two streams.*

draught /drăft/ *or* draft *n.* 1. A gulp, swallow, or drink of some liquid. 2. The amount taken in a single swallow. *The **draught** of well water refreshed me.*

E

ethereal /ĭ thîr′ ē əl/ *adj.* Pertaining to ether, which the ancients believed was a purer form of air or liquid in the atmosphere. *I know that there is no **ethereal** layer in space.*

exult /ĭg zŭlt′/ *v.* exulted, exulting To rejoice greatly. *The crowd was **exulting** at the sight of the prince.*

F

fanatic /fə năt′ ĭk/ *or* fanatical *adj.* Characterized as extreme. *Birds can be **fanatic** about guarding their nests.*

fashion /făsh′ ən/ *v.* fashioned, fashioning To shape or form; to mold. *I **fashioned** the wet clay into animal figures.*

firmament /fûr′ mə mənt/ *n.* The expanse of the heavens; sky. *The **firmament** was glowing with stars.*

flange /flănj/ *n., pl.* flanges A protruding rim or edge used to attach one object to another. ***Flanges** held the metal gutter to the roof.*

flaw /flô/ *n.* 1. A defect, often hidden. *We discovered a **flaw** in his plan.* 2. Nautical term for a sudden gust of wind. *A **flaw** puffed out the mainsail of the boat.*

forecastle /fōk′ səl/ *n.* The deck area located at the bow of a ship. *The captain paced the **forecastle**.*

H

haphazard /hăp hăz′ ərd/ *adj.* Lacking any plan or order. *The streets were laid out in a **haphazard** way.*

hemisphere /hĕm′ ĭ sfîr′/ *n., pl.* hemispheres One half of a sphere or ball. *The equator divides the earth into two **hemispheres**.*

hubris /hyoo′ brĭs/ *n.* Too much pride; arrogance. *Greek gods would punish any human that was guilty of **hubris**.*

humiliated /hyoo mĭl′ ē āt′ ĭd/ *adj.* degraded; humbled; disgraced. *I felt **humiliated** when you scolded me in front of my friends.*

I

idler /īd′ lər/ *n.* One who is not working or devoted to working. *He is an **idler** when it comes to chores.*

inactivity /ĭn ăk tĭv′ ĭ tē/ *n.* Idleness; a lack of activity. *His **inactivity** was a result of laziness.*

indebtedness /ĭn dĕt′ ĭd nĭs/ *n.* The condition of owing something, such as money or gratitude, to another. *I felt a sense of **indebtedness** to the firefighter.*

inevitably /ĭn ĕv′ ĭ tə blē/ *adv.* Unavoidably; not preventable. *I will **inevitably** be tired after the race.*

intelligible /ĭn tĕl′ ə jə bəl/ *adj.* Understandable; comprehensible. *Not much of his speech was **intelligible**.*

interim /ĭn′ tər ĭm/ *n.* The time between one event, process, or period and another. *Dusk is the **interim** between day and night.*

interrogation /ĭn tĕr′ ə gā′ shən/ *n., pl.* interrogations The art of questioning in detail in a formal manner. *The **interrogations** of the witnesses took ten days.*

intrigue /ĭn trēg′/ *v.* intrigued, intriguing To arouse the interest or curiosity of. *The theory of motion **intrigued** me.*

inundation /ĭn′ ŭn dā′ shən/ *n.* A complete covering with water; a flood. *A tidal wave caused the inundation of the coastal town.*

J

Jacob's Ladder /jā′ kəbs lăd′ ər/ *n.* A ship's ladder; named after the biblical Jacob. *I climbed the Jacob's Ladder.*

L

lame /lām/ *adj.* Disabled in one or more legs or feet, making walking difficult. *The lame conductor used a crutch to help her walk.*

M

man-rope /măn′ rōp′/ *or* **manrope** *n., pl.* man-ropes Ropes used as guardrails or supports. *The sailor held onto the man-ropes to keep from falling overboard.*

maxim /măk′ sĭm/ *n., pl.* maxims A short, meaningful saying regarding a truth or rule of conduct. *My aunt tells maxims about behavior.*

mould /mōld/ *or* **mold** *v.* molded, molding To form into a desired shape around a frame or model. *We moulded the clay over a wire frame.*

N

naturalist /năch′ ər ə lĭst/ *n.* An expert in the study of plants and animals in their natural environments. *She studied biology in order to become a naturalist.*

nymph /nĭmf/ *n.* In mythology a graceful female spirit or goddess that dwells in the woods and waters. *That tree was the home of a woodland nymph.*

P

palpable /păl′ pə bəl/ *adj.* 1. Recognizable; noticeable. 2. Capable of being handled or felt. *There was a palpable rise in the room's temperature.*

patron /pā′ trən/ *n.* Anyone who supports, fights for, or protects. *The goddess Athena was the patron of wisdom.*

pauper /pô′ pər/ *n., pl.* paupers An extremely poor person. *Paupers begged for coins.*

pose /pōz/ *v.* posed, posing To present, raise, or put forward. *The students posed a number of difficult questions.*

preposterous /prĭ pŏs′ tər əs/ *adj.* Contrary to nature, reason, or common sense. *I didn't believe your preposterous story.*

principality /prĭn′ sə păl′ ĭ tē/ *n.* A territory ruled by a prince. *The principality celebrated the arrival of the princess.*

prophecy /prŏf′ ĭ sē/ *n.* A warning of something to come often stated by a god-inspired human. *The god's prophecy told him what would happen.*

proverb /prŏv′ ərb/ *n.* A short, popular saying expressing a well-known belief. *"Waste not, want not" is a famous proverb.*

R

rack /răk/ *n.* The stress of a storm. *The sturdy old ship survived the rack.*

rash /răsh/ *adj.* Bold or hasty; careless. *Don't make rash decisions.*

ratio /rā′ shō/ *n.* A relationship between the amounts or sizes of two things; a proportion. *Mix flour and water in a ratio of five to two.*

repose /rĭ pōz′/ *n.* The act of resting; relaxation. *The child was lying in repose on the sofa.*

rigging /rĭg′ ĭng/ *n.* The ropes, chains, and tackle used to support and control the masts and sails of a ship. *I climbed the rigging to the top of the mast.*

royal /roi′ əl/ *n., pl.* royals   A sail set on the royalmast just below the skysails. *The sailors hoisted the royals.*

S

satyr /sā′ tər/ *n., pl.* satyrs   A creature of Greek myth with goat's legs, pointed ears, and a human face. *I loved the painting of satyrs dancing and playing flutes.*

shroud /shrowd/ *n., pl.* shrouds   A rope steadying the top of a mast. *We tightened the shrouds to the main mast.*

smith /smĭth/ *n.*   A blacksmith; a metalworker. *The smith hammered hot irons on her anvil.*

spat /spăt/ *n., pl.* spats   A cloth or leather covering for the ankle and the top of the shoe. *Years ago, men wore spats over their shoes.*

speculation /spĕk′ yə lā′ shən/ *n.*   The act of giving thought to some idea, theory, or subject. *There is speculation that Columbus did not discover America first.*

spirited /spĭr′ ĭ tĭd/ *adj.*   Characterized by energy or courage. *The governor gave a spirited speech.*

squall /skwôl/ *n., pl.* squalls   A brief, sudden, violent storm. *Squalls caused the sails to rip from their masts.*

surly /sûr′ lē/ *adj.*   Rude, sullen, and bad-tempered. *The surly waiter annoyed us all.*

sustain /sə stān′/ *v.* sustained, sustaining   To keep from falling or sinking. *A gentle breeze sustained the balloons overhead.*

T

tar /tär/ *n., pl.* tars   *Informal* A sailor. *After the ships dock, the old tars sit around and tell stories.*

technology /tĕk nŏl′ ə jē/ *n.*   The application of scientific knowledge in industry and commerce. *Tech-nology has led to many advances in medicine.*

temperament /tĕm′ pər ə mənt/ *n.*   The manner of thinking or behaving typical of a certain individual; disposition. *The child has a calm temperament.*

threadbare /thrĕd′ bâr/ *adj.*   1. Old, shabby clothing. 2. Poverty stricken. *The refugees wore threadbare clothing and shabby shoes.*

tread /trĕd/ *v.* treaded, treading   To walk on or over. *Water–skiing gives you the feeling of treading on water.*

truck /trŭk/ *n.*   The round tip of a mast. *He raised the flag to just below the truck.*

V

vainly /vān′ lē/ *adv.*   Without success; to no avail. *Marco tried vainly to catch the ball.*

vastly /văst′ lē/ *adv.*   Being great in degree or extent. *His health has improved vastly.*

W

weather /wĕth′ ər/ *v.* weathered, weathering   To pass through safely; to survive. *We weathered the storm and sailed into the harbor.*

windlass /wĭnd′ ləs/ *n.*   A device for raising or lowering sails. *It took two sailors to work the huge windlass.*

winnow /wĭn′ ō/ *v.*   To separate by means of a current of air; to cause to fly. *The airplane could winnow the air like a soaring eagle.*

Z

zeal /zēl/ *n.*   High enthusiasm in pursuit of a cause, ideal, or goal. *He approached his homework with great zeal.*

abstract noun names an idea, a feeling, or a quality.

active voice when the subject of a verb performs the action.

adjective describes, or modifies, a noun or a pronoun.

adjective clause a subordinate clause that modifies a noun or a pronoun.

adjective phrase a prepositional phrase that modifies a noun or a pronoun.

adverb modifies a verb, adjective, or other adverb. It usually tells *how, when, where,* or *to what extent.*

adverb clause a subordinate clause used as an adverb.

adverb phrase a prepositional phrase that modifies a verb, adjective, or adverb.

among a preposition used to refer to more than two persons, things, or groups.

antecedent a noun or pronoun to which a pronoun refers.

appositive a noun that identifies another noun.

beside a preposition that means "next to."

besides a preposition that means "in addition to."

between a preposition used to refer to two persons, things, or groups.

clause a group of words that has a subject and a predicate.

collective noun names a group of people, animals, or things that act as a unit.

colon used after a greeting in a business letter, between the hour and the minute in time, and before a list.

comparative degree of an adjective used to compare two things. Add *-er* or *more* to the adjective.

comparative degree of an adverb used to compare two actions or qualities. Add *-er* or *more* to the adverb.

complete predicate tells what the subject is, does, has, or feels.

complete subject tells whom or what the sentence is about.

complex sentence a sentence with one or more subordinate clauses and an independent clause.

compound noun a noun that is made up of more than one word.

compound predicate made up of two or more simple predicates that have the same subject.

compound sentence two or more related simple sentences usually joined with a comma and a conjunction.

compound subject made up of two or more simple subjects that have the same predicate.

concrete noun refers to material things, to people, or to places.

coordinating conjunctions words such as *and, but,* and *or* that join words or word groups with the same function.

correlative conjunction a pair of conjunctions that connects related words or word groups such as *neither . . . nor,* or *either . . . or.*

dash used to set off and show a sudden change of thought.

declarative sentence makes a statement and ends with a period.

demonstrative pronoun points out something (*this, that, these, those*).

direct object a noun or a pronoun in the predicate to which the action of the verb is directed.

double negative the incorrect use of two negatives to express one negative idea.

essential clause   identifies the noun or the pronoun it modifies and is necessary for the sentence to make sense. It is not set off by commas.

exclamatory sentence expresses strong feelings and ends with an exclamation point.

gerund   the present participle of a verb used as a noun.

gerund phrase functions as a noun. It is used as a subject, a direct object, an object of a preposition, or a predicate noun.

helping verb   helps complete the meaning of the main verb.

hyphen   used to divide a word at the end of a line, to join the parts of compound numbers, and to join words that work together as an adjective before a noun.

imperative sentence makes a command or a request and ends with a period.

indefinite pronoun   does not refer to a specific person or thing.

independent clause expresses a complete thought and can stand alone as a simple sentence.

indirect object   a noun or a pronoun in the predicate that tells *to* or *for whom* or *what* the action is done.

infinitive   formed with *to* and the base form of the verb. It is used as a noun, an adjective, or an adverb.

infinitive phrase   made up of an infinitive and the words that complete its meaning. It acts as a noun, an adjective, or an adverb.

intensifier   an adverb that tells *to what extent*.

intensive pronoun   ends in *-self* and *-selves* and emphasizes another word in the sentence.

interjection   a word or a group of words that expresses feeling or represents a sound.

interrogative sentence asks a question and ends with a question mark.

intransitive verb   a verb that does not send its action to a word in the predicate.

inverted order   when the subject of a sentence follows all or part of the predicate.

irregular verb does not follow rules for forming the past tense and past participles.

linking verb   links the subject with a word in the predicate that describes or identifies the subject.

main verb   expresses action or being.

nominative case used for pronouns used as subjects and predicate pronouns.

nonessential clause   gives extra information about the noun or the pronoun it modifies. It is set off with commas.

noun   names a person, place, thing, or idea.

noun clause   a subordinate clause that acts as a noun.

object   the word to which the action of the transitive verb is directed.

objective case   used for pronouns used as direct objects and indirect objects (*me, her, him, us, them*).

parentheses   used to enclose unnecessary information.

participial phrase   made up of a participle and its accompanying words.

participle   a verbal that is used as an adjective.

passive voice   when the subject of a verb receives the action.

personal pronoun has different forms to show person, number, and gender.

possessive noun   shows ownership or relationship. Add an apostrophe and *s* to a noun that does not end in *s* and an apostrophe only to a plural noun that ends with *s*.

possessive pronoun   can replace a possessive noun.

predicate adjective follows a linking verb and describes the subject.

predicate noun follows a linking verb and identifies or renames the subject.

preposition a word that shows a relationship between a noun or a pronoun and another word in the sentence.

prepositional phrase includes a preposition, its object or objects, and all of the modifiers of the object.

progressive verb form expresses continuing action. It is formed with an appropriate tense of *be* plus the present participle.

pronoun used to replace a noun.

proper adjective an adjective formed from a proper noun.

proper noun names a particular thing.

reflexive pronoun ends in *-self* or *-selves* and refers to the subject of the sentence.

run-on sentence two or more sentences that run together.

semicolon used to connect independent clauses that are closely related in thought or that have commas within them.

sentence fragment does not express a complete thought.

simple predicate the verb or verb phrase in the complete predicate.

simple subject the key noun or pronoun in the complete subject.

singular noun names one person, place, thing, or idea.

subordinate clause does not express a complete thought and cannot stand alone as a sentence.

subordinating conjunction usually begins a subordinate clause. It introduces an adverb clause.

superlative degree of an adjective used to compare three or more things. Add *-est* or *most* to the adjective.

superlative degree of an adverb used to compare three or more actions. Add *-est* or *most* to the adverb.

tense form of the verb that expresses time.

transitive verb expresses action that is directed toward a noun or pronoun in the predicate.

verb expresses physical or mental action or being.

verb phrase includes a main verb and one or more helping verbs.

verbal a word that is formed from a verb but used as a noun, an adjective, or an adverb.

Numbers in **bold type** indicate pages where skills are taught.

488, 495–496, 499, 526, 586, 629
good, well, 624
Graphs, 546–547, 549

H

Helping verbs, 148–149, 153–154, 167, 187, 189
Homographs, 578
Homophones, 577
Hyphens. *See* Punctuation

I

I, me, 628
Idioms, 580
Imagery, 285, 596
Indexes, using, 544
Indirect objects. *See* Objects
Inferences, 573
Infinitives and infinitive phrases, 469, **478–481,** 482–483, 487, 488, 497, 498, 499, 526, 587
Information: evaluating sources of, 353–356; in books, **434–435,** 448–449, 543–545, 600, 602; in dictionaries, **435,** **537–539,** 576; in encyclopedias, **434,** 436, 437; listening for, **123–124;** scanning for, 550
Instructions: following, 557; giving, 488, **558;** writing, 604–605
Intensifiers. *See* Adverbs
Interjections, 34–35, 39, 51, 304
Interrupters, 310, 336
Interrupted order in sentences, 176–177, 199, 629
Interviewing, 5, 142–143, 175, 177, 390, 399, 403, 406, 425, **427–429,** 447
Introductions: to book reports, 84; personal, **562;** to research reports, 440–441
Inverted order in sentences: agreement in, **176–177,** 199, 629; identifying subjects in, **20–21,** 22
Italics, 317
its, it's, 624

J

Journals, 4, 87, 145, 235, 269, 417, 458, 459, 461, 470

L

Language: figurative, **286–287,** 596, 608; formal, 279, **561;** informal, 279, **561;** literal, 285, 287
Language Terms, 654–656
less, fewer, 624, 626
Letters: activities for writing, 311, 313, 332, 374, 382, 407, 599, 607; business, 319–320, 357, **358–360,** 372, 598–599; friendly, 312–313, 360, 372, 376, **606–607;** persuasive, 313, 345, **353–377,** 382, 598–599; punctuation and capitalization in, **312–313,** 330, 337, 360, 372, 524, 606, 619, 620, 622; the writing process and, **366–373**
Library, using the, 540–542
lie, lay, **178,** 183, 184, 200, 624
Listening: critical, 78, 136, 226, 294, 370, 452; detecting signals of meaning, **65;** distinguishing fact from opinion, **353–354;** following instructions, **557–558;** guidelines for, **556;** during interviewing, **427–429;** predicting outcomes, **211;** for a speaker's purpose, 556; to take notes, **123–124;** TRACK method for, 556
Listening and Speaking Strategies, 556–568
Listing, 4
Literary terms. *See* Alliteration; Characters; Climax; Conflict; Dialogue, writing; Flashback; Idioms; Metaphor; Mood; Myths; Nonfiction; Onomatopoeia; Parable; Personification; Plot; Point of view; Repetition; Resolution; Rhyme; Rhythm; Setting; Similes; Stanza; Symbols; Theme; Tone

Literature: autobiography, 56–61; discussing, 3, 55, 61, 62, 116, 119, 120, 206, 208, 274, 275, 276, 347, 350, 419, 420, 424; letter, 348–350; myth, 114–116, 117–119, 120, 140; nonfiction, informational, 421–424; nonfiction book excerpt, 421–424; novel excerpt, 270–274; poetry, 54–55, 62, 275, 276, 346–347, 418–419, 420; responding to, 63, 121, 209, 277, 351, 425; short story, 2–3, 204–206, 207–208; writing about, 84–85, 140, 230, 232, 298. *See also* Literary terms
Literature Vocabulary, 650–653

M

Main idea, 127–128, 592, 600, 604
many, much, 626
Maps, 300–301, **548–549**
Mechanics. *See* Capitalization; Punctuation
Metaphor, 276, 286–287, 596, 608
Models. *See* Composition, models
Modifiers: 235, 260, 261; dangling and misplaced, 243, 484; infinitive phrases as, 480–481; infinitives as, 478–479; prepositional phrases as, 465–466, 486; for variety, 252. *See also* Adjectives; Adverbs; Usage
Mood, 274, 590, 594
Myths, 114–116, 117–119, 120, 140

N

Narrative poem, 608–609
Narratives. *See* Literature; Personal narrative; Stories
Negatives, 248–249, 255, 266, 626
Newspapers, using, 435
News reports, activities for writing, 91, 329, 385, 489
Nominative case. *See* Pronouns

Nonfiction, 421–424, 435. *See also* Literature
Notes, in texts, 545
Note-taking, 123–124, 437–438, 600, 602, 604
Noun clauses, 513–515, 516, 518, 521, 527, 534
Nouns: abstract, **88–89,** 102, 105, 107, 257; collective, **90–91,** 102, 108, **173–175,** 629; common, **88–89,** 102, 105, 107, 257; compound, **90–91,** 102, 108, 326–327; concrete, **88–89,** 102, 105, 106, 107, 257; of direct address, **310–311,** 336, 621; exact, **100, 130,** 285; gerunds as, 473–474, 495–496; identifying, 87, 106; infinitive phrases as, 480–481, 498; infinitives as, 478–479, 497; kinds of, **87–91,** 102; plural, irregular, **93,** 102, 105, 109, 257, 522; plural, regular, **92,** 102, 105, 109, 257, 522; possessive, **95–96,** 103, 105, 110, 257, 324–325, 522, 629; predicate, **167–168,** 183, 195, 258, 387, 523, 582; proper, **88–89,** 102, 105, 107, 257, **305–307,** 330, 334, 372, 524, 618–619; singular, **92,** 94, 102, 105, 257, 522; suffixes to form, 278. *See also* Usage
Novel. *See* Literature, novel excerpt
Numbers, as words or numerals, 322–323, 324–325, 331, 341, 372

O

Objective case. *See* Pronouns
Objective tests, taking, 553–555
Objects: compound, **387;** direct, **162–163, 164–166,** 183, 194, 258, 523, 583–584; gerunds and gerund phrases as, **473–474, 475–477,** 487, 495–496, 526; indirect, **164–166,** 183, 194, 258, 523, 584; of a preposition, **462–464**

V

Verb phrases, **148–149,** 182, 187, 258

Verb tenses: 150–152, 180, 182, 188, 228, 258, 630; perfect, **151–152;** from principal parts of verbs, **150–152;** shifts in, 228, 630; simple, **151–152**

Verbals, 469–470. *See also* Gerunds; Infinitives; Participles

Verbs: action, **146–147,** 182, 185, 186, 258, 523; agreement with subject, *see* Agreement, subject-verb; auxiliary, *see* Verbs, helping; of being, **146–147,** 148, **153–154,** 155, 167, 169, 199, 523; exact, 178–179, 221, 285; helping, **148–149,** 153–154, 167, 187, 189; intransitive, **162–163,** 164, 178, 183, 193, 523; irregular, **153–159,** 182, 189–191, 258, 523, 630; linking, **146–147,** 163, 167, 182, 186, 195, 258, 523, *see also* Predicate nouns and adjectives; main, **148–149,** 153–154, 187, 189; principal parts of, **150–159,** 182, 185, 189–191; progressive forms, **160–161,** 182, 192; tenses of, *see* Verb tenses; transitive, **162–163,** 164, 178, 183, 193, 523. *See also* Usage

Vocabulary: antonyms, 122, **426;** base words, **352;** borrowed words, **210;** connotation, **64,** 351; content area, 83, 141, 231, 299, 375, 457; context clues, **122;** denotation, **64;** etymologies, 63, 121, 538, **576;** homographs, **578;** homophones, **577;** idioms, **580;** Old English, **579;** onomatopoeia, 277; prefixes, 278, **352, 575;** suffixes, **278,** 296, **352, 575;** synonyms, 122, **426;** word roots, **352, 575;** writing definitions, 425. *See also* Words

Vocabulary Strategies, 575–580

Voice, active and passive, **169–170,** 183, 184, 196, 629

W

who, which, that, 504–505

who, whom, who's, whose, 389–390, 506–507, **514–515,** 531, 534, 625, 628

whoever, whomever, **514–515,** 534, 628

will, shall, 624

Word roots, 352, 575

Words: base, 352; borrowed, **210;** division at end of line, **326–327;** etymologies, 63, 121, 538, 576; exact, 100, 130, 178–179, 221, 285, 596, 608; guide, **537;** often misspelled, **611;** sense, 596, 608; order, 66, 604; transitional, 442–444. *See also* Vocabulary

Writing across the curriculum. *See* Content area, writing in

Writing conferences, 7–8, 452

Writing process: prewriting, **4–5,** 74–75, 132–133, 222–223, 290–291, 366–367, 446–447; planning a report, **448–449;** first draft, **6,** 76, 134, 224, 292, 368, 450; revising, **7–9,** 77–78, 135–136, 225–226, 293–294, 369–370, 451–452; proof-reading, **10,** 79–80, 137–138, 227–228, 295–296, 371–372, 453–454; publishing, **11,** 81, 139, 229, 297, 373, 455

Writing prompts: comparison and contrast paragraph, 593; description, 597; friendly letter, 607; instructions, 605; narrative poem, 609; personal narrative, 591; persuasive argument, 603; persuasive letter, 599; research report, 601; story, 595

Y

your, you're, 625

(Acknowledgments continued.)

from *Readers' Guide to Periodical Literature,* copyright © 1984, 1985 by The H.W. Wilson Company. Material reproduced by permission of the publisher.

from *The World Book Encyclopedia,* © 1986 World Book, Inc.

from "Animal IQ's," in *How Animals Learn* by Russell Freedman and James E. Morris. Copyright © 1969 by Russell Freedman and James E. Morris. Reprinted by permission of the authors.

from "You, whose day it is . . ." in *Nootka and Quileute Music* by Frances Densmore. Bureau of American Ethnology Bulletin 124. Reprinted by permission of The Smithsonian Institution Press, Smithsonian Institution, Washington, D.C. 01939.

dictionary entries from *Houghton Mifflin Students' Dictionary.* Copyright © 1981 by Houghton Mifflin Company. Reprinted by permission of Houghton Mifflin Company.

dictionary entries from *Houghton Mifflin Student Dictionary.* Copyright © 1986 by Houghton Mifflin Company. Reprinted by permission of Houghton Mifflin Company.

from *The American Heritage Dictionary: High School Edition,* copyright © 1982 by Houghton Mifflin Company. [Definition and pronunciation key] Reprinted by permission of Houghton Mifflin Company.

Grateful acknowledgment is given to Chad Burns, Jerry Hufford, Doug Kertscher, Emily Raimes, Lucy Raimes, and Ed Vietor, for permission to adapt and reprint original material as student writing models in The Writing Process lessons. Special thanks to the Gwinnett County School System, Georgia, for help in obtaining some of these models.

The publisher has made every effort to locate each owner of the copyrighted material reprinted here. Any information enabling the publisher to rectify or credit any reference is welcome.

Credits

Illustrations

Anthony Accardo: 591–609
Ann Bisset: 547, 548
Higgins Bond: 54, 55, 62
Pat and Robin Dewitt: 204–210, 221, 230
William Dippel: 360, 438
Graphics Etcetera: 546, 547 top
Laurie Jordan: 2–3
Mary Keefe: 76, 77, 79, 134, 135, 137, 224, 225, 227, 292, 293, 295, 368, 369, 371, 448–451, 453
Meg Kelleher Aubrey: 4, 7, 11
Stephan Marcarchesi: 114–122, 128, 140, 165, 218, 270–277, 282, 286, 288, 298
Claudia Sargent: 575–580, 640–648
Blanche Sims: 541 top
Jane Sterret: 346–352, 374
Jim Stout: 547 right
Gary Tong: 214, 291, 300, 437, 438 frame
Eva Burg-Vagreti: 22, 75, 85, 96, 133, 143, 223, 233, 301, 367, 377, 391, 418–426, 447, 456, 457, 459
Nina Winter: 40, 41, 106, 184–185, 260–261, 332, 406–407, 488–489, 528

Hand marbleized French and Swedish paper from Andrews/Nelson/Whitehead Corporation, Long Island City, New York: 36–37, 54–64, 100–101, 180–181, 252–253, 328–329

Photographs

1 Don Smetzer/TSW/Click/Chicago.   13 Fredrik D. Bodin.   15 National Theatre for The Deaf.   17 Ralph Wetmore/Index

Stock. 21 Historical Pictures Service, Chicago. 29 Dr. E.R. Degginger. 31 Milt & Joan Mann/Cameramann Intl. 34 Martha Swope. 52–53 Robert Holland. 56 Don Congdon Assoc. 59 printed by permission of the estate of Norman Rockwell © 1935 estate of Norman Rockwell. 72 Don Congdon Assoc. 82 Russ Lappa, Russell Baker portrait by Beverly Hall. 83 Lou Jones. 86, 87 Earth Scenes/G.I. Bernard. 89 Adam Woolfitt/Woodfin Camp & Assoc. 95 Focus on Sports. 112, 113 Judy Poe. 129 *The Berlin Painter*, Dionysos, ca. 480 B.C. Bequest—Frederick M. Watkins 1972.44, Fogg Art Museum, Harvard University. 144, 145 Edith G. Haun/Stock Boston. 153 Lee Foster/Bruce Coleman Inc. 157 Southern Stock Photos. 161 Carl Roessler/Bruce Coleman Inc. 168 Alex Von Koschembahr/Photo Researchers Inc. 171 Leonard Lee Rue III/Photo Researchers Inc. 176 S.J. Craig Jr./Bruce Coleman Inc. 202, 203 Palmer/Kane Inc./The Stock Market. 213 Four X Five. 231 (left) Animals Animals/Stouffer Prod. 231 (top right) Joseph Van Wormer/Bruce Coleman Inc. 231 (bottom right) G.C. Kelley/Tom Stack & Assoc. 234–235 J. Boutin/The Picture Cube. 237 Peter Kaplan/The Stock Shop. 244 The Bettmann Archive. 268, 269 Steve Lissau/Rainbow. 299 (left, right) The Bettmann Archive. 299 (middle) Historical Pictures Service, Chicago. 302, 303 Roy Morsch/The Stock Market. 315 Tom McHugh/Photo Researchers Inc. 316 Animals Animals/Michael Dick. 325 Camilla Smith/Rainbow. 378, 379 Julie Habel/Woodfin Camp & Assoc. 388 The Granger Collection. 401 Herb Snitzer/The Stock Shop. 416, 417 James Sugar/Black Star. 424 The Granger Collection. 460, 461 Randy O'Rourke/The Stock Market. 463 Jack Vartoogian. 473 Jerry Howard/Stock Boston. 483 The Granger Collection. 500, 501 Llewellyn. 505 Walter Chandoha. 511 Tom Bean. 512 Willard Clay/Click/Chicago. 517 Leo deWys Inc.

Nancy Sheehan: 81, 136, 139, 141, 226, 228, 229, 293, 297, 369, 373, 375, 451, 455 Elliot Varner Smith: 344, 345

Fine Art

37 *Bedroom at Arles*, Vincent van Gogh. Collection of the Louvre. Photo: Service de Documentation Photographique de la Reunion des Musees Nationaux. 59 Printed by permission of the estate of Norman Rockwell © 1935 Estate of Norman Rockwell 101 *Double Portrait of the Artist in Time*, Helen Lundeberg, 1935, oil on fiberboard, 47¾ × 40 inches (121.3 × 101.6 cm) 1978.51, *National Museum of American Art*, Smithsonian Institution, Museum Purchase. 181 *Mandolin and Guitar*, Pablo Picasso, 1924. Solomon R. Guggenheim Museum, New York. Photo: David Heald. 253 *The Polish Rider*, Rembrandt, Copyright The Frick Collection, New York. 284 Maurice Brazil Prendergast: *Franklin Park, Boston*, watercolor. Daniel J. Terra Collection, Terra Museum of American Art, Chicago, Illinois. 329 *Parade*, Jacob Lawrence, Hirshhorn Museum and Sculpture Garden, Smithsonian Institution. 403 *Relativity*, Escher, M.C., Photo Courtesy: Collection Haags Gemeentemuseum-The Hague. © M.C. Escher Heirs c/o Cordon Art, Baarn, Holland. 421 Detail (see page 485). 423 Ornithopter sketches, Notebooks of Leonardo daVinci, Historical Pictures Service, Chicago. 485 *The Fall of Icarus*, Bruegel. Musees Royaux des Beaux-Arts de Belgique, Brussels. 519 *Mont St. Michel: Staircase in the "Merveille,"* Frederick Evans. English, 1853–1943. Photo-

graph 9⅛ × 6⁷⁄₁₆ inches. Gift of David H. McAlpin. Courtesy, Museum of Fine Arts, Boston.

Cover Photographs

Cover and title page photograph: Ken Osborn

The photograph shows Oak Alley, a grove of trees on St. Simon's Island, Georgia.

Back cover: Jon Chomitz